Contents

The Michelin maps you will need with this guide are:

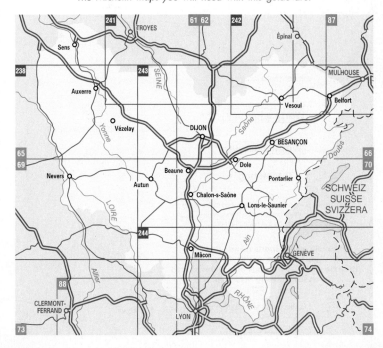

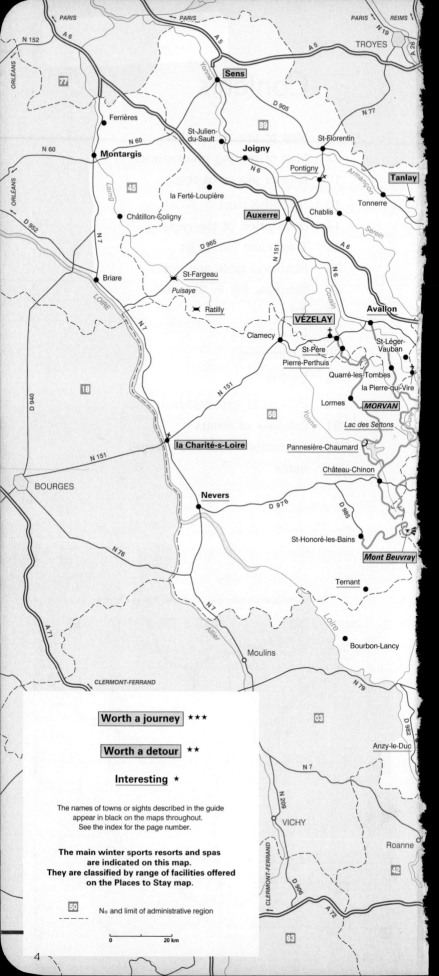

Worth a journey ★★★

Worth a detour ★★

Interesting ★

The names of towns or sights described in the guide
appear in black on the maps throughout.
See the index for the page number.

The main winter sports resorts and spas
are indicated on this map.
They are classified by range of facilities offered
on the Places to Stay map.

50   No and limit of administrative region

0   20 km

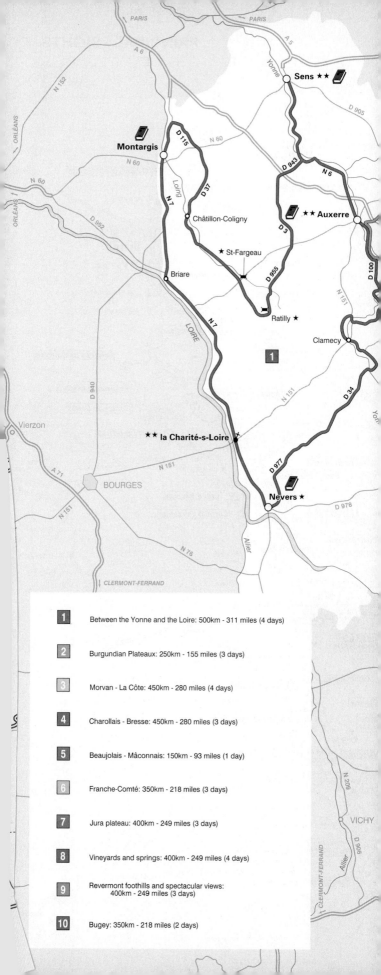

1	Between the Yonne and the Loire: 500km - 311 miles (4 days)
2	Burgundian Plateaux: 250km - 155 miles (3 days)
3	Morvan - La Côte: 450km - 280 miles (4 days)
4	Charollais - Bresse: 450km - 280 miles (3 days)
5	Beaujolais - Mâconnais: 150km - 93 miles (1 day)
6	Franche-Comté: 350km - 218 miles (3 days)
7	Jura plateau: 400km - 249 miles (3 days)
8	Vineyards and springs: 400km - 249 miles (4 days)
9	Revermont foothills and spectacular views: 400km - 249 miles (3 days)
10	Bugey: 350km - 218 miles (2 days)

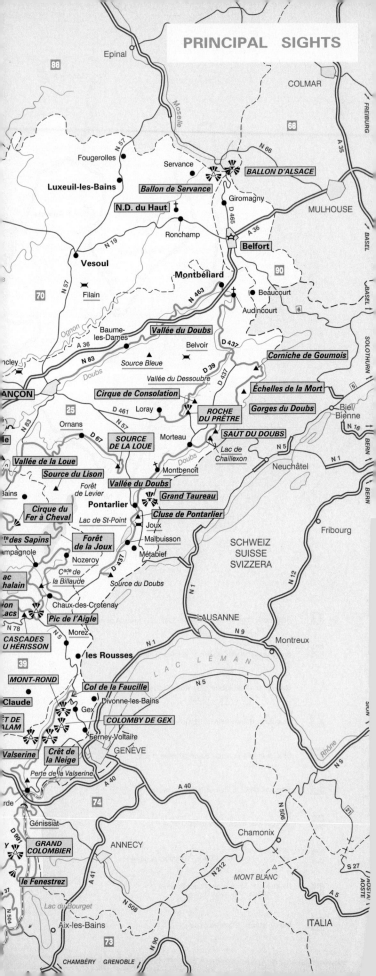

PRINCIPAL SIGHTS

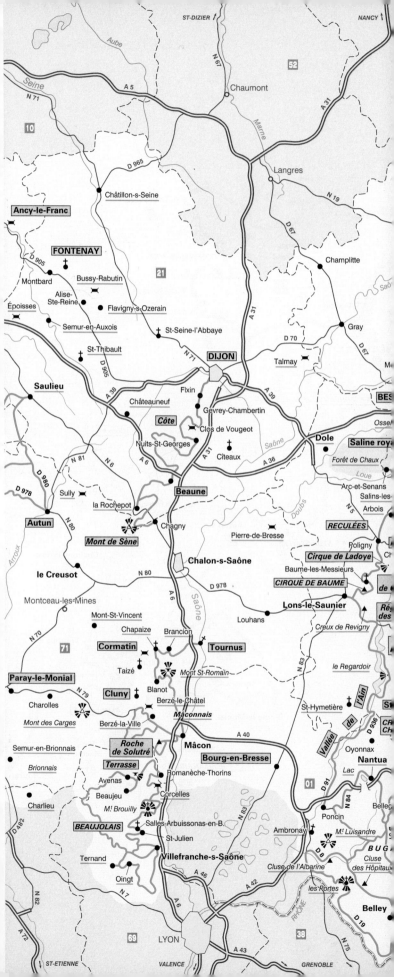

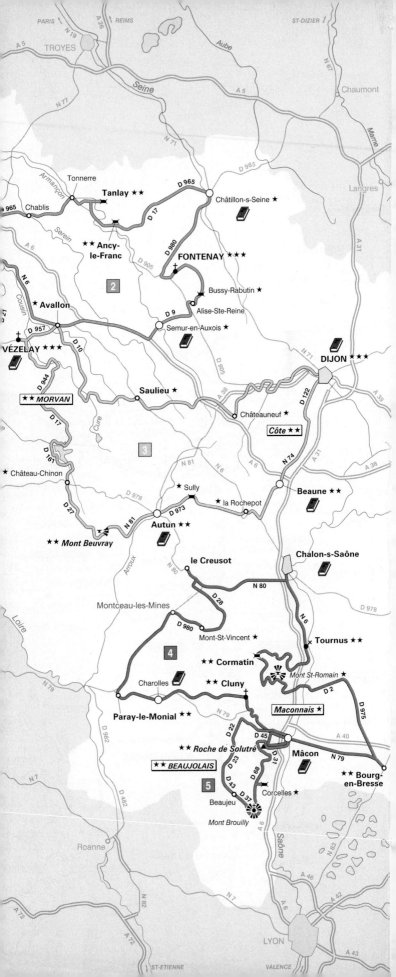

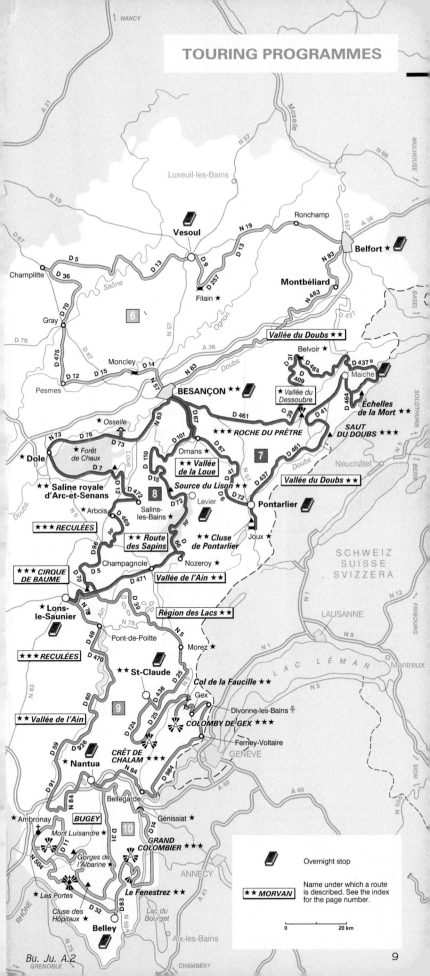

NANCY

A 31

MULHOUSE

Moselle

N 57

N 66

Luxeuil-les-Bains

N 19

Ronchamp

N 19

D 437

D 36

BASEL

Vesoul

N 19

D 13

N 83

Belfort ★

D 13

Champlitte

D 5

Montbéliard

D 36

Saône

D 9

N 463

Gray

D 70

Filain ★

D 257

D 431

6

Ognon

SOLOTHURN

D 475

D 67

Moncley

D 14

N 57

A 36

Vallée du Doubs ★★

Belvoir ★

D 31

Maiche

D 464

D 437 B

Pesmes

D 12

D 15

N 83

Doubs

Vallée du
Dessoubre

D 464

Échelles
de la Mort ★★

SOLOTHURN

Osselle

N 73

D 76

D 73

BESANÇON ★★★

D 67

D 461

D 39

D 41

SAUT
DU DOUBS ★★★

Dole ★

Forêt
de Chaux

D 7

Loue

D 110

D 101

Ornans

★★★ ROCHE DU PRÊTRE

D 461

Doubs

BERN

Saline royale
d'Arc-et-Senans

D 12

D 472

D 15

★★ Vallée
de la Loue

D 67

D 41

7

D 437

Vallée du Doubs ★★

Neuchâtel

N 5

Arbois

D 469

Source du Lison

D 72

D 6

Pontarlier

★★★ RECULÉES

D 96

RF

Salins-
les-Bains ★

8

D 72

Levier

N 57

RF

Route
des Sapins

★★ Cluse
de Pontarlier

Joux ★

SCHWEIZ
SUISSE
SVIZZERA

★★★ CIRQUE
DE BAUME

D 5

D 10

Champagnole

D 66

Nozeroy ★

D 471

Vallée de l'Ain ★★

N 1

LAUSANNE

Lons-
le-Saunier

N 78

Ain

D 39

Région des Lacs ★★

N 12

FRIBOURG

Pont-de-Poitte

N 78

N 5

Morez ★

LAC LÉMAN

Montreux

★★★ RECULÉES

D 470

★★ St-Claude

D 25

D 25

Col de la Faucille ★★

N 1

N 5

SION

D 60

9

D 436

Gex

Divonne-les-Bains

D 124

D 25

COLOMBY DE GEX ★★★

Ferney-Voltaire

N 504

★★ Vallée de l'Ain

D 936

D 984

GENÈVE

D 59

Nantua ★

CRÊT DE
CHALAM ★★★

N 84

N 504

N 84

Bellegarde

A 40

A 40

BUGEY

D 14

Génissiat ★

Ambronay ★

D 11

Mont Luisandre ★

D 31

GRAND
COLOMBIER ★★★

ANNECY

N 504

Gorges de
l'Albarine ★

RHÔNE

Les Portes ★

D 32

Le Fenestrez ★★

Lac du
Bourget

N 504

Cluse des
Hôpitaux ★

D 83

Belley

N 75

Aix-les-Bains

Legend

Overnight stop

★★ MORVAN — Name under which a route
is described. See the index
for the page number.

0   20 km

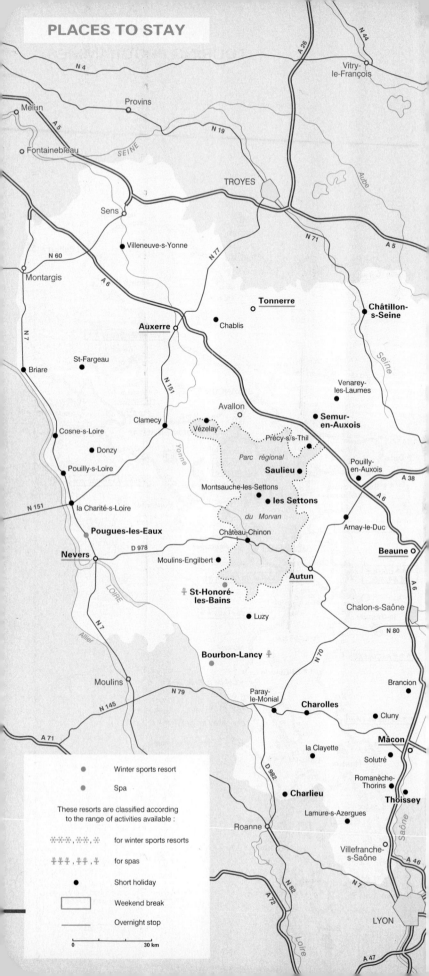

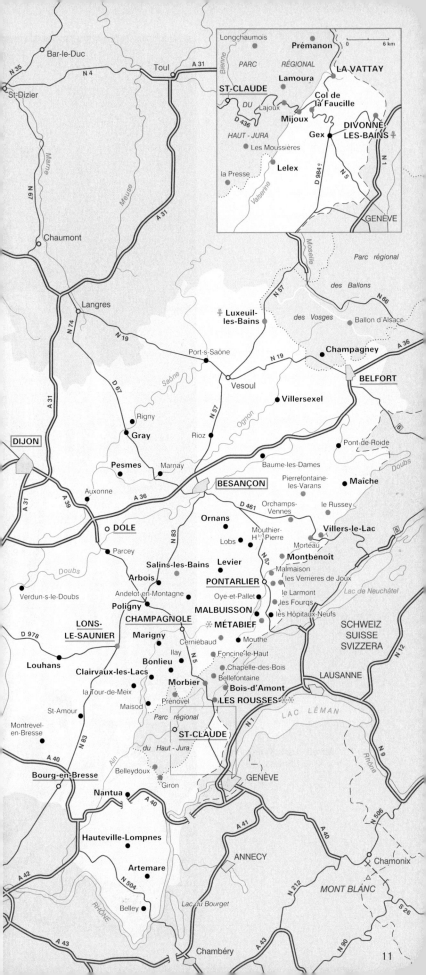

The splendour falls
on castle walls
And snowy summits
old in story:
The long light shakes
across the lakes,
And the wild cataract
leaps in glory.

Alfred, Lord Tennyson
The Princess (1847)

Cascade de l'Éventail

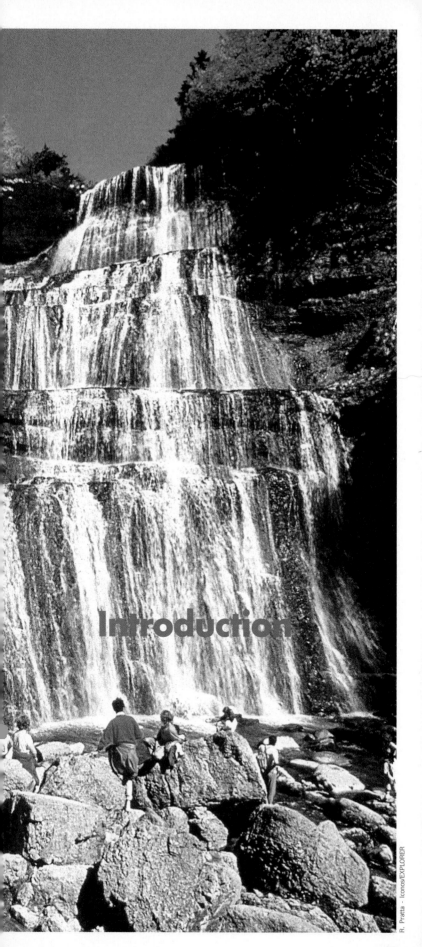

Introduction

Description of the region

The region described in this guide is not characterised by any particular geographical unity, as in the case of the Alps or the Paris basin, but comprises various types of physical relief:
– in the west, **Burgundy** can be divided into four basic areas: to the east, the wide river plains along the Saône valley; to the north and west, the fertile plains of the sedimentary basins forming Basse Bourgogne (the Auxerre and Chablis areas); at its heartland, the limestone plateaux terminating in escarpments to the east (the Arrière-Côte and Côte); and to the south, ancient granite massifs and uplands (the Morvan, the Charollais and the Mâconnais).
– in the east, the French **Jura** stretches across the Ain, Doubs and Jura *départements*, covering most of the old free province of Burgundy known as Franche-Comté. The 250km - 155 mile long Jura range runs from Rhine to Rhône, reaching a maximum width of 61km - 38 miles. Although the Jura range is only of medium height (highest peak: Crêt de la Neige 1 717m - 5 633ft), it has a striking relief, characterised by long parallel ridges and valleys running northeast-southwest and converging at either end. This pattern of folds steps down to an undulating plateau to the west, which rises again at around Montbéliard to meet the Vosges.

FORMATION OF THE LAND

Primary Era – Began about 600 million years ago. Modern France was entirely under water, until the tremendous "Hercynian fold" in the earth's crust pushed up a number of high mountain ranges: the Armorican Massif, the Massif Central, the Vosges, the Ardennes and the Morvan, formed of impermeable crystalline rocks (granite, gneiss, micaschist) mixed with rocks of volcanic origin (porphyry). The seas covering the Paris

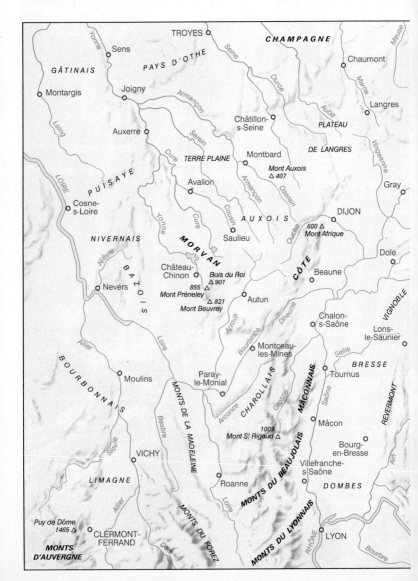

and Rhône basins were linked by a strait – the modern "threshold of Burgundy". Erosion by the elements gradually wore the Morvan heights down to their rocky base. A warm, humid climate gave rise to luxuriant vegetation, which was eventually buried under thick layers of alluvial deposits. Pressure slowly turned it into coal – the making of modern towns such as Autun and Blanzy.

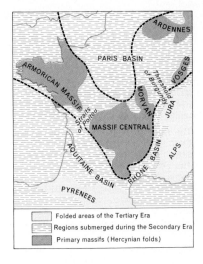

Folded areas of the Tertiary Era

Regions submerged during the Secondary Era

Primary massifs (Hercynian folds)

Secondary Era – Began about 200 million years ago. The seas flooded the Paris basin and the Jura region, covering even the highest land (Morvan, Beaujolais and Charollais) and depositing layers of sedimentary rocks – marl and limestone. The formation of such sedimentary rock strata was so prolific in the Jura in particular (some rock beds reach a thickness of about 1 300m - 4 300ft), that geologists have named the middle period of the secondary era, which lasted about 45 million years, the "Jurassic" period.

The waters then retreated from the high ground, and erosion once again wore away at the Morvan, reducing it in height by at least 1 000m - 3 280ft and washing away the marl and limestone deposits towards the centre of the Paris basin.

Tertiary Era – Began about 60 million years ago. The parallel rock strata of the Jura region were still covered with water (now the lakes of Biel, Neuchâtel and Geneva). The great Alpine folding movement forced the land upwards, causing the seas to fall back. The Massif Central was split; its eastern edge was pushed up to form a series of parallel folds – the uplands of the Autunois, Charollais, Mâconnais and Beaujolais regions.

Pressure during the Alpine-building period folded the Jura rock strata into their characteristic northeast-southwest crescent of ridges and valleys, curving between the Vosges and the Massif Central and sloping down towards the River Saône. Nearer the Alps, pressure folded the thick sedimentary layers into the Jura mountains. The western layers, not so thick, split along the faults formed by the movements of the earth's crust into a series of stepped plateaus. Not far from the slopes overlooking the Saône valley, a layer of salt formed – the resource of the later salt works.

Quaternary Era – Began about 2 million years ago. Erosion continued to shape the region into its present relief: ancient massifs (Morvan, Beaujolais); limestone plateaus (La Côte, l'Arrière Côte); sedimentary basins (Bazois, Terre-Plaine, Auxois); valleys (surrounding the Jura); and low-lying plains of subsidence (Saône valley). The quaternary era was marked by two significant events; the appearance of man, and coming of the Ice Age with its enormous glaciers, which invaded the Jurassic valleys from the Alps. Receding glaciers left in their wake a huge amount of debris, including glacial moraine, which blocked the drainage of water in many places, forming the Jurassic lakes.

THE REGIONS OF BURGUNDY

From the Auxois to the Beaujolais regions, from the River Saône to the River Loire, the many and varied regions which make up Burgundy have preserved their own particular appearance, economy and way of life.

The historical links which united them during the 15C have proved strong enough, however, for several common characteristics still to be apparent. Administrative divisions and modern economic demands may have caused a proportion of local activity to be moved to Paris, but the ties holding together the constituents of this province, of which Dijon is capital in more than name, remain unbroken.

The Alluvial Plains – The **Sénonais**, **Gâtinais** and **Puisaye** plains are situated on the northern borders of Burgundy. These are well-watered, fertile lands, rich in alluvial deposits, in which the forests and lakes provide a rich catch for hunters and anglers alike. The Sénonais is furthest to the north, and its varied and productive agriculture is reminiscent of the Brie region. The Gâtinais extends from Gien (in the Loire valley) to just north of Montargis and, apart from dairy cattle, its resources are somewhat limited, and it tends to identify more with the Paris region than with Burgundy. The Puisaye is quite similar to the Gâtinais in many ways, but it also produces fodder crops. The region is further distinguished by its abundant woodlands. The population is widely dispersed, and the isolated houses are often half-hidden among lines of trees.

The Nivernais – This region of plateaux and hills, essentially a crossroads, stretches away to the west of the Morvan massif and slopes gently down to the Loire valley.

To the west of Château-Chinon is the fertile, well-watered **Bazois** countryside. Cereal and fodder crops are cultivated on its slopes, while the lower lying land is given over to rich pasture for stock-breeding. This is where the white Charollais and Nivernais cattle are fattened for the Parisian meat market.

To the north of the Bazois stretches the hilly region of Clamecy and Donzy, with some peaks up to 450m - 1 476ft high, watered by a fairly dense network of rivers. The land is used for stock-breeding and crop farming.

From Nevers to Bonny the River Loire marks the boundary between the Nivernais and the Berry region. Stock-breeding pasture land alternates with wooded spurs.

Between Sancoins and Decize the boundary with the Bourbonnais region is not very clearly delimited. However, the architectural style of the farmhouses and châteaux indicates how strong the Bourbonnais influence is here.

Pouilly lies at the heart of a well-reputed vineyard which stretches over the hillsides overlooking the Loire valley.

The Morvan – In the aftermath of the great Alpine thrust, the edges of the great Morvan granite massif were broken up; erosion wore away at the softer limestone strata bordering the massif, scouring out a hollow surrounding it on three sides. This depression is surrounded in turn by limestone plateaux which tower at its outer edges. The Morvan is distinguished above all by its abundant forest cover and densely woven network of rivers.

Despite the extent of the forest, the countryside is essentially a mixed one; fields and meadows sectioned off by hedges form an ever shifting mosaic of greens, browns and yellows. There are few large towns in the Morvan. Instead hamlets are surprisingly far-flung. Morvan houses typically stand side by side with their farm buildings and stables. The isolation imposed on this region by its forests and relief have meant that the Morvan's economy has remained closed.

Nowadays, however, people's increasing mobility and a marked improvement in their standard of living have had a profound effect on the Morvan. The region is opening up to tourism and offers a number of possible holiday destinations for nature lovers in particular.

The Auxois – To the east of the Morvan lies the Auxois region, a rich and fertile land of lias, crisscrossed by many rivers, which is given over to pasture for stock-breeding. Rocky outcrops are occupied by fortified towns, such as Semur, Flavigny-sur-Ozerain and Mont-St-Jean, or ancient oppidums, such as Alésia on Mont Auxois. These isolated sentinels of the past watch over the roads and other communications routes.

The Charollais and the Brionnais – These regions of sweeping hillsides and plateaux, with superb rich pasture, are the home of the Charollais breed.

The Autun Basin – During the Primary Era, this depression was a vast lake, which was gradually filled in with the coal-bearing deposits and bituminous schists later to fuel the industrial development of this region. There are still a few spoil heaps around Autun, bearing witness to past industry.

The Dijonnais – The region around Dijon reunites all the characteristics of Burgundy's various regions in a striking synthesis. It is an area of limestone plateaux, isolated outcrops, rich pasture land, wide alluvial plain and "escarpments" covered with vineyards. Dijon, once the capital of the Duchy of Burgundy and now the regional capital, is the economic centre of the Châtillonnais, Haute-Bourgogne, the Côte, the Saône river plains, the Morvan and part of southern Burgundy. The Charollais and Mâconnais regions, however, are drawn more towards Lyon.

The Côte – This is the edge of the last slope of the "mountains" ("La Côte d'Or") overlooking the Saône plain. This escarpment was caused by the cracks which appeared as the Saône's alluvial plain subsided. Whereas the plateau of the hinterland, the Arrière-Côte, is given over to crops, woods and pasture land, the eastern slope is covered with vines. The villages are located at the heart of the vineyards, at the mouths of the combes which lead back into the hinterland. They are sited low enough to benefit from the abundant supply of spring water commonly found at the foot of such slopes.

The wine growers have large, comfortable houses, vertical in construction; the wine vats and storerooms are on the ground floor, while the living quarters are on the first floor. An outside staircase protected by a roof leads from ground to first floor level. Certain criteria determine on what kind of land the vineyards are sited: limestone warms up quickly in the spring; slopes should be sheltered and facing in the right direction to benefit from enough sun.

At the foot of the Côte, ashlar and marble are worked in the quarries of Comblanchien and Corgoloin.

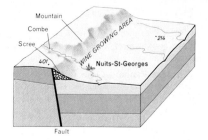

La Côte-d'Or

The Mâconnais – This is where the mountain range formed by the Côte d'Or extends southwards. But this region is different in that the steep faces of the escarpment are turned towards the interior, whereas along the Côte d'Or they overlook the valley of the Saône. This is a region of vine-covered hillsides or stock-breeding pasture land. The plains to the south of Chalon are highly productive thanks to the Grosne valley. Cereal crops, beet and vegetables are cultivated and poultry is bred here, as in the Bresse region.

The Saône Valley – Major communications routes run through this valley which stretches along the foot of limestone cliffs. The alluvial river plains of the Saône, which are frequently flooded during winter, are covered with rich pastures and arable land.

In addition to traditional wheat, beet and potato crops, there are now market gardens and fields of maize, tobacco and oilseed.

The Saône valley is in full economic expansion. Industrial activity is centred mainly in Chalon and Tournus. It is hoped that the Saône will become a major shipping route from the Rhine to the Rhone, now that the Mâcon penstock is operational.

The Bresse – The Bresse plain, in which the soil is composed of clay and marl, stretches from the Saône to the foothills of the Jura, the Revermont. Numerous streams cut

across the rolling countryside, which is dotted with spinneys. The farmhouses, often standing in solitary splendour in the middle of the fields, look pretty much the same as they always did, although the cob walls and thatched roofs have gradually given way to bricks and tiles. The houses are low, with a wide overhanging roof for drying maize and roofs featuring as often as not a Saracen chimney *(qv)*. Inside, there

Farmhouse in Saint-Trivier-de-Courtes

is the traditional "stove room". The land is used mainly for stock breeding: cattle, pigs and above all poultry, of a quality which has made Bresse poultry highly sought after by gourmets.

The Burgundy Plateaux – From the northern edge of the Morvan to the Langres plateau and from Auxerre to Dijon stretches a region of limestone plateaux forming the real heartland of Burgundy. In fact, this region is the threshold to Burgundy and the point of contact between the Seine and Saône basins, and between the Vosges and the Morvan. The state of Burgundy came into being at this junction of the very different regions it was to take under its control.

The plateaux rise to a relatively low altitude (400-500m - 1 312-1 640ft) sloping gently to the northwest but dropping abruptly in the southeast. Their dry appearance contrasts with the much greener, richer one of the valleys of the rivers which intersect them; the Yonne, Serein and Armançon. The plateaux are, from west to east, the Auxerrois, the Tonnerrois and the Châtillonnais.

The **Auxerrois** is a rocky plateau, split across by numerous valleys, in which the limestone can often be seen dazzling white. The sunny slopes have lent themselves to the cultivation of vines, in the region of Chablis, Auxerre and Irancy, and cherry trees.

The **Tonnerrois** plateau has similar characteristics to that of Langres, but it is at a lower altitude and has a climate not unlike that of the Paris basin.

The **Châtillonnais** is a series of monotonous plateaux, for the most part bare with the occasional rocky outcrop or dry river valley. Soil here is permeable. Water seeps down into the limestone surface and resurfaces in the form of resurgent springs *(douix)*, such as the Seine at Châtillon. There is a whole network of streams underground.

These plateaux used to be covered almost entirely by forests. Monks from the abbeys of Molesmes, St-Seine, Fontenay and Clairvaux were active in clearing areas of them. Later on, the iron ore deposits were exploited, and numerous forges, foundries and nail works were in evidence in the 18C.

Nowadays, reafforestation is being officially coordinated. Coniferous forests (larch, black pine, Norwegian pine, silver pine and spruce) stand side by side with deciduous ones (oak, beech, elm and ash), and the timber industry plays an important role in the local economy.

THE REGIONS OF THE JURA

From the majestic outline of the mountains to the natural beauty of the forests, lakes and rivers and the more muted colours of the hillsides, the Jura encompasses a wide variety of landscapes.

The Jura Range – From the Swiss plain the Jura appears as a high wall, a formidable unbroken fortified barrier across the horizon. From the crest, however, valleys and meadows give the countryside a less harsh appearance. Lake Geneva and the alps of Berne and Savoy can be seen in the distance. Poets such as Ruskin, Goethe and Lamartine have sung of the splendour of this sight. Each valley constitutes a little world of its own, in which the inhabitants congregate near springs, or on the banks of rivers or lakes. The **meadows**, on which glaciers deposited a layer of clay, contrast with the bare limestone, which looks almost like a desert in places. In between the meadows here and there are fields of crops (barley, rye, oats and potatoes). But at this altitude, winter lasts a long time, so cereals ripen fairly late and fruit trees are few and far between.

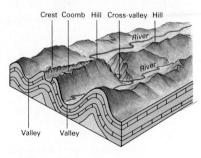

Diagrammatic section of a Jurassic fold
The parallel valleys (**vals**) are separated by the hills (**monts**) . The slashes made by erosion on the flanks of the hills form the **ruz** (a term derived from the name Val de Ruz). The cross-valley (**cluse**) cuts across the hill, connecting two valleys. The coomb (**combe**) runs longitudinally along the top of a hill; its escarped edges are called crests (**crêts**).

Besides the traditional "**chalets**" (wooden buildings on a stone foundation) scattered across the Alpine meadows, there are "**mountain houses**" which consist of living quarters, stable and barn all under the same roof. These houses are squat and compact; they are built close to the ground the better to shut out the wind. The low, thick stone walls have tiny windows; those on the sides exposed to wind and snow are protected by wooden slats known as *tavaillons*. Roofing materials are the tiles typical of the Franche-Comté or more commonly steel sheeting. The living quarters occupy the ground floor: the *houteau*, or kitchen, in which there is almost always a huge fireplace, and the *poêle*, a vast heated room used as a bedroom or, on special occasions, a dining room. The stable next door is linked to the house so that it can be entered without having to go outside. The barn is on the first floor and has a special opening through which fodder can be thrown down into the stable below. The barn can also be accessed from outside up a short steep slope.

Mountain house

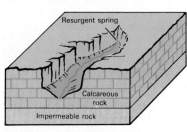

A "Reculée"

The Jura Plateaux – The best view of the Jura plateaux is from the summit called the Pic de l'Aigle. They drop down in steps of ever decreasing altitude (900-400m - 2 953-1 312ft) from Pontarlier to Besançon before reaching the Bresse region and Burgundy itself. To the north, they extend as far as the Belfort Gap, or "Trouée de Belfort", between the Jura and Vosges mountain ranges, which acts as the threshold to Burgundy. The rocky nature of these plateaux might at times appear rather monotonous, but they have their fair share of interesting natural features nonetheless. Most notable of these are the so-called "**Reculées**" *(qv)*, blind valleys ending at the foot of a cliff. Other impressive sights awaiting the visitor include gorges, river valleys, waterfalls, lakes, caves and forests. The typical dwelling of the plateaux shares similarities with that of the mountains, not least the accommodation of man and beast under the same roof. However, these houses are usually taller and have a rectangular roof with edges that slope steeply downwards, covered in the tiles typical of the Franche-Comté or else ordinary red tiles.

Typical Jura plateau dwelling

Two partition walls divide the ground floor interior lengthwise to separate the living quarters from the stable by the barn in between. The barn can be entered through a side door with a semi-circular arch. The main rooms are as above, but the first floor is often also given over to bedrooms.

The "Vignoble" – The road from Besançon to Bourg-en-Bresse, leading between the rivers Doubs and Ain, runs along the continuous slope on the western rim of the Jura plateaux, part of the Revermont. The vines cultivated here for centuries have earned the region its local name, the "Vignoble" (vineyard). It is also known as the "Bon Pays" (good land) in reference presumably to the wealth brought to the region by the wine industry.

Wine-grower's house in the Jura "Vignoble"

CAVES

Caves are common feature of the Jura plateaux, where they frequently occur at the foot of the steep rocky cliffs enclosing a *reculée (qv)*. They offer visitors to the region a chance to explore an underground world full of caverns, crystal clear subterranean rivers, intricate rock formations unknown at ground level and prehistoric deposits indicating the presence of early man.

Caves in the Jura region which have been adapted to accommodate visitors include the Grotte de Baume, with its great high chambers, the Grotte de la Glacière, frozen all year round, the Grottes des Moidons (concretions), Grottes d'Osselle (multiple columns), Grotte des Planches (good examples of features produced by limestone erosion) and the Gouffre de Poudrey (huge caved in gallery). A visit to these caves also makes people aware of the dangers of water pollution and the difficulties of protecting these fragile environments.

Underground rivers and limestone erosion – Jurassic rivers do not always flow exclusively at ground level. As in any limestone region, rain water, charged with carbonic acid, infiltrates the rock and dissolves the carbonate of lime, creating networks of cracks and fissures within and between the rock strata. The action of the carbonic acid and erosion by the water itself enlarges existing fissures to form subterranean galleries, wells

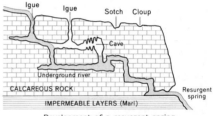
Development of a resurgent spring

and chimneys. The water collects along these underground courses, to emerge at ground level in the form of a spring, such as the source of the Cuisance in the Reculée des Planches. In some cases, subterranean rivers are formed by an existing river disappearing into a chasm at ground level (known locally as a *"perte"*), flowing for a stretch underground and then reappearing at ground level as a **resurgent spring** further downstream, as is the case with the rivers Loue and Lison. This difference in the original water supply explains why, during dry seasons, resurgent springs do not dry up entirely, whereas springs do, since their water supply is an underground lake, the level of which may sink in the absence of rain water until it is blocked by naturally formed dams, or *gours*, in the cave.

Chasms are formed either by the continued hollowing out of a depression at ground level until it collapses into a cave below, or by the caving in of the roof of the cave itself, as it is eroded upwards by the dissolution of the limestone in the cave walls.

Caves – As it circulates underground, water deposits the lime with which it has become charged, building up concretions of fantastic shapes, which seem to defy the laws of gravity. In some caverns, the seeping waters deposit calcite (carbonate of lime) to form pendants, pyramids and draperies. The best known formations of this type are stalactites, stalagmites and eccentrics.

Stalactites are formed on the cave roof, as every droplet of water seeping through to the ceiling deposits some of the calcite with which it is charged before dripping off. The concretion builds up slowly, layer by layer, as the drops are attracted and run down its length, depositing particles before falling.

Stalagmites are formed in the same way, but rising from the cave floor towards the roof. Drops of water dripping from the roof onto the same place on the floor below deposit the calcite particles they are carrying, which build up into a candle-like shape. This rises towards the stalactite above, with which it eventually joins to form a pillar linking the cave floor with the roof.

Concretions like these form very slowly indeed; the rate of growth in a temperate climate is about 1cm-half an inch every 100 years.

Eccentrics are very delicate protruberances, formed by crystallisation, which seldom exceed 20cm-8in in length. They emerge at any angle, seeming to disregard the laws of gravity, either as slender spikes or in the shape of small translucent fans.

VINEYARDS

Burgundy

While the name Burgundy conjures up masterpieces of the Middle Ages and the Renaissance for art lovers, it evokes good wine to all gourmets. The wines of Burgundy are some of the finest in the world and their fame is universal.

The history of Burgundy wine – The cultivation of vines was introduced to the region by the Romans and spread rapidly. Wine from Burgundy was quick to win accolade, a historical fact confirmed by the names of certain vineyards (Vosne-Romanée) which recall the popularity of the wines with the Roman prefects of the province of Maxima Sequanorum.

In the 12C, Cistercian monks built up the vineyards, in particular the famous "Clos de Vougeot". The local historian, Claude Courtépée, records that in 1359 Jean de Bussières, the Cistercian abbot, made a gift of 30 barrels of wine from the Clos de Vougeot vineyards to Pope Gregory XI. The grateful pope did not forget this handsome gift and made the abbot cardinal four years later.

In the 15C the Dukes of Burgundy took to styling themselves "lords of the best wines in Christendom" and supplying their wine to royalty. Louis XIV is known to have contributed to the fame of Côte de Nuits, while Madame de Pompadour favoured Romanée Conti, and Napoleon Chambertin.

In the 18C, the wine trade began to evolve; the first commercial warehouses opened at Beaune, Nuits-St-Georges and Dijon, sending representatives all over France and abroad (Britain, Belgium, Scandinavia, Switzerland, Germany) charged with the mission of finding new markets for Burgundy wines.

One of the enemies of the vine is a small aphid from America, phylloxera, which made an appearance in the Gard *département* in 1863. In 1878, it was found at Meursault and within a short time it had completely ravaged all the Burgundy vineyards, ruining all the local wine-producers. Luckily, the disaster was checked by grafting French vines onto American root stock, resistant to phylloxera, enabling the Burgundy vineyards gradually to be reconstituted without impairing the quality of their wines.

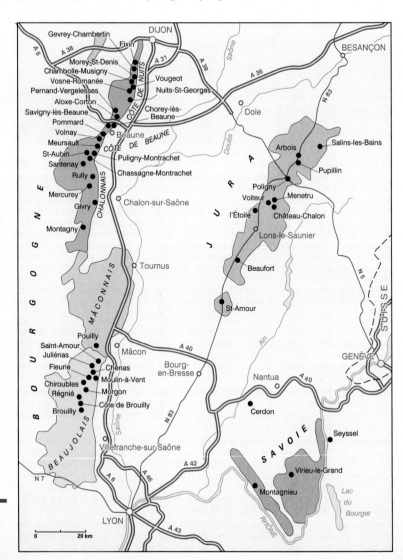

Distribution of vineyards – 37 500ha - 15 172 acres of vineyards producing officially registered vintages are to be found in the Yonne, Nièvre, Côte-d'Or, Saône-et-Loire and Rhône *départements*. Average annual production of high quality wines is about 1 800 000hl - 40 000 000 gallons.

In the Yonne, the region of **Chablis** produces some excellent crisp, dry white wines, and the hillsides of the Auxerrois some pleasant rosés and reds **(Irancy, Coulanges-la-Vineuse)**. Well-known wines such as **Pouilly-Fumé** come from Pouilly-sur-Loire in Nièvre. These wines have a flinty taste not unlike that of the neighbouring Sancerre wines. In the **Côte d'Or** highly reputed vineyards stretch from Dijon to Santenay. The **Côte de Nuits** produces almost exclusively top vintage red wines, some of the most famous of which are **Gevrey-Chambertin, Morey-St-Denis, Chambolle-Musigny, Vougeot, Vosne-Romanée, Nuits-St-Georges**. The **Côte de Beaune** wines include both magnificent reds, such as **Aloxe-Corton, Savigny-lès-Beaune, Pommard** and **Volnay**, and very fine whites, such as **Corton-Charlemagne, Meursault, Puligny-Montrachet, Chassagne-Montrachet.**

In Saône-et-Loire, the Mercurey region (Côte Chalonnaise) produces high quality red **(Givry, Rully)** and white wines **(Rully-Montagny)**, while the Mâconnais is justly proud of its **Pouilly-Fuissé**, which many consider to be one of the greatest white wines of France.

What makes good wine – The quality of a wine depends on grape variety *(cépage)*, and the type of soil and climate in which the vines grow. The work put in by the wine-grower also affects the final result.

Grape varieties – All the great red Burgundy wines are made from the **Pinot Noir**, long regarded as the "aristocrat" of grapes. It was already highly prized at the time of the Great Dukes, as illustrated by an ordinance issued by Philip the Bold in 1395 defending it against the more common Gamay. The Pinot Noir is native to Burgundy but has been successfully cultivated in Switzerland, and even in South Africa, in Cape Province. The juice of the Pinot Noir grape is colourless, and a special *vinification* (process for turning the grapes into wine) produces Champagne.

The **Chardonnay** grape is to white wines what the Pinot Noir is to red. It makes all the great white wines of the Côte d'Or (Montrachet-Meursault), the famous vintages of the Côte Chalonnaise (Rully), of the Mâconnais where it grows best (Pouilly-Fuissé) and the wines of Chablis (where it is known as the "Beaunois" grape).

Other grape varieties include the Aligoté, which has been cultivated for centuries in Burgundy, as it grows in the areas where the Pinot Noir and Chardonnay grapes do not thrive, and which produces white wines which are popular, even if they do not have quite the same reputation for character and quality as those from the more famous vineyards. These are the wines that are combined with blackcurrant liqueur *(cassis)* to make the popular French *apéritif* known as **"kir"** after the man who is credited with its invention, a mayor of Dijon, Canon Kir.

Soil – The soil type plays an important role in allowing the particular characteristics of the vines to develop, establish themselves and finally to come to fruition. It is in these dry, stony soils, which are well-drained and easily warmed by the sun, that vines grow best. Limestone soils produce wines with rich bouquets and a high alcohol content, which can be laid down for many years (Côte de Nuits, Côte de Beaune), while mixed soils of silicas, limestone and clay yield lighter wines (Chablis).

Climate – The general climate prevailing in Burgundy is due to its setting in a temperate zone, but one where the possibility of winter frosts cannot be excluded, giving rise to a number of factors which must be taken into consideration by the wine-grower for the best results. Burgundy vineyards are usually laid out in terraces on the hillsides at altitudes of between 200-500m - 656-1 640ft. They seem to thrive best when facing southeast, in the case of the Chablis vineyards, southwest, in the case of those at Pouilly-sur-Loire, eastsoutheast for the Côte d'Or (Côte de Nuits and Côte de Beaune) and east and south for the Côte Chalonnaise and the Mâconnais. In each village, the vineyards are divided into *climats*, or sections, and the names of the best-situated sections, which should normally produce the best wines, have the honour of being added to the name of the village: thus, Beaune-Clos des Mouches. Some of the *climats* have earned such an excellent reputation over the years that their name alone suffices to identify them: Chambertin, Musigny, Clos de Vougeot and Richebourg.

Beaujolais wine – The Beaujolais vineyards cover an area 60km - 37 miles long and 12km - 7.5 miles wide from the Mâcon escarpment to the north to the Azergues valley to the south. This area is about 22 500ha - 54 225 miles and yields an average of 1 250 000hl - 27 375 000 gallons of wine a year. The majority of these (99%) are red, exclusively from the **Gamay** grape. Beaujolais wines are divided into three categories: the ten best (and most famous) vintages, or *crus*; **Beaujolais-Villages**; and **Beaujolais or Beaujolais supérieurs**.

Top of the list of *crus* is **Moulin-à-Vent**, an elegant wine with plenty of substance, which can be kept for 5-10 years, closely followed by **Morgon** with its fine bouquet, which has often been described as the "Beaujolais most like a Burgundy". Firm and fruity **Juliénas**, well-rounded **Chénas**, classy **Fleurie** and **Côte de Brouilly** all have a keen following, while the fresh and lively **Saint-Amour, Chiroubles** (which the French consider to be a "feminine" wine), **Brouilly** and **Régnié-Durette** (the baby of the *crus*, having been promoted in 1988) should be drunk while quite young.

Wines of the Beaujolais-Villages are delicious, and their fruity flavour is at its best after about a year in the bottle. Beaujolais or Beaujolais supérieurs (the only difference being that the latter have a slightly higher alcohol content) are best drunk when very young and, unusually for a red wine, when slightly chilled.

Various local wine fraternities, such as the "Compagnons de Beaujolais" or the "Gosiers secs (dry throats) de Clochemerle", voluntarily take it upon themselves to spread the good reputation of these wines abroad.

Jura

The vineyards of the old Franche-Comté extend southwest of Salins, along a narrow strip of land 5km - 3 miles wide, covering the limestone and mixed clay and limestone slopes of the western edge of the Jura. Four vintages are produced from these vineyards: **Arbois**, the most famous, **Château-Chalon**, **Étoile** and those of the **Côtes du Jura** *appellation*, which includes local wines such as Poligny and Arlay (which are the principal ones). Wine-growers have their work cut out in this region, where they regularly have to carry soil that has been washed down the hillside back to their vineyards.

The major annual Jura wine festival is held in Arbois *(qv)* – the "Fête du Biou" *(see the Calendar of Events at the end of the guide).*

Château-Chalon vineyards

Jura wines – These can have quite knee-buckling effects, which does not however prevent local followers of Bacchus from singing their praises thus: "Du vin d'Arbois, Plus on en boit, Plus on va droit" (Wine of Arbois, the more of it you drink, the straighter you walk). Presumably one becomes hardened to their effect with regular consumption...

Grape varieties – The grape varieties cultivated in the Jura include the Trousseau, from which red wines are made, the Poulsard, for rosé wines, the Chardonnay, for white wines, and the Savagnin, from which the famous Vin Jaune of the Jura is made.

Red wines are produced in small quantities and are fresh and fruity when young, developing a subtle, characteristic bouquet with age. The best local red wines are said to come from Pupillin. The most famous **rosé wines** come from Arbois and Pupillin. With age, the wines take on a pretty colour, like that of an onion skin. These lively but not over-powering wines have a pleasant fruity flavour. Local **white wines** are dry, yet supple, and fairly heady. They are produced essentially in the Arbois and Étoile regions. They are excellent drunk on their own as well as with food. The Jura also produces some **sparkling** wines, both white (Étoile, Arbois, Côtes du Jura) and rosé (Arbois, Côtes du Jura).

Good years for Jura wines: 1976, '79, '82, '83, '85, '88, '89, '90, '92.

Vin jaune is a speciality of the Jura region (Château-Chalon and Arbois), made from the Savagnin grape only. The wine is left to age in barrels for 6-10 years, where it begins to oxidise and acquires its characteristic deep yellow colour and distinctive bouquet and flavour beneath a film of yeasts which has formed over its surface (rather like the production of sherry). A good vintage can be kept for over a century. Vin jaune is relatively rare and expensive, and a degree of circumspection is required when choosing what to drink it with, because of its strong flavour (which has been likened to hazelnuts). It is particularly good drunk at room temperature with another speciality of the Jura region, Comté cheese.

Vin de paille, or so-called straw wine, also particular to the Jura region, earns its name from the fact that the almost over-ripe grapes are dried on a bed of straw for a couple of months before being pressed. This produces a strong, sweet dessert wine, which is however quite rare (it takes about 100kg - 220lb grapes to produce 18l - 4 gallons of vin de paille!) and therefore expensive.

Macvin is another Jura dessert wine, made from grape must blended with Franche-Comté eau-de-vie, and it can reach up to 16-20 per cent alcohol content. It is usually drunk chilled as an *apéritif.*

Red and rosé **Bugey wines** are light and fruity, but it is the white Bugey wines which are the best. Particularly good examples of these are Roussette and Seyssel, followed by more rare wines such as Virieu or Montagnieu. This region also produces some sparkling wines, for example Seyssel and Cerdon.

Use the Principal Sights Map to plan an itinerary.

FOREST

In Burgundy and the Jura, an area of 1 500 000ha - 3 615 000 acres is covered by forest; 1 000 000ha - 2 410 000 acres in Burgundy (about 30% of its total area) and 500 000ha - 1 205 000 acres in the Jura (about 40% of its total area). This is a degree of forest cover well above the average for France (25%).

Vegetation – Altitude affects the distribution of the different types of tree in the forest. Deciduous trees generally give way to conifers at about 800m - 2 624ft, although this can vary according to the amount of sunlight to which the slope is exposed. Beeches predominate between 500-800m - 1 640-2 624ft. Higher up are the magnificent evergreen forests of the Joux *(qv)*, and above 1 000m - 3 281ft, forests of spruce alternating with wooded upland pastures.

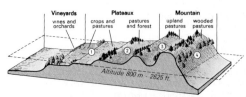

Vegetation at different altitudes
① Oak and beech trees – ② Conifers – ③ Spruces
④ Deciduous forest and chestnut trees

Trees – The various kinds of tree need their own particular conditions of light, temperature, humidity and soil type in which to grow. Deciduous trees lose their leaves every autumn, and grow new ones in the spring. The main trees in this group are beech and oak, and to a lesser extent ash, maple, cherry, elm and birch.

Conifers have thin, needle-like leaves which do not all die and fall from the tree at the same time, but a few at a time throughout the year. The sap of such trees is resinous, and they bear cones as fruit. Pines, firs, cypresses and spruce make up this group, and also larch, one of the few coniferous trees to lose its leaves in winter.

Spruce	Fir	Beech

Spruce – This is exclusively a mountain tree, which grows best on north-facing slopes. It has a pointed top shaped like a spindle and a bushy appearance, with downward curving branches reminiscent of spaniels' tails. The chocolate-brown bark becomes deeply cracked with age. The dark green needles are rounded and sharp and grow all the way round the branches and twigs. The cones hang below the branches, and when they are ripe their scales separate to release the seeds. Later, the cones themselves drop to the ground.

Timber from spruces is used mainly for roof beams and musical instruments.

Fir – This has a broad top, flattened into a "stork's nest" in older trees. The bark remains a darkish grey colour, with blisters of resin here and there. The cones stand upright on the branches, rather like candles, and scatter their seeds when ripe by disintegrating on the branch. The needles are soft and grow in rows along the branches, like the teeth of a comb. They are a paler green colour on their undersides, which have a double white line marking (hence the name "silver fir"). Fir trees are found on the deeply folded ridges of the mountain range.

Beech – This tall tree is easily recognised by its trunk, which is generally cylindrical with grey and white bark, and its regularly shaped, slightly wavy, thin, oval leaves. A beech tree can grow up to 1 700m - 5 577ft tall and live for 150 years. It grows best on well-watered slopes. In the autumn it bears beechnuts, which are quite oily. The beech tree occupies a special place in the forest of the Jura. Its timber is used primarily for industry and handicrafts.

Other types of tree – The **larch** can be found on the sunnier slopes. It has small cones, and its delicate pale green foliage does not cast so much shade that grass is unable to grow. The **Norway pine,** with its tall, slender trunk, has bunches of 2-5 needles growing together, held together by a scaly sheath, and cones with hard scales.

The elegant **birch**, with its slender trunk, trembling leaves and white bark which comes off in shavings, thrives in moist soil. It provides excellent firewood. The **oak** is a beautiful tree which can grow up to 30m - 98ft tall. Oak wood is valued highly by carpenters, and oak bark by tanners. Finally, the **durmast oak**, or white or truffle oak, grows well in the dry conditions of the grassy, limestone "garides". It can be found growing in copses above the vineyards, where its typically thick trunk is protected by a deeply ridged bark which sheds itself in square-shaped chunks.

The Jura forest

Nowadays, the forest cover is spreading of its own accord over all the areas abandoned by man. It is also gaining ground thanks to a deliberate policy of reforestation. The forest covers 42% of the land in this region. Deciduous trees (such as oak, beech, wild cherry, ash, maple) grow in the plains and at the level of the lowest plateau, where they have been nurtured by foresters for decades. Conifers (such as fir and spruce) are cultivated over-weeningly from the second plateau upwards.

State-owned and larger private forests have been organised so that the quantity of wood cut down every year matches new growth. Lines are marked out to divide the forest into numbered parcels of land. The area to be cut down is defined as early as June. The healthy trees are marked by a round sign (and the letters AF for "administration forestière"), while dried out, damaged or uprooted trees – dead wood – are given a different marking.

In parish forests, the trees destined for firewood are divided by local councils into lots which residents have the right to cut down; these lots are allocated by head count or number of fireplaces per home (very occasionally they are given out according to the size of the roof of the house, which is quite considerable in some of the villages of the Jura). Another possibility is that the wood is sold in its entirety by the national forestry office and the profit given to the parish. In times gone by, the sale of the wood made enough money to cover the residents' taxes in some parishes. Lots used to be larger, as there were fewer people sharing them; naturally, the arrival of new residents in the area was badly viewed by the local people. In state forests, virtually all the timber is sold in lots before the trees have been felled.

The exploitation of the forest in this way is subject to tight controls. The use of the State symbol in marking out the forests is protected by law in the same way as bank notes.

The Burgundy forest

There are forests scattered all over the province of Burgundy, but they are most extensive on the Châtillonnais, Tonnerrois and Sénonais plateaux to the north, in the Morvan and on the Nivernais plateau in central Burgundy, and around Charolles, Cluny and Mâcon to the south. The main timber areas are the forest of Othe, Châtillon, Bertranges, Planoise and St-Prix.

In the Morvan the forest is impressive for the sheer area it covers – about 137 000ha - 338 540 acres – more than 50% of some parishes. The most common trees are beech, oak, hornbeam and birch. The forests of the Morvan were exploited by monks from the 10C onwards. In the 17 and 18C, the wood was floated down to Paris to be used as firewood, or converted into charcoal where it was felled. Nowadays, the Morvan has a good reputation for the quality of the wood from its conifers. Tall stands of spruce and fir are to be found particularly round Haut-Folin, and, for the last twenty or so years, the Douglas fir has been increasingly used in replanting schemes.

The alluvial land along the banks of the Saône is covered with oak forests (Auxonne, Seurre and Chalon regions) which yield high quality timber, as does the magnificent oak forest of the Nivernais plateau. Large areas of the Côte have been replanted as broad-leaved forests, such as the Châtillon beech woods, or as plantations of black Austrian and Scots pines.

Several large industries are dependent on forestry: **wood distilling** and **charcoal making** (factories in Leuglay and Prémery) for the production of charcoal, acetic acid, methylene and their by-products; **sawmills;** manufacturers of veneer and chipboard (at Auxerre, St-Usage, Prisse-lès-Mâcon) and so on. In addition, Burgundy produces the largest number of young trees of any region in France in the tree nurseries near St-Florentin in the Yonne and Leuglay in the Côte d'Or which supply the French and European markets.

Traditional industries

There are many traditional industries in Burgundy and the Jura besides wine-growing *(see Vineyards above)*. The rich, fertile terrain of Burgundy and the pastureland of the old Franche-Comté make these ideal regions for raising cattle. Timber *(see Forest above)* and metallurgy industries also play an important role in the local economy. In the Jura, cheese-making, precious stones and diamonds, clock and watch-making and salt industries have evolved.

Stock-breeding and the dairy industry in the Jura

Country life – During the summer months, there are many traditional scenes of country life to be seen in the Jura. On the plateau, each farmer leads his herd to a meadow *("châtenage")* enclosed by a dry stone wall or a picturesque fence of pine slats. At set times of the day the herd heads for the drinking troughs in the meadow, the village or the farm. The animals are milked in the meadow itself, if the herd is spending the summer outside, without returning to the cattle sheds.

Cattle are still put out to graze on mountain pastures higher up, following traditional Alpine farming methods. The beasts are led up to their summer pastures by a shepherd in early June. These are located above 1 300m - 4 265ft, where the mixed pasture and forest gives way to the bare mountain peaks. Most of the livestock's nourishment comes from the pastures, which are cultivated using traditional, extensive agricultural methods. Since stock-breeding and dairy farming are the main sources of income for the region, farmers select their livestock with great care, with a view to improving the quality of their herd and its production. Local agricultural associations have been set up with this in mind, such as that at Morteau founded in 1862. Even now, there are annual competitions in each canton of the Haut-Doubs which bring together 300-400 cattle selected among the best.

Cheese, the pride and joy of the Jura

This is a direct product of the significant amount of stock-breeding there is in Jura, and the dairy industry represents a major proportion of the region's economy. This used to be a family industry, which evolved in step with that of stock-breeding during the 19C. It grew more refined with more rigorous selection of stock, rationalisation of working methods, modernisation of equipment and by professional organisation of the dairy industry from family cooperatives to associations and finally to companies. Nowadays, a professional cheese-maker will usually rent a cheese dairy *("fruitière")* in one of the villages, buy in his milk and sell the finished product on; warehouses for maturing cheese have been set up in larger towns and cities.

Cooperative cheese dairies – The production of Comté Gruyère cheese is one of the major industries on which the economy of this region depends. This production is based on the *"fruitière"*, or cooperative cheese dairy, formed by the milk producers of one or more villages. This is one of the oldest and most traditional features of life in the Jura. A cooperatively made cheese, *"froumaige de fructères" (fromage de fruitière)*, was being produced in the Doubs uplands in as early as 1264. Cooperative production was essential in areas where adverse weather conditions frequently made travelling difficult, if not impossible during winter. The number of cows per producer is tending to increase (10 to 20, and sometimes more), and the amount of milk produced by each cow is almost 4 000l - 876 gallons on average for every 300 days lactation. It takes 600l - 131 gallons of milk to make a 48kg - 105lb Comté Gruyère cheese.

At milking time, you still see women, children and the occasional man heading towards the cooperative dairy, carrying their milk in buckets, milk-cans, on the back of a donkey, in hand-carts or dog-carts, or even using more up-to-date means such as trailers pulled by tractors or motorcycles, or in small vans. In times gone by, the very basic modes of transport limited the dairy's catchment area and consequently the number of members of the cooperative, which was never more than fifty. Nowadays, however, the system for collecting milk has tended to favour larger cheese dairies, leaving the smaller ones to decline in numbers. Nonetheless, the traditional twice daily milk delivery has to survive, as it is fundamental to a certain quality of cheese. The **Poligny** dairy education centre (Centre d'enseignement laitier) promotes this kind of dairy production. Tourists can visit one of the 500 Comté chalets.

How Comté cheese is made – "Comté" is a registered product subject to quality control. The cheese is made from the milk of Montbéliard stock or red and white cows from the east of France, which have been fed exclusively on grass and hay. The milk is skimmed of 5-15% of its cream content to produce a cheese which has a fat content of about 48-50g – 1.7-1.8oz per 100g – 3.5oz of dry mass. The milk is then poured into huge copper cauldrons, with a capacity of 800, 1 400 or even 2 500l (177, 311 or 555 gallons), where it is heated to about 32°C – 90°F and curdled with rennet. It is then drained, and the curds are beaten and heated to between 54-56°C – 129-133°F, put into a linen cloth, placed into a mould and then pressed. The resulting round of cheese can weigh up to 40-50kg – 88-110lb. The cheese is put into a cold cellar for a few days, where it is salted and rubbed to speed up the formation of the rind. After this, the maturing process begins. The cheese is kept for three to nine months maximum in a cellar, initially at a temperature of 16-18°C – 60-65°F for two months, and thereafter at between 10-12°C – 50-54°F. The rind is rubbed with a cloth soaked in salt solution to encourage the growth of the moulds which give the Comté cheese its characteristic hazelnut flavour.

The uninitiated believe that the more holes there are in a Gruyère cheese, the better it is. However, this is certainly not the case with Comté. The finest, richest Comté cheese is that with no (or at least, very few) holes.

Other cheeses – **Morbier** cheese comes from Morez and the surrounding area, while the blue cheese Bleu de Haut-Jura comes from Septmoncel and Gex. **Vacherin** or Mont d'Or is a soft cheese made during the winter in the region of Champagnole, which was already being savoured in Levier in the 13C. Since 1917, factories at Lons-le-Saunier and Dole have been manufacturing various **processed cheeses** based on pasteurised pressed cheeses (Emmenthal, Gruyère, Comté), pasteurised non-pressed cheeses (Cheddar, Gouda, St-Paulin and Cantal) and blue cheeses (Roquefort, Bleu), and in the manufacture of which other dairy products such as butter, cream and milk may be used.

N. Thibault/EXPLORER

Comté cheese maturing in the cellar

Clock and watch-making in the Jura

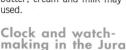

From hand to machine manufacture – The first French watch was made towards the end of the 15C. It was in fact a scaled down version of a portable clock with the weights replaced by a spring. It was not long, however, before the movements were refined, and there were many models available by the second half of the 16C.

At the courts of Henri II and Henri III, women would often wear watches as pendants, and men even had them set into the handles of their daggers as decoration. These timepieces only had one hand, the hour hand. A major turning point in the clock and watch-making process was reached in 1674 with the invention of the spiral spring balance-wheel by Dutch astronomer and physicist Christiaan Huygens.

Twenty years later the Dumont brothers, master watch-makers, brought out the first watches manufactured in Besançon. They were entirely hand-made.

Three quarters of a century after that, in 1767, Frédéric Japy of the village of Beaucourt manufactured some rough models of watches mechanically, using machines he had invented. This was immediately a success, and his production was soon turning out 3 000 to 3 500 watches per month.

In 1793, a Swiss clock-maker, Mégévand, and eighty of his fellow countrymen, all master craftsmen who had been banished from their country for their advanced ideas, sought refuge in Besançon. The town craftsmen were furious at the arrival of this new competition and were in favour of hanging the foreigners. However, the Convention took them under its wing and advanced them some money to enable them to set up a factory and a national school of clock and watch-making. They were to take in 200 apprentices per year, funded by the Convention. Mégévand went on to perfect assembly line production.

The boom – From then on, sales expanded rapidly. In 1835, 80 000 watches were produced in Besançon and in 1878, 240 000. The clock and watch-making industry spread to many towns in the Franche-Comté. In the winter, people in the small mountain villages would work at home, producing components or assembling clocks or watches themselves.

Competition and new growth – At the end of the 19C, however, competition from Swiss clock and watch-makers was becoming particularly tough. The Jura's annual production, which had reached 2 500 000 timepieces, began to falter. The work, which had assumed the nature of a rural handicraft, could not keep up with the demand, and manufacture was henceforth concentrated in specially designed, well equipped factories. All the same, the clock and watch-making industry found a new lease of life after the Second World War, until 1977. Since then, production has declined in the face of opposition from Japanese manufacturers.

Besançon nevertheless continues to fight for its share of the market with a tenacity typical of the region, supported by its various training centres in the field (Lycée technique d'horlogerie, École nationale supérieure de chronometrie et de micromécanique, Centre technique de l'industrie horlogère), its adult education centre and its national observatory specialising in the adjustment and monitoring of chronometers. This example is followed by other watch-making centres, on the Maîche plateau and at Morteau and Villers-le-Lac, for example. Since the 17C, Morez and Morbier have specialised in the production of grandfather and monumental clocks.

Centuries of iron-working in Burgundy

Burgundy has been an important iron-working centre since Antiquity, owing to its outcrops of iron-ore and vast reserves of timber for fuel. Archaeology has shown that even in the Gaulish era towns such as **Bibracte** and **Alise-Ste-Reine** contained many metal-workers whose output was gladly exploited by the Romans. Evidence of extensive Gallo-Roman and medieval metal-working has also been discovered in the vicinity of Vézelay.

The **Cistercians,** who produced a great deal of iron until the middle of the 14C, played a cardinal role in the development of techniques: their invention of the camshaft enabled them to use hydraulic energy to drive small metal hammers and, by the beginning of the 13C, forge bellows. This made it possible to attain high temperatures and thus a better amalgamation of carbon and iron, which led to the discovery of cast iron. The forge building at Fontenay abbey is one of the very rare relics of this industry in the Middle Ages. Production grew from the 16C onwards owing to the invention of blast furnaces; the forges at **Buffon** are one of the last examples of the so-called classic metallurgy, which was dependent on the combination of charcoal and hydraulic power.

Modern metallurgy was born in England in the 18C with the bringing together of coke as a fuel, the invention of the steam engine and the process of puddling (purifying cast metal by stirring). In 1785 the blast furnaces at the **Le Creusot** royal foundry were the first in France to be fired by coke. Unfortunately the technical success was not exploited for lack of financial support. English-style forges were not introduced in France until 1819; two years later they appeared in Burgundy in **Fourchambault** (1821) and then in **Ste-Colombe-sur-Seine** (1822). In 1836 the Le Creusot collieries, forges, foundries and workshops were bought by Schneider and in forty years became the largest metallurgical and mechanical centre in France.

In the late 18C and early 19C the development of the ironworks and related coalmines led to the founding or growth of several towns such as **Le Creusot, Montceau-les-Mines, Montchanin,** and **Blanzy** in Saône-et-Loire and **La Machine, Decize, Imphy, Fourchambault** and **Guérigny** in the Nièvre (where metallurgy was already well-established). In the 20C foreign competition and increasing use of energy sources other than coal led to a decline in certain centres. The metallurgical tradition survives, however, as is shown by the success since the 1950s of three big Burgundian companies: SEB (Société d'Emboutissage de Bourgogne), established in Selongey near Dijon, Vallourec, first French steel converter (Montbard) and Framatome, a branch of the Schneider group (Le Creusot and Chalon-sur-Saône).

Other industries

In addition to plying their traditional industries, Burgundy and the Jura are currently undergoing significant industrial expansion. In the Jura, industry is dominated by the great **Belfort-Montbéliard** complex with **Peugeot motors** manufactured at Montbéliard-Sochaux and the production of high speed (TGV) and electric trains by **GEC-Alsthom** at Belfort. **Besançon,** once the capital of the clock-making industry, is now channeling its energies into micro-technology.

Burgundy is the birthplace of the industrial miracle of **Le Creusot,** which is being repeated by the subsidiary of Usinor-Sacilor, CLI, Alsthom Creusot Rail and Framatome. Industrial activity at Le Creusot has furthermore diversified with the establishment there of SNECMA, the development of the textile industry and the founding of a pool of technological skill specialising in high-potential energy and electronics.

Assembly line for TGV and EUROSTAR high speed trains at GEC-Alsthom, Belfort

Historical table and notes

Prehistory

BC	The many bone fragments discovered at Solutré indicate that there was a human presence there between 18 000 and 15 000 BC.

Antiquity

6C	During the Gaulish period Burgundy is inhabited by the **Aedui**, the most powerful tribe in Gaul with the Arverni; their capital is Bibracte.
4C	The **Sequani**, originally from the Haute Seine region, settle in the Jura region. They build fortified camps, the most famous of which is Vesontio (Besançon).
59-51	*Caesar's conquest of Gaul.*
58	Under threat from the Helvetii the Aedui ask for help from Caesar, who promptly begins his conquest of the Gauls. The Sequani also request his help, this time against the Germanic threat. Caesar drives out the Helvetii and the Germanic tribes... but stays on in Gaul himself.
52	The whole of Gaul rises up against Caesar. The Sequani and the Aedui join forces under Vercingetorix, but are forced to concede victory to Caesar at Alésia, the decisive battle for the whole of Gaul.
51	*End of the Gallic War*
AD	*Roman civilization spreads throughout Gaul.*
1-3C	Autun, "city of Augustus", becomes capital of northeast Gaul and supplants Bibracte.
313	*Edict of Milan: the Roman Emperor Constantine grants freedom of worship to Christians.*
Late 4C	Christianity gradually spreads into Burgundy. *The Roman Empire falls under pressure from the Barbarians to the east.*

Burgundy

5C	Burgundians, natives of the Baltic coast, settle in the Saône plain. Evidence of their civilization shows that they were more advanced than the other Barbarians. They give their name to their new homeland: Burgundia (which evolved in French into Bourgogne).
534	The Franks seize the Burgundian kingdom.
800	*Charlemagne becomes Emperor of the West.*
814	The death of Charlemagne plunges the Empire into a period of instability. The sons of the Emperor Louis the Pious dispute his legacy.
841	Charles the Bald defeats his brother Lothar at Fontanet (Fontenoy-en-Puisaye).
843	*Treaty of Verdun: Charlemagne's empire is divided between the three sons of Louis the Pious.* Frankish Burgundy reverts to Charles the Bald. It is separated by the Saône from imperial Burgundy, Lothar's territory, the north of which becomes the County of Burgundy (or "Comté"), as distinct from the Duchy of Burgundy (or "Duché").
Late 9C	Frankish Burgundy becomes a Duchy and takes in Langres, Troyes, Sens, Nevers and Mâcon.

The Duchy of Burgundy

987-996	Reign of Hugues Capet.
996-1031	Reign of Robert II the Pious.
1002-1016	The King of France occupies the Duchy of Burgundy.
1032	The Germanic Emperor becomes Suzerain of the Comté. But both his power and that of the Count decline as the great feudal landowners gain influence, headed by the Chalons. Henri I, son of Robert II the Pious, to whom Burgundy returns, hands it over as a fief to his brother Robert I the Old (a Burgundian branch of the Capet family which survived until 1361). Under the Capetian dukes Burgundy is one of the bastions of Christianity; Cluny, then Cîteaux and Clairvaux reach the height of their influence.
1095	*First Crusade.*
1270	*Death of St Louis at the siege of Tunis.*
1295	Philip the Fair buys the Comté as an apanage for his son Philip the Long and his descendants. This is the beginning of a period of peace and prosperity.
1337-1453	*Hundred Years War.*
1349	The Comté is devastated by the Black Plague in "l'année de la grande mort".
1353	*Switzerland frees itself from imperial domination.*
1361	Duke Philippe de Rouvres dies young without issue, bringing the line of the Capet dukes to an end. The Duchy of Burgundy passes to the King of France, John the Good, who was regent during the duke's minority.
1366	The name "Franche-Comté" appears for the first time, on an official decree proclaiming the value the inhabitants attach to their rights, as had been done in the "Franche-montagnes" of the Swiss Jura.

1384-1477	Philip the Bold (son of the King of France, John the Good), who had already been given the Duchy in apanage, marries the heiress to the Comté and thus takes possession of the whole of Burgundy. He is the first of the famous dynasty of the "great Dukes of Burgundy", whose power came to exceed that of the Kings of France. He is succeeded by John the Fearless, Philip the Good and Charles the Bold. In the Comté, these rulers keep a tight rein on the feudal lords, enforce the authority of Parliament and the State bodies and become patrons of art and literature.
1429	*Orléans is saved by Joan of Arc.*
1453	*Constantinople falls to the Turks.*
1461-1483	*Reign of Louis XI.*

GENEALOGY OF THE HOUSES OF FRANCE AND BURGUNDY IN THE 14 AND 15 C

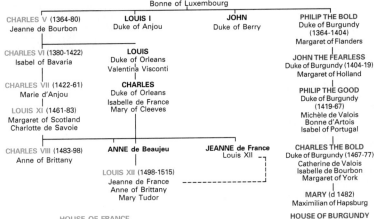

VALOIS

PHILIP VI (1328-50)
Jeanne de Bourgogne
Blanche de Navarre
|
JOHN II THE GOOD (1350-64)
Bonne of Luxembourg

CHARLES V (1364-80) Jeanne de Bourbon	LOUIS I Duke of Anjou	JOHN Duke of Berry	PHILIP THE BOLD Duke of Burgundy (1364-1404) Margaret of Flanders
CHARLES VI (1380-1422) Isabel of Bavaria	LOUIS Duke of Orleans Valentina Visconti		JOHN THE FEARLESS Duke of Burgundy (1404-19) Margaret of Holland
CHARLES VII (1422-61) Marie d'Anjou	CHARLES Duke of Orleans Isabelle de France Mary of Cleeves		PHILIP THE GOOD Duke of Burgundy (1419-67) Michèle de Valois Bonne d'Artois Isabel of Portugal
LOUIS XI (1461-83) Margaret of Scotland Charlotte de Savoie			
CHARLES VIII (1483-98) Anne of Brittany	ANNE de Beaujeu	JEANNE de France Louis XII	CHARLES THE BOLD Duke of Burgundy (1467-77) Catherine de Valois Isabelle de Bourbon Margaret of York
	LOUIS XII (1498-1515) Jeanne de France Anne of Brittany Mary Tudor		MARY (d 1482) Maximilian of Hapsburg
HOUSE OF FRANCE			HOUSE OF BURGUNDY

THE GREAT DUKES OF BURGUNDY

It was under this dynasty, a branch of the House of Valois, that Burgundy reached the height of its power and prestige, where it remained for over a century (1364-1477).

Philip the Bold (1364-1404) – Though scarcely more than a child, Philip fought heroically at the side of his father, King John II the Good of France, at the battle of Poitiers (1356). He earned the nickname "the Bold" when, although wounded and a prisoner, he landed a well-aimed blow on an English lord who had made insulting remarks about the King of France. By the time he became Duke of Burgundy (1364), Philip was a superb knight, who loved sport and women, and who devoted himself heart and soul to his Duchy and the interests of his House. His marriage in 1369 to Margaret of Flanders, the richest heiress in Europe, made him the most powerful prince in Christendom. He lived in great splendour, dressed magnificently and kept a large and luxurious household in the palace he had built, where he employed painters and sculptors from Flanders.

Philip founded the Chartreuse de Champmol in Dijon as a mausoleum for himself and his descendants. The finest marble from Liège and alabaster from Genoa were provided for the tomb, designed in 1384 by the sculptor **Jean de Marville**. On his death, the decoration was entrusted to **Claus Sluter**. Philip the Bold spent so much money that, when he died in 1404, his sons had to pledge the ducal silver to pay for his funeral. In accordance with Burgundian custom, his widow came and placed her purse, her keys and her belt on his coffin as a sign that she renounced succession to any of her husband's goods.

John the Fearless (1404-1419) – John succeeded his father, Philip the Bold. Although puny and unprepossessing to look at, he was brave, intelligent and ambitious. He had already shown his prowess in the crusade against the Turks. No sooner had he become Duke of Burgundy than he started a quarrel with the royal council against his cousin, Louis d'Orléans, brother of the mad king, Charles VI. As Louis had a knotted stick as his emblem, John took that of a plane to signal his intention to "plane that stick smooth". This he achieved in 1407 by having his rival assassinated. John took control of Paris, where he was staunchly opposed by the Orleanist faction which controlled the mad king. When the Orleanist leader, the poet Charles d'Orléans, was captured at

Agincourt (1415) and taken off to England, where he was imprisoned for 25 years, his father-in-law, Count Bernard VII of Armagnac took over his leadership.

During the struggle between the Armagnacs and the Burgundians, in which the French were drawn into fighting each other in a civil war from which the English were able to profit considerably, John the Fearless, realising the potential harm of the struggle for French interests, sought to negotiate an agreement with the Dauphin, the future King Charles VII. He agreed to meet Charles on 11 September 1419 on the bridge at Montereau, but there he was "traitorously felled by an axe and murdered".

Philip the Good (1419-1467) and the Order of the Golden Fleece – Filled with desire for vengeance, Philip the Good, son of John the Fearless, allied himself with the English and in 1430 handed over to them Joan of Arc, whom he had captured at Compiègne, for the enormous sum of 10 000 *livres*. A

few years later, however, Philip came to an understanding with Charles VII at the Treaty of Arras, which enabled him further to enlarge his territory. In this way, Dijon became the capital of a powerful state which included a large part of Holland, almost all of modern Belgium, Luxembourg, Flanders, Artois, Hainaut, Picardy and all the land between the Loire and the Jura.

Philip, who had an even greater taste for magnificence than his predecessors, lived like a king. Five great officers of state, the Marshal of Burgundy, the Admiral of Flanders, the Chamberlain, the Master of the Horse and the Chancellor, were part of the Duke's immediate entourage, in a court that was among the most sumptuous in Europe. On the day of his marriage with Isabella of Portugal, 14 January 1429, Philip founded the sovereign Order of the Golden Fleece (Toison d'Or) in honour of God, the Virgin Mary and St Andrew. The Order originally had 31 members, all of whom swore allegiance to the Grand Master, Philip the Good and his successors. They met at

Philip the Good by Rogier Van der Weyden; Musée des Beaux-Arts, Dijon

least once every three years and wore magnificent, fur-trimmed scarlet cloaks, over a similar robe. The neck chain of the Order was made of sparkling firestones and quartz. The headquarters of the Order was for a long time the ducal Holy Chapel at Dijon, which was destroyed during the Revolution. The Order is now one of the most prestigious and exclusive. When one of the members dies, his heirs must return his neck chain and fleece to the Grand Master.

Charles the Bold (1467-1477) – This was the last, and possibly the most famous member of the House of Valois and the Dukes of Burgundy. Tall, vigorous and strongly-built, Charles loved violent exercise, and in particular hunting. He was also a cultured man, however, and spent much of his time in study. Above all he was passionately interested in history. He was a proud, intensely ambitious man, as Commynes (historian and chronicler 1447-1511) said of him, "He was very pompous in his dress and in all other things, and altogether a little too exaggerated... He wanted great glory." As his father had borne the same name as Philip of Macedonia, Charles dreamed of becoming a second Alexander and was constantly waging war in an effort to underline the power of Louis XI, who in turn did everything possible to break up the Burgundian state. Charles was killed during the siege of Nancy, which was defended by René of Lorraine. His body, half eaten by wolves, was found in a frozen pool.

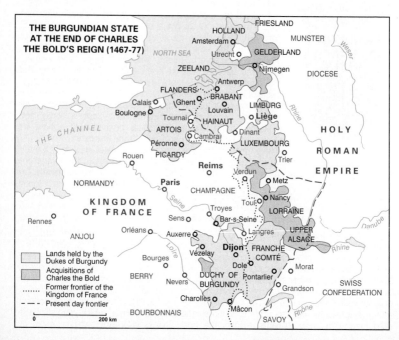

THE BURGUNDIAN STATE
AT THE END OF CHARLES
THE BOLD'S REIGN (1467-77)

FRIESLAND
HOLLAND
Amsterdam
MUNSTER
NORTH SEA
Utrecht
GELDERLAND
ZEELAND
Nijmegen
DIOCESE
Antwerp
FLANDERS
BRABANT
Calais
Ghent
LIMBURG
Boulogne
Louvain
Liège
Tournai
HAINAUT
ARTOIS
Dinant
HOLY
Péronne
Cambrai
LUXEMBOURG
Rouen
PICARDY
Trier
ROMAN
Reims
Verdun
EMPIRE
THE CHANNEL
NORMANDY
Paris
Metz
CHAMPAGNE
Nancy
KINGDOM
OF FRANCE
Troyes
Toul
LORRAINE
Rennes
Sens
Bar-s-Seine
ANJOU
Orléans
Auxerre
Langres
UPPER
ALSACE
Vézelay
Dijon
FRANCHE
COMTÉ
Bourges
Dole
Morat
BERRY
Nevers
DUCHY OF
BURGUNDY
Pontarlier
Grandson
SWISS
CONFEDERATION
Charolles
Mâcon
BOURBONNAIS
SAVOY

Lands held by the
Dukes of Burgundy
Acquisitions of
Charles the Bold
.... Former frontier of the
Kingdom of France
– – – Present day frontier

0   200 km

Return to the French Crown

1477	On the death of Charles the Bold, Louis XI invades the Comté. He annexes Burgundy and the Burgundian towns in Picardy to the royal territory. Mary of Burgundy, the daughter of the dead duke, deprived of a large part of her inheritance, marries **Maximilian of Habsburg** who thus acquires the rest of the old Duchy. Their union produces Philip the Handsome whose son, the future Emperor Charles V, will continue the struggle against the Kingdom of France ruled by François I.
1519	The Comté enjoys a period of prosperity under Charles V. He includes people from the Comté, such as the Granvelles, in his immediate circle.
1556-1598	Emperor Charles V bequeaths the Comté to his son, Philip II King of Spain, who proves to be far less sympathetic a ruler to the people of the Comté.
1589-1610	*Reign of Henri IV.*
1598	On the death of Philip II, the Comté passes to his daughter Isabelle, who marries the Archduke of Austria. The province of the Comté belongs to the Archdukes until it is seized by the French in 1678.

The French Conquest

	In order to understand the resistance to French rule of a French-speaking country with an economy closely linked with that of France, one must remember that, finding itself on the borders of the Holy Empire, Austria and Spain, the Comté had become accustomed to directing its own affairs. The independent people of the Comté regarded the rule of a Richelieu or a Louis XIV with some degree of trepidation.
1601	Henri IV acquires the territories of Bresse, Bugey, Valromey and the Gex region from the Duke of Savoy, in return for some Italian territory.
1609	*After 50 years struggle, the Netherlands wins independence from Spain.*
1610	Beginning of the reign of Louis XIII, who dies in 1643.
1618	Beginning of the Thirty Years War between the House of Austria and France allied with Sweden. The war finishes in 1648 with the Treaty of Westphalia.
1635	Richelieu gives the order to invade the Comté which gave refuge to his enemy, Gaston d'Orléans. The Ten Years War brings the country to ruin.
1643-1715	*Reign of Louis XIV.*
1648	Mazarin withdraws French forces and restores the Comté's neutral status.
1668	Louis XIV reclaims the Comté as part of the dowry of his wife Marie-Thérèse, daughter of the deceased King of Spain. After a brief campaign, he is forced to abandon the country and return it to Spain.
1674	Louis XIV, at war with Spain, makes a fresh attempt to take control of the province, and this time is successful. His conquest is ratified by the Peace of Nimègue (1678). Besançon takes over from Dole as capital. From now on, the history of the Comté follows that of the rest of France.

From the Revolution to modern times

1715-1774	*Reign of Louis XV.*
1789	*Fall of the Bastille.*
1793	The Montbéliard region is annexed to France.
1804	*Consecration of Napoleon I as Emperor of France.*
1815	*The battle of Waterloo.* Heroic defence of Belfort by Lecourbe.
1822	Invention of photography by Nicéphore Niepce at St-Loup-de-Varenne.
1870	Colonel Denfert-Rochereau resists attack by 40 000 Germans during the siege of Belfort.
1871	General Bourbaki is defeated at Héricourt, having won victory at Villersexel, and has to fall back to Besançon.
1878	Vines devastated by phylloxera aphid.
Late 19C-early 20C-	As industrialisation gains pace, the Franche-Comté is transformed. Great industrial dynasties such as Peugeot and Japy are born, compensating for the decline in the clock-making industry, which is exasperated by the war of 1914 in favour of the Swiss.
1914	Joffre *(qv)* gives his famous order of 6 September at Châtillon-sur-Seine.
1940	Occupation of the Franche-Comté by the Germans, who use the region to block the retreat of then retreating French forces trying to reach central France along the Swiss border.
1940-1944	The Resistance movement is active is Burgundy: Army children from Autun in combat; Châtillonnais forests are used as a hide-out.
14 Sept 1944	Leclerc's division joins De Lattre de Tassigny near Châtillon-sur-Seine.
Nov 1944	The Allied conquest of the northern part of the Doubs *département* completes the liberation of the Franche-Comté.
1948	Génissiat reservoir is filled with water.
1970	The A6-A7 motorway from Paris to Marseille opens up the west of Burgundy (Auxerre, Beaune, Mâcon).
1981	High speed rail service (TGV) links Paris-Le Creusot-Mâcon-Lyon and Paris-Dijon-Besançon.
1986	Setting up of the Haut-Jura regional nature park.

Monastic life in Burgundy

After the turmoil of the Carolingian decline, the church used its not inconsiderable influence and long-established cultural tradition to resume a leading role in society; there was a great renewal of fervour for the monastic life throughout western Europe. The church owed its importance mainly to the position held by the religious orders – in particular the order of St Benedict – which became more numerous from the 10C onwards. France was in the vanguard of this religious revival and, in France, it was Burgundy that provided the driving force.

The first religious orders – St Benedict and his Rule – In 529 Benedict, who was born in Norcia in Umbria, Italy, moved from Subiaco where he had at first led the life of a recluse to Monte Cassino where he worked out his "Constitution", soon to be adopted by many monasteries. The famous "Benedictine Rule" showed great moderation, recommending fasting, silence and abstinence, but condemning mortification and painful penances. St Benedict allocated a large proportion of time to manual labour in the monks' working day (six to eight hours, compared with four hours for reading and four for divine office). The abbots of the Benedictine monasteries, who were elected for life, had absolute authority. All relations with the outside world were to be avoided, and the community had to make itself completely self-supporting. The flexibility of this rule explains its later success in Italy, Gaul and Germany, especially from the 10C onwards.

Cluny and the triumph of Benedictine Rule – In 910, the founding of a monastery in the region of Mâcon by the Duke of Aquitaine, Guillaume le Pieux, marked the beginning of an important religious reform associated with the name of Cluny. The period was certainly propitious for such a change. The social "climate" – birth of the feudal system, political turmoil and instability of royal power – provoked a move towards mysticism and an influx of men to the cloistered life. A return to the spirit of the Benedictine Rule was marked by the observance of three cardinal rules – obedience, chastity and fasting – but divine service occupied the greater part of the day, reducing and almost eliminating the time for manual labour and intellectual work. The great innovation was the complete independence of the new abbey from all political power. Under its foundation charter Cluny was directly attached to the Holy See in Rome; given the remoteness of pontifical authority, this arrangement effectively conferred complete autonomy on the order. The Cluny order expanded rapidly; by the beginning of the 12C there were 1 450 monasteries with 10 000 monks, scattered all over France, Germany, Spain, Italy and Britain, all dependent on Cluny. Among its Burgundian filials were the abbeys or priories of St-Germain-d'Auxerre, Paray-le-Monial, St-Marcel-de-Chalon, Vézelay, Nevers (St-Sever and St-Étienne) and La Charité-sur-Loire.

This great expansion is largely explained by the personalities and the length of the "reign" of the great abbots of Cluny (Saints Odo, Mayeul, Odilo, Hugh and Peter the Venerable), who chose their own successors and were themselves supported by extremely competent men. The abbot in those days was a person of very considerable standing, sometimes more powerful than the pope himself, whose guide and counsellor he was. Kings were not above coming to him for arbitration. For two or three generations Cluny was the centre of essentially an empire. Its organisation, however, was based on extreme centralisation, with the whole weight of power vested in the abbot of Cluny. Were this supreme power to be abused, the entire structure of the order would come under threat.

Cîteaux and St Bernard – It was precisely to fight against the luxury and the slack discipline among the monks of Cluny that St Bernard spoke out. This young nobleman born at the château of Fontaine near Dijon, followed an unexpected destiny when at the age of twenty-one he renounced all riches and honours and went with thirty-two companions to the monastery of Cîteaux in search of God's mercy. On his arrival in 1112 the monastery, founded 14 years earlier by Robert de Molesmes, was undergoing a great crisis which seemed to be threatening its very future. In a short time Bernard turned this very difficult situation around by the example and influence he exercised on all around him. In 1115, leaving Cîteaux to continue its progress, he went to settle in a poor area along the borders of Burgundy and Champagne. Absinthe valley became "Clairvaux" (clear valley). Bernard, now an abbot, accomplished a huge amount of work there. Initially, he was completely destitute, and he had to contend with enormous difficulties: harsh climate, sickness and physical suffering due to a life of self-denial, which he imposed as strictly on himself as he did on of his monks.

The monastic foundations – Reward was not slow to follow; the fame of Bernard soon attracted so many applicants for the monastic life to Clairvaux that the abbey of Trois-Fontaines was founded in the Marne in 1121. On Bernard's death in 1153, Cîteaux had 700 monks and exercised considerable influence; 350 abbeys were attached to it, including the first four "daughters": La Ferté, Morimond, Pontigny and above all Clairvaux, which, thanks to St Bernard, maintained a leading role at the heart of the Cistercian order. During Bernard's abbacy, Clairvaux was exceptionally prosperous; from 1135, a total of 1 800ha - 4 448 acres of forest land and 350ha - 865 acres of fields and meadows belonged to the abbey, where stone buildings had replaced the wooden structures of the earlier years. Thus the man who seemed destined to lead a life of contemplation, a mystic convinced of the superiority of monastic life, was forced to play a political role of primary importance. Up to his death in 1153, his name recalled one of the greatest religious figures that the church had produced. Writer, theologian, philosopher, monk, military leader, statesman and arbiter of Europe, St Bernard was all of these things at once.

Cistercian law – St Bernard's interpretation and application of Benedictine Rule were uncompromising. He forbade the collection of tithes or the acquisition or purchase of land, and he imposed on his monks at Clairvaux, and in a wider sense on all the monks of the Cistercian order, rigorous living conditions. They wore a simple wool tunic whatever the season; their diet was frugal; seven hours a day were set aside for repose, when the monks slept fully dressed in a common dormitory on a simple straw pallet with a single woollen blanket. Every hour of the day was planned with precision. The monks were roused between one and two in the morning and as the day progressed sang matins, then lauds, celebrated private Masses, recited the canonic hours (prime, tierce, sext, nones, vespers and compline), and took part in the community Mass. Divine service thus took up to six or seven hours per day, and the rest of the time was divided between manual labour, intellectual work and reading religious texts. The abbot, leader of the community, lived and ate with his monks, presided over their worship and also over the chapter and any other meetings. He was assisted by a prior, who took over his duties in his absence.

The Cistercian Order in the 20C – The organisation of the Cistercian Order is still based on the "Charter of Charity" established about 1115, uniting the various abbeys, of equal status. Nowadays there are some 3 000 reformed Cistercians, governed by an Abbot General resident in Rome, throughout the world in about 92 abbeys, 15 of which are in France. The abbots of the Order meet regularly for the General Chapter. There are a further 2 000 monks belonging to 61 abbeys or priories, of which 12 are in France, ruled by the same Abbot General but with their own General Chapter.

Layout of a medieval abbey

The monastic buildings were arranged around the cloisters as in the plan below.

Cloisters – Generally composed of four galleries surrounding a central garth or courtyard often laid out as a garden. Some monasteries made this central area their herb garden. The east gallery opened onto the sacristy, the chapter house and the calefactory. In the south gallery there was the lavabo, usually a large stone basin with water flowing from a central fountain, in which the monks washed their hands before eating or praying. The west gallery bordered the lay-brothers' (who did the manual and domestic work) range or the cellars. The north gallery bordered the church, giving access to it through the monks' doorway, at the east end, and the lay-brothers' doorway, at the west end.

Abbey church – The monks spent the better part of their day in the church for Mass or other day- or night-time religious offices. The abbey church was characterised by a very long nave. In Cistercian churches, a rood screen or pulpitum separated the monks' choir near the high altar from the lay-brothers' choir.

Sacristy – Room where ecclesiastical robes and altar vessels were stored, and where the priest leading the service would robe.

Chapter house – For daily monastic business, including prayers before the day's work and a reading of a chapter from the monastic rule. This was where the abbot imposed penance on those who had transgressed the rule.

Calefactory – The only heated room in the monastery, for the use of all the monks (in carefully regulated moderation).

Scriptorium – The room allocated for the copying out of manuscripts, happily usually situated next to the calefactory.

Refectory – The large bare room where the monks ate, often with astonishing acoustics. At mealtimes, the reader would read from the Bible in the elevated pulpit.

Dormitories – There were generally two, one for the monks to the east above the chapter house, and one for the lay-brothers to the west above the lay-brothers' range. In the Cistercian order seven hours were set aside for rest. The monks slept fully clothed in a communal dormitory.

Outbuildings – Other conventual buildings included the barns and the porter's lodge or gatehouse, often quite a grand building with a huge gateway to allow the passage of both carriages and people on foot. The porter's lodge had living quarters on the first floor, in which alms were distributed and justice dispensed to the public.

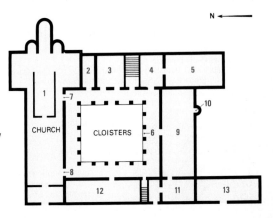

Plan of medieval abbey
1) Monks' choir
2) Sacristy
3) Chapter house
4) Calefactory
   (warming room)
5) Scriptorium
   (writing room)
6) Lavabo
7) Monks' doorway
8) Lay-brothers' doorway
9) Refectory
10) Reader's pulpit
11) Kitchen
12) Lay-brothers' range
    or cellars
13) Guesthouse or hostel

Art

ABC OF ARCHITECTURE

To assist readers unfamiliar with the terminology employed in architecture, we describe below the most commonly used terms, which we hope will make their visits to ecclesiastical, military and civil buildings more interesting.

Ecclesiastical architecture

illustration I ▶

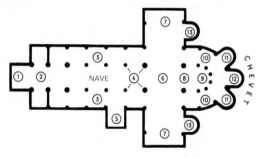

Ground plan: The more usual Catholic form is based on the outline of a cross with the two arms of the cross forming the transept: ① Porch – ② Narthex – ③ Side aisles (sometimes double) – ④ Bay (transverse section of the nave between 2 pillars) – ⑤ Side chapel (often predates the church) – ⑥ Transept crossing – ⑦ Arms of the transept, sometimes with a side doorway – ⑧ Chancel, nearly always facing east towards Jerusalem; the chancel, often vast in size, was reserved for the monks in abbatial churches – ⑨ High altar – ⑩ Ambulatory: in pilgrimage churches the aisles were extended round the chancel, forming the ambulatory, to allow the faithful to file past the relics – ⑪ Radiating or apsidal chapel – ⑫ Axial chapel. In churches which are not dedicated to Our Lady this chapel, in the main axis of the building, is often consecrated to her (Lady Chapel) – ⑬ Transept chapel

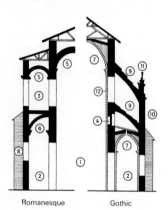

Romanesque   Gothic

◀ illustration II

Cross-section: ① Nave – ② Aisle – ③ Tribune or Gallery – ④ Triforium – ⑤ Barrel vault – ⑥ Half-barrel vault – ⑦ Pointed vault – ⑧ Buttress – ⑨ Flying buttress – ⑩ Pier of a flying buttress – ⑪ Pinnacle – ⑫ Clerestory window

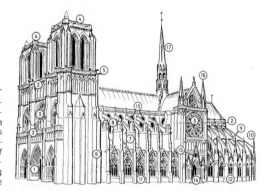

illustration III ▶

Gothic cathedral: ① Porch – ② Gallery – ③ Rose window – ④ Belfry (sometimes with a spire) – ⑤ Gargoyle acting as a waterspout for the roof gutter – ⑥ Buttress – ⑦ Pier of a flying buttress (abutment) – ⑧ Flight or span of flying buttress – ⑨ Double-course flying buttress – ⑩ Pinnacle – ⑪ Side chapel – ⑫ Radiating or apsidal chapel – ⑬ Clerestory windows – ⑭ Side doorway – ⑮ Gable – ⑯ Pinnacle – ⑰ Spire over the transept crossing

◀ illustration IV

Groined vaulting:
① Main arch –
② Groin –
③ Transverse arch

illustration V ▶

Oven vault:
termination of a
barrel vaulted nave

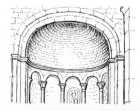

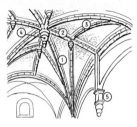

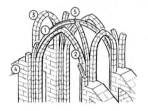

illustration VI
Lierne and tierceron vaulting:
① Diagonal - ② Lierne -
③ Tierceron - ④ Pendant -
⑤ Corbel

illustration VII
Quadripartite vaulting:
① Diagonal - ② Transverse -
③ Stringer - ④ Flying buttress -
⑤ Keystone

▼ illustration VIII

Doorway: ① Archivolt. Depending on the architectural style of the building this can be rounded, pointed, basket-handled, ogee or even adorned with a gable - ② Arching, covings (with string courses, mouldings, carvings or adorned with statues). Recessed arches or orders form the archivolt - ③ Tympanum - ④ Lintel - ⑤ Arch shafts - ⑥ Embrasures. Arch shafts, splaying, sometimes adorned with statues or columns - ⑦ Pier (often adorned with a statue) - ⑧ Hinges and other ironwork

illustration IX ▶

Arches and pillars: ① Ribs or ribbed vaulting - ② Abacus - ③ Capital - ④ Shaft - ⑤ Base - ⑥ Engaged column - ⑦ Pier of arch wall - ⑧ Lintel - ⑨ Discharging or relieving arch - ⑩ Frieze

Military architecture

illustration X
Fortified enclosure: ① Hoarding (projecting timber gallery) - ② Machicolations (corbelled crenellations) - ③ Barbican - ④ Keep or donjon - ⑤ Covered watchpath - ⑥ Curtain wall - ⑦ Outer curtain wall - ⑧ Postern

illustration XI
Towers and curtain walls:
① Hoarding - ② Crenellations - ③ Merlon - ④ Loophole or arrow slit - ⑤ Curtain wall - ⑥ Bridge or drawbridge

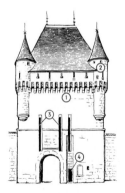

◀ illustration XII
Fortified gatehouse:
① Machicolations - ② Watch turret or bartizan - ③ Slots for the arms of the drawbridge - ④ Postern

illustration XIII ▶
Star fortress: ① Entrance - ② Drawbridge - ③ Glacis - ④ Ravelin or half-moon - ⑤ Moat - ⑥ Bastion - ⑦ Watch turret - ⑧ Town - ⑨ Assembly area

◀ illustration XIV

Dome on squinches:
① Octogonal dome –
② Squinch – ③ Arches of
transept crossing

illustration XV ▶

Dome on pendentives:
① Circular dome – ② Pendentive
– ③ Arches of transept crossing

◀ Illustration XVI

**Altar with retable or
altarpiece:**
① Retable or altarpiece –
② Predella – ③ Crowning
piece – ④ Altar table –
⑤ Altar front

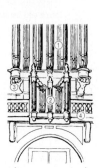

illustration XVII ▶

Organ:
① Great organ case –
② Little organ case –
③ Caryatid – ④ Loft

◀ illustration XVIII

Rood beam or tref: This supports the triumphal
(chancel or rood) arch at the entrance to the
chancel. The rood carries a Crucifix flanked by
statues of the Virgin and St John and sometimes other personages from the Calvary.

illustration XX ▼

Stalls: ① High back – ② Elbow rest ③ Cheek-
piece – ④ Misericord.

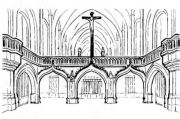

illustration XIX

Rood screen: This replaces the rood beam in larger
churches, and may be used for preaching and reading
of the Epistle and Gospel. Many disappeared from
the 17C onwards as they tended to hide the altar.

THE FINEST ROMANESQUE CHURCHES IN BURGUNDY

★★★

Fontenay	abbey church
Vézelay	Ste-Madeleine basilica

★★

Autun	St-Lazare cathedral
La Charité-sur-Loire	Notre-Dame church
Paray-le-Monial	Sacré-Cœur basilica
Tournus	St-Philibert church

★

Anzy-le-Duc	village church
Beaune	Notre-Dame collegiate church
Chapaize	St-Martin church
Cluny	St-Pierre-et-St-Paul abbey church
Nevers	St-Étienne church
Saulieu	St-Andoche basilica
Semur-en-Brionnais	village church

Other Burgundian Romanesque churches *(see index)*

Avallon (St-Lazare), Blanot, Bois-Ste-Marie, Brancion, Châteauneuf (Saône-et-Loire), Châ-
tillon-sur-Seine, Chissey-lès-Mâcon, Clessé, Iguerande, Montceaux-l'Étoile, Mont-St-
Vincent, Nuits-St-Georges, La Rochepot, St-Julien-de-Jonzy, St-Laurent-en-Brionnais,
St-Point, Taizé, Varenne-l'Arconce.

ARCHITECTURAL TERMS USED IN THE GUIDE

Altarpiece or retable: illustration XVI.
Ambulatory: illustration I.
Apsidal or radiating chapel: illustration I.
Archivolt: illustration VIII.
Arrow slit: illustration XI.
Axial or Lady Chapel: in the axis of the church; illustration I.
Barrel vaulting: illustration II.
Basket-handled arch: depressed arch common to late-medieval and Renaissance architecture.
Bay: illustration I.
Bracket: small supporting piece of stone or timber to carry a beam or cornice.
Buttress: illustration II.
Capital: illustration IX.
Chevet: illustration I.
Ciborium: canopy over the high altar or a receptacle for the Eucharist.
Coffered ceiling: vault or ceiling decorated with sunken panels.
Corbel: illustration VI.
Credence: side table, shelf or niche for eucharistic elements.
Crypt: underground chamber or chapel.
Curtain wall: illustration X.
Depressed arch: three-centred arch sometimes called a basket-handled arch.
Diagonal ribs: illustration VII.
Dome: illustrations XIV and XV.
Entombment or Holy Sepulchre: compositions covering this theme show the Placing of Christ in the Tomb and usually include seven figures around the crucified Christ.
Flamboyant: latest phase (15C) of French Gothic architecture; name taken from the undulating (flame-like) lines of the window tracery.
Fresco: mural paintings executed on wet plaster.
Gable: triangular part of an end wall carrying a sloping roof; the term is also applied to the steeply-pitched ornamental pediments of Gothic architecture; illustration III.
Gallery: illustration II.
Gargoyle: illustration III.
Glory: luminous nimbus surrounding the body.
Groined vaulting: illustration IV.
High relief: haut-relief; applies to a sculpture or carved work when it projects more than one half of its true proportions from the background.
Jetty: overhanging upper storey.
Keep or donjon: illustration X.
Keystone: illustration VII.
Lintel: illustrations VIII and IX.
Lombard arcades: decorative blind arcading composed of small arches and intervening pilaster strips; typical of Romanesque art in Lombardy.
Loophole or arrow slit: illustration XI.
Low relief: bas-relief; sculpture projecting only slightly from the background.
Machicolations: illustration X.
Mandorla: almond-shaped Glory *(see above)*.
Misericord: illustration XX.
Modillion: small console supporting a cornice.
Mullion: a vertical post dividing a window.
Oven vaulting: illustration V.
Parclose screen: screen separating a chapel or the choir from the rest of the church.
Pepperpot roof: conical roof.
Pier: illustration VIII.
Pietà: Italian term designating the Virgin Mary with the dead Christ on her knees.
Pilaster: engaged rectangular column.
Pilaster strip: decorative feature characteristic of Romanesque architecture in Lombardy consisting of shallow projecting pilasters and blind arcading.
Pinnacle: illustrations II and III.
Piscina: basin for washing the sacred vessels.
Pointed arch: diagonal arch supporting a vault; illustrations VI and VII.
Postern: illustrations X and XII.
Recessed arches and orders: illustration VIII.
Rood beam or tref: illustration XVIII.
Rood screen: illustration XIX.
Rose or wheel window: illustration III.
Semicircular arch: round-headed arch.
Sexpartite vaulting: six compartments formed by three intersecting diagonals.
Stalls: illustration XX.
Timber framing: method of construction using a timber framework with interspaces filled with brickwork or plaster.
Tracery: interesting stone ribwork in the upper part of a window.
Transept: illustration I.
Triforium: small arcaded gallery above the aisles; illustration II.
Triptych: three panels hinged together, chiefly used as an altarpiece.
Tympanum: illustration VIII.
Voussoir: illustration VIII.
Watch path or wall walk: illustration X.

RELIGIOUS ARCHITECTURE

In Burgundy

It is not surprising that Burgundy has an incomparably rich artistic tradition, since the necessary stimulation has always existed in the area. Since Antiquity, the region has been a crossroads where a wide variety of peoples and influences have met. The treasure found near Vix shows that strong currents were active in the region of Châtillon-sur-Seine in about the 6C BC.

In the 15C, on the initiative of the Great Dukes, many groups of artists from Paris and Flanders settled in Dijon, which they made one of the most important artistic centres in Europe.

This penetration of foreign influences, and the enduring qualities of Roman civilization and ancient traditions, combined with the expression of the Burgundian temperament led to the blossoming of a regional art that holds an honoured place in the artistic history of France.

Pre-Romanesque – After a period of artistic eclipse in the early Middle Ages, the Carolingian epoch (8-9C) witnessed a period of architectural revival in Burgundy in particular. The plans of the religious buildings were simple, and the buildings of poorly dressed stone were basic. Part of the former crypt of the cathedral of St-Bénigne at Dijon and the crypts of Flavigny-sur-Ozerain and St-Germain of Auxerre are among the oldest examples of these monuments.

Capital in the crypt of the church of Saint-Bénigne, Dijon

LAUROS GIRAUDON

Romanesque – Numerous towns, wealthy abbeys and abundant building material were favourable conditions in which the Romanesque school of Burgundy flourished, showing an extraordinary vitality in the 11 and 12C, not only in architecture, but in sculpture and painting *(see below)*. Furthermore, the influence of the school spread far beyond the geographic boundaries of Burgundy.

In the year 1000, the desire to build was given fresh impetus by the end of invasions, the strengthening of royal power and the evolution of new building techniques.

Raoul Glaber, a monk of St-Bénigne at Dijon, commented that, "As the third year after the millenium was about to begin, people all over Christendom, but particularly in Italy and Gaul, set about rebuilding the churches... the Christians replaced even those which did not need to be replaced with more beautiful buildings... it seemed as if the world had shaken the dust off its old clothes to clothe everything in the white robes of its young churches...".

The first Burgundian Romanesque churches – Among the great builders of this period, Abbot **Guglielmo da Volpiano**, of Italian origin and related to some of the greatest families of his time, built a new basilica in Dijon on the site of the tomb of St Bénigne. The building, begun in 1001, was consecrated in 1018.

Though this abbey was completely destroyed by fire in the 12C, the church of St-Vorles in Châtillon-sur-Seine – considerably modified in the first years of the 11C by the Bishop of Langres, Brun de Roucy, a relation of Guglielmo da Volpiano – provides an example of the features of Romanesque art during this period: slipshod building methods with badly placed flat stones, massive thick pillars, crude decoration of mural niches and cornices with Lombard arcades.

The most striking example of the architecture of this time is the church of **St-Philibert** in Tournus *(qv)*. The narthex and the upper storey of the narthex, built at the beginning of the 11C, are the oldest extant parts to date. The most striking aspect of this solid, powerful architecture is its sober, almost austere style.

Cluny and its school – Although in the beginning Romanesque art owed much to foreign influences, the following period witnessed the triumphant emergence of a new style from Cluny, which was to spread throughout Burgundy, eventually reaching as far as Switzerland.

It was at Cluny that the principal characteristics of Burgundian Romanesque architecture were united for the first time.

Until St Peter's was built in Rome in the 16C *(see the Michelin Green Guides to Rome and Italy)*, the abbey of Cluny was the largest church in all Christendom; its total internal length greatly exceeded that of the Gothic cathedrals that were built from the 13C onwards.

In 1247 an Italian churchman travelling through France remarked that "Cluny is the noblest Burgundian monastery of the Benedictine Black Monk Order. The buildings are so extensive that the Pope with his cardinals and entire retinue and the King and his court may be accommodated together, without upsetting the monks' routine or putting them out of their cells."

The extent and exceptional size of the remains of the abbey, which was started by St Hugh in 1088 and completed about 1130 *(see Cluny)*, are still impressive and allow one to recognise the general characteristics of the School of Cluny: the broken-barrel vaulting is an innovation of the period.

Burgundian architects avoided the use of semicircular vaulting as much as possible and substituted broken-barrel vaulting which was far more efficient at withstanding the strains and stresses of the building. This style of vaulting consists of each bay having a transverse arch; the use of broken arches reduces stress and thereby the weight on the walls, thus making it possible to raise the vaulting to a far greater height. The pillars are flanked by fluted pilasters in the Antique style; a false triforium of alternating bays and pilasters, surmounted by a clerestory, runs above the narrow arches. This arrangement of three storeys rising to a pointed vault is found in many churches in the region.

The completion of so large a building, in which a great many architects and artists participated, was to have a profound effect on the construction of other churches in the Mâconnais, Charollais and Brionnais districts.

Cathedral nave, Autun

The priory church of **Paray-le-Monial** is a smaller replica of the great abbey church at Cluny. It was also conceived by St Hugh and has an identical plan of construction. At **La Charité-sur-Loire** another abbey dependent on the great abbey also shows the influence of Cluny. Other Burgundian monuments take their derivation more or less directly from the abbey of Cluny. In the church of St-Lazare at **Autun**, consecrated in 1130, a much simplified plan of Cluny is to be found. However "Roman" influence is often in evidence: fluted pilasters copied from the antique style have replaced engaged columns on the piers; the decoration of the triforium arcade is similar to that on the Arroux gateway, although this ornamentation is not without a certain heaviness *(see illustration)*.

At **Semur-en-Brionnais**, home of the family of St Hugh, the church is almost as high as that at Cluny. On the interior of the west front, the overhanging gallery recalls a similar gallery in St-Michel in Cluny. The collegiate church of St-Andoche in Saulieu is associated with the Cluny family of churches: Notre-Dame in Beaune has more points in common with St-Lazare in Autun. Among the many village churches built under the inspiration of Cluny, particularly in the Brionnais region, those of Bois-Ste-Marie, Blanot, Montceaux-l'Étoile, Varenne-l'Arconce, Vareilles, Châteauneuf and Iguerande are particularly interesting.

Vézelay and its influence – The Cluny school was repudiated by a whole "family" of churches, the purest example of which is the basilica of Ste-Madeleine in Vézelay, although there are others that display characteristics even further removed from Cluny. Built at the beginning of the 12C on a hill overlooking the valley of the Cure, Vézelay constitutes the synthesis of true Burgundian Romanesque architecture. The essential difference between this church and earlier Romanesque buildings is that the nave has groined vaulting whereas up to that time only the side aisles had this feature, their small size mitigating the risk of the vaulting subsiding as a result of lateral pressure.

This design, originally without the support of flying buttresses which were added in the Gothic period, required the incorporation of iron bars to prevent the walls of the nave from bulging outwards.

Clerestory windows were placed directly above the main arches and opened onto the axis of each bay, shedding their light into the nave. The pilasters were replaced by engaged columns, as opposed to the Cluny style. The vaulting is supported by semicircular transverse arches. To break the monotony of this style of architecture, differently coloured building materials were used; vari-coloured limestone and alternating white and brown archstones.

The church in Anzy-le-Duc appears to have served as a model for the building in Vézelay; it is probable that Renaud de Semur, who came from the Brionnais region, wished to rebel against the all-powerful influence of Cluny and took as his model the church in Anzy-le-Duc, which at that time was the most perfect piece of architecture of the region. There is no shortage of points of comparison: the elevation of the storeys is the same; both have a solitary window above the main arches; both share the same style of semicircular vaulting and cruciform pillars flanked by engaged columns. This style, created in Anzy-le-Duc and perfected in Vézelay, has been copied in St-Lazare in Avallon and St-Philibert in Dijon.

Fontenay and the Cistercian school – Cistercian architecture first appeared in Burgundy in the first half of the 12C (Cistercium was the Latin name for the town of Cîteaux). It is characterized by a spirit of simplicity in keeping with the teaching of St Bernard, whose influence on his times was considerable. He objected bitterly to the luxury displayed in some monastic churches, opposing the theories of some of the great builders of the 11 and 12C with extraordinary passion and vehemence. His argument against the belief of abbots such as St Hugh, Peter the Venerable and Suger, who believed that nothing could be too rich for the glory of God, was expressed for example in the letter he wrote to William, Abbot of St-Thierry, in which he asks, "Why this excessive height in the churches, this enormous length, this unnecessary width, these sumptuous ornaments and curious paintings that draw the eye and distract attention and meditation? ... We the monks, who have forsaken ordinary life and renounced worldly wealth and ostentation for the love of Christ, ... in whom do we hope to awaken devotion with these ornaments?"

There is nonetheless a certain grandeur even in the sobriety and austerity that he advocated. The uncluttered style and severe appearance truly reflected the principles of Cistercian rule, which regarded everything that was not absolutely indispensable to the development and spread of the monastic way of life as harmful.

The Cistercians almost always insisted on the identical plan of construction for all the buildings of their order and directed work on new abbeys themselves. The abbey of Fontenay is a good example of the standard plan. Its design and architectural techniques are to be found throughout Europe from Sicily to Sweden. Every new monastery was another link with France, and craftsmen followed the monks. It was the turn of the Burgundian Cistercian monasteries to spearhead the expansion of European monasticism. In 1135, the Cistercians adopted Fountains Abbey in Yorkshire, recently founded (1132); there

Nave of the abbey church, Fontenay

they were to build on a large scale what was to become the wealthiest abbey in England.

In **Cistercian churches** the blind nave is covered by broken-barrel vaulting, as at Cluny; the side aisles are generally arched with transverse barrel vaulting, and their great height enables them to take the thrust of the nave. This style is to be found in many Burgundian churches of the 12C. The transept, also of broken-barrel vaulting, juts far out and has two square chapels opening into each transept arm. The choir, of broken-barrel vaulting, is square and not very deep. It ends in a flat chevet lit through two tiers of three windows. Five windows are placed above the chancel arch, and each bay of the side aisles is also lit through a window. The fact that most Cistercian churches have no belfry is evidence of St Bernard's desire to adhere to poverty, humility and simplicity. Living far from their fellow men, away from the frequented highways, the religious communities did not wish to attract the faithful from far and wide. Belfries, which drew attention to the existence of a church by their silhouette and shape, were thus banned.

By avoiding all decoration, be it painting or sculpture, and by eliminating every kind of superfluous ornamentation (such as stained glass windows, or illuminated paving stones), Cistercian art achieved a remarkable purity of execution.

Gothic – About the middle of the 12C and perhaps even earlier, pointed vaulting made its appearance in Burgundy, the prelude to a new development in architecture. The Gothic style, which originated in the Paris region (Ile-de-France), penetrated slowly into Burgundy, where it was adapted according to circumstances and trends.

Period of transition – In 1140, the gallery of the narthex at Vézelay was given pointed vaulting. The Cistercians were among the first to adopt this style of architecture and used it at Pontigny in about 1150. The choir of Ste-Madeleine at Vézelay, the work of the abbot Gérard d'Arcy, was started in the last years of the 12C; the flying buttresses were not added until the 13C. It was in the 13C that a Burgundian Gothic style emerged in religious buildings.

First half of the 13C – The church of Notre-Dame in Dijon, built without interruption between 1230 and 1251, represents the most perfect and best known example of this style. Its characteristics are to be found in many religious buildings of the period in Burgundy; beyond the transept, the fairly deep choir is flanked by apsidal chapels (there are generally two) and ends with a high apse. The use of sexpartite vaulting permitted the replacing of the uniformly sized pillars with alternating thick and thin pillars. A triforium runs above the great arches; at the clerestory level, the nave wall is set back slightly allowing for a gallery above that of the triforium.

In the external decoration, the presence of a cornice – its form varying from one building to another – goes round the choir, the nave, the apse, or the belfry and is a typically Burgundian mode of decoration.

Among the buildings constructed in this style, the most important are: Auxerre cathedral, the collegiate church of St-Martin in Clamecy and the church of Notre-Dame in Semur-en-Auxois. In the latter, the absence of a triforium further enhances the effect of dizzying height created by the narrow nave.

End of the 13C – Architecture now became much lighter and developed a boldness, seeming to defy the laws of gravity.

The choir of the church of St-Thibault in Auxois *(illustration above opposite)* appears in such a style, with its keystone at a height of 27m - 89ft. The five-sided apse rising to a height of four storeys is of an amazing lightness. Below the highest windows there is a clerestory composed of three tiers reaching to the ground: the top tier is a gallery, the middle tier is composed of pairs of radiant windows and the bottom tier consists of blind arcades. The church of St-Père shares certain similarities with Notre-Dame in Dijon, but it differs in its height, being of two storeys with a gallery in front of the windows.

14C – It was at this time that the Flamboyant Gothic style, characterized by the ogee arch, appeared; the number of ribs multiplied and the capitals were reduced to a simple decorative role or were sometimes even dispensed with completely.

This period did not produce any really fine buildings in Burgundy. The church of St-Jean in Dijon has a single nave surrounded by many chapels.

Renaissance – Under the influence of Italy, Burgundian art took a new turn in the 16C, marked by a revival of the antique styles.

In architecture the transition from Gothic to Italian art met with some resistance. The church of St-Michel in Dijon shows evidence of this: while the nave (started at the beginning of the 16C) is an imitation of Gothic art, the façade (built between 1537 and 1570) is a perfect example of the Renaissance style, with two towers divided into four storeys, on which Ionic and Corinthian orders are superimposed alternately, three semicircular doorways and the porch with its richly sculpted coffered vaulting all reflecting a strong Italian influence.

In the Franche-Comté

The religious architectural heritage of the Franche-Comté is indebted to the numerous monastic communities which were to be found in the region during the Middle Ages. The **monks** certainly played a vital role in the development of this

Choir of the church of Saint-Thibault

rugged, primitive country. By the Merovingian period, two abbeys were already making waves throughout the region: Luxeuil-les-Bains *(qv)* in the north and Condat *(qv)* in the south. The former rapidly became an intellectual centre exerting an influence on the whole of Gaul (in particular in Lure), while the latter devoted its energies to spreading the Christian message and to the enormous task of clearing space in the forests of the Jura. Unfortunately, the anarchy which greeted the end of Carolingian rule sounded a death knell for both these abbeys. In the 10C, the Benedictines thus faced the task of winning back territory in Burgundy. They were followed by the Cluny order (founded by the monks of the abbey at Baumes-les-Messieurs – *qv*), which soon dominated the province. However, in the 12C the Cluny order itself had to give way to the innumerable Cistercian communities which were springing up all over the region. At the same time, communities were being set up by the Premonstratensians, the Augustinians and the Carthusians who all threw themselves into clearing the forest and draining the soil, thus attracting their share of local residents, who set up communities round their abbeys. The churches, which are now used as parish churches, were originally monastery churches most usually built according to the rules of religious order which was to use them: thus, the Benedictine order introduced a primitive architectural style influenced by early Italian basilicas; the Cluny order preferred Burgundian style churches; and the Cistercians built churches with a flat chevet, like that at Cîteaux, and generally paved the way for Gothic art.

Romanesque – There is in fact no Romanesque art specific to the Franche-Comté; the primitive churches built there during the Romanesque period drew on Burgundian and Lombard architecture for their inspiration. They generally have a basilical floor plan with a transept hardly wider than the nave itself. The chancel ends in a semicircular apse, flanked by two apsidal chapels opening into the transept, or it ends in a flat chevet (as in the church at Courtefontaine). Large arcades are supported by heavy pillars, which can be square, round or octagonal, with no capitals. The actual fabric of the building, including the pillars, is often of small quarry stones. The nave and side aisles were originally covered by a timber roof, which was later replaced by ogive vaulting. The roofs over the side aisles are sometimes groined vaulting. The apse and apsidal chapels are closed off by half domes. The roof above the transept crossing is either a dome, or a bell tower when there is none above either of the transept arms. The bell tower never features as part of the façade.

Church of St-Hymetière

The churches of the Franche-Comté are typically understated, and the absence of almost any decoration further underlines their austerity. The only decoration is provided by tall Lombard bands joined by one or two arcades. The churches of St-Hymetière *(photograph previous page)*, St-Lupicin (early 12C), Boussières, and the crypt of St-Denis at Lons-le Saunier are the best preserved examples of this.

The cathedral of St-Jean at Besançon is virtually the only remaining trace of Rhenish Carolingian influence in the Franche-Comté; it has an apse at either end of its nave. Inside, square sturdy pillars alternate with round slender ones, creating a regular, harmonious division of space. There are also small churches by this school, which have a single nave and a bell tower on their façade.

Gothic – Romanesque art continued to exert its influence in the Franche-Comté for some time; one might take this as evidence of the distrust of innovation and change for which the region's inhabitants have acquired a reputation in the rest of France.

Thus, at the end of the 13C, which marked the culmination of the great period of creativity in Gothic art elsewhere, there were still numerous Romanesque features evident in buildings in the Franche-Comté which had adopted the "new" style. The most typical and best preserved example of this period of transition is the church of St-Anatoile at Salins. This has a semicircular arched doorway, large pointed arches in the nave and a triforium with Romanesque arcades. It is in fact this long-lasting preference for semicircular arches that gives the churches of the Franche-Comté their distinctive character. The Gothic style did not really become widespread in the Franche-Comté until the middle of the 15C, when Flamboyant Gothic features were adopted. It did not reach its apogee there until the following century, even surviving into the middle of the 17C, when the Renaissance style was already starting to decline in other parts of France.

Flamboyant Gothic churches in the Franche-Comté typically have three tall blind naves separated by elegant pointed arches supported on round pillars. The ribs from the vaulting and the moulding from the arches run down these pillars. The church is topped by an enormous bell tower. Large windows shed light into the deep, five-sided choir (Cathédrale St-Pierre in St-Claude, Collégiale St-Hippolyte in Poligny), which is flanked by two chapels. These open onto the transept, which is a little wider than the nave. The moderation and sobriety so dear to local people's hearts are probably responsible for the avoidance of the more excessive features of Flamboyant Gothic, which characterised the style elsewhere. In the Franche-Comté, vaulting is generally uncluttered by lierne and tierceron ribs (although the basilica of Notre-Dame at Gray is an example of this kind of decoration), and only seigneurial chapels, such as the Chalon family chapel at Mièges, feature large, ornate hanging keystones.

Renaissance – The Italian Renaissance did not have a very marked effect on the religious architecture of the Franche-Comté, which adhered to Flamboyant Gothic until quite late on. The new style was applied, once it began to make its influence felt, for the most part to church annexes, such as chapels (Pesmes) or entrance doorways (Collège de l'Arc at Dole). Sculpted decoration, in particular woodwork, adapted more successfully to the new style.

Classical to modern periods – As the Renaissance before it, so **Classical** art was slow to catch on in the Franche-Comté, where the influence of the Gothic style was still strong; it only really began to make its mark from 1674 onwards, when the churches destroyed during the Ten Years War (1633-1643) and the destructive campaigns of Louis XIV were being rebuilt. The small size and run-down nature of the churches which had survived from the Middle Ages, coupled with a huge rise in population figures from the middle of the 18C, may explain the great number of construction projects undertaken up until the Revolution.

The most characteristic feature from this period, which typifies the religious architecture of the region as a whole, is the way the porch is incorporated in a bell tower, which is surmounted by an "imperial style" dome, that is, a pointed dome with sides formed of four reversed curves covered with glazed tiles.

There are three common layouts: a church with a single nave, with or without a transept; a church with a centralised floor plan, either octagonal or in the shape of a Greek cross; or a hall church with three naves of equal height, generally without a transept. The naves are covered by pointed vaulting, and needed strong buttresses outside to counteract the powerful outward pressure which might otherwise have made the walls bulge at the top. The interior is often painted white, apart from the columns, pillars and ribs, which are picked out in grey. The regular façade is enlivened by frontons, pilasters and columns.

In the late 18C and early 19C, the neo-Classical style took over, with consciously simple, almost austere ornamentation. As in the Antique temples, the straight line replaced the curve, and side aisles with ceilings took the place of the side naves with pointed vaulting of the hall churches. The central nave was covered with a barrel vault, in which tall windows let in the light.

After 1850, the neo-Gothic style reintroduced pointed arches.

During the **contemporary** period, Franche-Comté is proud of the fact that it has been the setting for a revival of religious art. Since the 1950s and 1960s, some important architectural projects have been undertaken, for example, at Audincourt, Ronchamp and Dole (the church of St-Jean-l'Évangéliste). A desire to emphasize the spirituality of such places is often evident in the powerful movement of the line of the building and in the masterful way the decorative effects of light have been exploited.

Many artists, such as Manessier, Gabriel Saury, Bazaine, Le Moal and Fernand Léger, have contributed in the same spirit as the architecture, giving a new or renewed vitality to religious buildings with their stained glass windows, sculptures, mosaics or tapestries.

CIVIL AND MILITARY ARCHITECTURE

In Burgundy

Gallo-Roman art – During their occupation, the Romans were responsible for the building of numerous monuments in Burgundy. To this day the town of Autun, built at the order of the Emperor Augustus to replace Bibracte, capital of the Aedui tribe, recalls Roman civilization with its two monumental gateways and its vast theatre.

Excavations undertaken at Alésia, at the presumed site of the camp where Vercingetorix made his last stand before the Roman legions of Julius Caesar in 52 BC, have led to the discovery of a complete town built a little later: paved streets, the foundations of temples and a forum, as well as many dwellings have been uncovered. Other excavations carried out at the source of the Seine have revealed the ruins of a temple and a number of bronze statuettes and unusual wooden sculptures. Numerous pieces of pottery dating from Gallo-Roman times as well as examples of gold and silver work of great value were found more than fifty years ago at Vertault, not far from Châtillon-sur-Seine.

At Dijon, the remains of an entrenched camp *(Castrum Divionense)*, built about AD 273, have been uncovered. Excavations at Fontaines-Salées near St-Père-sous-Vézelay have revealed very extensive Gallo-Roman baths.

Gothic – Fine mansions and houses built by wealthy merchants in the 15C have survived in Dijon and some other towns, such as Flavigny-sur-Ozerain and Châteauneuf. Part of the palace of the Dukes of Burgundy in Dijon (the tower on the terrace and the ducal kitchens), the synodal palace in Sens and the hospital in Beaune, a triumph in wooden architecture, all date from this period. Among the fortified castles of the 13C, those of Châteauneuf, built by Philippe Pot the Seneschal of Burgundy, Posanges and the ducal palace at Nevers are particularly interesting.

Renaissance – There was no "blossoming" of great Renaissance châteaux in Burgundy, as there was in the valley of the Loire; however, towns such as Ancy-le-Franc, Tanlay and Sully boast some magnificent mansions.

Classical – The reunion of Burgundy with the crown of France marked the end of the duchy's political independence, but its artistic expression, albeit unobtrusive, survived. Classical art, initially imitated from Paris and later Versailles, is to be seen in Dijon in the layout of the Place Royale, the alterations to the old Palais des Ducs and in the building of a new Palais des Ducs. Many fine mansions were built by the families of parliamentarians who were in favour at Court at the time and who held high positions. Although retaining the characteristics of the Renaissance period, the Hôtel de Vogüé (built 1607-1614) features the new design where the living quarters are set back behind a courtyard having access to the street only through the coach gateway, with the opposite façade of the house opening onto the gardens.

Among the numerous châteaux built in the 17C and 18C, those of Bussy-Rabutin *(illustration p 113)*, Commarin, Grancey, Beaumont-sur-Vingeanne, Menou and Talmay deserve a special mention. The sculptors – Dubois in the 17C and Bouchardon and Attiret in the 18C – were very influential on their times. This applies also to painters and draughtsmen such as Greuze and François Devosge and above all Mignard, master-painter at the court of Louis XIV.

Burgundy prides itself on its contribution to the musical world, **Jean-Philippe Rameau,** born in Dijon at the end of the 17C. He was a contemporary of Bach and Handel and ranks as one of the great French classical composers. Besides many pieces for the harpsichord, he composed some operas, of which one, *Les Indes Galantes*, is still included in the contemporary repertoire.

19 and 20C – In architecture, **Gustave Eiffel** (1832-1923), an engineer from Dijon, specialised in metal construction: bridges, viaducts etc. The mention of his name conjures up the famous tower he erected in Paris for the universal exhibition in 1889, with a structure based on a web of girders.

In the Franche-Comté

The architectural heritage of the Franche-Comté reflects its turbulent history even now, after centuries as a point of meeting and exchange of ideas and people passing through, not to mention the strategic value its position was perceived to give it, regardless of which particular power claimed to have authority over it at the time. The region was regularly subjected to the ravages of war and invasion, and it spent most of its infrequent periods of peace rebuilding its ruins. For this reason, there are relatively few real architectural masterpieces. However, the restrained style of the buildings of the Franche-Comté lends them their own particular charm, which is supplemented from time to time by foreign influences. During the **Gallo-Roman** period, Sequania was wealthy, but little trace of this glorious past remains after the invasions of the 9 and 10C, which cost the Sequani dear as they struggled to defend themselves. The Roman triumphal arch which the inhabitants of Besançon call Porte Noir (the black gate), the Roman road at Boujailles, the remains of a theatre at Mandeure near Montbéliard are about all that is left from this period.

The Middle Ages – After the Carolingian invasions and the subsequent disintegration of Carolingian rule, power devolved into the hands of local lords. These immediately felt the need to protect themselves and their property, and turned to the Scandinavians for a design of fairly crude castle: the **keep** or **castle mound** (11C). This construction consisted of a mound (of earth) surrounded by a moat, and surmounted by a square wooden tower, which was later replaced by a stone tower.

At the same time, **stone fortresses** (Pesmes, Champlitte) made their appearance, generally built on existing hills. The surrounding fortified wall – a stone embankment with a moat around its outer edge – enclosed the living quarters and outbuildings, while the keep remained the stronghold. This kind of fortress reached its apogee in the late 12C and the 13C.

At this point, a new kind of seigneurial dwelling evolved with the rise of the middle-ranking class of knights: the **fortified house** (especially after 1250). This would be located just outside the village near a stream or river, and would be constructed on a man-made platform surrounded by a water-filled moat. The buildings – residential wings and outbuildings – are arranged around a central courtyard.

Fortresses did not fare at all well during the 14 and 15C, as first the Hundred Years War, then the guns of Louis XI's troops wreaked devastation. However, the Château du Pin (15C), which is very well preserved, is an interesting example of medieval military architecture.

At the end of the Gothic period, town houses began to feature more prominently, and were decorated in particular with mullioned windows surmounted by ogee arches.

Renaissance – The return of peace and prosperity to the Franche-Comté during the 16C was marked by numerous castles being modified to reflect the new style, while at the same time having their defences reinforced to withstand the new metal cannon balls, which were much more destructive than the old stone ones (reinforcement of the ramparts, piercing of loopholes for guns, construction of gun towers to protect in particular the entrance, etc.). But the aristocracy tended to prefer their mansions in town where Renaissance art really came into its own.

Unlike religious architecture, civil architecture drew very little inspiration from Gothic art, whereas it was wide open to the graceful, attractive lines and forms which arrived from Italy. Emperor Charles V's Chancellor, Perrenot de Granvelle, set the example by building himself a mansion at Besançon from 1534. The Franche-Comté gradually began to be taken over by buildings with façades with superimposed orders (the Hôtel de Ville at Gray) or at least with moulded string courses separating the different floors. Frontons replaced ogee arches above windows. On the ground floor, the basket-handle arch was used for doorways or open arcades, introducing a regular movement clearly Spanish in inspiration (the interior courtyard of the Palais Granvelle at Besançon). The architectural renewal made itself equally strongly felt in floral decoration as the façade of the Château of Champlitte illustrates. The decorative artist and architect Hugues Sambin (1518-1601), born near Gray and well known for the projects he completed in Burgundy, left a magnificent example of his energetic artistic creativity on the polychrome

Château de Champlitte

façade of the Palais de Justice at Besançon (1581), which is his finest piece of work in the Franche-Comté.

Classical – In the 17C, the Franche-Comté was crushed by the Ten Years War *(qv)*. It was not until after 1674, the date when the province was incorporated into France, that a new architectural impetus came to life. The strategic position of the region, in between the Vosges and the Jura mountain ranges, compelled the French kingdom to consider implementing a comprehensive project of fortification without further ado. The task was entrusted to Vauban, who paid particular attention to the defence of the points along the routes leading to Switzerland which were the only possible way to get through. Although part of it has been destroyed, Vauban's monumental work has left an indelible impression on parts of the Franche-Comté countryside. The royal architect's greatest achievement is to have developed the concept of bastion layout (adopted during the 16C) to its maximum potential, the underlying principle being to run a curtain wall between two bastions in such a way that the two protect each other. This idea had undergone significant development before Vauban, but he not only refined it to its definitive form *(see illustration XIII, p 35)*, but was able to adapt it to suit the terrain of any site, whether it be a fortified town wall (Belfort, Besançon – which also has an impressive citadel) or an isolated fortress (Fort St-André near Salins-les-Bains).

Civil architecture flourished in its turn in the 18C, which was a richly productive period for art in the Franche-Comté. The most original work of this period is the royal salt works at Arc-et-Senans, designed as an ideal town by visionary architect Ledoux *(qv)*. Châteaux (typically on a horseshoe layout, as at Moncley), private houses and civil buildings display perfectly symmetrical façades, pierced with large windows surmounted by triangular or rounded frontons. Another characteristic of these monuments, which some consider to be on a level of perfection with the Louis XVI style, is their traditional high roofs.

19 and 20C – In the Franche-Comté, military architecture continued to evolve throughout the 19 and 20C. In the 19C, a number of fortresses were built, including the large fort at Les Rousses) on sites that were vulnerable now that the potential for gun warfare was being developed. Most of these constructions have survived, although they are not easily seen nowadays. The invention of the torpedo shell in 1885, then of the double-action fuse meant that forts were abandoned in favour of semi-underground concrete bunkers. During the Second World War, the French High Command even went so far as to build thirty or so blockhouses to protect Swiss neutrality. Modern architecture has produced some great works of art in the region; in the 19C, impressive viaducts such as that at Morez were built to span some of the Jura gorges. Since the war, engineers have been concerned mainly with constructing dams; the Génissiat dam (1948) on the Rhône and the Vouglans dam (1968) in the Ain valley are two particularly impressive examples.

PAINTING AND SCULPTURE

In Burgundy

Pre-Romanesque – During this period, sculpture was clumsily executed: the crypt of Flavigny-sur-Ozerain, all that remains of an 8C basilica, contains four shafts of columns, of which three appear to be Roman and the fourth Carolingian. The capitals are of great interest: they carry a decoration of fairly crudely executed flat foliage. Two of the capitals in the crypt of the cathedral of St-Bénigne at Dijon are decorated on each face by a man with his arms raised in prayer.

The capitals, which were sculpted *in situ*, reflect the experimental nature of the work; some sides are no more than rough outlines *(see photograph p 38).*

During the same period, frescoes and glazed surfaces were used in the decoration of the walls of religious buildings. In 1927, fine frescoes representing among other scenes the stoning of St Stephen were discovered in the crypt of St-Germain in Auxerre.

Romanesque sculpture – The Cluny school of sculpture is the most significant development in the Romanesque period. The great Benedictine abbey of Cluny attracted large numbers of sculptors and image-carvers, thus becoming almost the only creative centre from 1095 to 1115.

An art form was born that paid great attention to form and detail. Artists revealed a new interest in nature in the variety of vegetation and keenly observed poses of the human figures they carved on the capitals in the choir (rare examples survive – *see photograph p 132).* The figures are draped in flowing tunics, creating an outline which is in keeping with the serenity they were desired to express. The influence of Cluny's sculpture was at first apparent in the church of Ste-Madeleine at Vézelay – both in the carved capitals and in the tympanum of the doorway in the narthex, which shows Christ sending out his apostles before his ascension into heaven. The composition contains a sweeping movement which represents the Holy Spirit; the bodies and draperies seem to be caught up in a wind. This sculpture (1120) has much in common with the doorway of the church of St-Lazare in Autun, where the Last Judgment (1130-1135) contains elongated figures draped in pleated robes more closely moulded on the bodies than at Vézelay.

Both here and in his work in general Gislebertus, the sculptor at Autun, tried to express the full range of human attitudes and sentiments. The capitals in the nave and choir, which are slightly earlier (1125-1130), depict scenes from the Bible and the lives of the Saints; they provided inspiration for the vigorous talent of the artists who created St Andoche in **Saulieu.**

The two doorways of the church of St-Lazare in **Avallon,** which date from the mid-12C, reveal a desire for a new style: luxuriant decoration including wreathed columns, an expression of the "Baroque tendency" of Burgundian Romanesque art, is depicted side by side with a column statue which recalls Chartres. The gravity and troubling presence of the round bosses on the tomb of St Lazarus in Autun (1170-1184) already point forward to the Gothic style.

The Brionnais, where there is an unusual profusion of sculpted doorways, seems to have been the oldest centre for Romanesque sculpture in Burgundy. From the mid-11C to the great projects of Cluny this region produced a slightly crude and gauche style; the figures are bunched and their movements lack elegance. After working in Cluny, where they were summoned by Abbot Hugh of Semur who was related to the lords of the Brionnais, the Brionnais artists introduced a new grace into their work, elongating the figures and creating less rigid compositions. These sophisticated trends appeared beside traditional elements, such as a taste for short compact figures, and evolved towards a certain mannerist decorative style (tympanum of St-Julien-de-Jonzy – *qv).*

Romanesque painting – The crypt of the cathedral in Auxerre contains some 11C frescoes depicting Christ on horseback, holding a rod of iron in his right hand. At Anzy-le-Duc, restoration work carried out in the choir in the middle of the 19C uncovered a large collection of mural paintings which had different characteristics from those at Auxerre: very subdued, dull tints with dark outlines covering a background composed of parallel bands.

Another style (blue backgrounds) appears at Cluny and at Berzé-la-Ville, in the chapel of the "Château des Moines", where one can see a fine collection of Romanesque mural paintings. These frescoes, brought to light at the end of the 19C from beneath a layer of distemper, were painted in the early years of the 12C. The use of bright paints, which are also not as matt as at Anzy-le-Duc, is the distinctive feature of a different technique from that used up to that time. As Berzé-la-Ville was one of the residences of the abbots of Cluny where St Hugh came to stay on several occasions, it appears certain that these frescoes were painted by the same artists employed in the building of the great abbey. The gigantic Christ in Majesty, surrounded by six apostles and numerous other figures, is of Byzantine inspiration and seems to have been copied from the mosaics of the Empress Theodora in the church of San Vitale in Ravenna.

Frescoes, Chapelle des Moines, Berzé-la-Ville

This similarity between Cluniac and Byzantine art is explained by the leading role played by St Hugh, who used examples furnished by the Roman and Carolingian basilicas, which were strongly influenced by Byzantine art. Thus, in architecture, sculpture and painting, the influence of Cluny was the determining factor in the art of the 12C, and the destruction of the majority of the great abbey at the end of the 18C can be viewed as an irreparable loss. The remains that have survived give a very incomplete idea of what was without doubt the synthesis of Romanesque art.

Gothic sculpture – This concedes nothing in vitality and quality to Romanesque sculpture.

13C – The influence of the Paris and Champagne regions is evident in the composition and presentation of subjects, but the Burgundian temperament appears in the interpretation of some scenes, where local artists have given free rein to their fantasy and earthy realism.
A great part of the statuary of this period was destroyed or damaged during the Revolution; some examples of this 13C art survive in Vézelay, St-Père, Semur-en-Auxois, St-Thibault, Notre-Dame in Dijon and Auxerre.
In Notre-Dame in Dijon, some masks and faces are treated with an extremely elaborate realism, while others have an authenticity and an expression of such good nature that one is forced to think that they are portraits of Burgundians taken from real life. The doorway of St-Thibault-en-Auxois presents a number of scenes depicting the Virgin Mary but, more noticeably, five large statues portraying Duke Robert II and his family, among others. This rare example of lay personalities represented on the doorway of a church of this period is explained by the important part played by the Duke in the building of this church.
At St-Père the sculpted decoration of the gable on the west front is repeated in an interesting floral decoration on the capitals. It is probable that the gable of Vézelay basilica was inspired by that at St-Père, but the statutes in St-Père are of a much finer workmanship than those in Vézelay.
The tympanum of the Porte des Bleds in Semur-en-Auxois depicts the legend of St Thomas: the figures are heavy and the draperies lack elegance – characteristics of the Burgundian style. This style was modified at the end of the 13C and became more plastic: the low reliefs on the base of the doorways on the western side of Auxerre cathedral are of a delicacy and grace never achieved before. These masterpieces were unfortunately badly damaged during the Revolution.

14C – The advent of the "Great Dukes of Burgundy" in 1364 coincided with a period of political expansion and the spread of artistic influence in the Duchy of Burgundy.
In 1377, Philip the Bold began the construction of the Chartreuse de Champmol at the gates of Dijon, destined to be burial place of the new dynasty. The duke spared no expense in the decoration of this monastery, bringing to Burgundy from his northern territories a large number of artists, many of whom were of Flemish origin.
Of the artists who in turn worked on the magnificent tomb now to be seen in the guard room in the Dijon museum, **Claus Sluter** (c1345-1405) is incontestably the greatest. He knew how to give the personalities he depicted an outstanding poise, movement and vitality. His work was continued by his nephew, **Claus de Werve**, who abandoned the brutal realism of his uncle's style in favour of a more gentle approach. The draperies and clothes on the statues of Philip the Bold and Margaret of Flanders in the doorway of the Chartreuse de Champmol, which are regarded as authentic portraits, are treated with consumate artistry, and the faces have a striking realism. The tableau includes the Virgin and Child against the central pillar and the donors' patron saints: St John the Baptist and St Catherine.
A new trend in sculpture emerged: statues ceased to be part of pillars and doorways; facial expressions were treated with realism, and the artist, searching for authentic representation

Head of Christ, Puits de Moïse, Dijon

first and foremost, did not hesitate to portray ugliness or suffering.
Claus Sluter was also the artist of the great cross that was to have surmounted the well in the charterhouse cloisters (Puits de Moïse). The fine head of Christ *(see illustration)*, which luckily escaped destruction, is kept at the archaeological museum in Dijon. The faces of Moses and the five prophets represented on the base of the calvary are striking in their realism, and the costumes are long flowing draperies in broken folds. In both cases the subjects have been carefully studied and then portrayed in extraordinary detail, giving the composition an outstanding vitality and great intensity of expression, which have won the work acclaim as one of the great masterpieces of 14C sculpture.

15C – The tomb of Philip the Bold has given rise to many imitations: the mausoleum of John the Fearless and Margaret of Bavaria is a faithful replica; the tomb of Philippe Pot, Seneschal of Burgundy, shows more originality, since it is the mourners who support the flagstone bearing the recumbent figure.
Sculpture now turned to a different style from that of the 13C; proportions were more harmonious and the draperies simpler. The Virgin Mary in the Musée Rolin at Autun is a good example of this particular Burgundian style.
Representations of the Entombment or the Holy Sepulchre became more popular. The most remarkable of these compositions, grouping seven figures around the dead Christ, are to be found in the hospital at Tonnerre *(qv)*, in the church of Notre-Dame in Semur-en-Auxois and in the hospital at Dijon.

Some carved and gilded wooden retables were executed at this time by Jacques de Baërze: the retable of the Crucifixion and the retable of the Saints and Martyrs are on display in the Salle des Gardes of the Dijon museum.

Two other 15C Flemish retables, one depicting the Passion and the other the Virgin Mary, are preserved in the little church at Ternant (qv).

Gothic painting – The great Valois dukes surrounded themselves with painters and illuminators whom they brought from Paris or from their possessions in Flanders. In Dijon, Jean Malouel, Jean de Beaumetz and André Bellechose, natives of the north, created an artistic style remarkable for its richness of colour and detail of design, a synthesis of Flemish and Burgundian styles.

Among the best-known works, the polyptych in the Hôtel-Dieu at Beaune by Rogier van der Weyden and the paintings in the Dijon museum are of great interest.

During the Gothic period, frescoes came into favour again. Apart from the frescoes in the church of Notre-Dame in Beaune by **Pierre Spicre**, a painter of Dijon, the curious *Dance of Death* in the little church at La Ferté-Loupière (qv) is also noteworthy. Pierre Spicre designed the cartoons on which the tapestries in the church of Notre-Dame at Beaune were based. These works are remarkable brightly coloured.

The tapestries in the Hôtel-Dieu at Beaune, commissioned by Chancellor Nicolas Rolin in the 15C, are among the most beautiful of this period.

Renaissance sculpture – While Burgundian Renaissance architecture was characterised by the triumph of horizontal lines and semicircular arches, sculpture of this style used the antique form of medallions and busts in high relief, and gradually replaced sacred subjects with the profane.

In the second half of the 16C, ornamental decoration such as that conceived by Hugues Sambin, artist of the gateway of the Palais de Justice in Dijon and probably also of large number of mansions, was much in vogue in the city. In the 16C, decorative woodwork – door panels, coffered ceilings, church stalls – became increasingly important. The twenty-six stalls in the church of Montréal, carved in 1522, are a work of local inspiration in which the Burgundian spirit is plain for all to see.

Classical to modern – The transition from the 18 to 19C is marked by **Girodet**, the famous citizen of Montargis (qv). Prud'hon and Rude, both pupils of Devosges and attached to the academic tradition, were producing paintings and sculpture at the beginning of the 19C; the work of the former is characterised by muted tones and dreamy, sensual figures; that of the latter recalls his neo-classical debut, and the force of his subsequent expression of his romantic temperament in the Marseillaise on the Arc de Triomphe in Paris.

They were followed by Cabet, Jouffroy, and, nearer the present, the animal sculptor François Pompon (qv) who all contributed to the artistic reputation of Burgundy.

In the Franche-Comté

The Franche-Comté cannot pride itself on having been home to a regional school of painting of sculpture. However, despite having been under the influence mainly of Burgundian and Flemish artists, local artists produced numerous works of art which reflect their talent.

Unlike painting, sculpture was overlooked by local artists as a way of expressing their ideas during the Romanesque period, and only appeared in very rare cases on capitals (Besançon cathedral) or church doorways.

Romanesque painting – The art of painting underwent significant development during the 12 and 13C, while sculpture was making little progress. During the Romanesque and Gothic periods, artists turned to frescoes in particular to decorate the interiors of churches.

Gothic sculpture – During the 13C, craftsmen produced wooden statues in a naïve style, mainly of the Virgin Mary, which were moving for all their somewhat crude execution. It was not until the 14C that a real surge of creativity burst onto the scene, inspired by Burgundian art and in particular the work of Claus Sluter. The influence of the master's realism and expressive power can be clearly seen in the art of the Franche-Comté of the 15 and even 16C (several examples at the collegiate church of Poligny, splendid statue of St Paul at Baume-les-Messieurs). The production and decoration of religious furniture also developed during this period; the magnificent choir stalls at St-Claude (15C) and the even more elaborate ones at Montbenoît (16C) are some interesting examples.

Gothic painting – In the 14 and 15C, the art of painting altarpieces spread at the same time as the fresco technique. Painters of altarpieces were primarily inspired by Flemish artists (see the Passion altarpiece in the museum at Besançon). Unfortunately, in the 16C, the initial impetus of the primitive artists of the Franche-Comté petered out. Jacques Prévost, trained in Italy, was the only artist to produce works of any quality (triptych at Pesmes).

The aristocracy and merchant classes took advantage of their travels abroad to buy Flemish and Italian paintings, some of which are still part of the artistic heritage of the Franche-Comté (church at Baumes-les-Messieurs, cathedral and Musée des Beaux-Arts at Besançon).

Renaissance sculpture – In the 16C, sculptural forms became less tortured, and Italian sculptors were brought in to participate in projects in the Franche-Comté. The Gothic tradition was gradually dropped as local artists such as Claude Arnoux, known as Lullier (altarpiece of the Chapelle d'Andelot in the church at Pesmes), and Denis le Rupt (pulpit and organ loft in Notre-Dame at Dole) adopted the new style.

Classical to modern sculpture – During the Classical period, religious statuary became bogged down in academism. Only furniture still showed signs of the originality and good taste of the local artists (Fauconnet woodwork at Goux-les-Usiers). Later, some sculptors achieved a certain degree of fame, such as Clésinger, Luc Breton and above all Parraud (1819-1876), who were inspired by the Romantic movement to produce sensitive, emotive works (see the museum at Lons-le-Saunier).

At the end of the century, Bartholdi immortalised the resistance of the city of Belfort in 1870, by sculpting an enormous lion out of rock.

Classical to modern painting – From the 17C, French art became less regionalised. Famous artists from the Franche-Comté include Jacques Courtois (1621-1676), who specialised in painting battle scenes, Donat Nonotte (1708-1785), a portrait painter from Besançon, and above all Courbet (1819-1877), an ardent defender of realism.

DECORATIVE ARTS IN THE FRANCHE-COMTÉ

Clocks – The first rustic "grandfather" clocks appeared in the Franche-Comté in about 1670. Their case, either with straight, parallel sides or curved ones according to the prevailing fashion at the time of their manufacture, was made of oak or cherry wood, embellished with fairly ornate mouldings. From 1850, they were made increasingly with pine wood and decorated with naïve motifs. Initially, there was just one iron hand on the plain, varnished clock face to indicate the hour. Later, the face might be decorated with a central medallion or surmounted by a stylised fronton in copper or brass. Sometimes a small round glazed opening was made in the case so that the movement of the iron or worked copper pendulum which regulated the weights could be seen inside.

Wrought iron – The development of wrought iron flourished in the 18C. Works such as the wrought iron gate at the Hôpital St-Jacques at Besançon and that of the hospital at Lons-le-Saunier vie with Jean Lamour's works of art in Nancy. Other examples can be found at Dole (Palais de Justice) or Conliège. Strolling along the old streets of Dole or Besançon, notice the bulbous wrought iron balconies protecting the windows. Not least their name – "rejas" – suggests that they are a trace of Spanish influence. Their shape is no doubt designed to enable inquisitive inhabitants of Besançon, as of Seville, to stick their heads out of the window, but the climate in the Jura is hardly ideal for the moonlit serenades for which these balconies are generally the setting in Andalusia.

FOUNTAINS IN THE FRANCHE-COMTÉ

Fountains are particularly common in the Doubs and Haute-Saône *départements*, and with the churches are one of the most distinctive features of villages in the Franche-Comté. Most were built between about 1850 and 1870 and are characterised by their architectural design and monumentality. They provided a meeting point for local residents and their animals, and were for a long time the focal point of rural life, as their prime position in the centre of squares illustrates. They generally combined the various functions of a fountain – washplace and water trough – in an infinite variety of designs. The main period of construction of such fountain-cum-wash-troughs began around 1820, introducing a classical architectural feature inspired by Greek Antiquity into village centres. The most simple fountains were not covered, and many had a central column with some form of decoration on it. Others were sheltered beneath tall roofs supported on straight pillars, columns or even arches (the fountain at Gy). Some even take the form of a miniature circular temple or a semi-circle of water nymphs. Beaujeu is an example of a village where the town hall was built above the fountain.

Fountain, Thervay

Local heroes

	PERSON	Place
1090-1153	**Bernard de Clairvaux** – Born at the Château de Fontaine near Dijon. His strength of character and genius dominate the 12C. Considered the greatest writer of his time.	Cîteaux-Cluny
1486-1550	**Nicolas Perrenot de Granvelle** – Chancellor to Emperor Charles V. Builds a magnificent palace at Besançon.	Besançon
1517-1586	**Antoine Perrenot de Granvelle** – Son of Nicolas. Prime Minister of the Netherlands, Vice-Roy of Naples and Minister for Foreign Affairs under Philip II of Spain.	Besançon
1519-1605	**Theodore Beza** – Follower of Calvin from Vézelay. This highly cultured humanist succeeded Calvin in Geneva.	
1580-1637	**Pierre Vernier** – Inventor of the precision measuring device that bears his name, which can be attached to the scale of a larger mathematical instrument and used for taking more minute measurements.	Ornans
1627-1704	**Jacques B. Bossuet** – Prelate and theologian born in Dijon.	
1633-1707	**Sébastien le Prestre de Vauban** – Born in the Nivernais. Great military engineer and also a talented writer.	St-Léger-de-Vauban
1707-1788	**Georges L. Leclerc, Comte de Buffon** – Born in Montbard. Played a major role in the spread of French science.	Montbard
1708-1785	**Donat Nonotte** – Born in Besançon. Painter of excellent portraits. Brought his expertise to the School of Painting at Lyon of which he was the head.	
1734-1806	**Nicolas Restif de La Bretonne** – Prolific novelist and sometime philosopher born in Sacy near Vermenton. His work, often licentious but overflowing with an imagination that was based on reality, is a valuable source of information on late-18C society.	
1751-1832	**Claude François, Marquis de Jouffroy d'Abbans** – Born in Roches-sur-Rognon (Haute-Marne). Invented steamship navigation.	Baume-les-Dames
1755-1826	**Jean-Anthelme Brillat-Savarin** – Gastronome famous for his work on the "physiology of taste".	Belley
1760-1836	**Claude-Joseph Rouget de Lisle** – Born in Lons-le-Saunier. Captain of Génie at Strasbourg, composed a war song for the Army of the Rhine which went on to become France's national song, "La Marseillaise".	Lons-le-Saunier
1765-1833	**Joseph Nicéphore Niepce** – Father of photography.	Chalon-sur-Saône
1769-1832	**Georges Cuvier** – Zoologist, pioneer in comparative anatomy and palaeontology.	Montbéliard
1771-1802	**Marie François Xavier Bichat** – Physiologist born in Thoirette. Renowned for his Treatise on General Anatomy, in which he details the role of tissues in the functioning of organs.	
1772-1837	**Charles Fourier** – Philosopher and economist born in Besançon. His theories denounced the "vices of civilization" and advocated a society of "phalanxes", or communities, in which consumption was inseparable from production.	
1780-1844	**Charles Nodier** – Poet and writer born in Besançon. Wrote numerous fairy stories, mainly inspired by dreams. Contributed to the spread of Romanticism and the birth of Surrealism.	
1790-1869	**Alphonse de Lamartine** – Born in Mâcon. This poet and politician was one of the greatest figures in French Romanticism.	Mâcon, Milly-Lamartine
1795-1869	**Désiré Dalloz** – Legal consultant and politician born in Septmoncel. With his brother Armand, he founded a publishing house specialising in legal collections and codes and political economics.	
1801-1877	**Augustin Cournot** – Mathematician, economist and philosopher born in Gray. His research concentrated principally on the idea of chance and the calculation of probabilities.	
1802-1861	**Jean-Baptiste-Henri Lacordaire** – Famous preacher and writer who, in association with the Breton Lamennais, founded a liberal Catholic movement. He also reintroduced the Dominican Order to France.	
1802-1885	**Victor Hugo** – The famous poet, novelist and playwright, a leading figure in the Romantic movement, was born in Besançon.	

1807-1891	**Jules Grévy** – Lawyer and politician, born in Mont-sous-Vaudrey. Succeeded MacMahon as President of the French Republic in 1879.	
1808-1893	**Victor Considérant** – Political theorist and follower of Fourier ; born in Salins. His socialist theories were to be of crucial importance in 1848. Exiled by Napoléon III.	
1809-1865	**Pierre-Joseph Proudhon** – Sociologist with socialist tending towards anarchic views, born in Besançon.	
1819-1877	**Gustave Courbet** – Master painter, born in Ornans. Founder of the Realist school.	Ornans
1822-1895	**Louis Pasteur** – Chemist; biologist; invented rabies vaccine.	Dole and Arbois
1839-1924	**Hilaire Bernigaud, Comte de Chardonnet de Grange** – Chemist and industrialist; inventor of artificial silk.	Besançon
1862-1954	**The Lumière Brothers, Auguste and Louis** – Born in Besançon. They undertook research in the filed of photography and invented cinematography in 1895 and colour photography in 1903.	Besançon
1908-1988	**Edgar Faure** – Politician, adopted the region of the Franche-Comté as his own. Became deputy, then senator of the Jura and Doubs *départements* in turn, mayor of Pontarlier and Port-Lesney and president of several regional authorities. Several times a Minister, and as President of the Assemblée Nationale he nonetheless took an active part in international politics.	
Late 19C-20C	Over the last century, famous local authors have sung the praise of their native region: **Tristan Bernard** (Besançon), **Louis Pergaud** (Belmont dans le Doubs), **Colette** (St-Sauveur-en-Puisaye), **Marie Noël** (Auxerre), **Gaston Roupnel** (Gevrey-Chambertin), **Maurice Genevoix** (Decize), **Henri Vincenot** (Dijon), **Romain Rolland** (Clamecy) and **Bernard Clavel** (Lons-le-Saunier).	

Gastronomy

In Burgundy

Burgundy's reputation as a gastronomic paradise has been established for a very long time. Dijon has been a city of fine food ever since Gallo-Roman times, if one is to judge from the culinary inscriptions and signs engraved on the stone tablets that are now kept in the archaeological museum. In the 6C, Gregory of Tours praised the quality of Burgundian wines, and King Charles VI, who was still sane at the time, proclaimed the gastronomic delights available from Dijon, both good wines and special local dishes. During the age of the Great Dukes of Burgundy, great importance was attached to cooking at the palace of Dijon. Nowadays, the States-General of Burgundy and the gastronomic fair at Dijon perpetuate this tradition of good food and wine in the region.

The raw materials – Land of many blessings, Burgundy is home to some first-class beef cattle in the regions of Auxois, Bazois and Charollais, as well as some of the tastiest game in France. It produces incomparable vegetables, many varieties of fish (white fish from the Saône and Loire and trout and crayfish from the rivers and springs of the Morvan), the most delicious mushrooms *(cèpes, girolles, morilles* and *mousserons)*, snails which are famous the world over and mouth-watering fruit (cherries from the Auxerre region, for example).

Burgundian cuisine – This is both rich and substantial, reflecting the Burgundian temperament and robust appetite; people here expect both quality and quantity at table. Wine, the glory of the province, naturally plays an all important part: the wine sauces called *meurettes* are the pride of Burgundian cuisine; basically, they are made from wine thickened with butter and flour with flavourings and spices added. These sauces blend well with fish – carp, tench and eel – brains, poached eggs and the famous *bœuf bourguignon* (Burgundian beef casserole).
Cream is used in the preparation of many dishes: *jambon à la crème* (cooked ham in a cream sauce), *champignons à la crème* (mushrooms in a cream sauce), *saupiquet* (a spicy wine and cream sauce that accompanies ham; the sauce dates back to the 15C, and its name is derived from the old French verb *saupiquer* – to season with salt).

Burgundian specialities – These are numerous and include (besides those already mentioned above): *escargots* (snails cooked in their shells with various stuffings, for example garlic, butter and parsley), *jambon persillé* (ham seasoned with parsley), *andouillette* (small sausages made from chitterlings), *coq au vin* (chicken in a wine sauce), *pauchouse* (stew of various types of fish cooked in white wine) and *poulet en sauce* (chicken cooked in a sauce half cream and half white wine). In the Nivernais and Morvan regions, home-cured ham and sausage, ham and eggs, calf's head or *sansiot*, eggs cooked in wine, roast veal and *jau au sang* (a young pullet fried with bacon and pearl onions) figure among the traditional dishes. Dijon is also famed for its mustard *(moutarde)*.
All these delicious dishes may be accompanied by the wide range of excellent red or white Burgundy wines available.

Cheeses – Although Burgundy is famed more for its beef than its dairy products, it nonetheless produces some tasty cheeses. The countryside round the river Yonne produces St-Florentin, which should be eaten when the heart is still white and moist. The town of Époisses has given its name to a soft cheese which develops a smooth reddish-orange surface after two or three months, while the inside becomes the colour of butter and is smooth and creamy with a distinctive flavour. The goat cheeses of the Morvan region are small and make a perfect accompaniment to the dry white wines of Pouilly-sur-Loire.

Taste-bud ticklers – Some of the more famous local sweetmeats include the ginger-bread and *cassissines* (blackcurrant sweets) of Dijon, the aniseed balls of Flavigny, the nougat of Nevers and the pralines (almonds browned in sugar) of Montargis.

Those in search of a *digestif* to round off a good meal might consider *cassis*, the blackcurrant liqueur from Dijon, or a Burgundian brandy *(marc)* that has been aged in an oak cask.

In the Franche-Comté

Poultry and freshwater fish go particularly well with Jura wines, and *coq au vin jaune* or *truite au vin jaune* are classic local specialities. Game is in abundant supply throughout the Franche-Comté, and there are many traditional local recipes for hare, young wild boar, venison, woodcock etc. Wild hare in a white wine sauce with diced bacon, venison casserole with cream, and roast thrush (yes, really!) flambéed in Marc d'Arbois are just a few popular local dishes. *"Potée"* is made with a variety of vegetables cooked slowly in a casserole, with a strong smoky flavour added by the inclusion of delicious Morteau sausage, a speciality of this region, as is Montbéliard sausage. Local *charcuterie*, such as "Jésus" from Morteau and the numerous smoked hams (Luxeuil-les-Bains), is also widely appreciated.

Pork and bacon were for centuries the only meat eaten in the mountain regions. The pig was therefore the object of great care and attention on the farms, and careful calculation went into the diet on which it was fattened. Pig-killing day was the occasion for a great family celebration, with a "pig feast" of black pudding *(boudin)*, tripe sausages *(andouilles)*, brawn (head-cheese), chops and various other "bits and pieces" from the pig.

In the Franche-Comté, there are as many types of fish as there are rivers and lakes for them to thrive in: char and trout from the Loue; carp and pike from the Doubs; tench and perch from the Ain. In the lakes there are fish from the salmon family (coregonidae), white fish and small fry (roach, bleak and gudgeon). **"Meurette"**, with red wine, and **"pauchouse"**, with white, are fish casseroles made with chunks of freshwater fish. Mushrooms from the forests – *morilles, chanterelles* and *cèpes* – add their delicate flavour to aromatic sauces or blend with unctuous creamy sauces and a good local wine.

It would be a crime to leave the Franche-Comté without first having at least tasted some of the local cheese: Comté, with its hazelnutty flavour, which is melted in a saucepan with white wine to make a **fondue**, into which people dip chunks of bread; mild and delicate Emmenthal; rich and creamy Morbier; Mont d'Or, a subtly flavoured cheese made from milk from cows that have been kept on mountain pastures; Gex Septmoncel, a blue cheese with a delicate parsley flavour; and the famous **"cancoillotte"**, one of the region's oldest and most typical specialities.

Last but not least, all the local vineyards produce good quality **marc** spirits, but the kirsch from the Loue valley (Mouthier-Haute-Pierre, Ornans) is particularly well regarded. Pontarlier, generally acknowledged as the capital of absinthe, produces an apéritif based on green aniseed, "Pontarlier Anis". Liqueurs made from gentian and pine in the Haut-Jura plateaux are also popular.

"Cancoillotte" – a speciality of the Jura

Cook your own snails...
Tempted to buy a tin of snails, but not sure what to do with them once you get them home? Mix up some garlic butter with plenty of freshly crushed garlic (4-6 cloves 3-4oz butter) and lots of chopped parsley. Put each snail into its shell (these can be improvised out of tinfoil if necessary) and seal it in with a generous dollop of garlic butter mix. Put snails open side upwards (propping them up on a slightly scrunched tinfoil lining helps) into an oven dish (with sides – to catch the butter) and cook in a fairly hot oven for 5-10min (until butter sizzles). Eat immediately with fresh bread and... of course, a glass of red wine!

"Les Trois Glorieuses"
a charity auction
with a difference

The great wine fair
of the Côte d'Or
takes place during
the third weekend
in November:
*   on Saturday -*
Château du
Clos de Vougeot;
*   on Sunday -*
auction at the
Hospices de Beaune;
*   on Monday -*
"Paulée" de Meursault.

Hôtel-Dieu, Beaune

Sights

Vallée de l'AIN★★

Michelin map 170 folds 5, 4 and 14 and 74 folds 4, 3 and 13
or 243 folds 31, 30 and 42 and 244 fold 5.

The Ain is a beautiful, powerful river. Only 15km - 9 miles separate its source from that of the Doubs, which flows into the Rhône making an immense detour of 430km - 267 miles via the Saône, while the Ain joins the Rhône more directly, after covering only 190km - 118 miles.

The river flows through the Jura region almost entirely at the bottom of a deep gorge, tumbling down waterfalls, churning along as rapids or threading its way among rocky crags.

The Ain and its tributaries supply energy to about fifteen hydroelectric plants, the largest of these being the Vouglans (qv) plant.

Now you see it, now you don't – The Ain rises at an altitude of 750m - 2 467ft, on the Nozeroy plateau. From here (the *Source de l'Ain*), the river flows down a narrow valley with steep, wooded sides. It disappears from view for a short distance, as it vanishes into a deep rift known as the *"Perte de l'Ain"*, then flows on down to the Champagnole plateau, which is more than 100m - 328ft lower than that of Nozeroy. It is this great drop in height which explains the many waterfalls and rapids.

Crossing the Champagnole plateau – The Ain flows through a pleasant valley after Bourg-de-Sirod, with pretty meadows rising up to wooded slopes. It is here that the river Lemme, which forms a lovely waterfall at Billaude, flows into the Ain, having been swollen by the waters of the Saine. This torrential river, which drops 320m - 1 050ft in only 17km - 10.5 miles, itself forms a superb waterfall at Planches-en-Montagne, before carving out the Gorges de la Langouette

The river Ain cuts through a wooded spur before watering the area around Champagnole. 10km - 6 miles further on, its path is blocked by the steep slopes of the Côte de l'Heute, which force it to make a sharp bend and flow southwards along the edge of the hillside. The valley, 2-4km - 1-2.5 miles wide, is known as the Combe d'Ain as far as the Cluse de la Pyle. It is in fact the bed of an old lake which has been partially refilled with water by the damming of the Vouglans. Small tributaries draining the lakes region (*Région des LACS DU JURA* – qv) feed into the river from the east.

From gorges to lakes – The Ain once flowed through striking gorges after the Cluse de la Pyle, until it left the Jura region; the walls of the gorges now rise up on either side of several broad lakes created along the river's course by a series of dams. The confluence of the Bienne, a tributary from the east, and the Ain divides the valley into two sections, reflecting the different types of relief that the river is flowing through. To the north of the confluence lies the plateau through which the Ain has carved a course. To the south lies the Bugey mountain range. The river cuts through the folds of the southern Jura in a series of stunningly beautiful transverse valleys or *cluses*. At Neuville-sur-Ain, the Ain breaks through the edge of Jura mountain massif, known as the Revermont, and then flows on through the plain in sinuous loops parallel to the Rhone for while, before finally joining the great river itself.

Ain Valley

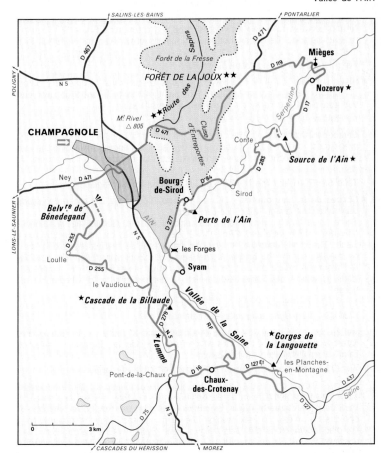

The events of 1944 – On 11 July 1944, the southern section of the Ain valley was the backdrop for military conflict, as three thousand German troops coming from Bourg attempted to cross the river at Neuville, heading towards the Bugey *(qv)* mountains. They were held off until the evening by two hundred men from the secret armies of Neuville-sur-Ain and Poncin, who formed the front guard of the *maquis*.

At the beginning of September soldiers of the US Seventh Army (Patch), coming from Bourg, crossed the Neuville bridge (since the Résistance had been unable to hold the bridge at Pont-d'Ain) on their way into Jura, in hot pursuit of the German Army retreating northwards.

★★UPPER VALLEY OF THE AIN

Leaving from Champagnole

84 km - 52 miles – allow 4 hours – local map above

Champagnole – Facilities. This industrial town, which was rebuilt after a fire at the end of the 18C, is a good departure point for excursions into the lakes region *(Région des LACS DU JURA - qv)*. The **Musée archéologique** ⊙ in the Rue Baronne-Delort contains objects discovered during excavation work in several Gallo-Roman necropolises. The collection of jewellery includes most notably some bronze and iron **buckles★** from the Merovingian period.

Leave Champagnole heading southwest on the D 471. At Ney, take the D 253 to the left; after 2.5km - 1.5 miles take the unsurfaced road, in poor condition, to the left for about 2.4km - 1.4 miles, until you reach a car park.

Belvédère de Bénedegand – *15 min Rtn on foot.*
A pretty forest path leads to this viewpoint. There is a lovely view of the Ain valley, Champagnole, Mont Rivel and, in the distance, the forest of Fresse.

Retrace your steps to the main road (D 253), go through Loulle and Vaudioux and turn right into the N 5. Take the first road on the left, the D 279, and leave the car in the car park at the side of the road, on a level with the Billaude waterfall.

There is a good view of the waterfall and its setting from the platform below.

★ Cascade de la Billaude – *30 min Rtn on foot.*
Take the path marked "Saut Claude Roy" which leads down to the waterfall. Take the steep, sharply twisting footpath down into the ravine, keeping to the right. Then there is quite a stiff climb uphill (100 steps, many of which are very high).

At the top, the Lemme can be seen tumbling from a narrow crevice in a wooded setting between towering rock faces, dropping a total of 28m - 92ft in two successive cascades. Delicately perfumed cyclamens grow near the waterfall in summer.

Return to the N 5 and follow it to the left.

★ **River Lemme** – The N 5 follows the valley of the river Lemme, a tributary of the Ain, as far as Pont-de-la-Chaux. The sight of this turbulent little river gushing between pines and rocky crags is fresh and exhilarating.

At Pont-de-la-Chaux, take the D 16 on the left.

Chaux-des-Croteney – This town, built on a triangular rocky plateau with precipitous rock faces dropping away at the edges, providing a natural defence, is thought by some archaeologists to be the site of ancient Alesia (qv).

Take the D 16 and the D 127^{E1} to Les Planches-en-Montagne.

★ **Gorges de la Langouette** – *30 min Rtn on foot. Leave the car in the shady car park after the bridge called "La Langouette".*
There is a lovely view from this bridge of the Gorges de la Langouette, only 4m - 13ft wide and 47m - 154ft deep, cut into the limestone by the river Saine. The three **viewpoints** ★ over the gorge can be reached by taking the path on the left before the bridge *(access also possible by car: follow the road indicated from the village of Les Planches).* The rather steep footpath is signposted and leads to where the Saine cascades into a narrow crevice, the beginning of the gorge.

Return to Les Planches and turn right at the church; then just before Chaux-des-Crotenay, turn right again into a forest road.

Vallée de la Saine – The route continues along a pretty road, running through forest along the top of the cliffs which form the sides of the narrow valley of the Saine, a small tributary of the Lemme.

Turn right after coming out of the gorge and cross the bridge.

Syam – Excavations in the Syam plain, near the confluence of the Lemme and the Saine, have enabled a team of archaeologists to say they believe they have located the site of the Battle of Alésia (qv). Having been besieged by Caesar's troops in the oppidum of Alésia for six weeks, the army of the Gauls is thought to have stormed down from the Gyts heights near Syam, where Vercingetorix had an observation post, in an attempt to join up with the Gallic relief forces which were attacking the Roman field camps defending the Crans threshold. In the ensuing battle, in which 400 000 men were involved, the Gauls were unable to break through the Romans' double line of defence fortifications and suffered a crushing defeat.
To the north of the village, near the Ain, there is a pretty little spot with an old mill and a forge which prospered during the First Empire.

North of Syam, turn right towards Bourg-de-Sirod.

Bourg-de-Sirod – This village owes its pretty site to the many waterfalls and rapids formed by the Ain as it covers the 100m - 328ft drop in altitude between the Nozeroy and Champagnole plateaux.

Leave the car in the car park near the Bourg-de-Sirod town hall (mairie). Follow the path marked "Point de vue, Perte de l'Ain".

Perte de l'Ain – There is a superb view of the waterfall formed by the Ain as it disappears into a crevice between fallen rocks.

Carry on through Sirod and Conte.

★ **Source de l'Ain** – Leave the car at the end of the access road (through forest) which leads off the D 283 after Conte. Continue on foot *(15 min Rtn)* to the river's source, which is at the bottom of the thickly wooded, rocky amphitheatre. This is in fact a resurgent spring *(qv)* and has a very variable flow. During the droughts of 1959 and 1964 the mouth was completely dry, and it was possible to climb up a part of the Ain's underground course.

Return to the D 283, turn left and continue to Nozeroy.

★ **Nozeroy** – See NOZEROY.

Mièges – This town grew up around a 16C priory. The inhabitants earn their living mainly from stock-raising and cheese-making. The **church** contains the late Gothic funerary chapel of the Dukes of Chalon; note the ornate pendant keystones on the ceiling.

Return to Champagnole by taking the D 119, then the D 471 to the left, which crosses the pleasantly green Entreportes ravine.

For details of leisure activities such as
  Rambling
  Canoeing
  Cycling
See under "Recreation" in the Practical Information section at the end of the guide.

★★ THE AIN RESERVOIRS

From Pont-de-Poitte to Poncin

109km - 68 miles - allow 2 hours 30 min

The Vouglans dam flooded 35km - 22 miles of the Ain gorge with water, forming the Lac de Vouglans. The lake is at its most attractive in the late afternoon. Tourists coming from Lons-le-Saunier begin this tour at Pont-de-Poitte; those from St-Claude join the tour having first travelled along the valley of the Bienne *(qv)*; and those who have based themselves at Bourg-en-Bresse or Nantua reach the gorge at Serrières-sur-Ain. Several parts of the Vouglans reservoir have been adapted for sport and recreation, at Surchauffant and Bellecin on the west bank and Mercantine on the east bank.

Pont-de-Poitte – There is a view of the river Ain from the bridge. When the water is low the "giants' cauldrons" are very much visible. When it is high, the rocky bed disappears under the foaming torrent, making an impressive scene.

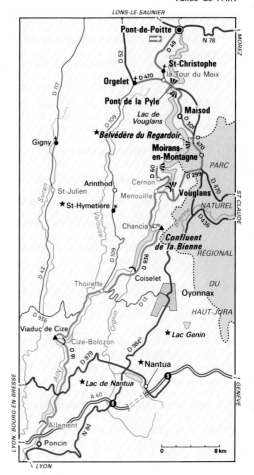

Leave Pont-de-Poitte on the D 49. 6km - 4 miles further on, take the D 60 to the left, then turn left again towards St-Christophe.

St-Christophe – This little village is set against a high cliff, overlooked by the remaining walls of a château as well as the **pilgrimage church of St-Christophe**. This was built in the 12C and 15C and contains interesting works of art and wooden statues. The 15C St Christopher shows German influence. In the single side chapel there is an alabaster Christ, a fragment of a 16C naïve wooden altarpiece, and a 15C Virgin and Child of the Burgundian School.

Go down to the village of Tour-du-Meix and take the D 470 to the right.

Orgelet – To the west of the church lies a large, grassy square with beautiful plane trees. The interior of the **church** is surprisingly spacious, with a tall Gothic vault and wide galleries across the west end of the nave (the organ loft) and above the first arches of the aisles on either side of the nave. The balustrade is extended by an arch which seems to close off the bay of the transept.

Carry on along the D 470 to the Pyle bridge.

Pont de la Pyle – The bridge is in prestressed concrete and is 351m - 384yds long and 9m - 10yds wide. The waters of the reservoir partially hide the three piles, each 74m - 243ft high. The view upstream is of the beautiful stretch of water which now occupies the old Pyle ravine.

From the Pyle bridge, follow the D 301 to the right (200m - 220yds after crossing the bridge).

As you turn, there is a lovely **view★** of the whole stretch of water contained by the dam. More **glimpses★** of the reservoir appear in between the oaks and evergreens which line the twisting road as you continue.

Maisod – Facilities. There is a signposted footpath in Maisod by the entrance to the château. A pleasant, shady walk *(1 hour Rtn on foot)* leads to the cliff overlooking the reservoir, and then continues along its edge.

Carry on along the D 301. A road leading to the edge of the lake leads off 1.5 km - 1 mile beyond Maisod.

Turn right into the D 470 towards Moirans.

★ Belvédère du Regardoir – *15 min Rtn on foot.*
There is a superb **view** from the platform overlooking the crescent-shaped section of reservoir, against a background of greenery.

Moirans-en-Montagne – This small industrial town tucked in a wooded combe has an interesting 16C church, which was partially rebuilt in the 19C. It houses a 17C wooden Pietà. Moirans itself is a centre for crafts and toy manufacture.

Musée du Jouet ⊙ – *5 Rue Murgin.* This toy museum presents a historical overview of the techniques of toy manufacture from the earliest days of this activity. The second half of the exhibition includes a collection of more than 5 000 toys displayed thematically in showcases on two floors. Children's play area.

Take the winding D 299 to the right after Moirans.

Belvédère du barrage de Vouglans – *2km - 1.2 miles from the D 299. Platform and shelter.*

There is an interesting view here of the Vouglans dam and the electricity (E.D.F.) plant which was built at its base.

At Menouille take the D 60 right, which leads to the level of the top of the dam.

Barrage de Vouglans – *See the Practical Information section at the end of the guide.*

There are boat trips available on the **Lac de Vouglans** ⊙. The 103m - 338ft high and 420m - 1 378ft high arch dam, which was first put in service in 1968, is only 6m - 20ft thick at the top. Containing 600 million m^3 - 21 190ft^3, it is the third largest reservoir in France after the dams at Serre-Ponçon and Ste-Croix in Haute-Provence *(see the Michelin Green Guide in French Alpes du Sud).* The underground electricity plant at the foot of the dam has an average annual production of 280 million kilowatt-hours.

One of the most beautiful meanders of the flooded valley can be ssen after Cernon, shortly before the intersection with the D 3. There is a **view**★★ of a wild landscape, including the wooded peninsula which extends to the middle of the lake *(car park right of the road).*

Turn back and follow the D 60 south. The road runs along the gorges beyond Menouille. Turn left towards Chancia and continue to the junction with the D 936, which you take to the right.

Confluent de la Bienne – This stretch of the valley, where the Bienne flows into the Ain, was flooded in 1971 to form a reservoir contained by the **Coiselet** dam.

After Thoirette the road is initially almost level with the bottom of the gorge for a while, then it climbs until it is overlooking it on the west bank.

Leave the D 59 and take a road on the left heading to Cize-gare.

This route follows a meander of the Ain, offering a view of the graceful curve of the 280m - 306yd long **Cize viaduct** which carries the railway line running from Bourg to Nantua.

After the viaduct, take the D 91 on the right.

The forests and meadows give way to thin scrub, surrounded by a majestic amphitheatre of cliffs; then the valley opens and the landscape becomes more cheerful. The last stretch of the itinerary runs along virtually at water-level beside the reservoir created in the Ain valley by the Allement dam, taking you to Poncin.

ALISE-STE-REINE

Population 667
Michelin map 65 north of fold 18 or 243 fold 2 – 16km –
10 miles northeast of Semur-en-Auxois

Alise-Ste-Reine is situated on the steep slopes of Mont Auxois (407m - 1 335ft) between the Oze and Ozerain valleys overlooking the plain of Les Laumes. The first part of the village's name is derived from Alésia, a Gaulish, then Gallo-Roman settlement on the plateau. The second part recalls a young Christian woman, Reina, who was martyred locally *(see Additional Sights below)* in the 3C; her feast day in September attracts many pilgrims.

Siege of Alésia – After his defeat at Gergovie (near Clermont-Ferrand in the Auvergne) in the spring of 52 BC, **Caesar** retreated towards the north to join forces with the legions of his lieutenant, Labienus, near Sens. Once the legions were united they began marching towards the Roman base camps, but on the way they were intercepted and atttacked near Alésia by the army of the Gauls, under **Vercingetorix**. Despite the surprise of their attack and their superior numbers, the Gauls suffered a crushing defeat, and Vercingetorix, fleeing from Caesar, decided to retreat with his remaining troops to the camp at Alésia.

A memorable siege began. Caesar's legions worked with pick and shovel to surround the camp with a double line of fortified earthworks, such as trenches, walls, palisades of stakes and towers; the inner ring of earthworks faced Alésia and was designed to prevent any attempts on the part of the besieged to escape, and the outer ring faced outwards to fight off any attacks from Gaulish armies trying to relieve the besieged camp. For six weeks Vercingetorix tried in vain to break through the rings that Caesar had set up. A rescue army of Gauls, 250 000 strong, was also powerless to reach the besieged and finally withdrew, abandoning them to their fate. With all hope of escape gone, Vercingetorix was forced to surrender and, to save his army, gave himself up to Caesar, who paraded him in triumph and eventually had him strangled after imprisoning him for six years in the Tullianum in Rome.

A battle of experts – During the last century, the site of Alésia as the scene of the siege was hotly disputed by some historians, who placed the combat between Caesar and Vercingetorix at Alaise, a little village in the *département* of Doubs, near the road from Ornans to Salins. To put an end to the controversy, Napoleon III had excavations carried out at Alise-Ste-Reine from 1861 to 1865. These revealed the presence of extensive military works built by Caesar's legions in the whole region of Mont Auxois, as well as the bones of men and horses and a mass of objects left behind during the siege: silver coins, millstones for cereals, weapons and weaponry. However, the erection of a huge statue to Vercingetorix on the site in 1865 by no means put an end to the polemics.

The opposing theory had a keen advocate in the erudite **Georges Colomb** (1856-1945) who, under the pseudonym of "Christophe", was also the author of two well-known books for young people, *La Famille Fenouillard* and *L'Idée fixe du savant Cosinus*. More recently excavations at Chaux-des-Crotenay to the southeast of Champagnole in the Jura have revealed another site which also claims to be Alésia.

Modern technology – aerial photographs and sample bores – has been pressed into service in support of the Burgundian claim. Information panels and markers at the side of the roads around Mont Auxois show where these roads intersect the ditches recognised by archaeologists as Roman trenches, or more precisely, the circumvallation and contravallation Caesar had built around Alésia.

★ MONT AUXOIS *time: 1 hour*

★ **Panorama** – There is a good viewpoint from beside the bronze statue of Vercingetorix by Millet. The panorama *(viewing table)* extends over the plain of Les Laumes and the site of the Roman outworks as far as the outskirts of Saulieu.

Les Fouilles (Excavations) ⊘ – The summit of the fortified settlement *(oppidum)* was occupied by a Gallo-Roman town which derived its prosperity from its metallurgical activity. The tour *(signs and numbered sites)* indicates the different districts grouped round the forum.

The western district contained the theatre (which in its final form dates from the 1C AD), the religious buildings and a civilian basilica. The northern district was prosperous and has shops, the bronze-workers' guild house and a large mansion, heated by a hypocaust (an ancient form of central heating beneath the floor), where a statue of the mother goddess was found in the cellar, hence the name "Cave à la Mater". The craftsmen's district to the southeast is composed of small houses, some with a yard where the craftsman plied his trade. To the southwest, the ruins surrounded by a cemetery belong to a Merovingian basilica dedicated to St Reina; this was the last building to be constructed on the plateau before the population moved down to the site of the present village.

The finds uncovered during the excavations are on display in the Musée Alésia.

Musée Alésia ⊘ – The museum is owned by the Société des Sciences of Semur-en-Auxois and contains all the objects found during the excavation of the Gallo-Roman town: statues and statuettes, fragments of buildings, reconstructed façade of a Gallo-Roman chapel, coins, pottery and other objects made of bronze, iron or bone. The 4C set of sacred vessels is dedicated to St Reina. In addition, various exhibits evoke the siege of Alésia.

ADDITIONAL SIGHTS

Fontaine Ste-Reine – Legend has it that a miraculous fountain gushed up from the spot where St Reina, a young Christian woman condemned to death for refusing to marry the Roman governor Olibrius, was beheaded. Up to the 18C, the curative powers of its waters were much esteemed; the fountain still attracts many pilgrims even now. The nearby chapel contains a much venerated 15C statue of the saint.

St-Léger – This 7-10C church, now restored to its original appearance, was built on the usual basilical layout with a timber roof over the nave and an over-vaulted apse. The south wall is of Mervingian construction; the one facing it dates from the later Carolingian period.

Théâtre des Roches – The theatre was built in 1945, modelled on ancient theatres, for performances of the mystery play performed as part of the annual pilgrimage in honour of St Reina *(see the Calendar of Events at the end of the guide).*

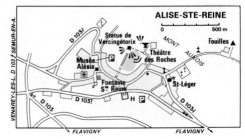

59

AMBRONAY★

Population 1 996
Michelin map 74 fold 2 or 244 fold 5 – 6km - 3.7 miles north of Ambérieu

Ambronay developed around a Benedictine abbey founded in the 9C by St Bernard, one of Charlemagne's knights (ruins of the old Carolingian church have been found under the choir and chancel).

Ancienne abbaye ⊘ – The church, cloister and chapter-house, as well as most of the conventual buildings, remain of the **abbey**, which has been rebuilt several times.

★ **Church** – This dates mainly from the 13C and 15C, with one or two even older remains. Many of the figures on the façade were destroyed during the Revolution. The lintel of the doorway on the left represents scenes from the Life of the Virgin. The Resurrection of the Dead can be seen on the lintel of the central doorway (13C, extensively restored): at the centre, Abraham is gathering souls into the fold of his cloak.

There is a beautiful line of smooth round columns (15C) along the south side of the nave, topped with simple ring capitals, which support the arches of the vaulting. A 15C polychrome stone Pietà can be seen in a wall niche in the north side aisle.

The **Chapelle Ste-Catherine**, north of the chancel, contains the 15C **tomb** ★ of Abbot Jacques de Mauvoisin, who had the church restored.

Cloisters (Cloître) – *Access through a door in the south side aisle*. The cloisters, a beautiful 15C construction, consist of arcades with graceful tracery, surmounted by a gallery which one can reach by taking the substantially restored, Louis XIV corner staircase.

Château d'ANCY-LE-FRANC★★

Michelin map 65 fold 7 or 243 fold 1 – 18km – 11 miles southeast of Tonnerre

The **château** ⊘ of Ancy-le-Franc is considered to be among the most beautiful Renaissance mansions in Burgundy. The sumptuous interior decoration, restored in the 19C, has a marvellous unity of style.

Antoine III of Clermont-Tonnerre, Grand-Master of Waters and Forests and husband of Anne-Françoise of Poitiers (sister of the celebrated Diane), had the château built in 1546 according to plans prepared by the Italian architect Sebastiano Serlio, who had come to the court of François I. He entrusted the interior decoration to II Primaticcio (1504-1570; Italian painter, sculptor and architect who did some of the ornamentation at Fontainebleau). In 1684 the château was sold to Louvois, Minister of War under Louis XIV. His descendants kept it until the middle of the last century, when the Clermont-Tonnerre family regained possession. On the death of the last duke, the château passed to this nephews, the princes of Mérode.

Exterior – A fine avenue leads to the entrance courtyard. The château consists of four wings connected by corner pavilions. The four façades are similar, lending symmetry to the ensemble.

This style of classic Renaissance architecture was the first to be seen in France. The simple, almost austere character of the external façades gives no hint of the sumptuous decoration of the inner courtyard, a vast square big enough to belong to a proper palace. The north and south wings have galleries composed of three arches running along their length opening out into the courtyard. Between the ground

Chambre des Arts

floor pillars are tablets which when read together reproduce the Clermont-Tonnerre family motto, *"Si omnes, ego non"* (Though all betray you, I will never betray you). This recalls the occasion when Count Sibaud de Clermont helped to reclaim the papal throne for Calixtus II, elected at Cluny, during the 12C Investiture Controversy (he was more successful at keeping the above promise than St Peter). In recognition of his support, Sibaud was granted the honour of bearing the pontifical tiara and keys of St Peter on his coat of arms.

Apartments – The tour of the galleries and apartments - 25 rooms - provides a chance to admire the sumptuous decoration by Il Primaticcio and also Niccolo dell'Abbate and other pupils of Il Primaticcio. The 16-19C furniture, for the greater part original, contributes to the harmony of the overall effect.

On the ground floor of the east and north wings are the following rooms: the Salle des Césars, the Salle de Diane (which has a beautiful ceiling painted in the Pompeian style in 1578), the Chambre de Vénus and the vast kitchens.

The first floor, starting in the north wing, houses the following rooms: the Galerie des Sacrifices (decorated with 16C monochrome panels), the Salle de Judith et Holopherne (Judith is depicted as Diane de Poitiers and Holofernes as François I), the **Cabinet du Pastor Fido** (the favourite retreat of Madame de Sévigné, panelled in carved chestnut and painted with pastoral scenes by Philippe Quantin in the 17C). There are also the library, several living rooms including the Salon Bleu, which was used by Louis XIV, the dining room, the huge Salle des Gardes (west wing) with an equestrian portrait of Henri III over the chimneypiece and finally the **chapel** with decorated woodwork and frescoes (1596) by the Burgundian painter André Ménassier.

In the south wing, the **Galerie de Pharsale** contains some enormous mural paintings in shades of ochre, giving an account of Caesar's victory over Pompey during the Roman civil war (48 BC), seen from the 16C perspective. The delightful Chambre des Fleurs takes its name from the many delicately portrayed species of flower; the painting above the fireplace shows a Clermont-Tonnerre as the huntress Diana. The Galerie de Médée (east wing) is followed by the splendid **Chambre des Arts**, decorated with oval medallions depicting the Liberal Arts, beneath an Henri II coffered ceiling richly decorated with arabesques.

Musée de l'automobile et de l'attelage ⊘ – The outbuildings to the right of the courtyard house about twenty **veteran cars** (pre-1914: Truffault 1900, Niclaux 1903, Renault and Dion Bouton 1905) and a selection of old bicycles, a 1926 Michelin poster as well as a collection of sixty carriages.

ANZY-LE-DUC★

Population 458

Michelin map 69 fold 17 or 238 fold 48 – 20km –12 miles south of Paray-le-Monial –
Local map under PARAY-LE-MONIAL: Excursion

This village in the Brionnais region possesses one of the most beautiful Romanesque churches in the area.

★ **Church** ⊘ – This harmonious church in golden stone was probably built in the early 11C. The tympanum from its fine doorway is now on display in the Musée du Hiéron in Paray-le-Monial *(qv)*. The building is surmounted by a magnificent Romanesque belfry, a polygonal tower with three storeys of bays. The outbuildings of the old priory, now occupied by a farm, are overlooked by a square tower. The tympanum of a very early **doorway** in the precinct wall shows the Adoration of the Magi *(left)* and Original Sin *(right)*. The lintel portrays the separation of the blessed from the damned at the Last Judgment. The main doorway (mentioned above) is still very beautiful, although its decoration has been badly damaged; it depicts Christ in Majesty.

The nave, remarkable for its purity of style and harmony of line, is roofed with groined vaulting and lit through the clerestory windows. The capitals have been well preserved; those in the nave represent biblical and allegorical scenes. The frescoes of the apse, now in poor condition, portray the lives of St John the Baptist and Hugues d'Anzy. Those in the choir show the Ascension of Christ. One fresco alludes to Letbaldus, the provost of Semur, who donated his property at Anzy-le-Duc in the 9C for the foundation of a Benedictine community.

ARBOIS★

Population 3 900

Michelin map 170 east of fold 4 or 243 fold 30 – Facilities –
Local map under Les RECULÉES

Arbois is at the entrance of one of the beautiful blind rift valleys known as *"reculées"* in the Jura, on either bank of the Cuisance. It is a picturesque little town surrounded by vineyards, and is a very popular holiday centre. It is possible to taste some of the famous local wine in several winegrowers' cellars which are open to the public. From the path winding along the west bank of the Cuisance there is a beautiful view of the church of St-Just, the Château Bontemps (once the residence of the Dukes of Burgundy), several old mills and the town.

Henri IV lays siege to Arbois – Henri IV invaded the province in 1595, using as his pretext the support the people of the Comté had given to the Catholic League. He claimed he had no objection to lands where the Spanish tongue was spoken staying under Spanish rule, or to those where German was spoken staying under German rule, but he insisted that all land where French was spoken should belong to him. The Maréchal de Biron, who led the campaign, laid siege to Arbois, which was defended by a **Capitaine Morel**. After three days of fruitless assaults, the Maréchal offered safe passage to the little garrison and its leader if they would surrender without further ado. The people of Arbois capitulated, but despite all the promises, the unfortunate Morel was immediately seized and hung. It required all the diplomacy Henri IV, a great lover of Arbois wine, could muster to mollify the outraged townspeople.

Hot tempers – The people of Arbois are renowned throughout the Comté for their particularly irreverent and independent spirit. The Arbois winegrowers have always been acknowledged to have a relatively short fuse. People have lost count of the number of times they have staged some sort of uprising. So it was that they were quick to proclaim the Republic in 1834, when Lyon rose in revolt. But they were disconcerted to realise that the new régime did not extend beyond the walls of their own little town. They were forced, albeit reluctantly, finally to accept Louis-Philippe. This particular uprising gave rise to the famous remark "We are all the leader" *(No san tou tchefs)*, when the Arbois citizens who had come to collect some gunpowder from Poligny were asked to name those who had led them in their revolt. The winegrowers have since revealed their explosive temperament only in connection with the proposed state monopoly on spirits in 1906, 1907, 1921 and 1922. Then they did not hesitate to voice loud and clear their criticism of the state, but once they had given vent to their spleen, they returned to work.

The "Fête du Biou" – This is the great Jura wine festival. On the first Sunday in September, the wine-growers of Arbois parade with an enormous bunch of grapes weighing 80-100kg - 176-220lb, which is made of many smaller bunches of grapes bound together. It is carried by four men, who march along behind fiddle-players, and behind these march the local dignitaries and wine-growers, escorted by "soldiers of the *garde-fruits*" carrying halberds festooned with vine shoots. After the procession, the "Biou" is hung in the nave of the church as an offering to St Just, the patron saint of Arbois.

PASTEUR IN ARBOIS

Pasteur's youth – Although Louis Pasteur was born in Dole, his true home in the Comté was the town of Arbois. After his parents moved there in 1827, he spent his youth there, his parents died there, and to the end of his days Pasteur never failed to spend his holidays in Arbois. When the Pasteur family moved to Arbois, they settled in a tannery which the scientist later turned into a large comfortable residence. The father did all types of leather work; the mother ran the household, raised the children, and kept the accounts. The close family life in which a high moral code was adhered to marked the young Louis for life.

Louis Pasteur

He attended primary school, then secondary school (where the sundial he made is still in the school yard). He was a conscientious, serious worker, who devoted so much careful thought to things that he gave the impression of being rather slow, and he was never considered more than a slightly above average student. His greatest interest was drawing. He drew portraits in pastels and pencil of his parents and friends, in which a certain talent is apparent. To be able to study for his baccalauréat, the young man entered the grammar school of Besançon as a teaching assistant.

A scientific genius – With his admission to the École Normale in 1843, Pasteur embarked on the career which was to distinguish him as one of the greatest minds in the history of mankind. He began with the study of pure science, where his studies of the geometry of crystals soon attracted attention. He then turned to practical problems. His study of various types of fermentation led him to discover the "pasteurization" process by which wine, beer and vinegar could be prevented from going off; his work on the illnesses of silkworms were invaluable to the silk industry. He produced vaccines to cure rabies in man and anthrax in animals. He put forward theories in the field of microbiology which were to revolutionise surgery and medicine in general, leading to the use of antiseptic, sterilisation, and isolation of those with contagious diseases. Pasteur also paved the way for immunization therapy (using antiserums).

Holidays – Every year the great scientist returned to Arbois with his family for the holidays, where he nonetheless continued his work, as vital to him as the air he breathed. However, whereas his Paris office and laboratory were strictly out of bounds to visitors, his Arbois home was open to all comers. Visitors flocked to ask for his support or advice; local winegrowers considered him a kind of viticultural magician and came knocking on his door as soon as a bottle developed some kind of problem. Pasteur's patience and goodwill were inexhaustible. He was also believed to be a great doctor, and the hope of a free consultation brought many a thrifty Arbois citizen to his office. He would participate enthusiastically in the parade for the "Fête du Biou" and the harvest celebrations.

In 1895, illness prevented the great scientist from going to Arbois as usual. On 28 September of that year, he died.

SIGHTS

★ **Maison de Pasteur** (Y) ⊙ – The house where Pasteur spent his youth has been preserved in such a way that visitors might almost think the great scientist was still in residence. The penholder stands ready on the desk; the inkwell and blotting pad are in their usual place; the cap might have been taken off just a few seconds ago. Photographs recall the faces of those Pasteur loved.

The instruments and apparatus used by the illustrious scientist during his stays in Arbois are on display in the laboratory. Even the culture mediums, which he used for his experiments on "spontaneous generation", have been preserved.

Not far from Pasteur's house stands a memorial statue (**Y E**) to the great scientist, under the lime trees of the Promenade Pasteur.

Place de la Liberté (Z) – This square still contains some 18C houses with arcades and wrought-iron balconies.

Hôtel de ville (Z H) – The town hall was once a convent. The chapel is now used as a law court. The 15C and 18C cellars **(caves ⊙)** now house temporary exhibitions. To mark the centenary of the great scientist Pasteur's death, during 1995 the cellars will be devoted to an exhibition on bacteria, "Mille Milliards de Microbes". This will study the role played by bacteria in the fermentation process, their use in the production of agricultural fertilisers, as well as looking at the ways in which they can both harm and be of benefit to humanity.

St-Just (Z) – The church, which dates from the 12-13C, stands on a large open square from where there is a view of the Cuisance. The most striking feature of this former priory church is its bell tower, which overlooks the town from the height of 60m - 197ft.

It was built in the 16C, using a yellow ochre coloured stone and has a bell shaped top, fairly common in the Franche-Comté. A lantern campanile contains the chimes.

Inside, great semicircular arches and massive pillars separate the side aisles from the narrow, Gothic vaulted nave. The sculpted wooden pulpit dates from 1717; the flat east end of the chancel is pierced by a large Flamboyant window, on which the twelve apostles are depicted. At the south door there is an epitaph to Capitaine Morel *(qv)*. The sculpted confessionals and the organ case date from the 18C. There is a particularly beautiful late 14C Virgin with Child in the north side aisle.

Pont des Capucins (Z) – From this bridge there is a lovely view of the Cuisance, the hills, the old houses and the remains of the fortifications with two old towers, the Tour Gloriette and the Tour Chaffin.

ARBOIS

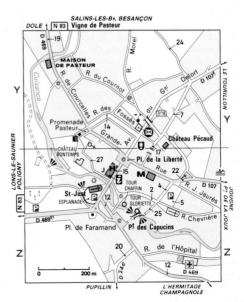

Arbois

Musée Sarret-de-Grozon (Z M) ⊘ – This old 18C mansion still has original furniture and woodwork, which evoke the atmosphere of a relatively well-to-do home of the period. Beautiful collections of paintings (works by the Jura artist A Pointelin), china and silver ware (from Dole and Besançon) are also on display.

Château Pécaud (Y) – These restored traces of the old fortifications of Arbois now house the institute of Jura wine and the **Musée de la Vigne et du Vin** ⊘. An outdoor display illustrates the various activities of the wine-grower, while inside there is a collection of exhibits evoking the history of local viticultural activity.

Vigne de Pasteur – *2km - 1.2 miles on the N 83, to the north of town plan.* Pasteur's vineyard is located to the east of the N 83 in the angle it forms with the road leading to Montigny-lès-Arsures. Pasteur bought these vines in 1874 and conducted his famous experiments on fermentation in grapes in 1878. The vineyard is remarkably well-kept and still produces an excellent wine, which is reserved for special ceremonies in memory of Pasteur.

EXCURSIONS

Pupillin – *3 km - 1.9 miles to the south.* One of the most famous local vineyards.

★★ **Reculée des Planches** – *21km-13 miles – see Les RECULÉES.*

ARC-ET-SENANS

Population 1 277
Michelin map 170 fold 4 or 243 fold 18 –
Local maps under Forêt de CHAUX and Vallée de la LOUE

Not far from the river Loue stands the old royal saltworks of Arc-et-Senans, one of the most unusual architectural essays in the classical style and a rare example of 18C industrial architecture.

An "ideal town" in the 18C – In 1773, the King's Counsel decreed that a royal saltworks should be founded at Arc-et-Senans, drawing on the salt waters of Salins which could be directed there in wooden conduits. The decision to built a saltworks at Arc-et-Senans was based on the fact that the nearby forest of Chaux would provide the fuel necessary for the processing of the salt. **Claude-Nicolas Ledoux** (1736-1806), inspector general of the saltworks in the Lorraine and Franche-Comté regions and already a famous architect, was commissioned to design the new saltworks. He had not yet designed the toll-houses in the so-called Farmers General fortified wall around Paris – most notably the rotundas in the Parc de la Villette and the Parc Monceau – but the private houses he had designed had won him a reputation for bold and ambitious ideas. He built the royal saltworks at Arc-et-Senans, his masterpiece, between 1774 and 1779. Only the cross-axis and half the first ring of buildings (workshops and workers' accommodation) envisaged by Ledoux were actually completed. What we see today is however enough to evoke the idea of an ideal 18C city. His plan was ambitious; a whole town laid out in concentric circles with the director's residence at the centre, flanked by storehouses, offices and workshops, and extending out to include a church, a market, public baths, recreational facilities etc. Ledoux's vision makes him one of the forerunners of modern architecture and modern design.

Unfortunately, the saltworks never produced as much salt as had been forecast – 40 000 hundredweight per annum instead of 60 000. Partially due to improved technology elsewhere, but mainly due to defective pipelines which led to the pollution of the drinking water with leaking salt water, the saltworks were closed down in 1895. Part of the buildings now houses a cultural centre, the **Fondation Claude-Nicolas Ledoux,** which organises a number of events.

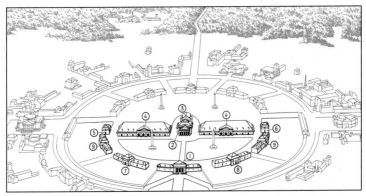

① Gatehouse (entrance)	④ Salt storehouses	⑦ Coopers' building
② Director's residence	⑤ Clerks' building	⑧ Farriers' building
③ Director's stables	⑥ Excise building	⑨ Dog handlers' building

The ideal town as designed by Claude-Nicolas Ledoux
All that was completed were the buildings to do with the saltworks, drawn in black above.

★★ SALINE ROYALE (ROYAL SALTWORKS) ⊘ *time: 1 hour*

Gatehouse ① – The road to Salins leads straight to the entrance of the gatehouse, which features a peristyle of eight Doric columns. Artificial grottoes recall the origins of salt. The building once housed the guards, and also the communal oven (which could be used for a fee), the wash house, the law court and the prison for the saltworks community. The building now houses the reception, a book shop and another shop selling miscellaneous items.

Courtyard – The semicircular courtyard, now a lawn, gives a good impression of the beauty and originality of the design of this complex. All the buildings around its perimeter face the director's residence, which is symbolically placed at the centre of the enterprise. They are decorated with carved motifs: petrified water flowing out of the necks of urns, evoking the source of the saltworking industry. This stylistically unified complex is all the more striking for the beauty and solidity of its masonry. The influence of Palladio, the 16C Italian architect, makes itself felt in the antique style columns and pediments, while the roofs are constructed in the manner typical of the Franche-Comté region.
Firewood was once unloaded for storage in this courtyard.

Director's residence, Saline royale

Coopers' building ⑦ – The cooper's building houses the **musée Ledoux**, a collection of about sixty architectural models at a scale of 1:200 and 1:100 which reveal Claude-Nicolas Ledoux's ideas about life in the ideal society. The right wing contains buildings by Ledoux which are only partially extant, or even not at all: the theatre at Besançon, of which only the façade remains; the saltworks at Arc-et-Senans; and the Château de Maupertuis. In the left wing, the "ideal city" of Chaux, the gun forge and the guardians' house at the source of the Loue are all projects that Ledoux was never able to realise. Prints and photographs complete the exhibition of the architect's work. On the first floor, there is a display of toll-houses.

Salt storehouses ④ – The old salt storehouses have been converted and during the summer now host concerts, temporary exhibitions and other events.

Director's residence ② – The director's residence has been the object of much needed restoration work, having been badly damaged by fire in 1918 and, as if that were not enough, the victim of a dynamite attack which wrecked the façade just as the building was about to be listed as a historical monument. The columns of the peristyle consist of alternating cylindrical and square drums. The salt warehouse was in the basement, while management occupied the ground and first floors. The landing of the main staircase was fitted out as a chapel, and above that was the administration department.

The rooms of the director's residence are now used for conferences and presentations. In the basement, the "**lieu du sel**" contains a display explaining why this place was chosen as the site of the royal saltworks and how the saltworks operated, and also a slide show and a film on the saltworkers of the early 20C.

AUTUN★★

Population 17 906
Michelin map 69 fold 7 or 243 fold 25 – Facilities – Local map under MORVAN

The city of Autun is flanked by wooded hills overlooking the valley of the Arroux and the vast plain that extends westwards. The cathedral, the museums and the Roman remains bear witness to the city's past greatness.
The remaining forests (Forêt des Battées and Forêt de Planoise, which is mainly oak trees) have enabled Autun to develop a high-quality furniture industry.

HISTORICAL NOTES

The Rome of the Gauls – Autun, derived from Augustodunum, was founded by the Emperor Augustus as a prestige Roman town, with the purpose both of honouring the Aedui, the local tribe, and of making them beholden to Rome. The splendour of the new town, which was known as the "sister and rival of Rome", soon eclipsed the contemporary Gaulish settlement at Bibracte *(qv)*. The city's location on the great commercial and military road between Lyon and Boulogne brought it wealth and prosperity. By the 3C, however, this extraordinary focus of Roman civilization suffered several disastrous invasions. All that remains today of the fortified enclosure and the numerous public monuments are two gates and traces of a Roman theatre.

The century of the Rolin family – In the Middle Ages Autun became prosperous once again, largely because of two men: Nicolas Rolin and one of his sons. Born in Autun in 1376, **Nicolas Rolin**, whose name is linked with the foundation of the Hôtel-Dieu at Beaune *(qv)*, became one of the most celebrated lawyers of his time. He attracted the attention of the Duke of Burgundy, Philip the Good, who made him Chancellor. Despite rising to such heights, he never forgot his native town, helping to restore its economic activity to a level it had not attained since Roman times. One of his sons, **Cardinal Rolin**, who became bishop of Autun, made the town a great religious centre. The completion of the cathedral of St-Lazare, the building of the ramparts to the south of the town and the construction of many private mansions date from this period.

★★CATHÉDRALE ST-LAZARE (BZ) ⊙ *time: 30 min*

Construction – In the 12C the Bishop of Autun decided to supplement the existing cathedral (destroyed in the 18C) with a new church to house the relics of St Lazarus, which had been brought back from Marseille by Gérard de Roussillon in about 970, hoping to create thereby a place of pilgrimage to rival the Basilique Ste-Madeleine in Vézelay *(qv)*. Construction took place from 1120 to 1146, and the cathedral was consecrated in 1130 by Pope Innocent II.
The exterior of the cathedral no longer looks particularly Romanesque because of later modifications. The belfry was destroyed by fire in 1469, and when it was rebuilt later that century, a Gothic spire was added to it. The upper part of the choir and the chapels in the right aisle date from the same period. Those in the left aisle are 16C. The two towers flanking the main front, which resemble those at Paray-le-Monial *(qv)*, were added in the 19C during large-scale restoration work by Viollet-le-Duc. The building was seriously damaged in the 18C, during the French Revolution; the cathedral canons demolished the rood screen and the tomb of St Lazarus which stood behind the high altar *(see below)*. They also plastered over the tympanum of the central door, which they found grotesque, and removed the head of Christ, which they thought stuck out too much. Happily, under this

protective covering the tympanum survived the Revolution unscathed and was rediscovered in 1837; the handsome head was found among the exhibits in the Musée Rolin and returned to its rightful place in November 1948.

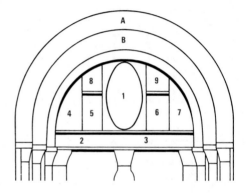

★★★ **Tympanum of the central doorway** – The tympanum (1130-35), one of the masterpieces of Romanesque sculpture, bears the signature of its creator, **Gislebertus**, beneath the feet of Christ. Nothing is known about him, except that his work suggests he was trained in Vézelay, and perhaps also in Cluny. Unlike his contemporaries, he did not conform to the Cluniac tradition, but produced his own distinctive style. His creative genius, his sense of form and his individual power of expression are evident in all the cathedral sculpture. The composition of the central tympanum is a masterly solution of the problems posed by the decoration of such a large area. The theme is the Last Judgement. Despite its apparent complexity, the design is impeccably thought out. At the centre, dominating the composition, is the tall figure of Christ in Majesty (**1**) surrounded by a mandorla supported by four angels. Below are the dead rising from their graves, summoned by four angels blowing trumpets (**4, 7, 8, 9**); in the centre of the lintel, an angel is separating the blessed (**2**) from the damned (**3**). At the left hand of Christ, the Archangel Michael confronts Satan, who is trying to upset the weighing of souls by pressing on the beams of the scales (**6**). Behind him yawns the mouth of Hell, which is squeezed to the extreme right of the tympanum (**7**), while Heaven occupies the whole of the upper register with *(right)* two Apostles or Enoch, the patriarch, and Eli, the prophet, transported straight to Heaven (**9**) and *(left)* Mary (**8**) in the heavenly Jerusalem (**4**) and the Apostles (**5**) attending the weighing of souls. St Peter, distinguished by the key on his shoulder, lends a hand to one of the blessed, while a soul tries to escape by clinging to the robe of an angel.

The human figure, which is the dominant subject of the tympanum, is treated in very diverse ways. The figures of God, His heavenly host, and the biblical characters are all dressed in light finely pleated garments. The diaphanous material, fluted at the hem, emphasises the insubstantial essence of the owners and the spiritual harmony of the heavenly kingdom. The smaller figures of the dead, sculpted in high relief, present a very different picture; the state of their souls is revealed through the simple but varied attitudes of their naked bodies; the more numerous blessed progress in a peaceful and orderly file, their faces turned towards Christ. By contrast, the fear and agony of the damned are expressed in the chaotic poses and irregular composition of the figures. Out of the parade of human beings, a few prelates and lords among the blessed *(left)* are draped with a cloak, which still leaves them largely naked like their fellows; the cloak is a distinguishing attribute and not a symbol of grace like the clothing of the divine figures in the upper register of the tympanum. Two pilgrims can be identified by their bags; one is decorated with a scallop shell, and the other with the cross of Jerusalem. Among the damned, on the right of the person in the clutches of the devil, is an adulterous woman with serpents (the symbol of lust) at her breast, while on the left is a miser with his money bag round his neck. The angular lines of the procession of the damned are repeated more forcefully in Hell, where the monstrous faces of the devils and the straining muscles of their misshapen limbs express their cruelty.

The whole composition is crowned by three orders of rounded arches. The outer order (**A**) represents the passing of time, the labours of the months alternating with the signs of the zodiac in the medallions; in the centre, between Cancer and Gemini, is a small crouching figure representing the year. The middle order (**B**) bears a serpentine garland of leaves and flowers. The inner order, destroyed in 1766 when the tympanum was plastered over, showed the elders of the Apocalypse.

Interior – *(Illustration p 39, plan overleaf)*. The pillars and vaulting date from the first half of the 12C. The Cluniac Romanesque style survives in spite of much alteration: three rows of elevation (large pointed arches, false triforium and high windows), massive cruciform pillars divided by fluted pilasters, broken-barrel vaulting with transverse ribs in the nave and rib vaulting in the aisles.

The chancel conforms to the early Christian design of an apse flanked by two apsidal chapels. The oven-vaulting disappeared in the 15C when the tall windows were inserted by Cardinal Rolin (the stained glass in the pointed windows dates from the 19C, that in the Romanesque windows from 1939). In 1766 the canons demolished the tomb of St Lazarus and used the marble to cover the chancel and the apse; the marble was removed in 1939.

The use of fluted pilasters surmounted by foliated capitals, which are to be found throughout the upper gallery, gives a sense of unity to the interior of the cathedral; these elements would have been familiar to the local masons from the many ancient buildings in Autun.

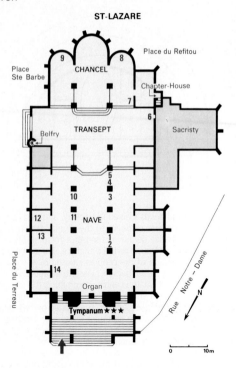

ST-LAZARE

Place du Refitou

Place Ste Barbe

9 8

CHANCEL

Chapter-House

7

6

Belfry

TRANSEPT

Sacristy

5
4

10 3

12 11 NAVE

13 1
2

14

Place du Terreau

Organ

Tympanum ★★★

Rue Notre – Dame

N

0   10m

The majestic effect is enlivened by the carved capitals. The most admirable features are:

1) and 2) Simon the Sorcerer tries to ascend to Heaven watched by St Peter, key in hand, and St Paul. Simon falls head first under the approving eye of St Peter. The devil (visible from the main nave) is beautifully portrayed.

3) The stoning of St Stephen.

4) Symbolic representation of Samson pulling down the temple.

5) The loading of the Ark, with Noah supervising from an upper window.

6) 16C sacristy door.

7) Statues of Pierre Jeannin, who died in 1623, President of the Burgundian Parliament and a Minister of Henri IV, with his wife.

8) The relics of St Lazarus are placed under the high altar.

9) White marble statue of the **Virgin and Child**★ dating from the late 15C.

10) Jesus appearing to Mary Magdalene against a background of curled foliage.

11) The second temptation of Christ. Oddly enough the devil is the only figure placed high up on the roof.

12) A 16C stained glass window representing the Tree of Jesse in the burial chapel of the bishops of Autun.

13) Painting by Ingres (1834) representing the martyrdom of St Symphorian by the Porte St-André.

14) The Nativity. St Joseph meditating in a strange, arched chair.

Chapter house – The chapter house was built in the early 16C, using some fine **capitals**★★ made of heavily grained stone containing mica, which originally capped the pillars in the chancel.
The most remarkable are on the right of the doorway:
– The hanging of Judas between two devils who are pulling the ropes.
– The Flight into Egypt, which should be compared with the representation of the same scene at Saulieu.
– The Magi asleep, all in the same bed with their crowns on. An angel is waking them to show them the star in the shape of a daisy. The scene is depicted with delightful simplicity.
– The Adoration of the Magi. St Joseph has been relegated to the right and seems to be waiting for the end of all the ceremony.

Belfry ⊙ – The belfry (80m - 262ft high) was built by Bishop Jean Rolin in 1462, when an earlier structure was struck by lightning. From the top *(230 steps)* there is a good **view**★ of the old roofs of the town, the bishops' palace, the unusual conical silhouette of the two old spoil heaps at Les Télots (relics of bituminous schist mines which once made an important contribution to the local economy) and *(east)* the blue hills of the Morvan.

Fontaine St-Lazare – This charming fountain stands to the north of the cathedral. It was built in 1543 by the cathedral chapter and has a dome and small lantern. The first dome of the Ionic order supports a second smaller one of the Corinthian order, and the whole is crowned by a pelican, a copy of the original of which is in the Musée Rolin.

ADDITIONAL SIGHTS

★ **Musée Rolin** (BZ M[1]) ⊙ – The museum is housed in a wing of the 15C mansion built for Chancellor Nicolas Rolin and in the Hôtel Lacomme, which replaced the main block of the Rolin mansion in the 19C.
Seven rooms on the ground floor of the Hôtel Lacomme house the Gaulish and Gallo-Roman collections. Relics of the oppidum at Bibracte are on display (large collection of tombstones). Gallo-Roman culture is illustrated through dress, jewellery and toilet articles (Roman helmet with a human face), through religious cults of Roman, oriental or traditional local deities such as Epona, and through art (handsome statues and a mosaic said to be of Naval Victory). The last room is devoted to late Antiquity and the Middle Ages.

Cross the courtyard to the ground floor of the Rolin mansion.

Two rooms are devoted to masterpieces of Roman **statuary★★**; most of it is the work of the two great sculptors of the Burgundian school, Gislebertus and Martin, a monk. Gislebertus's **Temptation of Eve** expresses sensuality through the curves of the body and the plants; the carving adorned the lintel of the north door of the cathedral before 1766. Martin created part of the **tomb of St Lazarus**, which took the form of a miniature church and stood behind the altarpiece in the chancel of the cathedral until it was destroyed during the changes made by the canons in 1766. The surviving figures from the main group, which depicted the resurrection of Lazarus, are the slim and poignant figures of St Andrew and Lazarus's sisters, Martha (who is holding her nose) and Mary. The rest of the work is represented by a few fragments supplemented by a sketch.

The first floor houses 14 and 15C sculptures from the Autun workshops (15C Resurrection of Lazarus in polychrome stone) and works by French and Flemish Primitive painters. The room devoted to the Rolin family contains the famous 15C painting of the **Nativity★★** by the Master of Moulins; the attention to detail and the muted colours betray the Flemish origin of the painter but the serene and solemn beauty and plasticity are characteristic of French Gothic painting. 15C Burgundian statuary is represented by the **Virgin★★** of Autun in polychrome stone and a St Catherine attributed to the Spanish sculptor Juan de la Huerta who worked in the region during the reign of Philip the Good.

Paintings, sculptures and furniture from the Renaissance to the present are displayed on the first floor of the Hôtel Lacomme. Note the curious 17C pharmacy sign.

Temptation of Eve, Musée Rolin

★ Porte St-André (**BY**) – This gate is where the roads from Langres and Besançon meet. It is the one survivor of four original gates in the Gallo-Roman fortifications, which were reinforced with fifty-four semi-circular towers. It has two large arches for vehicles, flanked by two smaller ones for pedestrians, surmounted by an upper arcade of ten even smaller arches. One of the guard-houses has survived by being converted into a church in the Middle Ages. Tradition has it that St Symphorian was martyred near this gateway.

Lycée Bonaparte (**AZ B**) – This was once a Jesuit college, built in 1709, and provides a noble focal point for the Place du Champ-de-Mars. The splendid wrought-iron **grille★**, dating from 1772, is adorned with gilded motifs of medallions, globe, astrolabes and lyres. On the left, the 17C church of Notre-Dame was originally the college chapel. Notable pupils included the whimsical Bussy-Rabutin and the three Bonaparte brothers, Napoleon, Joseph and Lucien. Napoleon spent only a few months here in 1779 before going on to the military school at Brienne.

Hôtel de Ville (**BZ H**) – The town hall houses a large **library** ⊙ including a rich collection of **manuscripts★** and incunabula.

Théâtre romain (**BYZ**) – The remains reveal the size of the largest theatre in Gaul (capacity: 12 000). Gallo-Roman stone fragments are incorporated into the wall of the porter's house.

Porte d'Arroux (**AY**) – This gateway was the Roman Porta Senonica, leading towards Sens and the Via Agrippa which ran from Lyon to Boulogne.

Musée Lapidaire (**BY M**) ⊙ – The lapidary museum is housed in the Chapelle St-Nicolas, a 12C Romanesque chapel with a Christ in Majesty painted in the apse. Some exhibits are also in the galleries around the adjoining garden. The stone fragments on display include architectural features, mosaics and tombstones from the Gallo-Roman period; sarcophagi, capitals and a "fossilized" boat from the Middle Ages; and pieces of statuary, both ancient and modern.

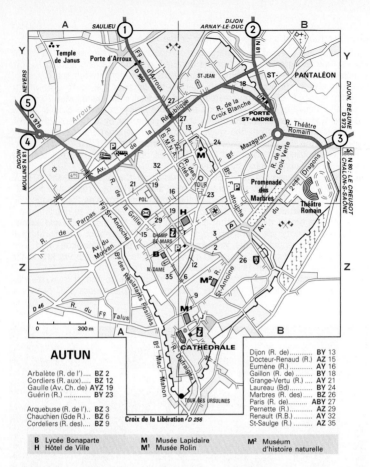

AUTUN

Arbalète (R. de l').... **BZ 2**
Cordiers (R. aux).... **BZ 12**
Gaulle (Av. Ch. de) **AYZ 19**
Guérin (R.) .... **BY 23**

Arquebuse (R. de l').. **BZ 3**
Chauchien (Gde R.).. **BZ 6**
Cordeliers (R. des).... **BZ 9**

Dijon (R. de) .... **BY 13**
Docteur-Renaud (R.) **AZ 15**
Eumène (R.) .... **AY 16**
Gaillon (R. de) .... **BY 18**
Grange-Vertu (R.) .... **AY 21**
Laureau (Bd) .... **BY 24**
Marbres (R. des).... **BZ 26**
Paris (R. de)......... **ABY 27**
Pernette (R.)........... **AZ 29**
Renault (R.B.) .... **AY 32**
St-Saulge (R.) .... **AZ 35**

B Lycée Bonaparte	**M** Musée Lapidaire	**M²** Muséum
H Hôtel de Ville	**M¹** Musée Rolin	d'histoire naturelle

Temple de Janus (**AY**) – The two walls of a square tower (24m - 80ft high) which stand alone in the plain on the far bank of the Arroux, are probably the remains of the sanctuary *(cella)* of a temple dedicated to a god who has not been identified (despite the name).

Promenade des Marbres (**BY**) – Near the broad tree-lined promenade, in a French-style garden, stands a fine 17C building. It was designed by Daniel Gitard, architect to Anne of Austria, as a seminary, but was later converted into a military training school.

Les Remparts – The walk round the ramparts begins at Boulevard des Résistants Fusillés to the west of town. Follow the ramparts south as far as the Tour des Ursulines (**BZ**), a 12C keep.

Muséum d'Histoire naturelle (**BZ M²**) ⊘ – The museum of natural history concentrates on the geological evolution of the Autun basin, the Morvan and Burgundy. On the ground floor, amidst the mineralogical collection, there are specimens of quartz (gemstones) and coal with the imprints of plants and animals (Actinodon) from the Primary Era. On the first floor there are fossils from the Secondary Era and the bones of a now extinct species of wild ox (auroch) and mammoths from the Quaternary Era. There is also a display on the birds and insects (butterflies) or Burgundy.

▶▶ **Cascade de Brisecou** – *2km - 1.2 miles south.*
A pleasant walk *(45min Rtn from Couhard)* along a stream to this waterfall, tumbling over rocks in a pretty wooded setting.

▶▶ **Croix de la Libération★** – *6km - 4 miles south.*
From this granite cross, put up in 1945 to commemorate the liberation of Autun, there is a good **view★** of Autun and the surrounding area.

▶▶ **Couches** – *25km - 16 miles southeast.*
Handsome 17C Maison des Templiers in town, and on outskirts of town the much restored 15C château of Margaret of Burgundy, with many of its early defensive features (drawbridge, traces of curtain wall and towers), 15C chapel and medieval keep (containing weapons and Aubusson tapestries).

▶▶ **Monastère tibétain Kagyu-Ling** ⊘ – *32km - 20 miles southwest.*
This Buddhist monastery, founded in 1974 in the 18C Château de Plaige, is an unexpected find in deepest Burgundy. The community of 4 Tibetan lamas and 30 or so western bonzes aims to explain Buddhist doctrine and Himalayan culture. The monastery includes a Buddhist temple and a centre for the study and translation of the Tibetan language and sacred texts.

AUXERRE★★

Population 38 819
Michelin map 65 fold 5 or 238 fold 10 – Facilities –
Plan of the conurbation in the Michelin Red Guide France

Auxerre (pronounced "Oh-ssair"), the capital of Lower Burgundy (Basse Bourgogne), is built on a sloping site on a hillside beside the river Yonne, at the beginning of the Nivernais canal. The site has also lent itself to the building of a pleasure boat harbour. The town's fine monuments are proof of its great past; its shady boulevards, its steep and busy streets and its old houses contribute to its overall interest. From the bridges, most particularly from Pont Paul-Bert (statue) and the right bank of the river, there are some very fine **views ★** of the town, made all the more striking as the chevets of the churches rise straight up along the river bank. The town is at the centre of a vineyard area, of which the most famous wines are Chablis and Irancy.

HISTORICAL NOTES

Near a simple Gaulish village (Autricum), the Romans built the town of Autessiodurum, which, like Autun, lay on the great road from Lyon to Boulogne. From the 1C it was a large town, as objects found during excavation in the area demonstrate.

The importance of Auxerre as an intellectual and spiritual centre in the Middle Ages rested largely on the influence of the bishops who ruled it, in particular St Germanus in the 5C. The saint's tomb became the object of pilgrimages, and Auxerre was declared a "Holy City" by the pope in the 12C.

Two great figures in French history have visited Auxerre. In 1429 **Joan of Arc** passed through the town twice, first with the handful of brave followers who accompanied her from Vaucouleurs to Chinon, and then a few months later at the head of an army of 12 000 men with Charles VII, whom she was taking to Reims for his coronation. On 17 March 1815, **Napoleon** arrived in Auxerre on his return from Elba: Maréchal Ney, who had been sent to oppose him, embraced him and the Maréchal's troops swelled the ranks of the Emperor's small army.

Auxerre was the birthplace of the physiologist **Paul Bert** (1833-86), who was later to enter politics and become Minister during the Third Republic, and of the poet **Marie Noël** (1883-1967) whose works were full of hope and serenity.

PRINCIPAL SIGHTS *time: 1 hour 30 min*

★★ **Cathédrale St-Étienne (BY)** ⊙ – The fine Gothic cathedral was built between the 13-16C. An earlier building, dating from the foundation of a sanctuary by St Amâtre *c*400, succumbed to fire. In 1023, Hugues de Chalon began to construct a Romanesque cathedral. In 1215 Guillaume de Seignelay started all over again with a Gothic one. By 1400 the chancel, the nave, the aisles, the chapels and the south transept were complete. The building was practically finished by 1560.

West front – The Flamboyant style façade is framed by two towers with sculpted buttresses. The south tower is incomplete. The façade is composed of four storeys of arcades surmounted by gables. Above the centre doorway is a rose window (7m - 23ft across) slightly recessed between the buttresses.

The sculptures on the entrance doorways (13-14C) were mutilated in the 16C during the Wars of Religion, and the soft limestone has weathered badly. The tympanum over the centre door shows Christ enthroned between the Virgin Mary and St John. The lintel depicts the Last Judgment. Christ presides with the Wise Virgins on his right and the Foolish Virgins (lamps upside down) on his left. These twelve statues are placed on the engaged piers. Beneath the niches of the base (containing seated figures), there are low reliefs in two sections: on the left, the Life of Joseph (read from right to left); on the right, the parable of the Prodigal Son (read from left to right).

View from the Pont Paul-Bert

The sculptures framing the north door trace the lives of the Virgin Mary, St Joachim and St Anne. The Coronation of the Virgin is on the tympanum. The medallions along the base are masterly representations of scenes from Genesis. The sculptures round the south door are 13C. The tympanum, divided into three, and the recessed arches are dedicated to the childhood of Christ and the life of John the Baptist.

Six scenes of the love of David and Bathsheba are on the upper section of the base - eight statuettes placed between the gables of the trefoiled arches symbolise Philosophy (on the right with a crown) and the seven Liberal Arts.

On the right of the doorway, a high relief represents the Judgment of Solomon. The more interesting of the side entrances is the 14C south door, which is dedicated to St Stephen; the north door is dedicated to St Germanus.

Interior – The nave, built in the 14C, was vaulted in the 15C. On the end wall of the south transept are four consoles supporting amazingly realistic figures. The glass of the rose windows, dating from 1550, shows God the Father surrounded by celestial powers.

The rose window of the north transept (1530) represents the Virgin Mary surrounded by angels and her own emblems.

The choir and the ambulatory date from the beginning of the 13C. In 1215, Guillaume de Seignelay, Bishop of Auxerre, who was a great admirer of the new architecture then known as the "French style" (the term Gothic was not used until the 16C), decided to pull down the cathedral's Romanesque choir; rising above the 11C crypt is the beautiful piece of architecture which he had built to replace it, which was completed in 1234.

The ambulatory is lit by a magnificent array of **stained glass windows**★★ composed of 13C medallions in which blue and red are the dominant colours. They represent scenes from Genesis, the stories of David, of Joseph and of the Prodigal Son and many saintly legends. The base is emphasised by a blind arcade decorated with sculpted heads, mostly representing the prophets and sibyls.

On the left side of the ambulatory, there is a 16C painting on wood representing the Stoning of St Stephen.

The beautiful stained glass of the rose window dates from the 16C.

★ **Romanesque crypt** – The crypt, a fine architectural unit and the only remaining element of the 11C Romanesque cathedral is decorated with fine 11-13C frescoes. The scene on the vault, showing Christ on a white horse surrounded by four mounted angels, is the only example of such a representation in France. The fresco in the apse shows Christ in Majesty surrounded by the symbols of the four Evangelists and two seven-branched candlesticks.

★ **Treasury** – The many interesting exhibits include a collection of 12-13C chased enamels, manuscripts, books of hours and miniatures.

Tower – From the top there is a fine **view** over the town.

To reach the old abbey of St-Germain, go along the north side of the cathedral and own the **Rue Cochois** which is part of the Quartier de la Marine *(see below)*. Pass the Préfecture, once the residence of the bishops of Auxerre *(explanatory plaque)*, then the entrance doorway of the old bishops' palace.

★ **Ancienne abbaye St-Germain** (BY) ⊘ – This celebrated Benedictine abbey was built in the 6C by Queen Clotilda, the wife of Clovis, on the site of an oratory where St Germanus, the 5C Bishop of Auxerre, was buried. In the times of Charles the Bald the abbey had a famous school which attracted such teachers as Héric and Rémi of Auxerre; the later was tutor to St Odo of Cluny.

Abbey Church – The upper part of the church was built from the 13-15C and is Gothic in style; it replaced a Carolingian Romanesque church. The ten-sided Lady Chapel, dating from 1277, is linked to the ambulatory by a short passageway and overlies two semi-underground chapels *(see below)* from the same period. In 1811, a number of bays were demolished at the western end of the church isolating the beautiful 12C Romanesque **bell tower** (51m - 167ft high), known as the tower of St-Jean. The square base, surmounted by the belfry, makes a strong contrast with the soaring stone spire.

The interior of the church is of fine proportions.

★ **Crypt** – The crypt forms a semi-underground church consisting of a nave and two aisles; the barrel vaulting dates from the Carolingian period. The confessio, raised on three steps in the centre of the crypt, provides a fine view of the Carolingian, Romanesque and Gothic vaulting; four Gallo-Roman columns, capped by composite capitals (acanthus leaves and crockets), support two millenial beams made of oak. The ambulatory is decorated with **frescoes**★ which date from 850 and are some of the oldest in France; they depict the life and martyrdom of St Stephen, and four bishops, in shades of red and ochre.

The vault (5m - 16ft deep), where St Germanus's body was enshrined, is covered by a ceiling spangled with painted suns (symbol of eternity), reminiscent of the mosaics in Ravenna where St Germanus died.

The axial chapel, dedicated to St Maxime, was rebuilt in the 13C on the site of the rotunda of the Carolingian crypt. The vaulted roof is divided by ribs into ten panels. Below is the Chapelle St-Clément, which can be reached via a narrow staircase *(to the right on leaving the Chapelle Ste-Maxime)*. The steeply sloping ground means that only part of the chapels are underground, so there are good views of the valley from some windows.

AUXERRE

B   Tour de l'Horloge
M¹   Musée Leblanc-Duvernoy
M²   Musée d'Histoire naturelle
M³   Musée St-Germain

Musée St-Germain (M³) – This museum is in the old conventual buildings of the abbey, including the abbot's residence rebuilt at the beginning of the 18C *(entrance to abbey and museum)*, the 14C cellars, the monks' dormitory and the 12C chapter house. The latter's beautiful façade was discovered behind the cloisters and the sacristy.

The main staircase leads to the monks' dormitory, which houses an **archaeological collection**. On the second floor, the room on pre- and proto-history contains displays on the four major eras (Palaeolithic and Neolithic eras, Bronze and Iron Ages) with explanatory panels. In the centre, a large display case exhibits reconstructions for each of these periods. Note in particular a small Gaulish horse from Guerchy, a cauldron from Cravant, an Etruscan tripod and various imported Etruscan receptacles discovered at the site at Gurgy. On the first floor, in the Gallo-Roman room, the infiltration of the Roman way of life into Autessiodurum (Auxerre) is illustrated through examples of architecture, town planning, lifestyle, occupations (reconstruction of a kitchen and a pottery workshop), religion and funerary rites (equestrian statue, stone statue of the god Mercury).

ADDITIONAL SIGHTS

St-Eusèbe (AZ) ⊘ – This church is all that remains of an old priory. It has a lovely 12C tower decorated with multifoil arches. The stone spire dates from the 15C.

Inside, note the rib vaulting in the high hexagonal drum above the Renaissance chancel, the beautiful axial chapel and the 16C stained glass windows.

St-Pierre (BZ) – A Renaissance doorway from an old abbey, flanked by two modern buildings, leads off Rue Joubert into the courtyard in which this church stands. It is a classical buildings which still bears traces of Renaissance decoration. The Flamboyant tower, which has had a lot of work done on it, draws its inspiration from the north tower of the cathedral.

Musée Leblanc-Duvernoy (**AZ M**[1]) ⊘ – This museum in an 18C residence is mainly devoted to *faïence* ware, with many exhibits from French or local *faïence* makers (there is a particularly large collection of *faïence* from the time of the Revolution). The museum also houses a series of magnificent 18C Beauvais tapestries depicting scenes from the life of the Emperor of China, a collection of Italic and Greek (black figure and red figure) pottery as well as earthenware from Puisaye.

Musée d'histoire naturelle (**Conservatoire de la nature "Paul Bert"**) (**AY M**[2]) ⊘ – The natural history museum is housed in a pavilion surrounded by a small botanical garden and contains exhibitions on subjects related to the natural sciences of the world at large. One room contains a display on the life and work of Paul Bert.

Quartier de la Marine – This part of town with its narrow winding streets was once home to the boatmen. From the **Rue Cochois**, take the strange little Rue de l'Yonne (note nos 6 and 10), then the Rue de la Marine to see the remains of the northeast tower of the Gallo-Roman fortified wall. Retrace your steps to the pretty little Place St-Nicolas (nos 3 and 4), overlooking the Quai de la Marine. The square is named after the patron saint of boatmen. The Rue du Mont-Brenn leads to the Place du Coche-d'Eau (no 4). At no 3, a 16C houses is host to temporary exhibitions as part of the local **musée du Coche-d'Eau**. Go up Rue du Docteur-Labosse (no 10) to rejoin Rue Cochois.

Town centre – There are still many interesting old houses here, most of which are 16C with half-timbering.

Rue du Temple (**AZ**): nos 19, 3 and 1.

Place Charles-Surugue (**AZ 33**): note the fountain in honour of Cadet Roussel *(see below)* and the houses at nos 3, 4, 5 and 18.

Place Robillard (**AZ**): no 5, dating from the 14-15C, is the oldest house in Auxerre.

Rue de Paris (**AY**): nos 37 and 67 (lovely Renaissance *hôtel* called "de Crole" with dormer windows and a sculpted cornice).

Rue de la Draperie (**AZ 10**): note the houses occupied by a bank and a jeweller's.

Rue de l'Horloge (**AZ 16**): no 6 (sculpted corner post) and the four houses opposite.

Tour de l'Horloge (**AZ B**): This Flamboyant clock tower was built in the 15C on Gallo-Roman foundations (old fortified wall). It was also called the Tour Gaillarde, after the gateway it defended, and was part of the fortifications. The belfry and the clock were symbols of the communal liberties granted by the Count of Auxerre. The clock (17C) has two faces showing the apparent movements of the sun and moon. The astronomical dial was mentioned by Restif de la Bretonne, a prolific 18C novelist (Nicolas-Edme Restif 1734-1806), who spent several years of his youth working as a printer's apprentice in the workshop at the base of the tower. A vaulted passageway beside the clock tower leads to the Place du Maréchal-Leclerc. Beneath the vault a plaque commemorates **Cadet Roussel** (1743-1807), a court official whose blighted ambitions are immortalised in a famous French song.

Place de l'Hôtel-de-Ville (**AZ 17**): a polychrome figure recalls the poet Marie Noël; note also nos 4, 6, 16, 17, 18.

Rue Fécauderie (**ABZ 12**): intersects with Rue Joubert; two half-timbered houses have a sculpted corner post.

Rue Sous-Murs (**BYZ**) : earns its name from the walls of the Gallo-Roman city which surround it; nos 14 and 19.

▶▶ **Seignelay** – *10km - 6 miles north*. Charming town in a hillside setting. Note in particular the 17C covered market on the Place Colbert and the church of St-Martial.

Massif du BALLON D'ALSACE★★★

Michelin map 66 fold 8 or 242 folds 35 and 39

The Ballon d'Alsace is the southern peak of the rounded granite summits *(ballons)* of the Vosges range. The massif has beautiful forests of pines and larches, delightful woodland, spectacular gorges and, on the uplands, huge mountain pastures covered in colourful Alpine flowers. From the highest peak (1 250m - 4 101ft) there is a magnificent panorama; in fine weather, you can see as far as the Alps. Unfortunately, the view is often obscured by fog.

★★MOUNTAIN ROAD

From Giromagny to the Ballon d'Alsace

Giromagny – This small town, on important crossroads in the upper valley of the Savoureuse, was for many years a major centre for the textile industry. The **fort** at Giromagny, built between 1875 and 1879, has a sizeable weaponry and constituted the link in the line of defensive fortifications between the upper Moselle valley and the fortress at Belfort. The fort here is now open to the public, having been the object of several restoration projects after years of disuse.

Musée de la Mine et des Techniques minières ⊘ – This small museum of mining and mining technology is to be found in the cultural centre *(Place des Commandos d'Afrique)*. It retraces the history (15-19C) of mining for copper and lead glance. Having passed **Lepuix**, a small industrial town, the road follows a narrow gorge.

Roches du Cerf – These rocks line the end of an old glacial valley. They have deep horizontal stripes scoured out by the lateral moraine of the glacier. A rock-climbing school exploits the challenging natural features of this site.

Maison forestière de Malvaux – The forester's lodge is in a pretty setting at the end of the rocky gorge.

Saut de la Truite – The Savoureuse tumbles over a rocky fissure as a waterfall known as "the trout's leap".

Cascade du Rummel – *15 min Rtn on foot.*
A signposted footpath leads to a bridge and then the waterfall, not far from the D 465.

Continue along the D 465 (leaving the Masevaux road to your right).

The road leads upwards through pretty countryside. The rocky slopes to either side are covered with magnificent pine and beech trees. In the distance, you should be able to see the lakes of Sewen and Alfeld, then across the Alsace plain and the valley of the Doller.

★★★ **Ballon d'Alsace** – *30 min Rtn on foot.*
The footpath to the summit leads off the D 465, from in front of the "Ferme-Restaurant du Ballon d'Alsace". It leads across the meadows to a statue of the Virgin Mary. Before Alsace was returned to France, this statue marked the frontier. The Ballon d'Alsace (1 250m - 4 101ft high) is the most southerly peak of the Vosges range. Its grassy crest towers above the last foothills of the Vosges. From the viewing terrace, there is a **panorama★★** as far as Donon, to the north, the Alsace plain and the Black Forest, to the east, and Mont Blanc, to the south.

BAUME-LES-DAMES

Population 5 237
Michelin map 166 east of fold 16 or 243 fold 20 – Facilities —
Local map under Vallée du DOUBS

Baume-les-Dames is prettily located against a backdrop of greenery at a point where the valley of the river Doubs *(qv)* widens. The town earns its livelihood in part from small businesses (printing, machine building, furniture, food industry); the famous Ropp pipes are made here.
Famous local figures include the Grenier brothers: Édouard (1819-1901), the poet, and Jules (1817-1883), the painter. The house they were born in is at 1 Rue Barbier.
The physicist Jouffroy d'Abbans (1751-1832) first tested a steamboat at Baume-les-Dames in 1778; a monument near the Doubs bridge commemorates the event.
As is the case with Baume-les-Messieurs *(qv)*, Baume-les-Dames, once Baume-les-Nonnes, owes its name partly to an old Celtic word meaning "cave", and partly to an old abbey run by Benedictine nuns. It is possible to visit the restored abbey church, **église abbatiale** ⊙, on Place de la République via the vault leading inside the old outer walls of the abbey. The abbey was founded in the 7C on the site of a castle, where St Odilia, blind from birth and driven from Alsace on that account by her father, is said to have lived and recovered her sight through baptism.
In the 18C the "canonesses" of Baume-les-Dames represented the cream of the aristocracy; in order to be admitted, they had to prove that they had sixteen noble ancestors (reflected in the quarterings on their coats of arms).

St-Martin – This church was rebuilt at the beginning of the 17C. The two chapels on either side of the chancel are adorned with Louis XIII altarpieces with 17C twisted columns. The chapel to the south contains a 1549 Pietà, while the north chapel has two statues: a 16C polychrome wooden statue of St Barbara, and a late 18C statue of St Vincent, patron saint of wine growers. There is a beautiful marble, bronze and wrought-iron lectern in the chancel by Nicole (1751).

There are some beautiful 18C houses around Place de la République, to the south of the church. A little further on, a Renaissance house with a beautiful door and a corbelled turret graces the corner of Place du Général-de-Gaulle and Place de la Loi.

▶▶ **Grotte de la Glacière** ⊙ – *20km - 12 miles south.*
Glacial cave 66m - 217ft deep *(260 steps).*

BAUME-LES-MESSIEURS

Population 196
Michelin map 120 south of fold 4 or 243 fold 30 – Local map under Les RECULÉES

Baume-les-Messieurs stands in a very pretty **setting** at the convergence of three valleys, one of which is the magnificent "blind valley" *(reculée)* of the Baume *(qv)* amphitheatre. The village is famous for the ruins of its old abbey, which make a very interesting visit. There is a beautiful view of the site from the viewpoint at the foot of the church of Granges-sur-Baume *(4km - 2.5 miles north).*

Monks and "Gentlemen" – The abbey at Baume was founded in the 6C by the Irish monk, St Columban, and adopted the Benedictine rule. One of its claims to glory is that in 910 twelve of its monks founded the illustrious abbey at Cluny. Monastic life, however, grew increasingly lax, as it did at St-Claude *(qv)*; from the 16C onwards, the humble monks of the abbey's beginnings were replaced by canons of noble birth, who had a much more worldly view of life. These high and mighty "Messieurs" lost no time in modifying the name of their home, thus Baume-les-Moines became Baume-les-Messieurs. This state of affairs lasted until the Revolution; in 1790 all the possessions of the abbey were seized and sold off at public auction.

The adventurous life of Jean de Watteville – Jean de Watteville was one of the abbots of Baume in the 17C, as well as one of the most extraordinary characters of his age, if one is to believe the Memoirs of Saint-Simon. His numerous adventures have almost certainly been embellished by hearsay.

Part the first: Soldier, Franciscan friar, Carthusian monk, Turkish Pasha... – Watteville initially followed a military career. While a minor officer in the Burgundy regiment during the Milan campaign he fought a duel with a Spanish nobleman in the service of the Queen of Spain and killed him. He was obliged to flee and went to ground in Paris. While there, he overheard a sermon on the dangers of hell in a church one day and, overcome with remorse, converted to Christianity. The ex-soldier became a Franciscan friar, then entered the abbey of Bonlieu as a Carthusian monk.

It was not long before Watteville tired of monastic life. However, he was caught climbing the wall in his bid for freedom by the prior himself. Without a second's hesitation, Watteville shot the man with his pistol and made good his escape. After many an adventure, he crossed the Pyrénées into Spain.

Leaving behind a second noble Spanish corpse, the victim of our hero's prowess in another duel, Watteville fled to Constantinople. The ex-monk converted to Islam and put his military talents to the service of the Sultan, who was so impressed with him that he promoted him first to Pasha, then to Governor of the province of Morea.

Part the second: ... Abbot of Baume ... – After several years of living the high life surrounded by a sizeable harem, Watteville made an offer to the Venetians, whom he had been engaged by the Sultan to fight: if they could promise him papal absolution for his past crimes as well as the abbey of Baume as a reward, he would surrender his troops. This outrageous deal was struck, and our opportunist ex-Pasha shaved his head for the second time and took charge of the abbey of Baume and its resident monks, directing them very much as if they were soldiers in a military campaign.

The abbot remained as impetuous as ever, as several anecdotes from this stage of his life illustrate. For example, Watteville had the series of ladders, which had previously been the only way of getting to the bottom of the valley from Crançot, replaced by steps cut into the rock (the Échelles de Crançot - *qv*). Seeing his monks taking infinite pains not to break their necks on the steep, slippery steps, the abbot flew into a rage, had his mule brought to him, leapt onto the long-suffering animal's back and drove it down the steps, berating the anxious monks as he went for their cowardice.

Part the third: ... Parliamentary Intermediary – When Louis XIV invaded the Franche-Comté, Watteville, after cunningly weighing up the French chances of winning, offered his services to the French king. Thanks to his skilful use of language and his clever scheming, he won over the last centres of resistance (Gray, Ornans, Nozeroy) to the French king's cause without a single shot being fired, greatly simplifying Louis XIV's 1668 campaign.

After the Nijmegen peace treaty of 1678, Watteville returned to his abbey, where he led a life of luxury and splendour more befitting a great lord. His eventful life finally came to an end in 1702, when he was 84.

C. Cuny/RAPHO

Baume-les-Messieurs

ABBAYE (ABBEY) ⏱ *time: 1 hour*

A vaulted passageway leads into the first courtyard, around which are the old guesthouse, the abbot's residence, the keep, the tower used as a court ("tour de justice") and the church.

Church – The 15C façade has an interesting doorway: God the Father giving Blessing is depicted on the central pillar and angels enthusiastically playing musical instruments in the side niches. The nave was once paved with tombstones, of which about forty remain; the most interesting are leaning against the wall of the north side aisle. The Chapelle de Chalon, the mausoleum of the aristocratic Chalon *(qv)* family, is to the north of the chancel. It contains a 16C statue of St Catherine and a 15C stone **statue of St Paul**, as well as various tombs of the Chalon family. The tomb of Abbot Jean de Watteville is in the north side aisle. There is a beautiful painted and sculpted early 16C Flemish **altarpiece with volets★** in the 13C chancel. A door in the middle of the nave on the south side leads to what used to be the cloisters. The monks'

Detail of altarpiece,
Abbey church of
Baume-les-Messieurs

dormitory and refectory overlooked this courtyard, which still has its fountain.

Abbey buildings – Go through an arch on the left. This leads into another courtyard surrounded by buildings which once contained the apartments of the aristocratic canons.
Return to the old cloisters and the first courtyard through a vaulted passageway through the 13C cellars.

Musée de l'Artisanat jurassien ⏱ – This museum of local crafts is located on the ground floor of the "tour de justice", on the right in the first courtyard. A forge has been reconstructed and is on display here, along with the tools of the blacksmith, the locksmith and the edge-tool maker. The cooper's workshop looks out onto the same courtyard. There is an audiovisual commentary of the two workshops which describes the various crafts and techniques involved.

★ Grottes de Baume – *See Les RECULÉES.*

BEAUCOURT

Population 5 569
Michelin map 166 fold 8 or 243 fold 10

Since the Franco-Prussian War, Beaucourt has become the third-ranking city of the Territoire de Belfort *département*, having previously been part of the Montbéliard principality, then of the Haut-Rhin *département*. The founding of a Japy clockmaking factory here largely contributed to the town's prosperity in the 19C.

Japy – Jacques Japy was a farmer and a blacksmith, who also knew something about locksmithing and the repair of various tools. His son Frédéric Japy founded a clock and watch-making workshop in the area in 1777, a business which was to be at the forefront of the region's industrial development for 180 years *(see Introduction, p 26)*. Factories were opened in Feschotte, Isle-sur-le-Doubs, Voujeaucourt, Anzin near Lille and Arcueil in the Paris suburbs. Their activities have diversified over the years; the manufacture of clock parts led to the production of hardware items and electro-mechanical devices, having also made diverse articles such as dancing dolls and mirrors for hunting larks. In 1910 Japy was manufacturing typewriters under a foreign license, and by 1955 the firm began production in its own right, taking the name Société Belfortaine de Mécanographie in 1967. SBM is still located in Beaucourt, but no longer manufactures typewriters since production was transferred to Switzerland in 1973.

Musée Frédéric-Japy ⏱ – The original clock-making workshop has been turned into a museum. The industrial genius invented the first machines for manufacturing clocks, at a time when clocks were being made entirely by hand. The display includes examples of the first watches manufactured in Beaucourt, as well as all sorts of clocks: alarm clocks, travelling clocks, mantelpiece clocks etc. The diversity of the Japy company's production is illustrated by the many types of screws and bolts, chandeliers, enamel items, typewriters, motors and pumps on display. Explanatory panels describe the evolution of the Japy enterprise.

*The current **Michelin Red Guide France** offers
a selection of pleasant hotels in convenient locations.
Each entry specifies the facilities available (gardens,
tennis courts, swimming pool, beach facilities)
and the annual opening and closing dates.
There is also a selection of establishments recommended for their
cuisine – well-prepared meals at moderate prices; stars for good cooking.*

BEAUJOLAIS★★

Beaujolais has been recognised as the most southerly of the Burgundy vineyards since 1930. The region's name is derived from that of the aristocratic Beaujeu family who were powerful between the 9-11C, founding Villefranche-sur-Saône *(qv)* and Belleville abbey. In 1400, Edouard de Beaujeu gave his property to the House of Bourbon-Montpensier. Pierre de Bourbon married Louis XI's daughter, who was known thereafter as Anne of Beaulieu. Marie-Louise de Montpensier, a niece of Louis XIII, left the property to the House of Orléans on her death, and this family kept it until the Revolution.

GEOGRAPHICAL NOTES

The Beaujolais is a mountain massif which stretches between the Loire and Rhône valleys, on the line where the Mediterranean and Atlantic watersheds meet. This region is clearly delimited only to the east and west; to the north it gradually gives way to the Charollais region, and to the south to the mountains of the Lyon region.

The Upper Beaujolais to the north cuts into granite, forming steep-sided cliffs. The highest point is at St-Rigaud (1 009m - 3 310ft). The Lower Beaujolais to the south is formed essentially from sedimentary rock of the Secondary Era, with hills reaching 650m - 2 133ft at the most. The distinguishing features of the Beaujolais region are the plateaux criss-crossed by narrow sinuous valleys and the asymmetrical relief between east and west. To the east, the land drops steeply down to the river plain of the Saône, while to the west it falls in gentle slopes. The cliffs caused by the sinking of the Saône river bed are home to the "Côte beaujolaise" vineyards, while the rest of the area forms "la Montagne" (the mountain).

La Montagne – This is a very pretty region with a wonderful variety of relief to add interest to the landscape. Vast panoramic views unfold from the tops of ridges or from the many lookout points over the valley of the Saône as far as the foothills of the Jura and the snow-capped Alpine peaks on the horizon. The upper slopes of the mountain regions are covered in pine forests and broom, further down there are stands of oak with large clearings in between them. Geographically, the area is ideally placed for trade and transport, situated as it is near Lyon between the Loire and Rhône valleys. Other economic activities include the textile and timber industries. A high quality, popular wine is produced from the vineyards at the edge of the Saône valley.

BEAUJOLAIS WINES

Wine has been produced in the Beaujolais region since Roman times. Beaujolais wines were very popular during the Middle Ages, then sank into relative obscurity in the 17C, before enjoying renewed popularity in the 18C. The construction of a road and rail network in the 19C meant that Beaujolais wines were able to reach new markets. Vines became more or less a monoculture on the sunny slopes of the Saône valley. Nowadays, the vineyards extend from the Mâcon escarpment south to the Azergues

Gaudeamus in vino

valley. The widespread Gamay grape yields a fresh, fruity red wine, with a bouquet which varies depending on the soil type in which the vines were grown. "Beaujolais Villages" comes from the granite slopes north of Villefranche, the **Coteaux du Beaujolais**. There are ten *crus*: Moulin-à-Vent, Fleurie, Morgon, Chiroubles, Juliénas, Chénas, Côte de Brouilly, Brouilly, St-Amour and Régnié. The golden sedimentary rock between Villefranche and the Azergues valley gives rise to "Beaujolais" and "Beaujolais Supérieur".

Unlike other red wines, Beaujolais is drunk while young, and chilled. It is possible to taste the various wines in many places – look out for signs advertising *dégustations* in wine cellars large or small *(caveaux, celliers, châteaux)*.

There are several local wine-tasting brotherhoods *(confréries)*, of which the "Gosiers secs de Clochemerle" are perhaps the most active in promoting the glories of local wine.

Gourmands or gourmets
*Each year the **Michelin Red Guide France** gives an up-to-date selection of establishments renowned for their cuisine.*
Local gastronomic specialities and fine wines are described in the Introduction.

★THE VINEYARDS

1 From Villefranche-sur-Saône to St-Amour-Bellevue

98km - 61 miles - allow 5 hours - local map opposite

The road winds its way through the vineyards, at first climbing the granite escarpment, then dropping down towards the Saône valley.

Villefranche-sur-Saône – *See VILLEFRANCHE-SUR-SAÔNE.*

Leave Villefranche on the D 504, take the D 19 right and then the D 44 left.

Montmelas-St-Sorlin – Drive round to the north of the feudal castle *(not open to the public)*, which was restored in the 19C by Dupasquier, a pupil of Viollet-le-Duc. The castle looks very imposing perched in solitary splendour on a rocky crag, with its high crenellated walls, its turrets and its keep.

Carry on from Montmelas as far as the Col de St-Bonnet. From the pass, to the right, an unsurfaced road leads to the Signal de St-Bonnet (30 min Rtn on foot).

Signal de St-Bonnet – From the east end of the chapel there is a broad view over Montmelas, the Beaujolais vineyards and the Saône valley in the background. To the southwest lie the mountains of the Lyon and Tarare regions.

Return to the pass and take the D 20 right.

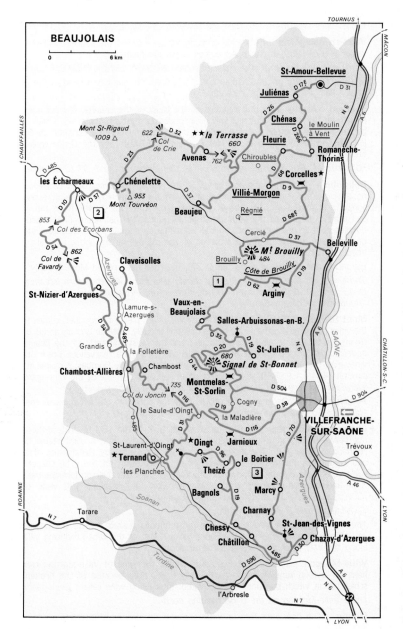

The wine-producing area is shown in green – Names of grands crus are underlined in red

St-Julien – This pretty little wine-growing village is the birthplace of the doctor Claude Bernard (1813-78). He was born the son of a wine-grower and earned part of the money for his studies by working in a chemist's. He became a professor in the Collège de France and a member of the Académie Française. The **Musée Claude Bernard** ⊙ recalls his work in the field of physiology, in particular on the absorption of fats and sugars by the liver. The museum garden leads to the house where Claude Bernard was born.

Take the D 19 to Salles-Arbuissonnas.

Salles-Arbuissonnas-en-Beaujolais – The monks of Cluny founded a **priory** in Salles as early as the 10C. This was taken over by nuns of the Benedictine order in the 14C, who ran it until they were replaced by "aristocratic" canonesses in the 18C. The 11C chancel contains the prior's chair (16C) and the choir stalls (18C). The 15C chapter house *(access through the garden and the cloisters to the south of the church. Light switch near the door on the left)* has been converted into a **museum** ⊙; note its vaulting, supported on a central pillar, and the elegant keystones decorated with the symbols of the four Evangelists. An elegantly arcaded gallery is all that remains of the Romanesque **cloisters** *(access through the little Flamboyant doorway to the south of the church's west end)*. Around the **Place du Chapitre**, shaded by plane trees, stand the houses once inhabited by the canonesses. There is a good view of the plain east end of the church and of the Romanesque tower with a pyramidal roof, a very common feature of churches of this period in the Beaujolais region.

From Salles take the D 35, then the D 49ᴱ to the right.

Vaux-en-Beaujolais – This wine-growing village inspired the satirist Gabriel Chevallier (1895-1969) to write his acerbic novel *Clochemerle*.

Carry on along the D 49ᴱ through Le Perréon and then take the D 62 to Charentay.

The unusual shape of the Château d'Arginy comes into sight in a bend to the right 1km - half a mile east of Charentay.

Château d'Arginy – All that remains of the castle is the chunky, red brick tower known as the Tour d'Alchimie. This is shrouded in mystery; some say it was used by the Knights Templar to hide their treasure, brought here by Guichard de Beaujeu, the nephew of Jacques de Moley, the Grand Master of the Order who was burned at the stake in Paris.

Follow the D 68, turn left into the D 19, then right on the D 37 to Belleville.

Belleville – This wine-growing town is situated on the crossroads between the north-south and east-west communications routes. Apart from wine, it produces agricultural machinery. The **church** ⊙ dates from the 12C (tower from the 13C) and used to be one of the Augustinian abbeys under the patronage of the lords of Beaujeu. The geometric motifs on the Romanesque doorway and the naïve scenes on the theme of the Deadly Sins carved on the capitals in the Gothic nave are particularly interesting.

Beyond Cercié *(carry on along the D 37)*, the road goes round Mont Brouilly.

Those wishing to climb Mont Brouilly should take the D 43, then turn left into the D 43ᴱ and, 100m - just over 100yds further on, left again into a road marked "Route de la Côte de Brouilly".

Mont Brouilly – Côte de Brouilly, a fruity wine with plenty of bouquet, comes from the vines harvested on the sunny slopes of Mont Brouilly. Côte de Brouilly and Brouilly (from the villages around Mont Brouilly) are the most southerly of the Beaujolais *appellations*. From the Mont Brouilly esplanade, there is a marvellous **view★** of the vineyards, the Beaujolais mountains, the Saône plain and the Dombes. A chapel at the summit (484m - 1 588ft) is the object of an annual pilgrimage by the wine-growers every autumn *(see the Calendar of Events at the end of the guide)*.

Return to Cercié. On leaving the village, take the D 68ᴱ to the left towards the old village of Corcelles, then continue on the D 9 (to the left).

★ **Château de Corcelles** ⊙ – The fortress was built in the 15C to protect the border between Burgundy and Beaujolais. It was converted into a comfortable ducal residence in the 16C. The inner courtyard was surrounded by Renaissance arcades and contains a fountain with a wrought-iron decoration on top. The chapel has some remarkable Gothic woodwork. The tour of the main building includes the kitchen and the old weapons room, now a cellar. The spacious 17C wine cellar *(Cuvier)* is one of the most handsome in Beaujolais.

Continue on the D 19 to the right.

The road crosses the vineyards of the most famous *grands crus* of the Beaujolais and affords pleasant views of the Saône valley. Most of the wine-producing villages along the way offer wine-tastings *(dégustations)*.

Villié-Morgon – Unlike most Beaujolais wines, the wine of Villié-Morgon can be kept for a long time. It has a particularly fruity taste because of the broken up schist soil in which the vines are cultivated. Interesting wine cellars *(wine-tasting)*.

Leave Villié-Morgon on the D 68 heading north.

Fleurie – The fine, light Fleurie wines are best drunk young. Interesting wine cellars *(wine-tasting)*.

In Fleurie, take the D 32 east, then turn left into the D 186.

Romanèche-Thorins – Facilities. The famous Moulin-à-Vent grows here and in the neighbouring village of Chénas. The **Maison de Benoît Raclet** ⊙ makes an interesting visit. Raclet's empirical discovery of a preventative measure against the pyralis worm, namely pouring boiling water over the vines *(échaudage)*, was used until 1945. The **Musée du compagnonnage Guillon** ⊙ displays exhibits from days of the traveling craftsman; there are some particularly fine examples of their work.

Take the D 266, which goes through Moulin-à-Vent, to the D 68.

Chénas – Home of robust, top-quality Moulin-à-Vent and the lighter Chénas.

Juliénas – The strong wines from this locality can be tasted in the **Cellier de la Vieille Église** ⊙. The tasting cellars in an old deconsecrated church converted for this purpose. The church walls are covered with charming pictures of baccanalian revels. By the exit to the village on, the D 137 there is a beautiful old 16-17C tithe house *(maison de la Dime)*. It is easily recognised by its arcaded façade.

Drive to St-Amour-Bellevue.

St-Amour-Bellevue – This village at the northerly tip of Beaujolais produces dark red wines with lots of body and high quality white wines.

★ **"LA MONTAGNE"**

② **From St-Amour-Bellevue to Villefranche-sur-Saône**

134km - 83 miles - allow 6 hours - local map p 79

This pretty drive climbs through the vine-clad hills to dark pine forests, then drops down to the Azergues valley, in which a number of sawmills have been set up.

St-Amour-Bellevue and Juliénas – *See above.*

From Juliénas, take the D 26 uphill, going through two passes one after the other (Col de Durbize at 550m - 1 804ft and Col du Truges at 445m - 1 460ft).

Beaujeu – The capital of the Beaujolais lies amidst vine-covered hillsides.

Musée des traditions populaires Marius-Audin ⊙ – Audin (1872-1951) was a printer from Beaujeu who founded this museum of traditional folk art in 1942. The first floor houses a collection of dolls, some dressed in 19C French fashions and others in folk costumes from French and Italian regions. Dolls' furniture, toys and knick-knacks surround this miniature society. The section on folklore contains the reconstructed interior of a 19C farmer's house, as well as the various tools used by cobblers, tanners, coopers, winegrowers and farmers, and furniture and other objects from the hospice at Beaujeu: bed, enamel ware, porcelain night-lights and enema syringes. Above the entrance to the wine cellar, called the "Temple of Bacchus", where there is the opportunity of tasting some local Beaujolais Villages wine, a handsome Antique head of the Roman wine god watches over the proceedings.

St-Nicolas – All that remains in its original state of the church built in 1130 from uneven black rocks is the Romanesque tower.

Take the D 26 and the D 18 to La Terrasse, from where there is a wonderful view.

★★ **La Terrasse** – Alt 660m - 2 165ft. *Viewing table.* The broad **view** from a bend in the D 18 about half a mile after the Col du Fût d'Avenas takes in the Saône valley, with behind it the Bresse plateau, the Jura peaks and (in clear weather) the Alps, with Mont Blanc, the Vanoise massif and the Pelvoux.

Avenas – The Roman road from Lyon to Autun once passed through this village. The late 12C church contains a lovely 12C white limestone **altar★**, which depicts Christ seated in Majesty in a mandorla, surrounded by the symbols of the Evangelists on either side. The sides show scenes from the life of the Virgin Mary *(left)* and King Louis, the donor *(right)* – this is assumed to be Louis VII, although the inscription does not clarify this.

Altar in the church of Avenas

Take the D 18ᴱ, then D 32.

Shortly before the pass (Col de Crie), there is a beautiful view north down the Grosne Orientale valley. As the road carries on downhill, it passes **Mont St-Rigaud** on the right, at an altitude of 1 009m - 3 310ft, the highest peak in the region.

Chénelette – This small village lies in a charming wooded setting. The **Tourvéon** (alt 953m - 3 127ft) towers above it. This summit was once the site of the great fortress of Ganelon. According to the *Chanson de Roland*, Ganelon betrayed the army of Charlemagne, bringing about its defeat and the death of Roland at Roncevaux. For this, he was put into a barrel lined with nails, which was then cast off the Tourvéon peak. His castle *(to visit the ruins: 45 min on foot Rtn)* was probably destroyed on the orders of Louis the Pious.

Les Écharmeaux – This small holiday resort (alt 720m - 2 632ft) is set against a backdrop of woods and meadows, near the mountain pass that bears its name. It is a junction for several main roads through the Beaujolais region. The view of the steep slopes of the Haut Beaujolais to the north is impressive.

The D 10 towards Ranchal crosses the Col des Aillets, then goes through a wooded area and over the Col des Ecorbans. Charming **views★** into the valley of the Azergues are revealed from the D 54 between Ranchal and St-Nizier-d'Azergues. After the **Col de Favardy** (862m - 2 828ft) there is a lookout point with a good **view★** opening out to the north: in the foreground lies the Azergues valley and in the distance loom the Tourvéon and the foothills of the Beaujolais.

St-Nizier-d'Azergues – Small but charming village above the Azergues valley.

The road carries on through picturesque countryside as far as Grandis.

Turn left onto the D 504 to La Folletière, then turn left onto the D 485.

The road follows the upper valley of the Azergues and goes through Lamure-sur-Azergues *(facilities).*

In Le Gravier, turn right onto the D 9.

Claveisolles – This small village perched on a spur is well known for its evergreen forest. In the 19C, the Comte de Sablon introduced Douglas firs from America. The present forest cover is amongst some of the most beautiful in France.

Go back to the D 485 and turn left towards Chambost-Allières.

Chambost-Allières – An amalgamation of two very different villages: Allières, in the valley, quite a busy place with a lot of through traffic; and **Chambost**, a charming rural hamlet reached via the D 116 climbing up from the valley.

The **route★★** from Chambost-Allières via Le Saule-d'Oingt to Cogny is very pretty indeed. The road climbs to an altitude of 735m - 2 411ft at the Col du Joncin. Then it runs along the ridge, offering a lovely **view★** of the Alps in clear weather.

In Le Saule-d'Oingt turn left onto the D 31, then right onto the D 19.

As the road goes downhill, the Saône valley, the Bresse region and the foothills of the Jura unfold to view.

Take the D 504 to Villefranche.

Villefranche-sur-Saône – *See VILLEFRANCHE-SUR-SAÔNE.*

★★ IN THE LAND OF GOLDEN STONE

③ Round tour leaving from Villefranche-sur-Saône

59km - 37 miles – allow 4 hours – local map p 79

In the so-called **Pays des Pierres Dorées** ⊘ the village and vineyards are built from the pretty local golden stone.

Villefranche-sur-Saône – *See VILLEFRANCHE-SUR-SAÔNE.*

From Villefranche take the D 70 south.

Views of the Saône valley from this charming **ridge-top road★** *("route de crête").*

Marcy – Outside this market town *(take the small road to the left, signposted "Carrières Piani, Montézain")* stands a restoration of the telegraph with moving arms invented by Claude Chappe, which was used 1799-1850 to transmit optical signals. From the foot of the tower there is a sweeping view of the Saône valley, the flat marshy Dombes region and the Lyonnais and Beaujolais mountain chains.

Charnay – This town lies at the peak of a hill. It still contains the vestiges of a 12C fortress. The village square is lined with 15-16C houses built from local golden stone. Inside the church there is a beautiful Gothic polychrome stone statue (12C). The imposing 17C castle set slightly above the village now houses the town hall.

Follow the narrow road south of Charnay to St-Jean-des-Vignes.

St-Jean-des-Vignes – There is a good view of the area around Lyon from the pretty church perched on the hillside.

Take the D 30 to Chazay-d'Azergues.

Chazay-d'Azergues – This small fortified village perched high above the Azergues valley still contains vestiges of the old ramparts. The gateway called the Porte du Baboin is named after a juggler who, dressed as a bear, rescued the lord of the manor's niece from a fire and was subsequently allowed to marry her. The 15C **castle** *(not open to the public)* was once the residence of the abbots of Ainay.

Carry on along the D 30 to Lozanne, then take the D 485 to Châtillon.

Châtillon – A fortress built in the 12 and 13C to protect the Azergues valley towers masterfully over the village. The **Chapelle St-Barthélemy** ⊘ *(follow steep signposted route to the left of the parish church)*, which was once part of the castle, was enlarged in the 15C by Geoffroy de Balzac. The chapel houses paintings by Lavergne and H. Flandrin (19C). The cantilevered east end is a most unusual feature. The Esplanade du Vingtain, running below the church, gives a good view of the village. As you leave the village, on the D 76 towards Alix, there is a pretty covered well (the *Puits Sarrasin*).

Carry on along the D 485 in between red spoil heaps.

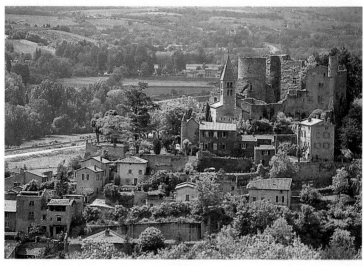

Châtillon

Chessy – The Flamboyant Gothic **church** ⊘ contains a beautiful 16C font and a naïve statue of St Margaret of Antioch subduing a dragon known as the "tarasque". Nearby Chessy a rich seam of copper, the property of Jacques Cœur, was once mined. The ore obtained was known as "chessylite" and was a variety of azurite with a beautiful blue glint to it.

Take the D 19 towards Bagnols.

Bagnols – In this village is a 15C castle. The village **church** ⊘, dating from the same period, contains a beautiful pendant keystone. There are some pretty old (15-16C) houses with porches on the village square.

Go back to the D 19 and follow it to the left.

Le Boitier – As you leave this hamlet, the road takes you past the Clos de la Platière, which belonged to the Rolands, a couple who became famous during the Revolution. Mme Roland de la Platière stands out from her contemporaries as an exceptionally cultured, well educated woman who forged numerous close connections with the politicians of her age. However, she made no secret of her antipathy towards Danton and Robespierre and paid for this in 1793 by being sent to the guillotine. Her husband, who as Home Secretary (since 1791) had tried to save the life of Louis XVI and had been forced to flee when he failed, committed suicide on receiving the news of his wife's death.

Theizé – The village is overlooked by the robust outline of its fortress, the **Château de Rochebonne** ⊘. The classical façade has a triangular pediment and is framed between two round towers. Note in the 16C **church** ⊘, now deconsecrated, a funerary band *(qv)* halfway up the chancel, recalling the burials of the local lords.

★**Oingt** – All that remains of the once mighty fortress here is the Porte de Nizy through which you enter the village. Little streets lined with very pretty houses lead to the **church** ⊘, the old castle chapel (14C). Note on the brackets supporting the arches of the chancel the carved faces of Guichard IV, his wife and their six children. From the top of the **tower** ⊘ there is a marvellous panorama of the Tarare and Beaujolais mountains and of the Azergues valley. In the town itself, note the two pedestrian streets and the 16C Maison commune (community centre), restored.

Carry on along the D 96.

Note the church with the porch in **St-Laurent-d'Oingt**.

When you get to the D 485, turn right.

On the left stands the old fortified town of Ternand.

★**Ternand** – Once the property of the archbishops of Lyon, Ternand retains some of its earlier fortifications, such as the keep and the watchpath, from which there is a good view of the Tarare mountains and the Azergues valley. The most interesting features of the **church** ⊘ are the Carolingian capitals in the chancel and the mural paintings, dating from the same period, in the crypt.

Turn back through Les Planches and take the D 31.

The **pass road**★★ over the Col du Saule-d'Oingt is very pretty. Picturesque farmhouses overlook the meadows from the hillside. From Saule-d'Oingt, heading down towards Villefranche, there is a good view of the Saône valley.

At La Maladière turn right towards Jarnioux.

Jarnioux – The **castle** *(not open to the public)*, built between the 15 and 17C, has six towers. The parts of it which date from the Renaissance are particularly charming. The grand entrance gateway, on which the traces of the drawbridge can still be seen, leads into two courtyards, one after the other.

Return to Villefranche on the D 116 and the D 38.

BEAUNE★★

Population 21 129

Michelin map 69 fold 9 or 243 fold 27 – Facilities – Local map under La CÔTE

At the heart of the Burgundian vineyards lies Beaune; the name is synonymous with good wine, and a visit to the city is not complete without also touring the vineyards on La Côte *(qv)*.

HISTORICAL NOTES

The birth of a town – First a Gallic centre and then an outpost of Rome, Beaune was the residence of the Dukes of Burgundy up to the 14C, before they moved permanently to Dijon. The original charter of communal liberties granted by Duke Eudes in 1203 is still in the town's archives.

The fortifications and towers that exist today were built from the 15C onwards. After the death of the last Duke of Burgundy, Charles the Bold, in 1477, the town stubbornly refused all efforts to annex it by Louis XI and surrendered only after a siege lasting five weeks.

There has always been a degree of rivalry, if not outright animosity, between the citizens of Dijon and Beaune. This was particularly pronounced during the 18C and was an ample source of inspiration to the Dijon poet **Alexis Piron** (1689-1773), who did not restrict himself merely to penning offensive odes about the residents of Beaune, but actually went there to insult them in person. His audacity almost cost him dear, however; he was cornered by an angry crowd baying for his blood and would certainly have been set upon, had a kindly citizen not rescued him and smuggled him out of the town at night.

Wine auction at the Hospices de Beaune – This is certainly the main local event of the year and draws a large crowd to the town. The Hospices de Beaune (this name includes the Hôtel-Dieu, the Hospice de la Charité and the hospital) acquired a very fine vineyard (58ha - 143 acres) between Aloxe-Corton and Meursault through Chancellor Rolin. The wines from this vineyard have won international acclaim, and the honour of being a wine-producer for the Hospices is highly sought after. The proceeds of the auction sales, **"Les Trois Glorieuses"** *(qv)*, which are known as the "greatest charity sale in the world", go to the modernisation of the surgical and medical facilities and the maintenance of the Hôtel-Dieu.

Courtyard of the Hôtel-Dieu

★★★ HÔTEL-DIEU (AZ) ⏱ *time: 1 hour*

The Hôtel-Dieu in Beaune, a marvel of Burgundian-Flemish art, was founded as a hospital by Chancellor Nicolas Rolin in 1443. The medieval building with its perfectly preserved medieval décor has survived intact and was used as a general hospital until 1971, when it became a geriatric hospital.

Street façade – The principal decorative elements of this sober façade with its tall and steeply-pitched slate roof are the dormer windows, the weather vanes, the delicate pinnacles and lacework cresting of lead. The roof line is broken by the bell turret surmounted by a slim Gothic spire 30m - 98ft high.

The lovely, delicate roof above the entrance porch is composed of three slate gables terminating in worked pinnacles. Each weather vane bears a different coat of arms. On the beautifully panelled door, note the ironwork grille with sharp points and the door knocker, a magnificent piece of chased wrought-ironwork.

Courtyard – The courtyard is surrounded by buildings which give it a charming overall effect in which cheerfulness, wealth and homeliness combine to make this seem more like a dwelling fit for royalty than a hospital for the poor. The wings to the left and the rear have magnificent roofs of coloured glazed tiles (recently restored) arranged in striking geometric patterns. These roofs are punctuated by turrets and a double row of dormer windows, surmounted by weather vanes adorned with heraldic bearings and small spires of worked lead.

A timbered gallery at first floor level rests on light stone columns forming cloisters on the ground floor. The building on the right, erected in the 17C, on the site of out-buildings, does not mar the beauty of the overall effect. On the reverse side of the façade, the pavilions that frame the entrance doorway were built during the last century. The old well, with its wrought-iron well head and its stone curb, is graceful.

Grand'Salle or Chambre des Pauvres – This immense hall (46m long by 14m wide by 16m high - 151ft x 46ft x 52ft), used as the poor ward, has a magnificent timber roof in the shape of an upturned keel which is painted throughout; the ends of the tie-beams disappear into the gaping months of monsters' heads. The paving is a reproduction of the original flag stones. All the furniture is original or else copied from the original models.

In earlier times on feast days the twenty eight four-poster beds were covered with fine tapestry bedspreads, now displayed in the Salle du Polyptyque. Even without the tapestries, the double row of beds with their red and white bedclothes, hangings and testers makes a striking impression. At the end of the room stands an arresting, larger than life-size polychrome wooden statue (15C) of **Christ seated and bound★** carved from a single piece of oak. Th death's head peeking out from underneath his tunic is a reminder of man's mortality. The Flamboyant style screen separating the Grand'Salle from the chapel was reconstructed in the 19C together with the large stained glass window. The famous altar-piece by Rogier van der Weyden, now in the Salle du Polyptyque, used to be above the altar. The chapel exhibits a copper funerary plaque in memory of Guigone de Salins, wife of Nicolas Rolin and co-founder of the Hôtel-Dieu. The Clermont-Tonnerre collection of sacred art (priestly vestments and objects) is displayed in showcases.

Salle Ste-Anne – The linen room, visible through the windows, was originally a small bedroom reserved for "the nobility". The work of the nursing nuns is illustrated by life-size models dressed in the habits worn by the staff until 1961.

Salle St-Hugues – This ward, which was taken out of use in 1982, has been partially refurbished with its 17C décor; the beds are those which were in use from the end of the 19C. The frescoes, by Isaac Moillon, depict St Hugues, as bishop and Carthusian monk, and the nine miracles of Christ.

Salle St-Nicolas – This ward, where those in danger of death were nursed, now houses a permanent exhibition on the history of the Hôtel-Dieu and the healing of the body and mind which it offered to the poor and sick. A glass slab in the centre reveals the Bouzaise stream which flows beneath the hospital and which carried away the waste.

Cuisine – *Son et lumière presentation every 15 min.*
In the kitchen, an old-fashioned scene has been set up round the huge Gothic fireplace with its double hearth and automatic spit, which dates from 1698.

Pharmacie – The first room of the pharmacy contains pewter vessels displayed on a handsome 18C dresser; the second, which is panelled, contains a collection of 18C Nevers porcelain and a huge bronze mortar.

Salle St-Louis – The walls are hung with early-16C tapestries from Tournai depicting the parable of the Prodigal Son and a series woven in Brussels early in the 12C illustrating the story of Jacob.

Salle du Polyptyque – This room was designed to exhibit the famous **polyptych of the Last Judgment★★★** by Rogier van der Weyden. This masterpiece of Flemish art was commissioned by Nicolas Rolin in 1443 to grace the altar in the Grand'Salle. It was extensively restored in the 19C and sawn in two so that both faces could be displayed simultaneously. A huge mobile magnifying glass enables viewers to study the smallest detail on the highly expressive faces of the subjects.

In the central panel Christ presides at the Last Judgment; he is enthroned on a rainbow surrounded by golden clouds suggestive of Paradise; four angels carrying the instruments of the Passion stand at his sides in the flanking panels. St Michael is weighing the souls, with angels sounding their trumpets on either side of him. In attendance on the central figures are the Virgin Mary and St John the Baptist appealing to the Saviour for mercy. Behind them are the Apostles and a few important people (including the donors) who are interceding on behalf of humankind.

At the bottom of the panels the dead rise from the earth; the just make their way to the Gates of Paradise, a sparkling golden cathedral, while the damned writhe at the entrance to the fiery pit of Hell.

The reverse side of the polyptych is on the wall to the right. In the past, only this face was usually visible, as the polyptych was opened only on Sundays and feast days. The fine portraits of Nicolas Rolin and his wife are accompanied by monochromes of St Sebastian and St Anthony, the first patrons of the Hôtel-Dieu, and the Annunciation. On the wall to the left hangs a beautiful early-16C *mille-fleurs* tapestry depicting the legend of St Eligius.

The tapestries hanging opposite the Last Judgment belonged to Guigone de Salins; against the deep rose-coloured background, scattered with turtle doves, are the arms of the founder of the hospital, an interlaced G and N and the motto "Seulle" (you alone) expressing Nicolas Rolin's faithful attachment to his wife. In the centre is St Anthony the hermit, patron saint of Guigone de Salins.

★COLLÉGIALE NOTRE-DAME (AY) ⓧ time: 30min

The daughter house of Cluny, begun about 1120, was considerably influenced by the church of St-Lazare in Autun *(qv)*; it is a fine example of Burgundian Romanesque art despite successive additions.

Exterior – The façade is concealed by a wide 14C porch with three naves. The sculpted decoration was destroyed during the Revolution, but the 15C carved door panels have survived.

Walk clockwise round the church to get the best view of the chevet. Three different phases of construction – the pure Romanesque of the ambulatory and absidal chapels, the 13C refurbishment of the chancel and the 14C flying buttresses – can be detected in the handsome proportions of the whole. The crossing tower, which is formed of Romanesque arcades surmounted by pointed bays, is capped by a dome and a 16C lantern.

Interior – The lofty nave of broken-barrel vaulting is flanked by narrow aisles with groined vaulting. A triforium, composed of open and blind bays, goes round the building, which is strongly reminiscent of Autun with its decoration of arcades and small fluted columns. The transept crossing is covered by an octagonal dome on squinches. Behind this, the ambulatory, with three semi-domed apsidal chapels opening into it, leads off around the harmoniously proportioned choir.

Besides the decoration of the small columns in the transept, it is worth noting the band of rosettes under the false triforium in the choir, and the sculptures on certain capitals in the nave representing Noah's Ark, the Stoning of St Stephen and a Tree of Jesse. The second chapel in the north aisle contains 15C frescoes depicting the Resurrection of Lazarus, which are attributed to Burgundian artist Pierre Spicre, and a 16C *Pietà*. There are two altar-pieces in the third chapel.

Note the Renaissance chapel with the fine coffered ceiling off the south aisle.

★★ **Tapestries** – In the choir behind the high altar there are some magnificent tapestries which mark the transition from medieval to Renaissance art. Five richly coloured panels, worked in wool and silk, trace the whole life of the Virgin Mary in a series of charming scenes. They were commissioned in 1474, woven from cartoons by Spicre based on outlines supplied by Chancellor Rolin and offered to the church in 1500 by Canon Hugues le Coq.

Cloisters – A Romanesque doorway in the south transept leads to what remains of the 13C cloisters and the chapter house, which have both been restored.

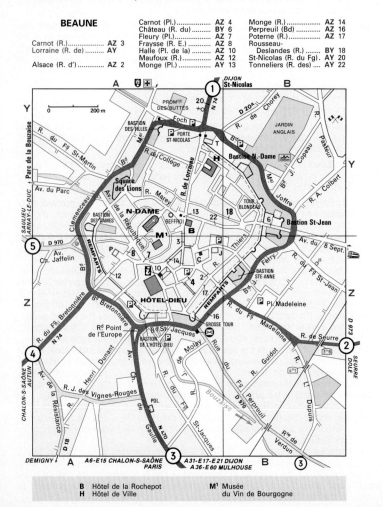

B	Hôtel de la Rochepot	**M¹**	Musée
H	Hôtel de Ville		du Vin de Bourgogne

ADDITIONAL SIGHTS

★ **Musée du Vin de Bourgogne (Burgundy Wine Museum)** (AZ **M¹**) ⊘ – The museum is laid out in the former mansion of the Dukes of Burgundy, a building of the 15 and 16C in which stone and woodwork complement each other harmoniously. The inner courtyard recalls the décor of a theatre and displays a reduced scale model (1:200) of the town's ramparts. The porter's lodge, to the right of the entrance doorway, dates from the 15C. The wine cellar (14C), reached through a large door, contains an impressive collection of wine presses and vats.

The entire history of Burgundian vineyards and the cultivation of the vine is explained in a comprehensive exhibition on the ground floor. The 16C polychrome statue is known as the Virgin Mary with a Bunch of Grapes or Notre Dame de Beaune. On the first door, a large room decorated with two immense Aubusson tapestries, one by Lurçat and one by Michel Tourlière, is the headquarters of the Ambassade des Vins de France (Embassy of the Wines of France).

Other rooms contain collections of pitchers, bottles, wine-tasting glasses, coopers' tools and also gold plate and souvenirs of the master craftsmen and journeymen of the Compagnons de Tour de France, a medieval guild.

★ **Hôtel de la Rochepot** (AY **B**) – *Not open to the public.*
This 16C building possesses a pretty Gothic façade.

In Place Monge stand a 14C belfry and a statue by Rude of **Gaspard Monge** (1746-1818), a local shopkeeper's son who became a famous mathematician. He is considered to be the founder of descriptive geometry (application of geometry to construction problems).

Hôtel de Ville (AY **H**) ⊘ – The town hall occupies the buildings of a 17C Ursuline convent. The right wing houses two **museums.**

Musée des Beaux-Arts – This fine arts collection includes numerous works by local artist **Félix Ziem** (1821-1911), 16C and 17C Flemish and Dutch paintings, medieval (14C bagpipes player) and Renaissance (16C St Anne) sculpture and a small Gallo-Roman section (statue of a river goddess discovered in Gissey-le-Vieil).

Musée Étienne-Jules Marey – The doctor and physiologist Étienne-Jules Marey was passionately interested in the phenomenon of movement. He invented a number of medical instruments (exhibited here), including the sphygmograph – a machine for recording the pulse graphically. From 1867 he held the chair of natural history in the Collège de France. He also contributed to the development of the motion picture, inventing a drum in which there was a series of photographs which, when the drum was turned, seemed to represent motion (he studied birds in flight with this). The Lumière brothers went on to develop his makeshift motion picture camera further. Several other inventions of his are on display, including the photographic rifle camera.

St-Nicolas – *Leave by ① on the town plan, the N 74.*
This 13C church in the midst of the wine-growers' area has a Romanesque tower with a fine stone spire. A 15C timber porch, covered with tiles and supported by pillars of dressed stone, shelters a 12C doorway. The monolithic tympanum depicts the Golden Legend of St Nicholas, in which he saves three young girls, whose father was too poor to provide them with a dowry, from a life of prostitution by giving them each a golden ball.

Old houses – Among the many picturesque old houses, note those at nos 18, 20, 22 and 24 **Rue de Lorraine** (**AY**), which form a fine 16C ensemble. At no 10 **Rue Rousseau-Deslandes** (**BY 18**) there is a house with its first floor decorated with trefoiled arcades; at no 2 **Rue E.-Fraysse** (**AZ 8**) the Maison du Colombier is a pretty Renaissance house which can be seen from the square in front of the church of the Notre-Dame; 13 **Place Fleury** (**AZ 7**) is the Hôtel Saulx, a mansion with a pretty little tower and an interior courtyard; 4 **Place Carnot** (**AZ 4**), is a 16C house with attractive sculptures.

Parc de la Bouzaise – *Take Avenue du Parc* (**AY**).
The fine shady trees and artificial lake fed by the river make this an agreeable spot for a walk.

★ **Les Remparts** – *An external tour of the ramparts is possible on foot or by car.*
The relatively well-preserved ramparts form an almost continuous wall walk (2m - 1 mile) – parts of which are now private property. The wall was built between the end of the 15C and the middle of the 16C, of roughly rectangular blocks. It is adorned with a few surviving towers and eight rusticated bastions of various shapes – the double one, originally a castle, is known as the **Bastion St-Jean**. In places the ramparts are hidden by bushes or private houses; the encircling moat is now occupied by gardens, tennis courts etc.

Tour of the ramparts – *From the Bastion St-Jean follow the outer boulevards, beginning with Boulevard Joffre, anti-clockwise.* The north tower of the Bastion St-Jean has several gargoyles and a niche occupied by a Virgin and Child. It overlooks a cherry orchard in the moat. Pass the Blondeau tower, which protrudes from the ramparts, to get to the **Bastion Notre-Dame**, with its trees and a charming turret covering the spur. The line of the ramparts is broken by the 18C Porte St-Nicolas at the end of Rue Lorraine. Next come the Bastion des Filles, spoilt by the addition of an ugly new roof, and the now filled-in Bastion St-Martin forming a triangular terrace (**Square des Lions**) overlooking a shaded garden.

The route now takes you past the Bastion des Dames (pretty house and trees), the **Rempart des Dames** (walkway bordered by fine plane trees) and the now-abandoned Bastion de l'Hôtel-Dieu, with a stream at its foot which served the washhouses in days gone by. The 15C Grosse Tour (great tower) on the Rempart Madeleine is followed by the overgrown Bastion Ste-Anne sporting a turret overlooking the moat. The tour ends in front of the castle's south tower overlooking the hedges and bamboo in the moat. Stand back a little to obtain a better view of this outwork crowned by a small house against a background of varnished tile roofs.

▶▶ **Archéodrome** ⊘ – *7km - 4.5 miles south.*
Panorama of the history of Burgundy from Paleolithic to Gallo-Roman times through reconstructions of sites and artefacts.

BELFORT★

Population 52 739
Michelin map no 155 fold 3 or 243 fold 10 – Facilities –
Plan of conurbation in the Michelin Red Guide France

Belfort is divided by the river Savoureuse into two distinct parts. On the river's west bank are extensive industrial and commercial areas and housing estates; on the east bank, at the foot of the rock on which the castle is sited, is the "impregnable" citadel built by Vauban.

The Belfort Gap – Lying at an altitude of 350m - 1 148ft between the Jura mountain plateaux (ranging from 800-1 000m to 2 625-3 281ft) to the south and the Vosges range (Ballon d'Alsace *(qv)* summit: 1 247m - 4 091ft) to the north, the 30km - 19 mile wide Belfort Gap (or "Trouée de Belfort", sometimes known as the Burgundian Gate) provides a natural passage between the two great valleys of the Rhine and the Rhône.
A river once flowed through this gap from southwest to northeast, but now the water tables divide at the level of Valdieu, halfway between Belfort and Altkirch. The gap has attracted all sorts of communications routes – roads, railways, the Rhône-Rhine canal – and, in the past, many invading armies.

Belfort's site – The best view of the Belfort Gap and the site occupied by the town of Belfort is from the **Fort du Salbert** *(8km - 5 miles northwest; see below).*
Leave the town on the Avenue Jean-Jaurès. Turn left into the Rue de la 1ʳᵉ Armée française, which runs into the Rue des Commandos-d'Afrique, then take the Rue du Salbert off to the right. The D 4, a winding forest road, leads to the fort, which is at an altitude of 647m - 2 123ft. The vast terrace *(200m - just over 200yds to the left - viewing table)* gives a marvellous **panorama★★** over Belfort, the Swiss Alps, the Ballon d'Alsace and the surrounding mountains.
Whereas the "mountain" (nearest hill in the foreground to the south) and the rocky escarpment on which the fortress and Lion of Belfort are built consist of Jurassic limestone, the hill on which the Fort du Salbert stands is still part of the Vosges, and therefore consists of granite and sandstone.

HISTORICAL NOTES

An invasion route – The Belfort Gap has drawn successive waves of invaders; Celts, Germanic tribes, soldiers of the Holy Roman Empire... in short, Belfort's history is a battered one. The town was subject to Austrian rule (the Habsburgs) from the mid-14C until the French conquest, but the citizens of Belfort took all this philosophically, knowing that their civil rights were protected by a charter dating from 1307.
During the Thirty Years War, in 1638, the town was taken by the French, under the leadership of the Count of La Suze for Montbéliard, who managed to break through the fortifications in a bold nocturnal attack. Suze was made Governor of Belfort by Richelieu and went down in the local annals for his succinct instructions to the commander of the garrison – "Ne capitulez jamais" (Never surrender). The French conquest was ratified by the Westphalia treaties in 1648, and Louis XIV ordered Vauban to make Belfort impregnable. The resulting fortified town is the great military engineer's masterpiece. Subsequently, the town was able to withstand the three sieges commemorated by Bartholdi's monument (in 1814, 1815 and 1870).

The Verdun of 1870 – In the course of the Franco-Prussian War of 1870, forty thousand German troops were held up for a month before Belfort by the Mobile Guards commanded by Colonel Denfert-Rochereau. Rather than shutting himself and his troops up in the fortress, as expected, he and his 16 000 courageous but inexperienced men retired in good order to the citadel, defending all approaches tenaciously as they went. This leisurely retreat took a month, and once in the fortress, they withstood a 103-day siege. During this time the enemy employed 200 huge cannon, unleashing a hail of shells onto the beleaguered town; they fired over 400 000 rounds in 83 days – that is about 5 000 per day, which is an huge number for that day and age. Denfert-Rochereau and his men only consented to march out (with full battle honours) on the direct orders of the French government, 21 days after the armistice signed at Versailles. In the struggle between President Thiers and Bismarck, the German Chancellor, over the cession of French territory, this exemplary resistance made it possible for Belfort to escape the fate of Alsace-Lorraine; it became instead the capital of its own tiny "territory", which was to acquire considerable economic importance.

Rapid Expansion – After 1870, Belfort underwent a radical transformation. Until then it had been essentially a military town (it produced more generals to serve France than any other town: twenty in a single century), with only 8 000 inhabitants. Within thirty years, Belfort had become a thriving conurbation with 40 000 inhabitants. One reason for this dramatic growth was the implantation of a number of subsidiaries of businesses belonging to residents of Alsace-Lorraine, anxious to keep up their connections with France in the wake of the German annexation. As pressure built up on the town to expand, Vauban's ramparts were demolished. The new districts, with their wide streets and huge squares, give Belfort the appearance of a small capital city.

The capture of the Fort du Salbert – On 14 November 1944 the First French Army, having been blocked for two months in its advance towards the Rhine by the bristling defences of the retreating Wehrmacht at Belfort, began the offensive which would break through to upper Alsace and the Rhine. Fort du Salbert, northwest of the town, was in the way, so they attacked it on the night of 19 November. Fifteen hundred Commandoes of the Army of Africa slipped into Salbert forest and put the German sentries out of action. They used ropes to drop into the deep moats surrounding the fort, without raising the enemy's alarm, and then managed to take the garrison by surprise and subdue it. Belfort was finally liberated on 22 November, after tank battles and street fighting, and the French Army's thrust in the direction of Mulhouse could now continue.

Industry in the 20C – 1926 and 1990 are dates which reflect the main thrust of Belfort's industrial activity this century. In 1926, the first electric train was produced in the Belfort workshops of the Société Alsacienne de Constructions Mécaniques; on 18 May 1990, the high-speed train TGV-Atlantique, built in Belfort (GEC-Alsthom), broke the world rail speed record by reaching 515.3kph - 320mph.

The group GEC-Alsthom in Belfort is concerned with electrical engineering, the production of railway fittings and the construction of thermal or nuclear power stations. These industries, along with firms which manufacture computer parts, have given the town and surrounding region an excellent reputation in the field of technology, which has been further enhanced by the founding of a technical university (Louis Neele) and an polytechnical institute in Sévenans.

★★ THE BELFORT LION

The great beast (22m - 72ft long and 11m - 36ft high), carved from red Vosges sandstone, just below the castle symbolises the spirit and strength of Belfort's defenders in 1870 and marks the response of the French people to their heroism. It is the work of **Frédéric Bartholdi** (carved from 1875-1880 and put together bit by bit on site), who here gave free rein to his patriotic fervour and ardent creativity. A path leads from the **viewing platform** ⊙ at the base of the Lion to the memorial *(take the stairs from the car park and turn right into the tunnel, from which a doorway opens almost immediately on the left to the memorial)*. The Lion is floodlit at night, which makes it look even more awe-inspiring. The view from the viewing platform is similar to that from the terrace of the fortress.

Frédéric Auguste Bartholdi (1834-1904) – This sculptor was born in Colmar and showed his artistic prowess from an early age. He won a competition held by his home town in 1856 to find someone to execute a memorial statue of General Rapp. His travels in Egypt and the Far East affected his later work. After the Franco-Prussian war in 1870, he sculpted a large number of patriotic monuments, the most famous of which are the Belfort Lion and the statue of Liberty lighting the World at the entrance to New York harbour *(see also the Monument des Trois Sièges below)*.

The Belfort Lion

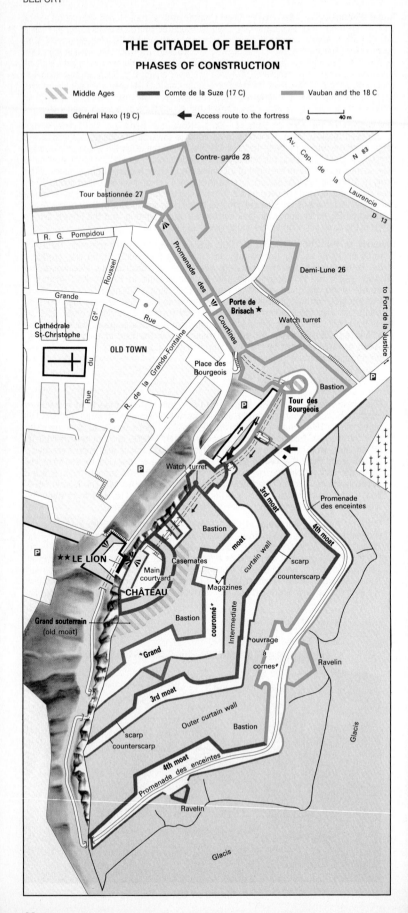

THE CITADEL OF BELFORT

PHASES OF CONSTRUCTION

Middle Ages   Comte de la Suze (17 C)   Vauban and the 18 C

Général Haxo (19 C)   ← Access route to the fortress   0   40 m

Contre-garde 28

Av. Cap. de la Laurencie   N 83

Tour bastionnée 27

R. G. Pompidou

Roussel

Demi-Lune 26

D 13

Grande

Rue

Gd.

du

Porte de Brisach ★

Watch turret

to Fort de la Justice

Cathédrale St-Christophe

OLD TOWN

R. de la Grande-Fontaine

Place des Bourgeois

Rue

Bastion

P

P

Promenade des Courtines

Tour des Bourgeois

Watch turret

P

Bastion

Promenade des enceintes

3rd moat

4th moat

★★ LE LÍON

P

Bastion

moat

Casemates

Main courtyard

CHÂTEAU

Magazines

curtain wall

scarp

counterscarp

Grand souterrain (old moat)

Bastion

couronné

Intermediate

★Grand

★ouvrage à cornes★

Ravelin

3rd moat

scarp

counterscarp

Outer curtain wall

Bastion

4th moat

Promenade des enceintes

Glacis

Ravelin

Glacis

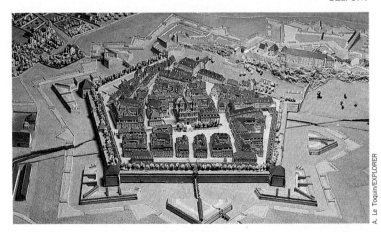

A. Le Toquin/EXPLORER

Belfort in 1703

★★ THE CITADEL

A key strategic position – As early as 1625 Richelieu, anxious to secure himself an access route into Alsace and the German Empire, had tried to annex Belfort. However, Tilly defended the fortress successfully with the help of Croatian troops. From 1687 Vauban began his master work; he surrounded the existing fortress and town with several pentagonal fortified walls anchored to the rocky cliff on which the buildings stood. Construction lasted about twenty years. Belfort played the role assigned to it by Vauban – of major military garrison between Alsace and the Franche-Comté – until the end of the Napoleonic Empire. Commandant Legrand was another heroic defender of this fortified site in 1814.

As military strategy developed away from the idea of entrenched warfare towards that of mobile warfare, first Général Lecourbe (from 1815) and then Général Haxo (from 1825) undertook not only to build at Belfort a means of protecting the town, but also a fortified military site that would enable resident troops to guard the Belfort Gap. In this way, they increased Belfort's military role considerably.

This plan was still in force at the time of the siege in 1870. It was further endorsed by the plans of Général Séré de la Rivière, who sought to fortify Verdun, Toul, Épinal and Belfort and link them together in a line of fortifications.

After 1885, in the wake of progress made in the development of efficient weaponry, many forts were modernised. Concrete replaced stone walls, and smaller batteries less easy to spot than fortresses were built for the artillery.

Shortly before the outbreak of the First World War, Belfort had reached the capacity to accommodate 7 500 men in peace time and ten times that number in the case of war. The line of fortifications between Épinal and Belfort was ready to play its role in the defence of the nation.

FORTIFICATIONS ⊙

The terrace of the fort – This terrace, open to everyone, is at the top of the barracks which houses the museum of art and history. It is an excellent viewing point, from which you will be able to place the fortress in its geographical context and gain a better understanding of its comprehensive system of defence.

The **panorama★★** reveals to the south the Jura mountain chain on the horizon, to the west the old town, the industrial zones and the Fort du Salbert, to the north the southern Vosges with the peaks of the Ballon de Servance, the Ballon d'Alsace, the Baerenkopf and the Rossberg, and to the east the curtain walls of the fortress and the Belfort Gap. At the foot of the barracks to the east, the **main courtyard** (Cour d'honneur) is surrounded by the Haxo casemates, which have been converted into art galleries. You can make out the outline of the **Grand souterrain**, a covered moat dating from the reign of Louis XV, which was used to provide troops and horses with shelter during attacks, and further to the east the moat known as the **Grand Couronné**, with its bastions, and the moat round the intermediate curtain wall (3rd moat) and that round the outer curtain wall (4th moat).

The curtain walls (Enceintes) – *Allow 1 hour. Follow the path at the foot of the fortress through the tunnel beneath the Lion and carry on along it until you get to the 4th moat (4ᵉ fossé).* Note the impressive proportions of the moats and, towards the motorway, the **glacis**, a vast area of bare land which slopes gently away. Walking along the 4th or 3rd moats, between the mighty scarp and counterscarp walls, is a good way to see the defence system in detail: numerous embrasures allowed soldiers to fire down into the moats, fortifications with horn-shaped projections (*"ouvrages à cornes"*), bastions. The tour ends at the **Tour des Bourgeois**, the old tower from the medieval curtain wall demolished by Vauban.

Promenade des Courtines – Walkway reached through the semi-circular room in the Tour des Bourgeois *(if the room is closed, go via the Place des Bourgeois).*

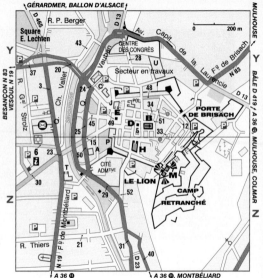

B Cathédrale St-Christophe
D Statue « Quand même »
E Monument des trois sièges
H Hôtel de Ville
M Musée d'Art et d'Histoire

The terrace above the Porte de Brisach gives a good view of the demi-lune fortification in front of the gateway. The double line of fortifications from Vauban's time are also visible.

Carry on to the **Tour bastionnée 27**, from where there is a view back to the fortress and its grass-covered walls, dating from Haxo's modifications.

Musée d'Art et d'Histoire ⊘ – The basement contains artefacts from the Neolithic, Gallo-Roman and Merovingian periods, found in the vicinity of the Burgundy Gap (earthenware, weapons, tools from the Cravanche cave, a mosaic from a villa in Bavilliers, belt buckles and a reconstruction of a tomb from a Burgundian cemetery). 19C rural, religious and domestic life is also evoked. The first floor is used for temporary exhibitions. The second floor is devoted to history. Exhibits include a reproduction of Vauban's relief model of his fortifications in 1687, and numerous military artefacts (weapons, helmets, trophies, documents, swords, medals). Articles which belonged to Colonel Denfert-Rochereau or to French and Prussian officers bear witness to the resistance against the 1870-71 siege.

On the other side of the courtyard, in the Haxo battery, collections of paintings (by Gustave Doré, Heim, Maximilien Luce, Guillaumin, as well as engravings by Dürer), sculptures (Camille Lefèvre, Dalou, Barye, Rodin) and photographs (A. Villers) are on display.

ADDITIONAL SIGHTS

★**Old Town** – It was not until the end of the last century that Belfort was able to get rid of its fortifications and link its old town with the new districts springing up on the west bank of the Savoureuse.

The old town has been undergoing restoration since 1986, and the colourful façades of the houses, in blue-green, green, pink or ochre coloured washes, with pale stone decoration around the windows lend a much friendlier atmosphere to the streets and squares of the once austere garrison town. Particularly charming examples are to be found in the Place de l'Arsenal, the Place de la Grande-Fontaine, the Grande-Rue and the Place de la Petite-Fontaine.

★**Porte de Brisach** (Y) – This gateway, constructed by Vauban in 1687, has been preserved in the original. It features a pilastered façade decorated with the Bourbon coat of arms with *fleurs de lys* and, on the pediment, the coat of arms of Louis XIV: the sun surmounted by the famous motto *Nec pluribus impar*.

Cathédrale St-Christophe (Y B) – The church, built of red sandstone, has an 18C classical façade. The exterior architecture and the interior decoration are highly unified in style. The frieze of angels' heads in relief runs all around the nave. The beautiful **gilded wrought-iron grille** enclosing the choir is similar to the railings by Jean Lamour in Place Stanislas in Nancy. The polychrome Italian marble altar dates from the 17C. Note in the transept paintings by the Belfort painter G Dauphin: an *Entombment of Christ* (on the right) and *The Ecstacy of St François-Xavier* (on the left). The 18C **organ★**, by Valtrin, has a beautifully carved and gilded wooden case.

Monument des trois sièges (Y E) – This work by Bartholdi depicts France and the city of Belfort with their three defenders (Legrand in 1814, Lecourbe in 1815 and Denfert-Rochereau in 1870). It stands in the middle of Place de la République, which houses the Préfecture, the Palais de Justice (law courts) and the Salle des Fêtes (festival hall), not far from the covered market or **Marché couvert Fréry**.

Hôtel de Ville (Z H) ⊘ – The town hall was built in the Classical style. The beautiful "Salle Kléber" on the ground floor is a good example of late 18C French art (rococo style). There are paintings depicting Belfort's history in the main hall (Salle d'honneur) on the first door.

"Quand même" (Y D) – This statue, erected on the Place d'Armes in memory of the siege of 1870-71, is the work of Mercié (1884).
There is a beautiful view of the Belfort Lion from Avenue du Général-Sarrail, south of the Hôtel de Ville.

On the west bank of the Savoureuse – Since the 1970s, a modern town has sprung up on the west bank of the Savoureuse between Les 4-As and the Faubourg de France. It has a lively pedestrian shopping zone.
In a car park on the Rue de l'As de Carreau there is an unusual **fresco★** by Ernest Pignon-Ernest, painted onto the walls of a U-shaped building: 47 life-size figures of men and women represent the art and science of Latin and Teutonic countries, with Beethoven and Picasso rubbing shoulders with Rimbaud and Goethe.

Square E.-Lechten (Y) – A great variety of plants and flowers and also a floral mosaic can be seen here.

EXCURSIONS

Fort du Salbert – *See above under Belfort's site.*

The Hills around Belfort – *You should allow about 2 hours for this walk. Leave the town through the Porte de Brisach and turn right alongside the fortress as far as a car park. Take the foot bridge on the left over the Avenue de la Laurencie.*
The path brings you first of all to the **Fort de la Justice**. On the left, there are lookout points which give a good overall view of the Vosges. One of these is directly opposite a dovecot for carrier pigeons with examples of some of the messages carried by the pigeons fixed to its façade. Beyond this is the **Fort de la Miotte**, distinguishable by its tower. This fort was rebuilt in 1947 after a succession of disasters had befallen it in 1724, 1835, 1870, 1875 and 1940.

Étang des Forges – *Park near the sailing base.* A nature trail leads round this lake, at times right by the water's edge, at others cutting through the reed beds. Information boards explain about the flora and fauna to be found in this area (the little bittern, the smallest heron in Europe, the crested grebe and the coot).

Etueffont: Forge-Musée – *15km - 9.3 miles northeast. Leave Belfort on the N 83; after 10km - 6.2 miles, turn left onto the D 12.*
Four generations of the Petitjean family, plying the two trades of blacksmithing and farm labour, lived between 1844 and 1975 in a house at the heart of the village.
Many tools are displayed in the forge, which is still in working order. Numerous agricultural tools, generations old, are to be seen in the attics, the barn and the stable. Other trades such as that of the sabot-maker, the ironmonger or the joiner are also represented. The house is furnished as it would have been at the turn of the century.

BELLEY

Population 7 807
Michelin map 74 northeast of fold 14 or 244 fold 17 – Facilities –
Local map under BUGEY

The town, which was destroyed by a fire in 1385, was rebuilt and surrounded by fortifications by Amadeus VII of Savoy (the Bugey *(qv)* region and its capital Belley had belonged to the House of Savoy since 1077; they were not to become part of France until the Treaty of Lyon in 1601). The gateway (Vieille Porte) at the end of Boulevard du Mail is a remnant of these ramparts.
Belley, in a charming little valley watered by the Furan, is a good central location for excursions into the green and pleasant Bugey region. This peaceful town, essentially an administrative centre, is nonetheless home to some industrial and commercial concerns. The poet Lamartine went to secondary school in Belley (a statue of him stands in front of the Collège Lamartine in honour of this). The town also won fame in the world of gastronomy for being the birthplace of the great toast of taste-buds everywhere, Brillat-Savarin.

The Physiology of Taste – When **Jean-Anthelme Brillat-Savarin** was born in Belley in 1755 his career was already mapped out for him; he would be a lawyer like his father. He settled into the quiet way of life typical of Belley, visiting family or entertaining friends in town or at his country home in Vieu, all of which left him plenty of time to indulge his interest in the sciences as well as the arts. In 1789, the year of Revolution, he was elected deputy of the Third Estate and executed this role with kindness and tolerance. Nonetheless, even he was not above suspicion during the years of the Terror and in 1794, back in Belley having been elected mayor, he was forced to flee, first to Switzerland, then to the United States. He returned to France under the Consulate and became councillor to the Supreme Court of Appeals in Paris. In his free time he wrote, initially judicial or political works, then the little masterpiece which earned him his fame: *The Physiology of Taste*. In thirty essays he examines the various aspects of and problems associated with good living and good food; philosophical principles appear side by side with reflections on gluttony, sleep and dreams; he passes from scientific theories to culinary precepts, adopting the light-hearted, entertaining tone characteristic of all his scholarly writings. He died in 1826, and Belley, in recognition of his achievements, put up a statue on the "Promenoir" bearing the inscription of one of his maxims: "Inviting guests into your home means looking after their wellbeing as long as they are under your roof."

SIGHTS

Cathédrale St-Jean – Although the cathedral was almost entirely rebuilt in the 19C, it still features its original north portal, dating probably from the 14C: a door beneath a pointed arch, between two blind arcades.

Inside, the spacious six-bayed chancel★ (1473) and the triforium with its pretty openwork balustrades are also original. Five richly decorated chapels open onto the ambulatory. The Lady Chapel, behind the high altar, contains an imposing marble statue of the Virgin Mary by Chinard (1756-1813).

There is a shrine reliquary to St Anthelme, bishop of Belley from 1163 to 1178 and patron of the town, to the left of the altar. It is made of gilded bronze decorated with enamel work and depicts 12 scenes from the saint's life. The blue globe, the cross and the stars above the shrine evoke the Carthusian Order to which he belonged.

Maison natale de Brillat-Savarin – *No 62 Grande-Rue.*
Brillat-Savarin's birthplace is a beautiful, two-storied house decorated with round arches on the façade. An inner courtyard

Brillat-Savarin,
after a drawing by Stanley

leads into a garden graced by a loggia, and in which an old well is also to be seen. The façade of the garden wing features three floors of galleries and balustrades. The bust of Brillat-Savarin is at the northern end of the Promenoir, opposite the Grand Colombier mountainside he loved, where he had his country château at Vieu.

Rue du Chapitre – There is a beautiful 15C Renaissance house with a turret at no 8; a Gothic inscription can be seen above the door.

Palais épiscopal ⊙ – A bishop was in residence in Belley from 555. The 18C bishop's palace is thought to have been constructed following designs by Soufflot. It now houses the municipal library, the music school and a concert and exhibition hall.

Château de BELVOIR★

Michelin map 166 fold 17 or 243 fold 21 – 24km – 15 miles to the west of Maîche

The **fortress** ⊙ of Belvoir, built in the 12C by the barons of Belvoir, is perched on a promontory overlooking the Sancey valley south of the Lomont mountains. It remained the property of the Belvoirs and their descendants (the House of Lorraine and the Princes of Rohan) until the 19C. Vincent de Belvoir, to whom St Louis entrusted the writing of the first encyclopaedia, was born here. Restoration began in 1955, and the many rooms of the Château de Belvoir now house costly furnishings.

The visit includes the kitchen with its gleaming copper utensils, the guards' room, the former arsenal, and the weaponry in which arms and armour from the Middle Ages to the 19C are on display.

The castle has two towers, both of which give a beautiful panorama of the surrounding countryside: the Lomont mountains to the north; the Maîche plateau to the south; and a landscape of hills and plateaux to the east and west.

A living room and study have been attractively furnished in the Madge-Fà tower, which owes its curious name to the strange bearded character crouching on a monster's head beneath the cul-de-lampe which supports the turret overlooking the road.

The village of **Sancey-le-Long**, 2km - 1.2 miles south of Belvoir, was the birthplace of St Jeanne-Antide Thouret, founder of the Besançon Sisters of Charity; there is a pilgrimage church in her memory.

BERZÉ-LA-VILLE★

Population 511
Michelin map 69 fold 19 or 243 fold 39 — 12km - 8 miles to the southeast of Cluny
– Local map under MÂCONNAIS

Towards the end of his life St Hugh of Cluny lived in the Château des Moines, a country house near the priory in Berzé owned by the abbey of Cluny.

Chapelle des Moines ⊙ – This Romanesque chapel belongs to the priory and is well known for its frescoes, a magnificent example of the art of Cluny *(qv)*.

★★**Frescoes** – The 12C chapel, built at first floor level in an earlier (11C) building, was decorated with Romanesque frescoes *(photograph p 45);* only those in the chancel are well preserved.

On the oven-vaulting of the apse, Christ in Majesty is depicted in the centre of an almond-shaped glory. The figure is almost 4m - 13ft high and is surrounded by Apostles, bishops and deacons as he hands a parchment of the Law to St Peter; below the windows are groups of saints and martyrs venerated at Cluny. The south wall of the apse shows the legend of St Blaise, and the north wall the martyrdom of St Vincent of Saragossa on a gridiron in the presence of Dacius, the Roman prefect. The Byzantine influence evident in the murals, which are painted on a blue background, is probably due to the fact that the Cluniac artists who worked at Berzé were directed by Benedictine painters from Monte Cassino in Latium, where the influence of the eastern Roman empire survived until the 11C.

BESANÇON★★

Population 113 828
Michelin map 66 fold 15 or 243 fold 19 – Facilities –
Local map under Vallée du DOUBS

The capital of the Franche-Comté lies in an almost perfect ox-bow meander of the Doubs, overlooked by a rocky outcrop on which Vauban built a fortress.
The strategic advantages of the site were appreciated early on by Caesar, who described it in his account of the Gallic Wars.
Over the centuries Besançon's role expanded from the purely military to include that of an ecclesiastical and then industrial centre. During the Revolution, the town became the hub of the French clock-making industry, and local manufacturers of modern high-precision instruments draw on this early expertise.
There has been an annual international music festival here since 1948, which takes place in September, during which a prize is awarded to the best young conductor (prize-winners include Seiji Ozawa in 1959 and Michel Plasson in 1962).
Famous people born here include: the portraitist Donat Nonotte (1708-1785); the philosopher and economist Charles Fourier (1772-1837), who envisaged an ideal society composed of cooperative working communities known as "phalanxes"; the novelist Charles Nodier (1780-1844); the great poet and writer Victor Hugo (1802-1885); the sociologist Pierre-Joseph Proudhon (1809-1865); and the Lumière brothers, Auguste (1862-1954) and Louis (1864-1948).

Donat Nonotte, Selfportrait;
Musée des Beaux-Arts, Dijon

The site★★★ – This is best appreciated from the citadel, but there is also a good view from the Fort-de-Chaudanne.

Chaudanne (**BX**) – *2km - 1 mile south, and then a 15 min walk Rtn (see the town plan). Leave Besançon on the Charles-de-Gaulle bridge towards Planoise, go under a bridge and turn right 100m afterwards into the Rue G.-Plançon. Take the first on the right into the Rue de Chaudanne. Follow the Rue du Fort-de-Chaudanne until you get to the lookout point in front of the entrance to the fort.*
There is a lovely **view** of Besançon and the Doubs meander; at 419m - 1 375ft, this is one of the most interesting lookout points in the area.
From right to left, the view takes in the cathedral and the old town of Besançon, at the foot of the citadel, then the church of St-Pierre and the business district. On the far bank of the Doubs, the old wine-producing district of Battant can be seen. Directly below Chaudanne lies the administrative centre around the prefecture. Note the formidable Ruty barracks, general staff headquarters, by the Bregille bridge.

HISTORICAL NOTES

A centre for Christianity – Vesontio, as Besançon was called by the Romans during their occupation of Gaul, was converted to Christianity by two missionaries of Greek origin: **St Ferréol** and **St Ferjeux**, who set up home *c*180 in a cave in the middle of the woods, now the site of a basilica which was built there in their memory. For thirty years they preached the Gospel throughout the region. They were finally beheaded in the amphitheatre, because they refused to make sacrifices to the old pagan gods.
However, religious persecution did not prevent the new religion from gaining ground, and finally being adopted by the Emperor Constantine himself. The town subsequently became an important archbishopric. Thanks to this ecclesiastical role, further strengthened by Besançon's proximity to Protestant countries at the time when it set itself up as the bastion of the Counter-Reformation, the city is home to numerous churches and convents.

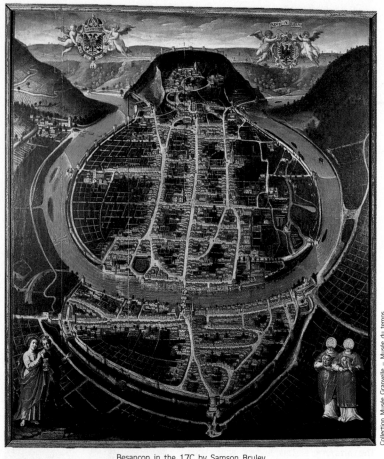

Collection Musée Granvelle – Musée du temps

Besançon in the 17C by Samson Bruley

Archbishop Hugh – When **Hugh of Salins** was made archbishop of Besançon in 1031, virtually the whole of France was in the grip of a terrible famine. Hugh came from one of the most illustrious families in the Franche-Comté and had been chaplain to Rudolph III, King of Burgundy. When Rudolph died in 1032, he left his estate to the Germanic Emperor Konrad II. Hugh proved to be an astute politician and was quick to begin forging connections with the new sovereign. In 1042, Konrad's successor **Heinrich III** presided over a diet at Besançon. He granted a degree of autonomy to Burgundy and appointed a chancellor, Hugh, who had won the emperor's confidence. Now that Hugh was second only to the emperor, Besançon gained the status of an imperial city, no longer answerable to the Comté, with the power to administer its own justice and mint its own money.

The archbishop's power was increased still further when a friend of his, Brunon de Toul, acceded to the Papal Seat as **Pope Leo IX**. Hugh entered the services of the pope and sat in on all the Church Councils of the day, where he initiated many reforms. He also carried out a number of construction projects in Besançon, until his death in 1066. The city owes the church of St-Étienne (1050) and the cathedral of St-Jean (1061) to him.

The rise of the Granvelle family – In the 16C, the fame of the Granvelle family cast a reflected glow on Besançon also. This family's success was touched with genius. The Granvelle forebears were the Perrenots, humble peasants from the Loue valley, who saved up enough to buy their liberty and set themselves up as craftsmen in Ornans. One of them managed to become a notary and sent his son to the university of Dole. This gifted young man, having qualified as a doctor of law and become a lawyer, married the daughter of a wealthy Besançon merchant, who brought a substantial dowry with her. In 1518, at the age of 32, he was appointed Parliamentary adviser. This might have been enough to fulfil most people's ambitions, but young Perrenot, now Lord of Granvelle, did not allow himself to be content with this honour. He carried on working, and his career continued its meteoric climb, until finally, at the age of 46, he was appointed Chancellor to Charles V, who placed such trust in him that he referred to his chancellor as "my bed of rest".

As was the custom of his age, Granvelle had made a fortune from his various offices. He had a vast palace built in Besançon and collected sumptuous works of art to put in it. Having ensured that his five sons and six sons-in-law held the most coveted positions in the Franche-Comté and at Court, this humble village boy from Ornans had indeed reached the pinnacle of his potential.

With infinite care, the chancellor groomed his son Antoine to succeed him. He desired his son not only to inherit material wealth and power, but also to win spiritual prestige by becoming a leading figure in the Church. Antoine de Granvelle went on to become Cardinal, Prime Minister of the Netherlands, where he advised the ruler Margaret of Parma, Viceroy of Naples, and as Minister for Foreign Affairs he was the only nobleman from the Franche-Comté whom Philip II of Spain would allow into his presence. Despite all these honours, Granvelle never forgot the town of his birth. He liked nothing better than to return to Besançon and his magnificent family seat, which he continued to embellish with works of art and other treasures.

Besançon falls under Spanish rule – In 1656, unbeknown to its inhabitants, the imperial city of Besançon was traded for Frankenthal and became Spanish territory. A turbulent period in the city's history ensued.

In 1668, 10 years after the death of Charles V, Condé took over the city after Louis XIV had laid claim to the Franche-Comté and Flanders as his inheritance. He had hardly done this, when the Treaty of Aix-la-Chapelle, signed the same year, returned the Franche-Comté to Spanish rule.

Nonetheless, in 1674 Louis XIV's troops, 20 000 men strong, assembled once more at the gates of Besançon. The siege was commanded by Vauban. In the meander of the Doubs, 5 000 men put up a heroic defence, withstanding the hail of French cannon balls which rained down of them from Chaudanne and Bregille for 27 days. Finally they had to admit defeat, although their leader, the **Prince de Vaudemont**, did not give himself up for another week.

In 1677, Louis XIV made Besançon the capital of the new French province, and the Treaty of Nijmegen (1678) annexed the Franche-Comté to France once and for all.

Capital of the Franche-Comté – Parliament, treasury, university and Mint all now moved from Dole to Besançon. At first the city's residents were delighted, but their pride soon changed to dismay when they were presented with a bill of 15 000 to 30 000 *livres* for each transfer by royal officials, who on top of that more than trebled their taxes. Nevertheless, local trade, industry and the arts all made greater strides than ever before thanks to the city's new status. Besançon owes much to one of the royal commissioners in particular, the **Intendant de Lacoré**, who endowed the city with beautiful monuments and parks during the 18C.

Manufacture of artificial silk – This industry, which is now of great importance world-wide, has its roots in Besançon. In 1884, after lengthy research and experimentation, the **Comte de Chardonnet**, a famous civil engineer, produced a cellulose material with the appearance and the resilience of natural silk.

At the World Exhibition of 1889, Chardonnet displayed church furnishings which he had made; they caused a sensation. The following year, the first factory was set up in Besançon, and artificial silk – later called rayon – began its rapid rise to stardom.

★★OLD TOWN
time: 2 hours

The old town should be visited on foot (much of it is pedestrian zones). Park your car either in the car park on the Promenade Chamars, or on the northwest bank of the Doubs. Cross the Battant bridge.

Before going down the Grande-Rue, take a few steps back along the bridge to get a better view of the 17C residences with beautiful grey-blue stone **façades★** which line the banks of the Doubs.

The **Grande-Rue** (**AY-BZ**) is an old Roman highway which crossed Vesontio from one side to the other and which, 2 000 years later, is still the main road through the city. Part of it, between the Pont Battant and the Place du 8-Septembre, has been sectioned off as a pedestrian zone. Note at no 44 the Hôtel de l'Emskerque (**B**), a late 16C mansion and residence of Gaston d'Orléans for a time, with elegant grilles on the ground floor.

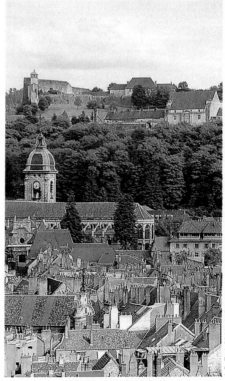

View of the old town and cathedral of Besançon with the citadel in the background

J.-P. Tupin/Mairie de Besançon

Opposite, at no 53, the interior courtyard has a remarkable stone and wrought-iron staircase. At no 67, the Hôtel Pourcheresse de Fraisans also has a lovely staircase in the courtyard. No 68, once the Hôtel Terrier de Santans (**D**), was built in 1770 and has a pretty interior courtyard. Number 86 used to be a convent for Carmelite nuns (**W**); it dates from the 17C and has an arcaded courtyard. At no 88 stands the old entrance doorway to the convent of the Great Carmelites (**E¹**) with a 16C fountain to the left of it. The sculptor Claude Lullier depicted the Duke of Alva, Philip II of Spain's military chief, as Neptune. No 103 has a lovely timber staircase in the courtyard.

Hôtel de Ville (**H**) – The town hall dates from the 16C. Its façade is decorated with alternately blue and ochre-coloured rustic work.

Opposite, the unusual façade of the **church of St-Pierre** is the work of Besançon architect Bertrand (late 18C).

Palais de Justice (**J**) ⊙ – The central park of the building which houses the law courts has a pretty Renaissance façade by Hugues Sambin. The wrought-iron gates in the entrance doorway are really beautiful. The Parliament of the Franche-Comté sat in session inside, on the first floor.

★ **Palais Granvelle** – The mansion was built from 1534 to 1542 for Chancellor Nicolas Perrenot de Granvelle. It has an imposing Renaissance façade overlooking the street, which is divided into three storeys and five bays. The high roof has crowstepped gables at each side and three dormer windows with richly sculpted frontons. There is a pretty rectangular interior **courtyard★** surrounded by porticoes with depressed basket-handle arches.

Musée du Temps ⊙ – A clock museum is going to be installed in the palace once renovation work is completed.

The Promenade Granvelle (**Q**) is a pleasant shady walk through the old palace gardens, which is particularly popular during the summer. It leads past the Kursaal, a concert and meeting hall.

Carry on along the Grande-Rue.

Victor Hugo was born at no 140 (**F**), and the **Lumière brothers**, inventors of the first motion picture camera, were born at no 1 Place Victor-Hugo.

Roman ruins – Rue de la Convention, the extension of Grande-Rue, offers a good view of the **Square archéologique A-Castan** (**L**), a pretty little park with a row of columns which once formed part of the peristyle of a nymphaeum. The channels of the aqueduct which supplied the basin can still be seen.

Opposite the square is the old archbishops' palace (**U¹**), dating from the early 18C, which now houses the local education authority.

Go through the **Porte Noire**, a Roman triumphal arch built in the 2C, which no doubt earned the name "black gate" from its very dark patina. It would have stood once upon a time in solitary splendour. The sculpture work on it, although partially restored in the 19C, has been very badly eroded by the weather.

Cathédrale St-Jean – The cathedral, most of which was built in the 12C, is dedicated to St John the Baptist. Interestingly, it has two apses, one at either end of the central nave. The bell tower collapsed in 1729 and was rebuilt in the 18C, along with one of the apses (Saint-Suaire, *left of entrance*) which was damaged when the tower fell in. In the south aisle, left of the great organ loft, is the famous painting by Fra Bartolomeo, the **Virgin Mary with Saints★**, executed in 1512 in Rome for the cathedral's canon Ferry Carondelet, abbot of Montbenoît *(qv)* and councillor to Charles V. The prelate is depicted on his knees on the right. Electric lighting *(switch located to the right below the painting)* enables viewers to appreciate fully the detail and colours of this work. The apse of Saint-Suaire is baroque in style and contains paintings from the 18C (Van Loo, Natoire, de Troy). The left apsidal chapel houses the marble tomb of Abbot Ferry Carondelet. On the north side of the nave is the beautiful Gothic pulpit, made of stone, from which St François de Sales is believed to have preached. The second chapel off the north aisle contains a round paleochristian altar in white marble, known as the "**Rose de St Jean**", which is decorated with a chrismon with, rather surprisingly, an eagle above it (since this is the symbol of St John the Evangelist). In the chancel is a replica of the throne used in the consecration of Napoleon I.

At no 5 Rue de la Convention is an old 18C town mansion, or *hôtel*, which now houses the Palais de l'Archevêché (archbishops' palace).

★ **Horloge astronomique** ⊙ – *On the ground floor of the bell tower.* The astronomical clock, a marvel of mechanics comprising 30 000 parts, was designed and made between 1857 and 1860 by A-L Vérité from Beauvais, and reset in 1900 by F Goudey from Besançon. It serves as a timepiece for the public, since it is connected to the clock faces on the bell tower. The 62 dials indicate among other things the days and seasons, the time in 16 different places all over the world, the tides in 8 ports, the length of daylight and darkness, the times at which the sun and the moon rise and set and, below the clock, the movement of the planets around the sun. Several automata are activated on the hour.

Take the pretty Rue du Chambrier down to the Porte Rivotte.

Porte Rivotte – This gate is the remains of 16C fortifications. After the French conquest, Louis XIV had the fronton decorated with a symbolic sun. The cliffs of the citadel rock with their horizontal strata tower above the gate. These cliffs once

BESANÇON

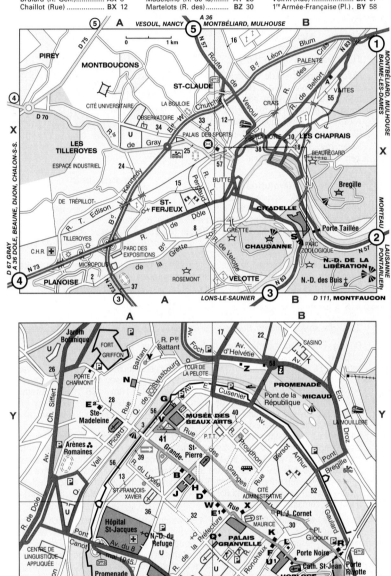

plunged straight into the river. The narrow strip of land along which the road passes was dug and blasted out of the rock face. A 375m - 1 230ft long canal cuts through the cliffs in a tunnel, providing a short cut past the Doubs meander.

Go down Rue Rivotte and Rue de Pontarlier.

Maison Mareschal (R) – *No 19 Rue Rivotte.*
This house dates from the 16C.

Place J-Cornet – The fountain, the old mansions and a convent now occupied by local administration help preserve the appearance that this square must have had two centuries ago.

Take the Rue des Granges to get to the bridge (Pont Battant).

Place de la Révolution (AY 41) – This lively square, better

Besançon street

known as the **Place du Marché**, is at a junction with the Musée des Beaux-Arts on one side and old buildings along the Rue des Boucheries. A passage underneath these buildings leads to **Promenade Vauban (G)** *(from where it is possible to walk along the quays on the banks of the Doubs north as far as the Pont de Bregille, or south as far as Faubourg Tarragnoz).*
On the northeast corner of the square stands the church of the **ancien hôpital du Saint-Esprit (V)**, which has been a Protestant place of worship since 1842. The courtyard has a carved timber gallery dating probably from the early 16C.

★★ CITADELLE ⊘ *time: 1 hour, not including the museums*

Take the steep, winding Rue des Fusillés-de-la-Résistance up behind the cathedral.

During Roman occupation this high ground was crowned with a temple, the columns of which now feature on the town's coat of arms. Later, a church dedicated to St Stephen stood on this spot. After the French conquest in 1674, **Vauban** had most of the earlier buildings demolished to make way for the fortress which now overlooks the River Doubs from a height of 118m - 387ft. The citadel of Besançon has played a variety of roles – barracks, military cadet academy under Louis XIV, state prison and fortress besieged in 1814 – and both its natural setting and historical interest have much to offer the visitor.
The fortress was built on a gentle ridge and has a more or less rectangular ground plan. Three bastions (or *enceintes* or *fronts*) with large esplanades in between them stretch across its width one after the other on one side: Front St-Étienne towards the town, Front Royal in the centre and Front de Secours nearest the fortress. The whole site is surrounded by fortified ramparts, along which a watch part runs. Several watch towers (**Tour du Roi** to the east and **Tour de la Reine** to the west) and bartizans remain.

Chemins de Ronde (Watch paths) – The watch path to the west, which begins at the Tour de la Reine *(on the right in the first esplanade)*, reveals a wonderful **view★★** of Besançon, the valley of the Doubs and the Chaudanne and Les Buis hills. The watch path which leads off towards the Bregille gives a good view of Besançon and the Doubs meander. On the side of the fortress away from the town the **Échauguette sur Tarragnoz (BX S)**, reached via the **Parc zoologique**, overlooks the valley of the Doubs.

★ **Musée Comtois (M¹)** ⊘ – This museum, in fifteen or so rooms in two buildings, houses a considerable collection of exhibits of traditional local arts, crafts and folklore from all over the Franche-Comté.
The ground floor of the right wing is given over to pottery, weaving and spinning. Note the display case of head-dresses. On the first floor, several rooms house a large collection of puppets from a so-called "mechanical theatre" dating from 1850. The left wing is devoted to the ironmonger's craft and contains some of the most original exhibits in the museum, including cast iron wall plates, andirons, kitchen ranges and cauldrons.

★ **Musée agraire (M²)** ⊘ – *The agricultural museum is located in an old gun depot, to the right of the entrance to the citadel.*
This museum contains agricultural equipment used in the Franche-Comté in days gone by (numerous different types of ploughs and even a complete oil press) as well as many very old tools and machines: yokes, collars, harrows, sickles, wooden forks and rakes, barrows for fodder and winnowing machines, one of which is made entirely of wood. Draught vehicles, some on wheels, some on rollers and some quite unusual, complete the exhibition: hay carts, hay sleds, travelling carts and sleds etc.

★ **Musée d'Histoire naturelle** (**M³**) ⊙ – The natural history museum is in two wings of the old arsenal and contains clear, up-to-date exhibitions on exotic fauna, with stuffed animals and birds, skulls and skeletons, and displays on insects, including a large butterfly collection. The art of Black Africa is represented by everyday objects and dance masks from the Ivory Coast.

Also of interest to visitors are:

– **Parc zoologique** (2.5ha - 7 acres) at the far side of the fortress, in the glacis of the Front St-Étienne and the moats of the Front de Secours (primates).

– **Aquarium Georges-Besse** in a large hall on the ground floor of the Petit Arsenal, where the aquatic fauna of the region's rivers are on show in fifteen 3 000l - 6 600 gallon tanks.

– **Insectarium**, a particularly original exhibition, on 300m² - 3 230ft² of the first floor of the Petit Arsenal.

Finally, there is a section on space travel and meteorology.

★ **Musée de la Résistance et de la Déportation** (**M⁴**) ⊙ – This museum on the French Resistance and deportation occupies 22 rooms and comprises an extensive collection of photographs, objects, posters and documents on the birth and rise of Nazism, the Second World War, the invasion of France in 1940, the Vichy régime, the French Resistance, deportation and the liberation of France. Pictures, paintings and sculptures done by inmates of German prison camps are also on display, along with contemporary works on this theme. An audio-visual room completes the visit. The statue near the entrance is by Georges Oudot.

Poteaux des Fusillés – These posts were put up in memory of the members of the French Resistance shot during the war.

A steeply sloping path leads down to the Faubourg Tarragnoz by the Doubs, which in turn leads to the Promenade Chamars.

ADDITIONAL SIGHTS

★★**Musée des Beaux-Arts et d'Archéologie** ⊙ – The museum of fine arts and archaeology is in the old grain hall, which dates from 1835. It has been extended since the 70s, by a follower of Le Corbusier, Louis Miquel, who built an original construction of concrete in the courtyard consisting of a succession of gently sloping ramps with landings in between them.

The museum contains some rich collections of works of art, some of which come from the Granvelle family, or more particularly from Nicolas de Granvelle.

At the heart of the building, the ground floor houses a collection of Egyptian antiquities and statues and objects from the Middle Ages and the Renaissance. In the side galleries, there is a chronological display of local archaeological finds (Gallo-Roman mosaic depicting a quadriga, a bronze bull with three horns, god with a hammer).

The section of paintings includes a wide variety of works by non-French schools, signed by some of the greatest names of the 14-17C. Some of the most remarkable works include: *The Drunkenness of Noah* by Giovanni Bellini (1430-1516) in Venice; *Deposition from the Cross* by Bronzino (1503-1572) in Florence; the central panel of the *Triptych of Our Lady of Seven Sorrows* by Bernard Van Orley (1488-1541) in Brussels; *Ill-assorted Pair* and *Nymph at the Fountain* by Lucas Cranach the Elder (1472-1553) in Germany; *Portrait of a Young Gentleman* by Tintoretto (1518-1594) in Venice; two studies of an old man's face by Jacob Jordaens (1593-1678) in Antwerp; *Child blowing soap bubbles* by Jean Lievens (1607-1674) in the Netherlands. At the top of the gallery is the Besson collection of paintings, watercolours and drawings, which includes some of Bonnard's best paintings, such as *Place Clichy* and *Café du Petit Poucet*, the portrait of Madame Besson by Renoir, *The Seine at Grenelle* and *Two Friends* by Albert Marquet and *Yellow Sail* by Paul Signac.

The old galleries on the first floor house ceramic ware (Rouen, Nevers, Moustiers, Delft). They also contain a lovely collection of 18 and 19C French masters: tapestry cartoons on a Chinese theme by Boucher; works by Fragonard and Hubert Robert; sketches by David; and, best of all, landscapes by Courbet (*The Conche Hill* and the monumental painting *Death of a Stag*).

In the gallery of 18C works, note the two panels illustrating *Scenes of Cannibalism* by Goya.

An adjacent gallery contains a relief model of Besançon – note the triumphal arch, no longer extant, which once stood on the Quai Vauban, and the old bell tower of the cathedral.

End your visit with a quick look at works by artists from the Franche-Comté (J. Gigoux, T. Chartran, J. A. Meunier) and at the interesting display of Neapolitan works (V. Codazzi: *Festival in the Villa of Poggioreale*).

The drawings room *(open by appointment only)* houses a comprehensive collection of over 5 000 works, including the famous red chalk sketches of the Villa d'Este by Fragonard. The drawings are exhibited in rotation, with only a selected few at a time on display.

★ **Préfecture** (**AZ P**) – The erstwhile Palais des Intendants was built in the 18C after designs by the architect Louis.

Outside, on the corner of the Rue Ch-Nodier, stands the pretty Fontaine des Dames (18C), or Ladies' Fountain, decorated with a mermaid (copy of a 16C bronze).

★ **Bibliothèque municipale** (**BZ X**) ⊙ – Marvellous illuminated manuscripts, incunabula, old books, drawings and bookbindings.

Besançon – Hôtel de Champagney

Jardin botanique (**AY**) ⊙ – These botanical gardens contain examples of the main flora of the region, an arboretum, medicinal plants and a floral rockery. In the tropical greenhouse are exotic plants such as epiphytes (orchids) and araceae (cuckoo-pint); in the temperate greenhouse is a large collection of ferns; and in the cold greenhouse, succulents and carnivorous plants.

Hôpital St-Jacques (**AZ**) – This hospital dates from the 17C. It has a splendid **wrought iron gate★** and a pretty 18C **pharmacy** ⊙.

Chapelle Notre-Dame-de-Refuge (**AZ**) ⊙ – This chapel owes its name to an establishment founded in 1690 by the Marquis de Broissia to shelter young girls in danger of falling into vice. It was built by the architect Nicolas Nicole in 1739, and became part of the hospital in 1802. Even the building's architecture takes on a religious significance: the shape of the interior gradually changes from an oval to a circle, the symbol of perfection. Note the beautiful Louis XV woodwork.

Promenade Micaud (**BY**) – There is a good view of the Doubs, the town and the citadel from this road, which has been reproduced by all of the local artists. In between the road and the river is the Jardin des Senteurs, a garden of fragrant plants which was designed especially for blind people. On the banks of the river stands a statue of Jouffroy d'Abbans (**BY Z**), who sailed one of the first ever steam boats down the Doubs.

Quartier de Battant (**ABY**) – This is the district on the northwest bank of the Doubs. The rather curious **Tour de la Pelote** (late 15C) was integrated into Vauban's defence system, thus saving it from destruction.
Take the Rue du Petit-Battant.
This lively district is one of the oldest parts of Besançon. It used to be the wine-growers' area, and the surrounding slopes covered with modern houses were once covered with vines.
*From the square containing the Bacchus fountain (**AY Y**) go down the Rue Battant.*

Hôtel de Champagney (**AY N**) – This mansion was built for Nicolas de Granvelle's widow in the 16C. The heads of its four gargoyles jut out over the pavement.
Pass through the archway to admire the inner courtyard with its arcades. The passage leads through the **Clos Barbusier**, a garden of old roses, to Fort Griffon from where there is a good view of the rooftops of Besançon.

Ste-Madeleine – This church was built in the 18C based on the designs of Nicolas Nicole, although both its towers were built later on in 1830. The interior is vast, with elegant vaulting supported on fluted columns. The great organ (restored) is the work of Callinet.
Take the Rue de la Madeleine to the right.
On the corner of the Rues du Petit-Charmont and du Grand-Charmont stands the **Hôtel Jouffroy** (**AY E²**) which dates from the late 15C-early 16C.

Porte Taillée – *See the map of the conurbation (**BX**). The gate is located southeast of Besançon on the N 57.*
The Romans cut this gateway into the rockface to gain access for the aqueduct which brought Besançon water from the Arcier spring.

▶▶ **Lookout point near Notre-Dame-de-la-Libération★** – *3.5km - 2 miles southeast.*

▶▶ **Musée de plein air des maisons comtoises** ⊙ – This open air museum of typical Franche-Comté houses is to be found near **Nancray** *(15km - 9 miles east).*

Mont BEUVRAY★★

Michelin map 69 folds 6 and 7 or 238 fold 36 – 8km – 5 miles west of
Saint-Léger-sous-Beuvray – Local map under MORVAN

Access to the summit via the D 274, a one-way loop from the D 3.
The road offers one or two fleeting views through the trees.

Oppidum Bibracte – The summit of Beuvray was the site of Bibracte, the capital of
the **Aedui** and a Gallic *oppidum* built in 150 or 120 BC. It was a sort of fortified camp,
the permanent living quarters of Gallic artisans and a refuge for the surrounding agricultural population in times of danger.

Vercingetorix made Bibracte famous by convoking a general assembly there – in effect
a council of war – of all the Gallic tribes that had risen against **Julius Caesar** in 52 BC.
It was there that he organised resistance to the Roman legions and was made commander-in-chief of the Gallic armies. After the capture of Alésia, Caesar twice went to
Bibracte. Under Augustus the *oppidum* was abandoned in favour of Augustodunum
(Autun) but its name was recorded in written history by Caesar in his "Commentaries"
on the Gallic Wars. As Bibracte was also the home of a Gallic divinity which drew
many faithful pilgrims every spring, there were markets held here during that period,
a tradition which continued until the 16C.

A monument commemorates Bulliot, whose 19C excavations were subsequently rebu-
ried; a new and ambitious programme of excavations was started in 1984. The Gallic
defences (5km - 3 miles long and 3-4m - 2-2.5 miles wide) are known as the Fossé
de Beuvray, or Beuvray Trench.
At the foot of Mont Beuvray, at the Croix-du-Rebout, there is an exhibition on the
excavations and Gallic culture. There are plans to convert this collection into a Bibracte
Gallic museum at some stage.

★★**Panorama** – From the viewpoint framed by age-old beech trees with twisted
trunks there is a magnificient panorama of Autun, the Uchon *(qv)* beacon and Mont
St-Vincent; when visibility is good, you can see the Jura and even Mont Blanc.

BOURG-EN-BRESSE★★

Population 40 972
Michelin map 74 fold 3 or 243 folds 40 and 41 – Facilities –
Plan of conurbation in the current Michelin Red Guide France

Bourg (pronounced Bourk) is and has always been the centre of the rich Bresse
region, noted for its poultry which make the local markets famous. On market days
or when there is a livestock fair, Bourg is picturesque and animated as crowds of farmers come into town. The annual exhibition *(see the Calender of Events at the end of
the guide)* of Bresse capons and roasting chickens is held in the Parc des Expositions.
The chickens' flesh is soaked in milk making it a pearly colour. The town has also got
a good reputation for the manufacture of Bresse country-style furniture *(meubles "rus-
tique bressan")* using fruit trees (cherry, wild cherry, pear and walnut) and ash trees.
The Meillonas pottery *(12km - 8 miles north east)* and attractive Bresse enamels
(émaux bressanes) are still produced locally. The town also specialises in mechanical
engineering.
The combination of traditional and modern industries contributes to Bourg's dynamic
image, while its reputation as an artistic centre rests on the many marvellous works
of art to which the town is home, not least of which are the outstanding art treasures
at the old monastery of Brou.

HISTORICAL NOTES

In the 10C, Bourg was still a little village of thatched cottages clustered round a castle.
When the family of the lords of the manor died out in the 13C, the dukes of Savoy,
powerful neighbours, took over the inheritance. They established the province of
Bresse and made Bourg, now a busy township, its capital.
In 1536 the Duke of Savoy refused François I permission to cross his lands to invade
the Milanese. The king forced his way through and, to secure his lines of communication, took possession of Bresse, Savoy and Piedmont. These territories were handed
back by Henri II with the Treaty of Cateau-Cambrésis (1559). In 1600 Henri IV invaded
the region. The Treaty of Lyon (1601) forced the Duke to exchange Bresse, Bugey,
Valromey and the Pays de Gex for the marquisate of Saluces, last of France's possessions in Italy. Bourg thus became part of France.

The Vow of Margaret of Bourbon – In 1480 Philip, Count of Bresse, later Duke of
Savoy, had a hunting accident. His wife, Margaret of Bourbon (grandmother of François I),
made a vow that, if her husband recovered, she would transform the humble priory of
Brou into a monastery. The Count recovered but Margaret died, leaving the task to
her husband and her son Philibert the Handsome. Her vow however remained unfulfilled.
Twenty years went by. Philibert, who had married Margaret of Austria, died suddenly.
His wife saw a heavenly punishment in this. So that her husband's soul should rest in
peace, she hurried to fulfil the vow of Margaret of Bourbon. She lost no time for two
reasons; firstly to affirm her sovereignty, and secondly to outshine her sister-in-law
Louise of Savoy, who was soon to become Regent of France. These motivations aside,
Brou has been a testament to the love of the two Margarets for their husbands for
over 400 years now.

Ill-fated Margaret of Austria – Margaret of Austria, the daughter of Emperor Maximilian of Austria and Mary of Burgundy (and grand-daughter of Charles the Bold), was two years old when her mother died. The following year she was taken to the court of Louis XI and, in a religious ceremony, married to the Dauphin Charles, heir to the French throne, also a child. The little girl's dowry was the Franche-Comté.

Five years later, quarrels over the succession to the duchy of Brittany began. Maximilian succeeded in winning the favour of the heiress, Duchess Anne, who had many suitors, and they were married by proxy. Unfortunately, once it became known that the bridegroom, who had had to borrow money to pay for his first wedding, would not be able to pay the 2 000 *livres* costs of his journey to Nantes for his latest wedding, Duchess Anne was quick to hand back her ring. Charles VIII took advantage of the predicament and proposed that Anne of Brittany become Queen of France instead of Empress of Austria. The two unconsummated marriages were annulled: Charles repudiated Margaret of Austria and Anne repudiated Maximilian, who thus suffered a double insult as father of the rejected Margaret and rejected husband himself.

At the age of seventeen the unfortunate Margaret was married to the heir to the Spanish throne, who died after only a few months, leaving her to bear a still-born child shortly afterwards. Four years later, her father gave her in marriage for the third time to Philibert of Savoy, a frivolous and fickle young man, who was however astute enough to acknowledge his wife as "intelligent enough for two" and remained content to let her practically govern in his stead. Margaret was to have three years of happiness at her handsome duke's side, before fate struck her another cruel blow: her young husband died after catching cold out hunting. Widowed for the second time, twenty-four year old Margaret was to remain faithful for the rest of her days to the memory of Philibert, whom she had loved dearly despite his weaknesses. This high-ranking woman, well-read and artistic, knew how to take care of herself, selecting trustworthy advisers and commanding absolute obedience. She now devoted herself to affairs of State. In 1506 she became Regent of the Low Countries and the Franche-Comté. Her wise and liberal policies won her the loyalty, respect and affection of all who lived in the Franche-Comté.

Fulfilment of the Vow – In 1506 work began on the construction of the monastery buildings in Brou. These were arranged around three cloisters, one of which was part of the original Benedictine priory.

The priory church was then pulled down to make way for the magnificient building which was to serve as the shrine for the three tombs of Philibert, his wife and his mother. Margaret, who was living in Flanders, entrusted the construction to a Flemish master mason, Loys Van Boghem, who was both architect and general contractor. This remarkable man brought life and strength to the faltering undertaking and succeeded in erecting the fabulous building in the record time of nineteen years (1513-1532). Sadly, Margaret died two years before the church was consecrated.

Brou was lucky enough to survive the Wars of Religion and the Revolution relatively unscathed. The monastery became successively a pig farm, a prison, a barracks, a home for beggars, a lunatic asylum, a seminary in 1823, and it now houses the museum of Brou (since 1921).

★★★ BROU *Southeast on the town plan. Time: 1 hour*

Brou was once a small village clustered round a Benedictine priory, attached to Bourg. It is now part of the southeastern suburbs of the town. The church and the monastery were built in the 16C in fulfilment of the vow made by Margaret of Bourbon.

A short history and the family tree of the founders are to be found in the south aisle of the church.

★★ Church ⊘

The church has now been deconsecrated. The building, in which the Flamboyant Gothic style is influenced by the Renaissance, was built at the same time as the Château of Chenonceau in the Loire valley. On the flat ground in front of the façade is there is a huge sundial which was reset in 1757 by the astronomer Lalande, a citizen of Bourg.

Exterior – The central park of the triangular façade is richly sculpted. The tympanum above the fine Renaissance **doorway★** shows Philibert the Handsome and Margaret of Austria and their patron saints at the feet of Christ Bound. On the pier is St Nicolas of Tolentino, to whom the church is dedicated (his feast falls on the day of Philibert's death). Surmounting the ornamental doorway arch is a statue of St Andrew; St Peter and St Paul flank the doorway on the arch shafts.

The decorative sculpture includes a variety of Flamboyant Gothic floral motifs (leaves and fruit), some showing a decidedly Renaissance influence (laurel, vine and acanthus), intermingled with symbolic motifs, such as palms interlaced with marguerites. The decoration at Brou comprises other motifs: The initials of Philibert and Marguerite linked by love-knots (twisted fillet moulding festooned between the two letters) and intermingled with crossed batons, the arms of Burgundy.

The simpler façade of the north transept has a pinnacled gable. The five storey square belfry stands on the south side of the apse.

Nave – On entering the church one is struck by the light which bathes the nave and its double aisles. The light entering through the clerestory windows falls on the false stonework marked on the surface of the walls. The pillars, formed by numerous little columns, thrust upwards in an unbroken line to the vaulting and open out into a network of ribs meeting at the carved keystones. A finely sculpted balustrade runs below the windows of the nave. The overall impression is one of elegance, magnificence and good taste.

In the second bay of the nave *(right)* is a 16C black marble font (**1**) bearing Margaret's motto (*"Fortune infortune fort une "* - see below).

The south transept is lit through a beautiful stained glass window (**2**) de-

picting Susanna being accused by the Elders *(above)* and being exonerated by Daniel *(below)*.

To the right of the rood screen is the Montécuto chapel (**3**) which contains models explaining the construction of the church.

★★ **Rood screen** – The richly decorated screen, which separates the nave and transepts (accessible to the faithful) from the chancel (reserve of the clergy and burials), is composed of three basket-handled arches supporting seven religious statues.

Chancel – Margaret spared no expense to make this, the most important part of the church, as perfectly resplendent as possible. Taken as a whole, the sculpted decoration might seem to border on the excessive, but the longer and closer one examines the ornamentation, the greater its charm, since the smallest detail is treated with quite extraordinary craftsmanship.

★★ **Choir stalls** – The 74 stalls, which line the first two bays of the choir, were carved from oak in the astonishingly short time of two years (1530-32). The master carpenter, Pierre Berchod, known as Terrasson, had to mobilise all the wood craftsmen of this locality, where woodcarving was, and still is, extremely popular.

The stalls are carved in the same manner as the sculptures on the tombs, and the designs appear to be those of the same artist, **Jean de Bruxelles**. The seats, the backs and the canopies have an extraordinary wealth of decorative detail and statuettes, which are considered to be masterpieces of their kind.

The stalls on the north side feature scenes from the New Testament and satirical characters. Those on the south side feature characters and scenes from the Old Testament.

★★★ **The tombs** – Many artists collaborated in the decoration of these three monuments, the high point of Flemish sculpture in Burgundy. The designs were sketched by Jean de Bruxelles, who furnished the sculptors with life-size drawings. The ornamentation and the statuary, much admired by visitors, are attributed for the most part to a Flemish workshop which was set up in Brou, in collaboration with French, German and Italian sculptors. The statues of the three princely personages are the work of Conrad Meyt, born in Germany but trained in Flanders. The effigies of the prince and princess are carved in Carrara marble. The great blocks were brought from Italy by sea and then transported up the river Rhône. The final part of their journey was in huge carts drawn by nine horses travelling at three to four miles per day. Philibert and the two Margarets are represented, each lying on the tomb on a slab of black marble, their heads on finely embroidered cushions. Following tradition, a dog, emblem of fidelity, lies at the feet of the two princesses, and a lion, symbol of strength, lies at the feet of the prince. Cherubim, symbolising the entry of the three in heaven, surround the statues. The tomb of Margaret of Bourbon (**4**) occupies a recessed niche hewn in the south wall of the choir. The two other tombs differ in that they have two recumbent effigies: the first depicted alive and the second dead in a shroud. That of Philibert (**5**), the most sober in conception but also the most moving, is in the centre. The tomb of Margaret of Austria (**6**), on the north of the chancel, with its huge canopy of chiselled stone, prolongs the parclose. Sibyls in the form of charming statuettes mount

105

Statuette from
the tomb of Philibert the
Handsome, Brou church

guard around the effigies. On the sole of her foot can be seen the wound which, according to legend, caused the princess's death by blood poisoning. Princess Margaret's motto is inscribed on the canopy: *Fortune infortune fort une,* or "Fate was very hard on one woman", recalling the sad destiny of princess whose constancy in adversity never wavered.

★★ **Stained glass windows** – The magnificent stained glass at Brou was made in a local workshop. The windows in the centre of the apse depict Christ appearing to Mary Magdalene *(upper part)* and Christ visiting Mary *(lower part),* scenes taken from engravings by Albrecht Dürer. On the left and right, Philibert and Margaret kneel before their patron saints. The coats of arms of their families are reproduced above them in glittering colours: Savoy and Bourbon for the Duke, and Imperial and Burgundian for the Duchess. The armorial bearings of the towns of the State of Savoy are also represented.

★★★ **Chapels and Oratories** – The chapel of Margaret (**7**) opens to the north of the choir. A retable and a stained glass window, both fine works of art, deserve to be admired.

The **retable** depicts the Seven Joys of the Virgin Mary. It is executed in white marble and is exceptionally well preserved. It is a masterpiece of delicate workmanship, a fantastic work of art which leaves the viewer quite stunned. A scene of the Seven Joys is set in each of the niches, designed for the purpose: on the left, below, is the Annunciation; on the right, the Visitation; above, the Nativity and the Adoration of the Magi; higher still are the Assumption, framed by Christ appearing to his mother, and Pentecost. The retable is crowned by three statues: the Virgin and Child flanked by St Mary Magdalene and St Margaret. On either side of the retable note St Philip and St Andrew.

The **stained glass window**, in magnificent colours, is inspired by an engraving by Albrecht Dürer representing the Assumption. The glass workers have added Philibert and Margaret kneeling near their patron saints. The frieze of the window, in monochrome, depicts the Triumph of Faith based on a design by Titian. Christ, in a chariot, is drawn by the Evangelists and characters from the Old Testament; behind them is a throng of scholars of the church and New Testament saints.

The oratories of Margaret were arranged for her personal use. They are next to the Chapelle de Madame (**8**) and are placed one above the other, linked by a staircase. The lower oratory is on the same level as the choir, the upper one is on a level with the gallery of the rood screen. These two chambers, decorated with tapestries and warmed by fireplaces, were effectively little drawing rooms. An oblique window, or squint, below a highly original arch, allowed the princess to follow the religious services.

The nearby chapel (**9**), which has the name of Laurent de Gorrevod, one of Margaret's councillors, has a remarkable stained glass window representing the incredulity of St Thomas and a triptych commissioned by Cardinal de Granvelle.

Leave through the doorway to the right of the choir to see the monastery.

★ Museum ⊘

The museum is housed in the monastic buildings which are ranged around three two-storey cloisters, unique in France. By 1506 the old Benedictine priory had become so damp and dilapidated that the monks obtained permission from Margaret of Austria to rebuild, beginning with the living quarters rather than the church.

Small cloisters – First of the three cloisters at Brou to be built, the small cloisters allowed monks to pass from the monastery to the church under cover. One of the galleries on the first floor gave access to the private apartment of Margaret of Austria, but she died before it was completed. The other gallery was to allow the princess to reach the chapel directly by way of the rood screen. On the ground floor the sacristy and the chapter house, now one room, are used for temporary exhibitions. From the galleries, now a stone depository with fragments of cornice and pinnacles, enjoy the view of the south transept gable and the spire.

Great cloisters – This is where the monks used to walk and meditate. It gives access to the second chapter house, now converted into the museum reception.

First floor – A staircase leads up to the dorter where the old monks' cells now house collections of paintings and decorative art. On the landing and in the recess in the middle of the great corridor are some fine pieces of Bresse furniture and a showcase of 18C Meillonnas earthenware.

The cells on the south side are devoted to 16-18C art. Among the Flemish and Dutch works is a fine **portrait of Margaret of Austria★** painted by B Van Orley *c*1518 and a triptych of the life of St Jerome (1518). The following rooms are hung with 17C and 18C examples of the Italian school (Magnasco: *Monks Practising Self-Flagellation*) and 18C examples of the French school (Largillière and Gresly), as well as Burgundian and Lyonnais furniture (Nogaret) and French religious *objets d'art.*

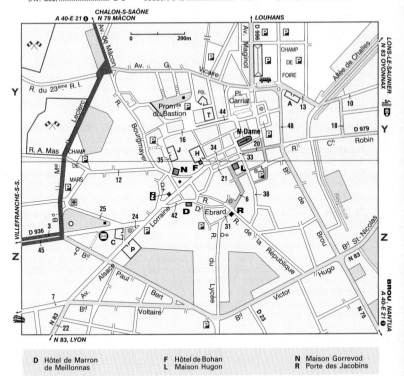

D Hôtel de Marron
de Meillonnas

F Hôtel de Bohan
L Maison Hugon

N Maison Gorrevod
R Porte des Jacobins

In the north gallery the rooms on the right are devoted to 19C French painting (Gustave Doré, Gustave Moreau, the Lyonnais school); those on the left exhibit the troubadour style and early-20C work. Margaret of Austria's great hall of State contains a collection of contemporary art.

In the southeast corner of the Great cloisters is the entrance to the refectory which displays 13-17C religious sculpture, in particular a black Madonna (13C), a Holy Sepulchre (1443) and Philibert and St Philibert from the tympanum of Brou church (early 16C). The refectory leads into the third cloisters.

Kitchen cloisters – Unlike the other two, these cloisters exhibit features typical of the region, such as the rounded arches and the gently sloping roof of hollow tiles. The far building contains archaeological collections.

ADDITIONAL SIGHTS

Notre-Dame (Y) – Although the church was begun in 1505, building was not completed until the 17C. The apse and nave are in the Flamboyant Gothic style, while a triple Renaissance doorway is the centrepiece of the façade. The central door is surmounted by a Virgin and Child, copied from a work by Coysevox (17C). The tall belfry was erected under Louis XIV, but the dome and the small lantern on top are modern. A carillon plays at 0750, 1150 and 1850.

Interior – The church contains interesting works of art and furnishings, in particular the finely carved 16C **stalls★** in the apse. The high altar, eagle-shaped lectern, the pulpit and organ loft are all fine examples of 18C woodcarving. The altar in the chapel north of the chancel is 19C. The chapel of St-Crépin *(third off the north aisle)* has a stained glass window depicting the Crucifixion, polychrome statues and a diptych showing the Last Supper, all dating from the 16C. The mid-20C stained glass in the aisles is by Le Chevallier *(north aisle)* and Auclair *(south aisle)*. Note the series of twelve 17 and 18C canvases depicting scenes from the life of the Virgin Mary.

The 13C Black Madonna, in whose honour the church was built, stands in the Chapelle de l'Annonciation to the south of the choir.

Old houses – There are two late-15C timber-framed houses: **Maison Hugon** *(on the corner of Rue Gambetta and Rue V-Basch - Z L)* and **Maison Gorrevod** *(Rue du Palais - Z N)*. Equally attractive are the fine 17C stone façade of the **Hôtel de Bohan** *(on the corner by the town hall - YZ F)* and the 18C **Hôtel de Marron de Meillonnas**, which houses the Trésorerie Générale *(Rue Teynière - Z D)*. A row of medieval half-timbered corbelled houses adjoins the Porte des Jacobins, built in 1437 *(Rue J-Migonney - Z R)*.

BRANCION★

The old feudal market down of Brancion is perched on a spur overlooking two deep
ravines, forming a picturesque and most unusual sight.

TOUR

*Since vehicles are not allowed into the town, visitors must park their cars in the
car park provided outside the town walls.*

Once through the gateway in the 14C ramparts, visitors will be pleasantly sur-
prised to find the imposing ruins of a fortress, narrow streets lines with medieval
looking houses – some of which have creepers growing all over them, 15C
covered markets *(halles)* and the church standing proudly at the end of the spur.
Some of the houses have been well restored.

Château ⊙ – This feudal castle dates back to the beginning of the 10C. The castle
was enlarged in the 14C by Duke Philip the Bold, who added a wing to lodge the
Dukes of Burgundy, and destroyed by the troops of Colonel d'Ornano on 11 June
1954, during the time of the Catholic League. The keep has been restored. From
the viewing platform *(87 steps)* there is a good view★ of the town and its church,
the Grosne valley and, to the west and northwest, the mountains of Charollais and
Morvan.

St-Pierre ⊙ – The church is a squat 12C building built in the Romanesque style,
surmounted by a square belfry. The simplicity and purity of line, the harmonious
colours of the stone and the roofing of stone tiles are all striking features. Inside,
there are 14C frescoes commissioned by Eudes IV, Duke of Burgundy, a recumbent
effigy of Josserand IV of Brancion (13C), a cousin and companion of St Louis, who
died on the Seventh Crusade, and numerous funerary stones. The 14 and 15C
mural paintings on the south wall of the apse have sadly deteriorated. They represent the Resurrection of the Dead.
There is an attractive view of the valley from the church terrace, built at the end
of the spur.

BRIARE

This little town on the banks of the Loire owed its prosperity at the beginning of the
century to the manufacture of porcelain-like buttons made from a paste of very pure
feldspar, imported from Norway. This activity produced not only a great quantity of
buttons but also pearl, jet, and in particular ceramic floor mosaics known as *Émaux
de Briare*. The ceramics industry is still going strong, despite competition from new
industries coming to Briare.

Briare Canal – The canal was begun in 1604 on the initiative of Sully by the "Compagnie des Seigneurs du Canal de Loyre en Seine", but it was not completed until
1642. It was the first junction canal (57km - 36 miles) to be built in Europe. The
canal links the Loire lateral canal to the Loing canal. The reach separating the Loire
and the Seine basins extends between Ouzouer-sur-Trézée and Rogny-les-Sept-Écluses
(seven locks which form a staircase).

Briare – Pont-Canal

B. Henry/CEDRI

SIGHTS

★★ **Pont-Canal** – The canal bridge, a work of art which dates from 1890, carries the Loire lateral canal over the river to join the Briare canal *(photograph previous page)*. The aqueduct (662m - 2 172ft long by 11m - 37ft wide including the towpaths) is made of metal plates held together by millions of rivets. The metal duct (2.2m - 7ft deep) and the towpaths are supported by 15 stonework piers constructed by the Société Eiffel. Steps lead down to the banks of the Loire, from where there is a fine view of the metal structure of the aqueduct.

►► **La Bussière** – *13km - 8 miles north.* Louis XIII style Château des Pêcheurs with interesting patterned brickwork and exhibition on **fresh-water fishing** ⊙.

MICHELIN GUIDES

The Red Guides (hotels and restaurants)

Benelux - Deutschland - España-Portugal - main cities Europe - France - Great Britain and Ireland - Italia - Switzerland

The Green Guides (fine art, historic monuments, scenic routes)

Austria - Belgium - Canada - England: The West Country - France - Germany - Greece - Italy - Mexico - Netherlands - New England - Portugal - Scotland - Spain - Switzerland
London - New York City - Paris - Rome

and 12 regional guides to France

BUGEY

Michelin map 74 folds 3, 4, 5, 14 and 15 or 244 folds 4, 5, 6, 16 and 17

The southern Jura region is known by this name. There are two natural divisions: the Haut-Bugey, delimited to the north by a series of transverse valleys, or *cluses*, which run from Nantua to Bellegarde, to the south by the *cluses* of Albarine and Hôpitaux, to the east by the Rhône and to the west by the Ain valley; and the Bas-Bugey, located in the great meander of the Rhône.

Historical background – The Bugey region was first joined to the kingdom of Burgundy in the 9C; then in 1077 a great part of the territory came under the rule of the Count of Savoy, who gradually managed to appropriate all of it. In 1601, the House of Savoy yielded both the Bugey and Bresse regions as well as the Pays de Gex to Henri IV, King of France, in exchange for the marquisate of Saluces.

The Ain Resistance movement – In 1943 the Resistance established several camps in the heart of the mountain massif protected by the Rhône and Ain valleys, overlooking the important road and railway routes. The main stronghold in the Valromey was the object of a German assault in 1944. At dawn on 5 February 5 000 Germans surrounded the mountains and then began the attack from the Hauteville, Retord and Brénod plateaux – in trucks, on foot and on skis. Snow made the going tough. The Resistance forces were forced to scatter after local skirmishes with the enemy. From 6 to 12 February the local villages and population were subjected to enemy violence. Another attack was launched against the Resistance, which had regrouped, in July. This time the fighting affected the entire Bugey region as the Germans sent in 9 000 men reinforced by aircraft and light artillery. The Resistance groups split up and retreated into the highest peaks.

Geographical background – As the Bugey region is located at the southern tip of the Jura "crescent", the mountain folds are closer and deeper than they are in the centre of the mountain chain. The highest range, which separates the Rhône from the Valromey, ends abruptly in the south in the Grand Colombier *(qv)*, the highest peak in the Bugey (1 531m - 5 022ft). The chain runs smoothly on into the high Retord plateau to the north.

It has a semi-continental climate where the Mediterranean nonetheless makes its influence felt. Its western exposure has made the cultivation of a few vineyards possible. Pastures abound in this well-watered region.

In the mountainous areas of the Haut-Bugey the main way of making a living is from stock keeping, while the valleys are given over to crop farming. The fertile Bas-Bugey is ideal for the cultivation of vegetable gardens and orchards.

A place of transit – It has always been easy to cross the Bugey region, marked as it is by the transverse valleys known as *"cluses"* linking the smaller mountain chains. Over the centuries the region's geographical location has brought it many sudden changes in fortune. In the 18C Spanish troops rode rough-shod through the region during the Spanish War of Succession; in the 19C, the allied nations rising against Napoleon used the Bugey as their main battleground. It was not until 1855, with the creation of the Lyon-Geneva railway line through the Cluse de l'Albarine, that the region could actually benefit from its position as a place of transit. In 1871 Ambérieu became an important communications node, with the cutting of a passage through Mont Cenis and the construction of the railway line to Italy.

The N 504 and the D 904, between Ambérieu and Culoz, together constitute the main route across the Bugey, which is also an important communications route with Geneva, Annecy, Chamonix, Aix-les-Bains and Italy. It passes through a series of transverse valleys which are grouped under the names of the Cluse de l'Albarine and the Cluse des Hôpitaux.

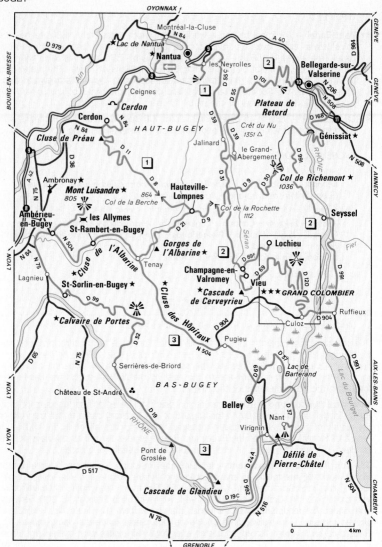

HAUT-BUGEY

① Round tour leaving from Nantua
139km - 86 miles – allow 4 hours

★ **Nantua** – *See NANTUA.*

Leave Nantua to the north on the picturesque N 84, which runs alongside the Lac de Nantua. Turn left at Montréal-la-Cluse; 2km - 1.2 miles after Ceignes, turn right onto a road leading off the N 84 and follow it for about 300m - 328yds.

Grotte du Cerdon ⊙ – This cave was hollowed out by a subterranean river which has now dried up (it was fed by the Lac de Nantua, which used to be a lot larger than it now is). The tour takes you past beautiful stalactites (the dais), stalagmites (the Cambodian statue) and draperies. It leads into an immense cavern in which a 30m - 98ft high arch is open to the sky. A gallery opened up in 1981 leads to the place where the vanished river emerged from the middle of the rockface as a resurgent spring. There is a view of the Reculée de Cerdon and the vineyard from this opening.

Cerdon – By the windswept Pont de l'Enfer a memorial has been set up to the members of the Resistance who fought in the Bugey (bust of a woman against a small wall).

At Pont Préau, take the D 11 on the left.

Cluse de Préau – This *cluse* is a small but typical example of this type of valley. It is so narrow that the last house in Préau seems almost to block it off, nevertheless leaving just enough room for the road to pass by.

The D 11 climbs through a charming valley.

Carry on, driving over two passes (the Col de Montratier and the Col de la Berche on the D 8), until Hauteville-Lompnès.

Hauteville-Lompnès – Facilities. The town is a popular holiday resort, well-known for its modern sanatoriums.

Take the D 21 on the right.

★ **Gorges de l'Albarine** – As the river Albarine flows southwest, it has cut many impressive **gorges★** along its course. Waterfalls tumble down the towering cliff faces at various points. As the road leaves the gorge, you can see the **Cascade de Charabotte★**, formed as the Albarine cascades down a 150m - 492ft drop on the edge of the Hauteville plateau.

Return to Hauteville-Lompnès and take the D 9 over the Col de la Rochette, altitude 1 112m - 3 648ft, as far as Ruffieu. The tour crosses part of the Valromey. Go towards Hotonnes at Ruffieu, and then take the D 30 on the left.

★ **Col de Richemont** – There is a **view** from the pass (alt 1 036m - 3 399ft) of the Michaille region, an undulating landscape stretching at the foot of the mountain as far as the Rhône, whose course is blocked by the dams at Seyssel and Génissiat; of the Grand Crêt d'Eau mountain range (1 534m - 5 062ft); the Défilé de l'Écluse, through which the Rhône flows into the Jura; and, in clear weather, the Mont Blanc mountain range.

Return to Ruffieu and take the D 31 north, the D 31^F at the Jalinard junction, the D 39 on the left and the D 55^C on the right. Then take the D 55^D through Granges-du-Poizat to reach Les Neyrolles. From here, take the D 39 on the left.

After a few sharp turns in the road there is a remarkable **view★★** of the steep slopes of the Nantua *cluse* and of the lake; this is a magnificent sight at sunset.

Return to the village of Neyrolles, from where the D 39 leads to the N 84, which leads off to the left back to Nantua.

2 Round tour leaving from Bellegarde-sur-Valserine

136km - 85 miles - allow 6 hours - local map opposite

This round tour, which is not described in detail, takes you from Bellegarde *(qv)* through the Rhône valley as far as the **Génissiat★** *(qv)* dam, then via Seyssel to Culoz. From here you drive to the summit of the **Grand Colombier★★★** *(qv)* from where there is a marvellous view. Carry on down the west face of the mountain to Vieu.

BAS-BUGEY

3 Round tour leaving from Belley

166km - 103 miles - allow one day - local map opposite

Belley – *See BELLEY.*

Leave Belley on the N 504, north of the map, then turn right onto the D 69, and after Billieu turn right again as far as the D 37.

Shortly after Pollieu, the road brings you to the **Lac de Barterand** *(see the table of lakes at the end of this guide)*, or Lac de St-Champ as it is sometimes called after the neighbouring village, a lake set in peaceful, green surroundings.

Take the D 992 on the left which runs alongside the canal, then take the D 37 on the right. Before reaching the N 504, turn right towards Chemillieu.

The view opens up to the Yenne basin, the Dent du Chat, Mont Revard (glimpsed through the gap of the Col du Chat), and the Chartreuse mountain range (the Grand-Som and Grande Sure summits).

Leave the car near the wash-house in the hamlet of Nant. Take the tarmac path on the immediate left, which soon becomes a stone track (closed to vehicles) leading along the rock face to the top of the gorge.

Défilé de Pierre-Châtel – *1 hour 30 min on foot Rtn.* There is a **view★** of the ravine from the top of a rocky outcrop left of the path. The Rhône has found a crack in the Jura mountains' armour; it cuts into the mountain range at the Col de Pierre-Châtel, forming a gorge, then flows on into a valley which it follows as far as its confluence with the Guiers. The buildings of an old Carthusian monastery tower above the ravine. The **Chartreuse de Pierre-Châtel**, founded in 1383, soon had fortifications added to it, before being fully converted into a fortress in the 17C, when it found itself situated on the frontier, as the Bresse and Bugey regions were handed over to France.

The elegant arch of the bridge spanning the Rhône at La Balme is eye-catching.

Return to the D 37 and take the N 504 which runs along the bottom of the ravine. Cross the Rhône on this road. At Virignin take the D 31^A on the left, then the D 24^A on the left, as far as Peyrieu, where you rejoin the D 992.

The road follows the course of the river as it once more changes its course, this time to bypass the Izieu mountain mass. At its confluence with the Guiers, it allows itself to be lead off to the northwest along a channel in the plateau.

Take the D 19^C on the right, then turn right again along the old D 19, which goes through the villages of La Bruyère, Brégnier-Cordon and Glandieu.

Cascade de Glandieu – During the week the waterfall is harnessed by two small hydroelectric plants at its foot.

Carry on north along the D 19.

Notice the suspension bridge at Groslée, a rare example of a lightweight metal alloy construction for unlimited tonnages. Shortly after Flévieu the road runs past the ruins of the **château de St-André**.

At Serrières-de-Briord take the D 32 to the right, then the D 99 to the left which leads to the Calvaire de Portes.

★ **Calvaire de Portes** – The mountain summit on which this calvary stands (alt 1 025m - 3 363ft) at the tip of a rocky spur can be seen from a long way off. *Park your car in the car park at the side of the road and take the path towards the calvary (15min on foot Rtn).* From the viewing table, the view encompasses the small, pointed mountain called Dent du Chat ("cat's tooth"; alt 1 390m - 4 203ft), to the left the towering form of the Grand Colombier (alt 1 531m - 5 023ft) and to the right the broad expanse of the plain through which the Ain flows on its way to the Rhône.

The D 99 leads down towards Lagnieu, providing a views of the Rhône valley as it goes.

★ **St-Sorlin-en-Bugey** – In season, there are flowers, particularly roses, wherever you go in this village. It occupies a picturesque site at the foot of a cliff which overlooks a curve in the Rhône valley. While the slopes are covered with vines, the plain is chequered with farmsteads. The village church has undergone several extension and restoration projects, the most ambitious of which completely rebuilt the interior, raising the roof vault and adding tall Gothic pillars supporting a network of ribs in the vault. There is a beautiful view of the whole village from the second hairpin bend in the road climbing beyond the church, from where the old château stands.

The Rhône at this point has returned to the same latitude as Culoz, although the broad meander south it has made in the meantime has taken it across the whole of the Bas-Bugey. It now flows into the Dombes plain, where it picks up the tributary of the Ain and flows on towards Lyon.

Ambérieu-en-Bugey – Ambérieu, an important junction for major railway lines and roads, is expanding in the Ain plain at the mouth of the Albarine gorge.

On reaching the church in Ambérieu, take a road on the left that climbs toward the Château des Allymes. Leave the car at the edge of the hamlet of Brédevent. From here you can take a walk to either Mont Luisandre or the Château des Allymes.

★ **Mont Luisandre** – *1 hour 15 min on foot Rtn.* Take the steep, stone track between two houses in the village, to the left of the wash-house. A 15 min walk brings you to a steep bank, where you take the path to the right which leads up through meadows and fallow land to the summit.

There is a cross at the summit (alt 805m - 2 641ft). Walk round the grove to obtain a sweeping **view★** of the Château des Allymes on one of the spurs of the Bugey, the Dombes plateau sparkling with reflected light from its lakes, the confluence of the Ain and the Rhône and the wooded summits of the Bugey region, slashed by the deep gorges of the Albarine.

Château des Allymes – *30 min on foot Rtn from Brédevent.* This fortified château was laid out as a square. The courtyard in its centre is protected by a solid, square keep in one corner, and a round tower with a lovely timber roof in the other. Walk round the second storey of the curtain wall to obtain glimpses through the openings of the Dombes plain and the Bresse region.

The tour continues through the Albarine and Hôpitaux *cluses*, which separate the Bugey region into two parts.

★ **Cluse de l'Albarine** – This valley cuts across from Ambérieu to Tenay. The Albarine, the railway line and the road wind along together between the steep slopes on either side. The lower part of these slopes is carpeted with vines here and there. The upper slopes, which are wooded, culminate in limestone ridges in which the rock strata run diagonally and at times almost vertically, in between crumbling boulders. The valley twists and turns, and then suddenly narrows off, giving you the impression that you are in fact in a cirque, and about to bump into its far side; it not until the last moment that you find the way out.

St-Rambert-en-Bugey – This little industrial town in a green valley on the banks of the Albarine houses a **Maison de Pays** ⊘, in which traditional industries are on display along with a reconstruction of the inside of a house from days gone by.

The road between Argis and Tenay, at the bottom of the *cluse*, passes one factory after another, surrounded by workers' homes. These factories used to specialise in handling silk byproducts, but now produce nylon and its derivatives.

★ **Cluse des Hôpitaux** – This valley opens up between Tenay and Pugieu. It is not as green as the Cluse de l'Albarine, as there is only a tiny stream trickling through it.

Its steep rocky sides, taller and craggier than those of the Cluse de l'Albarine, and its plunging gorge give the landscape a bleak and rugged air, accentuated by the almost complete lack of houses.

Return to Belley (qv) on the N 504.

Château de BUSSY-RABUTIN★

Michelin map 65 south of fold 8 or 243 fold 2

A few miles north of Alise-Ste-Reine, halfway up a hill, stands the château of Bussy-Rabutin; its highly original interior décor is an eloquent testimony of the state of mind of its owner.

The misfortunes of Roger de Bussy-Rabutin – While his cousin, Mme de Sévigné, was very successful with her pen, Roger de Rabutin, Count of Bussy, caused nothing but trouble with his. Turenne, already irritated by his acerbic couplets, described him to the king as "the best officer in his armies – for writing verse". Having compromised himself, in company with other young libertines, in a now famous orgy in which he improvised and sang couplets ridiculing the love affair of young Louis XIV and Marie de Mancini, Bussy-Rabutin was exiled to Burgundy on the orders of the king.

Accompanied in exile by his mistress, the Marquise de Montglat, he passed his time composing an *Histoire amoureuse des Gaules*, a satirical chronicle of the love affairs of the court. This libellous work had its author clapped straight into the Bastille, where he languished for over a year. Then he was sent home to Bussy, where he lived in exile – alone this time, as the beautiful marquise had forgotten all about him.

TOUR ⊘ *time: 45 min*

The château is protected by a moat and four round corner towers. Since the 16C Bussy has consisted of only three ranges of buildings around a courtyard which opens onto gardens.

The wings, which take the form of galleries, were decorated in the Renaissance style under Henri II. The main block was rebuilt in 1649 by Roger de Rabutin in the early Louis XIV style.

Interior – It was Bussy-Rabutin himself who designed the interior decoration of the apartments, a gilded cage in which he spent his exile, indulging in nostalgia for army and court life and giving vent to his rancour against Louis XIV and his unfaithful mistress.

Château de Bussy-Rabutin

Cabinet des Devises – Numerous portraits and allegorical paintings along with pithy maxims (*devises*) composed by Roger de Rabutin are framed in the woodwork panels of this room, giving it a most unusual appearance.

The upper panels feature views of châteaux and monuments, some of which no longer exist, and are thus interesting as historical documents. Over the fireplace is a portrait of Bussy-Rabutin by Lefèvre, a student of Lebrun. The furniture is Louis XIII.

Antichambre des Grands Hommes de Guerre – Portraits of 65 great warriors, from Du Guesclin down to the master of the house as "Maistre de Camp, Général de la Cavalerie Légère de France", are hung in two rows around the room. Some of the portraits are very good originals, but most of them are only copies from originals of the period (17C) which are nonetheless of historical interest. The woodwork and ceilings are decorated with fleurs-de-lys, trophies, standards and the interlaced ciphers of de Bussy and the Marquise de Montglat.

Chambre de Bussy – Bussy's bedchamber is adorned with the portraits of 25 women. That of Louise de Rouville, second wife of Bussy-Rabutin, is included in a triptych with those of Mme de Sévigné and her daughter, Mme de Grignan. Other personalities portrayed include Gabrielle d'Estrées, Henri IV's mistress, Mme de la Sablière, Ninon de Lenclos, the famous courtesan, and Mme de Maintenon.

Tour Dorée – Bussy-Rabutin surpassed himself in the decoration of the circular room where he worked on the first floor of the west tower. The walls are entirely covered with paintings, on subjects taken from mythology and the gallantry of the age, accompanied by quatrains and couplets. A series of portraits of the great personalities of the courts of Louis XIII and Louis XIV completes the collection.

Chapelle – The Galerie des Rois de France leads to the south tower, which houses a small, elegantly furnished oratory (16C stone altarpiece depicting the Raising of Lazarus).

Gardens and Park – The park (34ha - 84 acres), shaped like an amphitheatre with beautiful stone steps linking the levels, makes a fine backdrop to the gardens wih their statues (17-19C), fountains and pools, apparently designed by Le Nôtre, Louis XIV's own gardener.

CHABLIS

Population 2 569
Michelin map 65 folds 5 and 6 or 238 fold 11 – Facilities

The little town of Chablis, or the "Golden Gateway" to Burgundy, washed by the waters of the River Serein, is the wine capital of Lower Burgundy. These vineyards are of ancient origin, and were at their most prosperous in the 16C. At that time there were more than 700 vineyard owners in Chablis and the surrounding region.

Nowadays, the light dry **wines of Chablis,** with their delicate taste and subtle bouquet, are highly prized. Their special fragrance develops in about the month of March following the grape harvest and preserves its remarkable freshness for a long time. The grape variety is the Chardonnay, known in the region as the Beaunois. The area in which the wine is produced extends from Maligny and Ligny-le-Châtel in the north to Poilly-sur-Serein in the south, and from Viviers in the east to Courgis in the west, taking in about 20 establishments. "Grand Cru" (best quality) wines come from the vineyards grouped on the steep hillsides of the east bank; these are Vaudésir, Valmur, Blanchot, Grenouille, Les Clos, Les Preuses and Bougros, whereas "Premier Cru" (good quality) wines come from both banks of the Serein on the land round Chablis. The *appellations* or vintages beneath these are classified as "Chablis", from vineyards covering a much wider area, and finally "Petits Chablis". There is an annual Chablis Wine Fair, and also a fair on the feast day of St Vincent, the patron saint of wine-growers *(see the Calender of Events at the back of the guide).*

St-Martin ⊙ – The church, which dates from the 12C, was the collegiate church of the canons of St-Martin-de-Tours, who set up a sanctuary for the relics of their saint after fleeing from the Norsemen. On the Romanesque doorway of the south entrance, note the 13C paintings and the horseshoes nailed to the door as ex-voto offerings from pilgrims to the shrine of St Martin. The interior forms an attractive and harmonious ensemble.

St-Pierre – Only three bays remain of this Romanesque church, which is an excellent example of the Burgundian transitional style *(see p 40).* It was the parish church until 1789.

Lac de CHALAIN★★

Michelin map 170 folds 4, 5, 14 and 15 or 242 folds 30, 31 – Local map under Région des LACS DU JURA

This lake, at an altitude of 492m - 1 614ft, is the most beautiful and impressive of all. It is particularly well suited for fishing and boating *(see the table of lakes at the end of this guide).* The western part of the lake is enclosed by an indentation in the Fontenu plateau and is thus surrounded by steep wooded slopes, while the other part, with swampy banks in places, stretches between gently rolling hills. It is fed by resurgent springs from lake Narlay and in turn spills into the river Ain via the Bief d'Œuf.

In June 1904 a severe draught combined with the effect of water catchment for an electricity plant to lower the water level by 7m - 23ft. This revealed a number of wooden posts on the west bank, which turned out to be the vestiges of a lake community, dating from five millenia ago — the Upper Palaeolithic period (polished stone age). During successive excavations the remains of dwellings were discovered along about 2km - 1.2 miles of the west and north shores, beneath the present water level. Among the objects discovered during the excavations and now exhibited at the Lons-le-Saunier municipal archaeology museum, there is a particularly beautiful canoe, 9m - 354ft long, hollowed out of the trunk of an oak tree, and also tools and utensils carved from deers' antlers, bone and stone.

Two Neolithic houses on pillars have been reconstructed on the shores of the lake, using prehistoric techniques.

The **Maison des Lacs** ⊙ in **Marigny** *(facilities)* exhibits objects and tools discovered during the excavations conducted since 1988, as well as the interior of a lake dwelling.

Crêt de CHALAM★★★

Michelin map 170 south of fold 15 or 243 fold 43 –
Local maps above opposite and under ST-CLAUDE: Excursion

This is the highest peak (1 545m - 5 069ft) in the range overlooking the Valserine from the west.

Access – *1 hour 30 min on foot Rtn. We advise the route leaving from La Pesse.*

Take the road opposite the church. After 4km - 2.4 miles you come to a cross-roads (signposted "La Borne au Lion").

A lion (for the Franche-Comté), some fleurs-de-lys (for the kingdom of France) and the date of 1613 can be seen on this milestone, located at the foot of a monument to the Maquis of the Ain and Haut-Jura. It used to mark the border between France, Spain and Savoy.

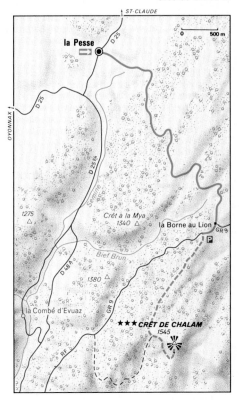

Turn right onto a forest road and park your car after about 250m. A sign (red arrows) on the left indicates an old road, now a footpath which leads to the summit.

The path soon crosses a plateau planted with spruces, from which the Chalam summit can be seen. The climb becomes very steep towards the end.

Panorama – The entire length of the Valserine valley can be seen from the summit.
The view to the east stretches as far as the great **Jura range**, the highest and final mountain chain before the land drops down to the Swiss plain. The gullied slopes of Roche Franche can be seen right in front of you; to your left are the Reculet and the Crêt de la Neige (1 717m - 5 633ft); to your right is the Grand Crêt d'Eau, beyond the Sac pass. In clear weather, even the Mont Blanc can sometimes be seen.
There is an extensive view to the west of the mountains and mountain plateaux of the Jura.

CHALON-SUR-SAÔNE

Population 54 575
Michelin map 69 fold 9 or 243 fold 27 – Plan of the conurbation in the current Michelin Red Guide France

Chalon, an inland port situated at the confluence of the river Saône and the Canal du Centre, is an active industrial and business centre; its commercial fairs are well attended. Chalon is also the capital town of an area of arable farming, stock raising and vineyards; the best wines are worthy of their great neighbours from the Côte d'Or.

The Côte Chalonnaise – The vineyards on the banks of the Saône link the Côte de Beaune and the Côte de Nuits to the north and the Mâconnais and the Beaujolais to the south. Famous wines such as Mercurey, Givry, Montagny and Rully (sparkling) come from this region, as do many fine table wines.
The eight-day long carnival festivities usually attract large crowds (see the Calendar of Events at the end of the guide).

Predestined as a crossroads – Julius Caesar chose Chalon as the main warehouse for his food supplies during his campaigns in Gaul, because of its situation on the banks of the Saône, a magnificent navigable waterway, and at the intersection of a number of major roads.
During the Middle Ages the annual pelt fairs (**Foires aux Sauvagines**), which lasted two months, were among the most popular in Europe. These two fur fairs still take place every year in Chalon and are picturesque events. Many collectors, trappers and game wardens come from the Alps, the Pyrénées, the Jura, the Vosges and the Massif Central, bringing every kind of pelt with them: fox, badger, polecat, stoat, otter, marten, mink etc. The winter fair, or Foire Froide, is the most important French fair for furs and always draws large crowds.

The father of photography – **Joseph Nicéphore Niepce**, born in Chalon in 1765, can well lay claim to the title of inventor of photography. After a short period with the Oratorians and a spell in the Revolutionary army, which he left for health reasons, he finally settled in Chalon in 1801, devoting himself to scientific research. After perfecting an engine along the same principles as the jet engine (the "pyreolophore"), along with his brother Claude, he then devoted his time to lithography and in 1816 succeeded in obtaining a negative image with the aid of a camera obscura, or pinhole camera, and then a positive one in 1822. Nicéphore Niepce died in Chalon in 1833. A statue in Quai Gambetta and a monument on the edge of the N 6 at St-Loup-de-Varennes (7km - 4 miles south of Chalon), where his discovery was perfected, perpetuate the memory of this great inventor.

Submarines for the Bolivian Navy – The building of the Canal du Centre in the late 18C-early 19C, as well as the canals of Burgundy and the Rhône-Rhine link, developed regional commerce on the waterways. In 1839 the Schneider company from Le Creusot set up a factory in Chalon at the east end of the Canal du Centre; it was initially known as "Le Petit Creusot", before becoming "Creusot-Loire" *(see Le CREUSOT)*. From 1839 the factory produced a series of torpedo boats, submarines and anti-torpedo boats for various countries' navies. Between 1889 and 1906 it produced 81 torpedo boats. The largest ship it produced was the anti-torpedo boat *Mangini*, launched in 1911 for the Bolivian navy. It was 78.10m - 256ft long and drew a depth of 3.08m - 13ft, making it too big to sail down the Saône. It had to be transported to the Mediterranean on a transport barge. The submarines produced here up until the Second World War were exported to Bolivia and Japan. This factory suffered the full force of the crisis in the steel industry in 1984. Since 1970, however, the economic activity of Chalon has been stimulated by the arrival of other industries such as Kodak, St-Gobain, Framatome, Air Liquide and Water Queen (European leader in the production of fishing gear).

SIGHTS

★ **Musée Denon** (BZ **M**[1]) ⊙ – The 18C building, once part of an Ursuline convent, had the neoclassical façade added to it when it was converted to house the museum which bears the name of one of Chalon's most illustrious citizens, Dominique Vivant **Denon** (1747-1825), a diplomat under the Ancien Régime, who was also a famous engraver and one of the first to introduce lithography to France. During Napoleon's campaign in Egypt he pioneered Egyptology and became artistic adviser to the Emperor, Grand Purveyor and Director of several French museums (including the Louvre), which he endowed with works of art.

The museum displays an important collection of 17-19C paintings. The Italian school is represented by three large canvases by Giordano, as well as works by Bassano *(Plan of Venice, Adoration of the Shepherds)*, Solimena and Caravaggio. The golden age of Dutch painting (17C) is represented by Hans Bollongier *(Bouquet of Tulips)*, Doomer and Davidsz de Heem *(Still Life)*. French painting is represented by Largillière, Carle Van Loo, Lagrénée, P de Champaigne and, from the 19C, Géricault (portrait of a *Black Man*) and the pre-Impressionist landscape painter Raffort, a native of Chalon.

Local history is illustrated by examples of domestic traditions, the life of the Saône boatmen and a collection of local furniture. Also on display are medieval pottery, various scale models, 12C religious artefacts, 16C religious sculptures and paintings, stained glass etc. The last room is devoted to Denon and artists of his period: terracotta figures by Clodion (female faun and children). The mezzanine gallery and its staircase are hung with contemporary works mainly by artists who won the Prix de Rome.

The ground floor is devoted to the rich archaeological collections: prehistoric flint implements from Volgu (Digoin-Gueugnon region – the largest and most beautiful stone-age relics discovered, dating from the Solutré *(qv)* period), many antique and medieval metal artefacts, a magnificient Gallo-Roman group in stone of a lion bringing down a gladiator. There are also Gallo-Roman and medieval lapidary collections.

St-Pierre (**BZ**) – The church was built between 1698 and 1713 (19C additions) as the chapel of a Benedictine abbey. It is in the Italian style and has a particularly impressive west front. The huge nave and domed chancel are furnished with statues, some of which date from the 17C: at the entrance to the chancel are St Peter and St Benet, in the transept are St Anne and the Virgin Mary overcoming a dragon. The choir stalls are attractively carved, and the Regency-style organ is surmounted by a figure of Saul playing the harp.

★ **Musée Nicéphore-Niepce** (**BZ M²**) ⊘ – This museum is housed in the 18C Hôtel des Messageries on the banks of the Saône. The rich collection includes photographs and photographic equipment, and some of the earliest cameras ever made, used by Joseph Nicéphore Niepce, and his first heliographs. There are also works by well-known contemporaries of Niepce in the world of photography.

The extensive ground floor displays photographic equipment from all over the world ranging from luminous projectors and Dagron equipment for microscopic photography (1860) to the camera used on the Apollo space programme. The Niepce room *(first floor)* contains family mementoes and the first camera (1816). The Daguerre room displays the machinery for producing daguerreotypes, and the following rooms are devoted to the first colour and relief photographs and the famous 19C cameras: Chevalier's Grand Photographe (*c*1850), the Bertsch cameras (1860) and the Damoizeau cyclographs (1890).

The last galleries *(ground floor)* are a huge room containing various old cameras (the Dubroni series, 1860; ferrotyping implements) and a small room of "photosculpture".

Cathédrale St-Vincent (**CZ**) ⊘ – The cathedral of the old bishopric of Chalon (suppressed in 1790) is not uniform in appearance. The oldest parts date from the late 11C; the chancel is 13C. The neo-Gothic façade (1825) is certainly the oldest in France in this style.

The pillars in the nave are composed of fluted pilasters and engaged columns. A 15C font and a Flamboyant vault adorn the third chapel in the north transept. The north apsidal chapel contains a large contemporary tabernacle in bronze gilt (1986). A finely sculpted canopy adorns the chancel, and a triptych of the Crucifixion (1608) the apse.

The 15C sacristy was divided horizontally in the 16C, and the lower chamber was covered with a vault supported by a central pillar. The ante-chapel is vaulted with five pendant keystones and lit through a beautiful stained glass window depicting the woman with the twelve stars of the Apocalypse.

The south transept opens into the chapel of Notre-Dame-de-Pitié (15C *Pietà* and Renaissance tapestry) and into the 15C cloisters (restored) which contains four wooden statues. The well in the cloister garth has also been restored.

The south aisle contains many burial stones; some chapels are closed off by stone screens (claustra); the last chapel contains a 16C polychrome *Pietà*.

Old houses – Some of the many old houses in Chalon have a particular charm. In the streets near the cathedral there are fine half-timbered façades overlooking Place St-Vincent (note also at the corner of Rue St-Vincent the statue of a saint), Rue aux Fèvres and Rue de l'Évêché. **Rue St-Vincent** (**CZ 39**) forms a picturesque crossroads at the junction of Rues du Pont and du Châtelet. No 37 **Rue du Châtelet** (**CZ 6**) has a handsome 17C façade with low reliefs, medallions and gargoyles. No 39 **Grande-Rue** (**BCZ 16**) is a fine 14C house (restored).

Hôpital (**CZ**) ⊘ – *On the island in the River Saône.*
The Flemish-style building was started in the 16C. The first door, the nuns' quarters, comprises several panelled rooms, including the infirmary which contains four curtained beds. The buildings were extended in the 17C, and in the 18C certain rooms were decorated with magnificent **woodwork★**. The nuns' refectory and the kitchen passage, which is furnished with dressers lined with pewter and copper vessels, are particularly interesting. The chapel (1873) has a metal structure and displays works of art from the buildings that have been demolished: woodwork decorated with coats of arms, 17C bishop's throne, rare late-15C statue of the Virgin Mary with an inkwell. A collection of 84 18C pots is displayed in the late-18C pharmacy.

Tour du Doyenné (**CZ**) ⊘ – The 15C deanery tower originally stood near the cathedral. It was dismantled in 1907 and rebuilt at the point of the island. Near the tower is a magnificent lime tree from the Buffon nursery.

★ **Roseraie St-Nicolas** – *4km - 2.5 miles northeast of Chalon-sur-Saône. Take the bridge, Pont-St-Laurent (*CZ*), and continue straight on across the two islands, then turn left into the Rue Julien-Leneuveu. A 5km - 3 miles trail through the rose garden (time: 1 hour 30 min) starts from the St-Nicolas recreation ground.*

The **rose garden** is laid out in a loop of the Saône, beyond the municipal gold course. The rose beds (25 000 bushes) are set in vast lawns shaded by conifers or young apple trees. The recommended route runs parallel with a keep-fit trail (2.5km - 1.5 miles). On the left of the main avenue are splendid banks of roses of contrasting and harmonious hues (in flower: June to July), which are judged in an annual international competition, a small garden of rare plants (talus de la Grande Rocaille) and an arboretum. On the right is an alley of old roses (mostly varieties obtained in the 19C), clumps of perennials (in flower: September), bulbs and rhizomes (irises, geraniums etc), water plants, an Erica garden and so on.

CHAMPLITTE

Population 1 906
Michelin map 166 southeast of fold 3 or 243 fold 5

Champlitte, an old fortified town, lies in tiers in the green Salon valley. It still has parts of its old fortifications, and also some Renaissance houses, called "maisons espagnoles". The festival of St-Vincent has been celebrated here since the 18C, in honour of the patron saint of wine-growers *(see the Calendar of Events at the end of the guide)*.

Church – This Classical building is flanked by an older Gothic tower (1437).

★ **Château** – *Illustration p 44.* The central part of this horseshoe-shaped building has a beautiful 16C Renaissance façade beneath a mansard roof. The low-relief decoration on this superposes Ionic and Corinthian orders, and is enhanced with arabesques and leafwork. The 18C wings are the work of Bertrand, who also created the Château de Moncley *(qv).*
The château nowadays houses the Hôtel de Ville (town hall) and a museum.

★ **Musée des Arts et Traditions populaires** ⊙ – Activities and objects of the past, from the Haute-Saône region and the hills south of the Vosges, are evoked in this museum. Visitors will discover the furniture and other typical local artefacts from days gone by – such as the bed-recess characteristic of the Champlitte region, mementoes of itinerant trades, carefully reconstructed craftsmens' workshops, and also reconstructions of various places once so central to village life such as the grocer's, the school, the café and the chapel. One section is given over in particular to folk medecine, the chemist's and the realities of the old almshouse. Finally, one of the halls (late-18C) on the ground floor contains some admirable Italian style decoration by Besançon sculptor Le Breton.
A subsection of this museum is to be found behind the church in the form of a sizeable collection of wine presses.

Musée 1900 – Arts et Techniques ⊙ – Two "streets" lined with workshops evoke the technical progress being made in such a town as this at the turn of the century.

CHAPAIZE★

Population 153
Michelin map 69 fold 19 or 243 fold 39 - 16km – 10 miles to the west of Tournus –
Local map under MÂCONNAIS

Situated on the river Bisançon, to the west of the magnificent forest of Chapaize, the little village of Chapaize is dominated by the high belfry of its Romanesque church. The church is all that remains of a priory founded in the 11C by Benedictine monks from Chalon.

★ **Église St-Martin** – *Time: 30 min.* This church was built between the first quarter of the 11C and the early 13C using the fine local limestone. The essentially Romanesque style building shows a strong Lombard influence – Italian stonemasons almost certainly worked on it – and features a strikingly robust, harmonious belfry.

Exterior – The original ground plan was basilical, and the central nave was made higher and had sturdy buttresses added to it in the mid-12C. The west front is fairly plain, with a triangular gable reflected in the pattern of the Lombard arcades. Beneath the gable is a round-arched window flanked with colonnettes and a large doorway with a small round-arched door to the left of it.

Église St-Martin, Chapaize

The mid-11C **belfry** is typical of those found in Lombardy, although this one is set above the transept crossing. It is surprisingly tall (35m - 115ft) for a building of such modest proportions. Certain architectural contrivances emphasize its soaring effect: the slightly rectangular shape; the imperceptibly pyramidal first storey as tall as the two storeys above it put together and adorned with Lombard arcades (stresses the vertical); upper storeys decorated with horizontal cornices, windows of different sizes placed at different levels, with width increasing upwards. An external staircase was added in the 18C leading up to the base of the belfry.

The chevet was rebuilt in the 13C, and its elegant simplicity harmonises well with the rest of the building.

In the late-14C, the church roof was recovered with stone slabs, known as *lauzes*. A few weathered sculptures, archaic in style and limited in number, carved with floral decoration or human faces, adorn the capitals of the windows and the belfry. On the north side of the latter a naïve figure carved on a column is a precursor of the statue-column.

Interior – The stark simplicity of the interior is quite striking. The great cylindrical pillars (4.8m - 15ft in circumference) are slightly out of line and are crowned with triangular imposts. Of the total seven bays, two belong to the choir. The nave arcade has very wide transverse arches which support 12C broken-barrel vaulting and also the groined vaulting of the aisles. The transept crossing is covered with an attractive **dome** on squinches and supported by semicircular transept arches. Both the apse and the apsidal chapels are oven-vaulted. The former is lit through three wide windows and the latter through openings flanked with columns; the one on the left is decorated with sculpted capitals. The side windows are 19C.

La CHARITÉ-SUR-LOIRE★

Population 5 686
Michelin map 65 south of fold 13 or 238 fold 21 – Facilities

La Charité, which is dominated by the belfries of its handsome church, rises in terraces from the majestic sweep of the Loire. The river is spanned by a picturesque 16C stone bridge which provides a good view of the town. In the days of navigation on the Loire La Charité was a busy port.

The port of La Charité-sur-Loire in 1830

The Charity of the Good Fathers – At first the small riverside town was called Seyr which, according to an etymology which seems to be Phoenician, means Town of the Sun. The conversion of the inhabitants to Christianity and the founding early in the 8C of a convent and a church marked the beginning of a period of prosperity which was interrupted by Arab invasions and attendant destruction.

It was in the 11C, when the present church was built, that the reorganised abbey began to attract travellers, pilgrims and poor people. The hospitality and generosity of the monks was so widely known that the unfortunate came in droves to ask for the charity *(la charité)* of the good fathers, and the town acquired a new name.

A check to Joan of Arc – The town, fortified in the 12C, was to be the prize in the struggle between the Armagnacs and the Burgundians during the Hundred Years War. La Charité was initially occupied by the Armagnacs, the allies of Charles VII, King of France. In 1423 the town was taken by the adventurer **Perrinet-Gressard** who was in the service of both the Duke of Burgundy, who wished to continue the struggle with Charles VII, and the English, who were anxious to delay for as long as possible a reconciliation between the Armagnacs and the Burgundians. In December 1429 Joan of Arc arrived from St-Pierre-le-Moutier and besieged La Charité on behalf of Charles VII, but lack of troops and cold weather obliged her to raise the siege. Perrinet-Gressard held the town until the Treaty of Arras in 1435, when he returned it to the King of France against payment of a large ransom and the office of town governor for life.

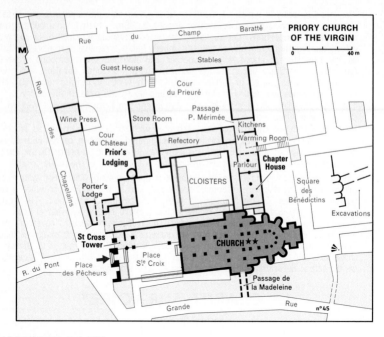

PRIORY CHURCH OF THE VIRGIN

★★ NOTRE-DAME ⏱ *time: 1 hour*

Despite the damage it has incurred over the centuries (a few bays, the transept and the chancel are all that remain), this **priory church** remains one of the most remarkable examples of Romanesque architecture in Burgundy.

Eldest daughter of Cluny – The church and its attendant Benedictine priory, a daughter house of Cluny, were built during the second half of the 11C. The church was consecrated in 1107 by Pope Paschal II. Its outline and decoration were modified in the first half of the 12C.
After Cluny the priory church of La Charité was the largest church in France; it consisted of a nave and four aisles (122m - 399ft long, 37m - 120ft wide, 27m - 89ft high under the dome). It could hold a congregation of 5 000 and carried the honorary title "Eldest daughter of Cluny". At the time, Cluny had at least fifty daughter houses.

Exterior – The façade, which was separated from the rest of the church by a fire in 1559, stands in the Place des Pêcheurs. Originally two towers framed the central doorway; only one *(left)*, the 12C **Tour Ste-Croix** has survived. It is square in design with two storeys of windows surmounted by a slate spire in place of the original one of stone. It is decorated with blind arcades and sculptured motifs including rosettes. The two doorways are walled up; one of them has preserved its tympanum and shows the Virgin Mary interceding with Christ to obtain protection for the monastery of La Charité, represented by the monk, Gérard, its founder and prior. Scenes from the life of the Virgin are portrayed on the lintels: the Annunciation, the Visitation, the Nativity, and the bringing of good tidings to the shepherds.
The steps of the Romanesque central doorway, of which very little is left and which was replaced by a Gothic construction in the 16C, lead to Place Ste-Croix, on the site of six bays of the nave destroyed in the fire of 1559.
Houses have been built into the former north aisle, which was transformed into a parish church from the 12C to the 18C. The arcades of the false triforium are still visible.

Interior – The present church consists of the first four bays of the original nave, the transept and the chancel. The nave, which was badly restored in 1695, has nothing of interest, but the transept and the chancel constitute a magnificent Romanesque ensemble.
The transept crossing is surmounted by an octagonal dome on squinches. The arms of the transept have three bays and two apsidal chapels dating from the 11C; this is the oldest part of the church. In the south transept, the second Romanesque tympanum of the Tour Ste-Croix is visible, representing the Transfiguration with the Adoration of the Magi and the Presentation in the Temple.
The choir, encircled by an ambulatory serving five radiating chapels, is of great elegance. The Lady Chapel dates from the 14C. The depressed arches of the ambulatory are sharp owing to the closeness of the high columns supporting the five historiated capitals. A bestiary of eight motifs accentuates the false triforium; its five-lobed arcades, of Arabic inspiration, are supported by ornamented pilasters. There are good modern stained glass windows by Max Ingrand.
Leave the church via the south transept.

★ **View of the chevet** – The 16C pointed-vaulted passageway (Passage de la Madeleine) emerges into the Grande-Rue. A covered passage, at no 45, leads into the Square des Bénédictins, which provides a good view of the chevet, the transept and the octagonal tower of the abbey church. Behind the chevet, traces of an 11C Cluniac priory are being excavated *(closed to the public)*.

From the square take the staircase leading down to the priory.

Prieuré – At the foot of the staircase, a passageway, which is reached from the warming room, leads into the courtyard of the old priory. Round this stand the main refectory, the kitchens and the stables. The prior's lodging (early 16C) with an attractive seven-sided turret overlooks the lower courtyard (now called Cour du Château).

Leave by the porter's lodge (porterie) to return to Place des Pêcheurs.

ADDITIONAL SIGHTS

Les Remparts – From the remains of the ramparts on the esplanade beside the college in Rue du Clos there is another attractive **view★** of the chevet with its circlet of apsidal chapels, the Loire, the old town and the ramparts.

Musée ⊘ – Considerable space is devoted to medieval objects found during the excavations behind the church: lapidary fragments and terracotta tiles, implements, pottery, keys, jewellery etc. There are also sculptures by Pina (1885-1966), a pupil of Rodin, and a fine collection of Art Nouveau and Art Deco: decorative objects by Louchet, glass by Lalique, Gallé, Duam and ceramics by Deck and Delaherche. A separate room traces the development of files and rasps; their production was an important local industry between 1830 and 1950. Every summer there are exhibitions of contemporary art.

CHARLIEU★

Michelin map 73 fold 8 or 239 fold 11 – Facilities

Ancient *Carus locus* was already an active market town in Gallo-Roman times on the road linking the Saône and Loire valleys. The pretty town of Charlieu still hosts important markets (livestock) and stands at the crossroads of several major communications routes. It is also a centre for the millinery and silk industries, on the scale of both factories and family-run cottage industries.

However, it is Charlieu's archaeological treasures in particular which have won the town its renown.

★ **ABBEY** **(ANCIENNE ABBAYE)** ⊘ *time: 1 hour*

The abbey was founded in 872, attached to Cluny in 932, converted into a priory in 1050 and then fortified on the orders of Philippe Auguste, its protector. The architects and artists from Cluny collaborated here with particularly happy results to rebuild the 11C church and add on the 12C narthex. Excavations thus show that

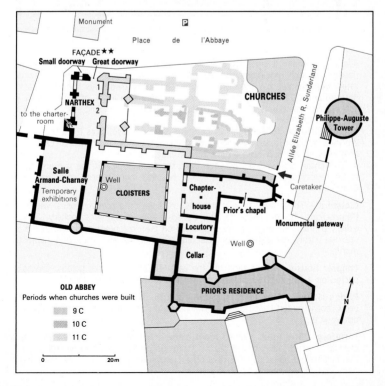

a small 9C church was replaced by a 10C church, which was replaced in turn by an 11C abbey church, on a slightly different axis. This church had a nave with four bays and aisles either side, a transept with transept chapels and an ambulatory with radiating chapels opening off it. The abbey was not to escape the ravages of the Revolution, however; the Benedictine priory, which at the time still housed two monks, was secularised in March 1789. The abbey buildings and the church of St-Fortunat, one of the finest of Cluny's daughters, were largely demolished. All that remains of the church are the narthex and the first bay, in which the capitals bear a resemblance to those of the Brionnais *(qv)*. The warm golden glow of the stone of the abbey buildings adds to the charm of the scene.

There is a good view of the two doorways, which are the abbey's best feature, from the Place de l'Abbaye.

★★ **Façade** – The north façade of the narthex is entered through a **great doorway**, dating from the 12C, which is decorated with some wonderful sculpture work. Christ in Majesty is depicted on the tympanum in a mandorla, supported by two angels and surrounded by the symbols of the four Evangelists. On the lintel, the Virgin Mary appears with two attendant angels and the twelve disciples. Sadly, the sculptures on the imposts of the engaged door posts are damaged; they depict on the left King David and Boson, King of Burgundy and Provence, and on the right St John the Baptist and Bishop Ratbert, the abbey's founder, with his brother Édouard and Boson.

Tympanum of the great doorway on the north side of the narthex, abbey of Charlieu

Above the archivolt note the Paschal lamb with its sharply defined thick curly fleece. The arch mouldings and the columns which frame the doorway are decorated with geometrical and floral motifs. The abbey owed this luxuriant plant-like decoration, of Eastern inspiration, to the Crusades. The inside of the left door post bears a representation of Lust, depicted as a woman grappling with frightful reptilian monsters.

The **small doorway**, to the right of the great doorway, also dates from the 12C. The Wedding at Cana is depicted on its tympanum, the Transfiguration of Christ on its archivolt and the sacrifice of rams on the lintel.

As you enter, you will see to your right the foundations of the various churches which have stood on this site. They can be seen more clearly from the Salle du Chartrier.

Cloisters – These were built in the 15C to replace the previous ones, which were Romanesque. An old well can still be seen against the west gallery. The east gallery contains six huge arches supported on twin colonnettes, on which the capitals are richly decorated with sculpted acanthus leaves, birds and geometrical motifs.

Chapter house – This dates from the early 16C and features pointed arches supported on a round stone pillar, into which a lectern has been carved.

Prior's chapel – This dates from the late 15C. The old terracotta floor tiling has been reconstructed based on the original. Above the chapel is a bell turret with a timber roof.

Parlatory – This lovely vaulted room dating from the early 16C houses a **lapidary museum** in which, next to old capitals from the priory, note two bas-reliefs: a 10C Carolingian one depicting Daniel in the Lions' Den and a 12C one depicting the Annunciation amidst interlaced arches.

Cellar – The cellar, beneath two semicircular vaults, houses a museum of sacred art (**musée d'art religieux**) including a lovely collection of polychrome wood statues from the 15-18C. Note in particular a Virgin Mary with Bird, from the church in Aiguilly (near Roanne), and a Virgin with Child, both Gothic dating from the 15C.

Narthex – This rectangular building, 17m - 56ft long by about 10m - 33ft wide, comprises two rooms, one above the other, with ribbed vaulting. To the east the wall is in fact the west wall of the old church of St-Fortunat, which was consecrated in 1094.

The narthex contains a **Roman sarcophagus** (**1**) which was found in the crypt of the Carolingian church. In the east wall of the narthex is the doorway to the 11C church of St-Fortunat (**2**), on which, on the tympanum framed by three well defined arch mouldings, Christ is depicted in Majesty in a mandorla held by two angels. The west façade has two twin windows with arch mouldings, and above, a pair of figures facing each other. You can get a closer look at the doorways from the narthex. After the narthex, in the first bay of the 11C church, note the interesting decoration on two of the capitals: Daniel in the Lions' Den and mermaids.

Charter room (Salle du Chartrier) – A spiral staircase leads up to this room, which is also known as the Salle des Archives. It contains an exhibition on the history of the abbey.

The great window to the east has two small blind arcades either side of it, and beautiful arch mouldings above it which are supported on engaged columns with capitals decorated with foliage. From here there is a good view of the site of the previous churches – the outline of each of their foundations shows up in the grass. The view also takes in the Philippe-Auguste tower, the prior's lodging and the rooftops of the town.

Before leaving the abbey, have a quick look down into the courtyard of the prior's lodging.

Prior's lodging (Hôtel du Prieur) – *Not open to the public.*

The 16C **monumental doorway** with a basket handle arch is surmounted by decorative crenellations and the coat of arms of the prior.

The prior's residence runs along an elegant courtyard to the south of the chapel, in the centre of which there is an old well with a wrought iron cover. The residence dates from 1510 and is a charming half-timbered building with two hexagonal corner towers and steeply sloping tiled roofs.

Philippe-Auguste tower – This imposing tower, of beautiful ochre coloured stone, was built c1180 on the orders of Philippe-Auguste, who considered the fortified town of Charlieu to be of great use to the French crown. The tower was part of the abbey's system of fortifications.

Salle Armand-Charnay ⊙ – *Entrance from the Place de l'Abbaye.*

This houses temporary exhibitions in the summer, on the subjects of archaeology, fine arts or handicrafts.

ADDITIONAL SIGHTS

★ **Couvent des Cordeliers** ⊙ – *Leave town on the Rue Ch-M-Rouillier to the west.*
This Franciscan monastery was founded in the 13C in St-Nizier-sous-Charlieu. Its unprotected site outside the town walls meant that it suffered quite a lot of damage both during the Hundred Years War and at the hands of roving bands of mercenaries. The monastery buildings have recently undergone restoration.

The **Gothic cloisters,** of pale gold stone, were sold to the United States and were to be taken down and rebuilt there, but luckily they were rescued at the last minute by the French State, which managed to buy them back in 1910. The arcades (late 14C-15C) are decorated with a fascinating variety of plant motifs. The capitals along the north arcade depict vices and virtues in an amusing series of figures and animals; one capital portrays the expressive face of a monk, another has the dance of death as its theme. The west arcade is adorned with a frieze of oak leaves with snails, rabbits and caterpillars on the capitals.

The single-naved church (late 14C), with no transept, has three side chapels on its south side (late 15C - early 16C) and has been partially restored. Originally, it was entirely decorated with paintings, but only a few mural paintings now remain in the chancel.

Hôtel de Ville ⊙ – The town hall occupies an 18C family mansion (the Hôtel de la Ronzière). The council chamber houses a lovely collection of 18C Aubusson tapestries depicting pastoral scenes, woven to fit the size of the panels.

Ancien Hôtel-Dieu – The 18C hospital has a beautiful façade overlooking the Rue Jean-Montel and consists of two huge rooms for the sick, separated by a chapel in which there is a handsome 17C gilded wood altar. The building now houses two museums.

Musée de la Soierie ⊙ – The silk museum, in the old men's ward, documents the history of the silk industry and silk weaving in Charlieu. The large room on the left houses the statue of Notre-Dame-de-Septembre, patron of the powerful weavers' guild, in whose honour there is an annual procession *(see the Calendar of Events at the end of the guide).* The exhibition includes samples of local silk production (sumptuous clothing, one-off creations commissioned by aristocratic families etc) and impressive old looms, giving a good overview of the technical developments in weaving from the 18C on.

Silk woven on a loom is made from the **warp**, a series of silk threads of the required length laid out on a warp beam, and the **weft**, which is wound in advance on a spooler and then interwoven with the warp.

All the equipment on display is still in working order, and from time to time there is a demonstration. Note in particular a large 18C vertical warp beam and some 20C looms which show how the weaving process is becoming increasingly automated.

On the first floor there is a display of materials and designer clothes as well as a video show on traditional and modern silk weaving techniques.

Musée hospitalier ⊙ – The hospital museum is in the women's ward, and includes also the room where patients were treated, the linen room etc. The apothecary's has its original woodwork and a nice collection of 18C porcelain pots.

St-Philibert ⊙ – This 13C church, which has no transept, has a layout typical of 13C Burgundian architecture: a nave with five bays, side aisles and a rectangular chancel. It houses some beautiful works of art, such as a 15C pulpit hewn from a single block of stone and 15C and 16C stalls with pretty painted panels. One chapel contains a 16C Madonna (Notre-Dame de Charlieu). In the chapel of Ste-Anne south of the chancel there is a 15C polychrome stone altarpiece depicting the Visitation and the Nativity. The chapel of St-Crépin north of the chancel contains a 17C Pietà and a statuette of St Crispin, patron saint of shoemakers and saddlers, in polychrome wood.

Old houses – Strolling round the streets near the Place St-Philibert, you will come across numerous picturesque houses dating from 13-18C.

Follow the tour marked on the town plan.

On the corner of the Place St-Philibert and the Rue Grenette stands a 13C stone house which has on its upper floor twin windows with colonnettes as mullions.

Go past the church of St-Philibert, then the Hôtel de Ville and the chapel of the Hôtel-Dieu into the Rue Jean-Morel. Stop outside no 32.

The **Maison des Anglais** dating from the 16C, has mullioned windows on its upper storey with Gothic niches in between them. Two watch turrets frame the façade.

Turn right into Rue André-Farinet.

No 29: 13C stone house; no 27: 15C half-timbered house, the **Maison Disson**; on the corner opposite, no 22: old 14C salt warehouse.

Turn right into the Rue Charles-de-Gaulle.

At no 9, the 13-14C **Maison des Armagnacs** has two twin windows surmounted by trefoil arches. That on the left is decorated with a floral motif, and that on the right with a human face. The upper storey is half-timbered and overhangs the street.

Take the Rue Michon and then the Rue Chanteloup, a shopping street, to the Rue du Merle.

On the corners of the Rue du Merle and the Rue des Moulins (no 11), and of the Rue des Moulins and the Place St-Philibert, stand old half-timbered houses.

▶▶ **La Bénisson-Dieu** – *12km - 8 miles southwest.*
12C **church** ⊙, a vestige of a Benedictine abbey.

CHAROLLES

Population 3 048
Michelin map 69 folds 17 and 18 or 243 fold 37 – Facilities –
Local map under PARAY-LE-MONIAL: Excursion

Main town of the Charollais region, the land of cattle breeding and fattening, Charolles is situated in a basin with ample pastureland and forests. The town is dominated by the ruins of a château which once belonged to the Counts of Charollais; the surviving main building now serves as the town hall. From the public gardens, laid out as a terrace along the wall of the old fortifications, at the foot of the ivy-covered tower of Charles-le-Téméraire, there is a pleasant view of the surrounding countryside. Since 1845 Charolles has possessed a pottery industry producing finely decorated artistic work. A small museum of sculpture (32 Rue Davoine, at the far end of Promenade St-Nicolas) commemorates the local artist René Davoine (1888-1962).

Cattle rearing in the Charollais – Charollais cattle now hold fourth place among French breeds, behind the black and white, Normandy and red and white breeds. Charollais now number 3 million and are distinguished by their uniformly white colouring. They are now the number one breed in France for beef production.

The herds go out to graze with the arrival of the better weather and are taken indoors again with the return of winter. Each week from April to December markets and fairs are held at which thousands of the great white cattle are sold: at St-Christophe-en-Brionnais and Charolles *(Wednesdays)*. These are always interesting, lively occasions. However, the only market on a truly European scale is held at Sancoins in the Cher, beyond the traditional rearing area.

EXCURSIONS

★ **Mont des Carges** – *12km - 8 miles east.*
From the esplanade where there are monuments to the underground fighters of Beaubery and the Charollais battalion an almost circular **view**★ takes in the Loire country to the west, all the Charollais and Brionnais regions to the south and the mountains of Beaujolais to the east.
North of the Mont des Carges the D 79 descends the wooded slopes of Mont Botey *(right)* and the Montagne d'Artus *(left)* through the heart of the Charollais.

Château de Chaumont – *16km - 10 miles to the northeast.* The Renaissance façade is flanked by a round tower, the other façade in the Gothic style is modern. The sheer extent and size of the outbuildings are quite remarkable.

CHÂTEAU-CHINON★

Population 2 502
Michelin map 69 fold 6 or 238 fold 36 – Facilities – Local map under MORVAN

The little town of Château-Chinon, main centre of the Morvan, occupies a picturesque **site**★ on the ridge that separates the Loire and Seine basins on the eastern edge of the Nivernais. Its favourable situation on the top of a hill, a natural fortress site easy to defend and from which one can see both the highlands of the Morvan and the Nivernais plain, made this position successively a Gallic settlement, a Roman camp and a feudal castle, which gave its name to the township. During centuries of battles, sieges and great feats of arms Château-Chinon has earned its motto *"Petite ville, grand renom"* (small town, great fame).

★★ **Panorama from the Calvaire** – *15 min Rtn from the Square Aligre.*
The calvary (609m - 1 998ft) is built on the site of the fortified Gallic settlement and the ruins of the fortress.
There is a very fine circular panorama *(viewing table)* taking in Château-Chinon and its slate roofs, and further off the wooded crests of the Morvan. The two summits of Haut-Folin (901m - 2 956ft) and Mont Préneley (855m - 2 805ft) can be seen to the southeast. At the foot of the hill the prévalley of the Yonne opens to the east, while to the west the view stretches beyond the Bazois as far as the Loire valley.

★ **Promenade du Château** – A road *(starting in Faubourg de Paris and returning via the Rue du Château)* encircles the hill halfway up the slope. Through the trees there are glimpses of the Yonne gorge and the countryside which is visible from the calvary *(above)*.

Musée du Septennat ⊙ – The buildings of an 18C convent of Poor Clares at the top of the old town now house the official presents received by François Mitterrand (who used to be mayor of Château-Chinon) in his capacity as President of the French Republic since 1981. There are photos of the heads of state he has met, of honorary insignia and decorations together with many examples of arts and crafts from all over the world.

Musée du Costume ⊙ – The costume museum, which is housed in the Hôtel de Buteau-Ravisy, exhibits a large collection of French civilian dress, fashion accessories and folk traditions (reconstructions).

Fontaine monumentale – The monumental fountain opposite the town hall, composed of independent articulated sculptures, is the work of Jean Tinguely and Niki de Saint-Phalle.

EXCURSION

★★ **Mont Beuvray** – *Round tour of 73km - 45 miles – allow 2 hours – local map under MORVAN. Leave Château-Chinon on the D 978 to the east.*
The winding and picturesque road passes through rolling countryside with numerous villages and hamlets scattered on terraces amidst a patchwork of fields enclosed by quickset hedges.

Arleuf – Almost all the western gable ends of the houses are slated to protect them against the rain.

Continue east.

Beyond the wood there is a good view of the highlands of the Forêt d'Anost to the left.

East of Pommoy turn right into the D 179 to the Gorges de la Canche.

The road runs along the ridge through a wild, rocky wooded area. There is a lookout point by a layby in a bend in the road with a view of the Canche gorge below and the white building of the electricity plant in it. As you cross over the Canche further on, you see the dam and the pretty reservoir on your right.

Drive southwest. In La Croisette turn right onto the Route forestière du Bois-du-Roi.

This forest road takes you through the magnificent stands of firs and spruces of the **forêt de St-Prix**.

At the roundabout turn right onto the Route forestière to Haut-Folin.

Haut-Folin – This is the highest point of the Morvan (alt 901m - 2 956ft) and is crowned by a telecommunications mast. Not far away is a small ski slope complete with ski-lift.

Go back to the Bois-du-Roi forest road and follow this southwest, and then south (the D 500). In Glux-en-Glenne follow the signs to Anvers and then on to Mont Beuvray.

★★ **Mont Beuvray** – *Access on the D 274, D 18 and D 3, from which you turn right onto the Chemin de la Croix de Rebout (one way). See Mont BEUVRAY.*

The road loops round the mountain to the south and east and carries on through Glux-en-Glenne and the Yonne valley (D 197) back to Château-Chinon. (It is also possible to take the crest road – the D 27 – between the Seine and Loire basins, which goes back to Château-Chinon through the forest of La Gravelle.)

CHÂTEAUNEUF★

Population 63
Michelin map 65 southwest of fold 19 or 243 folds 14 and 15

This old fortified market town, set in a picturesque **spot**★, is famous for its fortress, which commanded the road from Dijon to Autun and the whole of the surrounding plain.

★ **Château** ⊘ – The southern approach (D18ᴬ) provides a spectacular view immediately after crossing the Canal de Bourgogne.
In the 12C, the lord of Chaudenay, whose ruined castle stands on an attractive site in Chaudenay-le-Château *(6km - 3.5 miles south)*, built this fortress for his son. It was enlarged and refurbished at the end of the 15C in the Flamboyant Gothic style by Philippe Pot, Seneschal of Burgundy. In 1936 it was presented to the French State by its owner at the time, Comte G de Vogüé.
The impressive structure, enclosed by thick walls flanked by massive towers, is separated from the village by a moat. There used to be two fortified gates; now a single drawbridge, flanked by huge round towers, gives access to the courtyard and the two main buildings. Although partially ruined, the guest pavilion has retained its handsome ogee-mullioned windows. The other wing with its high dormer windows has been restored. The vast guard room, the chapel (1481) and several rooms decorated in the 17 and 18C are open to visitors. From the circular chamber there is a panoramic view of the Morvan plain.

★ **Village** – This forms a picturesque ensemble with its well-preserved old houses, built from the 14-17C by rich Burgundian merchants, its narrow streets and the remains of its ramparts. Note in particular an interesting old pewter workshop in the main street and carved or ogee door lintels.

▶▶ **Commarin**★ – *8km - 5 miles north*. **Castle**★ ⊘ with 16C tapestries.

CHÂTILLON-COLIGNY

Population 1 903
Michelin map 65 fold 2 or 238 fold 8

The town is situated on the banks of the river Loing and the Canal de Briare which are lined with old wash-houses. It was the birthplace, in 1519, of Admiral **Gaspard de Coligny**, a victim of the St Bartholomew's Day massacre in 1572. In 1937 a monument was erected (over the site of the room where he was born) in the park of the château, by Dutch subscription, to recall the marriage of Louise de Coligny, the admiral's daughter, to William the Silent, Prince of Orange. As the male line of the Coligny family died out in 1657, the Châtillon demesne reverted to the Montmorencys and then to the Montmorency-Luxembourg line.
In 1893 the French writer Colette married Willy (Henri Gauthier-Villars) at Châtillon-Coligny, where she lived with her brother Dr Robineau.

Château – When the Maréchal de Châtillon replaced his medieval castle with a magnificent Renaissance residence in the 16C, he retained the polygonal Romanesque keep (26m - 85ft high) built between 1180 and 1190 by the Count of Sancerre. The 12C keep and its underground access passages survived the Revolution, but all that remained of the 16C building were three huge terraces.

Not far from here are an old town gate and the church (16-17C) with a free-standing bell tower.

Musée ⊘ – The museum is in the 15C hospital. Besides portraits and literature on the history of the Coligny and Montmorency families, it contains a wonderful Louis-Philippe period pedestal table with Sèvres porcelain plaques which depict the Maréchal de Luxembourg and the Constables of Montmorency. A small room is devoted to local archaeology from the Iron Age to the Merovingian period.

CHÂTILLON-SUR-SEINE★

Population 6 862
Michelin map 65 fold 8 or 243 fold 2 – Facilities

The trim little town of Châtillon is set on the banks of the young Seine, which is joined here by the abundant waters of the river Douix, flowing from a resurgent spring. Sheep-breeding has for several centuries been the main source of wealth on the dry plateaux of the Châtillon region (Châtillonnais), and up to the 18C Châtillon was the centre of a very flourishing wool industry.

From one century to the next – A hundred years separate the two major events in the history of Châtillon.

In February 1814, while **Napoleon I** was defending every inch of the approaches to Paris, a peace congress was held in Châtillon between France and the countries allied against her (Austria, Russia, England and Prussia). Napoleon rejected the harsh conditions laid down, the fighting resumed, only to end soon afterwards with the downfall of his Empire.

In September 1914 French troops retreated in the face of a violent attack by the Germans. **Général Joffre**, Commander-in-Chief of the French armies, set up his headquarters at Châtillon-sur-Seine, where he issued his famous order of 6 September: "We are about to engage in a battle on which the fate of our country depends, and it is important to remind all ranks that the moment has passed for looking back..." The German advance was halted and the French counter-attack on the Marne became a great victory.

★ **Musée** ⊙ – This museum is in the Maison Philandrier, an attractive Renaissance building. There are several interesting Gallo-Roman exhibits – pottery, vases and statuettes – discovered in the 19C and early 20C during local excavations, particularly at Vertault *(20km - 12 miles west of Châtillon).* The pride of the museum is however the extraordinary archaeological find made in January 1953 at Mont Lassois near Vix.

N. Thibaut/HOAQUI

★★ **The Treasure of Vix** – The treasures were found in a 6C BC grave containing the remains of a woman: jewellery of inestimable value, the debris of a state chariot, countless gold and bronze items and a huge bronze vase (1.64m - 5ft high by 1.45m - 4.5ft wide and 208kg - 459lbs in weight). The rich decoration of the vase - sculpted frieze made of applied panels in high relief portraying a row of helmeted warriors and chariots and Gorgon's heads on the handles - reveals a highly developed art form influenced by the archaic Greek style. The showcases contain the order items found in the tomb

Bronze vase, Treasure of Vix

of the Gaulish princess: a massive golden diadem, bronze and silver goblets, wine jugs, bracelets and other jewellery.

★ **Source de la Douix** – The source of the river Douix is to be found in a spot of astonishing beauty, at the foot of a rocky escarpment (over 30m - 98ft high) set in lovely green scenery. This resurgent spring collects the waters of other small springs and infiltrations of the limestone plateau. The normal flow is 132 gallons a second but this can reach 660 gallons in flood periods. The promenade, laid out on a rocky platform, affords a view over the town, the valley and the swimming pool.

St-Vorles ⊙ – The church, built on a shaded terrace from which the view extends over the lower town and valley, dominates the Bourg district, city of the bishops which remained independent until the 16C.

The building probably dates from *c*991 and has retained one or two particularities of Carolingian architecture: double bell tower, double transept, upper chapel. The chancel has an archetypal Romanesque appearance, and in many places there are Lombard arches. The underground chapel of St-Bernard is where the miracle of lactation is supposed to have happened as the saint knelt before the statue of Notre-Dame-de-Toutes-Grâces. The north transept contains a Renaissance sculpture group of the Entombment.

Not far from the church are the ruins of the château and tower of Gissey. In the cemetery, you will find the tomb of Maréchal Marmont, who served under Napoleon and who was born at Châtillon.

Forêt de CHAUX★

Michelin map 170 fold 4 or 243 fold 18

This 20 000ha-49 420 acre forest, located between the rivers Doubs and Loue, is one of the largest forests in France. It originally belonged to the sovereigns, who hunted here; the nearby population also enjoyed extensive rights to the use of the land. These rights disappeared in the 19C, when the areas at the edge of the forest were given to the community *(forêts communales)*, while the central part (13 000ha-32 123 acres) became the property of the State *(forêt domaniale)*.

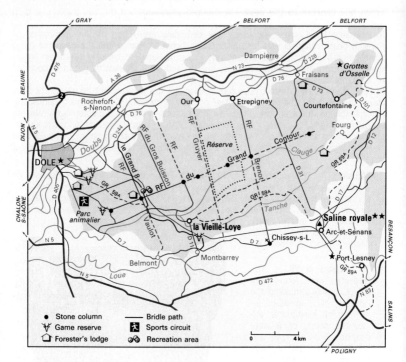

For centuries the forest has been a vital resource for the factories at its edge: salt works at **Salins** and **Arc-et-Senans**, forges at Fraisans, glass works at La Vieille Loye and so on. The previous layout of the forest in coppices no longer conforms to modern needs, and the forest is tending to be reorganised as regular forest. Oak predominates (60%), followed by beech (20%) and various deciduous (15%) and coniferous trees (5%).

A tourist zone has been established to the west of the forest, in order to protect the plants and wildlife of the rest of it. Facilities include a bridle path (the *bretelle du Grand 8*), forest footpaths, a keep-fit circuit, car parks and part of the long-distance footpath GR 59A from Dole to Arc-et-Senans, three game enclosures in which you can see various types of deer and wild boars and a nature reserve (88ha - 217 acres) where deer and wild boar roam at liberty. You can observe these from one of two raised observation posts, or by strolling around the forest. There is a 1 400ha - 34 594 acre game reserve *(closed to the public)* at the heart of the forest. The Grand Contour forest road between Dole and Fourg is marked with seven stone pillars, 4.5m - 177ft tall, which serve as milestones.

La Vieille Loye – The is the only village community in the forest. It used to be inhabited by woodcutters, who lived in huts, or *baraques*, at the centre of each forest area. A group of these woodcutters' huts, the "Baraques du 14", is currently being restored. A little further on are an old well and a communal village oven (the woodcutters used to have to pay the landlord a fee – *banalité* – to use the oven, which thus came to be called the *four banal*). In **Etrepigney** a *bacul* – small woodcutter's cottage – has been reconstructed, and in **Our** a 19C bread oven has been restored.

In the forest

STAND – A group of trees growing on a particular piece of land.

GROVE – A stand of trees grown from seed (unlike copses, where the new shoots grow from old stumps). A grove is called regular when the trees are obviously of about the same age.

ROUGH TIMBER – The trunk of a felled tree, stripped of its branches, ready to be turned into timber.

"ROND" – The French name for a point where forest roads meet. It may be named after a former forest warden or past event.

Abbaye de CÎTEAUX

Michelin map 65 south of fold 20 or 243 fold 16 –
14km - 9 miles east of Nuits-St-Georges.

Cîteaux ⏱, like Cluny *(qv)*, is an important centre in western Christendom. It was here, among the "cistels" or reeds, that Robert, Abbot of Molesme, founded the Order of Cistercians in 1098, an off-shoot of Cluny, which under the great driving force of St Bernard, who joined the community of Cîteaux in 1112 and eventually became abbot, spread its influence throughout the world.

The abbey of La Trappe *(see the Michelin Green Guide Normandy)*, which was attached to Cîteaux in 1147 and reformed in 1664, has given its name to several monasteries which joined the Strict Observance. They did not amalgamate however until 1898, following parallel courses. The Order is now divided into two branches; Cistercian monks who may devote themselves to a pastoral or intellectual life, such as teaching, and the more numerous Trappist monks who follow a strictly contemplative vocation.

During the Revolution, Cîteaux nearly perished in its entirety. The monks were expelled and did not return until 1898 (when the abbey was again proclaimed the mother house of the Order). The church containing the tombs of the first Dukes of Burgundy and of Philippe Pot (now in the Louvre, Paris) was completely destroyed. All that remains are relics of the library, faced with 15C enamelled bricks, which incorporates six arches of a Gothic cloister and a vaulted room on the first floor. There is also a handsome 18C building near the chapel and another late-17C building beside the river.

CLAMECY

Population 5 284
Michelin map 65 fold 15 or 238 fold 22 – Facilities

Clamecy is situated in the heart of the pretty country of the Vaux d'Yonne, junction point of the Morvan, the Nivernais and Lower Burgundy. The old town, with its narrow winding streets, is perched on a spur overlooking the confluence of the rivers Yonne and Beuvron. There are many pleasant walks along the hillsides.

Clamecy remains "the town of beautiful reflections and graceful hills" described by **Romain Rolland** (1866-1944), the French writer and philosopher, who is buried in the Nivernais not far from his native town.

Bethlehem in Burgundy – It is hard to understand why a bishopric existed at Clamecy, especially when there were already bishops at Auxerre, Nevers and Autun. One has to go back to the Crusades to find the answer.

Guillaume IV of Nevers, who left for Palestine in 1167, contracted the plague there and died at Acre in 1168. In his will he asked to be buried in Bethlehem and bequeathed to its bishops one of his properties in Clamecy, the hospital of Pantenor, on condition that it should be a refuge for the bishops of Bethlehem in the case of Palestine falling into the hands of the infidels.

When the Latin kingdom of Jerusalem fell, the bishop of Bethlehem took refuge at Clamecy in the domain bequeathed to the bishopric by Guillaume IV. From 1225 up to the French Revolution, fifty bishops succeeded each other at Clamecy. This episode is recalled in the dedication of the modern church (1927) of Our Lady of Bethlehem (Notre-Dame de Bethléem).

Corporations and brotherhoods – Corporations were once held in honour in Clamecy. Those of the butchers, tanners, cobblers, and apothecaries were prosperous. The Revolution put an end to these organisations but they later re-formed under the name of "Brotherhoods". There were seven of them, each of which carried the banner of its patron saint: St Crispin (cobblers), St Anne (carpenters), St Honoratus (bakers), St Fiacre (gardeners), St Nicholas (watermen and raftsmen), the Ascension (all trades using ladders), and St Eligius (blacksmiths). Only the brotherhoods of St Nicholas and St Eligius survive; they celebrate their corporative feast day each year.

Log floating – This method of moving timber, which goes back to the 16C, brought wealth to the river port of Clamecy for over three hundred years. It was first tried by Gilles Deffroissez and then organised on the river Cure by a rich timber merchant from Paris, **Jean Rouvet.**

The logs, cut in the forests of the Upper Morvan, were piled along the banks of the rivers and marked with their owners' signs. On an agreed day, the dams holding back the rivers were opened and the logs were thrown into the "flood" which carried them in a mass down to Clamecy. This was the floating of *bûches perdues* (free logs). All along the banks an army of workmen regulated the flow of logs as best they could.

At Clamecy, a dam stopped the wood, the timbermen with their long hooks "harpooned" the logs, dragging them from the water and putting them in piles according to their marks. This was known as the *triage*. In mid-March, at the time of the floodwater, immense rafts of wood, called "trains" and sometimes consisting of 7 063 cubic feet of wood, were sent by the Yonne and the Seine towards Montereau and Paris.

The building of the Nivernais Canal ended this method of transportation by "trains" with the introduction of barges. In 1923, the last "train" of wood left Clamecy.

Today all this logging activity has ended on both the Yonne and the Cure but Clamecy continued to operate the largest industrial charcoal factory in France until 1983 using supplies from the local forests.

SIGHTS

★ **St-Martin** ⊙ – The church was built between the end of the 12C and the beginning of the 16C. The rich Flamboyant decoration on the façade and the high platform tower contrasts with the austerity of the rest of the building. Episodes in the life of St Martin are illustrated on the arch stones over the door (damaged during the Revolution).

The interior reveals the rectangular plan and the square ambulatory. The rood screen was constructed by Viollet-le-Duc to counteract the bowing of certain pillars in the chancel. In the nave there are two small galleries: one in the triforium and one below the clerestory. The first chapel in the south aisle contains an early 16C triptych of the Crucifixion and two low-reliefs from the 16C rood screen (destroyed in 1773) which depict the Last Supper and the Entombment. The organ is by Cavaillé-Coll (1862).

Old houses – It is a pleasure to stroll through the picturesque streets looking for old houses. *From Place du 19-Août take Rue de la Tour and Rue Bourgeoise; turn right into Rue Romain-Rolland and Rue de la Monnaie. Take Rue du Grand-Marché and Place du Général-Sanglé-Ferrière to return to Place du 19-Août.*

Musée d'Art et d'histoire Romain-Rolland ⊙ – A bust of the writer stands in front of the museum. The museum is installed in the Duc de Bellegarde's mansion. Paintings include French and foreign works by Hell Bruegel, Pieter II, Vernet and Carracci. There is Nevers and Rouen pottery, ceremonial objects belonging to the corporations and an archaeological collection. One room is devoted to the floating of logs down the rivers while a second with a fine timberwork ceiling contains contemporary works. An underground passage leads to the Romain Rolland rooms which exhibit souvenirs of the author and various editions of his works.

Views of the town – The approach to Clamecy from Varzy (D 977) provides a glimpse of the old town with its red-brown roofs and the tower of the church of St Martin. From Quai des Moulins-de-la-Ville there is also an attractive view of the houses overlooking the mill-race. From Quai du Beuvron the picturesque Quai des Îles is visible.

The Bethlehem bridge, on which stands a tall statue in memory of the loggers, provides a good overall view of the town and its quays.

Upstream on the point overlooking the Nivernais Canal and the river stands a bronze bust of Jean Rouvet *(qv)*.

"L'homme du Futur" – Bronze statue of Caesar erected in 1987.

To find a pleasant country hotel
Consult the current **Michelin Red Guide France.**

Château du CLOS DE VOUGEOT★

Michelin map 65 fold 20 or 243 folds 15 and 16 – 5km – 3 miles north of Nuits-St-Georges – Local map under La CÔTE

The walled vineyard of Clos-de-Vougeot (50ha - 124 acres), owned by the abbey of Cîteaux from the 12C up to the French Revolution, is one of the most famous of La Côte.

Stendhal tells how Colonel Bisson, on his return from Italy, paraded his regiment in front of the château and made them present arms in honour of the celebrated vineyard. Since 1944 the château has been owned by the **Confrérie des Chevaliers du Tastevin** (brotherhood of the knights of the Tastevin). Ten years earlier in 1934 a small group of Burgundians met in a cellar in Nuits-St-Georges and decided to fight against the slump in wines and to form a society whose aim was to promote "the wines of France in general and, in particular, those of Burgundy". The Brotherhood was founded and its renown grew fast and spread throughout Europe and America.

Each year several chapter meetings of the order, well-known throughout the world, are held in the 12C Great Cellar of the château. Five hundred guests take part in these banquets, at the end of which the Grand Master and the Grand Chancellor, surrounded by high dignitaries of the Brotherhood, initiate new knights according to strictly observed rites that are based on the Divertissement in Molière's *Malade Imaginaire*.

During these plenary chapter meetings, the knights of the Tastevin celebrate the first of the "**Trois Glorieuses**" *(qv)* in the château on the eve of the sale of the wines of the Hospices of Beaune *(qv)*, which is held in the town on the following day. The Monday is devoted to the *Paulée de Meursault*.

Tour ⊙ – *Time: 30 min.* The château was built during the Renaissance period and restored in the 19C. The rooms visited include the Grand Cellier (12C cellar) where the "disnées" (banquets) and the ceremonies of the Order are held, the 16C kitchen with its huge chimney and ribbed vault supported by a single central pillar, and the monks' dorter which has a spectacular 14C pitched roof. *Presentation of slides (15 min) about the Confrérie des Chevaliers du Tastevin.*

The name of Cluny evokes the high point of medieval spirituality. The Order of Cluny exercised an immense influence on the religious, intellectual, political and artistic life of the West. Up to the time of the Revolution, each century left the mark of its style on Cluny. From 1798 to 1823 this centre of civilisation was ransacked but from the magnificence of what remains one can nevertheless get an idea of the majesty of the basilica. For a good overall view of the town, climb the Tour des Fromages.

CLUNY, LIGHT OF THE WORLD

The rise – The influence of the abbey of Cluny developed rapidly from the moment it was founded in the 10C, particularly through the founding of numerous daughter abbeys. In 1155 there were 460 monks resident in the abbey alone, and many young men from all over Europe flocked to this capital of learning. "You are the light of the world" said Pope Urban II, himself from Cluny, as were many other popes, to **St Hugh** in 1098. When St Hugh died in 1109, having begun the construction of the magnificient abbey church which **Peter the Venerable**, abbot from 1122 to 1156, was to finish, he let the abbey in a state of great prosperity.

The decline – Rich and powerful, the monks of Cluny slipped gradually into a worldly, luxurious way of life that was strongly condemned by **St Bernard** *(qv)*. He denounced the bishops who "cannot go four leagues from their house without a retinue of sixty horses and sometimes more... Will the light shine only if it is in a candelabrum of gold or silver?".

The 14C saw the decline of Cluny's influence and power. Its abbots divided their time between the abbey and Paris where, at the end of the 15C, Jacques d'Amboise rebuilt the mansion erected after 1330 by one of his predecessors, Pierre de Châlus. This private lodging (the Hôtel de Cluny) was often used by the kings of France, and gives an idea of the princely luxury with which the abbots of Cluny surrounded themselves.

Falling *in commendam* in the 16C, the rich abbey became nothing but a quarry for spoils. It was devastated during the Wars of Religion and the library was sacked.

Destruction – In 1790 the abbey was closed. Its desecration began when the Revolution was at its height. In September 1793, the local authority gave the order for the tombs to be demolished and sold as building material. In 1798 the buildings were sold to a property speculator from Mâcon who demolished the nave and sold off the magnificent abbey church bit by bit until by 1823 all that was left standing was what we see today.

★★ ANCIENNE ABBAYE ⊙ *time: 1 hour*

To visit the abbey, apply to the Musée Ochier.

Most of the abbey church of St Peter and St Paul, called Cluny III, was built between 1088 and 1130 by the abbots St Hugh and Peter the Venerable. The foundations of two previous 10C and 11C buildings have been uncovered, together with those of a Gallo-Roman villa, south of the 12C basilica on the site of the former cloisters in the southeast corner of the present cloisters.

Cluny III, symbol of the primacy of the Cluniac Order, then at its most powerful, was the largest Christian church (177m - 581ft long) until the reconstruction of St Peter's in Rome (186m - 610ft long). It consisted of a narthex, a nave and four aisles, two transepts, five belfries, two towers, 301 windows and 225 decorated stalls. The painted apsidal vault rested on a marble colonnade. It is difficult to imagine the full extent of the old building as only the south transepts remain standing.

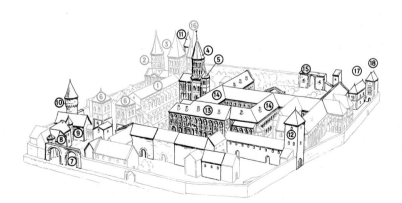

Cluny Abbey at the end of the 18C

1) Abbey Church of St Peter and St Paul – 2) Les Bisans Belfry – 3) Choir Belfry – 4) Holy Water Belfry – 5) Clock Tower – 6) The Barabans – 7) Main Gate – 8) Palace of Jean de Bourbon – 9) Palace of Jacques d'Amboise – 10) Fabry Tower – 11) Ronde Tower – 12) Cheese Tower – 13) Pope Gelasius' Façade – 14) Cloistral Ranges – 15) Garden Gate – 16) Lights Belfry – 17) Flour Store – 18) Mill Tower

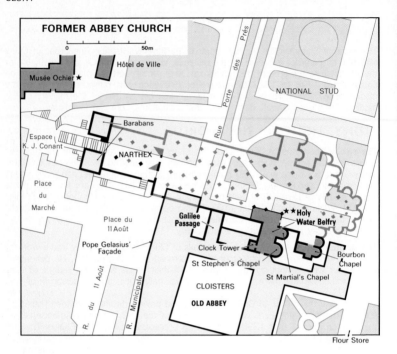

FORMER ABBEY CHURCH

0   50m

Hôtel de Ville

Musée Ochier ★

NATIONAL   STUD

Rue   Porte   des   Prés

Barabans

Espace
K. J. Conant

NARTHEX

Place
du
Marché

Place du
11 Août

Galilee
Passage

★★ Holy
Water Belfry

Pope Gelasius'
Façade

Clock Tower

Bourbon
Chapel

Rue   Municipale

R.   du   11 Août

St Stephen's Chapel

St Martial's Chapel

CLOISTERS

OLD ABBEY

R. Municipale

Flour Store

Narthex – The site of the narthex is now bisected by Rue Kenneth J Conant. During excavations in 1949 the base of the south end of the façade was uncovered, together with the footings of the doorway which was flanked by the square Barabans towers of which only the foundations survive. Subsequently the south aisle of the narthex was uncovered revealing a wall of uniform construction with pilasters attached to semi-columns.

The long Gothic façade (restored) in Place du 11-Août is named after Pope Gelasius who died at Cluny in 1119. By standing well back one can see the belfry and the high clock tower. To the rear are the Hugh stables.

Cloisters – The 18C monastic buildings form a harmonious group enclosing the vast cloisters; two great flights of stone steps with wrought-iron railings occupy two corners. There is a handsome sundial in the garth.

Galilee Passage – The 11C passage, which was used by the great Benedictine processions, linked the Galilee (a covered porch) of Cluny II with the south aisle of the great church of Cluny III.

Traces of the Church of St Peter and St Paul – From the dimensions of the **south transepts** it is possible to calculate the audacious size of the whole basilica. Its height (30m - 98ft under the barrel vaulting, 32m - 105ft under the dome) is exceptional in Romanesque architecture. The church consisted of three bays; the central bay, surmounted by an octagonal cupola on squinches, supports the handsome **Holy Water Belfry** (clocher de l'Eau-Bénite)★★. St Stephen's Chapel (St-Etienne) is Romanesque; St Martial's Chapel dates from the 14C. The right arm of the smaller transept contains the Bourbon Chapel with its late-15C Gothic architecture and a Romanesque apse. The contrast between them emphasises the transition from Romanesque to late-Gothic art.

Monastic buildings – The buildings, which house the School of Arts and Crafts, were nicknamed Little Versailles owing to the elegant classical east façade.

Flour Store (F) – The storehouse (54m - 177ft long) was built in the late 13C against the early-13C Mill Tower (tour du Moulin); in the 18C it was truncated (by about 20m - 65ft) to reveal the south end of the façade of the cloister building overlooking the gardens.

The low storeroom with its two ranges of ogive vaulting houses sculptures including a doorway with recessed arches from Pope Gelasius' palace *(see above)*.

The **high chamber,** with its beautiful oak roof, makes an effective setting for various pieces of sculpture from the abbey. The very fine **capitals** *(photograph right)* and column shafts saved from the ruins of the chancel of the

A. Wolf/EXPLORER

Capital from the chancel, Cluny abbey

abbey church are exhibited by means of a scale model of the chancel: the eight capitals on their columns are set in a semi-circle round the old Pyrenean marble altar consecrated by Urban II in 1095. They are the first examples of the Burgundian Romanesque sculpture which was to blossom in Vézelay, Autun and Saulieu. The two models, of the great doorway and of the apse of the basilica, were designed by Professeur Conant, the archaeologist who directed the excavations from 1928 to 1950.

ADDITIONAL SIGHTS

★ **Musée Ochier** (**M**) ⊘ – This museum is in the former abbey palace, a gracious building of the 15C, built by Abbot Jean de Bourbon, and is contemporary with the Cluny Mansion in Paris.

Pieces of the great doorway of the abbey church and capitals from the narthex, found during excavations carried out by the American archaeologist K. J. Conant are on display together with some outstanding works of lay sculpture. The rooms of the palace, complete with their chimney-pieces, house a certain number of items that belonged to the abbey (lectern, Paschal candlestick, chests) as well as 4 000 books, including the works of Prud'hon, who was born at Cluny. The cellars are devoted to the Gallo-Roman collections of the museum. There is also a centre for Cluniac studies.

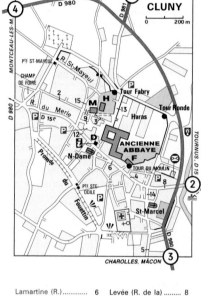

Hôtel de ville (**H**) – The town hall now occupies the building erected for Abbots Jacques and Geoffroy d'Amboise at the end of the 15C and beginning of the 16C. The garden front has an original decoration in the Italian Renaissance style.

Tour des Fromages (**D**) ⊘ – From the top (120 steps) of this curiously named 11C tower ("cheese tower") there is a good view of Cluny: the abbey, the Holy Water Belfry, the flour store and adjoining mill tower, the belfry of St-Marcel and Notre-Dame.

Lamartine (R.)	6	Levée (R. de la)	8
		Marché (Pl. du)	9
Avril (R. d')	2	Mercière (R.)	12
Conant (Espace K.-J.)	3	Porte-des-Prés (R.)	13
Filaterie (R.)	4	Prud'hon (R.)	14
Gaulle (Av. Ch. de)	5	République (R.)	15

D	Tour des Fromages	**H**	Hôtel de Ville
F	Farinier	**M**	Musée Ochier

Tour Fabry and Tour Ronde – The Fabry tower (1347) with its pepperpot roof is visible from the garden near the town hall, and the older Ronde tower can be seen from the Fabry tower.

Haras National ⊘ – In 1806 Napoleon I decided to establish 23 studs. The one at Cluny was constructed with the stones of the neighbouring abbey. The various stable buildings house about sixty stallions most of which are away during the breeding season (March to mid-July) at Burgundy's nine subsidiary stables.

Romanesque houses – Cluny has preserved fine Romanesque dwellings: at no 25 Rue de la République, a 12C house, and no 6 Rue d'Avril, the 13C mint (restored).

St-Marcel ⊘ – This church has a fine octagonal Romanesque **belfry**★ of three storeys, topped by a graceful 15C polygonal brick spire (42m - 138ft high). There is an excellent view of the belfry and the apse from the road (D 980).

Notre-Dame – The square in front of the church has an 18C fountain and old houses. The church, built shortly after 1100, was altered and enlarged in the Gothic period. It was originally preceded by a narthex of which only the flagging remains. The 13C doorway is badly weathered.
The interior is a good example of Cluniac architecture. The lantern tower has carved brackets. The stalls and panelling date from 1644. The stained glass in the choir is modern.

Promenade du Fouettin – Formerly part of the town's fortifications this promenade is bordered by centuries-old lime trees. There is a good view over the town and the Grosne Valley from the terrace at the southern end of the promenade.

▶▶ **Butte de Suin**★ – *About 20km - 12 miles west of Cluny.* **Panorama**★★.

Cirque de CONSOLATION★★

Michelin map 66 south of fold 17 or 243 fold 21 (13km – 8 miles north of Morteau)

The natural amphitheatre from which the Dessoubre, and its tributary the Lançot, spring takes the form of a double semicircle. Its rocky crags, partly wooded with ever-greens and beeches, tower majestically to over 300m - 984ft.

In one semicircle, the Dessoubre takes its source in a limestone wall (behind the Hôtel Joliot) and immediately forms a waterfall. The source of the Lançot is in the other semicircle. It appears in the park of Notre-Dame-de-Consolation, beneath a cave; when the water level rises, the river spills out of the cave itself.

★VALLÉE DU DESSOUBRE

From St-Hippolyte to the park of Notre-Dame-de-Consolation

33km - 21 miles – allow 45 min

St-Hippolyte – This town occupies a pretty **site★** on the confluence of the Doubs and the Dessoubre.

Leave St-Hippolyte on the D 39 heading southwest.

The D 39 follows the course of the Dessoubre quite closely, going through the villages of Pont-Neuf and Rosureux. The peaceful river valley runs between wooded slopes (fir, oak and ash; note several sawmills and furniture factories) crowned by limestone cliffs. Along the bottom of this charming valley, the river flows from pool to pool, sometimes over a bed of white pebbles. On either side of it stretch meadows, dappled by shade in places.

Gigot – The Dessoubre is joined here by a small tributary, the Reverotte, which wiggles its way west upstream of the village along a narrow steep-sided valley which is known as the **Défilé des Épais Rochers** ("rocky gorge").

After Gigot, the D 39 carries on along the banks of the Dessoubre, making a very pleasant drive indeed amidst woods and meadows with the river itself bubbling alongside. In rainy weather, the peaceful little river is transformed into a foaming torrent.

Notre-Dame-de-Conso-lation – This former Mini-mist convent was a small seminary until 1981, and now serves as a religious centre. The chapel is in the Jesuit baroque style and contains a beautiful marble mausoleum and an 18C carved wooden pulpit.

The **park** *(allow about an hour)* is a pretty place for a walk through fields dotted with trees, rocks, water-falls, springs (source du Lançot, source Noire and Source du Tabouret) and the Val Noir ("black valley").

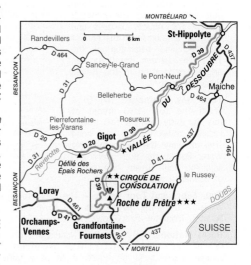

★★★ LA ROCHE DU PRÊTRE

La Roche du Prêtre – Grandfontaine-Fournets – Orchamps-Vennes – Loray

La Roche du Prêtre – This famous viewpoint is located on the edge of a cliff and offers an unforgettable view of the Cirque de Conso-lation and its surroundings. The summit towers 350m - 1 148ft above the fresh, green, wooded amphi-theatre in which the Des-soubre rises. Here and there craggy rocks break through the greenery. It makes a romantic scene of solitude and rugged gran-deur, in sharp contrast to the cosier landscape of the plateau covered with green pastures and dotted with farms.

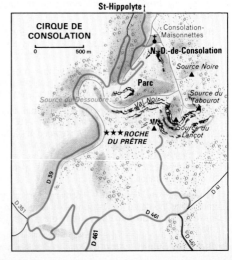

Grandfontaine-Fournets – This hamlet at the heart of the Haut-Doubs is typical of the Jura region. It is home to the Ferme du Montagnon, a farm dating from the 17 and 18C which contains evidence of age-old farming traditions. It still has its **smoking loft★** *(tuyé)* where meat, hams, bacon and sausages are cured (locally cured products are on sale in the old stables). The way of life on the farm in days gone by is evoked by furniture of the period.

Orchamps-Vennes – Facilities. This sizeable mountain village occupies a high plateau set back from the D 461 from Besançon to Morteau. Its low-roofed houses are scattered amidst a charming setting of green meadows and trees. Most of the village inhabitants earn their living in the timber, clock-making and dairy industries.

Église St-Pierre-St-Paul – This 16C church has a 19C belfry porch. There are some interesting tombstones in front of the church. Inside, there is a lovely 17C pulpit in carved oak attributed to Étienne Monnot from Orchamps-Vennes, who also executed the woodwork in the chancel. The south aisle contains an 18C carved font and, in a niche by the entrance to the chancel, a 16C polychrome wooden statue (restored) of St Anne teaching the Virgin Mary. A Stations of the Cross by Comtois sculptor Gabriel Saury in 1947 begins at the far end of the north aisle.

Loray – This village contains several houses typical of the region and a neo-Romanesque church with handsome 18C furnishings inside. Not far off stands a 12C **calvary** the upright of which (over 4m - 13ft tall) features a life-size statue of a figure holding a human head in its hand. Higher up are the Virgin Mary, Christ and St Michael overcoming the dragon. At the centre of the village square is a pretty, monumental 19C **fountain-washhouse** with fluted columns surmounted by Doric capitals.

Château de CORMATIN★★

Michelin map 69 fold 19 or 243 fold 39 – 13km – 8 miles to the north of Cluny – Local map under MÂCONNAIS

Cormatin was built in the aftermath of the Wars of Religion between 1605 and 1616 by the Governor of Chalon, Antoine du Blé d'Huxelles. The architecture is understated in the style of Henri IV and was probably designed by Jacques II Androuet du Cerceau, architect to the king. Originally the château consisted of three wings round three sides of a courtyard; the south wing collapsed in 1815 during conversion to a cloth weaving factory. The façades are in the "French rustic" style recommended by du Cerceau: absence of the classical orders (except for the two monumental doors in the courtyard), high stone base, matching quoins and window surrounds. The broad moat and the impressive cornerpavilions with watch-towers and cannon suggest a defensive concept confirmed by traces of a rampart (demolished in the late 17C) which closed the fourth side of the courtyard.

Interior ⊘ – The north wing contains a magnificent grand **staircase** in an open well (1610); the straight flights of steps, flanked by vigorous balusters, open directly on to the central well. It is the oldest and largest stair of this kind (25m - 82ft high), successor to the Renaissance stairs in two flights separated by a wall.

Cabinet de Sainte-Cécile

The sumptuous Louis XIII décor in this wing is the work of Marquess Jacques du Blé (son of Antoine) and his wife Claude Phélypeaux, who were close friends of Marie de' Medici and the literary salon of the Précieuses. They intended their summer house to reflect the sophistication of Parisian fashion, so used the artists and craftsmen who had worked for the Queen at the Luxembourg Palace. The gilt, the paintings and sculptures which cover the walls and ceilings are proof of an informed mannerism; each painting has an allegorical meaning reaffirmed in the symbolism of the decorative motifs and the colours used for the panelling.

The ante-chamber of the Marchioness (daughter and sister of Government ministers), which was created in the middle of the Protestant revolt (1627-8), is in homage to Louis XIII who is represented above the chimneypiece: the red panelling (colour of authority) celebrates the activites and virtues of the King. The Marchioness' room has a magnificent French ceiling in gold and blue, symbol of fidelity; the great painting of Venus and Vulcan, a work of the second Fontainebleau school, symbolises love and the baskets of fruit and flowers on the woodwork represent plenty. One of the oldest "heavenly" ceilings, made fashionable by Marie de' Medici, adorns the landscape room. The sumptuous baroque décor in the **Cabinet de Ste-Cécile★★★**, Jacques du Blé's tiny study, is dominated by very blue lapis-lazuli and rich gilding which reflected the glow of the candlelight so necessary in a study; the figure of St Cecilia accompanied by the cardinal virtues represents moral harmony. Also on view are the kitchens and the Neapolitan bed of Cécile Sorel in a room in the west wing which was refurbished at the turn of the 19C.

Park – There are fine views of the château from the grounds which have been laid out with various features: a box maze with a belvedere-aviary, a pond, an English garden, a grass theatre, a vegetable garden and a canal (200m - 219yds long).

La CÔTE★★

Michelin maps 65 fold 20 and 69 folds 9 and 10 or 243 folds 15, 16 and 27

The celebrated vineyards of the Côte d'Or (Golden Hillside) stretch from Dijon to Santenay (60km - 37 miles) forming a triumphal way for those who love good things to eat and drink. Each place bears a famous name; each village and each hillside has a claim to glory. This is the region of the great wines.

THE GREAT WINES OF BURGUNDY

Natural conditions – The Côte is formed by the eastern edge of "La Montagne", whose rectangular shape is cut by transverse combes in the same way as the blind valleys of the Jura vineyards. Between Dijon and Nuits-St-Georges, the cliffs and rocks of these combes are a favourite spot for the rock-climbers of Dijon. The vineyards cover about 8 000ha - 19 768 acres in the Côte d'Or and 10 000ha - 24 711 acres in the Saône-et-Loire and are planted with first-quality vines (Pinot Noir and Chardonnay). They are set in terraces overlooking the plain of the Saône at an altitude varying from 200m to 300m – 686ft to 984ft.

While the summits of the hills are covered with box-trees or sometimes crowned with small woods, giving a Mediterranean appearance, the vineyards occupy the limestone slopes, well exposed to the morning sun – the best – and sheltered from cold winds. This position makes the grapes extremely sweet which in turn gives the wine a high alcohol content. Only the southern and eastern-facing sides of the combes are planted with vines; the northern slopes are often covered with woods. In addition, the slopes facilitate drainage; vines like dry soil and the slope is therefore an important factor in the quality of the grape-harvest.

The great wines – For the greater part of its run through the vineyards the N 74 separates the "noble" wines from the others. The great wines are generally on terraces halfway up the slopes. The high-quality Pinot Noir, king of Burgundian vines, is the only plant for the great red wines. The great white wines are produced from the Chardonnay and Pinot Blanc vines. After the crisis brought about by the phylloxera aphid at the end of the 19C, the vineyards were entirely replanted with American rootstocks, onto which have been grafted the historic Burgundy vines.

South of the Dijon vineyards the Côte d'Or is divided into two parts, the Côte de Nuits and the Côte de Beaune. The wines of both are well known; those of Nuits for robustness; those of Beaune for their delicacy.

Each district has its own hinterland with vineyards higher up in the hills, where the wines are known as Hautes-Côtes, and although they do not pretend to be "noble", in a good year they may give pleasure to the most knowledgeable connoisseur. The **Côte de Nuits** extends from the village of Fixin to the southern limit of the Corgoloin region. Its production is almost entirely of great red wines. Its most famous wines, from north to south, are: Chambertin, Musigny, Clos-Vougeot, and Romanée-Conti. Particularly rich and full-bodied, the wines take eight to ten years to acquire their unequalled qualities of body and bouquet.

The **Côte de Beaune** extends from the north of Aloxe-Corton to Santenay and produces great white wines as well as excellent red wines. These wines mature more rapidly than those of the Côte de Nuits but grow old earlier. Its principal wines are: Corton, Volnay, Pommard and Beaune for the red wines, less full-bodied than those of the Nuits but very smooth, and Meursault and Montrachet for the rich and fruity whites. The great wines, enhanced by delicious cooking, make the Côte a celebrated roadway in the world of gourmets and connoisseurs.

★★ THE VINEYARDS

① From Dijon to Nuits-St-Georges

32km - 20 miles – about 1 hours 30min – local map overleaf

The road goes along the foot of hillsides covered with vines and passes through villages with world-famous names.

★★★ Dijon – *Time: 4 hours. See DIJON.*

Leave Dijon on the D 122, known as the "Route des Grands Crus" (Road of the Great Wines).

Chenôve – The Clos du Roi and Clos du Chapitre recall the former owners of these vineyards, the Dukes of Burgundy and the canons of Autun. The great wine cellar of the Dukes of Burgundy, **Cuverie des ducs de Bourgogne** ⊘ contains two magnificent 13C presses (some say they are early-15C replicas) which were capable of pressing in one go the contents of 100 wine casks.
Nearby *(on leaving the cellar turn left and first right)* there are picturesque vine-growers' houses, some dating from the 13C, in Rue Jules-Blaizet.

Marsannay-la-Côte – Part of the Côte de Nuits, Marsannay produces popular *rosé* wines, obtained from the black Pinot grapes.

Fixin – This is a famous wine-growing village which some believe produces wines among the best of the Côte de Nuits *appellation*. In the **Parc Noisot** ⊘ *(in the centre of town take the Rue Noisot for 500m to a car park and then go on foot via the Allée des Pins, which is signposted)* there is a memorial sculpture to Napoleon by **Rude**, *Éveil de Napoléon à l'Immortalité*, donated by a loyal officer from the Imperial Guard.

Brochon – Brochon, which is on the edge of the Côte de Nuits, produces excellent wines. The **château** was built in 1900 by the poet Stephen Liégeard who coined the phrase Côte d'Azur (the Azure Coast) for the Provençal coast and Mediterranean sunshine. The name has stuck long after his poet has faded into obscurity, together with his poem which was honoured by the French Academy.

Gevrey-Chambertin – *See GEVREY-CHAMBERTIN.*

At Morey-St-Denis rejoin the N 74.

Vougeot – Its red wines are highly valued.

★ Château du Clos de Vougeot – *See Château du CLOS DE VOUGEOT.*

Chambolle-Musigny – The road from Chambolle-Musigny to Curley (northwest) passes through a gorge, Combe Ambin, to a charming beauty spot: a small chapel stands at the foot of a rocky promontory overlooking the junction of two wooded ravines.

Reulle-Vergy – *8km - 5 miles west of Chambolle-Musigny.*
This village has a 12C church and a curious town hall, built on top of a washing house. Opposite the town hall a barn now houses a **museum** ⊘ describing the arts and traditions associated with the Hautes Côtes wines. Themes covered include the day-to-day work in the vineyards, archaeology (items from the Bronze Age, the Gallo-Roman and medieval periods), the flora and fauna, daily life in the 19C (costumes and everyday objects) and the history of the region (evocation of the medieval poem of the Mistress of Vergy).

From l'Etang-Vergy take the D 35 and D 25 south and east to Nuits-St-Georges.

Nuits-St-Georges – *See NUITS-ST-GEORGES.*

Vosne-Romanée – *2km - 1.25 miles north of Nuits-St-Georges.*
These vineyards produce only red wines of the highest quality; they are choice and delicate. Among the various sections *(climats)* of this vineyard, Romanée-Conti and de Richebourg have a worldwide reputation.

② From Nuits-St-Georges to Chagny

115km - 72 miles – about 4 hours – local map overleaf

The itinerary follows in part the N 74 and also some of the picturesque roads of the Burgundian part of "La Montagne".

Nuits-St-Georges – *See NUITS-ST-GEORGES.*

Comblanchien – *4.5km – 2.5 miles south of Nuits-St-Georges.*
This township is known for the limestone that is quarried from its surrounding cliffs. The stone is very beautiful and is often used for facings, replacing the more costly marble.

South of Comblanchien turn right to Arcenant, 9km - 5.5 miles northwest.

Beyond Arcenant raspberry and blackcurrant bushes border the road. During a fairly stiff climb, there is a good view over Arcenant, the arable land and the deep gorge of the **Combe Pertuis.**

From Bruant take the D 25, D 18 and D 2 south to Bouilland.

During the long run downhill, there is a view of **Bouilland** and its circle of wooded hills.

From Bouilland take the D 2 south.

Beyond the hamlet of La Forge the road is dominated on the left by the rocky escarpments crowning the hill and on the right by the rock known as the pierced rock *(roche percée)*. Soon after there is the cirque of the Combe à la Vieille on the left. The road then follows the fresh, green and narrow valley of the Rhoin, between wooded slopes. Shortly before **Savigny-lès-Beaune** the valley opens out.

From Savigny take the minor road west to Aloxe-Corton (3km - 2 miles).

Aloxe-Corton – This village (pronounced Alosse), the northernmost village of Côte de Beaune, is of ancient origin. The Emperor Charlemagne owned vineyards here and Corton-Charlemagne, "a white wine of great character", recalls this fact. Red wines are produced almost exclusively at Aloxe-Corton, "the firmest and most forward wines of the Côte de Beaune". The bouquet improves with age and the wine remains full-bodied and cordial.

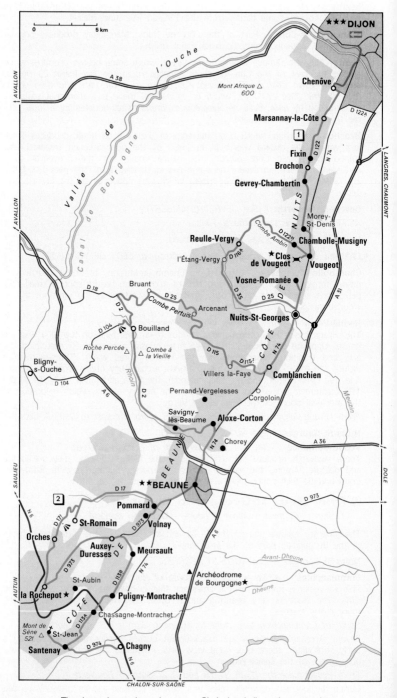

The vineyards are shown in green – Black dots indicate the great wines

★★ Beaune – *Time: 1 hour. See BEAUNE.*

Pommard – *3km - 2 miles southwest of Beaune on the N 74 and D 973.*
The fairly large village of Pommard takes its name from an ancient temple dedi-cated to Pomona, the goddess of fruits and gardens. These vineyards of the Côte de Beaune produce red wines that are "firm, dark red, full of candour and worth keeping". These wines were greatly appreciated by Ronsard, Henri IV, Louis XV and Victor Hugo.

Volnay – *1km - half a mile southwest of Pommard on the D 973.* Its red wines have a delicate bouquet and a silky taste. It is said that King Louis XI was fond of them. From the esplanade, below the small 14C church with its squat belfry, there is a good view of the vineyards.
Return to Pommard; take the D 17 west to St-Romain (9km - 5.5 miles).
The road follows the green valley floor between wooded slopes.

St-Romain – This township is made up of two quite distinct parts: St-Romain-le-Haut perched high on a limestone spur, surrounded by a semicircle of cliffs, with the ruins of its 12C-13C castle (short visitor trail marked out) on the southern edge. Lower down in St-Romain-le-Bas stands the mairie (town hall), which contains displays on **local archaeology and ethnology** ⊘.
North of St-Romain turn left into the D 17¹ to Orches and La Rochepot.
As the road approaches **Orches**, in its attractive rocky site, there is a fine **view**★ of St-Romain, Auxey, Meursault and the Saône Valley.

★ La Rochepot – *See La ROCHEPOT.*
From La Rochepot take the D 973 northeast skirting the château.
The road follows a narrow valley and prior to Melin crosses a series of lime-stone escarpments worn by erosion.

Auxey-Duresses – This village is set in a deep combe leading to La Rochepot and its château. The vineyards of Auxey-Duresses produce fine red and white wines which, before the law of nomenclature, were sold as Volnay and Pommard. The church, with its fine 16C triptych, is worth a visit.

Meursault – *2km - 1.25 miles southeast of Auxey.*
This little town, dominated by the beautiful Gothic stone spire of its church, is proud of producing both red and white wines of high quality. It owes its name to a valley that clearly divides the Côte de Meursault from the Côte de Beaune. This valley, known as the Rat's Leap *(Saut du Rat – in Latin* Muris Saltus*)* is said to have given the present name of Meursault. Its white wines, with those of Puligny and Chassagne-Montrachet, are considered "the best white wines in the world". They have a slight taste of hazelnuts and an aroma of ripe grapes which gives a freshness to the subtle qualities of taste and bouquet.
Meursault wines have the rarity of being both dry and mellow at the same time. The *Paulée de Meursault*, last of the **"Trois Glorieuses"** *(qv)*, is a well-known local fête. At the end of the banquet, to which each guest brings bottles of his wine, a literary prize is awarded. The happy laureate receives a hundred bottles of Meursault.

Puligny-Montrachet – *4km - 2.5 miles south of Meursault.*
The white wines of Puligny-Montrachet, like those of Meursault, are excellent. Alexandre Dumas, connoisseur of note, declared that this wine "should be drunk while kneeling with the head uncovered".
The red wines of this old walled vineyard are full-bodied and have subtle quali-ties of taste and bouquet.

Santenay – *6km - 3.5 miles southeast of Puligny.*
The three localities that go to make up Santenay – Santenay-le-Bas, Santenay-le-Haut and St-Jean – are spread along the banks of the river Dheune as far as the first slopes of Mount Sène or the Montagne des Trois-Croix. Santenay derives its reputation not only from its vast vineyards but also from the local mineral water, which contains lithia and is very salty. The church of **St-Jean** ⊘ stands at the foot of a semicircle of cliffs; a wooden porch protects the round-headed doorway which opens into the 13C nave; the 15C vaulting in the chancel contains an unusually high number of ribs. Two 15C painted wooden statues of St Mar-tin and St Roch contrast with a 17C Virgin and dragon by the local sculptor J Bésullier.

Chagny – *4.5km - 3 miles east of Santenay.*
This commercial and industrial town makes a good place to stop for a gastro-nomic meal. There are several interesting buildings.

Help us in our constant task of keeping up to date.
Send your comments and suggestions to
Michelin Tyre PLC
Tourism Department
The Edward Hyde Building
38 Clarendon Road
WATFORD - Herts WD1 1SX

Le CREUSOT

Population 28 909
Michelin map 69 fold 8 or 243 fold 26
Town plan in the current Michelin Red Guide France

The rural setting of Le Creusot, on the northeast border of the Massif Central, contrasts with its industrial character. The blast-furnaces and rows of brick-built workers' houses have been replaced by modern industrial plants.

LE CREUSOT BASIN

The basin is a natural depression containing the towns of Montceau-les-Mines, Blanzy, Montchanin and Le Creusot, from which it takes its name. It is an important passage, used by the Dheune and Bourbince rivers and now by the road, canal and railway, linking the Saône and the Loire river valleys.

Development of industry – Although iron ore was mined in the Middle Ages in the region of Couches, the discovery of vast coal deposits at Épinac, Le Creusot and Blanzy in the 17C marked the real origin of the industrial development of the whole area. Mining was pushed to its maximum during the last century to supply fuel for the growing steel industry of Le Creusot. Today, mining operations continue at the Blanzy pit to supply the thermal power station, Lucy III.
While certain localities, such as Couches and Perrecy-les-Forges, have seen their activity decline, Le Creusot has become in the 20C the focal point of the whole basin.

The Canal du Centre – In this hilly region, the canal is a vital artery, serving different industrial centres. The building of a canal was first envisaged at the start of the 17C but it was only in 1794, when Le Creusot began to develop as a steel town, that it was opened for navigation. From Chalon, where it leaves the Saône, to Digoin where it joins the Loire, the canal goes up the valley of the Dheune and then down that of the Bourbince.
Various industries are established along the banks of the canal. Although the canal's industrial importance has declined, the waterway now provides good possibilities for leisure cruising.

Promising beginnings – At the start of the 16C the inhabitants of Le Creusot began to exploit the outcrops of coal and to trade with the surrounding localities. The scarcity of coal-bearing deposits in Le Creusot itself forced the industries of this town into processing the primary materials, extracted from the iron mines and the quarries of the region, into finished products.
Industrial exploitation really began in 1769 and by 1782, "The Royal Foundry of Montcenis" consisted of a foundry and blast-furnaces.

City of steel – In 1836 **Joseph-Eugène Schneider**, forge-master at Bazeilles, and his brother, **Adolphe Schneider**, set themselves up at Le Creusot, at that time a little township of 3 000 inhabitants. The rapid expansion of the Schneider works was to contribute to the wealth of the town, which from that date increased its population tenfold. The construction of steam and marine engines began the following year. In 1843 the invention of the power hammer by one of the factory's engineers, M. Bourdon, resulted in the forging of heavy castings. From that time, besides products for the railways, the factories produced equipment for the great electrical power stations, for ports, factories and mines, etc.
About 1867 steel made its appearance and was used at that time mainly for sheets of armour plating and guns. The iron ore originally came from the Couches region. In 1924 the old power hammer was superseded by the great furnace (forge) equipped with 7 500 - 11 300 tonnes hydraulic presses. In 1949 the Schneider works were reconstituted as the Société des Forges et Ateliers du Creusot with factories in the communes of Le Creusot, Le Breuil, Torcy and Montchanin. In 1970 the company amalgamated with the Compagnie des Ateliers et Forges de la Loire to form Creusot-Loire. Following the European steel crisis, Creusot-Loire filed for bankruptcy in 1984. The works were acquired by CLI, a subsidiary of Usinor-Sacilor, by Alsthom Creusot Rail and by Framatome. The Creusot factory has also diversified with the establishment of SNECMA, the development of the textile sector and the creation of a nucleus of technological skills directed to high energy and electronics.

The industrial heritage and tourism – In a region rich in reminders of its industrial past (mines, foundries, factories, workshops and workers' settlements) there is now an effort to exploit this industrial heritage for tourism. The towns of Le Creusot and Montceau-les-Mines founded an association in 1983, which organises guided tours under the direction of former employees of Creusot-Loire or the Blanzy mines. There is also a **tourist train service** leaving from Combes station, where waste products from the Schneider factories used to be sent. Its route takes it along at the foot of Gros Chaillot hill, giving views of Mont Beuvray, the Mesvrin valley, and further south Le Creusot.

SIGHTS

Marteau-Pilon (Power hammer) – The 100 tonne power hammer, standing on the southern outskirts, symbolises the paramount importance of industry to the town. This particular machine was in use from 1876 until 1924 and enjoys a worldwide reputation.

Place Schneider – A statue of Eugène Schneider, one of the founders of the industrial empire, stands at the centre of the square. On the east side at the edge of a vast wooded park stands the Château de la Verrerie.

Château de la Verrerie ⊙ – The former home of the Schneider family was acquired by the municipality in 1971 and now houses a specialist **museum** and the headquarters of the Communauté Urbaine le Creusot-Montceau which covers 16 communes. The château is named after a glass factory, making crystal ware for Queen Marie-Antoinette, which was transferred in 1787 from Sèvres to Le Creusot where it prospered for many years; in 1833, when it was bought by the St-Louis et Baccarat group, the works in Le Creusot were closed down.

In front of the château and in contrast with its dazzling white façade stand two huge conical glass-firing ovens. They

Le Creusot – Marteau-Pilon

were converted in 1905, one into a delightful **miniature theatre** and the other into a chapel which is now used for temporary exhibitions. A collection of 18C and 19C bronze cannon is arrayed in the courtyard.

Nearby is the **Technical Centre** which displays examples of the metallurgical and mechanical activities of Le Creusot (articles, models, paintings).

The specialist museum **(écomusée** ⊙) is devoted to two themes: the history of Le Creusot, its locality and inhabitants (model of the metal works at the end of the 19C); the history of the Schneider dynasty and its achievements.

Promenade des Crêtes – *Follow Rue Jean-Jaurès, Rue de Longwy, the D 28 (towards Marmagne) and a sharp righthand turn to join this scenic mountain road.* The switch-back road overlooks the Le Creusot basin. A clearing in the woods *(viewing table)* provides an overall view of the town and its surroundings. Further on another viewpoint reveals the extent of the old Schneider works and the central position, in this context, of the Château de la Verrerie.

►► **Montceau-les-Mines** – *15km - 9 miles south.* **Fossil museum** ⊙ and **Blanzy Mine** ⊙.

►► **Signal d'Uchon**★ – *18km - 11 miles west.* Beacon from the summit of which there is an extensive view of the Morvan.

CUISEAUX

Population 1 779
Michelin map 170 fold 13 or 243 fold 41

Cuiseaux lies on the border between Burgundy and the Franche-Comté. It is set in a peaceful, green agricultural landscape and is well-known for its cooked meats and sausages *(charcuterie)*. The town was fortified in the 12C. There are a few vestiges left of the old fortifications, which originally included 36 towers. The area around Cuiseaux lends itself to pleasant walks in the forest or the countryside.

Church – The chancel is interesting; in addition to the 16C polychrome wood statues, there are two Italian primitive paintings to be seen. The lovely 15C carved wooden stalls further enhance the beauty of the interior. There is a highly venerated 13C black statue of the Virgin Mary in the north aisle.

Maison de la vigne et du vigneron ⊙ – This wine museum, part of the Écomusée de la Bresse bourguignonne at Pierre-de-Bresse *(qv)*, is inside the fortifications of the château which once belonged to the Princes of Orange. It recalls that Cuiseaux was an important winegrowing region until the end of the 19C. The museum has a display on Jura vineyards, along with winegrowers' tools and equipment and the reconstruction of a wine-grower's room ("chambre à feu").

►► **Gigny** – *15km - 9 miles southeast.* Beautiful **abbey church.**

Each year
the Michelin Red Guide France
presents a wealth of up-to-date information in a compact form.
It is the ideal companion for a holiday,
a long weekend or a business trip.

DIJON ★★★

Pop 146 703
Michelin map 65 fold 20 or 243 fold 16 – Facilities –
Local map under La CÔTE

Surrounded by magnificent vineyards, Dijon, the former capital of the Dukes of Burgundy, is famous for the many fine monuments which bear witness to its long and glorious history.

Dijon, an important regional centre on the confluence of the rivers Ouche and Suzon and the Canal de Bourgogne, is also a major junction on which converge the roads and railways of Europe. Spreading out from the city, a network of highways, railways and waterways lead off in all directions to Paris, the Mediterranean, Germany, Switzerland and Italy.

As a result of this privileged situation, Dijon has developed as an important commercial and industrial centre. The city's two main industrial zones are located to the south and northeast. Dijon is also home to a prestigious university.

DIJON

Aiguillettes (Bd des).......... A 2
Albert 1er (Av.) .... A
Allobroges (Bd des) .... A 3
Auxonne (Rue d') .... B
Bachelard (Bd Gaston) ..... A 5
Bellevue (R. de) .... A 8
Bertin (Av. J.-B.)............... B 9
Bourroches (Bd des) .... A
Camus (Av. Albert)........... B 12
Castel (Bd du) .... A 13
Chanoine-Kir (Bd) .... A 15
Châteaubriand (R. de)....... B 16
Chèvre Morte (Bd des) .... A 17
Chevreul (R.) .... AB
Chicago (Bd de)............... B
Churchill (Bd W.)............. B 18
Clomiers (Bd des) .... A 20
Concorde (Av. de la) .... B 21
Cracovie (R. de) .... B
Dijon (R. de) .... A
Dr Petit-Jean (Bd du) ...... B
Doumer (Bd Paul).............. B
Drapeau (Av. du)............... B
Dumont (R. Ch.).............. AB
Eiffel (Av. G.) .... A
Einstein (Av. Albert)......... B 24
Europe (Bd de l') .... B 25

Europe (Rd Pt de l').......... B 26
Faubourg-St-Martin
 (R. du)........................... A
Fauconnet (R. Gén.) .... AB 28
Fontaines-lès-Dijon (R.).... A 30
France libre (Pl. de la) ..... AB 31
Gabriel (Bd).................... B 32
Gallieni (Bd Mar.)............ AB 33
Gaulle (Crs Gén.-de) .... B 35
Gorgets (Bd des) .... A 36
Gray (R. de)..................... B
Jaurès (Av. J.)................. B
Jeanne-d'Arc (Bd)............ B 38
Joffre (Bd Mal.) .... B
Jouvence (R. de) .... A
Kennedy (Bd J.)............... A 40
Langres (Av. de)............... B
Longvic (R. de) .... A
Magenta (R.) .... B 42
Maillard (Bd)................... A 43
Malines (R. de) .... B
Mansard (Bd) .... B 44
Mayence (R. de)............... B
Mirande (R. de)............... B
Mont-Blanc (Av. du).......... B 46
Moulins (Rue des) .... A
Nation (Rd Pt de la).......... B 47
Orfèvres (R. des) .... A 48
Ouest (Bd de l') .... A 49
Parc (Cours du)................ B 50

Pascal (Bd)....................... B
Poincaré (Av. R.)............... B
Pompidou (Rd Pt G.)......... B 51
Pompidou (Voie G.) .... B
Pompon (Bd F.) .... A 52
Prat (Av. du Colonel) .... A 53
Rembrandt (Bd) .... B 54
Roosevelt (Av. F. D.)........ B 55
Saint-Exupéry (Pl.)........... B 56
Salengro (Pl. R.) .... B
Schuman (Bd Robert) ...... B 58
Stade (R. du) .... A
Stalingrad (Av. de) .... A
Stearinerie (R. de la)........ A
Strasbourg (Bd de) .... B 60
Sully (R.)......................... A
Talant (R. de) .... A
Trimolet (Bd) .... B 61
Troyes (Bd du)................. A
Université (Bd de l')......... A
Valendrons (Bd des) .... A
Valendrons (R. des).......... A
Victor-Hugo (Av.) .... A
1er Consul (Av. du) .... A
8 Mai 1945 (Rd Pt du) ..... B 65

M⁴ Musée Grévin

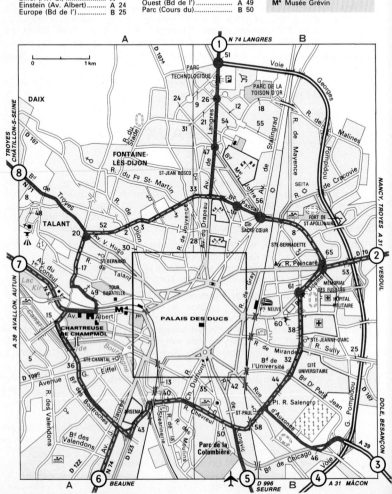

HISTORICAL NOTES

Creation of the Dukes of Burgundy – The Roman fortress that bore the name of Divio, set on the great military highway from Lyon to Mainz, remained a place of secondary importance for many centuries. Sacked, pillaged, burnt and rebuilt many times, Dijon played no great part in history until 1015, the year in which Robert I, Duke of Burgundy, chose it as the capital of his duchy.

In 1137 a terrible fire completely devastated the town. Duke Hugues II rebuilt it on a larger scale and enclosed it together with the abbey of St-Bénigne within a new city wall, composed of fortified ramparts, pierced by eleven gates. Porte Guillaume, the last gate to be demolished, was replaced in 1788 by the present triumphal arch.

The "Great Dukes of the West" – In 1364 Philip the Bold, fourth son of King John II the Good, of France, received the duchy of Burgundy as a legacy on the death of his father. He was the first member of the House of Valois which for the next 100 years was to transform Dijon, attracting many artists and giving it magnificent monuments. The reign of the Valois marked the most brilliant period in the history of Dijon. These four dukes of the House of Valois, Philip the Bold, John the Fearless, Philip the Good and Charles the Bold (Le Téméraire), were among the richest and most powerful princes in all Christendom. Their enormous wealth and the display of magnificence with which they surrounded themselves earned them the title of "the Great Dukes of the West" (see p 29 for the genealogy of the Houses of France and Burgundy in the 14C and 15C).

An argument without reply – On 7 December 1513 the town of Dijon was facing one of the greatest disasters in its history. An army of 30 000 Swiss, Germans and men of the Franche-Comté was at its gates. The Governor of Burgundy, La Trémoille, had only 6 000 or 7 000 men to defend the city. What could he do but negotiate? The Swiss however were inflexible.

They had opened fire and had already made breaches in the walls when La Trémoille had an inspiration of pure genius. Heading a procession of wagons all loaded with wine, a new group of negotiators was sent out to parley with the besiegers. What a godsend! The soldiers drank, they soon became fuddled and the Swiss agreed to lift the siege. France had to pay 400 000 écus and evacuate the Milan region. The king never really understood anything about this "marvellously strange" treaty and consequently refused to ratify it but Dijon and Burgundy had been saved.

The progress of the town – Although deprived of its position as capital of a State after the union of Burgundy and France, Dijon nevertheless retained an important administrative role. The Governors of the province still kept their headquarters there. The "States" of Burgundy (a regional assembly of deputies, clergy, the nobility and the Third Estate) held their meeting regularly every three years in the old ducal palace which was especially arranged for these solemnities; the town opened its richly decorated mansions in a series of brilliant civic receptions. At the end of the 18C, Arthur Young (English writer, 1741-1820) declared that "Dijon is a fine town; although the houses are built in old-fashioned style, the streets are well paved and have pavements, something that is very rare in France". At that time however Dijon had less than 20 000 inhabitants.

A centre of regional activity in Burgundy, Dijon is also proud of the great wines produced by the local vineyards and of several famous gastronomic specialities: mustard, gingerbread, blackcurrant liqueur and snails.

It is however to the development of communications, which began in 1850, that the town owes its present great progress. Dijon has become one of France's great rail junctions. The town is also served by an extensive motorway network and an airport.

★★PALAIS DES DUCS ET DES ÉTATS DE BOURGOGNE

time: 3 hours – plan overleaf

The old district around the Palace of the Dukes of Burgundy is quite charming. As you stroll along the streets, many of which are for pedestrians only, you will come across beautiful old stone mansions and numerous half-timbered 15-16C houses. In squares such as the Place François-Rude, the Place du Théâtre or the Place des Cordeliers, it is all too tempting sit and contemplate for a while on one of the café terraces.

The remains of the ducal palace are now surrounded by buildings in the classical style.

Place de la Libération – This is the former Place Royale. In the 17C, when the town was at the height of its parliamentary power, it felt itself to be a capital and decided to transform the ducal palace, which had stood empty since the death of Charles the Bold, and to re-arrange its approaches. Plans for the fine semicircular design were drawn up by Jules Hardouin-Mansart, the architect of Versailles, and were carried out by one of his pupils from 1686 to 1701: the arcades of the Place de la Libération, surmounted by a stone balustrade, enhance the main courtyard.

Cour d'honneur – The old "Logis du Roi" (King's House), a handsome ensemble marked by strong horizontal lines and terminating in two wings at right angles, is dominated by the tall medieval tower of Philippe-le-Bon.

The ducal palace houses, to the left, the various departments of the town hall and, to the right, the famous museum of fine art.

The vaulted passageway to the right leads you into the Bar courtyard.

MUSÉE DES BEAUX-ARTS (FINE ARTS MUSEUM)

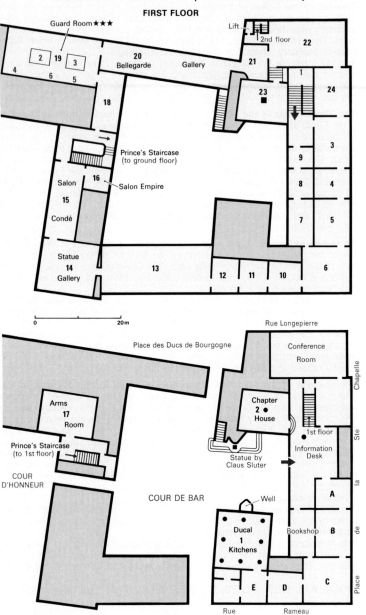

FIRST FLOOR

GROUND FLOOR

Cour de Bar – The **tower** (Tour de Bar, **B** *on town plan p 146*), built by Philip the Bold in the 14C, preserves the name of an illustrious prisoner who was kept there by Philip the Good: René d'Anjou, Duke of Bar and Lorraine, Count of Provence, who was known as "King René". The charming 17C **staircase** (**D** *on town plan p 146*) by **Bellegarde**, which goes round the tower, leads to the north gallery of the same period. Note the statue of the sculptor **Claus Sluter** by Bouchard and the old **well** backing on to the ducal kitchens.

Leave by the passage leading to the Rue Rameau and then turn left.

** **Musée des Beaux-Arts** ⊘ – The fine arts museum is installed in the former ducal pa-lace and in the eastern wing of the palace of the States-General. An engraved plaque, on the wall to the right of the entrance, shows the layout of the Gallo-Roman fortress which covered the central area of Dijon.

Ground floor – On the left, at the far end of the rooms devoted to temporary exhi-bitions (**A** to **E**), are the **ducal kitchens** (**1**), built in 1435. The six huge chimneys were scarcely sufficient for the preparation of feasts worthy of the Burgundian court; the vaulting converges on the central vent.

The **chapter house** (**2**) of the former 14C ducal chapel (missing together with its treasure) illustrates the evolution of religious sculpture – an art form held in high regard in Burgundy – from the 14C to the 17C; the two tombs by Dijon artist

Jean Dubois are of particular interest. Also on display are precious works of art: 15C stained glass windows, reliquaries, 16C silver gilt altarpiece together with St Robert's cross (11C) and a cup belonging to St Bernard.

On the grand staircase stands a statue of the Maréchal de Saxe (**1**) by **François Rude** (1784-1855).

First floor – On the landing is the old door of the Dijon law courts, carved by Hugues Sambin (16C), and some fine medieval and Renaissance pieces of religious gold and silver ware and carved ivory. Gallery (**3**) houses Italian painting from the 14-16C, with particularly good examples of the Primitive schools of Florence (Taddeo Gaddi) and Siena (Pietro Lorenzetti) and of the Florentine Renaissance (*St Peter walking on the water* by Vasari in 1574, the author of the famous artists' biographies). The next two galleries (**4** and **5**) contain paintings by 15 and 16C German (including Rhenish) and Swiss masters; the best of these include the works of the Master of the Darmstadt Passion (1425), Conrad Witz *(Emperor Augustus and the Tibur Sibyl)* and the Master of the Baden Carnation *(St Barbara and St Ursula)*. Note also the *Annunciation with St Christopher and St Anthony* (15C) and the *Entombment* (16C) by the German school.

In the next three galleries (**9**, **8**, **7** – *overlooking the courtyard*), the first two are devoted to Renaissance art: furniture, medals, enamels and paintings (*Woman at her Toilet* by the Fontainebleau school – late 16C); the third room is hung with 17C Burgundian paintings (Tassel, Quentin).

Galleries (**6**) and (**10**) are devoted to French painting of the 17C and works by painters under Louis XIV: Philippe de Champaigne *(Presentation in the Temple)*, Le Sueur, Le Brun and François Perrier. Note also in gallery (**10**) the *Portrait of a Painter* by P. Mignard and the *Holy Family resting on the flight to Egypt* by Sébastien Bourdon. Works from the late 17C and 18C are displayed in galleries (**11**) and (**12**): Rigaud, Coypel, Largillière, sculptures by Jean Dubois, Burgundian painters such as J.-F. Gilles, known as Colson (*Rest* 1759) and J.-B. Lallemand (Dijon 1716-Paris 1803), creator of landscapes and genre scenes. In the large gallery (**13**) there are paintings by La Fosse, Nattier *(Portrait of Marie Leszczynska)*, Van Loo *(St George and the Dragon)* and others.

The **Salle des Statues** (**14**) in the corner of the West Wing, which contains copies of ancient works and 19C pieces including *Hebe and the Eagle of Jupiter* by Rude, has a fine view of Place de la Libération; the ceiling depicting the fame of Burgundy and Prince Condé is by Pierre Paul Prud'hon after a Roman piece by Pietro da Cortona. The Salon Condé (**15**) is decorated with woodwork and stucco of the Louis XVI period; it displays 18C French art: furniture, terracottas and paintings, sculptures by Coysevox (bust of Louis XIV), Caffieri (busts of Rameau and Piron). The Salon Empire (**16**) presents furniture and paintings of the period (Prud'hon).

The Prince's Staircase, which is built against the Gothic façade of the old Dukes' Palace, leads down to the **Salle d'Armes** (Arms Room) (**17**) on the ground floor: weapons and armour from the 13C to the 18C; cutlery and knives dating from the 16C to 18C. On the first floor note the **Salle du Maître du Flémalle** (**18**) which contains 14-15C Flemish and Burgundian painting, including the famous *Nativity* by the Master of Flémalle and several works of art from the Chartreuse de Champmol *(qv)*.

The **Salle des Gardes**★★★ (**19**) overlooking the Place des Ducs is the most famous gallery in the museum. It was built by Philip the Good and used as the setting for the "Joyous Entry" of Charles the Bold in 1474; it had to be restored in the early 16C after a fire. It houses the art treasures from the Chartreuse de Champmol, the necropolis of the Dukes of Valois;

From 1385-1410 three men – Jean de Marville, Claus Sluter and his nephew, Claus de Werve – worked successively on the tomb of Philip the Bold (**2**). The magnificent recumbent figure, watched over by two angels, rests on a black marble slab surrounded by alabaster arches forming a "cloister" to shelter the procession of "mourners" composed of very realistic statuettes. The funeral procession consists of clergymen, Carthusians, relatives, friends and officials of the Prince, all hooded or dressed in mourning.

The tomb of John the Fearless and Margaret of Bavaria (**3**), dating from

Detail from the tomb of Philip the Bold, Musée des Beaux-Arts

LAUROS GIRAUDON

between 1443 and 1470, is similar in style. The two altarpieces in gilt wood commissioned by Philip the Bold for the Chartreuse de Champmol are very richly decorated. They were carved between 1390 and 1399 by Jacques de Baerze and painted and gilded by Melchior Broederlam.

Only the Crucifixion altarpiece (**4**) near the tomb of Philip the Bold has retained Broederlam's famous paintings on the reverse side of the wings: the Annunciation, the Visitation, the Presentation in the Temple and the Flight into Egypt. At the other end is the altarpiece of the Saints and Martyrs (**5**). In the centre, note an early 16C altarpiece of the Passion (**6**) from an Antwerp workshop. Above the central altarpiece, between two 16C wall hangings from Tournai, hangs a tapestry dedicated to Notre-Dame-de-Bon-Espoir, protector of the city since the raising of the siege of Dijon by the Swiss on 11 September 1513. A niche contains a handsome portrait of Philip the Good wearing the collar of the Order of the Golden Fleece, painted by the Rogier Van der Weyden workshop (c1455). A staircase leads to the tribune, from which there is a good view of the recumbent figures.

The **Galerie de Bellegarde** (**20**) contains some good examples of 17 and 18C Italian and Spanish painting, in particular *Moses in the Bulrushes* by Veronese and *Adam and Eve* by Guido Reni; there is an unusual panoramic landscape of the *Château de Mariemont* and its grounds by Velvet Brueghel, and a *Virgin and Child with St Francis of Assisi* by Rubens.

Galleries (**21**) to (**24**) return to the evolution of French painting in the 19 and 20C: paintings by Henner, Legros, Tissot *(Japanese girl bathing)*, as well as sculptures by Rude, Canova, Carpeaux and Mercié.

Second and third floors – These are devoted to modern and contemporary art, including the Granville bequest. Works by the great animal sculptor **François Pompon** (1855-1933, *qv*) are displayed in an old gallery in the Tour de Bar *(signposted)*.

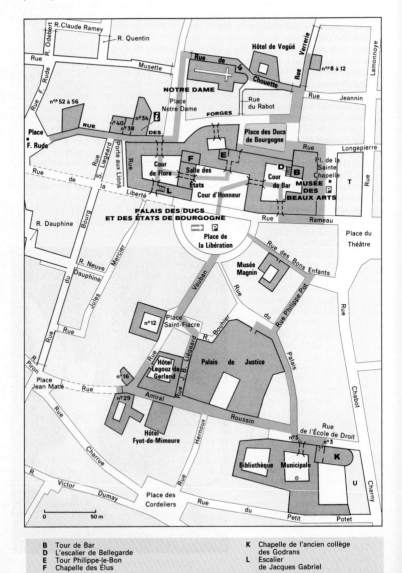

B	Tour de Bar	K	Chapelle de l'ancien collège
D	L'escalier de Bellegarde		des Godrans
E	Tour Philippe-le-Bon	L	Escalier
F	Chapelle des Élus		de Jacques Gabriel

The other galleries contain paintings, drawings, graphics and sculptures dating from the 16C to the present. Particularly famous names include Georges de la Tour *(Le Souffleur à la lampe)*, Géricault, Delacroix, Victor Hugo (imaginary landscapes in wash), Daumier, Courbet, Gustave Moreau and various painters from the Barbizon school (Daubigny, Th. Rousseau, N. Diaz de la Peña etc), Rodin, Maillol, Bourdelle and others.

The Impressionists and Post-Impressionists are represented by works by Manet (*Portrait of Méry Laurent* in pastel), Monet, Boudin, Sisley, Cross, Vuillard and Vallotton.

A remarkable collection of African sculpture and masks (Mali, Cameroon, Congo) gives an insight into the art forms which inspired Cubist painters and sculptors: Juan Gris, Marcoussis, Gleizes, Picasso *(Minotaur)*.

Among the rich collection of contemporary painting and sculpture note in particular works by artists in or linked with the Paris School and abstract artists of the 1950s to 1970s: Arpad Szenes and M.E. Vieira da Silva, his wife, C. Lapicque, N. de Staël *(Footballer)*, J. Bertholle, Manessier, Messagier, Mathieu and Wols; also several lovely sculptures by E. Hajdu.

Place des Ducs-de-Bourgogne – From this little square, one can imagine what the palace must have looked like at the time of the Dukes. The handsome Gothic façade is that of the Salle des Gardes, dominated by Philip the Good's tower.

Return to the main courtyard by the vaulted passageway which gives access to Philip the Good's tower.

Tour Philippe-le-Bon (**E**) ⊙ – The tower (46m - 151ft high) was built by Philip the Good in the 15C. From the terrace at the top *(316 steps)*, there is a fine **view**★ over the town, the valleys of the Ouche and the Saône and the first foothills of the Jura mountains.

Take the covered passageway to reach the Flore courtyard.

Cour de Flore – The buildings surrounding the courtyard were finished just before the Revolution in 1789. In the northeast corner is the **Chapelle des Élus** (Elect) (**E**); its interior decor and the doors date from the period of Louis XV. Mass was celebrated in the chapel during the sittings of the States of Burgundy. Under the porch which gives access to Rue de la Liberté (former Rue Condé) a magnificent staircase (**L**), designed in 1735 by Jacques Gabriel, father of the architect who designed the Petit Trianon at Versailles, leads to the **Salle des États** *(not open to the public)*.

Take the passageway north into Rue des Forges.

NEAR THE PALAIS DES DUCS

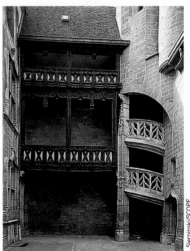

★ **Rue des Forges** – This is one of the most characteristic old streets of the town.

Hôtel Chambellan – *No 34 inner courtyard.* The 15C house, which was built by a rich family of drapers, has a very fine spiral staircase; the central column rises to a flamboyant palm-tree vault supported by the statue of a vine-grower carrying a basket.

Maison Milsand – *No 38.* The Renaissance façade is lavishly decorated in the style of Hugues Sambin.

Ancien Hôtel Aubriot – *No 40.* A classical doorway contrasts with the elegant 13C arcaded façade of the former Aubriot mansion, built by the first bankers of Dijon. This was the birthplace of Hugues Aubriot, provost of Paris under Charles V.

Inner courtyard of the Hôtel Chambellan, Dijon

He was responsible for building the Bastille, several of the bridges over the Seine, notably the St-Michel Bridge, and the first vaulted sewers.

Hôtel Morel-Sauvegrain – *Nos 52, 54 and 56.* 15C façade.

Place François-Rude (or Place du Bareuzai) – At the heart of the pedestrian zone stands this irregularly shaped, lively square, with one or two half-timbered houses overlooking it. When the statue by the fountain (the "Bareuzai") was erected in 1904, it provoked some raised eyebrows, but the grape-treading wine-grower, clad only in verdigris, has since been accepted as part of the scenery and is even looked on with some degree of affection by many. The product of his trampling is distributed only during the wine festival *(see the Calendar of Events at the end of this guide)*.

★ **Notre-Dame** – This church is a good example of 13C Gothic architecture in Burgundy. With only a restricted space in which to work, the master mason showed astonishing technical prowess.

Exterior – The façade is original. Above the great porch with its three bays, closed in laterally as is the porch at Autun, two delicately arcaded galleries are underscored by three tiers of gargoyles. Two graceful bell-turrets top the towers hidden by the façade: that on the right carries the Jacquemart clock brought from Courtrai by Philip the Bold in 1382 after his victory over the rebellious Flemish.

The clock has quite a history. It broke during the journey on an ox-wagon and on its arrival at Dijon had to be recast. The name of Jacquemart describing the figure of the man who strikes the bell of the clock with a hammer first appeared in 1500.

The people of Dijon were very fond of him and in 1610 considered that his continued celibacy must be weighing very heavily on the poor man. So he was given a female companion.

In 1714 the poet Aimé Piron took pity on this brave couple, who seemed to have undertaken a vow of chastity. They were given a son, Jacquelinet, whose hammer strikes the little bell for the half-hours; in 1881, a daughter was added, Jacquelinette, who strikes the quarter-hours.

Interior – The overall effect is harmonious; the triforium of small tapering columns is of great delicacy. Note the height of the transept crossing beneath the lantern tower. The boldly conceived choir, ending with a polygonal chevet, is sober and graceful.

The stained glass windows of the north transept date from the 13C. The 15C fresco has been restored. The chapel situated to the right of the choir houses the statue of Notre-Dame-de-Bon-Espoir (Our Lady of Good Hope). This Black Virgin, of the 11C, has been the object of particular veneration since the Swiss raised the siege of the town on 11 September 1513; the tapestry given at that time as a votive offering is now to be found in the fine arts museum *(Salle des Gardes, see above)*. After Dijon had been liberated without damage from the German occupa-

DIJON

tion on 11 September 1944, a second tapestry, made by Gobelins, commemorating the town's two liberations, was given as a new votive offering to Notre-Dame-de-Bon-Espoir. It is to be seen in the south arm of the transept.

Walking along the **Rue de la Chouette** gives a good view of the chevet; the owl which gave its name to this street can be seen at eye-level on one of the buttresses. Local legend has it that he will grant a wish to those who stroke him with their left hand.

Hôtel de Vogüé ⊙ – This early-17C mansion with its colourful tiled roof was one of the early meeting places of the representatives of the province. A portico richly decorated in the Renaissance style opens into an inner courtyard.
The mansion is now occupied by the offices of the city architect and the department of cultural affairs.

Rue Verrerie – Nos 8, 10 and 12 form an attractive group of half-timbered houses. Some of the beams have been richly carved.

Return by way of Place des Ducs de Bourgogne and the passageway through to the Cour d'honneur to reach Place de la Libération.

★THE LAW COURTS QUARTER *time: 1 hour*

Leave from Place de la Libération (plan p 146) by way of Rue Vauban to the south.

No 12 Rue Vauban has a classical façade adorned with pilasters and pediments, overlooking the inner courtyard.

Hôtel Legouz de Gerland – Take the Rue Jean-Baptiste Liégeard to the left to skirt this mansion with its Renaissance façade pinpointed by four watch-turrets. The classical inner façade may be seen from 21 Rue Vauban.

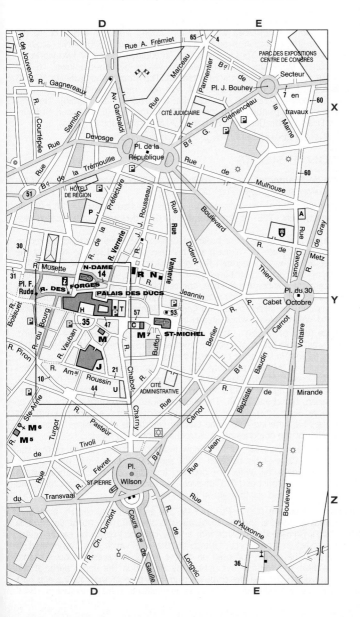

At the corner of Rues Vauban and Amiral-Roussin stands a half-timbered house (no 16) which once belonged to a carpenter. This craftsman embellished his shutters with linenfold panelling and some of the beams with scenes of his craft. The house almost opposite, at no 29, has an elegant courtyard which is screened off by a curved balustrade.

Hôtel Fyot-de-Mimeure – *No 23 Rue Amiral-Roussin.*
The façade in the pretty interior courtyard is in the style of architect and sculptor Hugues Sambin.

Bibliothèque Municipale ⊘ – *Enter by no 3 Rue de l'École-de-Droit.*
The 17C chapel of the former college of Les Godrans (**K**), founded in the 16C by the rich Dijon family of this name and directed by Jesuits, has been transformed into a reading room.
This large library contains amongst its 300 000 or more items precious illuminated manuscripts, including some executed at Cîteaux during the first thirty years of the 12C. The Well of Love (Puits d'Amour), from a house which was demolished when the lawcourts were extended, has been rebuilt in the courtyard *(enter by no 5 Rue de l'École-de-Droit).*
Follow Rue du Palais to reach the Law Courts.

Palais de Justice (Law Courts) – This building was formerly the Burgundian parliament. The gabled façade, in the Renaissance style, has a covered porch supported by columns. The door is a copy of a work by Sambin (the original is in the Musée des Beaux-Arts). The huge Lobby (Salle des Pas-Perdus) is covered by a **vaulted ceiling**★ like an upturned boat. Opposite the entrance the tiny chapel of the Saint-Esprit contains a screen of carved wood.

Musée Magnin ⊘ – This national museum is laid out in an elegant 17C mansion, which still has its period furnishings and obviously belonged to an art lover. The rooms are tastefully embellished with furniture dating from the early 18C to the Second Empire. The collection of paintings numbers almost 1 500 works, acquired at quite reasonable prices. Thus you will find, in addition to one or two works by famous masters, numerous carefully selected works by lesser known 16-19C artists, which are eminently worthy of attention. The ground floor exhibits 16-17C Flemish and Dutch works (J. Van Bijlert, A. Van dem Tempel) and Italian paintings (A. Allori, G. Cariani, Cerano, G.-A. Pellegrini, B. Strozzi, G.-B. Tiepolo). The first floor contains French painting from the late 16C to the 19C (E. Le Sueur, S. Bourdon, L. de La Hyre, Th. Géricault, E. Isabey, F.-M. Granet and E. Déria).
Take the Rue des Bons-Enfants back to Place de la Libération.

ADDITIONAL SIGHTS

★ **Chartreuse de Champmol** (**A**) ⊘ – *Town plan p 142. Entrance: 1 Boulevard Chanoine-Kir. Follow signs to the "Puits de Moïse".*

A psychiatric hospital now occupies the site of this monastery, destroyed during the French Revolution in 1793. At the entrance is a 15C doorway which escaped destruction.
The first Dukes of Burgundy were buried at Cîteaux but Philip the Bold wanted an almost royal burial place for himself and his heirs and in 1383 he founded the charterhouse which was consecrated five years later by the Bishop of Troyes. The best artists of the period contributed to the magnificent undertaking but nothing remains except the tombs of the dukes, the retables preserved in the Dijon Musée des Beaux-Arts, and two works by Claus Sluter (end 14C), the sculptor from Haarlem who became the leader of the Burgundian-Flemish school of art: the chapel doorway and Well of Moses which stands in a courtyard.

★★ **Puits de Moïse** (Well of Moses) – *Walk round the buildings to reach the courtyard.*
In fact the "well" is the socket of a polychrome Calvary made between 1395 and 1405 to decorate the font in the great cloisters *(the painting is barely visible).* It is named after the figure of Moses, probably the most impressive of the six huge and strikingly life-like statues which surround the hexagonal socket; the other five figures are the prophets *(going round the monument to the right from Moses)* – David, Jeremiah, Zachariah, Daniel and Isaiah. The angels beneath the cornice are the work of Claus de Werve, Sluter's nephew; with touching veracity each one through a different pose expresses his suffering before the Calvary (which has disappeared). The generous movement of the draperies brings baroque sculpture to mind.

★ **Chapel doorway** – The doorway, which is now inside the chapel, consists of five statues sculpted by Claus Sluter between 1389 and 1394. Duke Philip the Bold and Margaret of Flanders, his wife, are depicted kneeling, watched by their patron saints (St John the Baptist and St Catherine), on each side of the Virgin Mary and Child who are portrayed on the central pier.

Cathédrale St-Bénigne (**CY**) – *Plan p 148.* The ancient abbey church, pure Burgundian-Gothic in style, is the last to occupy this site. In 1001 Abbot **Guglielmo da Volpiano** built a Romanesque basilica with a large crypt to replace an earlier ruined church; he added a three-storey rotunda to the east which was consecrated in 1018. In 1271 the church collapsed on to the crypt. The present Gothic church was built against the rotunda but during the Revolution the upper parts of the rotunda were destroyed and the crypt filled in. The base of the rotunda and part of the crypt, the only relics of the Romanesque building, were excavated in 1843.

The **west front** of the Gothic church is supported by massive buttresses and projections flanked by two great towers crowned by two octagonal storeys with conical roofs of multi-coloured tiles. Within the porch, which is surmounted by a delicately pierced gallery, is the old 12C Romanesque doorway in the centre of the Gothic façade; it is topped by a tympanum, the work of the Bouchardon brothers, which came from the old church of St-Étienne (now the Chamber of Commerce – **DY**). The transept crossing is marked by a tall spire (93m - 305ft) in the Flamboyant style, restored in 1896.

The **interior** is quite austere; its lines are unadorned: plain capitals, simply moulded arcades in the triforium, little columns extending unbroken from the vault to the floor in the crossing and to the tops of massive round pillars in the nave. Since St-Bénigne lost its own works of art during the Revolution, it has provided a home for tombstones and pieces of sculpture from other churches in Dijon. The organ (1743) is by Riepp.

★ **Crypt** ⊘ – The only remaining traces of the Romanesque crypt consist of part of the transept with four apsidal chapels on the east side and a trench in the middle containing the remains of a sarcophagus which was probably used for the burial of St Benignus, the first Burgundian martyr who died in the 3C; there is a pilgrimage to his tomb on 20 November. The sarcophagus faces a broad opening in the lower storey of the **rotunda**★★ which echoes the highly symbolic architecture of the tomb of Christ in Jerusalem built in the 4C; only eight rotundas of this type are known in the world. Three circles of columns radiate from the centre; some have retained their original capitals decorated with palm leaves, interlacing, monstrous animals or praying figures, rare examples of pre-Romanesque sculpture. The eastern end of the rotunda opens into a 6C chapel which may be a "cella" (sanctuary).

★ **Musée archéologique** (CY M²) ⊘ – *Plan p 148*. The archaeological museum is housed in the west wing of the now non-existent cloisters of the old abbey of St-Bénigne. The 11C Romanesque cellars display a collection of Gallo-Roman sculptures; several tombstones, including those of a butcher and a wine merchant, represent the daily life of the period; a pillar depicting several divinities from Mavilly provides an interesting insight into Gaulish religion in Burgundy. The collection of ex-voto offerings, made of wood (in the Gaulish tradition), as well as of bronze and stone, includes human figures and parts of the human body; they come from a healing sanctuary near the source of the Seine which is personified by the bronze statuette of the goddess Sequana.

The monks' dorter (13C) on the ground floor is devoted to medieval sculpture from Dijon: a bust of Christ *(illustration p 46)* by Claus Sluter for the Calvary of the Chartreuse de Champmol is accompanied by architectural fragments; at the end of the bay is a Christ on the cross, attributed to Claus de Werve; flanking it are two Romanesque tympana from St-Bénigne.

The second floor presents household goods from different periods, from the Palaeolithic to the Merovingian period: pottery typical of the Chasséenne culture (Burgundian neolithic), a golden bracelet (1.3kg - 46oz) found at La Rochepot (9C BC), a hoard of Bronze Age objects found at Blanot (belt, greaves, leather and golden necklaces, bracelet), weapons consecrated at the Gaulish sanctuary at Mirebeau, several stone carvings of Gallo-Roman gods typical of the region (mother-goddesses from Alésia, a god with birds, a god with a mallet). Models showing major local archaeological digs in progress are on display.

St-Philibert (CY) – *Plan p 148*. This church, built in the 12C and altered in the 15C, has been deconsecrated.

Square Darcy (CY) – *Plan p 148*. The square takes its name from the engineer who brought drinking water to Dijon in 1839. The basins and fountains are complemented by a background of greenery.

At the entrance is Pompon's (1855-1933) imposing statue of a **polar bear.**

★ **Jardin de l'Arquebuse** (CY) – *Plan p 148*. This park owes its name to the Company of Harquebusiers, who occupied the site in the 16C. All the western part is taken up by the botanical gardens (3 500 different species), which were founded in the 18C and joined to the Promenade de l'Arquebuse. In addition there is an arboretum, tropical glasshouses and a vivarium. Magnificent trees surround the colourful banks of flowers.

★ **Muséum d'Histoire naturelle** (CY M³) ⊘ – The natural history museum, founded in 1836 by a nature lover from Dijon, Léonard Nodot, is housed in the old cross-bowmen's barracks (1608). The display case at the foot of the stairs labelled "Géologie au quotidien" contains a relief model of Burgundy. Explanations *(press the button on the left)* are given on the morphology and type of soil of this highly varied region. On the floor above, dioramas give a lively illustration of the different fauna of the various Burgundian habitats *(lighting, explanations and bird song available by pressing the button).*

Musée Grévin (A M⁴) ⊘ – *Plan p 142*. Historic tableaux composed of waxwork figures illustrating 17 episodes in the history of Burgundy between the 6C BC and the present.

Musée Rude (DY M⁷) ⊘ – *Plan p 149*. The transept and chancel of the cathedral of St-Étienne, which was deconsecrated at the Revolution, now house original works, plaster casts, copies and a few drawings by the sculptor of the

Marseillaise on the Arc de Triomphe in Paris, François Rude. Excavations in the chancel have revealed the foundations of the crypt of the 11C church and of the Gallo-Roman wall of enclosure (3C).

★ **St-Michel** (**DY**) ⊘ – *Plan p 149*. The church, which was begun early in the 15C in Flamboyant Gothic style, was consecrated in December 1529, although its façade was eventually completed in the full Renaissance style; the two towers framing it were finished in the 17C. The façade, on which the three classical orders are superimposed, is the most curious part of the building. The porch, which juts far out, is pierced by three doorways: a long frieze of ornamental foliage and grotesque decorations runs along the upper part of the porch for its whole length. Under it, in medallions, are busts of the prophets Daniel, Baruch, Isaiah and Ezekiel, as well as of David with his harp and Moses with the Tablets of the Law. The right doorway dates from 1537 and is the oldest of the three.
The Last Judgment, presented on the tympanum of the central doorway, is the work of a Flemish artist: Nicolas de la Cour. The 16C statue of St Michael on the pier replaces the original one which was destroyed during the Revolution. It rests on a finely sculpted console. The sculptures on the console were inspired by both pagan traditions and sacred texts; close together one can identify David, Lucretia, Leda and the Swan, Hercules, Apollo, Venus, Judith, the Judgment of Solomon, St John the Baptist and Christ appearing to Mary Magdalene.
The interior is Gothic in style. Note the height of the choir, which like St-Bénigne lacks an ambulatory, the 18C woodwork, and four paintings by Franz Kraus (18C German): *Adoration of the Shepherds* and *The Flight into Egypt* (deteriorated) in the north transept; *Adoration of the Magi* and *Presentation in the Temple* in the chapel of the Saint-Sacrement, which also has a fine Flamboyant altar. The far north chapel contains a fragment of a 15C Entombment.

Maison des Cariatides (**DY R**) – *Plan p 149. 28 Rue Chaudronnerie.*
This house built in 1603 has 12 caryatids on the street façade.

Rue Vannerie (**DY**) – *Plan p 149*. Nos 39 and 41 (**N**) are 18C mansions. At no 66 is a Renaissance mansion with ornamental windows flanking a watch-tower by Hugues Sambin.

Parc de la Colombière (**B**) – *Plan p 142*. This is reached by way of an avenue of magnificent trees. Clumps of flowering shrubs are intersected by paths and green lawns, all once part of the Condé Princes park. A section of the Roman road *Via Agrippa* which linked Lyon to Trier can be seen in this park.

Musée de la Vie bourguignonne (**DZ M⁵**) ⊘ – *Plan p 149*. An old Bernardine convent houses the regional and urban ethnographical collections of Perrin de Puycousin (1856-1949), a native Burgundian. Daily life, ceremonies and Burgundian traditions in the 19C are evoked through a lively display of costumes, furniture, domestic implements and other mementoes. Temporary exhibitions are held.

Musée d'art sacré (**DZ M⁶**) ⊘ – *Plan p 149*. The late-17C church of Ste-Anne, with its circular plan and dome, now houses a collection of 13C-19C sacred art: crucifix with delicate decoration in Limoges enamel, chalices, ecclesiastical vestments, wooden statues, including a 12C Virgin Mary in Majesty, a body of Christ in oak (late 13C) and an elegant monumental marble altar with stucco work sculpted by the Dijon artist Jean Dubois c1672. It depicts the Virgin Mary visiting St Elizabeth. The two bronze statues are beneath a Burgundian porphyry baldachin supported on black marble columns and enlivened by a group of white cherubim in flight.

A la Dijonnaise

Two Dijon specialities – mustard and blackcurrants – are used to flavour the local savoury and sweet dishes.
Dijonnaise sauce, which is served with meat and fish, is made with butter, mustard, white wine and vinegar, thickened with egg yolks.

DIVONNE-LES-BAINS⚓

Population 5 580
Michelin map 170 fold 16 or 243 fold 44 – Facilities –
Local map under ST-CLAUDE: Excursion

Divonne is a well-known spa town halfway between Lake Geneva and the great Jura mountain range, on the Franco-Swiss border. It is the only town in the Jura region equipped with luxury hotels, a golf course and a race-course. Many leisure activities can be enjoyed at the 45 ha-111 acre reservoir and the sailing base *(see the Practical Information chapter at the end of this guide)*.
Divonne (meaning "divine spring") was frequented long ago by the Romans. Then, for several centuries, the five springs, at a constant temperature of 6.5°C-44°F, bubbled forth undisturbed. It was not until 1848 that people thought of using them for medicinal purposes. Nowadays they are well appreciated by insomniacs, the overworked, the depressed, etc. The spa's park, with its shady areas and its springs, is very pleasant. Paths to the west of the town lead to beautiful walks around Mont Mussy.

DOLE★

Population 26 577
Michelin map 170 fold 3 or 243 fold 17 – Facilities – Local map under Forêt de CHAUX

The brown tile roofs of Dole's old houses cluster around the church and its imposing bell tower. The town is on a hillside overlooking the north bank of the Doubs, which is joined at this point by the Rhône-Rhine canal.

The citizens of Dole are proud of their city; it was the capital of the free province of Burgundy (the Franche-Comté) for many centuries. The present city is adorned with many splendid monuments which testify to its proud past.

HISTORICAL LANDMARKS

From the free county to the Franche-Comté – Dole was founded in the 11C, largely due to its position at the intersection of major communications routes. Until its annexation by the French, Dole forged links with both the Dukes of Burgundy and the Emperors of Germany – Friedrich Barbarossa endowed it with a civil charter in 1274. In the 15C, as seat of the parliament of the Comté and of a university, Dole was already playing the role of a capital city, and it was not long before the flourishing town was noticed – and coveted – by Louis XI and the French.

In 1479 Louis XI laid the town to siege. In spite of the heroic resistance of the inhabitants (which gave rise to a pithy summary of the exchange between the French, demanding surrender *"Comtois, rends-toi"*, and the citizens of Dole, refusing *"Nenni, ma foi!"*), Dole eventually fell and was methodically burned to the ground by its invaders. This is why there is so little architectural evidence left in the town predating the 16C. Furthermore, Louis XI, who was furious that the citizens of Dole had resisted him, forbade the townsdwellers to rebuild their houses. However, his son Charles VIII returned the Comté to the Habsburgs in 1493, and Dole soon rose to its position as capital again.

The golden age – The 16C and 17C were a period of great prosperity and also a great deal of construction. The collegiate church was built during this period, and a stronger fortified city wall with several bastions. Among the architects and artists responsible for introducing the Renaissance style to the city were Denis and Hugues Le Rupt, Jean Rabicant and the Lulliers.

Dole owed its development and influence up until French annexation primarily to its role as parliamentary, governmental and university seat.

The **Parliament** was set up by the Dukes of Burgundy from the House of Valois when they inherited the Comté in 1384. It exercised supreme justice – even the most noble landowner was not above its jurisdiction – and held major influence in the political, economic, diplomatic and military worlds. Apart from one or two members of the aristocracy, it consisted mainly of lawyers and legal experts from the merchant class. The **university**, founded in 1423, soon won a reputation for the excellent standard of its legal faculty. Lectures were attended by about 800 students, including many young men from abroad. It was customary for these foreign students to have "Valentines", young local girls who helped them improve their French. Dole's schools produced expert lawyers, providing the count and the emperor with reliable advisers who gradually replaced the members of the aristocracy.

The **States** (États) were formed of three classes of representative, the nobility, the clergy and the citizens. They decided how much tax the province should pay to the count.

Religious life also blossomed, with Dole becoming a leading bastion of the **Counter-Reformation** under Philip II of Spain, an ardent Roman Catholic. Churches and monasteries were built, which still enhance the present city.

The Siege of 1636 and the French Conquest – French attempts to annex the Comté were renewed under **Louis XIII** and his chancellor Richelieu. In 1636 the Prince of Condé, father of the Grand Condé, laid siege to Dole. The French soldiers subjected the town to a steady hail of newly developed, heavy bombs, which crashed through roofs and floors to explode in the basement, demolishing whole buildings. But even after three months of this, French troops were forced to withdraw in the face of the courageous resistance of the townspeople. This unexpected victory for Dole reaffirmed it in its position as independent capital. The episode passed into local legend and even today people recall, for example, the bravery of Ferdinand de Rye, Governor of the Comté and archbishop of Besançon, who despite being well over 80 years old had himself shut in with the beleaguered townspeople and became the heart and soul of their resistance.

However, in 1668 and 1674 Louis XIV's troops renewed the attack on Dole, which finally succumbed, and in the Treaty of Nijmegen (1678) town and province were officially annexed to France. The Sun King did not forgive Dole for having put up such strong resistance; he made Besançon the capital of the Franche-Comté in its place, stripping Dole of its parliament, its university and its ramparts.

LOCAL HEROES AND ENFANTS TERRIBLES

The Malet conspiracy – Général Malet, cousin of Rouget de Lisle, was born in Dole and embodied most of the characteristics that the French associate with a typical "Comtois"; he was independent-minded and stubborn, loved contention and espoused Republicanism. He was a prime target for Napoleon's suspicion and was eventually imprisoned in Paris on the latter's orders in 1808. Malet escaped during the night of

23-24 October 1812, along with a few supporters, and managed to bring the local barracks, several ministries and the town hall under his control. But a suspicious officer brought the attempted *coup* to an end. Malet was arrested and shot, along with nine of his comrades.

The Pasteur family – The great scientist Louis Pasteur was born in Dole on 27 December 1822. His father Joseph Pasteur has been a sergeant-major in the Imperial Army, but was discharged on the fall of Napoleon and took up his previous trade as tanner. He married Jeanne-Étiennette Roqui in 1816.

When the great scientist, at the peak of his fame, returned to Dole on 14 July 1883 for the unveiling of a commemorative plaque on the house where he was born, he made a vote of thanks, in which he above all expressed his gratitude to his parents. He spoke of his mother's enthusiasm and respect for learning, which she had passed on to him. He said his father had showed him what patience and tenacious application

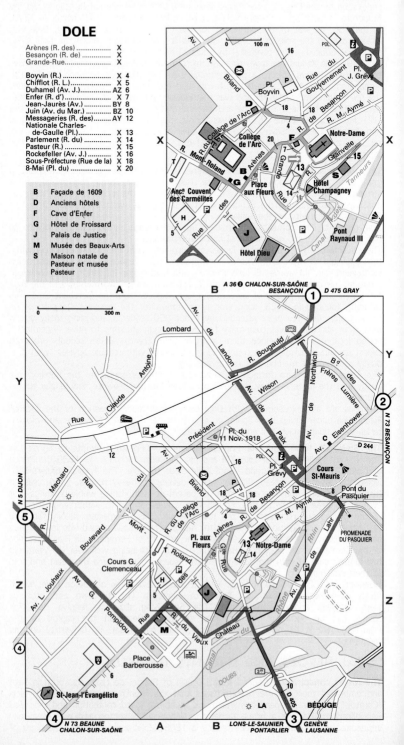

DOLE

B   Façade de 1609
D   Anciens hôtels
F   Cave d'Enfer
G   Hôtel de Froissard
J   Palais de Justice
M   Musée des Beaux-Arts
S   Maison natale de Pasteur et musée Pasteur

could achieve in even the hardest profession and described how his father had always admired great people and great achievements, teaching his son to be ever open to learning new things and to strive ceaselessly for self-improvement.
In 1827 the family left Dole to settle in Arbois *(qv)*.

Marcel Aymé's childhood in Dole – The writer and novelist **Marcel Aymé** (1902-67) was sent at the age of 7 from the little town of Villers-Robert in the Bresse region to his aunt's at Dole. He was a disruptive, mischievous child at school, but by the age of 17 passed his higher school certificate, specialising in mathematics, and left for Paris to study to be an engineer. Ill health forced him to break off his studies and return to Dole. Here he wrote his first novel *Brûlebois* in 1926. His talent was quickly recognised, and in 1929 he was awarded the Prix Renaudot for his *La table aux Crevés*. He followed this with works such as *La Jument Verte* and *La Vouivre*.
Dole is vividly portrayed in Aymé's novels. The fair ground, the hospital, the station, Rue Pasteur and the market place are just some of the parts of Dole which are evoked in his work. Indeed, the bell tower of Notre-Dame plays a significant role in the detective thriller *Moulin de la Sourdine...*

★★OLD TOWN *time: 2 hours*

The old town is clustered around the church of Notre-Dame. Its narrow, winding streets are closely packed with houses, dating from the 15C to the 18C, many of which have interesting details; coats of arms above doorways, turrets, arcaded inner courtyards, various types of stone or timber staircases, wells, statue-niches and wrought-iron window grilles and balustrades.

Leave from Place Nationale.

Place Nationale (**X 13**) – This charming square in the centre of the old town is surrounded by old houses.

Collégiale Notre-Dame (**X**) ⊘ – The collegiate church dates from the 16C and symbolises Dole's rise from the ashes of the fire of 1479. The sturdy bell tower (75m - 246ft tall) is a reminder also of the religious strife of the period.
The tympanum above the north portal depicts a Virgin with Child between two angels. The size of the church's interior is striking. Its clear sober lines are a resolute departure from the excessive ornamentation of the Late Gothic style, anticipating the Renaissance. It was furnished and decorated at the expense of local dignitaries and contains some of the first Renaissance works of art to manifest themselves in Dole, the beautiful **works in polychrome marble★**. These are characterised by motifs typical of those used by artists in the Dole workshops (foliage, tracery and birds) as, for example, on the façade of the Sainte-Chapelle, the organ case and the pulpit (Denis Le Rupt) and the holy-water stoup. The arch of the Carondelet mausoleum is attributed to a Flemish craftsman. The statues of the Apostles against the pillars either side of the chancel were executed by the Burgundian school (early 16C).
The marvellous carved wooden **great organ** dating from the 18C is one of the very rare examples of its type in France to have survived virtually intact. The organ builder was Karl Joseph Riepp.

The **Sainte-Chapelle** *(entrance at the far end of the south aisle)* was built in the 17C to house the miraculous Sacred Host of Faverney. In 1608 the church in Faverney burned to the ground, but the ostensory and the Sacred Host survived the fire intact, and have been kept at Dole ever since. The coffered vaulting is adorned with rosettes.

To the right of the old town hall, take the Rue d'Enfer, which leads into the Rue de Besançon. Carry on from here to Place du 8-Mai-1945, then into Rue des Arènes.

Place aux Fleurs (**X**) – There is a pretty **view** of old Dole, dominated by the bell tower of Notre-Dame church.
The fountain in the square, an Aquarius figure, was sculpted by François Rosset. There is also a modern work by Boettchen, *The Gossips*. A 1609 façade graces no 28 (**X B**).

Rue Mont-Roland (**X**) – Note the polychrome marble and stone doorway of the old

Place aux Fleurs with Notre-Dame
in the background, Dole

Carmelite convent (17C) and the façades of some of the private mansions, for example, the Maison Odon de la Tour (16C) and the **Hôtel de Froissard** (**G**) (early 17C), where you should pass through the gate to admire the double horseshoe staircase and the loggia in the inner courtyard.

Take Rue du Collège-de-l'Arc on the right.

Collège de l'Arc (**X**) – The Jesuits founded this school in 1582.

Go under the arch which spans the street.

The chapel, deconsecrated today, is distinguished by its beautiful, richly decorated Renaissance **porch**, surmounted by a loggia with arches supported by the figures of angels in flight.

Notice the two mansions (**X D**) on the left, one of which dates from 1738; they still have their small inner courtyards and beautiful balustrades.

Continue to Place Boyvin and from there take the Rue Boyvin, the Rue de la Sous-Préfecture and the Rue de Besançon to the right.

Cave d'Enfer (**X F**) – A plaque recalls the heroic resistance of a few Dole citizens during the attack on the town in 1479.

Turn back to reach Place Nationale, then take Rue Pasteur.

Rue Pasteur (**X 15**) – This street used to be called the Rue des Tanneurs, as it regrouped all the houses of the hemp and leather craftsmen along the banks of the canal. No 43 is the birthplace of Pasteur.

Maison natale de Pasteur and Musée Pasteur (**X S**) ⊘ – The house where Louis Pasteur was born still contains the evidence of his father's trade as tanner, with old tools and the tannery in the basement. In the living area, the room where Pasteur was born contains pastel drawings by the young Louis of furniture and other objects which belonged to his family.

Among the collection of original documents are the diploma of the Légion d'Honneur conferred on his father by Napoleon I, and several handwritten replies from Pasteur to people who had written to ask his advice (one of the letters begins, for example, with the words "Madame, où est le chien qui a mordu votre fils ?...").

From the terrace on the first door there is a view of the tanners' canal and the 16C fortifications.

The **Musée Pasteur** is located in another tanner's workshop next door to Pasteur's birthplace and illustrates the enormous significance of the great scientist's work. A room with old scientific equipment recalls the experiments of the chemist and physicist, who was neither doctor nor biologist, but whose discoveries about bacteria nonetheless made an enormous impact on the worlds of medecine and surgery. The famous dried bone marrow from a rabid rabbit still fascinates modern visitors.

Maison natale de Pasteur

Articles and photographs evoke the 27 Pasteur Institutes which there are now throughout the world, which carry out important scientific research particularly in the domain of immunology; a living testimony to this great man.

Take the passage on the right of Pasteur's birthplace, follow the canal walk and take the footbridges to get to Pont Raynaud III.

Pont Raynaud III (**X**) – View of a handsome architectural group: the Charité (18C hospital), the Hôtel-Dieu (17C hospice) and an 18C convent. The Grande Fontaine, an underground spring and wash house, can be seen under the last arch of the bridge *(to get to it, go down the Passage Raynaud III off the Rue de la Libération).*

Hôtel Champagney (**X**) – An 18C portal surmounted by a crest leads into a courtyard where two interesting staircases and a beautiful balcony on corbels can be seen.

Take picturesque Rue du Parlement, to the left and then to the right, from which there is a beautiful view of the Notre-Dame bell tower, which acts as a landmark to get back to Place Nationale.

ADDITIONAL SIGHTS

Musée des Beaux-Arts (AZ M) ⊘ – *85 Rue des Arènes.*
The museum of fine art is located in the 18C Officers' Lodge, hence the military nature of the decoration on the façade.
The lower level is devoted to local and regional archaeology (prehistoric, Gallo-Roman, Merovingian periods).
The ground floor rooms are reserved for temporary exhibitions.
On the first floor the museum houses, in addition to Burgundian sculpture, a collection of paintings mainly from France, dating from the 15C to the 19C: Simon Vouet, *Death of Dido*, Mignard, *Portrait of a Woman and Her Son*, several landscapes by Courbet and works by Auguste Pointelin (1836-1933) from Arbois, who was creating almost abstract landscapes with large patches of colour as early as 1870. There are also paintings evoking the sieges of various Franche-Comté towns, including that of Dole in the 17C.
The top floor exhibits the contemporary art collection.

Palais de Justice (X J) ⊘ – *The entrance is through the portal at no 39 Rue des Arènes.*
This was once a Franciscan convent. The portal is typical of the Renaissance style in Dole. A 16C well is to be found in what used to be the cloisters. The wrought-iron grilles and balustrades date from the 18C.

Hôtel-Dieu (X) – This 17C hospice was the last major construction project before the town fell to the French. The severity of the long façade and high roof of this stately building is softened by a remarkable balcony, supported by sculpted corbels, and the double windows with stone frames. The inner courtyard is laid out like cloisters with two storeys of arcades.

Cours St-Mauris (BY) – The esplanade was made into a public gardens at the turn of the 17-18C, when the town's fortifications were demolished. The area beneath the esplanade is a typically 19C landscaped garden.

St-Jean-l'Évangéliste (AZ) ⊘ – This church was built from 1961 to 1964 by architects Konrady and D. Cotter. It is strikingly original in style; the sail-like roof is made of two hyperbola-shaped parts. A beautiful wrought-iron **grille**★ by Calka, illustrating the Apocalypse, surrounds the glass walls; note particularly the *Lamb* and the *Woman and Dragon*. Extracts from the Revelation of St John are painted on the walls to the right of the altar and over the door. A wrought-iron eagle, the symbol of St John the Evangelist, adorns the base of the lectern. The baptistery and the altar were built from local stone.

▶▶ **Auxonne** – *13km - 8 miles north.* Facilities. **Napoleon Bonaparte Museum** ⊘.

Vallée du DOUBS★★

Michelin maps 170 folds 6 and 7 and 166 folds 15-18 or 243 folds 32, 33, 19-22

The numerous twists and turns it makes along its course make the Doubs an archetypal Jura river. The "uncertainty" (Lat.: *"dubius"*) which earned the river its name arises from the great variety of landscapes through which its beautiful valley passes.

From valley to valley – The river rises near Mouthe, at an altitude of 937m - 3 074ft. There are only 90km - 55 miles as the crow flies from the river's source to its confluence with the Saône, but the terrain in between consists of a series of mountain folds which force the Doubs to keep changing direction. The resulting detours bring the actual length of the river's course to 430km - 267 miles.
The way the course of the Doubs is determined is typical of rivers in this region: from its source in St-Ursanne it flows parallel with the folds in the mountain chain, that is, southwest to northeast. Whenever it comes to a transverse valley (*"cluse"* in French) the water run through this open gap into the next valley fold, in which it once more turns to flow parallel with the mountain chain until the next *cluse* offers it a chance to escape into the next valley. The upper reaches of the Doubs are the most interesting stretch of the river: in some places it surges through narrow green gorges, cut deep into the limestone (e.g. Entre Roches, Coin de la Roche, Goumois); in others it meanders sluggishly like a mature river on a plain (e.g. in the Bassin de Morteau or "dead water" basin); at certain points it forms lakes (St-Point, Chaillexon) or waterfalls (Saut du Doubs).

A dawdling river – If the Doubs continued to flow from southwest to northeast, it would eventually join the Rhine (which was indeed the case in the Tertiary era). However, at St-Ursanne the mountain chain alongside the river is cut by a curious horseshoe-shaped *cluse*. The Doubs flows into it, does a complete turnabout and heads back towards the Saône, flowing through a deep, steep-sided valley.
The Dessoubre flows into the Doubs at St-Hippolyte. Just before Pont-de-Roide the Doubs changes direction again, then heads directly north, as if it were aiming for the Alsace plain, and crosses a deep *cluse* in the Lomont mountain range. But it does not follow this course for long; at Audincourt its path is blocked by mountains which force the Doubs to twist one last time towards the southwest, that is, towards the Saône. The river has reached the last foothills of the Jura and finally emerges from this mountainous region, in which it has been forced so often to stray.

The river flows on in numerous meanders between steep slopes along the edge of the mountain massif as far as Besançon. Then it heads off towards Dole, where its main tributary, the Loue, joins it. The Doubs meanders along casually in the plain, before finally flowing into the Saône at Verdun-sur-le-Doubs (alt 180m - 590ft). From source to confluence, the river has thus dropped a total of 757m - 2 484ft.

① THE UPPER VALLEY

From the source to Morteau

68km - 42 miles – allow a half-day – local map below.

Source du Doubs – The road *(signposted - 2km - 1.2 miles)* which leaves from the war memorial in **Mouthe** *(facilities)* leads to the river's source; there is a car park nearby *(100m away).*

The Mouthe valley, where the Doubs rises, has a mixed landscape of meadows and fir trees. The crystal-clear spring gurgles forth from a cave at the foot of a steep slope in the forest of Noirmont, at an altitude of 937m - 3 074ft.

Take the D 437 for 15km - 9.3 miles in the direction of Pontarlier.

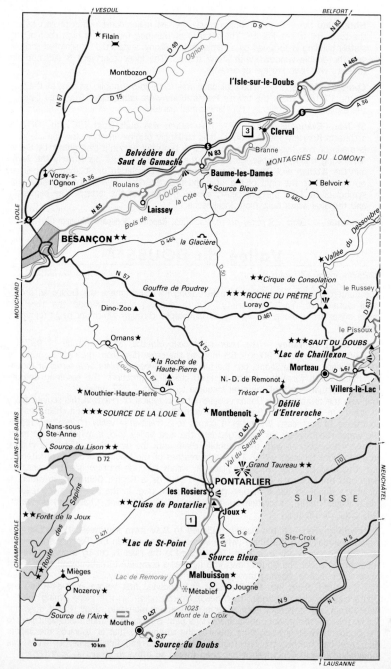

Before the Ice Age the Doubs left its present course at Gellin to flow directly into Remoray lake (near Malbuisson - *qv*). Then, it followed the Brey valley, as the D 437 now does, instead of, as it now does, flowing round Mont de la Croix (alt 1 023m - 3 356ft) and through a beautiful *cluse* to reach the plain at Labergement-Sainte-Marie.

★ **Malbuisson and the Lac de St-Point** – Facilities. This small holiday resort lies on the east bank of the lake of St-Point in a valley enclosed at both ends by mountains. Legend has it that there is a town at the bottom of the lake (6.3km - 4 miles long by 800m - half a mile wide), drowned because its inhabitants refused to give shelter to a young mother and her child. Since a dam has been built at the north end of the lake, it has been possible to regulate the flow of the Doubs. Sports facilities *(see the Practical Information chapter at the end of the guide)*.

Carry on from Malbuisson to Le Vézenay, leave the car at the exit to this village and follow the footpath to the right signposted "Source Bleue" (15 min walk Rtn).

Source Bleue – The waters of this spring are so pure and clear that it is possible to see right down into its crystal blue depths. Legend has it that Amaury de Joux returned from the Crusades after five years' absence and discovered that his wife

had been unfaithful to him, so locked her up. From her dungeon she could see the gallows where her lover had been hung. The unfortunate woman is said to have wept so much that her tears ran into the spring and dyed its waters blue. Another story goes that the waters took on the colour of the eyes of a young woman who used to use the spring as a mirror.

Continue to follow the D 437, then take the N 57 on the right.

★★ **Cluse de Pontarlier** – This is one of the most beautiful examples of a Jura *cluse*. The transverse valley through the Larmont mountain cuts a passage just wide enough for the road and the very important railway line running from Pontarlier to Neuchâtel and Berne. Two strongholds command the cliffs: that of Le Larmont Inférieur, to the north; and the Château de Joux to the south.

★ **Château de Joux** – *See Château de JOUX.*

Take the N 57 back the way you came.

Les Rosiers – There is an excellent **view**★★ of Cluse-et-Mijoux from the 1870 war memorial platform.

Pontarlier – *See PONTARLIER.*

Leave Pontarlier on ① on town plan p 226. The D 437 now runs along the Saugeais valley.

★ **Montbenoît** – *See MONTBENOÎT.*

Défilé d'Entreroche – The charming Saugeais valley upstream of Montbenoît becomes this twisting gorge. The road cuts between breathtaking craggy limestone cliffs, in which there are two caves:

– The **Grotte du Trésor**, with an incredibly high entrance arch. The cave is located 5 minutes from the D 437 on the rock face a little above road level. The beginning of the wooded path leading there is signposted where it branches off from the main road.

– The cave of **Notre-Dame de Remonot**, which has been converted into a chapel and place of pilgrimage, in which the water is said to heal illnesses of the eye. The opening is at road level; a grille protects the entrance.

The Doubs, the railway and the road twist along beside each other between Remonot and Morteau, squeezing between steep wooded slopes. It is easy to see how the river has gouged its course out of the rocks in many places.

The valley opens up again at the end of the gorge, to form the Morteau basin.

Morteau – Facilities. This village on the northwest bank of the Doubs grew up around a Benedictine priory during the 12C. There was serious fire in 1865, after which the village was completely rebuilt. Local people earn their living as clock makers or farmers. A famous gastronomic speciality of the town is the **smoked sausage** which shares its name, which goes down very well with potato salad.

★★ ② THE GORGES DU DOUBS
From Morteau to Montbéliard

115km - 71.4 miles – allow a day – local map previous pages

Morteau – *See above.*

Leave Morteau on the D 461, which runs along the northwest bank of the Doubs.

Villers-le-Lac – Facilities. There is a **boat service** ⊙ from here to visit the waterfall known as the **Saut du Doubs** *(see below)*. The boats follow the river's meanders as they gradually open up to form the Chaillexon lake; then they take their passengers through a gorge, the most picturesque part of the trip. From the landing-stage, take the path *(45 min on foot Rtn)* which leads to the two viewpoints overlooking the Saut du Doubs from a height of 27m - 88.5ft.
This excursion is less interesting during long periods of drought, when the Saut du Doubs has a tendency to dry up.

Leave Villers by taking Rue du Lac, just in front of the Hôtel de France, and continue alongside the Doubs for 2km - 1.2 miles, as far as the hamlet of Chaillexon.

There are beautiful views here of the valleys and gorges around Chaillexon lake.

★ **Lac de Chaillexon** – The two slopes on either side of the river Doubs crumbled in here and blocked a part of the valley, creating a natural dam which in turn formed the lake. There are two principal parts to it: in the first, the water is a single open stretch between the gentle slopes of the valley; in the second, it lies between abrupt limestone cliffs which divide this part of the lake into a number of basins. The serpentine lake is 3.5km - 2.1 miles long, and on average about 200m wide *(see table of lakes at the end of this guide).*

Return to Villers-le-Lac and take Rue Foch (the D 215) behind the Hôtel de France, towards Russey. Take the road on the right, 5km - 3.1 miles after Villers, towards Pissoux; then take a downhill road, which leads to a car park. From there it is possible to walk to the downstream end of Chaillexon lake (1 hour 30 min Rtn) or the Saut du Doubs.

★★★ **Saut du Doubs** – From a lake on a small shelf, the Doubs tumbles to its natural level in a magnificent cascade.
Take the path *(15 min on foot Rtn)* by keeping left after the souvenir shops; it leads to the main lookout point over the waterfall, directly opposite it.
There is a very beautiful view indeed of the impressive Saut du Doubs and, in the distance, the cascade a little further downstream, 27m - 88.5ft high, at the beginning of the lake contained by the Chatelot dam.
On the way back, head towards the left *(steep, slippery path)* to a viewpoint higher up, from which there is a very impressive sight of the water thundering into the narrow basin.
Return to the landing-stage or car park along the path along the riverbank.

Take the car to the road linking Villers-le-Lac and Pissoux and drive on to Pissoux.
At the entrance to the village, take the road on the right which leads to a viewpoint 70m - 230ft above the Chatelot dam and its reservoir.

Barrage du Chatelot – The dam, built in a horseshoe on the Franco-Swiss border, was a joint project realised by the two countries. It is an arch dam supported by the rocks on the two banks, standing 148m - 162yds wide, 73m - 240ft high, 14m - 46ft thick at the base and 2m - 6.5ft thick at the top. The crest serves as an overflow. The power plant, which is in Swiss territory along with the water intake and drainage tunnel, has a 30 000 kilowatt capacity and produces about 100 million kilowatt-hours in the average year; this energy supply is divided equally between the two countries.

Saut du Doubs

Lac de Chaillexon

Return to Pissoux and go straight on to Barboux; take the D 211 on the right, which runs along a ridge overlooking the Doubs. Take the D 464 on the right after Blancheroche.

★★ **Les Échelles de la Mort** ("The Ladders of Death") – Immediately after the La Cheminée customs *(let the customs official know you do not intend to go into Switzerland)* take the road on the left leading to the Le Refrain hydroelectric plant. This road leads downhill to the bottom of the gorge, in which there is an impressive **landscape★** of tall cliffs crowned by firs and spruces.

Leave the car left of the plant gates and take the signposted path on the left (45 min on foot Rtn) to the foot of the "Échelles de la Mort" (steep climb through undergrowth).

To reach the **viewpoint** the tourist must climb three steel ladders fixed into a rocky wall, which (despite their name...) have solid reinforced steps and are equipped with hand rails. The climb leads up to a viewpoint about 100m - 330ft high, overlooking the Doubs gorges.

Take the D 464 again, on the right, heading in the direction of Charquemont.

Belvédères de la Cendrée – Take the D 10^E in Charquemont to go to La Cendrée *(car park)*. Two paths 200m further on lead to the viewpoints, from which there are very beautiful views of the Doubs gorge and Switzerland. The first path *(30 min on foot Rtn)* comes to a rocky spur which rises sheer 450m-1 476ft above the Doubs valley. The viewpoint at the end of the second path *(45 min on foot Rtn; marked with arrows)* is at the top of the La Cendrée rocks.

Take the D 201 to the right in Charquemont. The D 437^A leads to the Col de la Vierge (altitude of pass: 964m - 3 163ft).

★★ **Corniche de Goumois** – This very picturesque road runs along the steep west side of the Doubs valley, where the river marks the border between France and Switzerland for a while. For 3km - 2 miles the drive overlooks the depths of the gorge from a height of about 100m - 330ft *(best viewpoints have protective railings)*. The steep slopes are wooded or rocky, or carpeted with meadows when they slope less steeply. The landscape exudes a calm grandeur, rather than any particular wild ruggedness. The Swiss Franches Montagnes range can be seen on the other bank of the Doubs *(linked to this itinerary by the Goumois bridge and the no 107 road)*.

Continue on the D 437^B and take the D 437 to the right after Thiébouhans.

St-Hippolyte – This little town is surrounded by pretty **countryside★**, where the Dessoubre flows into the Doubs.

Leave St-Hippolyte on the D 437^C.

The road follows the Doubs valley and runs through the beautiful *cluse* which the river cuts across the Lomont mountain folds.

Pont-de-Roide – Facilities. Pont-de-Roide, in a pretty spot on the banks of the Doubs, owes its living in part to the Ugine technical steel factories. There is a 15C bronze holy water stoup in the church, and some beautiful stained glass windows by the firm of J. Benoît in Nancy. In the neighbouring chapel of Notre-Dame-de-Chatey is a 14C Pietà. The woods of Chatey nearby are ideal for pleasant walks.

Mandeure – Ancient Roman Epomanduodorum still has the vestiges of its 2C theatre, a testimony to the past importance of this community, located on the trade route between the Rhine and the Mediterranean.

The road leads through Valentigney and **Audincourt** *(qv)*, part of the Montbéliard suburbs.

Montbéliard – *See MONTBÉLIARD.*

③ IN THE FOOTHILLS OF THE JURA

From Montbéliard to Besançon

69km - 42.8 miles – allow 6 hours, not including the tour of Besançon – local map pp 158 and 159

Montbéliard – *See MONTBÉLIARD.*
Leave Montbéliard on ⑥ on town plan p 200, the N 463.
The road runs along the north bank of the Doubs.

L'Isle-sur-le-Doubs – Interestingly, the Doubs divides this town into three districts: the "Ile" (island) in the middle of the river; the "Rue" (street) on the north bank; and "Le Magny" on the south bank. The banks of the Canal du Moulin are very picturesque.

The road twists between wooded cliffs and gentle foothills after Rang, straying from the river's edge when the valley is wide enough for it to do so, only to return and stick close to the river's winding course a moment later.

The river Doubs at Clerval

Clerval – Clerval is a small community between the forest of Côte d'Armont and Montfort mountain, in which a few small businesses have set themselves up. There are some particularly interesting works in the **church** ⊘: two 16C statues on each side of the crucifix and a 16C wooden Pietà in a side aisle.

The valley opens up considerably just after Clerval and then the river heads to the west at the foot of the Lomont mountains. After Branne small islands can be seen, with people walking or picnicking on their shores. The limestone cliff with its cap of green gives way to a very pleasant rolling country landscape. Little villages tucked into the valleys make a very pretty picture, their red roofs reflected in the river.

Baume-les-Dames – *See BAUME-LES-DAMES.*
Leave Baume-les-Dames on the N 83.
There is a pretty view looking back of the village in its leafy, wooded site.

Belvédère du Saut-de-Gamache – This viewpoint, left of the road, overlooks the valley from opposite the village of Esnans and the wooded slopes of the Bois de la Côte.

Laissey – *3.5km - 2 miles from Roulans on the D 30.* This pretty village lies in a quiet, sunny spot on the banks of the Doubs.
The N 83 leads to Besançon.

★★ Besançon – *See BESANÇON.*

A number of Touring Programmes is given on pp 7-9.
Plan a trip with the help of the Principal Sights Map on pp 4-6.

ÉPOISSES

Population 794
Michelin map 65 fold 17 or 243 fold 1 – 12km - 8 miles west of Semur-en-Auxois

Époisses is a pleasant village, on the plateau of Auxois, a livestock-rearing district which is known for its cheese.

It is said that Époisses was the seat of royal power in the 6C Kingdom of Burgundy, notably of Brunehaut and her grandson King Thierry II. It was the latter that the Irish St Columban (540-615) rebuked for his degeneracy. St Columban had founded a monastery at Luxeuil-les-Bains *(qv)* in the Vosges and having incurred the displeasure of Brunehaut he left for Gubbio in Italy via Switzerland.

★ **Château** ⊙ – The château is set slightly apart from the village and is enclosed by two fortified precincts ringed by dry moats. The buildings in the outer courtyard form a small village clustered round the church, once part of a 12C abbey, and a robust 16C dovecot.

To see the four towers which link the living quarters walk round the outside of the inner precinct before crossing the second moat. The entrance is in the keep; the Condé tower (named after the prince who lived there) is a 13C building of rubble and stone, a rare combination in Burgundy; the rustic octagonal tower was built in the 14C; the Bourdillon tower, at the end of the west wing, is the oldest tower (10C), restored in 1560.

A balustraded terrace precedes the court of honour, which is marked by the presence of a well with an attractive wrought-iron wellhead. The château was remodelled in the 16C and 17C and the southern range was demolished during the Revolution. The Guitaut family, owners of the château since the 17C, have preserved many mementoes of famous people who have stayed here.

Interior – In the entrance hall Renaissance portraits are set into the panelled walls. The small room beyond has a richly painted ceiling. The salon's Louis XIV furniture includes chairs covered with Gobelins tapestries.

On the first floor the portrait gallery is hung with paintings of 17C and 18C personalities (Charles de Sévigné, son of the famous marquise). Opening off this on one side is the less elaborately decorated King's Bedroom where Henri IV is said to have slept, and on the other side, Madame de Sévigné's Room with its attractive 16C painted ceiling. When in Burgundy she often stayed at Époisses, with the Guitaut family, as her own château, Bourbilly, was by then in a state of dilapidation.

Col de la FAUCILLE★★

Michelin map 170 folds 15 and 16 or 243 fold 43 –
Local map below and under ST-CLAUDE: Excursion

This famous pass is well known as one of the main passages through the Jura mountains. It is crossed by the N 5, one of the most important roads linking France and Switzerland.

The last German battalion went through the pass on 21 August 1944 on their way out of the Gex region, harried as they went by the Haut-Jura maquis. The Germans burned homes, the police headquarters and the customs point before moving on to Morez.

FROM LA CURE TO GEX 27km
17 miles - allow 30 min

The N 5 from La Cure leaves the forest of Massacre to the right, beyond the Valmijoux *(qv)* dip through which the Valserine flows. The Dôle (1 677m - 5 502ft) towers to the left in Swiss territory.

Near the pass, the road runs along for a while between two walls of fir trees. Suddenly Mont Blanc, the giant of the Alps, looms into view directly ahead. At the end of an afternoon of fine weather, the sudden appearance of this immense mound of sparkling snow blushing pink in the rays of the setting sun quite takes your breath away. There is a beautiful **view**★ down into the Valserine valley from the end of the pass road from a height of over 300m - 984ft.

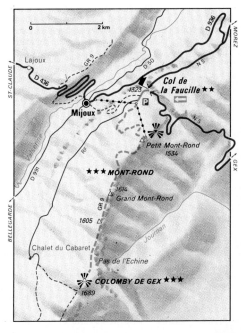

The pass – At an altitude of 1 323m - 4 341ft, the pass cuts a passage through the great mountainous Jura spine separating the Rhône valley and Lake Geneva to the east from the Valserine valley to the west.

The village of **La Faucille** *(facilities)* is a popular holiday resort and departure point for excursions to Mont Rond, the Colomby de Gex and into the Valserine valley.

The road leading to the Mont Rond cable-car *(télécabine)* leaves the N 5 at La Faucille, and then divides into three directions: left to Mont-Rond *(the long-distance footpath GR 9, closed to vehicles)*; straight on to the Colomby de Gex *(see below)*; and right towards Mijoux along the old La Faucille road *(road closed)*.

★★★ **Mont Rond** – *500m after the pass.* The left hand road *(closed to vehicles)* leads to the valley station of the cable-car to the Petit-Mont-Rond lookout point and then on to Mont-Rond *(details of both these under MONT-ROND)* itself.

★★★ **Colomby de Gex** – *500m to car park, then about 4 hours on foot to the peak. To cut down the length of the walk, take the cable-car up to the Petit-Mont-Rond, then follow the GR 9 footpath (signposted) along the ridge.* At 1 689m - 5 545ft, the Colomby de Gex is one of the highest points in the Jura range. It offers almost the same view as that from the Petit-Mont-Rond.

Extensive **view**★ of the valley in wich Lake Geneva lies, and beyond it a view of the Alps stretching 250km - 155 miles.

★★ **Valserine** – *61km - 38 miles from the pass to Bellegarde. Leave the pass heading north on the N 5 and about 2.5km - 1.5 miles north of the pass take the D 936 to the left. Take the D 991 at Mijoux (facilities).* The charming valley of the Valserine (also known as the Valmijoux) is typical of the Haut-Jura. It is bounded to the east by the highest Jura chain with the **Crêt de la Neige** (1 717m - 5 633ft); it is possible to get to the **peak**★★ of this mountain from Lélex *(facilities)* by cable-car *(Télécabine de la Catheline, allow 10 min journey time, then about 3 hours on foot Rtn. The footpath leads off to the right of the cable-car station, but is slippery; you are advised to wear climbing boots with proper non-slip soles).* As soon as the top of the Grand Crêt has been conquered, the Jura chain in the east, with Lake Geneva and the city of Geneva, comes into view. The peak also gives an impressive view of the **Alps**, from the Berne Alps to the Barre des Écrins in the Pelvoux massif.

The equivalent climb on the other side of the valley is that to the Crêt de Chalam *(qv - 1 545m - 4 069ft).* While the valley and lower slopes are covered with meadows, there are forests and heathland higher up. The valley narrows into a gorge in several places.

The main town in the region is **Bellegarde-sur-Valserine** – a small industrial town on the confluence of the gushing mountain river with the Rhône. Near a cemetery, signs indicate the footpath leading to the **Perte de la Valserine**★, where the Valserine disappears from view amidst a setting of rocky crevices and great cauldrons *(oulles)* scoured out in the rocks by the river *(45 min walk Rtn, the path leads downhill through forest and is cut into steps in places).*

★★ **Descent to Gex** – Having crossed the La Faucille pass, the road leads through pine forest. It opens up after the "La Mainaz" hotel, making a great hairpin meander round the green fields and houses of Le Pailly. Leave the car in the enlarged part of this bend, to enjoy the splendid **panorama**★★. Lake Geneva appears in a sort of mist, sometimes even disappearing entirely under a sea of clouds, while the peaks of the Alps stand out quite sharply. *It is possible to identify the mountains by referring to the diagram under MONT-ROND.*

The Fontaine Napoléon comes into sight further down, on the side of the road as it makes a tight hairpin bend around a house. The fountain dates from the construction of this road (1805) and recalls its originator. The countryside around Gex appears shortly afterwards, spread out at the bottom of the slopes, a less typically Jura scene with its landscape of cultivated fields laid out like a chess board.

Gex – Facilities. This small village (alt 628m - 2 060ft) not far from the mountains and Switzerland is a good departure point for excursions. The Mont Blanc can be seen from the village square, Place Gambetta, on a terrace. Gex was once a small principality, and until 1601 it belonged to the House of Savoy. It then passed into the hands of the French, who granted it duty-free status for tobacco and salt during the 18C. Modern residents still benefit from a special tax status exempting them from duty on all products imported from abroad.

FERNEY-VOLTAIRE

Population 6 408
Michelin map 170 fold 16 or 243 fold 44

Ferney-Voltaire lies on the Franco-Swiss border and is a literary Mecca for those interested in Voltaire. In 1758 the philosopher, who lived at Les Délices near Geneva, was having trouble with local residents and the strictly conventional Calvinistic city council in particular, who found his plays rather shocking. He therefore decided to buy the estate at Ferney, on French territory but near the border. Depending on whatever situation he found himself in, he would then be able to slip into exile easily from one country to the other.

From 1760, Ferney became his favourite home. He extended the château and laid out the park, taking his role as landlord very seriously. He had sanitation installed in the village, part of his estate, and endowed it with a hospital, a school and clock-making workshops. He had solid homes built for the residents out of stone, around a church in which Voltaire – who would have thought it? – had his own pew.

Life in Ferney – Voltaire as good as held court in Ferney for eighteen years, with great lords, merchants, artists and writers all enjoying his hospitality and attending the plays put on in his theatre. The immense fortune which Voltaire had amassed, owing to some fortunate speculation in military supplies, enabled him to entertain fifty guests at all times. The curious came from far and wide to catch a glimpse of him in the park. When he emerged from his château, he would be walking amidst a sort of guard of honour of admirers. He wrote his stories here, as well as numerous leaflets and pamphlets, led campaigns against abuse of any kind, particularly against the still-existing serfdom in the Haut-Jura *(see ST-CLAUDE)*. His correspondence was prolific: he wrote or dictated at least twenty letters a day at Ferney, of which over 10 000 were published. Shortly after

Voltaire

the eighty-four year old travelled without his doctor's permission to Paris, where he was rapturously received, he died, exhausted with all the honour (1778).

Château ⊘ – Among other paintings, it contains Quentin de La Tour's portrait of Voltaire at the age of 40.

FILAIN

Population 207
Michelin map 166 southwest of fold 6 or 243 fold 8

Filain, amidst the undulating countryside around Vesoul and the first foothills of the Jura, is marked out by its château.

★ **Château** ⊘ – In the 15C a stronghold flanked by four towers stood on this spur. The right wing of the château dates from this period; the windows were enlarged and mullions were added in the 16C. The central, Renaissance building was linked in the 16C to the earlier buildings. There are large mullioned windows between the two orders of superposed columns (the Roman Doric style can be seen on the ground floor, and the Ionic style on the first floor). The once open gallery on the ground floor was converted to its present state at the beginning of the 19C.

From the garden the 16C south facing façade is seen at is best, framed by two square towers each topped by a more recent, typically Comtois roof in the Imperial style. Under the First Empire, the old drawbridge was replaced by a staircase with balustrades.

The building is entered through a beautifully sculpted Renaissance doorway, which was carved out of one of the old stronghold corner towers in the 15C. The tour begins on the ground floor, in the kitchen where a beautiful collection of waffle irons and host moulds are displayed; then come two rooms containing an ornithological collection. On the first floor there is a particularly ornate Renaissance chimneypiece embellishing the Salle des Gardes (guards' room); the château's two façades have been reproduced at the top of the composition, to the left and in the centre. The tour now goes through the Grande Galerie and the parlours, before going down to the old kitchens, which have been converted into a library, and the barrel-vaulted passageway which was once the main entrance of the château.

D'après photo Larcher, Vesoul

Renaissance chimneypiece in the Salle des Gardes

The **Michelin Motoring Atlas France**
provides the motorist in France
with the best possible information
for route-planning and choosing where to go.

FLAVIGNY-SUR-OZERAIN★

Flavigny is built in a picturesque **spot**★, perched on a rock isolated by three streams. Seat of an abbey since the 8C and a fortified township in the Middle Ages, Flavigny no longer has its former importance. Its narrow streets, flanked by old mansions, its fortified gateways and the remains of its ramparts recall its past grandeur.

These days, Flavigny is chiefly known for the production of aniseed-flavoured sweets *("les anis")*, which were first made in the 9C.

SIGHTS

Park the car on the Esplanade des Fossés. No cars allowed beyond this point.

St-Genest ⊙ – This 13C church, built on the site of an even earlier religious building, was altered in the 15C and 16C.

It has a stone central gallery dating from the beginning of the 16C. Other galleries run along the top of the aisles and the first two bays of the nave, something that is very rare in Gothic architecture. They are enclosed by 15C wooden screens. The stalls are early 16C.

Among the many interesting statues, note the **Angel of the Annunciation**, a masterpiece of the Burgundian school, in the last chapel on the right in the nave, and a 12C Virgin nursing the Infant Jesus, in the south transept.

Ancienne abbaye – A Benedictine abbey, founded in the 8C, consisted of a great church, the basilica of St-Pierre, and the usual conventual buildings.

The latter were rebuilt in the 18C and now house the aniseed sweet factory. There are interesting remains from the Carolingian period of St-Pierre.

Crypte Ste-Reine ⊙ – The upper level of the double-decker Carolingian apse, reached by steps from the nave, contains the high altar. The lower chamber, built *c*758, contains the tomb of St Reina. Following her martyrdom at Alise-Ste-Reine *(qv)* her remains were buried here in 864. The finely carved pillar is a good example of Carolingian decorative work.

Chapelle Notre-Dame-des-Piliers – In 1960 excavations revealed the existence of a hexagonal chapel with ambulatory beyond the crypt. The style recalls the pre-Romanesque rotundas of St-Bénigne in Dijon and Saulieu.

Tour of the town – Starting from the 15C gatenay, Porte du Bourg, with its impressive machicolations, take Chemin des Fossés and Chemin des Perrières to reach the Porte du Val flanked by two round towers. Nearby is the Maison Lacordaire, a former Dominican monastery founded by **Father Lacordaire** (1806-61) *(qv)*.

Old houses – Many houses have been restored; they date from the late Middle Ages and the Renaissance and are decorated with turrets, spiral stairs or delicate sculptures.

Abbaye de FONTENAY★★★

The abbey of Fontenay, nestling in a lonely but verdant valley, is a particularly good example of what a 12C Cistercian monastery was like, self-sufficient within its boundaries.

A Second Daughter of St Bernard – After he had become Abbot of Clairvaux, Bernard founded three religious settlements one after the other: Trois-Fontaines near St-Dizier in 1115, Fontenay in 1118, and Foigny in Thiérache in 1121. Accompanied by twelve monks, he arrived near Châtillon-sur-Seine at the end of the year 1118 and founded a hermitage there. After he had returned to Clairvaux, Bernard found that the monks he had left under the direction of Godefroy de la Roche had attracted so many others that the hermitage had become much too small. The monks moved into the valley and established themselves where the abbey stands today.

Up to the 16C the abbey was prosperous with more than 300 monks and converts but the regime of Commendam – abbots nominated by royal favour and interested only in revenues – and the disorders caused by the religious wars brought about a rapid decline. The abbey was sold during the French Revolution and became a paper mill.

In 1906 new owners undertook to restore Fontenay to its original appearance. They tore down the parts which had been added for the paper mill and rebuilt the abbey just as it was in the 12C *(plan p 167)*. The many fountains from which the abbey takes its name are today the most beautiful ornaments of the gardens surrounding the buildings.

Cloister garth

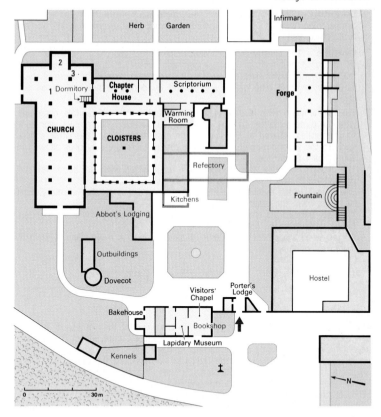

TOUR ⊙ *time: about 45 min*

The main doorway of the porter's lodge is surmounted by the coat of arms of the abbey; the upper floor dates from the 15C. On going under the archway, note the niche below the staircase: the opening made at the bottom used to permit the watch-dog, on guard inside, to keep an eye also on the hostel, the long building on the right of the inner courtyard, where pilgrims and travellers were lodged.

After the porch, walk along beside a large 13C building, which used to house the visitors' chapel and the monks' bakehouse, remarkable for its round chimney. Today this houses the reception area and a small lapidary museum. Further on to the right is a magnificent circular dovecot.

Abbey Church – Built during the lifetime of St Bernard, the church was erected from 1139 to 1147, owing to the generosity of Ebrard, Bishop of Norwich, who took refuge at Fontenay. The church was consecrated by Pope Eugenius III in 1147. It is one of the most ancient Cistercian churches preserved in France.

The expression "monastic simplicity" is particularly suited to the architectural art of the Cistercians *(details p 39)*.

The façade, stripped of all ornament, is marked by two buttresses and seven round-headed windows, symbolising the seven Sacraments of the church. The porch has disappeared but the original corbels that supported it are still in place. The leaves and hinges of the doorway are exact reproductions of the original folding doors.

Interior – The Cistercian rules and plans of design have been scrupulously observed *(see p 32)* and despite the relatively small dimensions of the building (length: 66m - 217ft, width of transept: 30m - 98ft), the general effect is one of striking grandeur.

The nave, of broken-barrel vaulting, has eight bays; it is supported by aisles of transverse barrel vaulting, forming a series of communicating chapels, lit by small semicircular bays. The blind nave receives its light from openings in the façade and from those set above the chancel arch.

In the huge transept, the arrangement of the barrel vaulting and the chapels in the transept arms is similar to that in the aisles. In the north transept arm, note the statue (**1**) of Notre-Dame de Fontenay (end of the 13C); her smile and ease of pose recall the Champagne school.

The square chancel (**2**) with its flat chevet, is lit by a double row of windows in triplets (symbol of the Trinity). Tombstones and the remains of the 13C paving of small squares of glazed stone, which once covered the floor of the choir and a great part of the church, have been assembled here. On the right, there is the tomb (**3**) of the nobleman Mello d'Époisses and his wife (14C). The stone retable of the former Gothic high altar (late-13C) has been damaged.

The night stair to the monks' dormitory is in the south transept.

Dormitory – The monks slept on straw mattresses on the floor and each sleeping compartment was screened off by a low partition. The magnificent oak timberwork roof is late 15C.

Cloisters – The cloisters, on the south side of the church, are a superb example of Cistercian architecture, both elegant and robust. Each gallery has eight bays marked by fine buttresses; the semicircular archways, except for those of the doorways giving on to the garth, are divided by double arches resting on coupled columns.

The **chapter house**, with quadripartite vaulting and water-leaf capitals, communicates with the eastern cloister by way of a splendid doorway. The monks' workroom or scriptorium is situated at the end of the east range. From the latter a doorway leads to the warming room. The two fireplaces were the only ones allowed in the abbey apart from those in the kitchen.

The prison is open to view; so too is the forge which was built beside the river to provide water power to activate the hammers and bellows.

The monks raised medicinal plants in the gardens next to the infirmary, which is set apart from the other buildings.

The path back to the entrance passes in front of the water tower, its fountain cascading down into the fish pond (trout).

A road which goes behind the abbey buildings leads to a very fine beech grove in the forest of Fontenay.

FOUGEROLLES

Population 4 167
Michelin map 66 fold 6 or 242 fold 34

The site of the little town of Fougerolles, in the valley of the Combeauté on the border between the old duchy of Lorraine and the Franche-Comté, meant that in the past, depending on the outcome of the various military skirmishes that took place, Fougerolles was ruled successively by the Dukes of Lorraine and the Counts and Dukes of Burgundy. In 1501, since the boundaries between France, Burgundy and Lorraine had still not been firmly established, a meeting was held to decide to which territory Fougerolles should be attached. Discussions got nowhere, and the final decision was therefore suspended, leading to a period of transition for the town until it was finally attached to France in the treaty of Besançon signed in 1704 by Louis XIV and Duke Leopold of Lorraine.

The modern town, which has an attractive late 18C church, has earned a reputation for its kirsch, which is produced on both a small and an industrial scale.

★ **Écomusée de la Distillation et du Pays fougerollais** ⊘ – *2km - 1 mile north on the C 201.*

This interesting local museum, located in the hamlet of Petit-Fahys on the premises of one of the region's earliest industrial distilleries (1831), aims to show visitors an authentic kirsch distillery as it would have been during the 19C and the early 20C. It includes the distiller's house with all its furniture, the maturing loft, the warehouse and the two large workshops with their rows of huge shining stills worked by boilers or steam. The agricultural setting of this activity, so closely linked with it, and various crafts associated with the distillery (cooperage, basketmaking, textiles) are represented by displays of tools and other equipment and reconstructions of workshops.

Adjoining the buildings is a conservatory containing orchards, in which the various local types of cherry are cultivated.

Barrage de GÉNISSIAT★

Michelin map 74 fold 5 or 244 fold 6 – Local map under BUGEY

Until January 1948, when the Génissiat dam was flooded, the river Rhône used to disappear in dry seasons into a 60m - 197ft deep fissure, known as the "Perte du Rhône", once it got to Bellegarde. The site is now a reservoir 23km - 14 miles long on which pleasure boats of all shapes and sizes can be seen in summer. The reservoir takes up all of the valley floor and fills the series of gorges the river has cut downstream of Bellegarde, flowing at the narrowest point between cliffs either side only 1.70m - 5.5ft apart. The Génissiat dam constitutes the most important power plant in the Jura stretch of the Rhône hydroelectric scheme.

The Rhône in the Jura – The river rises at an altitude of 2 200m - 7 218ft in Switzerland, in the glacial cirques of the Oberland between the Furka and Grimsel passes. The Rhône is a torrential mountain river with turbulent muddy waters until it flows into Lake Geneva (alt 309m - 1 014ft). From here it emerges into French territory as a remarkably clear, calm river, almost a different river altogether, as the dizzying descent from the high mountains is now over. In crossing the Jura the average drop in altitude is seven times less steep than it was in Switzerland. The river nevertheless flows irregularly; the depth of the water can vary from season to season from 0.30m to 5m (1ft-16ft).

The fast-flowing, swollen river Arve joins the Rhône shortly after Geneva, bringing with it water from the glaciers of Mont Blanc. 30km - 19 miles further on, the Rhône runs up against the steep ridge of the Jura mountain chain, a natural barrier which it must cross by flowing through a series of *cluses* taking it from one parallel ridge to the next. The first of these is the picturesque Défilé de l'Écluse. The Rhône, which was 350m wide when it left Geneva, is a great deal narrower here as it tries to force its way through - it is now only 20m wide.

The exploitation of the River Rhône – There are nine hydroelectric plants drawing on the resource of the Rhône, between Geneva and Lyon: two in Switzerland, at Verbois and Chancy-Pougny; and seven in France, at Génissiat, Seyssel, Chautagne, Belley, Brégnier, Sault-Brenaz and Cusset-Villeurbanne. Plans are underway to install a further plant at Loyettes.

TOUR

The site – The Rhône flows between tall cliffs upstream of the dam, which meant that the level of its waters could be raised by 69m - 226ft without risk of serious flooding.

A decisive criterion in the selection of this site for the dam was the density of the limestone, to which 600 000m^3 - 21 189 000ft^3 of concrete was to be anchored. There had to be no risk of water seeping under the dam through cracks in the rock beneath it. Once the surrounding limestone was confirmed as being sufficiently solid, work on the dam began in 1937. The reservoir was flooded in early 1948.

The dam – The Génissiat construction is a gravity dam, that is it resists the push of the water by its sheer weight alone. It measures 104m - 341ft high from the foundations to the top, 140m - 153yds wide along the crest and 100m - 328ft thick at the base.

The reservoir contains 53 million m^3 - 1 872 million ft^3 of water and extends over 23km - 14 miles, as far as the Swiss border. Two evacuation canals were constructed to accommodate the Rhône's violent spates, in which the river's rate of flow can change from 140 to 2 800m^3 per second (4 944-98 882ft^3 per second); one canal is above ground and makes a "saut de ski" (ski jump) to the west bank, while the other runs underground on the east bank. Between them, they can drain 4 000m^3 - 141 300ft^3 of water per second, or twice volume of water of the greatest spate ever recorded.

The **Léon Perrier power station** *(centrale)*, at the foot of the dam of which it is part, was named after the founder of the Compagnie Nationale du Rhône (in charge of the French part of the Rhône hydroelectric scheme). Six pressure pipelines, 5.75m - 19ft in diameter, lead through the concrete mass of the dam to six 66 000kW generators. The power station is capable of producing 1 700 million kWh in an average year.

The **salle des machines** (machine room) ⊘ is open to visitors interested in learning more about the workings of an energy plant.

The surrounding area – *Time: about 30 min.*

Leave the car in the car park next to the monument commemorating the construction of the dam.

A **kiosque touristique** (tourist information centre) has been set up at the first viewpoint, with explanatory and descriptive display boards giving information on the construction of the dam, the nature of the installation at Génissiat and the technical details of the other plants in the Upper Rhône hydroelectric power scheme.

There is a view from the second viewpoint (small garden) which overlooks the west bank evacuation canal with its "saut de ski". When it is in operation (usually in the early summer), it emits a majestic, foaming jet of water.

Boat trips are available on the reservoir in summer between Bellegarde and the dam.

GEVREY-CHAMBERTIN

Population 2 825
Michelin map 65 fold 20 or 243 folds 15 and 16 – 12km - 8 miles south of Dijon –
Local map under La CÔTE

This village is typical of the wine-growing community immortalised by the Burgundian writer, **Gaston Roupnel** (1872-1946). It is situated at the open end of the gorge, Combe de Lavaux, and surrounded by vineyards. The older part lies grouped around the church and château while the Baraques quarter crossed by the N 74 is altogether busier.

The famous Côte de Nuits, renowned for its great red wines, starts slightly to the north.

Chambertin – Among the wines of the Côte de Nuits, full-bodied wines that acquire their body and bouquet as they mature, Chambertin, which comes from the two vineyards of Clos de Bèze and Chambertin, is the most famous and one of the most celebrated wines of all Burgundy. The "Champ de Bertin" (Field of Bertin), which became "Chambertin", was the favourite wine of Napoleon I and was always to be found in his baggage-train, even on campaigns.

Today there are only 28ha - 69 acres producing this celebrated wine, while there are 400ha - 988 acres producing Gevrey-Chambertin.

Château ⊘ – In the upper village stands the square-towered fortress, lacking its portcullis; it was built in the 10C by the lords of Vergy. In the 13C it was given to the monks of Cluny who enlarged the windows and installed a fine spiral staircase, wider than the simple ladders used hitherto.

The great chamber on the first floor with its uncovered beams contains a beautiful late-14C credence table. The great tower has retained its watch room and bowmen's room. Beneath the basket-handle vaulting in the cellars past vintages are stored.

Church (Église) – Dating from the 13C, 14C and 15C the church still has a Romanesque doorway.

GRAND COLOMBIER★★★

Michelin map 74 fold 5 or 244 fold 17 – Local map under BUGEY

This is the highest peak (1 531km - 5 023ft) in the Bugey region, at the tip of the long mountain chain separating the Rhône from the Valromey.

FROM VIRIEU-LE-PETIT TO CULOZ

29 km - 18 miles – allow 2 hours – local map below

After leaving Virieu, the road climbs the slopes of the Grand Colombier along a series of hairpin bends weaving through a rural landscape. Once it reaches the forest's edge, the road makes its way through stands of magnificent fir trees. The gradient becomes 12% (1:8), then 14% (1:7) and finally even 19% (1:5). It passes to Lochieu road on the left and then comes to a broad shelf of beautiful mountain pastures, at the level of La Grange de Fromentel, from which there is a good view of the Champagne-en-Valromey valley.

After climbing about 1km – half a mile further up through the forest, the road branches off to the left towards the Colombier service station and hotel, while the final hairpin bend up the mountain leads to the pass.

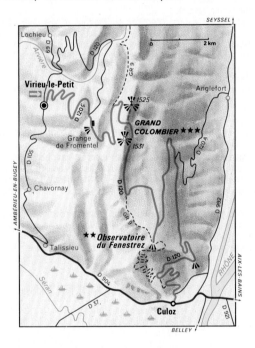

★★★ **Grand Colombier** – From the car park *(extension work in progress)*, there are easy footpaths up to both Grand Colombier peaks. On the rounded northern peak there is a cross and a viewing table *(30 min on foot Rtn)*; the south peak ends in a steep crest on the west face of the mountain and has a triangulation point *(45 min on foot Rtn)*.

There are magnificent, extensive panoramas of the Jura, the Dombes, the Rhône valley, the Massif Central and the Alps; in fine weather three lakes can be seen twinkling in the sun – Geneva, Bourget and Annecy.

On the east face of the mountain the road runs through mountain pastures before entering the forest. From the hairpin bend 5km - 3 miles from the Fenestrez summit, take the right turn.

★★ **Observatoire du Fenestrez** – A footpath leads to the edge of the cliff *(benches and hanggliding take-off strip; no parapet)* from where, at a height of about 900m - 2 950ft, there is a view of the Culoz plain.

The lakes of Bourget and Chambéry can be seen to the southeast and that of Annecy to the east. Beyond this, the view stretches as far as the Alps in the distance, from La Meije (French Alps) to the Matterhorn.

Return to the main and turn right (15% - 1:7 gradient downhill). After 4km - 2 miles keep right towards Culoz when the road forks left to Anglefort.

There are some impressive views of the Bugey region, the Rhône valley and the Culoz plain on the road downhill *(gradient of 12% - 1:8 in some places: 13 hairpin bends),* particularly when the road runs along the ridge of the crest, at the edge of the forest.

▶▶ **Lochieu** – *3km - 2 miles north of Virieu-le-Petit.*

Musée rural du Valromey ⊘ (local farming museum).

GRAND TAUREAU★★

Michelin map 170 west of fold 17 or 243 fold 33 (11km - 7 miles east of Pontarlier)

This is the highest point (1 323m - 4 340ft) of the Larmont mountains, less than 1km - half a mile from the Franco-Swiss border.

Take the road which branches off to the left from the N 57, just over 1km - half a mile south of the centre of Pontarlier, leading up to the ruins of the Larmont-Supérieur fortress.

The **view★** from here stretches over Pontarlier and the Jura plateaux to the west. The Larmont is equipped with all the necessary facilities for winter sports holidays. For a full panorama, continue to the very top.

Leave the car in front of the little chalet at the end of the road. Climb up the slope which borders it to the right and walk a little way along the ridge overlooking the Morte valley, continuation of the Val de Travers.

★★ **Panorama** – The all round view takes in the parallel mountain ridges of the Jura, as far as the last line of mountains looming on the other side of the Swiss border, from the Chasseral to Mont Tendre. The snow-capped Berne Alps can be seen in the distance on a clear day.

GRAY

Population 6 916
Michelin map 166 fold 14 or 243 fold 18 – Facilities

The houses of this small agricultural centre stand row upon row up the slopes of a natural amphitheatre on a hill overlooking the Saône. There is a pretty view of the town from the 18C stone bridge. **Boat trips** ⊘ are available on the Saône.

Gray is the birthplace of the mathematician Augustin Cournot *(qv)* and **François Devosge** (1732-1811), founder of the Dijon École des Beaux-Arts (attended by Prud'hon and Rude). It is also home to an Esperanto museum (Nacia Espéranto Muzéo) with comprehensive archives, literature and an exhibition on the history of the international language since its creation in 1887 to the present.

Hôtel de ville (Y H) – The town hall is an elegant building dating from 1566, with Renaissance arcades and a beautiful varnished-tile roof.

GRAY

Gambetta (R.)	Y 13
Thiers (R.)	Y 33

Abreuvoir (R. de l')	Y 2
Boichut (Pl.)	Y 3
Capucins (Av.)	Z 5
Casernes (R. des)	Z 6
Couyba (Av. Ch.)	Y 7
Curie (Rue P.)	Z 9
Devosge (R. F.)	Y 10
Eglise (R. de l')	Y 12
Gaulle (Av. Général de)	Z 14
Gaulle (Pl. Charles-de-)	YZ 15
Libération (Av. de la)	Z 17
Marché (R. du)	Z 18
Mavia (Quai)	Y 20
Neuf (Chemin)	Z 21
Nicolas Mouchet (Rue A.)	Z 22
Paris (R. de)	Y 24
Perrières (R. des)	Z 25
Perrières (R. du Fg des)	Z 26
Pigalle (Rue)	Y 28
Quatre-Septembre (Place du)	Y 29
Revon (Av.)	Z 30
Rossen (R.)	Z 31
Signard (Rue M.)	Z 32
Soupirs (R. des)	Z 34
Sous-Préfecture (Place de la)	Y 35
Vieille-Tuilerie (Rue de la)	Z 36

H   Hôtel de Ville
M¹   Musée Baron-Martin

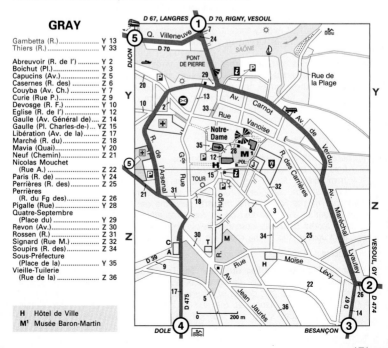

171

La Dame à l'Ombrelle
by James Tissot (detail)

Musée Baron-Martin

Musée Baron-Martin (Y M¹) ⊙ – This art museum is in the château of the Count of Provence, brother of Louis XVI, which in the 18C replaced the feudal fortress belonging to the Dukes of Burgundy. The Paravis tower and the cellars date from the original fortress. In the entrance hall there is a bust of Gauthier d'Ancier (1538). The first galleries contain works by Primitive artists from various western schools: the Italian (16-18C), Flemish (17C), Dutch (17C) – including some engravings by Rembrandt – and French (16-19C). A beautiful collection of **pastels and drawings★** by P Prud'hon (1758-1823) can be seen in one gallery, including three portraits which he executed during his stay at the château in 1795 and 1796. The first floor is devoted to late-19C and early-20C works –·extensive sets of prints by Albert Besnard and Aman Jean, Fantin-Latour's lithographic stones, paintings by Tissot and Steinlen – and to contemporary art.

The 13C vaulted cellars house, among other things, a collection of coins, fragments of earthenware discovered locally dating mainly from the Gallo-Roman era and a display case of Hellenic vases.

Basilique Notre-Dame (Y) – The church was begun at the end of the 15C. Above the transept crossing is an impressive baroque dome. The porch was not finished until the last century. The bays of the nave, three of which are square, have rib vaulting. The sculpted wooden organ case dates from 1746.

Cascades du HÉRISSON★★★

Michelin map 170 north of fold 15 or 243 fold 31 –
Local maps below and under Région des LACS DU JURA

The source of the Hérisson is at an altitude of 805m - 2 641ft, in the lake of Bonlieu to the south of the waterfalls, at the bottom of the western slopes of the Chaux-du-Dombief cirque. The upper course of the river through the Franois plateau takes it for barely 2km - 1 mile, before it drops down to the Doucier plateau (alt 520m - 1 706ft). The Hérisson covers the 280m - 920ft difference in altitude in only 3km - 2 miles, by cutting through narrow gorges, forming spectacular waterfalls. The river owes its picturesque stepped course to the differing textures of the horizontal limestone strata through which it wears its way. Each shelf is formed by strata of more resistant rock. Bear in mind that the flow of small rivers in the Jura, a terrain of mostly porous limestone, is very dependent on the weather.

The Hérisson is a magnificent spectacle during rainy periods. The sight of the water tumbling down in a mighty torrent or in a lengthy series of cascades is well worth the minor inconvenience of having to wear a raincoat and taking care not to slip on the wet ground.

After long periods of fine weather the river, which has no tributaries as it is so near its source, can virtually dry up. Although the falls themselves are not quite so interesting at these times, the river bed itself, especially between the Gour Bleu and the Grand Saut, features some fascinating evidence of erosion by the river's water: natural stone "steps", giants' cauldrons, multistoried systems of caves.

TOUR *time: about 3 hours*

There are three possible departure points:
– **from Ilay:** *park the car by the Auberge du Hérisson.*
– **from Bonlieu:** *follow the forest road for 2km - 1 mile; to the east of Bonlieu church take the signposted road, from which there is a lovely view of the lower reaches of the Hérisson to the left; park the car by the refreshment kiosk level with Saut de la Forge and go on foot straight to the Cascade de l'Éventail; from there follow the route described below from Doucier.*
– **from Doucier:** this is the route we recommend:

Doucier – Take the D 326 east.

Lac de Chambly and Lac du Val – The D 326 climbs the Hérisson valley downstream of the waterfalls, giving the occasional glimpse of these two lovely lakes through the trees *(for details of leisure facilities see the table of lakes in the Practical Information chapter at the end of this guide).* The valley floor is flat and green, the slopes steep and wooded. Once it has passed through the lakes of Chambly and Le Val, the river will flow into the Ain.

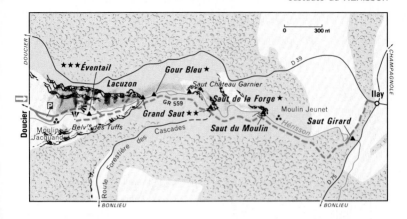

Continue on the D 326 as far as the Jacquand mill (moulin) and leave the car there.

The footpath (Sentier des Cascades) follows the gorges, almost continually through woods. It is sometimes very steep but not dangerous. *Allow 2 hours 30 min on foot Rtn.*

★★★ **Cascade de l'Éventail** – After about 400m the path brings you to the foot of this waterfall *(photograph p 13)*, from where there is the best view. The water tumbles down a total of 65m - 213ft in leaps and bounds, forming a monumental pyramid of foaming water (the name *éventail* derives from its *fan* shape).
The path then leads very steeply uphill to the top of the Éventail waterfall.
Take the Sarrazine footbridge across the Hérisson, and then follow the path on the right to the Belvédère des Tuffs, from where there is a beautiful view of the Hérisson gorge and the Éventail waterfall.

Return to the footbridge and continue upstream along the river course to the Lacuzon footbridge about 300m further on.

Grotte Lacuzon – *30 min Rtn on foot from the footbridge.*
Cross the Hérisson and follow the very steep path up to this cave.

Carry on upstream along the south bank, to the Grand Saut.

★★ **Cascade du Grand Saut** – The best view of the Grand Saut is from the foot of the waterfall. The water falls from a height of 60m - 200ft in a single cascade.

The footpath, now cut into the rock face, is very steep and quite narrow (but with handrails) in places as it leads to the Gour Bleu waterfall.

★ **Gour Bleu** – At the foot of the little waterfall known as the Gour Bleu lies a beautiful shallow basin ("gour") in which the water is a clear blue colour.

The path carries on to the **Saut Château Garnier** and the **Saut de la Forge** waterfalls.

★ **Saut de la Forge** – The river, flinging itself from the top of a curving, rocky overhang, makes a very pretty spectacle.

Saut du Moulin and Saut Girard – *1 hour 30 min walk Rtn from Saut de la Forge.*
From the path, which runs through woods at some points and meadows at others, the Saut du Moulin can be seen, near the ruins of the Jeunet mill, and, further on, the Saut Girard, falling from about 20m - 66ft.

The path crosses the Hérisson at the foot of Saut Girard and leads back to the Ilay crossroads, near the Auberge du Hérisson.

JOIGNY

Population 9 697
Michelin map 65 north of fold 4 or 238 fold 10

Joigny, whose townsfolk have the name of "Joviniens", is a busy, picturesque little town set at the gateway to Burgundy on the borders of the forest of Othe. It is built in terraces on the side of a hill, the Côte St-Jacques, overlooking the river Yonne. From the Yonne bridge, which has six 18C arches, there is a pretty view of the river, the quays, the shady promenades and the town built in the shape of an amphitheatre.

The Revolt of the Maillotins – In 1438 the people of Joigny rebelled against their lord of the manor, Count Guy de la Trémoille. They attacked and captured his castle, and put the Count to death with blows from their mauls or mallets, tools used by the wine-growers of those days. Since that event the "Joviniens" have been known as Maillotins (Maul-bearers) and the maul figures in the town's coat of arms.

SIGHTS

St-Thibault (A) – This church, built in both the Gothic and the Renaissance style between 1490 and 1529, is dominated by a 17C square tower crowned by a delicate belfry. Above the door is an equestrian statue of St Theobald (1530) by the Spanish sculptor Joan de Juni (Jean de Joigny). Inside the church, the chancel

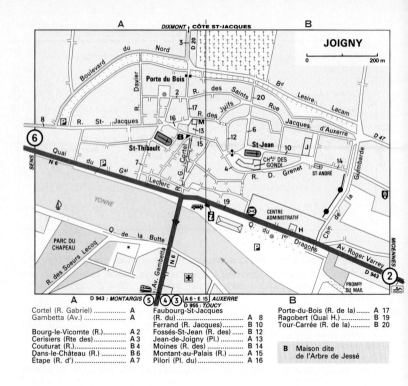

slants to the left; this rare asymmetry is emphasised by the chancel vaulting, which has an unusual hanging keystone. There are many works of art *(plan in the north aisle level with the pulpit):* paintings and sculptures including a charming **Smiling Virgin★**, a 14C stone statue *(against the 4th pillar on the right facing the pulpit),* and a series of low-relief Renaissance sculptures from the old rood screen including Christ in hell *(in the east chapel).*

St-Jean (**B**) – A belfry-porch precedes the west front of this church which lacks transepts but has a pentagonal chevet. The Renaissance-style coffered ceiling has carved medallions framed by decorated ribs.

The south aisle contains a 15C Holy Sepulchre in white marble, ornamented with low-reliefs and the 13C recumbent figure of the Comtesse de Joigny. The tomb is lavishly sculptured and includes the figures of the countess's children. The Louis XV woodwork and the furnishings of the sacristy came from Vézelay.

Porte du Bois (**A**) – This 12C gateway, flanked by two round towers, was once part of the medieval wall, part of which can be seen in Chemin de la Guimbarde (**B**).

Old houses – A stroll through the narrow streets in the vicinity of the churches of St-Thibault and St-Jean will reveal several half-timbered houses dating from the 15C and 16C. Most of these were badly damaged, either during the bombardments of 1940 or a gas explosion in 1981, but have been restored. The best-known house is the corner one (**A B**), called the Arbre de Jessé (Tree of Jesse).

EXCURSIONS

★ View from the Côte St-Jacques – Michelin map 61 south of fold 14 or 237 fold 10. *1.5km - 1 mile north by the D 20.*
The road climbs in hairpin bends round the Côte St-Jacques. From a right-hand bend there is a fine semicircular **panorama★** over the town and the valley of the Yonne.

★ Musée rural des Arts populaires de Laduz ⊘ – *15km - 10 miles south.* This folk museum at the southeast entrance to the village recalls rural working life before 1914; the tools and products of about fifty craftsmen are on display together with a large collection of old toys and many of the carved figures which were popular in the past.

La Fabuloserie ⊘ – *25km - 16 miles west by the D 943.*
At **Dicy** there is a museum of unsophisticated or "over the top" art which displays unusual and spontaneous works created from a variety of material by untrained people without reference to accepted artistic norms. The world of the irrational extends into the garden where more works are exhibited in the open air.

St-Julien-du-Sault – *10km - 6 miles north.*
This small village on the banks of the Yonne is home to a 13-14C **church** ⊘, parts of which were restored in the 16C. The side doorways are interesting. Inside, note the high Renaissance chancel and the stained glass windows dating from the 13C (oval) and the Renaissance (with figures). There is a pretty 16C **half-timbered house** in the Rue du Puits-de-la-Caille.

S. Chirol

Detail from the Dance of Death, La Ferté-Loupière

La Ferté-Loupière – *18km - 11 miles southwest.*
This **church** ⊘ (12C and 15C) in this old fortified market town contains remarkable 15-16C **mural paintings**★ depicting the parable of the three living and three dead men and a Dance of Death. This latter represents 42 figures from all walks of life and is thus an interesting historical document, as well as a moral lesson (death comes to all). Note also on the larger pillars the Archangel St Michael, Dragon-slayer *(left)*, and an Annunciation *(right)*.

Château de JOUX★

Michelin map 170 fold 6 or 243 fold 32 (4km - 2 miles south of Pontarlier) –
Local map under Vallée du DOUBS

This château reigns over the extreme end of the Pontarlier *cluse*, used since the Roman Empire as a route linking northern Italy with Flanders and Champagne. This great trade route also served for invading forces: Joux was besieged by the Austrians in 1814, and by the Swiss in 1815; the fortress was used to cover General Bourbaki's *(qv)* army in 1871, on its retreat into Switzerland; and the German invading army used it in 1940.

The château was built by the Lords of Joux in the 11C, and was enlarged under Emperor Charles V. Vauban fortified it, in view of its vulnerable position near the border, after France annexed the Franche-Comté in 1678, and the fortress was used as a prison until 1815. The last modernisations were carried out between 1879 and 1881, by the future field marshal, Joffre. The stronghold has seen many political prisoners, military figures and other famous personalities pass through its gates. **Mirabeau** was shut up here after his father, tired of bailing his son out of the debts he ran up with his profligate lifestyle, succeeded in obtaining an order under the King's seal to lock him up out of the reach of moneylenders. **Toussaint Louverture**, a black politician who played a major role in the fight against slavery in France, earned Napoleon's displeasure with his efforts to win independence for Haiti and was imprisoned in Joux in 1802. He died of a lung infection a couple of months later, thus missing the proclamation of Haitian independence read out by Dessalines on 1 January 1804. The German writer **Heinrich von Kleist** was also held here on charges of spying in 1806.

Leave the car in the car park at the château entrance.

J. Guillard/SCOPE

Château de Joux

Tour ⊙ – The tour of the five successive curtain walls covering 2ha - 5 acres, each separated by deep moats crossed by three drawbridges, unfolds ten centuries of fortification. There is a beautiful view of the Doubs valley and the Pontarlier *cluse*, from the terrace of the gun tower.

A **Musée d'armes anciennes**, comprising 650 antique weapons, has been installed in five rooms of the old keep. The collection ranges from the first regulation flint-lock rifle (1717 model) to the repeating fire-arms from the beginning of the Third Republic (1878). There is also an exhibition of military headgear – including a beautiful collection of shakos – and uniforms.

It is possible to visit the cells of Mirabeau, with a beautiful dowelled timber roof frame, of Toussaint Louverture, and the tiny dark cell of the legendary Berthe de Joux. A 35m - 115ft deep vertical gallery *(212 steps)* leads down to the underground section and the great well shaft, 3.70m - 12ft in diameter and 120m - 394ft deep.

Forêt de la JOUX★★

Michelin map 170 fold 5 or 243 fold 31

This splendid forest with stands of magnificent conifers is described under **Route des SAPINS★★**.

Région des LACS DU JURA★★

Michelin map 170 folds 4, 6, 14 and 15 or 243 folds 30, 31, 42 and 43

The Région des Lacs, or **Jura Lake District**, designates the area between Champagnole, Clairvaux-les-Lacs and St-Laurent-en-Grandvaux, in which there are some delightful lakes. They are set in peaceful, restful countryside, in which the light and colours are at their best on a summer afternoon.

The lake district extends over the Champagnole and Frasnois plateaux. The Champagnole plateau, home to the lakes of Chalain, Chambly, Le Val and both the lakes of Clairvaux in the Drouvenant valley, ends in a steep cliff overlooking the Ain valley.

The smaller, higher and more deeply ridged Frasnois plateau, at the foot of the Chaux-du-Dombief heights, has six lakes: Vernois, Narlay, Ilay, Grand Maclu, Petit Maclu and Bonlieu.

"Wicked as Weimar" – In 1635, Richelieu ordered his troops into the Comté, and in the subsequent campaign the lake district was decimated by Swedish troops, allies of the French, under the command of Bernard de Saxe-Weimar. Homes were torched, crops cut down before they could be harvested, and vines and fruit trees uprooted. The resulting famine was so great that people even resorted to cannibalism. Terrible tortures were devised to force people to reveal the whereabouts of their life savings. Entire families, discovered hidden in caves or underground passages, were walled in alive into their refuge. For over a century the expression *"Mauvais comme Weimar"* (Wicked as Weimar) was still enough to send shivers down anyone's spine.

The entire province was subjected to this nightmare, with the result that large numbers of Comtois fled to seek refuge in Savoy, Switzerland or Italy. 10 000-12 000 settled in a single district in Rome, where they had a church built, dedicated to St Claude.

Lacuzon, Hero of Independence – One of the caves in the valley of the Hérisson *(qv)*, near the Grand Saut, is called after the popular hero **Lacuzon** (1607-1681), who once sheltered here. His real name was Jean-Claude Prost, and for forty years he was a leading figure in the battle of the Franche-Comté for independence.

Prost was born in Longchaumois and had an established business in St-Claude when he took up arms at the time of the 1636 invasion. He soon realised that not everyone who wants to be a soldier is born one. He would be so terrified before the start of each battle that he would have to bite himself to get a grip on himself. He is said to have cried out as he did so, "Flesh, what have you to fear? You're going to rot one of these days anyway!", echoing the words of another French hero, Turenne, "You tremble, carcass…" Prost's serious, care-ridden expression earned him the nickname of Lacuzon (*cuzon* means "worry" in the local dialect).

The Bresse plain, in French hands from 1601, was systematically exploited by Lacuzon and his followers, who gave the new French landlords plenty to think about with their numerous successful forays. However, it was the people of the Bresse region who bore the brunt of his attacks; "Deliver us from the plague and from Lacuzon" was a prayer regularly offered up. Many of Lacuzon's ruses went down in local annals. One oft-quoted example is the siege during which he had one of his officers, Pille-Muguet, disguise himself as a Capuchin friar and enter the town. The false monk won the confidence of those defending the town with his constant outspoken criticism of the assailants and their leader and managed to persuade someone to give him the key to one of the gates, which he then opened during the night to his comrades.

The 1648 Treaty of Westphalia brought an end to the Thirty Years War and to Lacuzon's military activities. Despite his age, he took up the fight again, when Louis XIV invaded the Comté. The old soldier found a surprising follower in the priest Marquis of St-Lupicin, who mustered his parishioners and led them himself into battle. He would celebrate mass with a pair of pistols on the altar and during the sermon, he would outline the military exercises which would later take place in the square in front of the church. However, the French army proved too strong in battle for the Franche-Comté partisans, who were killed to a man. In 1694 Lacuzon escaped capture by a hair's breadth, managing to reach Milan, at the time under Spanish rule. He died there seven years later, as uncompromising as ever.

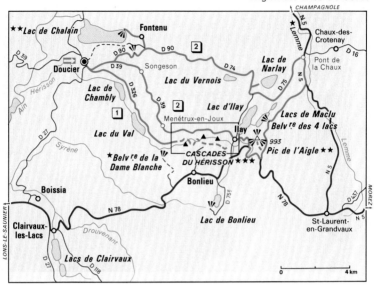

★★★① CASCADES DU HÉRISSON

8km - 5 miles beyond Doucier (D 326), then 2 hours 30 min on foot Rtn –
waterfalls *described under Cascades du HÉRISSON.*

★★② LAC DE CHALAIN and the PIC DE L'AIGLE

Round tour of 46km - 29 miles – allow 2 hours 30 min – local map above

Doucier – *See Cascades du HÉRISSON.*

Leave Doucier east on the D 39 towards Songeson and Menétrux-en-Joux; after Ilay turn left onto the N 78; leave the N 78 north of Chaux-du-Dombief, taking the Boissière road, and park the car 250m further on.

★★ **Pic de l'Aigle** – *45 min on foot Rtn along a path which is indicated initially but sometimes difficult to make out; it climbs steeply to the right, towards the wooded outcrop of rock called Pic de l'Aigle.*

The **view** from the top of the Pic de l'Aigle (993m - 3 258ft), often also called Bec de l'Aigle ("eagle's beak"), stretches across the entire Jura region, overlooking the Ilay *cluse*, through which the N 78 leads, and the Chaux-du-Dombief heights. The Jura mountain chains tower on the left, behind which the summit of Mont Blanc can be seen in fine weather; the plateaux extend to the right, as far as their rim above the Saône plain.

Leaving the road to Boissière to the right, take a narrow road uphill.

Belvédère des Quatre lacs – *15 min on foot Rtn.* The lakes of Ilay, Narlay, the Grand Maclu and the Petit Maclu can be seen from this viewpoint.

Return to the N 5 and take it to the left as far as Pont-de-la-Chaux, then take the D 75 to Le Frasnois. Then take the D 74 to the right.

Lac de Narlay – The lake *(see the table of lakes in the Practical Information section at the end of this guide)* is overlooked by wooded slopes. It has a distinctive triangular shape (the other lakes are elongated) and, at a depth of 48m - 157ft, it is the deepest lake in the lake district. Its waters drain into several gullies at the west end of the lake and flow underground for 10km - 6 miles, after which they re-emerge and feed into the Lac de Chalain.

Local hearsay has it that a good fairy cast a spell over the lake so that laundry washed in it came out white without the need to use any soap (– a useful tip for hard-pressed campers).

Lac du Vernois – The lake, surrounded by woods, comes into view suddenly at a bend in the road. There is not a dwelling in sight; the atmosphere is one of absolute peace and privacy. The waters from this little lake *(see the Practical Information chapter at the end of this guide)* spill into a gully and flow into those from the Lac de Narlay underground.

Continue along the D 74 and take the D 90 towards Fontenu.

Fontenu – The church in this village is surrounded by century-old lime trees. About 800m beyond Fontenu is the north shore of the Lac de Chalain, from which there is an excellent **view★★** *(car park, viewpoint, picnic area).*

★★ **Lac de Chalain** – *See Lac de CHALAIN.*

Turn back and keep right, without going down to the lakeside (one-way), but taking the D 90 towards Doucier.

There is a second **view★★** of the lake 500m after rejoining the road.

Return to Doucier on the D 90 and the D 39.

177

P. Corne/EXPLORER

Lakes of Maclu and Narlay

ADDITIONAL SIGHTS

Boissia – *3.5km - 2 miles northwest of Clairvaux-les-Lacs (N 78 and D 27).*
A monument has been put up in memory of the fifteen young Resistance fighters executed by the Nazis on 17 June 1944.

Bonlieu – Facilities. The restored church still has a beautiful Renaissance altarpiece, which probably came from the Carthusian monastery in Bonlieu. The village is a departure point for visiting the Hérisson waterfalls, the lake at Bonlieu and the Dame-Blanche viewpoint.

Lac de Bonlieu – *4.5km - 3 miles southeast of Bonlieu on the picturesque N 78, then the D 75^E to the right.*
This pretty lake is almost entirely hidden amidst the forest. It is overlooked by a rocky ridge, covered with conifers and beech trees and crisscrossed by numerous footpaths. Boat trips can be taken on the lake *(see the Practical Information section at the end of the guide)*.
The Carthusian monastery at the north end of the lake was founded in Bonlieu in 1170 by Thibert de Montmorot. Jean de Watteville *(qv)* was a monk here. The monastery buildings were demolished in 1944.
A forest road runs up above the east shore, leading to a viewpoint south of the lake, from where there is a beautiful view of the Pic de l'Aigle, the lakes of Ilay, Grand Maclu and Petit Maclu, and of Mont Rivel in the distance.

Clairvaux-les-Lacs – Facilities. The church here contains 15C sculpted stalls from the abbey in Baume-les-Messieurs, and paintings by 18C masters.

Lacs de Clairvaux – *300m south of Clairvaux on the D 118 and to the right, along a narrow road.*
These lakes are not quite as pretty as the others in the region. The greater and smaller lakes (Grand et Petit Lacs) are linked by a canal, and when the waters are high the two lakes become one. In 1870 the remains of a lakeside community, the first of its type to be found in France, were discovered in the mud of the Grand Lac. Nowadays visitors can swim, explore the Grand Lac de Clairvaux by boat, pedal craft or yacht *(see table of lakes at the end of this guide)*.

★ **Belvédère de la Dame-Blanche** – *2km - 1 mile northwest of Bonlieu, then 30 min on foot Rtn. Drive towards Saugeot from the N 78/D 67 crossroads, and after about 800m take the unsurfaced road to the right on leaving the forest. At the first crossroads turn left and park the car at the edge of the forest and follow the footpath.*
A rocky bank overlooks the Dessus and Dessous valleys. There is a view of the lakes of Chambly and Le Val to the left and of the Pic de l'Aigle to the right.

Ilay – Facilities. This is the departure point for visiting the Hérisson waterfalls and the lakes of Ilay and the Grand and Petit Maclu.

Lac d'Ilay or Lac de la Motte – The lake owes its alternative name to the small rocky island *(motte)* rising near the east shore, a pretty little spot shaded by fir trees and beeches. The priory built there was destroyed during the wars of the 17C. A causeway, now submerged, linked it to the lakeside; the rushes growing on it indicate where it once was. The Lac d'Ilay *(see the Practical Information chapter at the end of this guide)* lies in the centre of a long fault which it shares with the lakes of Narlay and Bonlieu. The waters of the lakes of Maclu flow into it through a canal. The Ilay's waters disappear underground into gullies at its southern end, to flow into the Hérisson, downstream from the Saut Girard.

Lacs de Maclu – These lakes, named after the nearby villages of Grand Maclu and Petit Maclu, lie in a valley overlooked to the east by the wooded cliffs of the Bans, to the west by a rocky outcrop separating them from the Lac d'Ilay, and to the south by the majestic cone of the Pic de l'Aigle.

The Petit Maclu lake empties into the Grand Maclu *(see the Practical Information chapter at the end of this guide)*, which in turns flows into the Lac d'Ilay through a 500m long canal.

Source du LISON★★

Michelin map 170 fold 5 or 243 fold 31

Some of the most interesting natural features of the Jura lie in the area described below, including the source of the river Lison, the Creux Billard and the Sarrazine cave.

Underground, overground... – The river Lison, a tributary of the Loue, actually rises on the slopes of the forest of Scay. Its course on its upper reaches, the Lison-du-Haut, is quite irregular. It will vanish underground for a short distance, only to reappear for a little while, then disappear once more into a gully or crevice. The underground course of the river can be seen at ground level in the largely dry, at times strangely shaped valley which follows it. The valley sides becomes steeper and steeper, forming a gorge which is spanned by the **Pont du Diable** ("devil's bridge") over which the D 229 from Crouzet-Migette to Sainte-Anne runs. After heavy rainfall, the river becomes a gushing torrent, filling the valley, before it cascades into the pool known as the Creux Billard.

TOUR *time: about 1 hour*

★★ **Grotte Sarrazine** – *30 min on foot Rtn.*
A gigantic natural "porch" in the steep wooded rockface marks the opening to this enormous cave (90m - 295ft high). The sheer size of it can best be appreciated in summer when the resurgent spring is dry and the cave can be visited. During rainy periods the resurgent spring, fed by an underground stretch of the Lison, flows out of the cave as a surprisingly swollen torrent.

Go back to the road on the right and after 200m take the footpath which climbs up to the source of the Lison.

★★ **Source du Lison** – *15 min on foot Rtn.*
The abundant fresh green foliage which surrounds this relatively large pool, going right down to the water's edge, makes a pretty scene. This is the second largest river source in the Jura after the Loue, and even when the water level is low, it flows at 6001 - 132 gallons per second. It is possible to enter the cave through a small tunnel in the rock *(take a torch; slippery underfoot)* which ends at a pulpit shaped rocky platform *("chaire à prêcher")*.

Slightly downstream, in the pretty village of Nans-sous-Sainte-Anne the Lison is joined by the Verneau, and they both flow into the Loue shortly afterwards, amidst a fertile, peaceful landscape.

Retrace your steps along the path and turn right into a signposted footpath which twists and turns its way up through the woods. The climb down to the Creux Billard can be a bit tricky.

★ **Creux Billard** – *30 min on foot Rtn.*
This deep rocky cirque (over 50m-164ft) is characterised by an unusually subtle light quality. The water in the pool is part of thè Lison's underwater course, although the river rises "officially" further downstream in a nearby cave *(described above)*. The discovery that the Creux Billard is linked with the Lison's source was made after a tragic accident: in 1899 a young girl drowned in the depths of the pool; three months later her body was found downstream of the river's source.

LONS-LE-SAUNIER★

Population 19 144
Michelin map 170 folds 4 and 14 or 243 fold 30 – Facilities –
Local map under Les RECULÉES

Lons-le-Saunier is an excellent base for tourists wishing to make excursions to the vineyards or the Jura plateaux. It is also a spa town, where mineral-enriched waters are used to treat rheumatism and problems of retarded growth.

Rouget de Lisle – The author of the French national anthem, the *Marseillaise*, was born in 1760 at no 24 Rue du Commerce, son of a king's counsellor. Rouget enlisted with the army and became a captain of the Engineers, although he was not all that enamoured of warmongering. His tastes ran rather to poetry and music. The products of his fertile mind - the Lons museum contains four whole volumes of his songs – charmed everyone who frequented the town's salons.

He composed the war song for the Army of the Rhine, later to become known as the *Marseillaise*, in April 1792 at Strasbourg, where he was garrisoned. But the poet-musician was then imprudent enough to write a hymn dedicated to Henri IV, for which he was put into prison as a Monarchist.

On his eventual release, Rouget lived on the verge of poverty, scraping a living by copying music and later returning to his family home in Montaigu and becoming a wine-grower (1811 to 1818). He did not meet with much success, so returned to Paris, as poor as a church mouse. He was imprisoned at Sainte-Pélagie for a debt of 500 francs and was only saved by the generosity of the songwriter Béranger, who paid off his debt to have him freed. In 1830 friends at Choisy-le-Roi took in the now half-paralysed, virtually blind artist. But his luck now finally changed for the better – Louis-Philippe awarded him a pension of 1 500 francs, which at least provided him with some comfort during the last six years of his life.

Maréchal Ney's desertion – Maréchal Ney rallied to Louis XVIII's side after Napoleon's departure for the island of Elba and was appointed commander of the Besançon military division. He was ordered to apprehend Napoleon, who had returned from exile, landed at Golfe Juan and was marching towards Paris via Grenoble and Lyon. Impulsive by nature, Ney declared, "I shall bring him back bound hand and foot in an iron cage!"

On his arrival in Lons on 14 March 1815, however, the field marshall once described by Napoleon as the "bravest of the brave" was assailed by fresh doubts as he reviewed his troops on the Chevalerie Promenade and was met with cries of "Long live the Emperor!" In the grip of powerfully conflicting emotions, Ney allowed himself to be swayed by memories of the past and changed camps once more, proclaiming: "The Bourbon cause is lost forever." He hurried after Napoleon to throw himself into his arms at Auxerre. When Louis XVIII recovered his throne in July 1815, Ney's career ended before a firing squad.

SIGHTS

★ **Rue du Commerce** (**Y**) – The arcaded houses along this street (146 archways onto the street and under cover) make it look very picturesque indeed. The houses were built in the second half of the 17C, after a terrible fire had literally cleared the space. Yet, in spite of the symmetrical balance dictated by the arcades, the people of Lons managed to manifest their taste for beauty as well as the independent spirit common to all Comtois people by varying the dimensions, curve and decoration on the arches. Note the large roofs, with a few dormer windows to let in the light and tall chimneys. The house in which Rouget de Lisle was born is at no 24 (**Y B**).

Hôpital (**Y**) – 18C. A very beautiful wrought-iron **gate★** closes off the main courtyard. There are porcelain, tin and brass pots in the dispensary (**pharmacie**) ⊙.

Place de la Liberté (**Y**) – This square contains the clock tower (Tour de l'Horloge), which once defended the entrance into the fortified town (the square is located on the site of the old moat). At one end of the square stands a statue by Étex of General Lecourbe (born in Besançon and buried at Ruffey, near Lons). To the east the square is closed by the imposing rococo façade of the theatre, with a clock which runs through two bars of the *Marseillaise* before ringing the hour.

Promenade de la Chevalerie (**Y 7**) – The statue of Rouget de Lisle is by Bartholdi.

Église St-Désiré (**Z**) – A beautiful 15C Burgundian School Entombment or Pietà is to the right of the chancel. The 11C crypt is one of the oldest in the Franche-Comté. The triple nave has six bays and is roofed with ribbed vaulting. The sarcophagus of St Desiderius is in one of the three apsidal chapels.

Église des Cordeliers (**Y**) – This Franciscan church is the burial place of the Chalon-Arlays *(qv)*, who were Lons' feudal lords in the Middle Ages. The church was restored in the 18C. Besides the Louis XVI woodwork in the chancel, note the 1728 pulpit executed by the Lamberthoz brothers of Lons.

Musée des Beaux-Arts (**Y M**) ⊙ – This museum exhibits paintings – by P Brueghel the Younger *(Massacre of the Innocents)*, Vouet, Courbet, etc. – and sculpture – by Falconet, Perraud and Franche-Comté artist Claude Dejoux.

Musée municipal d'archéologie (**Y M¹**) ⊙ – The archaeology museum's temporary exhibitions give an idea of its large regional archaeological collections (prehistory; Neolithic lakeside communities; the metal ages; the Gallo-Roman, Merovingian and medieval periods). An entire room has been devoted to exhibiting the Bronze Age dugout canoe found in the Lac de Chalain *(qv)*.

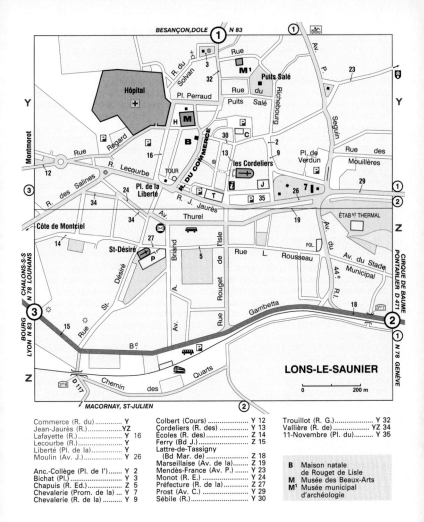

BESANÇON, DOLE   N 83

Hôpital

Puits Salé

LONS-LE-SAUNIER

0   200 m

MACORNAY, ST-JULIEN

B   Maison natale
        de Rouget de Lisle
M   Musée des Beaux-Arts
M¹ Musée municipal
        d'archéologie

Puits-Salé (**Y**) – The town developed around this salt-water spring, used as early as the Roman period.

Côte de Montciel (**Z**) – *1.5km - 1 mile west. Leave town on the Rue des Salines, which is an extension of Avenue de Montciel.*
The climb up leads to a plateau where expanses of grass alternate with magnificent avenues of trees. There is a very extensive view of Lons-le-Saunier from the viewpoint.

Colline de Montmorot (**Y**) – *2km - 1.2 miles west. Leave town on the Cours Colbert (12) and turn right in Montmorot.*
The Montmorot salt works, along with those at Salins, were the biggest in the Franche-Comté. Production stopped in 1966. There is a beautiful view of Lons-le-Saunier from the hilltop crowned with the ruins of a keep.

EXCURSION

★★★ **Cirque de Baume** – *19km - 12 miles east. Leave Lons-le-Saunier on the N 78, ② on the map; then take the D 471 on the left. 100m after going under a railway bridge. Full description under Les RECULÉES* ③
There is an extensive view of the Bresse region and Burgundian "Côte" from where the road bears right, on the climb up to the plateau.
Take the little road, leading to the **Belvédère des Roches de Baume**★★★ *(qv)*, which is on the left 1.5km - 1 mile after passing the D 39 turn on the right.

GREEN TOURIST GUIDES

Architecture
Fine Art
History
Geography
Picturesque scenery
Touring programmes
Town and site plans

Guides for the holidays

Vallée de la LOUE★★

Michelin map 166 folds 15 and 16 and 170 folds 5 and 6
or 243 folds 18, 19, 20, 30 and 31

The idyllic Loue valley has inspired many a painter, particularly Courbet *(qv)*, who painted numerous masterpieces on the wooded river banks. The most varied and picturesque landscapes can be found along this short stretch of river valley, of interest to amateur geographers and nature-lovers, drivers and walkers alike.

The Loue valley's history really began with the invasion of the Burgundians, until which the region had been nothing but an immense forest. From the 6C onward, monks retreated to this solitary place to clear and cultivate the region; their trace lingers on in the name of Mouthier-Haute-Pierre (*moûtier* means "monastery"). Then the Counts of Burgundy chose the Château d'Ornans as their summer residence, and other feudal lords came to rule over the Loue valley from the lofty heights of their fortresses, the ruins of which can still be seen. Thus the history of this part of the Jura is essentially made up of the rivalries, alliances and quarrels between these noble families.

Life in the valley was happy and prosperous under the generous Granvelle family *(qv)* in the 16C, but the 17C brought first the ravages of Richelieu's battle against Comté, then the plague. When it was all over Ornans had only 800 of its original 2 600 inhabitants left. All the châteaux were destroyed when Louis XIV annexed the Comté.

Martel's experiment – One day in the summer of 1901, André Berthelot, son of the famous chemist, was walking near the source of the Loue. He noticed that the water both looked and smelled like absinthe, and when he tasted it he discovered that the river Loue had indeed been transformed into a source of free aperitifs. It turned out that the day before a million litres of absinthe had poured into the river Doubs at Pontarlier, after a fire at the Pernod factory. The Loue therefore appeared to be a resurgent spring of the river Doubs. A scientific experiment was conducted by the great scholar Édouard-Alfred Martel to prove this. He located a fissure in the Doubs river bed near Pontarlier and put some vivid green dye into the water there. The source of the Loue was the same bright green sixty-four hours later. Factory owners along the Doubs began feverishly searching for all fissures along the river bed in order to cement them up, since the productivity of their factories dropped along with the water level in dry seasons. Those who lived on the banks of the Loue protested vigorously, in desperation lest their river should dry up. After arbitration it was decided to leave the cemented up places as they were, but to forbid the blocking up of any other fissures. A small dam was built at the northern end of what is now the Lac de St-Point on the Doubs, to regulate the Doubs' flow to everyone's satisfaction.

A tortuous course – The Loue was once known as the Louve ("she-wolf"). The river surges forth from a bed of rock and runs along the bottom of the imposing Nouailles gorge – narrow, deep and winding – dropping in a series of waterfalls. The gorge was in fact formed by the "roof" of what was once an underground river having caved in. Minor resurgent springs add more water, welling up in the river bed itself or from riverside caves. The cliffs gradually open out to form enclosed basins at Mouthier-Haute-Pierre and Vuillafans, on the slopes of which vines and cherry trees grow. Shortly after this, the Loue is no longer the gushing torrent it was initially, but rather a calm, more mature river reflecting the charming little town of Ornans in its mirror-like surface.

The Loue meanders between steep banks on its way from Ornans to Chenecey-Buillon. The limestone cliffs bear the evidence of the progressive deepening of the river's course, as it cuts its way into the plateau. After Chenecey the river comes within 3km - 2 miles of the Doubs, without however managing to pierce a way through the last mountain range which separates them. The Loue then wanders southwards to flow through the pretty Quingey valley. The river changes its course one last time shortly before Port-Lesney to meander lazily across the plain, before finally returning its waters to the river from which they originally came.

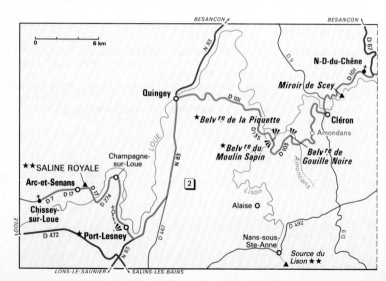

① FROM THE SOURCE TO ORNANS

40km - 25 miles – about 4 hours 30 min – local map below

The even course of the Loue from Mouthier-Haute-Pierre down to its confluence with the Doubs is easy to follow by canoe. The river's winding course, the few rapids encountered, the crystal clear waters and the picturesque charm of the banks all make for a very pleasant trip.

The valley is at is most interesting between the source of the Loue and Ornans; the river drops 229m - 4 507ft in altitude over a distance of 20km - 12 miles.

The water flows along the bottom of a deep, often wooded gorge in the Jura plateau. The region around Mouthier-Haute-Pierre is positively enchanting in May, when the slopes are white with cherry trees in blossom; in summer, the best light is at the end of the afternoon.

★★★ **Source de la Loue** – *After leaving Ouhans, head for the river's source along the D 443, which climbs steeply uphill. Leave the car in the car park next to the little refreshment stall, "Chalet de la Loue", and go down the path (30 min on foot Rtn) to the valley bottom.*

This spot is one of the most beautiful in the Jura.

A bend in the path suddenly brings you to an impressive semicircle in which the Loue rises. It has been proved that the Loue draws its waters from the Doubs. It also is fed by infiltrations from the Drugeon and by rain water draining off the plateau, with the result that the river's flow never falls very low.

The springs swells when it rains and stays muddy and turbulent for a while afterwards, although as a general rule the water is very clear.

The river rises from a vast cave at the bottom of a tall cliff about 100m - 328ft high. From the entrance to the cave, there is a good view of the power and size of the Loue's source.

Return to Ouhans and take the D 41 on the right towards Levier, then take the D 376 on the right shortly afterwards. On leaving of Renédale, leave the car near the entrance gate of the path leading to the viewpoint.

★ **Belvédère de Renédale** – *15 min on foot Rtn.*

This pleasant path overlooks the Nouailles gorge from a height of 350m - 1 148ft. It leads to a platform from which there is virtually a **bird's-eye view** down into the gorge; directly opposite are the cliffs with the D 67 winding its way along them.

Take the D 376 again to head north; after 2.5km - 1.5 miles the road ends at the foot of a television broadcasting station, at a viewpoint.

★★ **Belvédère du Moine de la Vallée** – Touring Club de France bench. There is a superb **panorama** of the Loue valley northwest to Vuillafans, Roche mountain and the village of Mouthier-Haute-Pierre.

Take the road back to Ouhans and carry on along the D 41 as far as the junction with the D 67; turn left into this towards Besançon.

★ **Gorges de Nouailles** – This gorge was the favoured haunt of the Vouivre, the winged serpent of Franche-Comté legend which flew as fast as lightning. Daring country folk eager for riches dreamed of stealing the carbuncle which it wore on its forehead.

The little café called "La Creuse" marks the start of the gorge.

There is a walk (1 hour 30 min on foot Rtn) from the "Café La Creuse" to the source of the Loue; take the path along the gorge which branches off from the D 67. This wooded path twists along the steep cliff.

The path gives beautiful **glimpses**★ of the gorge, which is over 200m - 656ft deep. The walk goes down to the bottom of the cirque in which the Loue rises *(see above)*. A footbridge leads to the cave from which the river springs.

★★ **Belvédères** – Two viewpoints come one after the other along the D 67, from which one of the most beautiful meanders in the river can be seen, from a height of 150m - 492ft.

Another viewpoint is 300m further on (Touring Club de France bench), known as the **Belvédère de Mouthier**. The **view**★★ is remarkable, taking in Mouthier as well as the upper Loue valley at the end of the Nouailles gorge. The Mouthier hydro-electric plant is visible in the dip.

Source du Pontet and Grotte des Faux-Monnayeurs – *45 min on foot Rtn from the D 67*. The walk is mostly through woods, climbing up slopes that are some-times quite steep. Iron ladders lead to these two caves; that of the Faux-Mon-nayeurs is not recommended to visitors with no head for heights. The source of Le Pontet is a resurgent spring welling up in a cave at the bottom of a wooded hol-low. The Faux-Monnayeurs cave ("Counterfeiters' Cave", so named as it is said that counterfeit money was made here in the 17C) is about 30m - 98ft higher up; this was the river's original source.

Cascade de Syratu – Visitors climbing back up the valley will see Syratu waterfall, just at the exit to Mouthier-Haute-Pierre, tumbling from a high cliff.

Mouthier-Haute-Pierre

★ **Mouthier-Haute-Pierre** – Facilities. This charming vil-lage set in a rocky amphi-theatre is, along with Ornans, one of the prettiest spots in the Loue valley. One or two old houses still stand near the church in the upper part of the vil-lage (Mouthier Haut). The village grew up around an old Benedictine priory, first recorded in 870 and decon-secrated during the French Revolution. The **village church** was built in the 15C and extended in the 16C; note the carved wood-work (altarpiece, stalls, confes-sional, pulpit) and the various wooden statues dating from the 13 and 14C. Mouthier is at its most delightful at the end of April, when the cherry trees are in bloom.

Excellent cherries are har-vested downstream of Mou-thier in the area known as the "Loue orchard"; they are also used to make a famous kirsch.

Lods – Facilities. This vil-lage (pronounced "Lo") is on the banks of the Loue, where the river is broken by waterfalls which are particularly beautiful when the water level is high. The old Lods forges are on the opposite bank.

Vuillafans – Old houses, once the homes of merchants or aristocrats, are still standing here. A charming 16C bridge spans the Loue.

The D 67 leads to Ornans.

★ **Ornans** – *See ORNANS.*

② **FROM ORNANS TO CHISSEY-SUR-LOUE**

65km - 40 miles - allow 5 hours - local map previous pages

Except for the last few miles along the N 83, this route follows some charming little roads along the banks of the Loue for the most part, but which wander away from the river in some places. The trip is at its most picturesque between Cléron and the confluence of the Loue and the Lison.

★ **Ornans** – *See ORNANS.*

Leave Ornans on the D 67 west; after 2.5km - 1.5 miles take the D 101 to the left.

Chapelle de Notre-Dame-du-Chêne – The chapel can be seen from the D 101. It was built to celebrate a miraculous revelation in 1803, when a young girl from the area claimed that there was a statue of the Virgin Mary in the trunk of a cer-tain oak tree. The tree was opened up, and an old terracotta Madonna was indeed found inside, the tree bark having grown over it. The statuette, kept in the chapel,

Château de Cléron

has drawn pilgrims ever since: on Whit Monday, the Sunday of Corpus Christi, 15 August (Assumption) and the following Wednesday and the first Sunday in September. A bronze Virgin now stands on the spot where the oak once grew.

Miroir de Scey – *Follow the signs from the road.*
This is the name given to a beautiful meander in the Loue, where the trees and plants on the river banks, and the ruins of a fortress, the Châtel-St-Denis, are reflected in the river's waters (*miroir* means mirror).

Cléron – From the bridge over the Loue a well-preserved 14-16C **château** ⊘ comes into sight downstream. With its reflection in the river and surrounded by its grounds, it makes a beautiful picture. There is a pretty view of the valley upstream.

There are three viewpoints *(car parks)* between Amondans and the confluence of the Loue and Lison, all at the edge of cliffs overlooking the river valley which is narrow and deserted at this point.

Belvédère de Gouille Noire – View of the Amondans stream directly below. This small tributary of the Loue flows between two rocky spurs.

★ **Belvédère de la Piquette** – *15 min on foot Rtn from the D 135. Follow a wide path for about 100m, then take the path on the right; turn right at the edge of the cliff.*
There is a **view** of a meander in the Loue, as it swirls around a wooded spur between steep banks.

★ **Belvédère du Moulin Sapin** – *Beside the D 135.* There is a beautiful **view** of the peaceful Lison valley.

The bridge crosses the Lison just after it flows into the Loue, in a lovely calm **setting**★. The source of the Lison *(qv)* near Nans-sous-Sainte-Anne is one of the most famous sights in the Jura. Soon, the old Châtillon forge come into sight from the road. Upstream of the dam, there is a pretty view of some little wooded islands.

Quingey – A path, bordered with plane trees, runs along the south bank of the Loue, offering a pretty view, especially in the morning, of the little market town on the opposite bank reflected in the water.
Take the N 83 south and then the D 48 on the right, by the bend in the river.

★ **Port-Lesney** – This pretty village on the charming river Loue is a popular place in summer for a country holiday. On Sundays, fishermen, boating enthusiasts and lovers of trout and fried fish flock to the village.
There is a footpath *(1 hour Rtn)* from the Chapelle de Lorette which leads through the undergrowth to the Belvédère Edgar Faure overlooking the village and the entire valley.

The D 274 follows the outer curve of the bend in the river at **Champagne-sur-Loue,** north of Port-Lesney. There is a beautiful view from the village of the slopes of the north bank.
Shortly before Cramans, take the D 17^E, which leads straight to Arc-et-Senans.

Arc-et-Senans – *See ARC-ET-SENANS.*

Chissey-sur-Loue – The interesting 13C church has a majestic-looking doorway, on which the tympanum features a sculpture of Christ Bound. The upper part of the walls is decorated with a frieze of small trefoil arches. Inside, note the stone baboons supporting the cornice of the main nave, the pulpit (18C), the gilded altarpiece of St Christopher (17C), the giant polychrome stone statue of St Christopher (15C) and a marvellous statue of the Virgin Mary.

LOUHANS

Population 6 140
Michelin map 70 northwest of fold 13 or 243 fold 29 – Facilities

Louhans is a picturesque little town and is an important centre for butter, eggs and Bresse poultry, which is known as Louhannaise poultry. The town is also known for its pig and cattle markets.

SIGHTS

Hôtel-Dieu ⊙ – The 18C hospital contains two large public rooms divided by a wrought-iron screen. Each curtained bed bears a plaque indicating for whom the bed was intended – usually the benefactors offered a bed to the inhabitants of a particular town.
The **pharmacy**, decorated with Louis XIV woodwork, displays a beautiful collection of hand-blown glass vessels and Hispano-Moorish lustreware. There is also a most unusual Burgundian wood-carving of the Virgin of Mercy kneeling before the dead Christ (early-16C).

★ **Grande-Rue** – The arches of the old houses with wood or stone pillars, which date from the late Middle Ages, provide a picturesque scene.

Church – This building has been greatly restored with stone and brick and is roofed with glazed tiles. On the left is a belfry-porch and large chapel with turreted pavilions.

L'Atelier d'un journal ⊙ – This annexe of the local museum, the Écomusée de la Bresse bourguignonne at the Château de Pierre-de-Bresse *(qv)* is housed in the old premises *(29 rue des Dôdanes)* of the Independent (l'Indépendant), a Bresse newspaper abandoned in 1984 after a hundred years of publication. The old machines are still in place; the offices have been reconstructed.

EXCURSION

Chaisiers et pailleuses de Rancy ⊙ – *12km - 8 miles southwest by the D 971 on the outskirts of Rancy.*
Chair-making, which at the beginning of the 19C was a long-established part-time occupation in Rancy and Bantanges, had become a full-time job by the end of the century. This centre is now the second most important French producer of straw-bottomed chairs. This annexe of the Écomusée de la Bresse bourguignonne at the Château de Pierre-de-Bresse *(qv)* illustrates the development of the different stages in this manufacture from the making of the wooden frame to the addition of the straw seat.

LUXEUIL-LES-BAINS✚

Population 8 790
Michelin map 66 fold 6 or 242 fold 38 – Facilities

Luxeuil-les-Bains is a well known spa town specialising in the treatment of gynaecological and venous illnesses.
The town is predominantly built in red sandstone and contains many interesting monuments and old residences. The construction of a large airbase near the town has opened up new possibilities for the town, which has also made great strides in recent years in the range of facilities it has to offer (concert hall, casino, tennis courts, golf course, swimming pool).
Luxeuil was the seat of a famous abbey founded by **St Columban**, an Irish monk who came to France in 590 with a dozen companions. He was forced to seek refuge at Bobbio in Italy after he rebuked the king of Burgundy for his loose living.

SIGHTS

★ **Hôtel du Cardinal Jouffroy** (**B**) – Cardinal Jouffroy, abbot of Luxeuil and later archbishop of Albi, was highly favoured by Louis XI throughout his life. The house in which he lived (15C) is the most beautiful in Luxeuil. In addition to its Flamboyant Gothic windows and arcade, it has some Renaissance features, including, on one of its sides, an unusual corbelled turret (16C) topped by a lantern. Famous figures such as Madame de Sévigné, Augustin Thierry, Lamartine and André Theuriet all lived in this house.
Beneath the balcony, the third keystone from the left depicts three rabbits, sculpted in such a way that each rabbit appears to have two ears, although only three ears in total have been carved.

★ **Hôtel des Échevins (Musée de la tour des Échevins)** (**M**) ⊙ – This large 15C building has crenellated walls. The decoration of the exterior and the splendid Flamboyant Gothic loggia contrast with the building's overall appearance. The museum inside houses on the ground and first floors some remarkable stone funerary monuments from the Gallo-Roman town (Luxovium), votive **steles**★, inscriptions, Gallic ex-votos, a reconstruction of a potter's kiln, sigillated pottery etc. The second and third floors are occupied by the **musée Adler** containing paintings by J Adler, Vuillard and Pointelin. From the top of the tower *(146 steps)* there is a good **view** of the town and, in the distance, the Vosges, the Jura and the Alps.

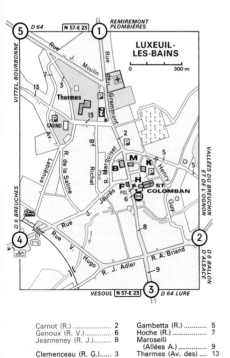

B Hôtel du cardinal Jouffroy	**H** Hôtel de Ville
F Maison François 1er	**K** Maison du Bailli
	M Hôtel des Échevins

★Ancienne abbaye St-Colomban
– This abbey has survived almost in its entirety, and much of it is recently restored.

Basilica – The present building, which replaced the original 11C church of which only traces are left, dates from the 13 and 14C. Of the three original towers, only the west bell tower remains. This was rebuilt in 1527 and the top of it dates from the 18C. The apse was rebuilt by Vauban in 1860. The north façade of the church, with a modern statue of St Colomban nearby, can be seen from the Place St-Pierre. A classical doorway with a pediment leads into the interior, which is in the Burgundian Gothic style. The organ case is supported by an atlas beneath which the floor is decorated with magnificent sculpted medallions. The pulpit, with sophisticated Empire style ornamentation, stands out from the decor of the rest of the church; it dates from 1806 and came from Notre-Dame, Paris. Lacordaire is among those who preached from it. There are some interesting 16C stalls in the chancel. The south transept houses the shrine of St Colomban, and the north transept a 14C statue of St Peter.

Cloisters – Three of the four red sandstone galleries remain. One arcade with three bays surmounted by an oculus dates from the 13C; the others were rebuilt in the 15-16C.

Conventual buildings – These include, to the south of the church, the 17-18C "bâtiment des moines" (monks' building) and, on Place St-Pierre, the 16-18C abbot's residence, now the town hall (**H**).

★ **Maison François-Ier** (**F**) – This Renaissance mansion (west of the abbey church) is named not after the king of France, but an abbot of Luxeuil.

Maison du Bailli (**K**) – The bailiff's mansion on the square north of the abbey church dates from 1473. The courtyard is overlooked by a Flamboyant stone balcony and a crenellated polygonal tower.

Thermes – The baths, rebuilt in red sandstone in the 18C, are set in a pretty park with plenty of shade. Besides facilities traditionally found in spas, it houses a very modern **centre d'aquathérapie** open to all comers.

"Sentier des Gaulois" – This walk *(4km - 2.5 miles)* beginning from the baths leads visitors past all the historical monuments of the town.

Luxeuil-les-Bains – Thermes

A. Le Toquin/EXPLORER

MÂCON

Population 37 275

Michelin map 69 fold 19 or 243 fold 39 – Facilities – Local map under MÂCONNAIS

Mâcon spreads along the west bank of the Saône between the river and the Mâcon-nais heights with their slopes covered in vineyards. The round roof tiles mark it as a southern town. Its lively atmosphere is due partly to the great reach of water, the marina and, not least, to the national French wine fair *(see the Calendar of Events at the end of the guide)* held here every year.

The Mâconnais wines complement the delicious culinary specialities of the region *(quenelles de brochet* – pike fish balls, *pauchouse* – fish stewed in white wine, *poulardes à la crème* – chicken in cream sauce, *coq au vin* – chicken in red wine sauce).

Mâcon is the meeting point of the main roads from the Paris basin to the Mediterranean coast and from Lake Geneva to the banks of the Loire. It has always been a busy crossroads; since ancient times waves of invasion have left their mark, such as the prehistoric civilization excavated at Solutré *(qv)*. At the end of the Roman period, Mâcon, then known as Matisco, was invaded by the Barbarians.

The Prince of French Romanticism – **Alphonse de Lamartine** *(see MÂCONNAIS* **3** *)* was born in Mâcon in 1790 and took an interest in literature and religious issues from an early age, reading among other things Châteaubriand's *Génie du Christianisme*. During his first trip to Italy (1811-12), he fell in love with a certain Antoniella, who inspired his later work *Graziella*. In 1816, he met a great love of his life, Julie Charles, the wife of the physicist Jacques Charles. Julie's premature death drove him to write the melancholy ode *Le Lac*. His *Méditations poétiques*, in which the poet extols Julie under the name of Elvira, were published in 1820, and it was these works which won Lamartine fame. In 1820 he married a young English woman, Mary Ann Birch, and began a very productive period of creativity. In 1829, he was made a member of the Académie Française, and from 1831-33 he fulfilled his childhood dream of making a voyage to the east to visit Nazareth and Jerusalem. However, his daughter Julia died during this voyage, which profoundly shook Lamartine in the religious beliefs which had guided him thus far. The result of this personal crisis was *Jocelyn*, published in 1836, which was enormously well received.

Lamartine's political career – Besides his brilliant literary career, Lamartine enjoyed a no less brilliant career in politics. When King Louis-Philippe came to the throne in 1827, Lamartine gave up his post as embassy secretary to pursue politics. He was elected Deputy of a town in the Nord *département* in 1833, and from 1837 onwards he represented Mâcon, retaining his seat in 1842 and 1846. The newssheet he founded in 1842, *Le Bien public*, in which he expounded his social theories, had a large readership. His historical work, *Histoire des Girondins*, was also very successful. Following the Revolution of February 1848, he was actively involved in founding the Second

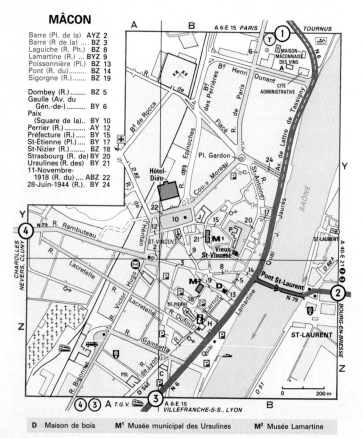

MÂCON	
Barre (Pl. de la) **AYZ** 2	
Barre (R de la) ... **BZ** 3	
Laguiche (R. Ph.) **BZ** 8	
Lamartine (R.) ... **BYZ** 9	
Poissonnière (Pl.) **BZ** 13	
Pont (R. du)........ **BZ** 14	
Sigorgne (R.)....... **BZ** 19	
Dombey (R.)........ **BZ** 5	
Gaulle (Av. du Gén.-de-).......... **BY** 6	
Paix (Square de la).. **BY** 10	
Perrier (R.)........... **AY** 12	
Préfecture (R.)..... **BY** 15	
St-Étienne (Pl.)..... **BY** 17	
St-Nizier (R.)........ **BZ** 18	
Strasbourg (R. de) **BY** 20	
Ursulines (R. des) **BY** 21	
11-Novembre-1918 (R. du) .... **ABZ** 22	
28-Juin-1944 (R.). **BY** 24	

D Maison de bois   **M¹** Musée municipal des Ursulines   **M²** Musée Lamartine

Republic and played an important role as Minister of Foreign Affairs. In the election of the French president by universal suffrage in December 1848 he won 18 000 votes, losing to Louis-Napoléon Bonaparte's 5 million.

In 1849 he retired from politics to his homeland, the Mâconnais. The end of his life was beset with financial problems and family grief. He died in Paris in 1869 and is buried in St-Point.

SIGHTS

Pont St-Laurent (BZ) – Mâcon was a border town until the treaty of Lyon in 1601, when the Bresse region came under the aegis of the kingdom of France. The existence of the fortified bridge of St-Laurent, part of the border town's fortifications, is first recorded in 1077. The bridge was restored and enlarged in the 18C. From the bridge, there is a good **view** of the banks of the Saône and the town itself, with the twin towers of the old cathedral of St-Vincent rising above the rooftops.

Upstream of the bridge the Saône opens out into the splendid broad reach of water (300m wide) which hosts the annual French rowing championships *(see the Calendar of Events at the end of the guide).*

★ **Musée municipal des Ursulines (BY M¹)** ⊘ – The museum, which is housed in a 17C Ursuline convent, contains sections on prehistory, Gallo-Roman and medieval archaeology, regional ethnography, painting and ceramics.

Ground floor – After the presentation of the history of Mâcon from antiquity to the present, the prehistory section displays articles from the excavations at Solutré *(qv)* and other regional sites: flint-cutting techniques, tools, weapons and ceramics from the palaeolithic period to the iron age. The following rooms are given over to the Gallo-Roman period (statuettes, tools, pottery kiln, collection of funerary urns from the Mâcon necropolis), medieval artefacts (Merovingian weapons and sepulchres, lapidary fragments) and sculpture from the 12-17C. The convent chapel houses temporary exhibitions.

First floor – The gallery is devoted to regional ethnography and local traditions and occupations, especially those linked with the river and the land (mason, winegrower, potter).

Second floor – This gallery contains 17 and 18C furniture, French and foreign glazed earthenware and painting: 16C Flemish works; Fontainebleau school; 17 and 18C French and Northern schools (Le Brun, Ph. de Champaigne, Greuze); 19C Romanticism (Corot), academics and symbolists (Busière); 20C post-Cubist canvases (Gleizes, M. Cahn) and contemporary works (M. Bill, G. Honneger, T.-L. Boussard).

Vieux St-Vincent (BY)– All that remains of the old cathedral of St-Vincent, after its destruction by fervent Revolutionaries, are the narthex, two octagonal towers and the intervening bay of the main nave. In the **narthex** the 12C tympanum features carvings which were already damaged during the Wars of Religion. Five rows of superimposed sculpture depict scenes from the Last Judgment; the Resurrection of the Dead, Paradise and Hell are still distinguishable. The cathedral building now houses a **lapidary museum** ⊘.

Musée Lamartine (BZ M²) ⊘ – The museum dedicated to the famous poet and politician is in the Hôtel Senecé (18C), an elegant, Régence-style mansion and seat of the Académie de Mâcon (founded 1805). It contains paintings, tapestries and furniture of the period. A collection of documents recalls the life and work, both literary and political, of Lamartine.

Maison de Bois (BZ D) – A charming half-timbered Renaissance house with finely sculpted small columns stands at no 22 Rue Dombey, on the corner of Place aux Herbes. Grotesque carvings and fantastic animals decorate the coping.

Hôtel-Dieu (BY) ⊘ – This 18C hospital was designed by Melchior Munet, one of Soufflot's pupils. The Louis XV **dispensary**★ has a fine collection of pottery of that period. The Louis XV style panelling is as remarkable as the woodwork of the windows which blends perfectly with the general decor.

MÂCONNAIS★

Michelin map 69 folds 19 and 20 and 73 folds 9 and 10 or 243 folds 39 and 40

The delightful and varied landscape of the Mâconnais extends from Tournus to Mâcon, between the valley of the Saône and the valley of the Grosne (west).

GEOGRAPHICAL NOTES *see also Introduction: Description of the region*

The terraced Mâconnais heights on the west bank of the Saône terminate at the northern end in the Chalon plain north of Tournus. On the west they are separated from the Charollais by the Grosne valley; in the south they merge imperceptibly into the Beaujolais country. The Mâconnais does rise to dramatic heights (Signal de la Mère Boitier 758m - 2 487ft) but the countryside is attractive and varied. The forested peaks and the barren sunless slopes contrast with the well-watered meadows in the valleys; the terraces bordering the Saône and the hillsides which catch the sun are planted with vineyards.

The Mâconnais contains features more typical of the Mediterranean region to the south: instead of high pointed roofs of slates or flat tiles one sees low-pitched roofs covered with rounded tiles known as Roman or Provençal. The region is a borderland between the north and the south. The climate is less harsh than in northern Burgundy.

THE WINES OF THE MÂCONNAIS

The monks of Cluny planted the first vines in the Mâconnais, of which the Chardonnay, the Pinot and the Gamay are the best known.

The king and the wine producer – Although he was only a simple wine-grower from Chasselas, **Claude Brosse** decided to try his local wines on the Paris market. He filled two hogsheads with his best wine, loaded them on to a cart drawn by two oxen and after a journey of 33 days arrived in the capital. In Versailles he attended mass in the presence of the King who noticed his great stature. After the service Louis XIV desired to see the unknown man. Unabashed, Claude Brosse explained the purpose of his journey and how he hoped to sell his wine to some noble lord. The King asked to taste the wine on the spot and found it much better than the products of Suresnes and Beaugency then being drunk at court. The wines of Mâcon became very popular with the courtiers and acquired their titles of nobility; the bold wine-producer continued to convey the produce of his vineyards for sale in Paris and Versailles.

The extent of the vineyards – The Mâconnais vineyards meet the Beaujolais vineyards on their southern border; they extend from Tournus in the north to St-Vérand in the south and include the region of Pouilly-Fuissé, which produces fine white wines. Annual wine production in the Mâconnais is about 200 000hl - 4 400 000 gallons, two-thirds of which are white wines.

The main wines – Up to the 19C the vineyards of the Mâconnais produced only a medium-quality wine known as "grand ordinaire"; now they produce good red wines and particularly good white ones.

The white wines: these come from the Chardonnay stock, the great white grape vine of Burgundy and Champagne. The most celebrated is Pouilly-Fuissé. This wine has a beautiful green-gold colour, it is dry and crisp; when young it is fruity but with age

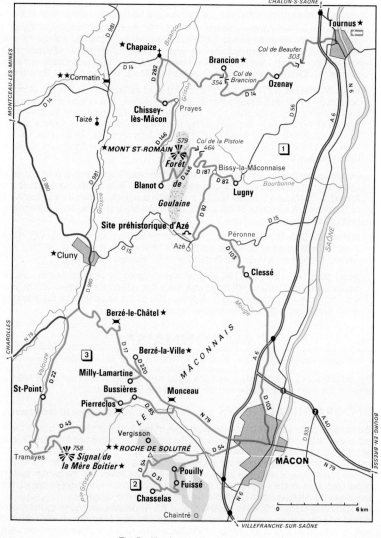

The Pouilly vineyard is shown in green

acquires a bouquet. Pouilly-Loché, Saint-Vérand, Pouilly-Vinzelles, Mâcon-Lugny and Mâcon-Viré, members of the same family as Pouilly-Fuissé, are also well known. The other white wines are sold under the names of White Burgundy, White Mâcon and Mâcon-Villages. They are produced from the Pinot-Chardonnay stock.

The red wines: without pretending to equal the great wines, these can be considered as excellent value. Fairly full-bodied and fruity, they are generally produced from the Gamay stock, which is a black grape with a white juice.

① LA MONTAGNE

From Tournus to Mâcon
71 km – 44 miles – about 3 hours 30 min – local map previous page

This drive passes through a picturesque region of fine views and wide panoramas, as well as Romanesque churches *(signposted itinerary)* and many other interesting buildings.

★ **Tournus** – *Time: 1 hour. See TOURNUS.*
Leave Tournus by ③ on the town plan, the D 14.

The road climbs rapidly, providing views over Tournus, the Saône valley and the Bresse region. Southwest of the Beaufer pass the countryside has many valleys and the crests are covered with boxwood and sometimes by conifers.

Ozenay – Set in a little valley, Ozenay has a small 13C castle and a rustic 12C church.
Beyond Ozenay outcrops of rocks appear here and there on the slopes.
Most houses have a porch and covered balcony forming a loggia.
From the Brancion pass, take the road to the old market town of Brancion, picturesquely perched on a promontory.

★ **Brancion** – *See BRIANCION.*
Returning to the pass, go as far as Chapaize, which is pinpointed at a distance by its fine belfry.

★ **Chapaize** – *Time: 30 min. See CHAPAIZE.*
Opposite the church in Chapaize take the road to Lys; turn left.

Chissey-lès-Mâcon – The 12C church with an elegant belfry, typical of Cluny, has curious historiated capitals.
Continue east to Prayes; turn right into the D 146.
Take the D 446 northeast.

Blanot – *8km - 5 miles south of Chissey.*
This old village at the foot of the Mont St-Romain is home to the fortified buildings of a 14C **priory★** which once belonged to Cluny. Three tombs dating from the Merovingian period were discovered here. The apse of the late 11C **church** is decorated with a pretty openwork frieze. The Romanesque bell tower is decorated with Lombard arcades and has a curious widely oversailing roof.
Carry on northeast. The pretty road (the D 446) leads through the beautiful forest of Goulaine (Forêt domaniale) before climbing steeply to Mont St-Romain.

★ **Mont St-Romain** – From the top of the tower there is a marvellous **panorama★★** of the Saône plain to the east, with the Bresse region and the Jura and Alpine ranges beyond it, the Mâconnais and Beaujolais regions to the south and the Charollais to the west *(viewing table).*
From Mont St-Romain, continue to the Col de la Pistole, then on to Bissy-la-Mâconnaise.
East of Bissy-la-Mâconnaise lies the Mâconnais vineyard country.
The D 82 leads to Lugny.

Lugny – Nestling amid green scenery, Lugny produces an excellent white wine and is situated on the Mâconnais Wine Trail *(Route des vins du Mâconnais).* The town has a modern wine co-operative.
Beside the ruins of a fortress stands the **church** ⊙ which has a 16C stone altarpiece portraying Jesus with the twelve Apostles.
Return to Bissy; take the D 82 south to Azé.

Site préhistorique d'Azé ⊙ – The **museum** displays over 2 000 artefacts found locally. An arboretum precedes the entrance to the **caves;** the first (208m - 682ft long) served as a refuge for cave bears (many bones), prehistoric man, the Aedui, the Gallo-Romans etc; the second cave contains an underground river which can be followed for a stretch (800m - 2 625ft).
Take the D 15 east; in Péronne take the D 103 southeast to Clessé.

Clessé – This wine-growers' village (co-operative) has a late-11C **church** ⊙ with a polygonal tower and varnished spire, similar to the one on the fine octagonal belfry with its twinned openings and arcading. The nave is covered with a timberwork roof.
Continue south on the D 103 to Mâcon.

Mâcon – *See MÂCON.*

② THE VINEYARDS

Round tour of 20km - 12 miles – about 2 hours – local map p 190

The circuit in the immediate environment of Mâcon is a pleasant drive in the very heart of the Mâconnais vineyards, through a countryside of varied and picturesque scenery.

Mâcon – *See MÂCON.*

Leave Mâcon by ④ on the town plan, the N 79; turn left into the D 54 to Pouilly.

Pouilly – This hamlet gives its name to various wines: Pouilly-Fuissé, Pouilly-Loché and Pouilly-Vinzelles. These wines are highly appreciated and go well with certain Burgundian specialities.

Beyond this village the orderly patterns of the vineyards spread over the gentle curves of the hillsides.

Fuissé – This is one of the communes (Chaintré, Fuissé, Solutré, Pouilly and Vergisson) producing Pouilly-Fuissé, classed as one of the world's great white wines.

Fuissé is a pleasing village, typical of a community of rich and prosperous wine-growers.

Between Fuissé and Solutré, the road affords splendid views over the neat patterns of the vineyards.

Chasselas – This village is dominated by an outcrop of grey rock which appears amidst the heath. The village has developed a vine that produces a well-known dessert grape.

The rock of Solutré, looking like the prow of a ship, stands out against the sky.

★★ **Roche de Solutré** – *See Roche de SOLUTRÉ.*

In the background appear the valley of the Saône, the Bresse countryside and the Jura mountains. After Solutré the road enters the heart of the vineyard and affords a pretty view of the village of **Vergisson** and its rocky outcrop, a fine limestone escarpment.

Return to Mâcon.

③ LAMARTINE HERITAGE TRAIL

70km - 44 miles – about 3 hours – local map p 190

All those who are interested in souvenirs of Alphonse de Lamartine or who appreciate the elegiac style of his poetry will be attracted by this tour which passes through the countryside he knew, the scenes and views from which he drew his inspiration.

Mâcon – *See MÂCON.*

Take the N 79 west.

Château de Monceau ⊙ – This château (now a convalescence home for the elderly) was one of Lamartine's favourite residences, where he lived as a great vineyard owner but where his creditors pursued him at the end of his life. It was in a little building, known as "La Solitude", in the middle of the vineyards, that he wrote his *Histoire des Girondins.*

Milly-Lamartine – An ironwork grille stands before the house where the poet spent his holidays as a child, free to enjoy the beautiful countryside nearby (**Maison d'Enfance de Lamartine** ⊙). The 12C church has been restored. At the top of the village, in front of the Town Hall, there is a bronze bust of the poet and a good view over the vineyards. It was at Milly that Lamartine composed his first meditation, *L'Isolement.*

★ **Berzé-la-Ville** – *See BERZÉ-LA-VILLE.*

From the road (D 17) one sees the imposing mass of Berzé-le-Châtel castle with its impressive fortifications.

★ **Château de Berzé-le-Châtel** ⊙ – This feudal castle was once the principal seat of the most important barony in the Mâconnais. Henri IV made it a county. The castle protected the southern approaches to Cluny from its highly attractive site on the vineyard covered slopes.

Take the D 17 and the N 79 west and the D 22 south up the Valouze Valley to St-Point.

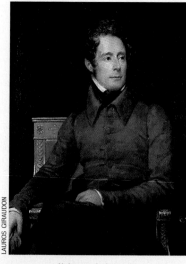

LAUROS GIRAUDON

Alphonse de Lamartine

St-Point – The **church**, in the style of Cluny, has a fresco of Christ in Majesty in the apse. It also possesses two pictures painted by Madame de Lamartine, who rests close to her husband and other relatives in the little chapel nearby. To the left of the church, a small door opens on to the park of the **château** ⊙. This château was Lamartine's favourite residence and was considerably altered between 1833 and 1855. Inside one can see his study, his bedroom and his salon, which contain many souvenirs. These include portraits by his wife, letters from personalities of the period and a 17C Gobelins tapestry (Battle of Zama).

South of St-Point beside the road (D 22) lies an artificial stretch of water which is used as a leisure and water-sports centre. East of Tramayes the picturesque road offers wide views.

★ **Signal de la Mère Boitier** – *A steep road leads up to a car park. 15 min Rtn on foot.*

From the signal station (758m - 2 487ft), the highest point of the Mâconnais region, there is a fine **panorama★** *(viewing table)* of the Butte de Suin to the northwest, the St-Cyr mountain to the west and the Bresse and Jura to the east.

Take the D 45 northeast to Pierreclos.

Pierreclos – *13km - 8 miles northeast from the Signal de la Mère Boitier.*
In this pretty village overlooking the Saône plain and the rocks of Vergisson and Solutré is the lovely **château** ⊙ in which Mademoiselle de Molly lived, who is generally thought to have been the model for Laurence, the priest's lover in *Jocelyn*. Inside, note the elegant and unusual spiral staircase, and in the inner courtyard the chancel and bell tower of an 11C church. Wine can be tasted and bought here.

Bussières – **Abbot Dumont**, Lamartine's first master and his great friend, whom he immortalised in *Jocelyn*, rests by the chevet of the little church.

Return to Mâcon by the D 45 and the N 79.

Château de MONCLEY

Michelin map 166 fold 15 or 243 fold 19
(14km - 9 miles northwest of Besançon)

This **château** ⊙ was built in the 18C by Bertrand, on the site of an ancient feudal fortress, in a pleasant spot overlooking the Ognon valley. The C-shaped façade is decorated with a group of four Ionic columns supporting a triangular pediment at its centre. The side facing the garden is embellished with a rotunda topped with a dome. Inside, the vestibule is interesting. A dozen Corinthian columns elegantly support a balustraded tribune, which is reached by taking the majestic double staircase. The first floor houses a number of admirable family portraits and Louis XVI furniture, as well as hunting trophies and various stuffed animals.

Château de Moncley

MONTARGIS

Population 15 020
Michelin map 61 south of fold 12 or 238 fold 8
Plan of conurbation in the current Michelin Red Guide France

Montargis, the chief town of the Gâtinais, a region known for shooting and fishing, is dominated by its château which is now occupied by a school. The pleasant town stands on the edge of a forest (4 000ha - 9 884 acres) at the junction of three canals – the Briare, the Loing and the Orléans – and at the confluence of three rivers. The main river, the Loing, widens out into **Lac des Closiers** (water-sports centre).

Confectionery and Canine Skill – Montargis has two claims to fame: the invention of **pralines**, grilled almonds with a sugar coating, which were first produced in the 17C by the Duke of Plessis-Praslin's cook and the medieval legend of a dog which by identifying its master's murderer was instrumental in the criminal's execution.

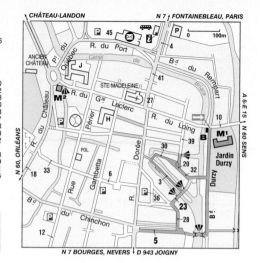

MONTARGIS

B   Stèle
    commémorative
M¹ Musée Girodet
M² Musée du Gâtinais

SIGHTS

The canals – *Round tour of about 1 hour.*
The old part of Montargis is criss-crossed by waterways – the Briare canal, smaller canals and branches of the rivers – which are spanned by 127 road and foot bridges.

*Take the Boulevard Durzy along the east bank of the canal from the bridge which is level with the Girodet museum (**M¹**).*

Canal de Briare – The sight of barges and locks filling and emptying attracts anyone out for a stroll. The canal, which was built in 1642 to link the Loing to the Loire (*commemorative stele* – **B**) skirts the town to the north and east; the water courses which embellish the old part of the town were used in the past to regulate the Loire which was always liable to burst its banks.

Boulevard Durzy – Shaded by plane trees the boulevard is bordered on one side by the Briare canal and on the other by the Durzy garden. At the southern end is an elegant metal hump-back footbridge over the canal. From this footbridge there is an attractive view of two locks.

Cross the canal by the bridge and carry straight on.

Boulevard Belles-Manières (**5**) – The boulevard runs parallel to a narrow canal with footbridges giving access to the houses, built on the foundations of the rampart towers.

From the east end of Boulevard Belles-Manières (retrace your steps) turn left into Rue du Moulin-à-Tan; leave Place de la République on the left and take Rue Raymond-Laforge.

Rue Raymond-Laforge (**23**) – The bridges over the two canals provide views of the old houses and the wash houses lining their banks and of the decorative barges, acting as large window boxes, which are tied up to the quays.

Return several yards to take Rue de l'Ancien-Palais up the finger of land.

At the end of Rue de l'Ancien-Palais turn right into an alleyway which is prolonged by a bridge offering a perspective along the second canal.

Turn right again into Rue de la Pêcherie.

The half-timbered houses in this district have been restored. From Place Jules-Ferry Rue Raymond-Tellier leads to a bridge providing another **canal landscape** which stretches as far as the Briare canal.

Turn around. Turn left into Rue de la Poterne and take the bridge over the Briare canal to reach the Boulevard Durzy.

A canal

Musée Girodet (M¹) ⊘ – The building, Hôtel Durzy, was designed in the 19C as a museum. It is surrounded by a charming garden, planted at the same time, which contains an arcade from a 13C building belonging to the Templars.

The museum is devoted to the painter, **Anne-Louis Girodet** (1767-1824), a native of Montargis, who was a pupil of David and a leading light of both neo-classicism and romanticism. There is also an important collection of work by the romantic sculptor, Henry de Triqueti (1804-74) who designed the doors of the church of La Madeleine in Paris. On the first floor the first gallery is hung with 15C to 18C French and Italian paintings, a St Jerome by Zurbaran and 16C and 17C Dutch and Flemish paintings.

★ **Collection Girodet** – The square salon and the second gallery are devoted to Girodet; among his 20 paintings are the extraordinary *Flood* on which the painter spent four years of study, portraits of Doctor Trioson, his adopted father, of Mustapha, together with the sketch and the replica, painted by Girodet himself, of two famous canvases in the Louvre: *The Sleep of Endymion* and *The Entombment of Atala*.

The second gallery, in which one of Girodet's pupils has painted the local monuments on the ceiling, is hung with works by 19C French artists such as Bonvin, Lancrenon, Chaplin, Ribot *(The Poacher)*, Carpentier *(Portrait of Girodet)*; the display case contains precious earthenware and porcelain including a 19C Sèvres service and a rare breakfast service by Dagoty (early-19C).

Musée du Gâtinais (M²) ⊘ – The archaeological museum is housed in a 15C tannery. The ground floor is devoted to the Gallo-Roman sites at Sceaux-en-Gâtinais and Les Closiers where excavations uncovered a necropolis and a cult complex near a theatre. The other section contains articles from Merovingian burial sites at Grand Bezout. The first floor is devoted to prehistoric regional archaeology; it also contains a small Egyptian section (two sarcophagi, a mummy) from the Campana collection.

EXCURSIONS

Ferrières – *11km - 7 miles north of Montargis.*
The Benedictine abbey of Ferrières, which was deconsecrated during the French Revolution, was an important monastic centre and fount of learning during the Carolingian period. *Park the car on the shady esplanade marked by the beautiful slim cross of St Apollina.*

Ancienne abbaye St-Pierre St-Paul – The Gothic **church** has an unusual **transept crossing**★ in the form of a rotunda rising from eight tall columns. It was built in the 12C and is thought to have been inspired by an earlier (9C) Carolingian building. The 13C chancel is illuminated through five Renaissance stained glass windows. In the north transept there is a collection of 14-17C statues and a curious baroque liturgical object, a sort of hanging pyx in the form of a gilt palm tree interlaced with vine tendrils, used to display the Holy Sacrament.

Old abbey buildings – The open space below the old cloisters gives a view of the south side of the church and the chapel of Notre-Dame-de-Bethléem, which has been rebuilt many times since the 15C and has long been a highly venerated place of pilgrimage.

Lower town – A stray arm of the Cléry gives this part of town a charming appearance. One of the old wash-houses (Lavoir de la Pêcherie) is still in use. The bridge affords a delightful **view** of the tanning mill's sluice, the old rooftops and the spire of the abbey church.

▶▶ **Égreville** – *25km - 16 miles north.*
16C **covered market** with an impressive chestnut timber roof.

MONTBARD

Population 7 108
Michelin map 65 southeast of fold 7 or 243 fold 1

Montbard rises up the slope of a hill that impedes the course of the river Brenne; it has become an important metallurgical centre specialising in steel tubes and pipes.
The memory of Buffon outshines that of the Counts of Montbard, who built the fortress that was to become a residence of the Dukes of Burgundy.

A GREAT SCHOLAR

Georges-Louis Leclerc de Buffon – Born at Montbard in 1707, Buffon was the son of a counsellor of the Burgundian parliament. At a very tender age he showed his passionate interest in science and went on several journeys to France, Italy, Switzerland and England in order to satisfy his desire to study nature. In 1733, when he was only 26, he entered the Académie des Sciences, where he succeeded the botanist, Jussieu. His nomination to the post of Administrator of the King's Garden (Jardin du Roi) and museum, now the Jardin des Plantes, in 1739 was to be decisive in his career. Hardly had he taken over his new position than he conceived the vast plan of writing the history of nature. From then on he devoted all his energies to this gigantic task. The first three volumes of his *Histoire Naturelle (Natural History)* were published in 1749 and in 1752 Buffon was elected to the Académie Française. However the honours that were showered on him, just reward for his work and his ability, never went to the great scientist's head.

The crowned heads of all Europe and all the leading figures of his times sought his friendship and were honoured to obtain it.

Helped by the naturalist, Daubenton (1716-99), Buffon reorganised the Jardin du Roi, extending it as far as the Seine, adding avenues of lime trees, a maze, and considerably augmenting the collections of the natural history museum.

Buffon at Montbard – Buffon did not really care for Paris as the distractions offered him in the capital did not allow him to work as he wished. So he came back to Montbard, his real home. He set up **forges** *(see opposite)* on his estate to the northeast of Montbard and took charge of running them himself. As lord of Montbard, he razed the central keep and the annexes of the château, keeping only the outer walls and two of the ten towers. Inside he laid out terraced gardens and planted trees of different species as well as flowers and vegetables. It was at Montbard, where he led the life he liked most, that Buffon wrote the greater part of his huge work, which eventually ran to 36 volumes.

He died in Paris, in the Jardin du Roi, in 1788.

MONTBARD

B   Hôtel de Buffon
D   Cabinet
    de travail de Buffon
M¹ Musée des Beaux-Arts
M² Musée des anciennes
    écuries de Buffon

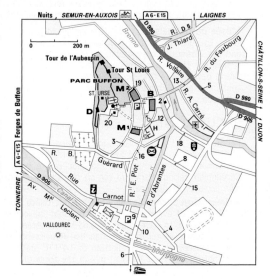

SIGHTS

★ **Parc Buffon** ⊘ – In 1735 Buffon bought the Château de Montbard, which dates from before the 10C and was by then in ruins; he demolished all but two towers and the fortified wall of enclosure. The gardens which he laid out, slightly altered over the years, now form the Parc Buffon. The paths and alleys provide a number of pleasant walks.

Tour de l'Aubespin – Buffon used the height of this tower (40m - 131ft) to conduct experiments on the wind. The gargoyles and merlons date from a 19C restoration. From the top there is a fine **view** of the town and its surroundings. The first of the three rooms contains souvenirs of local history.

Tour St-Louis – The mother of St Bernard was born in this tower in 1070. Buffon lowered the tower by one storey and used it as his library.

Cabinet de travail de Buffon (**D**) – It was in this small pavilion with the walls covered with 18C coloured engravings of various bird species that Buffon wrote most of his *Natural History*.

Chapelle de Buffon – Buffon was buried on 20 April 1788 in the vault of this small chapel adjoining the church of St-Urse (St Ursa) which stands outside the old castle precinct.

Hôtel de Buffon (**B**) – Buffon built the large and comfortable mansion from which he had direct access to his gardens and his study.

Musée des Beaux-Arts (**M⁴**) ⊘ – The fine arts museum is housed in the former chapel (1870) of the Buffon Institute. It contains a magnificent wooden triptych (Adoration of the Shepherds) by André Ménassier (1599), 19C and 20C paintings and sculptures. Three of the artists represented here are natives of Montbard: the sculptor Eugène Guillaume and the painters Chantal Queneville and Ernest Boguet. There are also works by Yves Brayer, Maurice Buffet and three sculptures by Pompon.

Musée des anciennes écuries de Buffon (**M²**) ⊘ – Buffon's stables now house a museum devoted to the great naturalist and to his place in the history of Montbard.

EXCURSIONS

Forges de Buffon ⊘ – *7km - 5 miles northwest.* In 1768 when Buffon, the great French naturalist, was 60 years old he built a forge for the commercial exploitation of his discoveries about iron and steel and to continue his experiments with minerals on a large scale.

His industrial complex was built on two levels: on the lower level were the production shops beside a channel containing water diverted from the River Armançon; on the upper level above the flood line were the houses and other facilities.

The **workshops** consist of three buildings separated by two water channels which supplied hydraulic energy to the bellows and trip hammers: the blast furnace was reached from the upper level by a huge internal staircase which divided into two flights serving platforms where the pig iron was drawn off; next came the refinery, the forge itself, where the pig iron was recast and beaten with the trip hammer into iron bars, and the slitting mill where the bars could be reworked into semi-finished products. Further on is the basin where the raw mineral was washed before being smelted.

Château de Nuits ⊘ – *18km - 11 miles northwest.* The castle was built in 1570 during the Wars of Religion. The attractive Renaissance façade of pediments and pilasters was formerly screened by a fortified wall. The east façade, facing Armançon (the old border between Burgundy and Champagne), has retained its austere defensive appearance. The vaulted cellars leading to the east terrace contain a kitchen with an indoor well which enabled the castle to hold out against a siege. Among the state rooms are a salon with a Renaissance chimneypiece, an 18C Venetian bedroom and a 19C dining room (neo-Baroque chimneypiece).

MONTBÉLIARD

Population 117 510
Michelin map 166 fold 8 or 243 fold 10 – Local map under Vallée du DOUBS

The majestic shape of the castle, framed between two round, fat towers, high above Montbéliard testifies to this city's rich past.

HISTORICAL NOTES

The fortified hilltop village of "Mons Beligardae" began to expand in earnest after the destruction of Mandeure *(qv)* in the 8C. It was ruled as an independent county by a succession of different noble families, including the Montfaucons. As the last Montfaucon died without male issue, the county was inherited by one of his granddaughters, Henriette d'Orbe. In 1397 she married Prince Eberhard IV of Württemberg, thus bringing Montbéliard under the rule of the Germanic Empire.

"Mömpelgard", a German principality – For the next four centuries the principality of Montbéliard was a small German enclave, known as **Mömpelgard**, within the borders of France and frequently quite a thorn in the flesh of French rulers. The territory covered an old Gallo-Roman *pagus* (administrative unit), encompassing the seigneurial domains of Héricourt, Châtelot, Clémont, Blamont and Etobon. The princes and dukes of Württemberg, who divided their time between the castle here and their palaces at Stuttgart and later Ludwigsburg, drew many German artists and craftsmen to the town. Although French continued to be the language spoken, German influence was soon evident in economic, cultural and religious fields.

The enclave of Mömpelgard became increasingly problematic for its French neighbours as the ideas of the Reformation began to spread after 1524. The principality officially declared itself Protestant in the mid-16C, and by the end of the century many Huguenots had sought refuge here. Various attempts by the French to seize control, however, met with failure.

The city flourishes – Under the rule of **Friedrich I of Württemberg** (1581-1608), the town blossomed into an elegant city worthy of its princely residents, imbued with the syle of the Renaissance. Much of its transformation was effected by the architect Heinrich Schickhardt *(see below)*. The influx of Huguenots refugees meant that the town had to be extended beyond the medieval fortifications, resulting in the construction of the Neuve Ville.

During the French Revolution Montbéliard was besieged and finally succumbed to the young French Republic on 10 October 1793.

Famous Montbéliard Citizens – The zoologist Jean Léopold **Cuvier** (known as Georges) was born in Montbéliard on 23 August 1769. His studies at the local École française and a period at the Karlsschule in Stuttgart, coupled with his keen early interest in the natural sciences, paved the way for his brilliant scientific career. He began teaching anatomy at the age of only 25 at the botanical gardens in Paris, then from 1799 at the Collège de France, then finally in 1802 at the natural history museum. He was elected a member of the Académie française in 1818 and received the title of baron from Louis XVIII, having established himself as the founder of comparative anatomy and paleontology.

Georges-Frédéric Parrot was a contemporary and friend of Cuvier. He followed a similar career path to that of the great scientist as far as Stuttgart, from where he chose to pursue his work in Russia, in the company of many of his fellow citizens who had followed in the tracks of Sophie-Dorothee of Württemberg when she left for Russia to marry Tsar Paul In in 1776. They set up colonies in major cities such as St Petersburg, Riga and Moscow, although many returned to end their days in their home country. Parrot made a career as vice-chancellor and professor of physics at the University of Dorpat (now Tartu) in Estonia. Once back in France Napoleon appointed him to the Imperial Conseil d'État. Parrot made a major contribution to the fields of modern biology and electrochemistry.

Fanny Durbach, a young Montbéliard woman, taught Tchaikovsky while she was in Russia, and the great musician would later always come and visit her when he was in France.

Heinrich Schickhardt (1558-1634) – During the reign of Friedrich I of Württemberg, the Swabian architect Heinrich Schickhardt played a major role in the construction of modern Montbéliard. Besides being a talented architect and town planner, he was an engineer, a technician, topographer and writer. The carpenter's son, born in Herrenberg in Swabia, learned his trade in the workshops of the architects to the court of the dukes of Württemberg, before being summoned into service of Friedrich I. The duke took him under his wing and accompanied him on a trip to Italy where the two men were able to perfect their knowledge of the Italian Renaissance. At the age of 42, Schickhardt was put in charge of architecture throughout Württemberg and was finally able to unleash his full creative potential. He introduced the Renaissance style to Montbéliard, as well as endowing cities such as Freudenstadt and Stuttgart with his work (his masterpiece, the "Neuer Bau" in Stuttgart, was destroyed by fire in the 18C). He was promoted architect to the ducal court on the death of Friedrich, but his life ended abruptly and tragically when he was assassinated in December 1634. *There is a 2.8km - 2 mile signposted tour of what remains of his work in Montbéliard (leaflet available from the tourist office).*

★OLD MONTBÉLIARD

Château (**AZ**) – All that remains of the castle built in the 15 and 16C are two massive round towers surmounted by lantern turrets, the Tour Henriette (1422-24) and the Tour Frédéric (1575-95). The rest of the castle was demolished in the mid-18C to make way for classical style buildings. A beautiful contemporary wrought iron gate by Jean Messagier closes off the doorway leading to the Tour Henriette.

Museum (**M**) ⊘ – *The castle museum is currently under restoration.* The most interesting departments are at the moment the zoological gallery, where the natural habitat of local animals has been recreated, and the paleontology exhibition which includes the splendid fossil of an ichtyosaurus.

The **Logis des Gentilhommes** (**AZ L**) stands on the Esplanade du Château. This town house was built by Schickhardt and has an elegant scrolled gable of Swabian influence.

Place Saint-Martin (**AZ**) – This square at the heart of old Montbéliard hosts most of the town's major events, such as the **Lumières de Noël**, a Christmas market in true German tradition (with bretzels, mulled wine and Christmas trees – *see the Calendar of Events at the end of the guide*). Many of the city's most important monuments are to be found on this square:

Château de Montbéliard

Office de tourisme Montbéliard

Temple St-Martin (**V**) ⊘ – This is the oldest Protestant church in France (built between 1601 and 1607 by Schickhardt). The architecture of the façade draws its inspiration from the Tuscan Renaissance. The inside would be quite plain, were it not for the original polychrome decoration, rediscovered recently, on the mid-18C **organ** and tribune.

Hôtel de ville (**H**) – The elegant pink sandstone town hall was built from 1776 to 1778. There is a commemorative statue of Cuvier *(qv)* by David d'Angers in front of the building.

Hôtel Beurnier-Rossel (**M¹**) – This is a typical example (1772-3) of the private town houses of the 18C. It now houses the **Musée historique**, which is currently closed for restoration *(scheduled to reopen 1995 or 1996).*

Montbéliard – Rue Diemer-Duperret

The museum collections include some beautiful pieces of 18C marquetry furniture, by the Montbéliard cabiner maker Abraham Nicolas Couleru *(exhibited in the museum in the château during restoration work)*, and traditional Montbéliard women's head-dresses.

Maison Forstner – This town house (probably dates from late 16C) now houses a branch of the Banque de France. The building is named after its former occupant, the Chancellor of Friedrich I of Württemberg. The stately Renaissance façade features four storeys of superposed columns.

Colourful old houses – Since 1987 there has been an ambitious restoration pro-ject implemented to restore the old town centre of Montbéliard to its former glory – the façades of the houses in this German style town were all originally painted. Almost 300 houses, in the **Rues de Belfort, Diemer-Duperret and Cuvier** in particular, have already taken on the subtle hues of pale reds or blues or pastel greens and greys, giving the old town a pretty new look.

Halles, Pierre à poissons – The 16-17C **covered market** has a distinctive roof and long façades with large windows with double mullions. The enormous building was the meeting hall for the town council prior to 1793, then was used to store the town's grain *("éminage")*, then as a market and also a customs post.
In Place Denfert-Rochereau, a 15C flagstone (**E**) can be seen, which is known in Montbéliard as the **"pierre à poissons"**. The stone was used by fishmongers on market day. In 1524, Swiss Reformer Guillaume Farel is said to have used it as a pulpit, to preach the Reformation to the people of Montbéliard.

Neuve Ville – Friedrich I commissioned Schickhardt to build this suburb in 1598, to accommodate the waves of Huguenot refugees fleeing France. Note the lofty site of the **Église St-Maimbœuf** (mid-19C) and the, in comparison to the nearby **Temple St-Georges** (late-17C), exaggerated ornamentations, both physical reminders of the Roman Catholic church's reconquest of this bastion of Lutheranism after Montbé-liard was reclaimed by France. The interior of St-Maimbœuf is also pretty lavishly decorated; monumental tribune with Corinthian columns, extravagant wooden stucco ornamentation, German baroque style altarpieces and so on.

ADDITIONAL SIGHTS

Près-la-Rose – This 10ha - 25 acre industrial zone near the old town centre has been redeveloped into a science and technology park. A number of large sculptures are dotted about the area, for example *Vaisseau* (Ship) and the eye-catching *Fon-taine Galilée* (Galileo Fountain).

Citadelle – *Take the street to the right of St-Maimbœuf church.* The citadel built on this hill by Schickhardt was demolished by the French in 1677. There is a good view of the town from here, as well as of the Lomont Jura chain to the southeast, the Pont-de-Roide *cluse* to the south and the dark mass of Mont Salbert to the north.

MONTBÉLIARD

SOCHAUX

This industrial suburb to the east of Montbéliard grew up around the Peugeot factories, after the company had established its largest car manufacturing plant on the Sochaux-Montbéliard plain in 1908.

The industrial development of the Montbéliard area – By the end of the 18C, Montbéliard had established itself as the economic hub of the Franche-Comté region.
Various factors combined to make the Montbéliard region an obvious location for industrial enterprises; good communication links, new opportunities offered by the region's annexation to France, dynamic neighbours in Switzerland, Baden and Alsace, the receptive attitude of Lutheran management towards Anglo-Saxon economic ideas.
It was not long before major firms such as Peugeot and Japy were attracted to the region.

The first Peugeot car – In the 18C, Jean-Pierre Peugeot was a weaver in Héri-moncourt. When his two oldest sons, Jean-Pierre and Jean-Frédéric, founded a steelworks in the mill at Sous-Cratet in 1810, no one dreamed that this small enterprise would be a huge international industrial concern by the 20C. Soon more factories were founded at Terre-Blanche, in the Gland valley, Valentigney and Pont-de-Roide, producing laminated steel, saw blades, tools, domestic appliances etc, while a factory in the old mill at Beaulieu turned out various types of velocipede and later bicycle. Finally, in 1891, Peugeot produced its first auto-mobile with a combustion engine, called the "Vis-à-Vis" (face-to-face) because its passengers had to sit facing one another. Since then, the company has manufac-tured over 600 car models.

★ **Musée Peugeot** (**AX**) ⊘ – The Peugeot museum, which opened in 1988 in the premises of an old brewery, houses an extensive collection of automobiles, cycles, tools and other objects (sewing machines, coffee grinders) illustrating the Peu-geot firm's output from the early days to the present.

Phaeton Lion Type V4C3

About 75 models are on show, illustrating the evolution of the car with the lion insignia. Among the "vis-à-vis" quadricycles and traps characteristic from about 1904 on, notice the elegantly decorated model made for the Bey of Tunis (1892). The 1906 Double Phaeton 81B, with four seats facing the way the car was going and inflatable tyres, shows how rapidly cars were evolving. The Bébé, a small car designed in 1911 by Ettore Bugatti, was a huge success; more than 3 000 were manufactured in just a few years. The Phaeton Lion Type V4C3 *(see illustration)*, with a folding back seat, dates from 1913. Beginning with the Peu-geot 201 in 1929, all Peugeot models were identified by a three digit number with zero in the middle. The 201 was Peugeot's main defence against the international economic slump; the 1932 "comfort" model was the first mass-produced car with independent front wheel suspension. Peugeot developed a name for being at the forefront of design; the streamlined bodywork of the Peugeot 402 which appeared at the end of 1935 embodied the latest develop-ments in the field of aerodynamics. A prototype of the 402, the 6 models of which were built by J. Andreau, launched in 1936 cut petrol consumption by 35%. The Peugeot 402 Limousine equipped with a gas generator and a coal box (consumption: 15kg - 33lb per hour!) bears witness to the extreme shortage of fuel in 1941.

After the war, Peugeot brought out another new model, the Peugeot 203, with an integral all-steel welded body. More recent models and racing cars include: the Darl'mat 302 Roadster, winner of the Le Mans 24 Hour Grand Prix in 1938; the Peugeot 205 Turbo 16, World Rallying Champion in 1989 and the Peugeot 205 Turbo 16 Grand Raid, which came first in the 1990 Paris-Dakar.

Among the cycles, note in particular the 1882 Gran-bi, the first bicycle. The tri-car and the scooter take you back to the 50s.

Tour of the Peugeot factories ⊘ – Sochaux is the largest Peugeot automobile production centre, above the factories at Mulhouse, Poissy and Valenciennes. The factory is still expanding. Recently, the company gained 12ha - 30 acres of land when the river Allan was diverted. The Peugeot 205, 605 and 405 are the main models manufactured at Sochaux.

The tour takes visitors through a pressing workshop with a programmable metal stamping machine, a sheet-iron works lit up by sparks, the accessories assembly plant, with robots at work everywhere (robot welders, robots for adjusting the windscreen, etc). As the car on the production line is built up before visitors' fascinated gaze, it becomes clear how many amazing technological developments there have been in car manufacture over just the last ten years.

▶▶ **Audincourt** – Northeast suburb of Montbéliard. The church of **Sacré-Cœur** (conse-crated in 1951) contains a particularly interesting **baptistery★**.

▶▶ **Fort on Mont Bart** ⊘ – *Southwest of the city (on the N 463).* Altitude 487m - 1 598ft.

MONTBENOÎT★

Population 238
Michelin map 170 fold 7 or 243 folds 21 and 33 –
Facilities – Local map under Vallée du DOUBS

This village is the tiny capital of the Saugeais valley. It stands on a hillside overlooked by rocky cliffs on the banks of the Doubs, which follows a peaceful pretty course at this point. The old abbey of Montbenoît is among the Jura's most beautiful architectural monuments and draws many visitors.

Saugeais valley – Montbenoît abbey was founded by the hermit Benedict (Fr.: Benoît) who came to live here, drawing crowds of followers with him. In 1150, the lord of Joux, the region's landlord, was seeking ways of winning Divine grace, of which he was much in need thanks to his immoral lifestyle (the Joux were little more than highwaymen). He offered Humbert, archbishop of Besançon, the stretch of sunlit valley through which the Doubs flows from Pontarlier, between Arçon and Colombière, to be used for the first inhabitants of Montbenoît. Humbert summoned Augustine monks from the Valais region in Switzerland to build a church and buildings, some of which are still standing. They called on some Swiss compatriots, known as Saugets, to help clear and cultivate the land. This name has been given to the valley (the spelling has altered over the years) and to the local residents. Modern "Saugets" and "Saugettes" are perceived as having retained the strong individuality of their Swiss forebears. The twelve villages surrounding Montbenoît have their own particular dialect, customs and style of houses. Brass bands and choruses still ring out the Sauget hymn at local festivals. These people are characterised by their lively sense of humour, which can at times border on the caustic.

The abbey – Montbenoît remained under the feudal suzerainty of the lords of Joux. To make his authority clear, every time a new abbot was elected, the landlord would present himself at the monastery gates, surrounded by his vassals and men-at-arms. The abbot, holding a cross and wearing his mitre, would come out and greet him and hand him the keys of the abbey on a silver plate. The landlord would then be in charge of the community for the rest of the day.

The abbey declined in the same way as the abbey of St-Claude. It was held *in commendam* from 1508 onwards; the abbots drew on the abbey's profits without having to either oversee the general administration of the abbey or even take part in the religious life of the abbey. The two most famous abbots were the Cardinal of Granvelle *(qv)* and Ferry Carondelet. Carondelet joined the order after being widowed, and became counsellor to Emperor Charles V. He was a luxury-loving patron who had the church chancel rebuilt and filled it with the most beautiful works of art. He also made generous donations to the cathedral of St-Jean in Besançon, where he was canon and where he is buried. During the Revolution, the abbey of Montbenoît was declared the property of the French state and its lands were sold.

★ OLD ABBEY *time: 45 min*

Ancienne église abbatiale – The nave of the abbey church dates from the 12C and the chancel from the 16C. The bell tower was rebuilt in 1903.

Nave – Against the first pillar on the south side is a monument (1522) to a local girl, Parnette Mesnier, who met her death while attempting to resist the unwelcome advances of a young man. Pretty Parnette fled him by clambering up the scaffolding above the chancel, which was under construction at the time. The young man was about to catch up with her at the top, whereupon Parnette threw herself to the ground below. Kindhearted Ferry Carondelet donated the monument in memory of the young girl's defence of her virtue.

Note also, the 17C pulpit and, opposite it, the 15C statues in wild cherry wood of the "Mater dolorosa" and St John at the foot of the Cross.

In the Chapelle Ferrée north of the chancel there is a 16C statue of St Jerome and a stone Pièta on the altar.

The beautiful sculpted doors at the entrance to the Chapelle des Trois Rois south of the chancel were part of the original 16C rood-screen.

Chancel – Abbot Ferry Carondelet had travelled all over Italy as ambassador to the court of Rome for the government of the Netherlands and Flanders and sought to re-create at Montbenoît some of the magnificence and refinement of the Italian Renaissance. He personally chose the craftsmen who took just two years to create this harmonious group of sculpture and stained glass, one of the great successes of the early Renaissance in the

Panorama from the Petit Mont-Rond

Franche-Comté. The brilliant colours of the ornamental foliage and arabesques are still visible on the pendentive vaulting, which is decorated with a delicate network of ribs.

The decoration on the magnificent **stalls★★**, dating from 1525 to 1527, is clearly the result of both a lively wit and great artistic talent;. unfortunately, very few motifs have survived intact. Note the delicacy and variety of the ornamentation on the upper part between the pinnacles.

One or two cleverly sculpted scenes contribute to the richness of the whole (such as "Women fighting", symbolising the triumph of Truth over Error) and illustrate ideas taken from the Middle Ages ("Lay of Aristotle", representing Science being punished by Truth).

There is a beautiful marble **abbatial recess★** to the right of the altar; a 1526 piscina, also in marble, is next to it.

Detail from the choir stalls of the abbey church

Above the sacristy door is a low relief commissioned by Ferry Carondelet in memory of the Joux landlords. The sculpted man's head sticking out of the socle is probably a representation of Ferry Carondelet.

Cloisters – The architectural indecisiveness typical of the Franche-Comté is in evidence in the 15C cloisters.

Round arches are still used, while the corner doors are surmounted by Flamboyant Gothic ogee arches and sculpted tympanums. The twin colonettes have archaic-style capitals, decorated with foliage, fish and animals.

Chapter-house – This chapter-house, which opens onto the cloisters, has diagonal groined arches springing from the door.

Note the 16C painted and gilt wood statuettes, of the Virgin holding Jesus as well as of the Three Kings.

Kitchen – Note a Louis XIV clock with one hand, a beautiful Louis XIII armoire and an enormous mantelpiece.

MONT-ROND★★★

Michelin map 170 fold 15 or 243 fold 43 – Local map under Col de la FAUCILLE

The Petit and the Grand Mont-Rond peaks constitute one of the Jura's most famous viewpoints. The view from the **Petit Mont-Rond** is the more interesting.

The usual way of reaching Petit Mont-Rond is from the Col de la Faucille (qv). Follow the wide road which leads down southwards from the pass. After about 500m, leave the car in the park and take the cable-car (télécabine) ⊙.

Another possibility is to take the chairlift (télésiège) ⊙ from Mijoux up to the bottom cable-car station at Col de la Faucille and then continue to the summit in the cable-car.

There is a French radio and television relay near the cable-car station at the top.

Panorama – The sweeping view from the viewing table is breathtaking. Beyond the rift valley in which Lake Geneva lies tower the Alps, extending over an area 250km wide by 150km deep (155 miles by 93 miles), as well as the Jura and Dôle (in Switzerland) chains.

In spring the summit is covered with a glorious carpet of blue gentians, yellow anemones and white crocuses; in summer and autumn Alpine asters and mountain thistles lend the peak more subtle tones.

(Distance from the viewpoint in brackets)

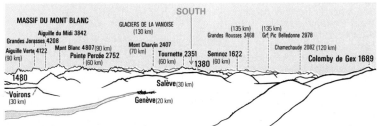

MONT-ST-VINCENT★

Population 335 – Michelin map 69 fold 18 or 243 fold 26

The Charollais village stands on a bluff, on the watershed between the Loire and the Saône. It is one of the highest peaks (603m - 1 987ft) in the Saône-et-Loire *département*, where an old Celtic mid-summer custom is perpetuated when a bonfire is lit on about St John's Day (24 June) to celebrate the return of summer *(see the Calendas of Events at the end of the guide)*.

SIGHTS

★★Panorama – At the entrance to the village a sharp righthand turn leads up to a TV and meteorological station. From the top of an old mill, converted into a belvedere *(telescope and viewing table)*, there is an almost complete panorama: the Morvan mountains (northwest), the Le Creusot and Autun basins (north), the mountains of the Mâconnais (southeast) and Charollais (southwest).

Church – The church, built at the end of the 12C, was once a priory of Cluny abbey. A gallery surmounts the square porch. Above the doorway is a carved tympanum, now badly damaged, showing Christ in Majesty between two figures, believed to be St Peter and St Paul. There is transverse barrel vaulting, similar to that in St-Philibert in Tournus, in the nave and groined vaulting in the aisles. The transept crossing is surmounted by a dome on squinches. From the open space beside the graveyard there is an attractive view of the many small valleys to the north.

Musée J.-Régnier ⊘ – The old 15C salt warehouse (restored) now houses a collection of articles (from the neolithic to the medieval period) found in regional archaeological excavations. One room is devoted to Romanesque art.

MOREZ★

Population 6 957
Michelin map 170 fold 15 or 243 fold 43 – Local map under ST-CLAUDE: Excursion

Morez lies in an unusual **setting★** in the bottom of a *cluse*. The town traditionally had a reputation for woodwork, but it has become associated with the watchmaking industry, and even more so, with the manufacture of spectacles. The village stretches for about 2km - 1 mile along the bottom of the Bienne valley, and the river provided its principal source of energy for centuries. The road up to the nearby passes, Col de la Faucille or Col de St-Cergue, goes through Morez and, as it continues to climb, it offers virtually a bird's-eye view of the town. It is fascinating to see the artistry with which the engineers have designed the route for the railway and the hairpin roads which pass through the town.

The town of spectacles – Spectacles have been worn to correct poor vision since the 13C. However, the first workshop for their manufacture did not appear on the outskirts of Morez until 1796. The spectacles manufactured there consisted of two heavy wrought iron side arms welded to two enormous circles. In spite of the primitive nature of this product, it met with resounding success locally. In about 1830, a Morez craftsman took his merchandise to the Beaucaire fair, where he established trade contacts and ended up by making Jura spectacles famous throughout France. Other factories sprang up. In about 1840 Morez introduced the pince-nez, took up the manufacture of optical glass, and gradually became the centre of the French optical industry. As such it can produce up to 12 million pairs of glasses per year.

Morbier cheese – Morbier cheese is manufactured throughout Morez and the surrounding area, rather than solely in the little holiday resort of **Morbier** *(facilities)*. The texture of Morbier cheese is not as refined as that of Comté, but the two cheeses are otherwise fairly similar. After the milk (about 70-801 - 15-18 gallons for a single cheese) has been left to curdle, it is stirred and heated to about 40°C-104°F, then poured into a circular mould. The

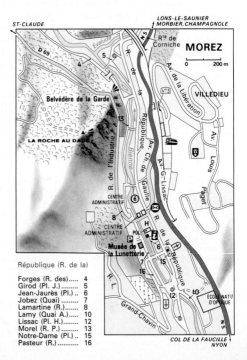

République (R. de la)

Forges (R. des)	4
Girod (Pl. J.)	5
Jean-Jaurès (Pl.)	6
Jobez (Quai)	7
Lamartine (R.)	8
Lamy (Quai A.)	10
Lissac (Pl. H.)	12
Morel (R. P.)	13
Notre-Dame (Pl.)	15
Pasteur (R.)	16

cheese is lightly pressed and drained and divided into two disks; their flat sides are dusted with ash, which will later appear as a bluish-black line through the middle of the cheese when the two circles are put together. The Morbier is then put into a press and stored in the cellar for two months to complete the maturing process. The cheese-makers of the Morez region uphold the Morbier tradition of using only fresh, unpasteurised milk from either Morbier or St-Laurent.

SIGHTS

Musée de la Lunetterie ⊙ – This spectacle museum presents the evolution of the most important industrial activity in Morez. Antique machines and tools give the visitor an idea of how the different elements of a pair of spectacles are made. The display cases contain a wide variety of spectacles, both antique (metal frames, frames with side arms, pince-nez) and modern (sunglasses, goggles for sports or industrial use). The visit ends with an audio-visual presentation on the modern spectacle manufacturing industry in Morez.

EXCURSIONS

Belvédère de la Garde – This viewpoint is 500m west of Morez, along the St-Claude road (the D 69). It gives a good view of the various levels of viaducts running between the hill-sides around Morez and, to the right, of the town itself, strung out along the valley.

★ **La Roche au Dade** – *30min on foot Rtn. Follow the little road leading off from the D 69 (northwest on the town plan) a little further west of the Belvédère de la Garde; then take the path indicated with red flashes which goes past the Lamartine family home.*
There is a good **view★** of the Bienne valley, Morez and its viaducts, and the mountain of Dôle just over the Swiss border.

Chapelle-des-Bois – Facilities. *Leave Morez to the north and turn right immediately onto the D 18, which leads into the N 5.*
This simple mountain village (alt 1 100m - 3 609ft) surrounded by meadows at the bottom of a vast coomb at the heart of the Haut-Jura national park, has become a major centre for cross-country skiing *(see the Practical Information at the end of the guide).* In the summer, the surrounding countryside is ideal for long rambles. Take the D 46 along the Combe des Cives to Maison Michaud, now an écomusée (open air museum). This sturdy building is one of the oldest farmhouses in the area. It was built in the late 17C and has been completely restored. The immense roof and pretty chimney are covered in the wooden slats known locally as *tavaillons.* The museum gives a good impression of what life in such an isolated dwelling would have been like. Most notably, it would have centred around the chimney, which occupies virtually a room of its own inside, in which the family would have gathered round the fire, cooked their bread, cured their meats and made cheese. *Bread and cakes on sale.*

MORVAN★★

Michelin maps 65 folds 15, 16 and 17 and 69 folds 6, 7 and 8 or 238 folds 23, 24, 35 and 36 and 243 folds 13 and 25

The Morvan massif is not served by any main roads but it receives a growing number of visitors who are attracted by the vast forests, rocky escarpments, valleys and picturesque sites; canoeists appreciate the mountain streams, fishermen line the banks of the rivers, lakes and reservoirs.
Although the Morvan is a distinct natural region between the Nivernais and Burgundy, it has never been a separate political or administrative entity; it has no historically-established borders. Only its physical characteristics distinguish it from its neighbours. From a distance it is recognisable by its vast and sombre forests; in Celtic etymology "morvan" means "black mountain" *(montagne noire).*

GEOGRAPHICAL NOTES *see also Introduction*

Lower and Upper Morvan – The Morvan covers a quadrilateral area (70km - 44 miles long by 50km - 31 miles wide) stretching from Avallon to St-Léger-sous-Beuvray and from Corbigny to Saulieu.
Seen from the north the Morvan appears as a vast, slightly undulating plateau, which rises slowly towards the south. The northern section (maximum altitude 600m - 2 000ft) descends in terraces sloping gently into the Paris basin; this is "Le Bas Morvan" (Lower Morvan).
It is the southern section, "Le Haut Morvan" (Upper Morvan), south of Montsauche, which contains the higher peaks: Mont Beuvray (821m - 2 694ft), Mont Preneley (855m - 2 805ft), the Massif du Bois du Roi or Haut-Folin (901m - 2 956ft). Although the peaks do not reach very great altitudes, it is because they end suddenly above the Autun basin that the region is said to be mountainous.

Countryside of water and forest – The Morvan is subject to heavy rain and snow fall because of its geographical location and altitude. Precipitation on the outskirts of the region is on average 1 000mm - 39in annually, but can reach over 1 800mm -71in in the Haut-Folin. It rains or snows for 180 days in an average year on the peaks. The heavy rainfall and the melting snow turns the smallest stream into a torrent. As the ground is composed of non-porous rock covered with a layer of granitic gravel (a sort of coarse sand), the Morvan is like a sponge full of water: the rivers – Yonne, Cure, Cousin and their tributaries – become turbulent watercourses. Dams and reservoirs (Pannesière-Chaumard, Les Settons, Crescent, Chaumeçon) have been built to regulate the flow when the rivers are in spate or the water level is low, so as to supplement the output of hydroelectric power when necessary; St Agnan provides a reservoir of drinking water.

The characteristic feature of the Morvan massif is the forest which covers a third and often half of the surface area. Gradually the beeches or oaks are being replaced by fir trees. Timber is no longer floated to Paris by water as tree trunks but is now transported by lorry to nearby factories for cabinet-making and particularly charcoal production.

LIFE IN THE MORVAN

A rough and unfertile country, the Morvan has for a long time been the butt of gibes from its neighbours. In Burgundy they say: "Nothing good comes from the Morvan, neither good people nor a good wind", an unjust statement which expresses the superior attitude of the rich Burgundians towards the Morvan people, whose countryside has neither vineyards nor fertile fields. Since they could extract only small profit from the soil of their native land, the Morvan men often "came down" to the surrounding plains of Bazois or Auxois, rich lands of cattle-breeding and cultivation, while the women found work as wet-nurses.

The Morvan wet-nurses – In the 19C in particular wet-nursing was a most profitable occupation for the ·Morvan women.

In the towns at this period it was not considered proper for young mothers to nurse their children and the Morvan women were excellent wet-nurses. Some went to Paris "to provide food", some stayed at home to nurse the babies entrusted to their care. Countless Parisian children spent the first months of their lives in the Morvan during this period.

Present resources – Today the Morvan is still far from being a rich and prosperous region and its population continues to decline. Cattle-rearing on a small scale is no longer a profitable proposition. Forestry, however, is a new resource instituted since the Second World War by the planting of conifers to provide raw material for the developing timber industries.

Another sector of commercial progress is tourism in the Avallonnais and the Morvan. In the highest parts of the Massif, southeast of Château-Chinon, a skiing centre has been established with downhill runs (Haut-Folin – *qv*) and cross-country routes.

Parc naturel régional du Morvan – The majority of the Morvan region was designated a regional nature park in 1970, which contributed a great deal to attracting tourists to the region. The park encompasses 74 *communes* from the départements of Côte-d'Or, Nièvre, Saône-et-Loire and Yonne. The image of a galloping horse, taken from an ancient Aedui coin, was adopted as the park's logo.

The park lends itself to numerous sports activities, such as hiking, cycling, riding or fishing. The long-distance footpath GR 13 crosses the Morvan from north to south (Vézelay to Autun). Shorter rambles are possible on the so-called GR de Pays *(yellow flashes on red background)*, which makes a tour of the Morvan via the big lakes, and a number of smaller footpaths *(marked by yellow flashes)* – detailed description of routes in the Topo-guides series; see the Practical Information section at the end of this guide. There are also plenty of possibilities for accommodation on offer (on local farms etc.).

The **Maison du Parc** ⊘ at **St-Brisson** houses the park's administration and an information and exhibition centre. The 40ha - 99 acre grounds are home to an arboretum, through which a forest track with 17 explanatory panels leads, and a "herbularium", containing about 160 species of local plantlife.

LE BAS MORVAN

A brief description of this northern area is given on the previous page.

① From Vézelay to Château-Chinon

97km - 60 miles – about 3 hours 30 min – itinerary ① on the local map p 208.

This road enters the Morvan from the north and the scenery becomes hillier and more varied after Lormes. The altitude increases southwards.

★★ **Vézelay** – *Time: 1 hour. See VÉZELAY.*

Leave Vézelay by the D 957 east towards Avallon.

Vézelay and its basilica, set high on their rocky outcrop, are still visible from St-Père.

★ **St-Père** – *Time: 15 min. See ST-PÈRE.*

Take the D 958 south.

The road follows the upper Cure Valley, which becomes a wooded gorge.

Fouilles des Fontaines Salées – *See ST-PÈRE.*

★ **Pierre-Perthuis** – This tiny village in its picturesque **site**★ is named after a rocky spur which can be seen from the modern bridge spanning the Cure.

Continue south on the D 958. Turn left into the D 453 and left to the dam.

Barrage de Malassis – This small dam and hydroelectric power station on the Cure are intended to regulate the flow of water and in particular any irregularities caused by the Bois-de-Cure power station upstream.

Continue southeast.

After Domecy-sur-Cure, the road becomes very winding; it overlooks the enclosed river valley.

After crossing the river in St-André-en-Morvan, take the road east to Chastellux.

Chastellux château comes into view, perched on a hillock dominating the Cure.

Château de Chastellux-sur-Cure – This château was altered in the 13C and restored in 1825 and has been the seat of the Chastellux family for over a thousand years.

The best view of the château is from the viaduct which carries the D 944 across the Cure. The building clings to a rocky slope amidst much greenery, overlooking the wooded gorge.

A track (left) descends steeply, affording views of the Crescent dam and reservoir, in a setting of lush meadows and wooded hillsides.

Barrage du Crescent – Built between 1930 and 1933 this dam impounds the Cure downstream from its junction with the Chalaux. By its sheer mass the dam retains the accumulated waters flowing from the Cure and the Chalaux. It has a maximum height of 37m - 122ft and a total length of 330m - 1 083ft.

The reservoir of water (14 million m^3 - 494 million cu ft) is used by the Bois-de-Cure power station to generate electricity and helps to regulate the flow of the Seine.

Drive south for 13.5km - 8 miles to Lormes.

Lormes – This small town on the border between the Morvan and Nivernais regions is an ideal departure point for day trips to the nearby reservoirs. Rue du Panorama, the steep road by the tax office *(Perception)*, leads up to the lookout point by the cemetery, from where there is a broad **panorama**★ of the wooded heights of the Morvan (to the southeast), and the farmland of the Bazois and Nivernais regions dotted with little villages and woods (to the southwest). On the horizon, roughly in the centre of the panorama, stands Montenoison hill.

Just south of Lormes, turn left onto the D 17 towards Ouroux-en-Morvan.

Ouroux-en-Morvan – There is a charming view from this village of the surrounding hills and a stretch of the Pannesière reservoir. Two paths *(15 min Rtn)* lead up to the **viewpoint**★ from the village square and the church.

After 1.5km - 1 mile turn right into the D 12 in the direction of Chaumard.

The last mile or so of this downhill run towards the Pannesière reservoir provides superb bird's-eye views of this stretch of water.

Before Chaumard, turn sharp right into the D 303, which runs along the bank of the reservoir and across the dam. Turn left into the D 944 and left again into the D 161 which leads to the reservoir.

★ **Barrage de Pannesière-Chaumard** – This 340m long by 50m high (1 115ft by 164ft) dam is supported on numerous slender arches and flanked by massive concrete embankments on either river bank. Twelve supporting buttresses rise from the bottom of the gorge. The dam controls the flow of water in the Seine basin. The hydroelectric power station downstream produces nearly 18 million kWh per year. The reservoir (7.5km - 5 miles long), with a capacity of 18 145 million gallons, forms a glorious expanse of water in an attractive **setting**★ amid wooded hills. A road runs all the way round it and along the top of the dam, giving a pretty **view** of the numerous inlets of the lake with the summits of the Haut Morvan outlined against the sky in the background.

Downstream of the main dam (near the D 944) is a control dam (220m - 722ft long) composed of 33 slender arches. While the turbines consume water at the rate of demand for electricity, the control dam enables the discharged water to be returned to the Yonne at a constant rate and also supplies water to the Nivernais canal.

Take the road south along the west shore of the lake to Château-Chinon.

★ **Château-Chinon** – *See CHÂTEAU-CHINON.*

② From Château-Chinon to Saulieu

59km - 37 miles – about 3 hours – itinerary ② on the local map overleaf.

The road affords charming views over Les Settons reservoir and the upper valley of the Cure.

★ **Château-Chinon** – *See CHÂTEAU-CHINON.*

Leave Château-Chinon by the D 944; turn right into the D 37.

After a bridge over the Yonne, you will see **Corancy** on the left, clinging to its hillside. The winding road follows the small valleys at mid-slope level.

North of Planchez turn right to the Lac des Settons.

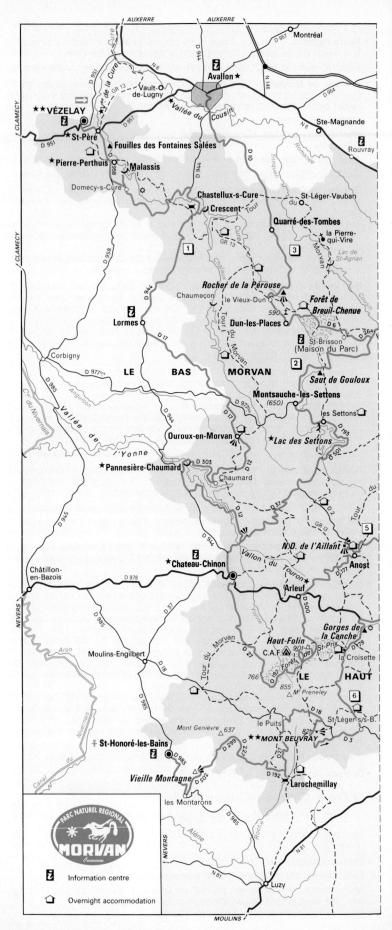

★ **Lac des Settons** – *See Lac des SET-TONS.*

After crossing the River Cure the road (D 501) follows the east shore of the reservoir. After turning north the road (D 193) climbs, offering pretty views over the reservoir and its wooded islands, to the charming resort of Les Settons which overlooks the reservoir and the dam.

Montsauche-les-Settons – Facilities. This village is the highest resort (650m - 2 133ft) in the massif. The village stands at the centre of the Parc naturel du Morvan. Like Planchez, this township was rebuilt following almost total destruction in 1944.

Take the D 977bis northeast.

The road descends rapidly into the Cure valley and crosses the river just before Gouloux.

Saut de Gouloux – *Access by a path (right) from the first bend in the road after the bridge over the Cure. 15 min on foot Rtn.*
Just upstream from its confluence with the Cure, the Caillot flows over an attractive waterfall.
The road continues east through the forest and across a plateau, dotted with woods and pools, before reaching Saulieu, on the eastern edge of the Morvan.

★ **Saulieu** – *Time: 30 min. See SAULIEU.*

③ **From Saulieu to Avallon**
55km - 34 miles – about 2 hours 30 min – itinerary ③ on the local map left

The proposed route between Saulieu and Avallon, both small towns situated on the borders of the Morvan, enters the massif through vast forests in picturesque scenery.

★ **Saulieu** – *Time: 30 min. See SAULIEU.*
From Saulieu take the D 977bis west; turn right into the D 26ᴬ to Dun-les-Places.

The road crosses a plateau dotted with woods and pools and then wooded countryside.

Forêt de Breuil-Chenue – West of Les Fourches *(2km - 1 mile)* a track (right) leads to the information centre in a former forestry lodge. Nearby there is a pen containing fallow deer with observation posts from which to view the animals. A nature trail *(1 hour)* and a forest trail lead to a fine beech wood.

Dun-les-Places – North of the village *(access by the minor road and a path to the campsite)* stands a calvary (alt 590m - 1 936ft); the road provides good views of the Morvan peaks.

Take the picturesque road north through Le Vieux-Dun. After crossing the River Cure turn right into a forest track.

Rocher de la Pérouse – *From the parking place a steep footpath climbs to the rocky summit (200m - 656ft); 30 min on foot Rtn.*

From the top there is an interesting **view** over the isolated Cure valley and the rounded summits of the massif.

Continue along the forest track; turn right then left into the D 10 to Quarré-les-Tombes.

Quarré-les-Tombes – *About 12km - 8 miles north of Vieux-Dun.*
This village owes its name to the numerous limestone sarcophagi dating from the 7-10C discovered near the church. It is thought that there must have been some kind of sanctuary to St George in Quarré, near which knights and other people of rank were buried.

Beyond Marrault, Avallon comes into view.
After passing through wooded country the road (D 944) runs parallel with the Cousin into Avallon, a picturesque town built on a rock spur.

★ **Avallon** – *Time: 30 min.* This pretty town, located on a rocky outcrop high above the Cousin valley, still has its old **fortified town centre**★. From the Promenade de la Petite Porte there is a lovely view of the Cousin valley.
The church of **St-Lazare** ⊘ has interesting **doorways**★ on the façade and a beautiful 15C clock tower.
The local museum, **Musée de l'Avallonnais** ⊘, contains an eclectic collection of exhibits, including a number of Gallo-Roman artefacts (a mosaic thought to be of Venus), and a particularly interesting graphics collection. Note the two series of lively, precise engravings by **Jacques Callot** (1592-1635) and the famous 58-plate expressionist series of the **Miserere**★ by Georges Rouault.
There is a **Musée du Costume** ⊘ in the old Hôtel de Condé (17-18C) which contains exhibitions of period costume which are rotated annually.

VALLÉE DU TERNIN

④ From Saulieu to Autun

45km - 28 miles – about 1 hour – itinerary ④ on the local map previous pages

Picturesque drive up the valley.

★ **Saulieu** – *Time: 30 min. See SAULIEU.*

Leave Saulieu by the D 26 going southwest.

The road climbs steeply and crosses a plateau before following the **Ternin valley.** There is an attractive view (left) of the water held back by the **Chamboux dam** (completed in 1985). The river winds between small green hills with wooded summits. South of Alligny-en-Morvan (D 20) the valley narrows but widens out again as the road (D 980) approaches Chissey-en-Morvan, the only place of any size, apart from Lucenay-l'Évêque.

★★ **Autun** – *Time: 30 min. See AUTUN.*

LE HAUT MORVAN

A brief description of this southern region is given on p 205.

⑤ From Château-Chinon to Autun

84km - 52 miles – about 2 hours 15 min – itinerary ⑤ on the local map, previous pages

This drive crosses several forested massifs and offers far-reaching views.

★ **Château-Chinon** – *See CHÂTEAU-CHINON.*

Leave Château-Chinon by the D 27 going south.

A view opens out towards the west of a landscape of meadows, arable fields and woods. The road then rises steeply before entering the **Forêt de la Gravelle.**
This is the threshold between the drainage basins of the Seine (Yonne to the east) and the Loire (Aron and its tributaries to the west).
At one point quite near to the summit (766m - 2 513ft) there is a view to the right of bleak broom-covered moorland. The road then leaves the forest. Another good panorama opens out southwards over a small dam nestling at the bottom of a green hollow dominated by the wooded crests which mark the limit of the Morvan.

Turn left into the D 197; turn right into the forest track (steep gradient 16% - 1:6) which passes through the state forest of St-Prix.

Haut-Folin – The slopes of this peak have been developed for skiing by the French Alpine Club.

Turn left into the Bois-du-Roi forest track and left again into the Haut-Folin forest track.

The Haut-Folin (901m - 2 956ft), the highest peak in the Morvan, is crowned by a telecommunications mast.
The Bois-du-Roi forest track continues west through the **Forêt de St-Prix,** a magnificent stand of spruce and fir trees with immense trunks.

Turn left into the D 500 to Arleuf.

Arleuf – See CHÂTEAU-CHINON; Excursion.

East of Arleuf turn left into the D 177; in Bussy take the D 88 to Anost.

Anost – Set in a pleasant and picturesque **spot,** Anost offers the tourist the choice of numerous walks, especially in the forests (signposted forest trails).

Notre-Dame-de-l'Aillant – Access by the D 2 north and 15 min on foot Rtn. From beside the statue there is a semicircular **panorama★** over the Anost basin and beyond the hills of the Autun depression.
Further north (D 2) are wild boar in an enclosure. Northeast of Anost the winding road (D 88) affords views of the hills and their wooded crests.

Cussy-en-Morvan – This small village is curiously built on a hillside in an attractive beauty spot. The **church** has an interesting statue of the Virgin and Child dating from the 15C.

Continue on the D 88 which descends steeply; in Mortaise turn right into the D 980.

Between Lucenay-l'Évêque and Reclesne the downhill drive affords views of Autun surrounded by an arc of wooded hills.

★★ **Autun** – Time: 30 min. See AUTUN.

⑥ From St-Honoré-les-Bains to Autun

79km - 49 miles – about 2 hours – itinerary ⑥ on the local map pp 208-209

This drive through the highest part of the Morvan is both varied and picturesque. After Les Montarons the route follows a succession of picturesque local roads and passes the Vieille Montagne and the foot of Mont Genièvre.

★ **St-Honoré-les-Bains** – Facilities. The sulphurous, radioactive hot springs of this small spa town were first used by the Romans and are now part of cures for asthma, bronchitis and diseases of the respiratory tracts.

Take the D 985 south; in Les Montarons turn left into the D 502.

Vieille Montagne – Car park. 30 min on foot Rtn.
From the clearing a path leads to the belvedere in its pleasant setting; there is an extensive view, partly through trees, of Mont Beuvray and the Forêt de la Gravelle.
Between Le Niret and Sanglier the road (D 299) skirts the foot of Mont Genièvre.

Turn right into the D 227, then left into the D 192 and right into the D 27.

The Château of Larochemillay comes into view perched high on its rocky site.

Larochemillay – This 18C **château** replaced an earlier feudal fortress. From its remarkable site the château dominates the Roche valley.

Take the D 27 north; in Le Puits turn right into the D 18; after 5km - 3 miles turn right into a one-way road with very steep gradients (20% - 1:5) to Mont Beuvray.

★★ **Mont Beuvray** – See Mont BEUVRAY.

Continue east to St-Léger; take the D 179 north.

Gorges de la Canche – The road follows the gorge along the side of a hill in a wild landscape of rocks and trees. There is a fine viewpoint in a bend to the left (partly screened by trees).
At the bottom of the gorge can be seen the white building of La Canche hydro-electric power station.

Turn right into the D 978 to Autun.

★★ **Autun** – Time: 30 min. See AUTUN.

NANTUA★

Population 37 602
Michelin map 74 fold 4 or 244 fold 6 – Facilities –
Local maps under Vallée de l'AIN and BUGEY

Nantua, tucked in a steep-sided, evergreen-forested **cluse★★** on the northern edge of the Bugey (qv) region, grew up around a Benedictine abbey founded here in the 8C. In the Middle Ages it was a free town surrounded by solid ramparts, which it certainly needed, as it was continually caught up in the turbulent religious and political disputes between the Bugey, the Franche-Comté, Savoy and Geneva, not to mention between France and the Germanic Empire.
Henri IV annexed Nantua to the kingdom of France in 1601.
During the age of stage-coaches, Nantua was a busy town as it was the relay post between Bourg-en-Bresse and Geneva. However, in the 19C, when the railway brought an end to handsome teams of horses, Nantua fell into decline and was forgotten.
Recently, the development of tourism and the growing popularity of mountain resorts as holiday destinations have injected new life into what is now a charming lakeside resort. Local gastronomic treats include freshwater crayfish (écrevisses) and a type of dumpling (quenelles à la Nantua).

NANTUA

B Statue de
Jean-Baptiste Baudin
M Musée départemental
de la Résistance
et de la Déportation
de l'Ain et du Haut-Jura

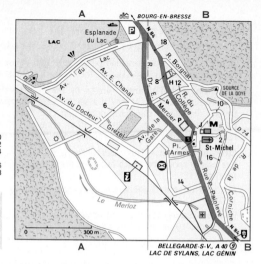

BELLEGARDE-S-V., A 40 ⑨
LAC DE SYLANS, LAC GÉNIN

★ **Lac de Nantua** (A) – The 2.5km - 1.5 mile long by 650m - 0.4 mile wide lake (*see table of lakes at the end of the guide*) is all that remains of a glacier from the Ice Age which was trapped in the *cluse* by moraine. The lake is fed by several springs, including that of Neyrolles, which comes from the Lac de Sylans (*see below*). Its waters flow into the Oignin, a tributary of the Ain, via the so-called "Bras du Lac".

There is a beautiful **view**★ from Avenue du Lac and from the lakeside promenade shaded by magnificent plane trees. The lake can be seen framed by the heights of the Haut-Bugey, with the cliffs on the northern side ending abruptly in a wooded scree slope.

Boat trips on the lake ⊘ – *See town plan for location of the landing stage.* Boat trips round the lake are organised during the summer.

St-Michel (B) – This church is the last trace of a 12C abbey destroyed during the Revolution. The beautiful Romanesque portal is unfortunately badly damaged, but the Last Supper can nonetheless be discerned on the lintel.

Inside, the height of the great arches of the nave and that of the octagonal lantern tower on pendentives above the transept crossing are striking. The first chapel in the north aisle dates from the Renaissance and is embellished with complex vaulting and a beautiful stone altarpiece.

Note the Martyrdom of St Sebastian by Delacroix on the wall of the north aisle. The chancel contains some beautiful carved woodwork and a pair of kneeling angels on either side of the altar (17C and 18C).

Near the church, on the Place d'Armes, Nantua has put up a statue in memory of one of its citizens. Deputy **Jean-Baptiste Baudin** (**B B**) served in the National Assembly during the Second Republic (1848-52) and was killed the day after Napoleon III's coup d'état (2 December 1851) at the Faubourg St-Antoine barricades in Paris, probably as he shouted the now famous words, "I'll show you how to die for 25 francs!", thereby attracting the opponents' attention to himself. (Deputies were at that time paid 25 francs a day.)

Musée départemental de la Résistance et de la Déportation de l'Ain et du Haut-Jura (**B M**) ⊘ – The museum collection (uniforms, weapons, flags, posters, letters and clothes of those deported, parachuting equipment, etc.) traces the rise of Fascism and Nazism and recalls the Vichy administration, the Occupation, the Resistance, the Maquis and deportation. Numerous documents and a film testify to the particularly tough struggle between the Nazis and the Maquis in the Bugey region.

NEVERS ★

Pop 41 968
Michelin map 69 folds 3 and 4 or 238 fold 33 – Facilities
Plan of the conurbation in the current Michelin Red Guide France

Situated a few miles from the confluence of the Loire and the Allier, Nevers is the capital of the Nivernais region and the town of fine pottery.

From the great bridge of reddish-brown sandstone that spans the river Loire, there is an overall **view** of the old town, set in terraces on the side of a hill and dominated by the high square tower of the cathedral and the graceful silhouette of the ducal palace.

Julius Caesar checked – In 52 BC, before undertaking the siege of Gergovie, Caesar made the fortified town into an important food and forage depot for his army. Noviodunum Aeduorum, generally considered to have been the Roman name for Nevers, was situated on the borders of the territory of the Aedui tribe. On hearing the news of his check before Gergovie, the Aedui immediately attacked Noviodunum and destroyed it by fire, thus imperilling Caesar's whole position in Gaul.

Pottery and spun glass – Luigi di Gonzaga, the Duke of Mantua's third son who became Duke of Nevers in 1565, brought artists and artisans from Italy.

He developed the glass industry as well as the art of enamelling, which became very fashionable. The town's products – spun glass was generally used in the composition of religious scenes – were sent by boat on the Loire to Orléans and Angers.

Luigi di Gonzaga introduced artistic earthenware in Nevers between 1575 and 1585. The three Italian brothers Conrade, "master potters in white and other colours", taught their art to a group of local artisans. Little by little, the shape, the colours and the decorative motifs, which at first reproduced only the Italian models and methods, evolved into a very distinctive local style. About 1650 the pottery industry was at its height – with twelve workshops and 1 800 workers.

The Revolution of 1789 dealt the industry a grave blow. Today, three **workshops** ⊘, two of them employing artisan craftsmen, maintain the reputation of this traditional craft.

"Ver-Vert" the parrot – The history of the parrot is told in a piece of light verse written by J.-B. Gresset in 1733.

The famous parrot once lived with the Visitandines in Nevers, coddled and spoiled but impeccably educated. When the Visitandine nuns at Nantes heard of the prodigious reputation of this marvellous parrot, they begged their sisters at Nevers to let them have him for a few days. The nuns at Nevers were reluctant but finally they agreed. Ver-Vert went off for his visit to Nantes but during his voyage in the river boat the Loire rivermen and some Dragoons taught him a vocabulary considerably less virtuous than that he had learned with the nuns:

> "For these Dragoons were a godless lot,
> Who spoke the tongue of the lowest sot,
> ... Soon for curses and oaths he did not want
> And could out-swear a devil in a holy font."

The nuns in Nantes were horrified at his lurid maledictions; Satan's myrmidon was quickly sent back to Nevers. Brought before the convent's Council of Order, Ver-Vert was condemned to a period of fasting, solitude and, worst of all, to silence. After honourably serving his sentence, Ver-Vert returned to favour once again among the nuns of Nevers but, as in the past, he was spoiled and he died of over-indulgence:

> "Stuffed with sugar and mulled with wine,
> Ver-Vert, gorging a pile of sweets,
> Changed his rosy life for a coffin of pine."

OLD TOWN *time: 2 hours*

Start from the Porte du Croux and follow the itinerary shown on the plan.

★ **Porte du Croux** (Z) – This handsome square tower gateway with machicolations and corbelled turrets, topped by a high roof, is one of the last remnants of the town's fortifications. It was built in 1393, at the time when the fortifications, set up two centuries earlier by Pierre de Courtenay, were being enlarged.

The tower houses the **Musée archéologique du Nivernais** ⊘ which contains ancient sculptures (Greek and Roman marbles) and a large collection of Romanesque sculptures.

Follow the rampart walk.

Musée municipal Frédéric-Blandin (Z M¹) ⊘ – The museum, which is housed in the buildings of an old abbey, has a fine collection of **Nevers pottery**★ including pieces in the Italian, Persian, Chinese and Nivernais traditions. Among the polychrome and monochrome earthenware there is a statue (1636) of the Virgin with an Apple and a Nevers blue dish depicting Venus and Mercury.

Other pieces include delicate enamels and spun glass from Nevers by Jean Baffier.

Return to the crossroads and turn right into Rue des Jacobins.

★★ **Cathédrale St-Cyr-et-Ste-Julitte** (Z) ⊘ – This vast basilica, displaying all the architectural styles from the 10C to the 16C side by side, was consecrated in 1331 before being completed and then altered several times. The plan is characterised by two apses at opposite ends of the nave: Romanesque to the west and Gothic to the east. This arrangement, which was common in the Carolingian period and is to be found in some cathedrals on the banks of the Rhine, notably at Speyer, Worms and Mainz, is rare in France.

Nevers faïence plate (late 17C-early 18C)

J. Guillot/C.D.A. EDIMEDIA

NEVERS

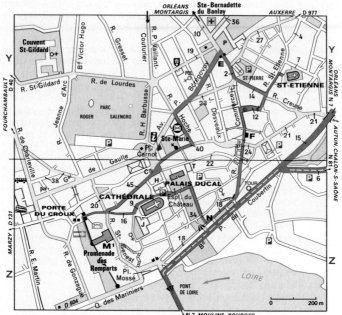

Exterior – Walk round the building which bristles with buttresses, pillars, flying buttresses and pinnacles to see the sequence of the different styles and to admire the square tower (52m - 171ft high) standing against the south arm of the transept. The tower is flanked by polygonal buttresses; the lower storey is 14C, and the other two, richly decorated with niches, statues and arcades, are 16C.

Interior – The most striking feature is the sheer size of the nave with its triforium and clerestory and the choir encircled by the ambulatory.

The Romanesque apse, named after St Julitta, raised by thirteen steps and with semi-domed vaulting, is decorated with a 12C fresco representing Christ surrounded by the symbols of the Evangelists. The 13C nave is off-centre. The 16C clock has a jack o' the clock. Statuettes decorate the base of the triforium columns. The chapels date from the 15C.

★ **Palais Ducal (Z)** – The former home of the Dukes of Nevers was begun in the second half of the 15C by Jean de Clamecy, Count of Nevers, who was eager to move out of his old fortress which stood on the site of the present town hall. The new ducal residence was completed at the end of the 16C by the Clèves and Gonzagas. The palace is a most beautiful example of early civil Renaissance architecture. The great round towers at the rear give on to a courtyard that overlooks Rue des Ouches. The ochre façade is surmounted by a slate roof and flanked by twin turrets; the beautiful canted tower in the centre rising to a small belfry contains the grand staircase; a most graceful effect is created by the placing of the windows which follow the spiralling of the stairs. The modern low-reliefs recall the legends of St Hubert and of the Knight of the Swan (Chevalier au Cygne), an ancestor of the house of Clèves, who inspired the tale of Lohengrin. The dormer windows are flanked by caryatids and the chimneys resemble organ pipes. On the left turret a plaque recalls that several princesses of the Nivernais became Queens of Poland.

Cross Place de la République in front of the Palais Ducal.

Montée des Princes (Z N) – From the terraced garden beyond the esplanade of the Palais Ducal there is a good view of the Loire.

Turn left into Quai de Mantoue then Rue du Commerce.

Beffroi (Y F) – The vast 15C belfry, which is dominated by a pointed belltower, once housed the covered markets and the council chamber.

Follow Rue du Commerce; turn right into Place Guy-Coquille; turn left into Rue St-Étienne.

★ **St-Étienne** (Y) – This beautiful Romanesque church, which once belonged to a priory of Cluny, has remarkable purity and homogeneity of style. It was built from 1063 to 1097, at the instance of Guillaume I, Count of Nevers.

The chevet, best seen from Rue du Charnier, has a magnificent tiered arrangement of apse and apsidals. The transept tower, of which only the base remains, was destroyed together with the two towers surmounting the façade, at the time of the French Revolution.

The façade is sober. A line of brackets indicate the former existence of a porch. Apart from the capitals in the ambulatory, the interior is devoid of sculpture but its attraction lies in its fine proportions and the golden colour of the stone. The six bays of the nave are covered by barrel vaulting with transverse arches; there is groined vaulting in the aisles. A Romanesque altar stands in the chancel (restored). The transept crossing is covered by a dome on squinches. The row of windows beneath the vault is of impressive boldness and the two galleries of the triforium open to the nave are also remarkable.

Return south; turn right into Rue Francs-Bourgeois and then Rue des Ardilliers.

Porte de Paris (Y E) – This triumphal arch was built in the 18C to commemorate the victory of Fontenoy; verses by Voltaire in praise of Louis XV are engraved on it.

North of the gate turn left into Rue du Rempart, left again into Rue Hoche and finally right into Rue St-Martin.

Chapelle Ste-Marie (Y) – This is the former chapel, now deconsecrated, of the 7th convent of the Visitandines founded in France. At the request of the bishop of Nevers, Mademoiselle de Bréchard, a lady of the Nivernais, who had become a nun of the Visitation and Mother Superior of the convent of Moulins, was sent by St Francis of Sales to found this convent.

The façade, of Louis XIII style, is covered with Italian-type ornamentation: niches, entablatures, columns and pilasters.

Promenade des Remparts (Z) – A well-conserved section of the town walls, built by Pierre de Courtenay in the 12C, stretches from the Porte du Croux southwards to the Loire. Several of the original towers (Tours du Hâvre, St-Révérien and Gogin) are still standing.

ADDITIONAL SIGHTS

Couvent St-Gildard (Y) ⊙ – *Pilgrimage from April to October.*

It was this convent that **Bernadette Soubirous**, acclaimed at Lourdes for her many visitations, entered in 1866. She died there in 1879 and was canonised in 1933. Her embalmed body rests in a glass shrine in the chapel of the convent which is the mother house of the Sisters of Charity and Christian Instruction of Nevers.

A small **museum** retraces the saint's life and work and displays some of her personal effects. The fine low-relief portraying scenes from the life of the Virgin originally belonged to the church of St-Gildard.

Ste-Bernadette-du-Banlay ⊙ – *Take Avenue Colbert* (Y 10) *and then Boulevard de-Lattre-de-Tassigny.*

From the outside this church (1966) has all the massive appearance of a blockhouse. Inside however the well-lit nave has a great feeling of spaciousness.

▶▶ **Circuit auto-moto de Nevers-Magny-Cours** ⊙ – *14km - 9 miles south.*

This motor and motor bike racing track hosts Grand Prix races every year.

NOZEROY★

Pop 416
Michelin map 170 fold 5 or 243 fold 2 –
Local maps under Vallée de l'AIN and Route des SAPINS

This old market town lies in a picturesque setting, on a solitary hilltop overlooking a vast, pasture-covered plateau. Nozeroy still has a certain old-style flair, along with the more concrete traces of its past such as a 15C gateway (the Porte Nods) and the vestiges of some ramparts north of the town.

Castle seat of the House of Chalon – Nozeroy is tucked up against the ruins of a château, which was built by the most famous member of the Chalon family, Jean l'Antique ("the Ancient", 1190-1267). This noble family had several branches – the Chalon-Viennes, Chalon-Auxerres, Chalon-Arlays – and played a very prominent role in the political life of the Franche-Comté. Their history is turbulent; family members fought one another for the leadership of the Comté, joined forces to fight feudal rivals and formed an alliance with the Comté aristocracy to resist the advances of foreign princes. Jean l'Antique put arms, money *(see Salins-les-Bains)*, alliances and diplomacy to his own personal use so skilfully that by the end of his life he had procured over five hundred fiefs. His many children, the Chalon-Arlays, inherited the Nozeroy seigneury and expanded its territory still further. Jean de Chalon-Arlay III acquired the title of Prince of Orange through his marriage in 1386. The château was razed in the 15C and replaced by a magnificent palace, decorated by artists from the court of Burgundy. A century later Philibert, the last of the Chalons, who had attained the rank of commander-in-chief of the Spanish armies and viceroy of Naples, laid on splendid feasts at Nozeroy which drew nobility from all over the province.

Nozeroy and Holland – Nozeroy hosted a number of illustrious individuals, such as St Colette, who founded a convent of the Order of St Clare at Poligny *(qv)* in 1415, the future king Louis XI and the last of the great Dukes of Burgundy Charles the Bold. When Philibert died without issue in 1530, the property of the Chalon family passed to the House of Orange-Nassau, which had links with them. In 1684, a creditor of William of Nassau, stathouder of the Netherlands and then king of England, was able to take possession of the prince's domains in the Comté. The Chalon estate is now divided between a number of different families, and the château was completely destroyed during the Revolution.

SIGHTS

Porte de l'Horloge – This gateway through a tall square machicolated tower is a remnant of the old fortified curtain wall.

Grande Rue – Several old houses are to be seen along this street.

Place des Annonciades – This square is shaded by a magnificent chestnut tree.

Walk along the tree-lined promenade (bust of Pasteur) which leads round the château ruins, providing some beautiful views of the surrounding area.

Église – Most of the church dates from the 15C. Note the 15C stalls and the sculpted wooden pulpit. Lovers of more unusual works of art will appreciate the 17C altar hanging in the right chapel, which was patiently embroidered in woven straw by Nozeroy's Annonciade nuns. Note also the 15C polychrome stone Virgin and Child, against a pillar in the south aisle.
Behind the church is the tomb of Général Pajol (1772-1844).

Promenade des Fossés de Trébief – This avenue runs alongside the most interesting section of the old ramparts.

NUITS-ST-GEORGES

Population 5 569
Michelin map 65 southwest of fold 20 or 243 fold 16 – Local map under La CÔTE

This friendly and attractive little town is the centre of the vineyards to which it has given its name. It is proud of the famous wines which have a world-wide reputation.
The fame of the wines of Nuits goes back to Louis XIV. When the royal doctor, Fagon, advised the king to take some glasses of Nuits and Romanée with each meal as a tonic, the whole court wanted to taste it.
Among the most famous of the wines Nuits-St-Georges, produced from the vineyards since the year 1000, is the best known.

St-Symphorien – This vast church was built at the end of the 13C although it is pure Romanesque in style. The flat chevet is pierced by a large rose window and three windows flanked by small columns and sculptures. A massive belfry surmounts the transept crossing.
The lofty nave, which is covered with groined vaulting, contains an 18C organ loft and a rare late-16C wooden cylinder decorated with open-work carving to enclose a spiral staircase. Traces of frescoes (including the martyrdom of St Christine) and 16C inscriptions are visible in the aisles.

Other buildings – There are two fine 17C edifices: the belfry of the former town hall and the St-Laurent hospital. The present town hall is 18C. The modern church of Notre-Dame has stained glass (1957) by J.-J. Borghetto.

Musée ⊙ – This museum occupies the premises of an old wine business. In the cellars is an exhibition of archaeological items discovered in the Gallo-Roman settlement excavated at Les Bolards near Nuits-St-Georges (ex-votos, funerary steles and urns, everyday household objects). The rooms on the first floor contain weapons, costumes, uniforms of the light infantry (1845-1945), and memorabilia of the victorious fight put up by Nuits-St-Georges against the united forces of Baden and Prussia on 18 December 1870.
One room is devoted to the Burgundian painter Jean François (1906-80), whose works take wine-growing and wine as their theme.

In recent years, 1985 and 1990 produced excellent vintage red Burgundies, while 1989 was the best for white Burgundies. The years 1979, 1982 and 1988 to 1993 have given rise to fine red and white Burgundies (1985 and 1986 were also fine years for white Burgundies).

ORNANS ★

Population 4 016
Michelin map 166 south of fold 16 or 243 fold 20 — Facilities —
Local map under Vallée de la LOUE

Ornans' history, number of inhabitants and industrial activity justifiably make it the small capital of the Loue valley. The stretch of river flowing between the double row of old houses on piles is one of the prettiest scenes in the Jura.

The "Magistrat" — Ornans, of which there is no record until the early Middle Ages, received its charter from the lord of Comté in 1244. The town was governed by a municipal council, called the "Magistrat", composed of the mayor, four aldermen (now deputies) and twelve members under oath (councillors). These individuals were elected annually by all family heads over the age of 25. The Magistrat designated twelve leading citizens from among the biggest taxpayers to oversee administration of the community. None of these posts was paid. The town had the right to grant sanctuary and made sure that this right was upheld, even by Parliament. In one case, where Parliament had seized a fugitive to imprison him in Dole, the Magistrat brought the affair before Emperor Charles V and had the prisoner returned to sanctuary. Pettifoggery was rife in Ornans, as it was throughout the Comté; the 1 500 inhabitants provided more than enough business for eight barristers, eight solicitors, seven bailiffs and six notaries.

The militia — The men of Ornans were all armed and formed a local militia to defend and keep watch over the château and, if need be, make up a garrison in case of attack. They were less than keen on occupying the feudal towers, which were so well ventilated that they were nicknamed "wind-gobblers", or more crudely, "bum-coolers". The militia assiduously practised use of the crossbow and the harquebus. There was an annual competition, the victor of which was exempted from the year's taxes. If the same man won three times in a row, he was exempted from paying taxes for the rest of his life.

Processions — Processions were major local events. The priest and twenty chaplains would be at the head, singing loudly, followed by members of the professional guilds in traditional costume with banners, various brotherhoods, penitents in black accompanied by a giant crucifix, young girls in white with flowers in their hair, and women in black with head-dresses. Next would come the town sergeants, then the members of the Magistrat, very dignified in their purple robes and caps. The militia would bring up the rear of the procession, with their motley clothes and weapons; despite the beating drums and their purposeful marching and frowning faces, the soldiers nonetheless had a good-natured air.

Famous citizens — Chancellor Perrenot de Granvelle *(qv)* came from Ornans. **Pierre Vernier**, the inventor of the vernier caliper, a measuring instrument, and also artilleryman, military engineer and captain of the château in the 17C, was born in here.
The great painter **Gustave Courbet**, master of French Realism, was born in Ornans in 1819. His parents were wine-growers and wanted their son to become a notary, but he eventually abandoned his law books for the painter's easel, teaching himself by studying the paintings in the Louvre. His work provoked a storm of both praise and criticism. He was strongly attached to Ornans and found most of his subjects in and around his birthplace. Landscapes such as *Château d'Ornans* and *Source de la Loue* capture the essence of nature in the Franche-Comté. The subjects of his portraits were friends or members of his family; *L'Après-Dinée à Ornans* and *Enterrement à Ornans* are particularly interesting as historical documents. He excelled at psychological portraits, especially of women, such as *L'Exilée polonais*. In 1868 he made the acquaintance of the painter Wilhelm Leibl, who had been honoured with a gold medal at the Paris Salon, and they became friends.
Courbet was as revolutionary in his politics as he was in his painting. In 1871 he took part in the Paris Commune. He was held responsible for the toppling of the Vendôme column and condemned to six months imprisonment and a 500 francs fine. In 1873, he was fined a further 323 000 francs for the cost of replacing the column. Financially ruined, revolted by the horrors he had witnessed, no longer able to exhibit his work — the Paris Salon, which was vitally influential in painters' careers at the time, returned his paintings without even looking at them — and all too conscious of the public censure surrounding him, he went into exile in Switzerland in 1873. He died there in 1877, at La Tour-de-Peilz near Vevey, a broken man. His body was brought back to the Ornans cemetery in 1919.
Special **festivities** ⊙ are put on in Ornans each summer in memory of this painter.

Portrait of Courbet by Cayat

SIGHTS

Grand Pont – This great bridge is the most famous spot in Ornans, with its picturesque **view★** of the town's old houses reflected in the Loue.

Musée Courbet ⊘ – The museum is in the house where Courbet was born, a beautiful 18C building which used to be the Hôtel Hébert. Works by the artist are exhibited (Jura landscapes, drawings, sculptures), as well as by his students and friends. There are also many objects evoking 19C artistic life in Paris and in the Franche-Comté. Note in particular the *Autoportrait à Ste-Pélagie*, his famous self portrait painted in prison, and the landscapes *Château Chillon* and *La papeterie d'Ornans sur le ruisseau de Bonneille*. The rooms downstairs are used for temporary exhibitions.

J. Guillard / SCOPE

Ornans

Hôtel Panderet de Velonne – This 17C town house has a lovely façade and gate.

Hôtel de Grospain – This 15C residence was used for a long time as the town hall.

Église – The church was rebuilt in the 16C, retaining only the lower part of the 12C bell tower from the original Romanesque building. The dome and the lantern turret date from the 17C. The church was funded by the Chancellor and the Cardinal of Granvelle, who furthermore ensured that it received a regular "contribution" for thirty years from the sovereign, in the form of revenue from the sale of ten loads of salt shipped from Salins every week.

Miroir de la Loue – *Beyond the church, take Rue du Champliman along the river bank.*
The pretty stretch of water seen from the bridge downstream of the old town is known as the "Loue Mirror". Church, town and cliffs are reflected in the water's silvery surface.

▶▶ **Trépot** – *12.5km - 8 miles north.* **Musée fromagerie** (cheese museum) ⊘.

▶▶ **Gouffre de Poudrey** ⊘ – *14km - 9 miles northeast.* Swallowhole *(150 steps).*

▶▶ **Dino-Zoo** ⊘ – *At Charbonnières-les-Sapins, 5km - 3 miles southwest of the Gouffre de Poudrey.* Life-size plastic dinosaurs.

To plan a special itinerary
- *consult the map of the region on pp 4-6 which shows the main towns, individual sights and recommended routes described in the guide;*
- *read the descriptions of the above which are described in the middle section of the guide in alphabetical order under their own name or are incorporated in the excursions radiating from a particular town or tourist centre;*
- *use the appropriate **Michelin Maps** which show places of interest, scenic routes, viewpoints and natural features...*

Grottes D'OSSELLE ★

The Osselle ⓥ caves are set in a cliff overlooking a meander in the Doubs. They were discovered in the 13C and have been visited since 1504. During the Revolution, the dry galleries were used as refuges and chapels by local priests; a clay altar can still be seen. A cave bear's skeleton has been assembled from bones found among the debris.

Out of 8km - 5 miles of long, regularly shaped galleries, leading in the same direction as the mountain ridge, 1 300m have been adapted and opened to visitors.

The first galleries, with walls somewhat blackened by the smoke of resin torches, contain concretions which are still being formed by running water. A low passage leads to galleries of stalagmites of almost pure white calcite, or which have been tinted various colours by iron oxide, copper or manganese. Some niches decorated with small, delicate stalactites make pretty tableaux by themselves or reflected in the pools of the cave. The underground river in one of the lower galleries is spanned by a small stone bridge (built in 1751), enabling visitors to see the so-called organ gallery and gallery of the white columns.

Salle des Trois Colonnes

A cave-dweller at heart ?
Other caves worth visiting in the region include: Grotte Sarrazine, Grottes de Baume, Grotte des Planches and Grotte du Cerdon (see the index for the page number).

OYONNAX

Population 23 869
Michelin map 74 north of fold 4 or 244 fold 6 –
Local maps under Vallée de l'AIN and ST-CLAUDE: Excursion

This industrial town is at the heart of a popular tourist region, between the valleys of the Ain to the west, the Bienne to the north and the Valserine to the east, and the Bugey region to the south.

From wooden hair combs to "Plastics Vallée" – Beautiful wooden combs have been crafted here for centuries by local mountain dwellers during the winter, using Jura boxwood as well as beech and hornbeam. By the end of the 18C other materials were gradually introduced, in particular horn.

The discovery of celluloid in 1869 in the United States opened up new opportunites for comb-makers in Oyonnax. In 1878 they began using this material to make not only new kinds of combs, but other accessories and toys. As fast as a new material (galalith, bakelite, cellulose acetate, etc.) was developed, Oyonnax craftsmen would adapt it to their products, thereby remaining at the forefront of the market. Rhodoid, a thermoplastic derived from cellulose acetate, played a particularly important part in the town's economic prosperity from 1924.

Oyonnax has now evolved into a production centre of European importance, turning out a wide variety of objects: household articles, toys, artifical flowers, combs, spectacles, car accessories, and parts for radios and other electrical appliances. The association "Plastics Vallée" was created in 1986, bringing together 1 200 specialised businesses within a 50km - 31 mile radius. In addition to the technical college for the science and manufacture of man-made materials (the Lycée technique Arbez-Carme) which has been located here for almost a century, the Pôle européen de plasturgie was opened here in 1991 to train plastics engineers from all over the country. Every year, the town hosts a number of international fairs and conferences for professionals in the plastic industry. All these factors combine to make Oyonnax one of the most important centres of the man-made materials industry in Europe.

Musée du Peigne et des Matières plastiques ⊘ – *Centre culturel Aragon, first floor, Square G.-Pompidou.*

The museum collections give a good overview of the evolution and variety of products manufactured in Oyonnax. Exhibits include combs made of boxwood, horn and celluloid, spectacles, buttons, buckles, jewellery, artificial flowers, etc. Many objects, such as celluloid mantillas and plastic spectacles, illustrate the manufacturers' skill at their craft and sense for aesthetic design. Machines which once made horn and celluloid combs complete the exhibition.

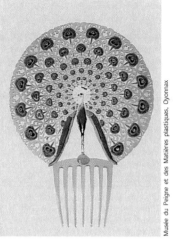

Musée du Peigne et des Matières plastiques, Oyonnax

Celluloid comb for fastening a mantilla (1920)

PARAY-LE-MONIAL★★

Population 9 859
Michelin map 69 fold 17 or 243 fold 37 – Facilities – Local map under Excursion below

Paray-le-Monial, cradle of the worship of the Sacred Heart of Jesus, is situated on the boundary between the Charollais and Brionnais regions, on the banks of the river Bourbince beside which flows the Canal du Centre.

The town's Romanesque basilica is a magnificent example of the architecture of Cluny. The building materials industry, which is concentrated in the valley of the Bourbince, is represented at Paray by factories producing tiles and sandstone pavings as well as fireproof products.

Marguerite-Marie Alacoque – Although her desire to become a nun was obvious at a very early age, Marguerite-Marie Alacoque, the daughter of a royal notary in Verosvres-en-Charollais, could not carry out her intention until she was 24.

On 20 June 1671 she entered the convent of the Visitation at Paray-le-Monial as a novice and two months later took the veil.

From 1673 onwards, Sister Marguerite-Marie received a succession of visitations that continued up to her death. Helped by her confessor, Father Claude de la Colombière, she revealed the messages she had received – writing out the revelations that were made to her: "Here is this heart, which so loved mankind" – thus initiating the worship of the Sacred Heart in France. She died on 17 October 1690.

Devotion to the Sacred Heart – It was not until the beginning of the 19C, when the turmoil of the French Revolution had died down, that devotion to the Sacred Heart made any significant progress. In 1817 hearings began before the Vatican Tribunals which ended in 1864 with the beatification of Sister Marguerite-Marie. In 1873, when the first great pilgrimage in Paray-le-Monial took place in the presence of 30 000 people, the decision was made to dedicate France to the Sacred Heart of Jesus. This event was linked to the vow made in 1870 to build a church dedicated to the Sacred Heart with money raised by national subscription; this was the basilica of Sacré-Cœur which now stands on the hill of Montmartre. Pilgrimages have been repeated each year since 1873. Sister Marguerite-Marie was canonised in 1920.

Many religious orders have communities at Paray-le-Monial which has become one of the great centres of Christianity.

★★BASILIQUE DU SACRÉ-CŒUR ⊘ *time: 30 min*

On the right bank of the Bourbince, approached by a promenade flanked by flowers and weeping willows, stands the church; it was originally dedicated to the Virgin Mary but in 1875 it was raised to the level of a basilica and consecrated to the Sacred Heart.

The church was built without interruption between 1090 and 1109 under the direction of St Hugues, Abbot of Cluny, and restored in the 19C and 20C; it constitutes a contemporary model on a smaller scale of the famous Benedictine abbey at Cluny. Only the architectural style is similar; the builders eschewed decorative splendour and large-scale design to the glory of God, in favour of abstract beauty, composed of the rhythmic combination of light and shadow, space and simplicity, which is conducive to contemplation. The rare sculptures make generous use of the geometric motifs found in Islamic art; its enchanting perfection was probably discovered by St Hugues during two visits to Spain.

From the bridge spanning the Bourbince there is a fine view of the basilica; its golden stone is used in many of the churches in the neighbouring Brionnais *(see Excursion below)*.

Exterior – The façade is of a great simplicity: two square towers surmount the narthex. Supported at the corners by powerful buttresses, the towers have four storeys of windows, of which the first tier lights the narthex.

The right-hand tower, built in the early 11C, has sober decoration; the tower on the left, which is of a later date, is more richly decorated: the upper storeys are separated by a moulded cornice and

Basilique du Sacré-Cœur

the third storey is pierced by two twinned openings, divided by columns ornamented with capitals; on the top storey, the arch of the opening is formed by two recessed orders instead of three, while the capitals of the small columns are joined by a cordon of ovoli (quarter-section mouldings) and lozenges. The octagonal tower which stands over the transept crossing was restored in 1860.

A good vantage point from which to admire the decorative harmony of the chevet is the top of the steps of the old Maison des Pages which now houses the Chambre des Reliques. Enter the basilica by the north arm of the transept; the beautiful Romanesque doorway is decorated with floral and geometric designs.

Interior – One is struck by the height of the building (22m - 72ft in the main nave) and the simplicity of its decoration. Here, one finds all the characteristics of the art of Cluny. Huysmans (French novelist 1848-1907) saw the symbol of the Trinity in the three naves, composed of three bays supporting above the great arches three arcades surmounted by three windows. The choir and its ambulatory with three small apses – the gallery of the Angels – make an elegant ensemble. The historiated capitals of the delicate columns are a typical example of 12C Burgundian art. The semi-domed apse is decorated with a 14C fresco, representing a benedictory Christ in Majesty, which was brought to light only in 1935. The transept crossing, covered by a dome on squinches, is of a well-proportioned height.

THE PILGRIMAGE

Chambre des Reliques (B) ⊘ – In the former house of the pages of Cardinal de Bouillon, many souvenirs of St Marguerite-Marie have been assembled in a relics chamber. The saint's cell has been faithfully reconstructed.

Parc des Chapelains ⊘ – It is in this large park, containing Stations of the Cross, that the great pilgrimage services take place. A **diorama** in the park depicts the life of St Marguerite-Marie.

Chapelle de la Visitation (E) ⊘ – It was in this little chapel, also called "Sanctuary of the Apparitions", that St Marguerite-Marie received her principal Revelations. The silver-gilt reliquary in the chapel on the right contains the relics of the saint.

PARAY-LE-MONIAL

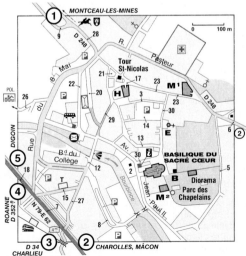

B	Chambre des Reliques	H	Hôtel de ville	M²	Musée de
E	Chapelle de la Visitation	M¹	Musée du Hiéron		la Faïence charollaise

ADDITIONAL SIGHTS

★ **Hôtel de ville** (**H**) – The façade of this fine Renaissance mansion, built in 1525 by a rich draper, is decorated with shells and medallion portraits of French kings.

Musée du Hiéron (**M¹**) ⊘ – The theme of this museum of sacred art is the Eucharist reflected in the life of Christ, the Virgin Mary and the saints. The collection of 13C to 18C Italian art includes primitive paintings; works from the schools of Florence (Donatello, Bramante), Venice, Rome and Bologna; sculptures including a 13C Tuscan Christ and a 13C and 16C ivory eucharistic tabernacle; gold and silver ware. There are also a few works from Flanders and Germany (engravings by Lucas of Leyden and Dürer) as well as from France: a very beautiful 12C **tympanum**★ from the Brionnais priory at Anzy-le-Duc *(qv)*. In the revolutionary turmoil of 1791 the doorway was transported to the park of Château d'Arcy and then given to the Hiéron museum. The tympanum shows Christ in Majesty enthroned in a mandorla supported by two angels. On the lintel the Virgin Mary bares her breast to the Infant Jesus in her lap; to the left are four virgins bearing a crown and to the right four apostles and disciples. The technical achievement of the sculpture is as remarkable as its iconographic richness.

Liturgical items: gold and silver ware, ivory, enamels.

Musée de la Faïence charollaise (**M²**) ⊘ – The museum is devoted to the history of a product which has altered many times in shape and decoration between 1836 and now. In 1879 Élisabeth Parmentier, a decorative artist who had worked with Majorelle, settled in Charolles and established a style which became the hallmark of Charollais earthenware: delicate bouquets flanked by insects or butterflies and bordered with a blue frieze. At the same time part of the production followed the stylistic development of the decorative arts.

The first room presents moulds, tools, raw material and firing errors *(diorama of the production process)*. The following rooms contain many pieces in chronological and thematic order; the last section is devoted to the factory archives.

Tour St-Nicolas – This square 16C tower was originally the belfry of the church of St-Nicolas, now deconsecrated. The façade which overlooks Place Lamartine is adorned with a beautiful wrought ironwork staircase and a corbelled turret at the apex of the gable.

EXCURSION

★ **The Brionnais** – The region south of Paray-le-Monial, enclosed by the rivers and Loire and Sornin, is known as the Brionnais. Semur-en-Brionnais is the regional capital. The rolling countryside is given over mainly to cattle rearing. There are about a dozen **Romanesque churches**★, inspired by the great abbey of Cluny, in the area *(see local map)*, which are well worth a visit.

The yellowish, fine-grain lime-stone of the region is relatively easy to work but at the same time very durable, making it the ideal medium for decorative sculpture on façades and doorways. It gives the churches a lovely warm ochre or yellow colour, which looks particularly beautiful in the rays of the setting sun. Harder stone like granite or sandstone, which cannot be worked in detail, is better suited to emphasise line or mass, as in the churches at Varenne-l'Arconce, Bois-Ste-Marie, Châteauneuf and St-Laurent-en-Brionnais. Certain themes predominate, although the attitudes and expressions of the figures do vary. The tympanum usually depicts Christ in Majesty, in a mandorla and surrounded by the four Evangelists or their symbols, or Christ ascending into Heaven. The decoration on the lintels is very elaborate (eg Last Supper scene at St-Julien-de-Jonzy); multitudes of tiny figures throng round the central figure of the triumphant Christ, who is depicted larger than everyone else in accordance with hierarchy.

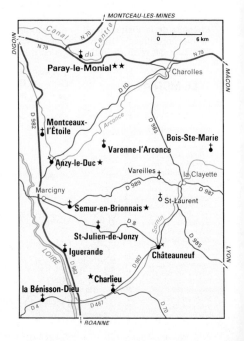

For details of the evolution of architecture in the region, see the Introduction.

Château de PIERRE-DE-BRESSE ★

Michelin map 70 fold 3 or 243 fold 29

The Château de Pierre is set in a park (30ha - 74 acres); it is a handsome 17C building constructed of limestone bricks with a slate roof. The moat and U-shaped plan, guarded by four round corner towers capped by domes, reveal that it stands on the foundations of a fortified building. The central block is ornamented by an arcade of round-headed arches opening into a gallery. The pediment above the delicate central section is detached from the high mansard roof. In the 18C the axis of the courtyard was extended by the addition of an outer court bordered by extensive outbuildings encircled by a second moat.

The left wing of the château houses the **Écomusée de la Bresse bourguignonne** ⊙. Only the stairs in the entrance lobby with their beautiful wrought-iron bannister and two rooms (18C and 19C) restored in period show how the interior of the château used to be. The exhibitions on three floors cover the natural environment, history, the traditional way of life and the present economic situation in Burgundian Bresse *(several audio-visual presentations including one 18 min long at the end of the tour)*. The museum, which illustrates the activities and traditions of Bresse, has established several branches throughout its territory at Louhans, Rancy, St-Germain-du-Bois, Perrigny, Verdun-sur-le-Doubs and Cuiseaux (Vines and Viticulture).

Château de Pierre-de-Bresse

J. Cartier, Pierre-de-Bresse

EXCURSIONS

Château de Terrans – *3km - 2 miles west by the D 73 and a left turn into a small road.* The sober, elegant façade of the château (1765), with two lions flanking the main steps, is visible through the beautiful wrought-iron railings around the courtyard.

St-Germain-du-Bois: L'Agriculture bressane ⊙ – *17km - 11 miles south by the D 13.* This branch of the Écomusée de la Bresse bourguignonne *(see above)* is devoted to the rural life of Bresse; it traces the development of agricultural machinery in the 19C and 20C and presents the traditional products of the region – predominantly maize and poultry. The section on horses includes a reconstruction of a saddler's and harness-maker's workshop.

Maison de la Forêt et du bois de Perrigny ⊙ – *27km - 17 miles southwest by the D 13, D 313, D 970 and D 35.* This branch of the Écomusée de la Bresse bourguignonne *(see above)* situated in the centre of the woodland of Bresse is devoted to the timber trade and its attendant crafts and to different aspects of the Bresse forest (sculptures by Alan Mantle).

Abbaye de la PIERRE-QUI-VIRE

Michelin map 65 folds 16 and 17 or 238 fold 24 – 10km - 6 miles east of Quarré-les-Tombes – Local map under MORVAN

This monastery, founded in the middle of the last century, is built in a wild and lonely part of the Morvan, on a hilly bank of the Trinquelin, the local name for the river Cousin, a small stream of clear water flowing at the foot of granite rocks in the middle of thick woods.

Foundation of the Abbey – The name of **Father Muard** is closely associated with the foundation of the abbey. He was born in 1809 in the diocese of Sens and showed a desire to enter holy orders at an early age. In 1850 Father Muard laid the foundations of his monastery on land donated by the Chastellux family. It took its name of "Pierre-Qui-Vire" (the Rocking Stone) from a druidic monument, an enormous block of granite, placed on another rock, which could be made to rock with a push of the hand.

Father Muard's death in 1854, when he was Superior of the abbey, did not stop the development of the community which joined the Benedictine Order in 1859. The present buildings – the church and monastery buildings – were built from 1850 to 1953. Although the rules of monastic enclosure forbid tours of the monastery, the **salle d'exposition** ⊙ is always open to visitors interested in the life of the monks and their work, mainly editing the Zodiaque books on religious art *(audio-visual presentation on the life of the monastery)*. The church is open for **services** and one can visit the **druidic stone** *("pierre plate")* which is outside the monastery walls.

POLIGNY

Population 4 714
Michelin map 170 fold 4 or 243 fold 30 — Facilities —
Local map under Les RECULÉES

Poligny lies at the entrance to a blind valley, the Culée de Vaux *(qv)*, and is over-looked by the Croix du Dan *(take the D 68 south, then the D 256)*, a cross which stands by a lookout point at an altitude of 450m - 1 476ft. This small town surrounded by rich farmland has justly earned itself a reputation as the capital of Comté cheese and has a dairy industry school as well as a research centre.

Good wines have been produced from the surrounding area for centuries. The early wine-growers built their homes inside a fortified curtain wall and were under the additional protection of the nearby fortress at Grimont, the ruins of which can still be seen. This fortress belonged to the Comté lords, who kept their records here along with a dungeon for rebellious vassals.

The Grimont dungeons certainly did not lie idle during the reign of the Great Dukes of Burgundy *(qv)*, since the independent lords of the Comté would keep taking up arms to resolve issues, without first obtaining the permission of their sovereign duke. To uphold their authority, the Dukes of Burgundy had declared the Comtois nobility subject to the jurisdiction of the Dole Parliament, which was quite capable of sentencing an insubordinate lord to a twenty-year spell in gaol, or even to death. The power struggle came to a head on one occasion in 1455, when Philip the Good imposed a tax of two francs on each household on each seigneury. This was greeted with universal outrage. In particular Jean de Grandson, seigneur of Pesmes, made no secret of his anger; he was forthwith seized and imprisoned in the Grimont fortress where, on being condemned to death by the Dole Parliament, he was suffocated between two mattresses. Jacques Coitier, Louis XI's crafty doctor, was born in Poligny. Once he fell out of favour, he had reason to fear for his life, until he persuaded his royal patient that he would die three days after his doctor. Richelieu ordered the invasion of the Franche-Comté in 1635, unleashing the Ten Years War. The town of Poligny was captured and burned by French troops three years later.

COLLÉGIALE ST-HIPPOLYTE (Y) *time : 30 min*

The main doorway beneath the porch features a 15C polychrome stone Virgin (a) on the central pillar. Above this, a low relief depicts St Hippolytus being quartered. On the doorway to the right of the main entrance, a 15C Pièta (b) stands on an emblazoned corbel. Inside, note the remarkable wooden calvary on the rood-beam above the chancel entrance, and the beautiful collection of 15C Burgundian school statues★.

1) St Blaise, polychrome alabaster statue
2) St Catherine, polychrome alabaster statue
3) St Stephen, alabaster statue
4) St Anne teaching the Virgin Mary, polychrome stone
5) St Bon, polychrome alabaster statue
6) A 1615 stone Pièta beneath a polychrome wooden altarpiece depicting Christ's Passion
7) St Paul, 15C statue
8) St John the Baptist (original in the Metropolitan Museum of Art, New York)
9) St James the Greater (original in the Metropolitan Museum of Art, New York)
10) St Anne teaching the Virgin Mary, 16C Brou school alabaster group
11) Virgin and Child, 16C Brou school alabaster work
12) St Leonard and St Nicholas (17C), either side of the altarpiece
13) From left to right, against the colonnettes of the chevet: Jean Chousat, the rich bourgeois sponsor of the church, represented with a falcon on his left fist and his right hand in his purse; A Virgin and Child holding a cloth with the imprint of Holy Face in his hand; St John the Evangelist; St Andrew
14) The Madonna of the Founder, stone statue

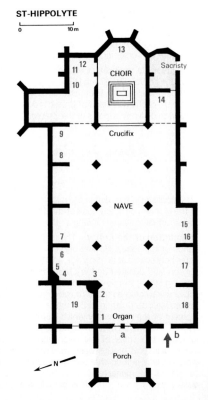

ST-HIPPOLYTE

0   10m

13

11 12

CHOIR

Sacristy

10

14

9   Crucifix

8

NAVE

15

16

7

17

6

5

4   3

2

19

18

1   Organ

a   b

Porch

N

15) Thomas de Plaine, president of the Burgundian parliament (original in the Louvre)
16) St Barbara, polychrome stone statue
17) Pierre Versey, bishop of Amiens
18) Jean Chevrot, bishop of Tournai
19) A group of damaged statues, which include a 14C Head of Christ, a 16C alabaster Pièta, five 15C stone statues, and a 17C statue

The church also has a large Cavaillé-Coll organ dating from 1859.

ADDITIONAL SIGHTS

Couvent des Clarisses (Y B) – *Behind the church.*
The entrance is through a great brown door. The convent was founded in 1415 by St Colette. Her relics are in a shrine in the **chapel** which was rebuilt after the Revolution.

Grande-Rue (Y) – This street contains old mansions with their original 17C carved wooden doors. The Croix de Dan can be seen following the line of the street.

Église de Mouthier-Vieillard (Z E) ⊙ – All that remains of this 11C Romanesque church are the chancel, part of the transept and the bell tower surmounted by a 13C stone spire. Of interest inside: a 1534 alabaster altarpiece, a 14C polychrome wooden calvary and some 13C and 15C statues, including one of St Anthony.

Hôtel-Dieu (Z) ⊙ – This 17C hospice still has its original cloisters, pharmacy (Nevers and Poligny faïence) and vaulted refectory.

Maison du Comté (Z K) ⊙ – This centre houses a cooperative committee for the promotion of Comté cheese and well as an exhibition outlining the various processes in the making of Comté *(qv)*, from the delivery of the milk to the final ripening of the cheese.

Technical progress in the production of this cheese can be followed in the display of machines and other equipment (copper tubs, presses, curd-cutters, churns). An audio-visuel presentation shows the landscapes and daily activities of the cheese-producing region.

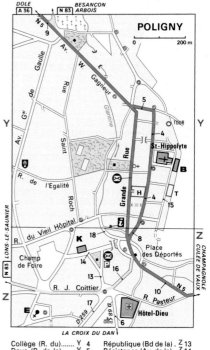

POLIGNY

Collège (R. du)	Y 4	République (Bd de la)	Z 13
Doye (R. de la)	Y 5	Résistance (Av. de la)	Z 14
Foch (Av.)	Z 6	Théâtre (R. du)	Y 15
Friant (R.)	Z 8	Travot (R.)	Z 16
Gare (Av. de la)	Y 9	Verdun (R. de)	Z 17
Genève (Rte de)	Z 10	4-Septembre (R. du)	Z 18

B Couvent des Clarisses
E Église de Mouthier-Vieillard
K Maison du Comté

PONTARLIER

Population 18 104
Michelin map 170 fold 6 or 243 fold 33 – Facilities – Local map under Vallée du DOUBS

Pontarlier lies near the Swiss border at the foot of the Jura mountains. It is a popular resort both for summer holidays and winter sports.

The town earns its living from wood, cheese, chocolate, knitted goods, and also distilleries (the manufacture of absinthe, an apéritif with a very high alcohol content, was an important industry here until it was banned in 1915).

From the Middle Ages to the 17C – From the 11C, the history of Pontarlier was closely linked to the turbulent relationships between the lords of Salins and of Joux, and between the abbeys of Montbenoît and Mont-Sainte-Marie.

In the mid-13C, Pontarlier and the eighteen nearby villages formed a small administrative and ecclesiastical community, the **Baroichage**. Pontarlier's merchant class were the driving force behind this move, which resulted in only minimal independence. The town's economy expanded until the 17C, largely due to the international trade route provided by the nearby pass over the Jura into Switzerland (the Col de Jougne) and four annual fairs.

The anni horribiles: 1639 and 1736 – During the Ten Years War, mercenary troops on the French payroll spread terror and destruction throughout the Franche-Comté. On 26 January 1639 Pontarlier surrendered after a four-day siege led by Bernard de Saxe-Weimar's *(qv)* Swedish forces. The town was pillaged, burned, and over 400 people died.

During the 18C, Pontarlier was damaged several times by fire, which caught hold quickly as the town's buildings were largely made of wood. The worst of the fires occurred on 31 August 1736, destroying half the town. As a result of this, Pontarlier was reconstructed following plans by engineer Querret.

Pontarlier became part of France in 1678, when Franche-Comté was officially annexed under the Nijmegen Treaty.

Mirabeau's romantic adventure – In 1776 the Marquis de Monnier, the former president of the Cour des Comptes, retired to spend the summer with his young bride Sophie de Ruffey at his country seat, the Château de Nans near the source of the Lison *(qv)*. The ex-president at the age of 75 had married this 20 year old, who, with only a small dowry, had presumably preferred marriage to a man old enough to be her grandfather to life in a convent. It is hardly surprising, therefore, that a regular guest at the couple's home, namely Mirabeau, supposedly imprisoned at the Château de Joux *(qv)* but nonetheless permitted considerable freedom, all too keenly struck up a "friendship" with Sophie. The liaison was discovered, and the lovers had to flee the wrath of the Marquis.

The pair had made contingency plans for just such an event. Sophie made a particularly daring escape; at dead of night she slipped through the grounds of the château disguised as a man, climbed over the wall by means of an opportunely placed ladder and leaped onto a conveniently tethered horse which carried her to meet Mirabeau waiting for her on the Swiss border. However, despite the 10 000 *livres* which were waiting safely for them in Switzerland, having been stolen from the Marquis de Monnier bit by bit and sent on ahead, the couple found they were not able to start an idyllic new life together as they had planned. The Pontarlier tribunal, unmoved by this tale of true love, sentenced, in their absence, the seducer to death and the unfaithful spouse to a lifetime's exile in a convent.

The fugitives were arrested on their way to Amsterdam and brought back to France. Sophie was packed off to the convent in Gien, while Mirabeau managed to save his skin by paying 40 000 *livres* compensation to the Marquis de Monnier and spending four years imprisoned in the castle at Vincennes. He got himself transferred to the prison at Pontarlier in 1782, and appeared before the tribunal pleading his own defence. After a long and difficult struggle, he got the original sentence annulled.

The flame of romance had died, however, and even Mirabeau's *Lettres à Sophie*, penned while he was incarcerated at Vincennes, could not persuade her to leave her convent for him.

B Ancienne chapelle
  des Annonciades
M Musée municipal

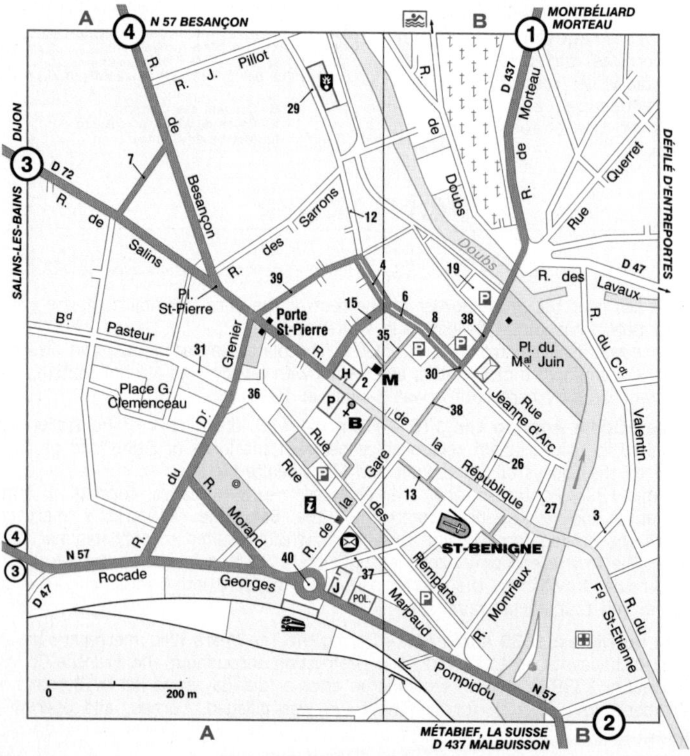

The end of the Bourbaki army – In December 1870 General Bourbaki's army of 130 000 men set out to cut off the Prussian army's passage through the Belfort Gap and thus force them to lift the siege of Paris.

Having won at Villersexel, Bourbaki was defeated at Héricourt (15-17 January 1871) and forced to fall back to Besançon. Caught between the armies of German Generals Werder and Manteuffel, he tried to escape along the Swiss border. He would certainly have been forced to surrender were it not for the noble sacrifice of General Billot's corps, who held back the enemy in the narrow Pontarlier pass while the rest of Bourbaki's army crossed into Switzerland, where they were disarmed (1 February 1871). Unbeknown to Bourbaki, Paris had fallen a few days beforehand (28 January) and the Versailles armistice had put an end to the Franco-Prussian war.

Porte Saint-Pierre

SIGHTS

Ancienne chapelle des Annonciades (A B) – This chapel, part of the Annunciade convent, was built in 1612. The doorway dates from the beginning of the 18C. The chapel, now deconsecrated, has been turned into an exhibition centre.

Porte St-Pierre (A) – This triumphal arch was built to celebrate the rebuilding of the town. It is comparable with the Porte St-Martin in Paris, which commemorates the French conquest of the Franche-Comté in 1678.

Église St-Bénigne (B) – The church was rebuilt in the 17C and then restored, but it still has an original 15C Flamboyant side doorway.

This curious building has a blind façade on its right side, built after the 1736 fire to make the church blend in with the new houses round the square. The bell porch is in the style of mountain churches designed to withstand heavy snowfall.

Inside are two particularly interesting paintings either side of the chancel: that to the left, which depicts Christ surrounded by angels bearing the instruments of the Passion; and that to the right, known as "The Miracle of Lactation" (the Virgin Mary is seen pressing her breast, from which a stream of milk flows to wet the lips of St Bernard). The Flamboyant vaulted chapel housing the font contains an early 16C wooden Virgin with Child and a beautiful crucifix. Note also the 1754 pulpit, skilfully carved by the Guyon brothers of Pontarlier; a 17C recumbent Christ; the 18C Black Madonna of Einsiedeln, which was worshipped throughout the Haut-Doubs region; and the 1758 organ case, also the work of the Guyon brothers.

Manessier's 1975 stained glass **windows★**, with the Paschal Symphony as their theme, harmonise well with the architecture of the church.

Musée municipal (A M) ⊘ – The museum is in what was a bourgeois home, built in the 16C and later modified several times (French style ceilings with painted beams, Art Nouveau windows). The three floors display an archaeological collection (Iron Age), 19C and 20C Comtois paintings (including *Autoportrait au Chien* by Courbet), 18C faïence ware, and objects related to the history of absinthe (posters, engravings, miscellaneous exhibits). The museum also puts on temporary exhibitions.

*The Michelin Red Guide France lists
the addresses and telephone numbers of the main car dealers,
garages offering a 24-hour breakdown service,
general repair garages and tyre specialists.*

PONTIGNY★

Population 737
Michelin map 65 fold 5 or 238 fold 11 – 18km - 11 miles northeast of Auxerre

This little village on the edge of the river Serein is celebrated for its former abbey, the second daughter-house of Cîteaux, founded in 1114. Whereas Cîteaux is now in ruins, the abbey of Pontigny (a retraining centre since 1968) has preserved its church intact.

HISTORICAL NOTES

The foundation – At the beginning of the year 1114 twelve monks with the Abbot Hugues de Mâcon at their head were sent from Cîteaux by St Stephen to found a monastery on the banks of the Serein, in a large clearing at a place known as Pontigny. The abbey was situated on the boundaries of three bishoprics (Auxerre, Sens and Langres) and three provinces (counties of Auxerre, Tonnerre and Champagne) and thus from its beginning benefited from the protection and the generosity of six different masters. An old saying recalls that three bishops, three counts and an abbot could dine on the bridge of Pontigny, each one remaining on his own territory. Thibault the Great, Count of Champagne, was the abbey's most generous benefactor: in 1150 he gave the abbot the means to build a larger church than that existing at the time (the chapel of St Thomas), which had become too small for the monks. He enclosed the abbey buildings with a wall (4m - 13ft high) of which sections still remain.

A refuge for archbishops – During the Middle Ages Pontigny served as a refuge for ecclesiastics fleeing from persecution in England; three Archbishops of Canterbury found asylum there. Thomas à Becket, Primate of England, came to Pontigny in 1164 having incurred the anger of his sovereign, Henry II. He returned to his country in 1170 but was murdered in his cathedral two years later.
Stephen Langton took refuge at Pontigny from 1208 to 1213 because of a disagreement with King John.
Edmund Rich, St Edmund of Abingdon, lived in Pontigny in saintly exile for several years until his death in 1240, when he was buried in the abbey church. He was canonised in 1247 and is venerated throughout the region (known locally as St Edme).

The decades of Pontigny – Abandoned during the French Revolution, the abbey served as a quarry for the nearby villages up to 1840. The ruins were then bought back by the Archbishop of Sens and put at the disposition of the Congregation of Missionary Fathers founded by Father Muard (see Abbaye de la PIERRE-QUI-VIRE), who restored the church and other buildings.
At the start of the 20C, the fathers were expelled and the property was bought by the philosopher, Paul Desjardins (1859-1940), who organised the famous "Décades" which brought together the most eminent personalities of the period including Thomas Mann, André Gide, T S Eliot and François Mauriac, who had lengthy literary conversations in the celebrated avenue of arbours.

★THE ABBEY time: 30 min

Opposite the War Memorial in the village an 18C entrance, flanked by small pavilions, opens into a shady avenue which leads past the conventual buildings to the abbey church.

★ **Church** ⊙ – Built in the second half of the 12C in the transitional Gothic style by Thibault, Count of Champagne, it is austere, in conformity with the Cistercian rule. Of impressive size (108m - 354ft long inside, 117m - 384ft with the porch, and 52m - 171ft wide at the transept), it is almost as large as Notre-Dame in Paris.

Exterior – A lean-to porch, festooned with arcades standing on consoles and small columns, takes up the whole width of the façade. Closed at the sides, it is pierced by twin, double-semicircular bays and a central doorway with a low arch.
The façade, decorated with a tall lancet window and two blind arcades, ends in a pointed gable with a small oculus. The sides of the church are typically bare; no belfry breaks the long line of the roof. The transept and the aisles are of a great simplicity; flat-sided buttresses and flying buttresses support the chevet and the north side.

Interior – The long, two-storey nave has seven bays; it is the earliest Cistercian nave with pointed vaulting to have survived to the present day. The perspective of the nave is interrupted by the wooden screen of the monks' choir.
The squat side aisles of groined vaulting contrast with the more unrestricted nave. The transept, lit at either end by a rose window, is very characteristic with its six rectangular chapels opening on to each arm of the transept.
The choir, rebuilt at the beginning of the 13C, is very graceful with its ambulatory and its eleven apsidal chapels. The crocketed capitals of the monolithic columns are more elaborate than those of the nave where water-lily leaves, of somewhat rudimentary design, constitute the main decorative element.
At the end of the choir under a heavy baldaquin is the 18C shrine of St Edmund; the earlier wooden shrine, made during the Renaissance, is kept in one of the apsidal chapels.
The beautiful **stalls★**, the transept grille and the organ case date from the end of the 17C. The organ loft, which is heavily ornamented, the choir parclose and the altar date from the end of the 18C.

Monastery buildings – All that is left of the 12C Cistercian buildings is the wing of the lay brothers' building; the rubblestone and delicate Tonnerre stone harmonise well in the façade, which is supported by buttresses.
Of the other buildings, only the southern gallery of the cloisters, rebuilt in the 17C, remains today (access via the church).

PUISAYE

Michelin map 65 folds 3, 4, 13 and 14 or 238 fold 9

The Puisaye is a region of forests, water and scrubland, which has a reputation for being monotonous and even austere. The uniformity is however only superficial and the visitor will find a variety of scenery; St-Fargeau is the chief town of the region.

The countryside – The word "Puisaye" appears to be the combination of two Celtic words: *poel*, meaning lake, marsh or pool, and *say*, meaning forest. The forest that once covered most of the area has now disappeared but the damp climate and the marl and sand soil still favour the existence of numerous pools. From Toucy to Bléneau and from Arquian to St-Sauveur, water is the dominant element and oozes everywhere: a multitude of rivers and pools are hidden in the greenery. From St-Sauveur through St-Fargeau and Bléneau to Rogny-les-Sept-Écluses runs a watery chain: Moutiers pool, Bourdon reservoir, La Tuilerie pool, La Grande Rue pool etc. The meadows and fields, enclosed by quickset hedges, the wooded hills and the silhouettes of the many châteaux – Ratilly, St-Fargeau, St-Sauveur and St-Amand – all add to the interest of a drive in the Puisaye.

The country of Colette – It was in **St-Sauveur** that Colette was born and spent her childhood. On the façade of a large house with a flight of steps, in Rue Colette, a red marble plaque carries a simple inscription commemorating the fact that Colette was born there.

She described this village, which she used to know so well, in *La Maison de Claudine* and in *Sido* with an exactitude and a reality that never sought to hide or embellish. Those days however have passed and St-Sauveur no longer has the appearance that the author knew.

On the wishes of Bel-Gazou, daughter of Colette and Henri de Jouvenel, a **museum** to Colette is planned *(scheduled to open during 1995)* in the Château St-Sauveur (17-18C). It is the reconstruction of her last apartment in the Palais Royal in Paris.

Pottery in the Puisaye – The soil of the Puisaye contains uncrushed flint coated with white or red clays which were used in the Middle Ages by the potters of St-Amand, Treigny, St-Vérain and Myennes.

It was in the 17C that the pottery trade really began to develop; the fine pieces of pottery, known as the "Bleu de St-Verain" (Blue of St Verain), were followed in the next century by utility products. In the late 19C craftsmen-potters built up a new reputation.

Pottery making is now concentrated in **St-Amand-en-Puisaye**, where there is a training centre, and on the outskirts of the town where several potters' shops produce first-rate stoneware. Moutiers, near St-Sauveur, is known for the earthenware and stoneware produced at La Batisse. At the Château de Ratilly *(see below)* those interested in ceramic art can observe the different stages of the potter's craft: casting, moulding and throwing on the wheel.

Château de RATILLY★

Michelin map 65 northeast of fold 13 or 238 fold 21

The first sight of this large 13C castle ⊘, placed well away from the main roads in a setting of magnificent trees in the heart of the Puisaye region, will charm visitors. Massive towers and high walls of an austere appearance overlook the dry moat surrounding the castle, which is built in fine ochre-coloured stone that time has mellowed.

In 1653 La Grande Mademoiselle (Mademoiselle de Montpensier), who had been exiled to St-Fargeau *(qv)*, stayed for a week at Ratilly. A little later Ratilly served as a refuge for the Jansenists, who published a clandestine paper there, safe from the pursuit of the royal police.

The left wing now houses a stoneware workshop (courses available). Both the workshop and the showroom, with its small exhibition on the original Puisaye stoneware, are open to the public. Other premises have been refurbished to house temporary art exhibitions.

▶▶ **Treigny** – *2km - 1 mile east.* 15-16C **church.**

Les RECULÉES★★★

Michelin map 170 folds 4, 5 and 14 or 243 folds 30, 31 and 42

On the road from Dole, a plateau can be seen looming on the horizon. This is the first step in the gigantic staircase formed by the Jura plateaux.

On reaching the vineyard region southeast of Arbois, Poligny and Lons-le-Saunier, you will see that the edge of this flat plateau is sharply incised by short truncated valleys with steep sides. These "blind" valleys, known as **reculées**, are a typical feature of the French Jura.

Each *reculée* ends in a rocky, steep-sided amphitheatre. The upper valley sides are tall sheer cliffs giving a vertical section through the porous limestone which has been gouged by erosion. The slopes at the foot of the cliffs may be scattered with scree or covered with shrubs or grass. Finally, the gentler lowermost slopes and the damp, green valley bottom consist of impermeable, marly soil. Resurgent springs well up from the caves at the base of the limestone cliffs, where the ground becomes marl.

The roads around the *reculées* are often very old ones used by the Romans to get to Helvetia (now Switzerland) or as trade routes between the mountains and the plains. At times they follow the bottom of the amphitheatre; at others they climb the sides to reach the rim at the top, from which there are breath-taking, virtually bird's-eye views. The Bresse plain, stretching to the horizon, can be glimpsed frequently between clefts in the rock face.

The "entrance" to a *reculée* may be marked as often as not by a fairly large market town, which has grown up around communications routes.

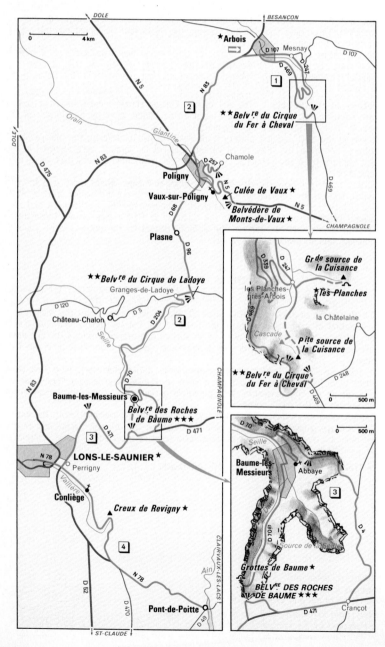

230

★★ ① RECULÉE DES PLANCHES
Round tour starting from Arbois
21km - 13 miles – allow one day – local map previous page

This *reculée* is also called the Reculée d'Arbois, because the town of Arbois lies at its opening.

★ **Arbois** – *See ARBOIS.*

Leave Arbois on the D 107, then take the D 247 to the right near the church in Mesnay. This picturesque road soon enters the Reculée des Planches, in which the village of Planches nestles. Go past the church on coming to Planches-près-Arbois, head past the stone bridge, and take the narrow surfaced road sharply to the left, along the foot of the cliffs. Leave the car 600m further on, near a little refreshment stand.

Grande source de la Cuisance – This is the more interesting of the two sources of the Cuisance, a tributary of the Loue. In rainy seasons the water cascades from a cave, which is also the entrance to the cave of Les Planches.

★ **Grotte des Planches** ⊙ – This cave was formed by the erosive action of water running between rock strata. Two of the galleries have been set aside for tourists, who can trace the underground path of the water as it flows through the rock.

In rainy seasons the Cuisance river course flows through the lower gallery in a series of spectacular thundering cascades. During dry periods, the floor of the gallery is occupied by a string of lakes, the innermost of which is over 800m from the entrance to the cave. The crystal clear waters of these lakes are strikingly blue.

The effects of erosion can also be seen during dry periods: long galleries almost completely bare of concretions, their ceilings polished by the underground river; vents enlarged by the pressure of whirlpools; underground pools and, more commonly, "giants' cauldrons" in various stages of development (mainly in the upper gallery).

The exploration, formation and modification for visitors of the cave, and also the formation of the *reculée*, are described in an adjoining cave. Excavations beneath the exit brought to light layers of evidence of habitation dating from the bronze, neolithic and paleolithic ages.

Petite source de la Cuisance – *500m from leaving Les Planches, then 1 hour on foot Rtn. On reaching Arbois take the direction "Auberge du Moulin"; leave the car in the park next to the river. Follow the path uphill.*

This waterfall in its pretty setting is formed by the young river and the spring itself during periods of heavy rainfall.

Retrace your steps. Straight after the bridge over the Cuisance, before the church in Les Planches, turn left onto the D 339, a narrow surfaced road leading uphill. Then take the D 469, cut into the rock face, on the left. The road goes through a tunnel in the rock face. Leave the car in the car park, which is 30m further on.

Retrace your steps to enjoy a view of the Fer-à-Cheval (horseshoe) amphitheatre, which closes off the Planches *reculée*.

Return to the car and take the D 469.

★★ **Belvédère du cirque du Fer-à-Cheval** – *Leave the car near an inn and take the signposted path (10 minutes on foot Rtn) on the left.*

The path goes through a little wood, at the edge of which the amphitheatre opens out *(protective barrier)*. There is a superb **view** of the *Reculée* from the viewpoint overlooking the valley floor from nearly 200m-656ft up.

Return to Arbois (qv) on the D 469.

② THE "VIGNOBLE"
From Arbois to Baume-les-Messieurs
40km - 25 miles – allow one day – local map previous page

★ **Arbois** – *See ARBOIS.*

Leave Arbois on the N 83 westwards.

The road runs along in view of the Jura plateau.

Poligny – *See POLIGNY.*

Take the N 5 towards Champagnole.

★ **Culée de Vaux** – There is a difference in height of 240m-787ft between Poligny and the top of the plateau.

The N 5 runs along the steep valley side of the Culée de Vaux. The Glantine, which flows through Poligny, rises in this valley.

Vaux-sur-Poligny – There is an old Cluniac church here with an unusual roof of multicoloured varnished tiles.

★ **Belvédère de Monts-de-Vaux** – This well-appointed viewpoint *(car park)* offers a beautiful **view** along the length of the *reculée*. The slopes are a pretty patchwork of meadows and woodland.

Rejoin the N 5 towards Poligny: after about 3.5km - 2 miles the D 257 towards Chamole leads off to the right.

As the road climbs there are **views**★ over the Culée de Vaux, Poligny and the Bresse region.

Return to Poligny. Leave the town on the D 68 south.

Plasne – A stroll around this hilltop village offers pretty **views**★ of the Bresse region.

Now take the D 96, a narrow, bumpy road.

★★ **Belvédère du Cirque de Ladoye** – *There is a car park for this viewpoint located above the reculée, to the right of the road about 40m beyond the intersection of the D 96 and the D 5. The* **view** *is impressive. A tributary of the Seille flows out from the bottom of the amphitheatre.*

Take the D 204 at Granges-de-Ladoye. This narrow, winding road first heads down to Ladoye-sur-Seille, before following the beautiful Seille valley. Turn left at the junction with the D 70, towards Baume-les-Messieurs.

Baume-les-Messieurs – *See BAUME-LES-MESSIEURS.*

★★★ ③ CIRQUE DE BAUME

21km - 13 miles – allow 6 hours – local map p 230

Baume-les-Messieurs – *See BAUME-LES-MESSIEURS*

Leave Baume-les-Messieurs on the D 70^{E3} over the Seille; then take the D 70^{E1} to the left, which goes down to the bottom of the amphitheatre along the banks of the Dard.

The tall rocky cliffs which form this amphitheatre are an awe-inspiring sight. Leave the car near the Chalet des Grottes de Baume.

Waterfall by the Grottes de Baume

★ **Grottes de Baume** ⊘ – The source of the Dard, a tributary of the Seille, was once to be found in these caves. Following heavy rainfall, the overspill from the Dard does still flow from here in a great cascade. The resurgent spring is below and to the left of the entrance to the caves.

Having gone along the entrance gallery, visitors are taken through tall, narrow chambers to the great hall, which has superb acoustics. Then the visit goes around a little lake containing small white blind shrimp of the niphargus genus. The ceiling of the Catafalque gallery is 80m-262ft high.

Return to the D 70 and then turn right to Crançot.

There is a view after the second hairpin bend of Baume and its abbey, which can be seen nestling at the bottom of the valley, at the foot of white limestone cliffs.

Further ahead turn right onto the D 4, then right again at Crançot onto the D 471, then right once more towards the Belvédère des Roches de Baume, also known as the Belvédère de Crançot.

★★★ **Belvédère des Roches de Baume** – Walk along the edge of the cliff which forms the famous viewpoint. At the last minute an astounding view of the entire amphitheatre unfolds though a gap in the rocks. The rocky outcrops crowning the cliff are surprisingly thick. Near the viewpoint furthest to the right there is a path down in the shape of steps cut into the rock. These steps, known as the **Échelles de Crançot,** lead to the floor of the amphitheatre and to the caves.

Return to the D 471 to take it to Lons-le-Saunier.

At a bend to the left in the road dropping down from the plateau there is a good **view** *(viewpoint)* of the Burgundy mountains.

4km - 2.4 miles further on turn right at Perrigny onto the N 78 to Lons-le-Saunier.

★ **Lons-le-Saunier** – *See LONS-LE-SAUNIER.*

4 **THE JURA PLATEAU**

From Lons-le-Saunier to Pont-de-Poitte

19km - 12 miles – allow 4 hours – local map p 230

★ **Lons-le-Saunier** – *See LONS-LE-SAUNIER.*

Leave Lons-le-Saunier on ② on the town plan, the N 78.

Conliège – The 17C **church** has beautiful wrought-iron chancel railings, a richly sculpted 17C pulpit, churchwardens' pews dating from 1525, and a 16C shrine containing the relics of St Fortuné.

★ **Creux de Revigny** – This is a beautiful amphitheatre enclosed by limestone cliffs, at the foot of which the source of the Vallière is to be found. This river flows on to Conliège and Lons-le-Saunier. There are many caves in the cliff, hidden amidst the dense foliage, which served as a refuge for the nearby inhabitants during the 17C (Ten Years War - *qv*). These people lived there on a virtually permanent basis; the region was so dangerous during the bloody attacks by the Swedes that even baptisms were held here.

The road then heads down into the Ain valley, which it reaches at Pont-de-Poitte.

Pont-de-Poitte – *See Vallée de l'AIN.*

In this guide the length of time indicated
– for sightseeing is the average time required for a visit
– for touring allows one to enjoy the views and the scenery.

La ROCHEPOT★

Pop 241
Michelin map 69 fold 9 or 243 fold 27 – 5km - 3 miles east of Nolay

The village, now by-passed by the main road, is set at the foot of a rocky promontory on which stands the feudal castle which has been restored. It was the birthplace of Philippe Pot (1428-94), famous statesman and ambassador in London of the Dukes of Burgundy. His tomb is a masterpiece of the Burgundian school and is now to be seen in the Louvre Museum.

Château ⊙ – The château is in an impressive **setting★**. The original 12C building was altered in the 15C but the keep was razed during the French Revolution. The complete rebuilding of the castle was undertaken by M. Sadi Carnot, son of Président Carnot. The outer defences are dominated by huge but graceful towers. The inner courtyard, beyond the drawbridge, contains a well with a wrought-iron wellhead; the turrets of the Renaissance wing are roofed with glazed coloured tiles.

Château de la Rochepot

The tour includes the Guard Room with its vast chimney and handsome ceiling beams, the chamber of the Captain of the Guards, the kitchens, the dining room, which is richly furnished and contains numerous *objets d'art*, the former chapel, the northern tower with its apartments and the watchpath. From a small terrace at the far end of the courtyard on the right, there is a view over the village and its encircling hills.

Church (Église) – This 12C priory church was built by the Benedictine monks from Flavigny. The historiated capitals are similar in style to those at Autun and represent Balaam's ass, the Annunciation, a knight and an eagle in combat. It contains a number of interesting works of art including a 16C triptych by the Dijon painter, Quentin, with a Descent from the Cross on the central section.

RONCHAMP

Population 3 088
Michelin map 166 fold 7 or 243 fold 9 - 12km - 8 miles east of Lure

Since the 50s the name of Ronchamp has evoked the chapel of **Notre-Dame-du-Haut**, designed by Swiss architect Le Corbusier in 1955 to replace a chapel destroyed during the Second World War. Until 1958 when the last colliery was closed down, Ronchamp was a mining town. A museum and archive testify to this industrial past.

★★ Notre-Dame-du-Haut ⊘ – *The chapel is 1.5km - 1 mile north of the town; access via a steep uphill road.* Le Corbusier's comment on this chapel, which is one of the most important works of contemporary religious architecture, was that he had intended his design to create a place of silence, prayer, peace and inner joy. The chapel was constructed on a hill (alt. 472m - 1 546ft) overlooking the industrial town of Ronchamp, which had been dedicated to the worship of the Virgin Mary since the Middle Ages. It is built entirely of concrete; the brightness of its whitewashed walls looks dazzling juxtaposed with the dark grey untreated concrete of the roof. The rigid geometric lines of the walls contrast strikingly with the softer plastic curves of the roof, which sweeps upwards in a graceful motion, and the rounded towers. In his conception of this chapel Le Corbusier broke with the rationalist movement and its inflexible designs, creating a work which has been described as architectural sculpture.

Inside, despite sloping walls and its relatively small size, the chapel seems spacious. The nave widens out up to the altar of white Burgundy stone, and the floor of the chapel follows the slope of the hill it is built on. The image of the Virgin Mary stands bathed in light in a niche in the wall. Light in the church filters through numerous different tiny windows randomly cut in the walls, allowing for a subtle interplay of light and shadow in the half darkness which softens the effect of the bare concrete walls. The three small chapels inside the three towers seen outside contribute to this subdued lighting effect.

Musée de la Mine ⊘ – This museum retraces two centuries of mining in the region. The first gallery contains a display on coal mining – equipment, mining lamps, collections of fossils – and reproductions of common underground catastrophes in the mines. The second gallery is given over to the life of the miners themselves, both pleasant aspects such as festivals, sports and musical activities, and the ever present threat of illnesses such as miners' silicosis.

Specialists in the field have access to a large archive on mining which includes information not only about the local mining industry, but also those in other countries in which mining is an important part of the national economy.

F. Jalain/EXPLORER

Notre-Dame-du-Haut

ST-CLAUDE★★

Population 12 704
Michelin map 170 fold 15 or 243 fold 43 – Facilities –
Local map under Excursion below

The town of St-Claude, tucked amidst delightful countryside, is the most important tourist centre in the Haut-Jura. It has always been famed for its charming setting (of which there is an excellent view from the Morez road, the D 69) and for the abbey which was once here. Since the town has been destroyed several times by fire, most notably in 1799, after which not much consideration was given to aesthetic appeal in its reconstruction, it has no buildings of any note apart from its cathedral. There are however some marvellous views of the surrounding countryside.

The capital of pipe-making – The Romans smoked hemp in terracotta or iron pipes. Pipes were not used in France, however, until 1560, when Nicot, the French ambassador to Portugal, first introduced them and tobacco to the court. The pipe itself consisted of a long tube ending in a little silver bowl. It was not terribly popular ini-

tially, but by the end of the 18C pipe-smoking had become quite the fashion, and craftsmen in St-Claude, who were already well reputed for their wood-turning, began to devote their professional interest to the problems of making pipes.

First of all, they fixed wooden or horn stems made locally to porcelain bowls imported from Germany, then they tried making pipes entirely of wood. Boxwood, wild cherry, walnut and pear wood all produced disappointing results, as they

Antique pipes

burned along with the tobacco, giving an appallingly bitter aftertaste. In 1854 a Corsican offered to supply a local pipemaker, Daniel David from the village of Chaumont near St-Claude, with briar root, which is far superior to boxwood for making pipes. David tried out this new material and came to settle in St-Claude, where he met with tremendous success. The pipemakers got their briar root from Corsica or countries on the shores of the Mediterranean in the form of lengths of root, weighing as much as 50kg - 110lb. These they dried themselves and then sawed into manageable chunks. Only after a process of about twenty different stages was the polished, varnished pipe ready for the smoker's delight and delectation. The town held a virtual monopoly on this manufacture until 1885, but the two World Wars favoured the development of foreign competitors. However, St-Claude is still an important pipe manufacturing centre. The town is home to related industries, such as the manufacture of cigarette-holders, pipe-cleaners, wooden snuff-boxes, pipe accessories in horn, etc.

Other industries in St-Claude include diamond cutting (also other precious stones), wood turning, the production of ebonite, production based on man-made and metal materials and the manufacture of high-precision instruments and spectacles.

HISTORICAL NOTES

Pioneers of the Jura – In c430 the future St Romanus, a young man wishing to lead a reclusive life, left his native village of Izernore (45km - 28 mile southwest of St-Claude) and went to live in the dense forest of the Haut-Jura. He chose a great fir tree, standing next to a spring, as his shelter (this would one day become the site of the cathedral of St-Claude). He lived off wild berries until he was able to harvest something from an area of ground which he broke up and cultivated.

He was joined by his brother Lupicinus (later also made a saint), and then by an ever-growing number of followers, attracted by the hermits' saintliness and the miracles they accomplished. St Lupicinus led a particularly austere life. He ate one vegetarian meal every two days, and never drank anything. When his thirst became unbearable he would plunge his hands into cold water and let the fluid seep through his pores into his dried out body. He wore animal skins and slept seated in one of the stalls in the chapel (if he fell ill, he would allow himself the luxury of lying on the rolled up bark of a fir tree).

By the time St Lupicinus died fifty years later, the monastery of **Condat** had grown up near St Romanus's original fir tree. Linked with it, numerous priories and more basic monastic communities known as *"granges"*, in which only two or three monks lived, were founded throughout the Haut-Jura and Switzerland. About 1500 monks now lived in the forest region and cultivated it. They used the boxwood from the forest to carve religious objects for pilgrims: statuettes, crucifixes, rosaries, etc. This was the origin of the turned-wood articles that were later to be so important economically to the region. The abbey and its extensive domains formed essentially an ecclesiastical principality from the 9C onward, which was only very loosely tied to the Holy Roman Empire. The abbot was both its spiritual head and its feudal lord.

Saintly monks – Abbey life was a model of piety and morality until the 12C. The monks adhered strictly to the austere rules of the Benedictine Order: ten hours of manual labour every day, in the fields or in the workshop, followed by two hours of reading and meditation, and long services both day and night. They lived in complete poverty, under the absolute authority of the abbot, practising silence, abstinence and mortification of the flesh. St Eugendus (Fr. Oyend), in the 6C, and St Claudius, in the 7C, made major contributions to the illustrious reputation of the abbey; the latter was a great lord and archbishop of Besançon, who gave up his wealth and rank to become a monk and who governed the abbey for over fifty-five years. During the reign of these saints the abbey gained its reputation for being a place of miracles. By the 12C the monastery and the town depending on it had taken the name of St-Claude, and pilgrims hurried along the roads of Burgundy to visit the relics of the holy monks. Louis XI himself came as well in 1482 to fulfil a vow.

Laxness – Religious discipline began to crumble during the 13C and 14C. The abbey had grown steadily in wealth, thanks to the generous donations from grateful pilgrims, and it simply became too rich. Absolute poverty became increasingly difficult for the monks to practise, and they finally succumbed to temptation. Money which had until then been used for the good of the whole monastic community ended up being shared out among a few individuals, and many of the new recruits to the abbey were motivated by worldly greed. To increase their individual share of the abbey's wealth, the monks in the know reduced the number of their community – that of the mother abbey at St-Claude fell from five hundred to thirty-six and finally to only twenty.

Aristocratic monks – The Comté aristocracy was envious of the rich inhabitants of the abbey, and began taking over places there as they became vacant. Once the nobility held the majority in the chapter, they decreed that admission to the abbey of St-Claude would henceforth be conditional on the applicant's having at least four generations of aristocracy on both maternal and paternal sides of his family. This recruitment policy had disastrous consequences for the abbey, as the monks from established noble families continued leading the life of luxury they were used to, and did not take their spiritual responsibilities at all seriously: religous offices were reduced to a minimum or cut out altogether; on days of abstinence or fasting the monks simply left the abbey to dine in town; monks were seen out hunting in lay clothes, wearing wigs on their heads and swords at their sides; friends and family of both sexes were welcomed into the abbey as visitors.

The Holy See and the episcopal authorities attempted on several occasions to reform the abbey, but were powerless in the face of the political influence of the monks. In 1737, the desperate pope decided to create an episcopal seat in the town, for which the monks became canons, thus freeing them of the duty to follow the Benedictine observance which was so foreign to them.

A lawyer's paradise – From the 15-18C, armies of lawyers made a living from settling the numerous, incredibly petty disputes between the abbey and the town of St-Claude. The question whether the bell in the monastery or that in the parish church should ring more loudly is just one example of the kind of issue which would provoke a lengthy legal wrangle – in this case forty years, until the problem was solved by the personal intervention of Emperor Charles V.

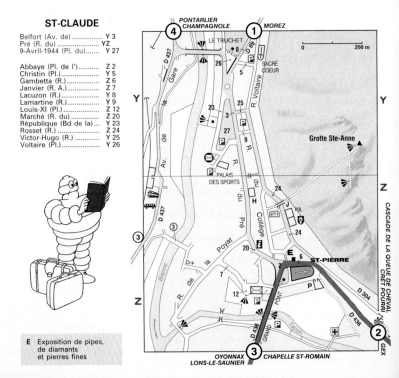

ST-CLAUDE

E Exposition de pipes, de diamants et pierres fines

The Revolution – The lordly canons, distinctly lacking the moral cachet of their saintly predecessors, were regarded by the 14 000 inhabitants of the abbey lands as nothing more than a handful of utterly shameless over-privileged layabouts. In 1770, shortly before the outbreak of the French Revolution, six Haut-Jura villages, with the help of their lawyer Christin, took out a lawsuit against the chapter to win their freedom. Their case made a tremendous impact; even Voltaire, living at Ferney at the time, came to the aid of the villagers by writing his acidly worded pamphlets. After a court case lasting five years, the canons, who refused point blank to give any ground, emerged victorious. The bishop suggested that, as their rights had been officially recognised, they might like to make the generous gesture of liberating their serfs on their own initiative, but the monks refused. The bishop appealed to the king, Louis XVI, but even he did not dare intervene in the face of the chapter's stubborn opposition. Finally, the problem was settled by the outbreak of Revolution: the religious principality of St-Claude was abolished, its goods and lands were confiscated and sold, and the serfs were freed. All that now remains of the once-glorious monastic community is the cathedral surrounded by the ruins of one or two buildings.

SIGHTS

★★ **The setting** – In order fully to appreciate the originality of St-Claude's setting on a narrow terrace in between the mountain torrents of the Bienne and the Tacon, stand on the bridge (Grand Pont) spanning the Tacon, from where there is an overall view of the town and the Cirque des Foules.
Then head to Place Louis XI (**Z 12**), from where there is a beautiful **view**★ above the old ramparts.

Other views – There is a view of the Tacon valley from the bottom of the steep, picturesque Rue de la Poyat. This street was once an important link between the upper district (around the abbey) and the suburb inhabited by workers and craftsmen. Before the modern bridges were built, it was also one of the routes taken by pilgrims on their way to revere the relics of St Claudius.
There is a beautiful view from the **Grotte de Ste-Anne** (**Y**), a cave which overlooks the town from a height of 200m - 656ft. Another good viewpoint is to be found on Place du 9-Avril-1944 (**Y 27**). Finally, from the middle of the viaduct (**Y**) the view shows clearly how the lack of level ground has made it necessary to expand the town upwards instead of outwards.

★ **Cathédrale St-Pierre** (**Z**) – This cathedral church, originally dedicated to Saints Peter, Paul and Andrew, was once the heart of the abbey community. The present building, originally built in the Gothic style in the 14C and 15C, was finished in the 18C with the addition of a classical façade. The 15C tower was extended higher in the 18C. The most interesting part of the exterior is the east end, with its watch turrets topped with spires.
The beautiful rectangular interior is plain, even austere, and is supported by 14 massive octagonal pillars. The chancel contains magnificent sculpted **wooden stalls**★★ which were begun before 1449 and finished in 1465 by the Geneva craftsman Jehan de Vitry. The apostles and the prophets are depicted alternately on the backrests, then the former abbots of the monastery; scenes from the abbey's history with the founders St Romanus and St Lupicinus, are represented on the large and small cheekpieces; the 19C restorers added scenes of everyday life to the elbow rests and misericords. Unfortunately the southern section of the stalls was destroyed by fire during the night of 26 September 1983.
St Claudius's tomb drew crowds of pilgrims until 1794. Emperors, kings and great lords all came to venerate him. Anne of Britanny had been unable to conceive until her pilgrimage to the Jura, after which she bore a daughter to Louis XII and named her Claude (later to become the wife of François I and Queen of France). St Romanus's shrine was burned during the Revolution, and the few remaining relics of the saint are kept in a reliquary in the chapel south of the chancel.
Left of the entrance, an **altarpiece**★ stands against the wall of the nave. It was donated in 1533 by Pierre de la Baume, the last Bishop of the Franche-Comté, who lived in Geneva, in gratitude to St Peter for protecting him through all the political and religious disturbances. Scenes from the life of St Peter are depicted on the predella. Above this are the three patrons of the church; St Peter in the centre, St Andrew on the right and St Paul on the left. Above this are St Claudius, to the right, and St Eugendus, to the left.

Exposition de pipes (**Z E**) ⊙ – This collection of 18C and 19C pipes is very varied, containing many examples of different materials (meerschaum, baked clay, brass, enamel, briar root, horn, etc.), different sizes and different origins (all over the world). Some pipes are very artistically decorated. The "Chancellerie" displays a collection of pipes marked with the names of those admitted into the famous pipe makers' guild of St-Claude. Note the sculpting machine, which works on the same principle as the pantograph.

Exposition de diamants et pierres fines (**Z E**) ⊙ – This exhibition includes displays on diamond-cutters themselves; precious stones, both natural and synthetic, cut and uncut; the diamond-cutter's and the lapidary's tools; and the various steps involved in cutting a precious stone. There are also one or two crowns and other ceremonial pieces from among the world's famous jewels and treasures.

EXCURSION

Parc naturel régional du Haut-Jura – As part of the French government's efforts to inject a new lease of life into the often flagging economies of many rural areas, a 75 672ha - 186 993 acre area of the Haut-Jura region was designated a regional nature park in 1986, to preserve the beautiful local forests and create a new source of income for the region's inhabitants. The park's administration (**Maison du Parc du Haut-Jura**) is located in **Lajoux** *(facilities)*, a small town east of St-Claude.

The park encompasses 46 communities *(communes)*, including St-Claude and Morez. The Crêt Pela, at 1 495m - 4 905ft the highest summit in the Jura, offers plenty of opportunities for ski enthusiasts in the winter, and nature ramblers in the summer.

There are several museums which give an insight into the development of crafts and industry in the region, which range from independent artisans and cottage-industries to factories. Besides the pipe-making and diamond-cutting workshops of St-Claude *(see above)*, activities include spectacle-making in Morez, the manufacture of earthenware in Bois-d'Amont and toys in Moirans-en-Montagne, and traditional cheese-making at "Les Moussières" in **Septmoncel**.

The tourist offices in St-Claude and Les Rousses *(facilities)* and the Maison du Haut-Jura in Lajoux give information on the park itself and the accommodation and leisure facilities it has to offer visitors *(further information in the Practical Information section at the end of the guide)*.

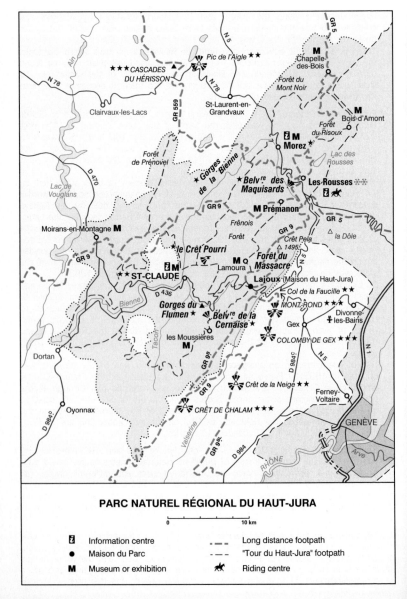

PARC NATUREL RÉGIONAL DU HAUT-JURA

0   10 km

🛈 Information centre	- · - · -	Long distance footpath
● Maison du Parc	- - - -	"Tour du Haut-Jura" footpath
M Museum or exhibition	🏇	Riding centre

ST-FARGEAU

Population 1 883
Michelin map 65 fold 3 or 238 fold 9 – Facilities

The clearing of the forests made possible the establishment of smelting works at St-Fargeau, chief town of the Puisaye *(qv)* to treat the minerals extracted from the ferruginous soil. St-Fargeau has a fine château filled with memories of Anne-Marie-Louise d'Orléans, cousin of Louis XIV, better known under the name of Mademoiselle de Montpensier or "La Grande Mademoiselle". She was an incorrigible supporter of the Fronde (a rising of the aristocracy and parliament, 1648-53).

★ **Château** – The present château is built on the site of a fortress erected at the end of the 10C; the system of fortifications was completed two centuries later. The present building was begun in the Renaissance period and was built in several stages. The largest tower was built by Jacques Cœur, treasurer to the royal household of Charles VII (reign 1422-61), who owned St-Fargeau for some time.

Antoine de Chabannes, who acquired the château when Jacques Cœur fell into disgrace, carried out many improvements but it is **"La Grande Mademoiselle"** who can claim the honour of completely changing the appearance of the buildings. Mademoiselle de Montpensier was exiled to St-Fargeau for several years on the orders of Louis XIV as punishment for her attitude during the rising of the Fronde. When she arrived in 1652 she had "to wade through knee-high grass in the courtyard" and found a dilapidated building. To make her place of exile more comfortable, she called in Le Vau, the king's architect, who laid out the inner courtyard and completely refurbished the interior of the château.

In 1681, Mademoiselle de Montpensier made a gift of St-Fargeau to the Duc de Lauzun, a man of questionable background, whom she later married in a secret ceremony.

In 1715 the property was bought by Le Pelletier des Forts. His great-grandson, **Louis-Michel Le Pelletier de St-Fargeau,** became deputy to the National Convention in 1793 and voted for the death of Louis XVI. He was assassinated on the eve of the king's execution by the Paris bodyguard and considered by the revolutionaries as the first martyr of their cause; his corpse is buried in the chapel.

Tour ⊘ – The warm rose-coloured brick does much to dispel the grim aspect that the massive towers of the main gateway and the corner towers give to this impressive building, surrounded by a moat. With the exception of the largest tower, known as that of Jacques Cœur, these squat towers are surmounted by slender, pierced lanterns.

Within the feudal enclosure is a huge courtyard of rare elegance bordered by five ranges of buildings (the most recent on the right of the entrance dates from 1735).

A semicircular stair in the corner between the two main wings leads to the entrance rotunda. The chapel is housed in one of the towers: on the left is the portrait gallery which led into the apartments of the Grande Mademoiselle until they were burned in 1752; on the right is the 17C guardroom. A grand stair leads to the rooms on the first floor.

In addition there are the timber-roofed attics. In the park (118ha - 292 acres) with its handsome groves there is a large lake, fed by the small Bourdon river.

Tour de l'Horloge – Brick and stone clock tower (late 15C fortified gateway).

Church (Église) – The church was built and altered or added to during the 11C, 13C and 15C. The Gothic west front has a radiant rose window set in a square. In the nave, note on the right a 16C polychrome *Pietà* in stone and the choir stalls of the same period. At the far end of the choir the wooden statue of Christ dates from the 14C. The chapel in the south aisle contains three sculptures in wood, a 15C triptych representing the Passion, a 16C painted statue of the Virgin Mary and a remarkable 16C carving of St Martin sharing his cloak.

Église de ST-HYMETIÈRE★

Michelin map 170 fold 14 or 243 fold 42

The beautiful Romanesque church *(photograph p 41)* west of St-Hymetière, a rural village in the Revermont, depended originally on the priory in Mâcon. It has several striking external features: old tombstones as flagstones on the floor of the porch; massive buttresses and narrow archaic windows on the south side of the church; tall pilaster strips; a protruding apse and a tall octagonal tower. Inside, the oven-vaulted chancel enclosed by plain arcading and the south aisle recall the original Romanesque building, while the main vault and the north aisle bear signs of the reworking of the masonry carried out in the 17C.

ST-LÉGER-VAUBAN

Population 394
Michelin map 65 fold 16 or 238 fold 24 – 5.5km - 3 miles northeast of Quarré-les-Tombes
– Local map under MORVAN

Sébastien le Prestre, who under the name of the **Marquis de Vauban** became one of the outstanding figures of the Grand Siècle (as the 17C is known in France), was born in 1633 in this little village which was then called St-Léger-de-Foucheret.

Vauban, "the most decent man of his century" – Sébastien le Prestre was left a penniless orphan early in life, and at the age of seventeen joined the army of the Prince of Condé, then in revolt against the court, and was taken prisoner by the royal forces.

From that time onwards, he entered the service of Louis XIV. As a military engineer, from the youthful age of 22, he worked on 300 ancient fortified places and built 33 new ones; he successfully directed 53 sieges, thus justifying the saying: "a town defended by Vauban is an impregnable town: a town besieged by Vauban is a captured town". Created Brigadier

General of the royal armies and then Commissioner General of fortifications, he was made a Field Marshal in 1704. He was extremely inventive in thinking up new tactics for breaking into fortresses and designed a number of weapons and other instruments of war which were revolutionary for his period. He also systematically fortified the north and east borders of France with a belt of fortresses entirely new in conception (Verdun, Metz, Strasbourg, Neuf-Brisach).

Saint-Simon (writer: 1675-1755), who was not renowned for his kind remarks, wrote of Vauban: "A man of medium height, rather squat, who had a very warlike air, but at the same time an appearance that was loutish and coarse, not to say brutal and ferocious. Nothing could be further from the truth; never was there a gentler man, more compassionate, more obliging, more respectful, more courteous, and most sparing in the use of men's lives, a man of great worth capable of giving himself in the service of others..."The last years of this man's life, who never denied his humble origin, were unhappy. Deeply affected by the great misery of the common people, he sent his *Projet d'une Dîme Royale* (Plan for a Royal Tithe) to the king, in which he proposed ways and means of bettering the living conditions of the lower classes. The work was banned and Vauban, relegated virtually to disgrace by Louis XIV, died of grief on 30 March 1707.

In 1808 Vauban's heart was placed in the Invalides in Paris by Napoleon I; the rest of his body lies in the church in **Bazoches**, a village in the Morvan *(20km - 12 miles southwest of Avallon)*, near the château which was in large part reconstructed by his efforts and from which the view extends to Vézelay.

SIGHTS

St-Léger – The church, in which Vauban was baptised, was originally built to a cruciform plan in the Renaissance period; it was transformed in the 19C and boasts some interesting modern additions by the sculptor Marc Hénard: carved wooden panels in the south door; the sculptures and stained glass window in the chapel of Notre-Dame-du-Bien-Mourir (1625), left of the chancel; the beautiful blue and pink ceramic **tiles★** (1973) which surround the high altar and depict the planets, animals, tools etc revolving round the triangle of the Holy Trinity.

Maison Vauban ⊘ – *In the Maison communale.*
In a small room information panels and an audiovisual presentation *(20 min)* retrace the life and work of this great Frenchman.

▶▶ **Ste-Magnance** – *12km - 8 miles north on the N 6.*
Church with beautiful 12C **tomb★** of St Magnance.

ST-PÈRE★

Population 348
Michelin map 65 fold 15 or 238 fold 23 – 2km - 1 mile southeast of Vézelay –
Local map under MORVAN

The little village of St-Père, standing at the foot of the hill of Vézelay, on the banks of the river Cure, is home to a beautiful Gothic church.

★ NOTRE-DAME ⊘ time: 15 min

The church, which was begun in about 1200 and completed in 1455, shows all the stages in the development of the Gothic style between the 13C and 15C. In the 16C it became the parish church in place of the church of St-Pierre (from which the name St-Père is derived) which burned down in 1567 during the Wars of Religion and was never rebuilt.

Exterior – The gable, surmounting a rose window of beautiful design, is hollowed out by arches forming niches. Those in the centre contain statues of Christ being crowned by two angels, and St Stephen, framed on one side by the Virgin and Saints Peter, Andrew and James, and on the other by St Mary Magdalene with St John and two Evangelists.

The delicately worked 13C belfry is graceful. At the corners angels sound trumpets. The porch added at the end of the 13C and restored by Viollet-le-Duc (1814-79) has three doorways. The centre one, which has a trefoiled archway, depicts the Last Judgment: on the right of Christ, the blessed are being welcomed by Abraham, while on His left the damned are being devoured by Satan.

Under the porch housing the tomb of the donors (dating from 1258) note the size of the arches and the design of the tracery of the large side windows.

Interior – The overall effect is one of great purity of style. Rebuilt in the 15C the choir is encircled by an ambulatory with five radiating chapels. On entering note the two 14C cast-iron fonts shaped like upturned bells.

The vaulting of the nave has painted bosses and corbels carved in the form of expressive faces.

A narrow gallery leads round the building at the height of the clerestory windows. In the north aisle there is a defaced recumbent figure dating from the 13C and in a chapel on the south side of the choir a 10C stone altar which probably belonged to the original church. On leaving the church note the curious painted baptismal font dating from the Carolingian period.

ADDITIONAL SIGHTS

Musée archéologique régional ⊙ – The regional archaeological museum is installed in the former presbytery, built in the 17C, and contains objects excavated at Fontaines-Salées, in particular sections of a water conduit made from tree trunks hollowed out by fire to carry mineral water from a spring; it dates from the Hallstatt period (First Iron Age). Also on display are a 4C Gallo-Roman weighing device, enamelled bronze fibulae in the form of seahorses or wild ducks, Merovingian weapons and jewellery found in the tombs at Vaudonjon near Vézelay, and Gratteloup near Pierre-Perthuis. The medieval room contains sculpture from the 12C to 16C from the Vézelay region including a statue of St James the Great and a 13C statue of Christ conferring His Blessing.

Fouilles des Fontaines-Salées ⊙ – *2km - 1 mile.* These excavations, which are near the D 958, have unearthed Gallo-Roman baths, built on to what was once a Gallic sanctuary (a 2C BC circular temple with a lustral basin) enclosed within a vast precinct dedicated to the gods of the springs.
These saline springs, which were used in the Iron Age, by the Romans and again in the Middle Ages, were filled in by the salt tax authorities in the 17C. Nineteen wooden casings dating from the first millennium BC have been preserved by the high mineral content of the water. A stone duct from the Roman period gives access to the waters of a spring which is once again being used for treating arthritic complaints.

ST-SEINE-L'ABBAYE

Population 326
Michelin map 65 fold 19 or 243 fold 15

This place, about six miles from the source of the Seine, perpetuates the name of a holy man who founded a Benedictine abbey on his land in the 6C. The abbey church has survived.

Église abbatiale – This early-13C abbey church marks the transition from the Burgundian-Romanesque style to the Gothic style which came from the Île-de-France. The church was restored in the 14C after a fire; the façade dates from the 15C. The porch is set between two towers, supported by buttresses; the right-hand tower is incomplete. The nave is lit by a clerestory; the flat chevet is pierced by a beautiful rose window, rebuilt in the 19C. The chapels in the flat-ended transept communicate with the side aisles of the choir by means of stone screens pierced by window apertures. There are numerous tombstones in the transept. At the end of the choir stands the former rood screen.
The 18C carved stalls are set against a Renaissance screen, on the reverse side of which are paintings representing the story of St Seine (Sequana).
On leaving the church, note the fountain of the Samaritan Woman; the basin is surmounted by an 18C bronze.

▶▶ **Sources de la Seine** – *10km - 6 miles northwest.*
It is hard to believe that this tiny stream becomes the world-famous river.

ST-THIBAULT

Population 142
Michelin map 65 fold 18 or 243 fold 14 – 19km - 12 miles southeast of Semur-en-Auxois

This Auxois village is named after St Theobald whose relics were presented to the local priory in the 13C. The priory church has a choir of great elegance and a main doorway which is considered among the most beautiful examples of 13C Burgundian architecture.

★CHURCH ⊙ *30 min*

The church is approached from the north side. The original church was built to house the relics of St Theobald at the expense of Robert II, Duke of Burgundy, and his wife, Agnes of France, daughter of St Louis; all that remains are the choir, an apsidal chapel and the carved doorway from the old transept which collapsed together with the nave in the 17C. The **doorway★** is a picture-book in itself. The sculptures of the tympanum, executed during the second half of the 13C, are devoted to the Virgin. Those in the recessed arches, dating from the same period, represent, on the inner arch, the Wise Virgins to the left and the Foolish Virgins to the right.
About the year 1310, five great statues were added: St Theobald stands with his back to the pier; the other four have been identified as true likenesses of Duke Robert II and his son, Hugh V, benefactors of the church, the Duchess Agnes, and the Bishop of Autun, Hugues d'Arcy. The expressions on the faces and the modelling of the features show great skill; the door itself has beautifully carved 15C panels.

Interior – The nave, which was rebuilt in the 18C, is decorated with period woodwork from Semur-en-Auxois. The chief interest lies in the choir and apse, masterpieces of bold and skilful design, which date from the end of the 13C and the beginning of the 14C.
The five-sided **choir★** is the most graceful Burgundian construction of that period. From the ground to the vault each slender column rises in an unbroken upward movement linking the blind arcades at the lowest level, the lower windows with their delicate tracery, the triforium and the clerestory *(illustration p 41).* In the choir (left) stands a late-14C painted wooden statue of St Theobald when young, in a slightly affected pose, one finger on the page of a book.

To the right, in a recess, is the 13C tomb of the founder of the church, Hugues de Thil. The low-reliefs on the back wall of the recess were restored in 1839. Nearby is the piscina for the high altar, with two 13C basins.

The **furnishings**★ are interesting; the altar is decorated with two carved wooden retables representing episodes from the life of St Theobald.

At the far end of the choir is a large 14C Crucifixion and above the high altar a beautiful crosier, decorated with a 16C eucharistic dove.

On the right of the nave, standing against the wall of the choir, is an attractive 14C statue of the Virgin watching Jesus playing with a bird.

In the chapel of St Giles, which is the oldest part of the church, stands the 14C wooden shrine of St Theobald and statues of characters from the Old and New Testaments.

SALINS-LES-BAINS★

Population 3 629
Michelin map 170 west of fold 5 or 243 fold 31 – Facilities

The town of Salins lies in a remarkable **setting**★, strung along the pretty, narrow valley of the Furieuse, beneath the fortresses of Belin and St-André.

Like Dole Salins still has some traces of its medieval fortifications and one or two towers. Lacuzon *(qv)*, hero of the Franche-Comté's fight for liberty, fired his last few cannon balls at the French from one of these in 1674.

Salins

White gold – In the past, salt was indispensible for preserving foodstuff. However, primitive mining methods made it so scarce and so costly that anyone caught stealing it was sentenced to be hung forthwith (a gallows stood in the central courtyard of the salt mine, which itself resembled a fortress). A salt mine was thus a real gold mine. Jean l'Antique, the most famous member of the Chalon *(qv)* family, seized the salt mine at Salins early in the 13C, procuring for himself a source of enormous wealth. The sale of the salt brought him huge sums of liquid currency, which was an exceptionally privileged situation to be in at the time. While most landlords paid for their purchases with goods (mainly grown on their lands), borrowing if necessary small cash sums from Jewish moneylenders and larger ones from the bankers of Lombardy, Jean l'Antique was able to put his ducats to astute use, buying fiefs, vassals and the goodwill of bishops, monks, soldiers and wealthy merchants. Delighted with his increased power, he bestowed a charter on the home town of the salt mine, source of his wealth, in 1249, according it a fair degree of autonomy.

The year of the Black Death – Bubonic plague wreaked havoc in Salins, and throughout the Franche-Comté, for six months of 1349. The victims were covered with black, red or bluish patches and died within two or three days. Stringent quarantine regulations were imposed by the town authorities in an attempt to contain the plague, but despite these about 80% of the town's inhabitants died.

The town's recovery from this disaster was slow. In 1374 a public lending house was founded, called the Mont-de-Salins. This is the precursor of the modern French lending houses called Mont-de-Pitié.

The timber trade – Huge quantities of wood, taken from the nearby forests, were needed to heat the cauldrons used to evaporate water in the salt extraction process, as well as for the increasing number of sawmills and industrial needs in general, with the result that the timber trade became almost as important for Salins as its salt mine. As many as 60 000 horse-drawn carts loaded with wood came into the town each year. The waters of the Furieuse were harnessed to drive twelve great sawmills. Salins soon developed a reputation for producing the best ships' masts on the market, with which it supplied the French Marines.

By the 17C Salins, with 5 700 inhabitants, was the second largest community in the Franche-Comté after Besançon, which had 11 500.

SIGHTS

A statue of General Cler, killed in Magenta in 1859 during the war between the Sardinians and French and the Austrians, stands in the middle of Place des Alliés.

Hôtel de Ville (Y H) – The town hall dates from the 18C. The 17C **chapel of Notre-Dame-de-la-Libératrice (Y B)**, crowned by a dome, is in the town hall complex.

Salines (Z) ⊙ – Salins is the only **salt mine** where visitors can see how salt water was once pumped out of the Jura soil.

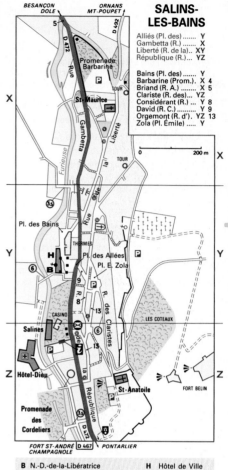

SALINS-LES-BAINS

Alliés (Pl. des)	Y
Gambetta (R.)	X
Liberté (R. de la)	XY
République (R.)	YZ
Bains (Pl. des)	Y
Barbarine (Prom.)	X 4
Briand (R. A.)	X 5
Clariste (R. des)	YZ
Considérant (R.)	Y 8
David (R. C.)	Y 9
Orgemont (R. d')	YZ 13
Zola (Pl. Émile)	Y

B N.-D.-de-la-Libératrice **H** Hôtel de Ville

Salt was already being mined in Salins under the Romans, who considered Sequanian salted meats to be a great delicacy. The salt mines then passed into the hands of the Chalon family, followed by the Spanish crown, the French crown before finally becoming, in 1843, a private business.

The salt waters of Salins-les-Bains are now used exclusively for salt water cures in the local spas.

It is interesting to visit the underground galleries, up to 400m long, where good lighting shows off the magnificent 12C vaults. The salt water was pumped up from the salt seams, 250m - 820ft underground, through boreholes 30cm - 15in in diameter. A system using a long beam and a hydraulic wheel activated the pump which drew up the water, which had a high salt content of 33kg - 71lbs of salt per 100l - 22 gallons. Enormous cauldrons (two of which are on display) were heated over coal fires to evaporate the water and obtain the salt.

Église St-Anatoile (Z) – This is the most interesting church in Salins, and one of the best examples of 13C Cistercian architecture in the Franche-Comté, in which there is nonetheless evidence of the local architects' predilection for round arches.

Two protruding Flamboyant Gothic style chapels frame the beautiful Romanesque doorway.

Inside, pretty round-arched arcades run along above the pointed Gothic arches separating the nave from the side aisles. Note the 17C pulpit to the right, the 16C choir stalls decorated with striking medallions and woodwork and the carved wooden organ case dating from 1737.

Église St-Maurice (X) – Inside this church there is a wooden statue of St Maurice on horseback in medieval costume at the back of the chapel on the south side. A niche in the south aisle contains a 16C alabaster Pietà.

Hôtel-Dieu (Z) ⊙ – This hospice dates from the 17C. The pharmacy has some beautiful woodwork as well as a collection of pots in Moustiers faïence.

Promenade des Cordeliers (Z) – This walk along the west bank of the Furieuse has one or two delightful shady spots.

★ **Mont Poupet** – *10km - 6 miles north on the D 492.*
A **view★** from an altitude of 803m - 2 635ft of Mont Blanc, the Jura plateau and the Bresse plain.

Route des SAPINS★★

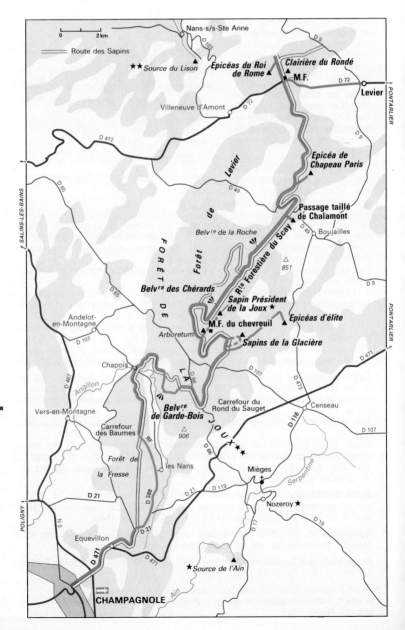

Michelin map 170 fold 5 or 243 fold 31

The beautiful 50km - 31 mile stretch of road known as the "Route des Sapins" (Evergreen Forest Drive) runs between Champagnole and Levier, through the forests of La Fresse, Chapois, La Loux and Levier. The itinerary below follows the most interesting stretch with the best facilities *(car parks, rest and picnic areas, signposted footpaths, nature rambles).*

FROM CHAMPAGNOLE TO LEVIER

55km - 34 miles – allow 3 hours – local map below

Champagnole – *See Vallée de l'AIN.*

Take the D 471 northeast. The Route des Sapins leads straight on from Equevillon.

The road climbs through the **Forêt de la Fresse,** offering glimpses of Champagnole to the left. *Turn right into the D 21, leaving the Route des Sapins to the left, and go as far as the junction with the D 288, into which you turn left.*

The road follows the line of the hillside, about halfway up, along the coomb through which the Angillon has cut its riverbed. To the east of the road lie the magnificent stands of the forest of La Joux, and to the west the 1 153ha - 2 849 acres of conifers which make up the forest of La Fresse. Just before the village of Les Nans, turn left onto the forest road known as Larderet aux Nans, which gives a good view of Les Nans and the Angillon coomb. The road rejoins the Route des Sapins at the crossroads, Carrefour des Baumes, then runs through the northern part of the forest of La Fresse, through the village of Chapois and into the forest of La Joux, climbing as it goes.

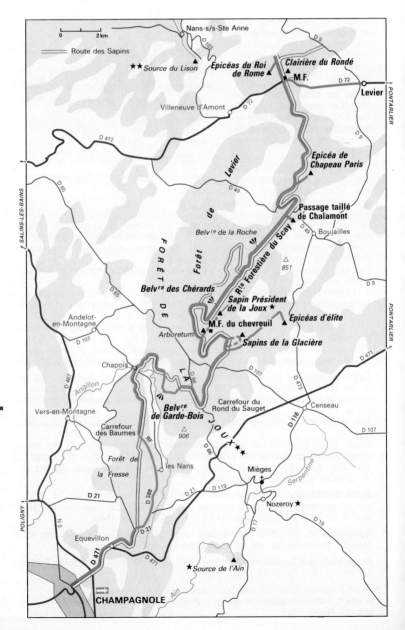

★★ FORÊT DE LA JOUX

This is one of France's most beautiful evergreen forests. The 2 652ha - 6 553 acres it covers are separated from the forest of La Fresse to the south by the river Angillon, and are met by the forêts of Levier to the north. Although the forest consists mostly of coniferous trees, it is nevertheless home to a few scattered deciduous trees. One or two conifers still grow to an exceptional size, on occasion up to 45m - 150ft high with a diameter of 1.20m - 4ft at a height of 1.30m - 4ft from the ground. Larger trees than this are to be found only in California or the tropics. The forest is laid out in regular rows, and is managed in such a way that the removal of timber in any one year does not exceed the annual increment of new growth. About 10 000 to 12 000 trees are cut down every year (equivalent to about 20 000m^3 - 706 300ft^3 of timber). The forest is officially divided into five administrative blocks

Autumn in the Forêt de la Joux

(cantons or *séries);* the most beautiful trees are to be found in the *cantons* of La Glacière and Les Sources.

Leave the Route des Sapins once more to take the road on the right to the Belvédère de Garde-Bois, which is near a chapel.

Belvédère de Garde-Bois – There is a pretty view of the deep Angillon valley as well as the forest of La Fresse in the distance.
Carry on east along the road that led to the viewpoint to rejoin the Route des Sapins. The stretch of road from the Rond-du-Sauget crossroads onwards is particularly pretty.

Sapins de la Glacière – *30 min on foot Rtn.*
Take the path which leads off to the right from the Route des Sapins as you come from Champagnole.
This *canton* earned its name from being the coldest part of the forest and the area where the snow lasts longest. Magnificent conifers, as straight as ramrods, grow around a deep hollow in the *canton's* centre. There is a particularly tall splendid tree next to the footpath. The peace and quiet in the forest combine with the subdued quality of the light filtered by the trees to create a soothing, meditative atmosphere.

Épicéas d'élite – *The Route de la Marine leads to this stand of spruces. Alternatively, there is a signposted footpath leading off from the D 473; the beginning of it is indicated about 1km - half a mile south of the level crossing at Boujailles station (30 min on foot Rtn).* These are the most beautiful trees in the Esserval-Tartre spruce forest, hence their name.

Maison forestière du Chevreuil – The clearing by this forester's lodge is a major tourist attraction in the region. Those interested in forestry will be able to visit the **Arboretum,** a test planting area for trees not native to the region.
Where the Route des Sapins divides into two, take the right fork, signposted *"Route des Sapins par les Crêtes".*

Belvédère des Chérards – There is a glimpse from here of wooded plateaux.

★ **Sapin Président de la Joux** – This fir tree, the most famous tree in the Chérards *canton,* is over two centuries old. It has a diameter of 3.85m - 13ft at a height of 1.30m - 4ft from the ground, is 45m - 148ft tall and represents the equivalent of 600 planks of wood or 22m^3 - 777ft^3 of timber.

The Route des Sapins carries on through the forest, offering a pretty view of the Chalamont dip to the left.

FORÊT DE LEVIER

This forest was once the possession of the Chalon family until it was confiscated in 1562 by Philippe II, King of Spain. It became the property of the King of France after Louis XIV's conquest of Franche-Comté in 1674. At that time the forest was used to provide timber for naval construction and for the Salins salt works. Local people also came here to obtain their firewood, so large areas were planted entirely with deciduous trees, in keeping with the forest's role as a useful resource.

The modern forest, at an altitude of between 670m - 2 198ft and 900m - 2 953ft, covers an area of 2 725ha - 6 733 acres and consists almost exclusively of coniferous trees (60% fir, 12% spruce). The forest area is managed in three blocks (the *"séries"* of Jura, Arc and Scay).

Route forestière de Scay – This slightly bumpy road, which crosses the forest of Levier through the so-called quiet zone *(zone de silence)* of Scay, offers some beautiful views of the surrounding area. At the **Belvédère de la Roche** there is a view over the forest of Levier and the clearing in which the village of Villers-sous-Chalamont lies.

Passage taillé de Chalamont – Shortly before the D 49, a footpath leads off to the right *(30 min on foot Rtn)*, along what was once a Celtic, then a Roman path. Note the steps cut into the sloping or slippery sections and the grooves which guided chariot wheels. At the point where the path leaves the forest, by the ruins of the medieval tower of Chalamont, it passes through a kind of trench, a technique which was imitated in the building of the nearby modern road linking Boujailles and Villers-sous-Chalamont.

Épicéa de Chapeau Paris – This tree is to the forest of Levier what the Sapin Président is to the forest of La Joux. It is 45m - 148ft tall with a diameter of 400cm-13ft and represents an equivalent volume of timber of about 20m^3 - 706ft^3.

Take the Route forestière de Ravonnet and then the Route du Pont de la Marine to the right.

Clairière du Rondé – This clearing contains an enclosure containing Sika deer and a forester's lodge *(maison forestière* – exhibitions in summer).

Épicéas du Roi de Rome – These spruces are over 180 years old and can reach heights of more than 50m - 164ft.

Turn back to take the D 72 on the left towards Levier.

SAULIEU★

Population 2 917
Michelin map 65 fold 17 or 243 fold 13 – Facilities – Local map under MORVAN

Saulieu is pleasantly situated on the boundaries of the Morvan and the Auxois, beside the N 6. The art lover will find interest in the basilica of St-Andoche and also in the works of François Pompon, the animal sculptor, who was born at Saulieu in 1855.

A gastronomic centre – The gastronomic reputation of Saulieu is linked to the history of road travel and goes back to the 17C. In 1651 the Burgundian States decided to restore to the old Paris-Lyon road, which passed along the eastern edge of the Morvan, the importance that it had before the Middle Ages. Saulieu set about increasing its prosperity by developing local industry and fairs. The town became a post house on the route and felt it its duty to treat travellers well. Rabelais had already praised Saulieu and its excellent meals. **Madame de Sévigné** stopped in the town on her way to Vichy on 26 August 1677, and she avowed later that for the first time in her life she had become a little tipsy.

The timber of the Morvan – Although Saulieu's economic activity has always been to a great extent based on forestry there has been a considerable transformation in this sector. There is an ever-growing trade in Christmas trees; each year more than a million of these trees (spruces in particular) are sent to Paris and other large towns in France, Europe and Africa. Despite this shift to conifers there are still large areas of oak and beech. Large tree nurseries now produce several hundreds of thousands of saplings for the French and foreign markets.

The state forest of Saulieu (768ha - 1 898 acres) now has many recreational facilities: picnic sites, adventure playgrounds, walks and trails, riding tracks and small lakes providing trout fishing.

★BASILIQUE ST-ANDOCHE
time: 30 min

The basilica stands in Place du Docteur-Roclore where there is a pretty 18C fountain. The church, which dates from the beginning of the 12C, is slightly later than the one in Vézelay; it was built to replace an abbey church founded in the 8C on the site of the martyrdom of St Andoche, St Thyrse and St Felix, and was influenced by St-Lazare in Autun of which it was a sister house.

This fine Romanesque building has been sadly maltreated; the main doorway was mutilated during the French Revolution and rebuilt in the 19C. Inside, the bases of the pillars are buried nearly three feet deep. The choir was burnt by the English in 1359 and rebuilt in 1704 without any attempt at coherence of style.

Capital in St-Andoche

SAULIEU

Interior – The main point of interest is the series of historiated or decorated **capitals**★★, inspired by those in Autun. Here one can see: the Flight into Egypt, the Temptation of Christ in the Desert, the Hanging of Judas, Christ appearing to Mary Magdalene, the false prophet Balaam.

The choir stalls date from the 14C and the organ loft from the 15C. After its restoration, the tomb of St Andoche was placed in the last chapel in the right aisle. To the right of the choir, note a Renaissance Virgin in stone and a 14C statue of St Roch. In the north aisle, there is a handsome tombstone and painted *Pietà*, presented, so it is said, by Madame de Sévigné as a penance for over-indulgence *(see above)*.

ADDITIONAL SIGHTS

Musée (M) ⊙ – The museum, which is housed in a 17C mansion abutting the basilica, contains archaeological and ethnological collections about Saulieu and its neighbourhood. Ground floor: in the entrance hall a collection of fragments offers a visual survey of the history of the site; the following rooms display Gallo-Roman tombstones from the old necropolis, fragments of the Romanesque doorway from St Andoche's basilica, a collection of sacred statues (12C-18C) and obsolete tools (hemp working, clog making, forge). First floor: one room is devoted to a Gallo-Roman water source (discovered near Saulieu) believed to have curative powers, as is evident from the considerable collection of small wooden votive offerings in the shape of human limbs and organs; the large oak casing of the well is on show together with a model of the site. Souvenirs of **François Pompon** (Saulieu 1855 - Paris 1933) as well as some of his original work are displayed in the following rooms; he was a pupil of Rodin *(Bust of St Catherine and Cosette)* and is best known for the smooth finish of his large animal sculptures (one of his masterpieces, the **Bull**★ (Taureau), was erected in 1948 in a square on the north side of the town). Old crafts, souvenirs of 19C Saulieu and a reconstruction of a traditional Morvan domestic interior complete the ethnological collections on the ground floor.

St-Saturnin – This charming 15C church, with its pointed belfry covered with shingles, stands in the middle of a terraced graveyard.

Beyond the east end of the church is the tomb of François Pompon, surmounted by one of his own works representing a condor.

Promenade Jean-Macé – A pleasant walk, shaded by age-old lime trees.

SEMUR-EN-AUXOIS★

Population 4 545
Michelin map 65 folds 17 and 18 or 243 fold 13 – Facilities –
Local map under MORVAN

The **setting**★ and the town of Semur, main centre of the Auxois agricultural and stock-raising region, form a picturesque scene if approached from the west or the north. From the Paris road, there is a good view of the ramparts and the town during the downhill run to the Joly bridge.

A tightly-packed mass of small light-coloured houses stands on the top of a rose-tinted granite cliff, overlooking a deep ravine at the bottom of which flows the river Armançon. Above the houses and cascade of gardens rise the great red-slated towers of the castle keep and the slender spire of the church of Notre-Dame.

A stronghold – Semur became the strong-point of the duchy in the 14C when the citadel was reinforced by ramparts and eighteen towers. The town was divided into three parts each with a perimeter wall. Occupying the whole width of the rock spur and towering above all else was the keep, a citadel in itself and reputedly impregnable

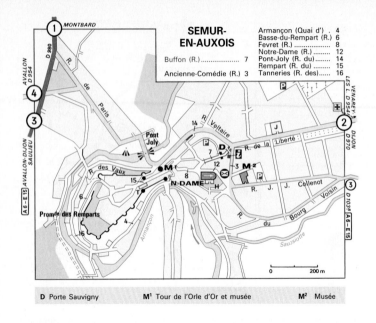

SEMUR-EN-AUXOIS

Buffon (R.) 7
Ancienne-Comédie (R.) 3

Armançon (Quai d') . 4
Basse-du-Rempart (R.) 6
Fevret (R.) 8
Notre-Dame (R.) 12
Pont-Joly (R. du) 14
Rempart (R. du) 15
Tanneries (R. des)...... 16

D Porte Sauvigny   **M¹** Tour de l'Orle d'Or et musée   **M²** Musée

It had a sheer drop both to the north and the south to the Armançon valley and was flanked by four enormous round towers: the Tour de l'Orle d'Or, the Tour de la Gehenne, the Tour de la Prison and the Tour Margot. The château stood to the west, on the upper part of the peninsula, encircled by a bend in the river – the ramparts can still be seen. To the east was the town, still the most densely populated district although the town has spread on to the west bank.

★ NOTRE-DAME *time: 30 min*

The church stands in Place Notre-Dame, flanked by old houses. It was founded in the 11C, rebuilt in the 13C and 14C, altered in the 15C and 16C, extended by the addition of chapels to the north aisle and restored by Viollet-le-Duc (1814-79).

Exterior – The 14C façade, dominated by two square towers, is preceded by a vast porch. In Rue Notre-Dame, the 13C door in the north transept (Porte des Bleds) has a beautiful tympanum depicting Doubting Thomas and the bringing of the Gospel to the West Indies. Surmounting the doorway is a statue of an angel, arms open in a welcoming gesture. On one of the slender engaged piers which flank the doorway are two sculpted snails, symbolising Burgundian cooking.
The 15C porch shelters three doorways. Although the sculptures of the recessed arches and the niches disappeared at the Revolution, various low-relief figures line the base of the engaged piers.
From the garden behind the church there is a view of the chevet which, with the narrow and steeply roofed apse and conically roofed chapels, show great purity of line.

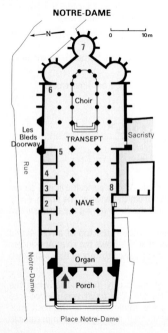

NOTRE-DAME

Place Notre-Dame

The octagonal transept crossing tower is surmounted by a beautiful stone spire

Interior ⊘ – The narrowness of the central nave, dating from the 13C and 14C, emphasises the soaring height of the vaulting supported by slender columns.
There are several interesting chapels opening off the north aisle. In the second chapel (1) is a polychrome Entombment dating from the late 15C with monumental figures typical of Claus Sluter *(qv)*. The third chapel (2) with its stellar vaulting has 16C stained glass illustrating the legend of St Barbara. The last two chapels contain panels of stained glass given in the 15C by local guilds: the butchers (3) and eight panels from the drapers (4).
Behind the pulpit is a 15C stone canopy (5), remarkably carved with a 5m - 16ft high pinnacle.
A blind triforium decorates the 13C choir and the transept; its elegant and slender columns are surmounted by capitals in the form of sculpted human heads. The hanging keystone of the choir is brightly painted and represents the crowning of the Virgin amidst foliage and angels' heads.

The choir is flanked by double aisles; the three chapels radiating from the ambulatory are separated by triple lancets. The Grantin-Riepp-Callinet organ dates from the 17C-19C.

In the last chapel of the outer north aisle is a painted retable (**6**) dating from 1554, representing the Tree of Jesse. The retable is surmounted by a Gothic canopy of carved wood. The Lady Chapel (**7**) is lit by very beautiful stained glass windows of the 13C restored by Viollet-le-Duc. In the ambulatory is a late-15C polychrome statue (**8**) of Christ bearing the Five Wounds; with a theatrical gesture He indicates the spear thrust in His side; two angels carry His mantle.

ADDITIONAL SIGHTS

Tour de l'Orle d'Or and Musée (**M**¹) ⊘ – This tower, which is now cracked on the north side, was once part of the keep which was razed in 1602. The tower owes its name to its battlements (demolished), which used to be covered with coppered lead *(ourlée d'or* – trimmed with gold). Its dimensions are impressive (44m - 144ft high, walls 5m - 16ft thick at the base tapering to about 2.2m - 7ft at the top). Prior to the construction of the Joly bridge (1787), this tower was one of the main entrances to the town. It now houses a local and natural history **museum**. The different floors provide good views of the keep and the town. The top floor has a fine chestnut timber ceiling.

Promenade des Remparts – The former ramparts along the edge of the granite spur have been converted into a promenade shaded by lime trees which overlooks the valley of the Armançon. To reach the promenade, go past the hospital, a pleasant 18C building, which was once the mansion of the Marquis du Châtelet, Governor of Semur, whose priggish wife was Voltaire's sweetheart.

Pont Joly – From the Joly bridge there is an overall **view★** of the little medieval city. It is particularly charming in the light of the setting sun. The bridge crosses the Armançon at the foot of the castle keep, which once guarded the narrow isthmus joining the rose-coloured cliff, where the city first started, to the granite plateau on which the town has now spread. In the foreground the view sweeps up the valley with gardens, rocks, parks and small cascades on either side.

Tour of the ramparts – Rue Basse-du-Rempart skirts the foot of the ramparts. Their grandeur is emphasised by the enormous blocks of red granite, sparkling with mica and quartz, which serve as the foundations of the keep.

Musée (**M**²) ⊘ – An old Jacobin convent houses the museum and library. The ground floor displays a collection of 13C to 19C sculpture, including many original plaster figures, mostly by Augustin Dumont, who created monumental sculptures and commemorative statues (*Spirit of Liberty* in Place de la Bastille in Paris). The first floor houses a rich collection on natural science, particularly zoology and geology (fossils – rare fish fossils – and mineral samples). The second floor contains articles found during the archaeological excavation of prehistoric, Gallo-Roman (votive offerings from the source of the Seine) and Merovingian sites. The gallery contains 17C to 19C paintings (*Portrait of a Prophet* by Vignon and three works by Corot) and a few 19C sculptures; a small room is devoted to the Middle Ages and the Renaissance (*Angels* by Le Moiturier).

Porte Sauvigny (**D**) – This 15C gateway, preceded by a postern, marked the main entrance to the district known as the Bourg Notre-Dame.

Semur-en-Auxois

SEMUR-EN-BRIONNAIS★

Population 636
Michelin map 73 north of folds 7 and 8 or 243 fold 37 –
Local map under PARAY-LE-MONIAL: Excursion

The village stands on a promontory which is covered with vines and fruit trees. The château, the Romanesque church, the former priory and 18C court room (now the *mairie*, or town hall) make an attractive ensemble in pinkish stone.

SIGHTS

★ **St-Hilaire** – The church, which was built in the Cluniac style, has a very fine chevet; its squat appearance is relieved by the height of the gable walls at the end of the chancel and the transept arms, and its austerity is offset by the carved cornice below the roof. The elegant octagonal belfry is decorated with a double band of twin Romanesque arcades; the upper band is framed by a series of recessed arches.

The west doorway is richly decorated although the sculptures show a certain lack of skill in the modelling. As at Charlieu, a haloed lamb is carved on the external key-stone. The lintel depicts a scene from the life of St Hilary of Poitiers: condemned by a council of Arian bishops, he sets off into exile, a begging bag on his shoulder; on the road he meets an angel who gives him hope and returns him to his place among the bishops; meanwhile the devil makes off with the soul of the Council President.

The nave is very attractive; at the west end the triforium, which consists of an arcade with twin arch stones, forms a bowed gallery which is supported by an impressive corbel springing from the keystone of the west door. The gallery may be an imitation of St-Michel above the west door of Cluny abbey church. The dome on squinches above the transept crossing is decorated with arcades similar to those of the triforium.

Château St-Hugues ⊘ – The 9C rectangular keep was the birthplace of the famous abbot, St Hugh of Cluny *(qv)*. The two round towers served as a prison in the 18C.

There is a view of the vineyard-covered slopes and in the distance the summits of Le Forez and La Madeleine.

Mont de SÈNE★★

Michelin map 69 fold 9 or 243 fold 27 – 10km - 6 miles west of Chagny

The Mont de Sène is also known as the **Montagne des Trois-Croix** after the three crosses which stand on the summit. It is approached by a turning (east) off the road between Dezize-lès-Maranges and the N 6 (north); the road is narrow with sharp bends and steep gradients near the top.

★★ **Panorama** – From the top one can see (north) the famous vineyards of the Côte beyond La Rochepot, (east) the Saône valley, the Jura and the Alps, (south) the Cluny district dominated by Mont St-Vincent and (west) the Morvan.

SENS★★

Pop 27 082
Michelin map 61 fold 14 or 237 fold 45 –
Plan of conurbation in the current Michelin Red Guide France

Now a simple sub-prefecture in the *département* of Yonne, Sens is the seat of an archbishopric, proof of its past grandeur. The old town is girdled by boulevards and promenades that have replaced the ancient ramparts. In the city centre stands the cathedral of St-Étienne. The approach from the west (D 81) provides a fine view of the town as the road descends from the heights on the left bank of the Yonne.

HISTORICAL NOTES

The Country of the Senones – The tribe of the Senones, who gave their name to the town, was for a long time one of the most powerful in Gaul. In 390 BC, under the command of Brennus, they invaded Italy and seized Rome. When the Romans were masters of all Gaul, they made Sens the capital of a province of the Lyonnaise, known as Lyonnaise IV or Senonia.

An Important Diocese – Up to 1622, the year in which Paris was elevated to the rank of an archbishopric, Sens had pre-eminence over the bishoprics of Chartres, Auxerre, Meaux, Paris, Orléans, Nevers and Troyes, giving the initials forming the device of the metropolitan church: "Campont". During the residence in Sens of Pope Alexander III in 1163-64 the city became the temporary capital of Christianity. The church council that condemned Abélard was also held at Sens and the marriage of St Louis and Marguerite of Provence was celebrated in the cathedral in 1234. With the elevation of Paris, the diocese of Sens lost the bishoprics of Meaux, Chartres and Orléans.

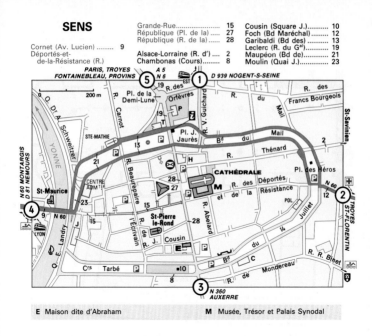

E Maison dite d'Abraham   M Musée, Trésor et Palais Synodal

★★ CATHÉDRALE ST-ÉTIENNE *time: 30 min*

Although the cathedral was started *c*1130 by Archbishop Henri Sanglier, most of the construction took place between 1140 and 1168; it was the first of the great Gothic cathedrals in France. Many other buildings have borrowed largely from the design (the layout, the alternating pillars, the triforium): William of Sens, architect, used it as his model when reconstructing the chancel of Canterbury Cathedral (1175-92).

Exterior – The west front, despite the loss of a tower, has nevertheless pre-served its imposing majesty and harmony of balance The north tower ("tour de plomb" or Lead Tower), built at the end of the 12C, used to be surmounted by a timbered belfry covered in lead, which was destroyed last century.
The south tower ("tour de pierre" or Stone Tower), which collapsed at the end of the 13C, was gradually rebuilt in the following century and was completed in the 16C. It is topped by a graceful campanile and is 78m - 256ft high. The tower houses two bells, weighing 13 3/4 tons and 15 3/4 tons.
The statues on the upper gallery, which were added in the 19C, represent the leading archbishops of Sens. An immense radiant window, a rose window of smaller size, and a Christ conferring His blessing, framed by two angels (modern statues), rise in tiers above the central doorway.

North doorway – The tympanum of this 12C doorway recalls the history of St John the Baptist. Generosity and avarice are portrayed at the bottom of the low-reliefs.

Central doorway – A beautiful statue of St Stephen, in the costume of a deacon and car-rying the Gospel, fortunately spared during the Revolution, stands with its back to the pier of the main doorway. This work, dating from the end of the 12C, marks the transition period between the sculptures of Chartres and Bourges and those of Paris and Amiens, and is thus an interesting sign of the beginning of Gothic sculpture.
The low-reliefs of the engaged piers framing the doorway represent the Foolish Virgins on the right and the Wise Virgins on the left. The statues of the Apostles, which used to occupy the twelve niches in the splaying of the doorway, have disap-peared. The original tympanum, which it is believed portrayed the Last Judgment, was remade in the 13C: it is devoted to scenes from the life of St Stephen. Sta-tuettes of saints decorate the arches.

South doorway – The tympanum of the right-hand doorway (early-14C) is devoted to the Virgin. The statuettes, representing the prophets, have been decapitated. A decoration of angels ornaments the arching.

Go round the cathedral to the north and take the passage (14C St-Denis doorway) to the Maison de l'Œuvre, the 16C chapter library. Carry on to the Impasse Abraham.

North transept – From the Impasse Abraham one can admire the magnificent Flam-boyant-style façade built by Martin Chambiges and his son between 1500 and 1513. The sculpted decoration is very graceful. The statue of Abraham, surmount-ing the gable, is modern.

Go back to the west front of the cathedral and enter by the south doorway.

Interior – The nave is impressive for its size and unity; it is divided from the aisles by magnificent arches surmounted by a triforium and roofed with sexpartite vault-ing. The alternating stout and slender pillars are characteristic of the early-Gothic style. The original appearance of the church has been somewhat lost in successive alterations: the clerestories in the choir were extended upwards in the 13C and in the nave in the 14C; in the 15C Archbishop Tristan de Salazar added the transept marking the division between the nave and the choir.

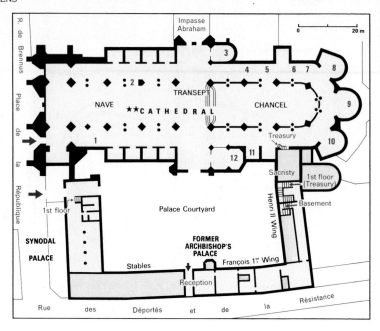

The **stained glass windows★★**, dating from the 12C-17C, are magnificent.

In the third bay of the south aisle is a window (**1**) by Jean Cousin, dating from 1530. On the north side of the nave is a Renaissance retable and a monument (**2**) given by Archbishop de Salazar in memory of his parents.

The stained glass windows of the south transept (1500-02) were made in Troyes: those portraying the Tree of Jesse and legend of St Nicholas are outstanding; the rose window represents the Last Judgment. Those in the north transept were made in 1516-17 by Jean Hympe and his son, glaziers from Sens; the rose window represents Paradise.

The choir is enclosed by handsome bronze screens (1762) bearing the arms of Cardinal de Luynes. The large high altar is 18C by Servandoni and the stained glass of the clerestory dates from the 13C.

In summer, it is possible to leave the cathedral via the north transept to admire its façade (see above).

Both St John's Chapel, which contains a fine 13C calvary (**3**), and the blind arcade round the ambulatory are part of the original building. The oldest stained glass, dating from the late 12C, is in the four windows overlooking the ambulatory: the story of Thomas à Becket (**4**), the story of St Eustache (**5**) and the parables of the Prodigal Son (**6**) and the Good Samaritan (**7**). The tomb (**8**) of the Dauphin, father of Louis XVI, by Guillaume Coustou is placed in the next chapel. The 13C apsidal chapel has stained glass windows (**9**) of the same period. In the chapel of the Sacré-Cœur (**10**) one of the windows is attributed to Jean Cousin. In summer, a 13C staircase leads up to the cathedral treasury (in winter, go via the museum, as the staircase is closed).

In the chapel beyond the sacristy is a Renaissance retable (**11**). The Lady Chapel contains a 14C seated statue of the Virgin (**12**) above the altar.

Leave by the south transept.

South transept – This was built by Martin Chambiges, master mason who had worked at both Beauvais and Troyes. It is a fine example of the Flamboyant style (1490-1500). The decoration of the Moses doorway is quite remarkable. The gable is surmounted by a modern statue of Moses.

★MUSEUM, TREASURY AND PALAIS SYNODAL (**M**) ⊙

The Musées de Sens are housed in the **ancien archevêché** (16C-18C) and the Palais Synodal which stand on the south side of the cathedral.

François I and Henri II wings – These galleries are devoted to the history of Sens and the Sens district. The first rooms display prehistoric and protohistoric articles: Palaeolithic stone tools, Neolithic house and burials (7 500 to 2 500 BC), Bronze Age objects (2 500 to 750 BC) including the treasure of Villethierry (jeweller's stock), many Iron Age weapons and ornaments.

The basement contains pieces of **Gallo-Roman stonework★** re-used in the construction of the town walls of Sens: architectural pieces, sculptures, tombstones. It is noticeable that the sculpture on the public monuments is in the official Roman style (façade of the baths) whereas funerary sculpture, a more popular art, displayed in the vaulted cellars, provides a picture of ancient Sens society. Excavations under the courtyard have revealed the foundations of a 4C bathhouse including a collection of bone combs.

18C sculpture is displayed on the first floor: reliefs from the Porte Dauphine which was erected in memory of the Dauphin, Louis XV's son, and of the Dauphin's wife, and parts of a rood screen removed from the cathedral in the 19C. The second floor is hung with 17C to 19C paintings.

★★ **Cathedral treasury (Trésor)** – *Access via the museum.*

This treasure house, along with that in Conques *(see the Michelin Green Guide Gorges du Tarn)* is one of the richest in France. It contains a magnificent collection of materials and liturgical vestments: the shroud of St Victor, a 13C white silk mitre embroidered with gold thread, St Thomas à Becket's alb; handsome 15C high warp tapestries *(Adoration of the Magi* and the *Coronation of the Virgin);* ivories (5C and 6C pyx, the 7C liturgical comb of St Lupus, an 11C Byzantine coffret and a 12C Islamic one) as well as goldwork (late-12C ciborium).

Palais Synodal – This beautiful 13C palace was restored by Viollet-le-Duc. The great vaulted chamber on the ground floor was the seat of the ecclesiastical tribunal *(officialité).* In the 13C two bays were converted into a prison and there are still traces of graffiti on the walls.

The magnificent hall on the first floor was where the bishops deliberated. The archaeological collection on the ground floor and the collections of the adjoining treasury (Lemoine paintings, tapestries...) will be rearranged once the rooms of the new museum are ready.

ADDITIONAL SIGHTS

Marché couvert – The metal framework filled with pink brick of the covered market standing opposite the cathedral is typical of the architectural style in fashion during the latter half of the 19C. The conspicuous pitched roof is ornamented with pinnacle turrets.

Old houses – Among the many old buildings in the town, two are particularly noteworthy. At the corner of Rue de la République and Rue Jean-Cousin, stands a 16C house (**E**), the **Maison dite d'Abraham.** The carved corner post is decorated with a Tree of Jesse. The house next door, at 50 Rue Jean-Cousin, known as the House of the Pillar (Maison du Pilier) (16C), has a curious porch. Further along, at no 8, the Maison Jean-Cousin with a garden façade overlooking the Rue Jossey also dates from the 16C. The pedestrian shopping street, the Grande-Rue, has numerous half-timbered houses along it, some of which have plaques indicating their former function. In Rue Abélard there are several 17C and 18C mansions.

St-Pierre-le-Rond ⊘ – Beside the church stands the bell tower (1728) and a building which in 1927 was faced with the 13C façade of the Sens charity hospital (Hôtel-Dieu). The high spear-shaped windows in the gables provide a point of harmony between the two façades. The wooden-roofed 13C nave of the church leads to a rectangular chancel. The aisle, built in the Gothic style, is lit by five windows which have largely retained their 16C stained glass. The wrought-iron screens date from the 17C.

St-Maurice ⊘ – The church was built in the latter half of the 12C on an island in the Yonne. The square east end is half-timbered; the slate spire rising from the asymmetrical roof is seen to advantage from the right bank of the river. The choir, which was refurbished in the 16C, contains a large low-relief sculpture composed of several panels dating from 1567.

St-Savinien ⊘ – *East of the town plan in Rue Alsace-Lorraine, 750m - 820yds from Boulevard du Mail on the left.*

The church was built in the 11C on the site of an earlier church. It is basilical in plan with a steep-pitched roof over the nave and three apsidal chapels but no transept. A flight of steps in front of the central apsidal chapel leads to a small crypt. The plain exterior of the building contrasts with the graceful belfry which has two storeys; the lower one in the Romanesque style is pierced by twin bays with round-headed arches; the upper one has tall bays with pointed arches.

Lac des SETTONS★

Michelin map 65 southwest of fold 17 or 238 fold 24 – Local map under MORVAN

The reservoir of Les Settons (34 359ha - 887 acres) was created in the Cure valley (alt 573m - 1 880ft) in one of the most isolated parts of the Morvan. It is a peaceful place, surrounded by fir and larch woods, where wildfowl congregate in the autumn. Footpaths and a lakeside road provide easy access for walking, fishing and water sports.

The dam (277m – 909ft long) was built in 1861; the dike (227m - 745ft) was added in 1901. The reservoir has a potential capacity of 4 619 million gallons of water. It was created originally to facilitate logging on the River Cure but is now used to regulate the flow of the River Yonne.

The small resort of **Les Settons** *(facilities)* is a pleasant place to spend the summer holidays.

Roche de SOLUTRÉ★★

Population 360
Michelin map 69 south of fold 19 or 243 fold 39 –
Local map under MÂCONNAIS

The **rock of Solutré**, a superb limestone escarpment with a distinctive profile which can be seen from miles away between Mâcon and Bourg-en-Bresse in the east, figures largely in prehistory. It was here that a particular type of flint tool was first identified and given the name Solutrean (18 000 to 15 000 BC). The tools were created by knapping, i.e. knocking off flat flakes to obtain bifaced stones with sharp edges, sometimes called "laurel leaves" (fine examples in the Musée Denon in Chalon-sur-Saône – *qv*). The end of this period is marked by the appearance of stone needles with eyes.

Roche de Solutré

A. Gaël

Excavations – The first excavations at the foot of the rock in 1866 brought to light a pile of horse bones which, together with a few bison, auroch, deer and mammoth bones, formed a layer between 0.5m - 2m (18in - 6 1/2ft) thick covering an area of 4 000m^2 - 4 784sq yds. This hunting ground was used for 25 000 years by the different generations of the Upper Palaeolithic Age (Aurignacian, Gravettian, Solutrean and Magdalenian).

At the end of the last century it was supposed that the horses were rounded up on the top of the rock and forced by noise or fire to jump to their death; this theory is no longer maintained. Excavations carried out between 1968 and 1976 suggest that the wild horses were hunted during their spring migrations to the foot of the rock where they were slaughtered and dismembered.

> **Panorama** – *From Mâcon take the D 54 southwest through Solutré (facilities); beyond the cemetery take the second road on the right to a car park; 45 min on foot Rtn.*
> A path leads through Crot du Charnier (where the museum is situated) to the top of the rock of Solutré (495m - 1 624ft). Although the range is limited the view embraces the valley of the Saône, the Bresse, the Jura and on a clear day the Alps.

> **Musée** ⊙ – The museum, which is buried at the foot of the rock, is devoted to the prehistoric archaeology of the south Mâconnais, the horses and hunting at Solutré in the Upper Palaeolithic Age and Solutrean man in the European context (numerous models).
> In between the three sections are two viewpoints over-looking the surrounding countryside: the valley of the Saône and the rock of Solutré.

Château de SULLY★

Michelin map 69 fold 8 or 243 fold 26 – 4km - 3 miles northwest of Épinac

The **château of Sully** ⊙ is a Renaissance mansion flanked by its outbuildings and set in a vast park; in its lay-out and decoration it is similar to the château of Ancy-le-Franc *(qv)*.

The building was begun early in the 16C by Jean de Saulx, who had already acquired the land at Sully, and continued by his son, the Maréchal de Tavannes.

The surrounding moat is fed by the River Drée. Four wings, flanked by four square corner towers set at an angle, enclose an inner courtyard.

The west façade, containing the entrance, consists of wide bays separated by pilasters at first-floor level. Two turrets flank the chapel in the south façade. From the north façade, which was rebuilt in the 18C, a monumental stair gives access to a terrace, bordered by a handsome balustrade, overlooking a stretch of water.

The château was the birthplace of Maréchal **Mac-Mahon**, Duke of Magenta and President of the French Republic from 1873 to 1879.

TAIZÉ

Population 118
Michelin map 69 fold 19 or 243 fold 39 – 10km - 6 miles north of Cluny –
Local map under MÂCONNAIS

The charming village of Taizé amidst the hills of the Grosse region hosts tens of thousands of young people from all over the world every summer, as they meet to pray.

Brother Roger – In 1940 Pastor Schutz (now called Brother Roger) settled at Taizé and established an ecumenical community which now numbers over 80 brothers, who take lifelong vows and are drawn from various Christian churches (Catholic and Protestant) and from about twenty different countries.

Their mission is to be involved worldwide with young people in the search for unity and reconciliation; the brothers organise youth meetings throughout the world. Pope John-Paul II visited Taizé in 1986.

The community is a highly active one with a tented village and group of bungalows to accommodate the visitors, and many craft workshops and stands.

SIGHTS

Église de la Réconciliation ⊙ – The low-lying, flat-roofed Church of the Reconciliation was consecrated in 1962 and serves as a place of worship. The five-bell peal is out in the open air. This concrete building has a large main doorway but small and narrow windows. There are 3 daily prayer services held here for the community.

The nave is flanked to the right by a passageway leading to the crypt. The stained glass in the 7 small windows opening into this passage represent the main feast days: the Easter Lamb, a yellow and flame-coloured composition in which the Lamb's eye stands out most clearly; the last window, of the Transfiguration, has ochre-coloured figures against a pale blue-green background with touches of red.

The first crypt, revolving round a central pillar supporting the choir, is a place of prayer and silence; the second crypt is an orthodox chapel.

Église paroissiale – This Romanesque church is starkly simple and is lit by narrow windows. The church is also used by the community, but is above all a place reserved for personal prayer and meditation.

Château de TALMAY★

Michelin map 66 fold 13 or 243 fold 17 –
6km - 4 miles north of Pontailler-sur-Saône

The great 13C square keep (46m - 151ft high), topped by a Louis XIV roof and surmounted by a lantern tower, is all that remains of the feudal castle destroyed in 1760 and replaced by the present charming **château** ⊙ in the classical style.

There is a curious decoration on the fronton of the 18C main building: the Phrygian goddess, Cybele, mother of the gods, stands in the centre with the sun and the moon on either side. The gardens, through which the Vingeanne flows, are laid out in the French style.

The different floors of the keep are furnished with taste; first there are fine Renaissance rooms with sculpted ceilings and 17C woodwork; on the upper floors are a library, a room decorated with Louis XIV wainscoting, and the guard room, which has a handsome fireplace.

From the top of the tower there is a wide panorama: La Côte to the west prolonged to the north by the Langres plateau with the Jura mountains rising to the southeast.

Château de TANLAY★★

Michelin map 65 fold 7 or 238 fold 12 – 9km - 6 miles east of Tonnerre

The château of Tanlay, built about 1550, is a magnificent architectural composition, and an unexpected surprise in this small village on the banks of the canal de Bourgogne, which draws fleets of houseboats every summer. The château was built shortly after Ancy-le-Franc *(qv)*, the first example of the classical Renaissance style, and is a fine monument to French Renaissance architecture at a time when it had broken away from the Italian influence.

Approaching Tanlay from the east by the D 965, there is a good general view of this handsome residence and its park; it is particularly attractive in the evening light.

TOUR ⊙ *time: about 1 hour*

Exterior – The small château (the "Portal"), an elegant building of Louis XIII style, leads into the "Cour Verte" (Green Courtyard), which is surrounded by arches except on the left where a bridge crosses the moat and leads to the great doorway opening onto the main courtyard of the large château.

Built by François de Coligny d'Andelot (1531-69) on the site of an ancient feudal fortress, the large château was completed and decorated by Michel Particelli d'Hémery (d1650), Superintendent of Finances. The architect Le Muet, who oversaw work on the château, designed the pyramidal obelisks which stand at the entrance to the bridge.

Château de Tanlay

The main living quarters are joined by two staircase towers to two lower wings at right angles to the main building. Each wing ends in a round domed tower with a lantern. The Tour des Archives is on the left, the Tour de la Chapelle on the right.

Interior – On the ground floor, the hallway (Vestibule des Césars), is closed off by a handsome 16C wrought-iron doorway leading to the gardens. Go through the great hall and the antechamber (note the beautiful Louis XVI desk).

Dining room – The dining room features an eye-catching monumental white stone Renaissance chimneypiece. Interesting items of furniture include a French Renaissance cabinet and a Burgundian chest.

Drawing room – The 17C woodwork bears the mark of sculptor Michel Porticelli d'Hémery. The pair of sphinxes with women's faces on the chimneypiece are supposed to depict Catherine de' Medici. In the centre, the face of the Amiral de Coligny can be seen.

Bedchamber of the Marquis de Tanlay – *First floor*. Note the late 16C German School painting on copper.

★ **Great Gallery** – The old ballroom on the first floor is decorated with monochrome trompe-l'œil frescoes.

Tour de la Ligue – The circular room on the top floor of this turret was used for Huguenot meetings during the Wars of Religion. Like his brother Gaspard de Châtillon (assassinated in 1572), François d'Andelot had embraced the Reformation, after which Tanlay, along with Noyers – the fief of the Prince de Condé, became one of the two main centres of Protestantism in the country.
The domed ceiling of the room is decorated with a distemper painting (Fontainebleau School), depicting major 16C Roman Catholic and Protestant protagonists in the somewhat frivolous guise of gods and goddesses.

Outbuildings – Now a **centre of contemporary art** (exhibitions in season).

Gardens – *Only partly open to visitors*. These lie either side of the long canal (526m – 1 726ft) built by Particelli, which is lined with ancient trees.

TERNANT★

Population 240
Michelin map 69 fold 6 or 238 fold 35 – 13.5km - 8 miles southwest of Luzy

The art lover visiting the Nivernais or the Morvan should not miss going to Ternant to see the two magnificent 15C Flemish triptychs in the little village **church**.

★★THE TRIPTYCHS IN THE CHURCH *time: 30 min*

The triptychs were given to the church between 1432 and 1435 by Baron Philippe de Ternant, Chamberlain to Philip the Good, Duke of Burgundy, and his son Charles de Ternant. They are made of wood – carved, painted and gilded.

Large triptych – This is devoted to the Passion of Christ. The centre panel portrays Christ's death. Below, a fainting Virgin Mary is supported by St John and the holy women; the donor Charles de Ternant and his wife Jeanne are shown kneeling in the foreground.
The left-hand panel is a *Pietà* including the figures of St John, Mary Magdalene and the holy women. To the right is the Entombment. The folding panels show scenes from the Passion: the Agony in the Garden, Christ carrying the Cross, the Resurrection, the Descent into Hell.

Small triptych – This triptych, which is older, is devoted to the Virgin Mary. In the centre of the carved panel is a scene from the Assumption: a little angel, his head covered by a hood, draws the Virgin's soul, depicted as a little girl at prayer, out from her head. Above this is shown the later scene of the Assumption of the Virgin, when she is carried to heaven on a crescent moon held by an angel: this particular detail is unique.

The last meeting of the Virgin with the Apostles is shown on the left of the central motif; on the right is her funeral procession.

The panel paintings are remarkable. Besides the scenes from the life of the Virgin Mary – the Annunciation, the crowning of the Virgin, Christ holding the world, the Virgin's funeral – one can see the donor, Philippe de Ternant, dressed in chequered material – the arms of his house – the Order of the Golden Fleece *(qv)* about his neck, and his wife Isabella, in full state dress, accompanied by the crowned Virgin Mary, her patron saint.

TONNERRE

Population 6 181
Michelin map 65 fold 6 or 238 fold 12 – Facilities

Tonnerre is a pleasant little town, terraced on one of the hills that form the west bank of the Armançon and surrounded by vineyards and green scenery. Both the old town and the newer quarters are dominated by the church of St-Pierre and the tower of Notre-Dame. From the terrace behind St-Pierre there is a good view of the town and its surroundings.

Few monuments have survived the fire that ravaged the town in the 16C but the old hospital and the beautiful sepulchre it contains are among the treasures of Burgundy.

The Knight of Éon – It was at Tonnerre that Charles-Geneviève-Louise-Auguste-Andrée-Timothée Éon de Beaumont, known as the knight or the lady-knight of Éon, was born in 1728. After a brilliant military and diplomatic career, during which he sometimes had to wear women's clothes, he met with reversals of fortune and was forced to flee to London. He was refused permission to return to France except dressed as a woman. Returning to England, he died there in 1810. To the end of his life, there was widespread speculation as to his sex. The announcement of his death gave rise to a wave of great curiosity ended only by an autopsy. Charles d'Éon was unquestionably a man.

ANCIEN HÔPITAL *time: 30 min*

This beautiful old hospital, erected between 1293 and 1295 by Margaret of Burgundy, widow of Charles d'Anjou, king of Naples and Sicily and brother of St Louis, has survived intact, apart from minor modifications.

From the outside, the walls of the hall, despite their buttresses, seem to be crushed by the tall roof which covers an area of 5 400 sq yds. The west face was changed in the 18C.

Interior – Although shortened by 20m - 66ft in the 18C, the great hall is of impressive size (80m - 262ft long and 18.2m - 60ft wide). The broken-barrel vaulting and the **oak timbering★** are remarkable. The forty beds for the sick were set in wooden alcoves built in lines along the walls as at Beaune, which was built 150 years later. The walls themselves were pierced by high semicircular bays, divided by pointed arches. From 1650, the hall was put to many different uses and often served as the parish church. Many citizens of Tonnerre were buried there, which explains the presence of the numerous tombstones.

Note the gnomon (sundial) on the paving, designed in the 18C by a Benedictine monk and the astronomer Lalande (1732-1807).

The chapel opens off the end of the hall. The tomb of Margaret of Burgundy, rebuilt in 1826, is in the centre of the choir. Above the altar is a 14C stone statue of the Virgin Mary. To the right of the high altar, a little door leads to the sacristy which contains a carved **Entombment★**, presented to the church in the 15C by a rich merchant of the town *(illustration below)*. The figures of this Holy Sepulchre make up a scene of dramatic intensity. In the north side chapel is the monumental tomb of the French statesman Louvois, who acquired the county of Tonnerre in 1684 and served as Minister of War under Louis XIV. The bronze statues represent Vigilance by Desjardins and Wisdom by Girardon (1628-1715). The wooden statues in the niches at the end of the hall, above the gallery, representing Margaret of Burgundy and Margaret of Beaumont, Countess of Tripoli, who withdrew here with the foundress, are late 13C.

Among the objects on view in the Salle du Conseil (consultation room) of the hospital are the original documents of the Foundation Charter (1293), the queen's will (1305) and a great golden cross in which is mounted a reputed piece of the True Cross.

Entombment, Ancien Hôpital, Tonnerre

TONNERRE

Hôpital (R. de l')	9
Hôtel-de-Ville (R. de l')	10
St-Pierre (R.)	23

Campenon (R. Gén.)	2
Colin (R. Armand)	3
Fontenilles (R. des)	4
Fosse-Dionne (R. de la)	6
Garnier (R. Jean)	7
Marguerite-de-Bourgogne (Pl.)	12
Pompidou (Av. G.)	14
Pont (R. du)	16
République (Pl. de la)	17
St-Michel (R.)	18
St-Nicolas (R.)	20

B Hôtel d'Uzès

ADDITIONAL SIGHTS

St-Pierre ⊙ – This church stands on a rocky terrace affording a good view of the town and its surroundings. With the exception of the 14C chancel and the 15C square tower, the church was rebuilt in 1556 following the fire that ravaged the town. There is a handsome doorway on the south side with a statue of St Peter on the pier.

Inside, note the interesting 16C paintings on wood, representing scenes from the Passion, and the 17C pulpit, churchwarden's pew and organ loft.

Fosse Dionne – This circular basin, filled with blue-green water, is used as a wash-house.

It is fed by an underground river that flows through a steeply-inclined rock gallery (45m - 148yds long) to emerge in the centre of the pool; its flow varies considerably according to season and rainfall. The pool overflows into the Armançon by way of a small stream.

Hôtel d'Uzès (**B**) – A savings bank occupies this Renaissance dwelling, birthplace of the Knight of Éon; note the design on the doors.

Promenade du Pâtis – Pleasant shady walk.

TOURNUS★

Population 6 568

Michelin map 69 fold 20 or 243 folds 39 and 40 – Local map under MÂCONNAIS

The town stands on the right bank of the Saône between Chalon and Mâcon, near the agricultural land of the Mâconnais hills; the region, which is blessed with a gentle climate, is rich in old buildings and famous wines.

The original Gaulish city of the Aedui tribe became a *castrum* under Roman rule. The few surviving traces of the old fortifications are dominated by the tall towers of the abbey church.

Tournus is one of the oldest and most important of the monastic centres in France owing to the architectural beauty and the harmonious proportions of the church and the conventual buildings, which date from the 10C.

Monastic centre – When St Valerian, a Christian from Asia Minor, escaped from persecution in Lyon in 177, he travelled to Tournus to convert the people but was martyred on a hillside above the Saône; a sanctuary was built beside his tomb. In the Merovingian period it was converted into an abbey and dedicated to St Valerian.

In 875 the monastery embarked on a period of development following the arrival of monks from Noirmoutier. They had led a wandering life fleeing from the Norsemen since the beginning of the 9C until they were invited by Charles the Bald to settle at St Valerian's abbey. They brought with them the relics of St Philibert, founder of the abbey of Jumièges in Normandy, who died at Noirmoutier in 685; the dedication of the abbey was eventually changed from St Valerian to St Philibert.

A Hungarian invasion in 937 checked the prosperity of the abbey which was destroyed by fire and rebuilt. In about 945 the monastery was abandoned by the monks who retreated to St Pourçain in the Auvergne. In 949 following a decision in council, Abbot Stephen, formerly prior of St Philibert, was ordered to return to Tournus with a group of monks.

The reconstruction which he set in motion was completed in the 12C; it produced one of the most beautiful parts of the church.

Over the centuries the building underwent damage, repair and modification; in 1562 it was sacked by the Huguenots.

The abbey became a collegiate church in 1627 and in 1790 a parish church, so that it avoided irrevocable damage during the Revolution.

★★ ANCIENNE ABBAYE (ABBEY)
time: 1 hour

St Philibert ⊙ – *Access from the main road by Rue Albert-Thibaudet.*
The street passes between two round towers, all that is left of the Porte des Champs, the main entrance to the old abbey precinct.

Exterior – The façade, dating from the 10C and 11C and built of beautifully cut stone, has almost the appearance of a castle keep with the dark loophole slits emphasising the warm colour of the stone. The bareness of the strong walls is broken by slightly projecting Lombard bands. The crenellated parapet with machicolations linking the two towers accentuates the military appearance of the building. Both this gallery and the porch are the work of Questel in the 19C.

Interior of the abbey church
of St-Philibert, Tournus

The right tower is topped by a saddle-back roof; the other was heightened at the end of the 11C by the addition of a two-storey belfry surmounted by a tall spire.
The two column-statues, which decorate the corners of the upper storey, are among the oldest of their kind.

Enter the church by the doorway to the right of the main façade.

Narthex – This is the place of transition from the outer world to the house of God, where reflection and preparation for prayer are encouraged by the half-light. Its rugged and simple architecture achieves a singular grandeur. Four enormous circular abacus pillars divide it into a nave and two aisles, each of three bays. The nave has groined vaulting while the two aisles are covered with transversal barrel vaulting.
One bay of the vault is painted in a black and white chequered pattern, the arms of Digoine, an old and powerful Mâcon family. On the wall above the entrance to the nave is a 14C fresco of Christ in Majesty (1); the end wall of the north aisle carries another 14C fresco portraying the Crucifixion (2).
The round tombstones are peculiar to this region.

The nave – The luminous and rose-coloured nave, which dates from the beginning of the 11C, is now devoid of decoration.
Magnificently tall cylindrical pillars made from the rose-coloured stone of Préty (a small place near Tournus) are surmounted by ordinary flat capitals, like those in the narthex; they divide the five bays of the nave from the aisles.
A most unusual feature is the central vault which consists of five transverse barrel vaults resting on transverse arches with alternating white and pink archstones; great columns surmounted by slim columns support the arches, which obscure the clerestory, through which light enters the nave.
Pronounced transverse ribs sub-divide the vaulting in the aisles.
The side chapels in the north aisle date from the 14C and 15C.
A 15C niche in the south aisle contains a 12C statue-reliquary of the Virgin (3), Notre-Dame-de-la-Brune, which shows the artistic influence of the Auvergne. The statue, which is made of painted cedar wood (regilded in the 19C) retains an aura of calm and majestic beauty.

Transept and choir – Built at the start of the 12C, the transept and choir contrast strongly with the rest of the building in the whiteness of the stonework; they show the rapid evolution of Romanesque art.
In the transept the contrast can be seen between the spaciousness of the nave and the narrowness of the choir which the architect restricted to the dimensions of the existing crypt.
The semi-domed apse is supported by six columns with capitals, surmounted by semicircular windows framed by delicately sculpted decoration. The ambulatory built at the beginning of the 11C has barrel vaulting and five radiating chapels with flat end walls; the axial chapel contains the shrine of St Philibert (4).

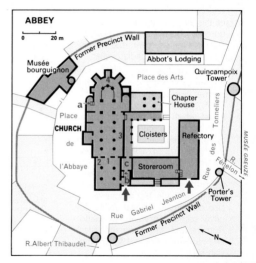

259

★ **Crypt** (**a**) – *Access by steps in the north transept.* The crypt with its thick walls was built by Abbot Stephen at the end of the 10C and restored by Questel in the 19C. The height of the crypt (3.5m - 12ft) is quite exceptional. The central part, flanked by two rows of slender columns (some have a typical archaic bulge) with delightful foliated capitals, is surrounded by an ambulatory with radiating chapels. The 12C fresco, decorating the chapel on the right and representing a Virgin and Child and a Christ in Majesty, is the best preserved in the whole church.

Chapelle St-Michel (**b**) – The chapel occupies the upper room in the narthex which was built before the nave. In plan it is identical with the ground floor but the astonishing height of the central section and the amount of light give it an entirely different feel. The ancient sculpture on the capitals and the blocks which they support have survived from the Carolingian period: the Gerlannus inscription half-way up the archivolt may refer to the year 1000 and confirm that the room was built earlier than the nave. The great arched bay opening into the organ loft was once the entrance to a small oven-vaulted apsidal chapel which was built out on corbels at first-floor level; the chapel was suppressed when the organ loft was built in 1629.

Conventual Buildings – To reach the cloisters one passes through the old alms room (**c**) or warming room (13C) adjoining the south wall of the narthex. It contains a lapidary collection including the column-statues and capitals from the north tower as well as a few sculptures from the cloisters.

Chapter House – This was rebuilt by Abbot Bérard following a fire in 1239 and now houses temporary exhibitions. The pointed vaulting is visible through the Romanesque apertures overlooking the cloisters.

The buildings on the south side, which hide the refectory, now house both the public and abbey libraries. They are dominated by the square Prieuré tower.

Leave the cloisters by Place des Arts.

Admire the east end with the chevet and five radiating chapels, all dominated by the 12C belfry over the transept crossing. This fine tower was inspired by Cluny.

Abbot's Lodging – This is a charming late-15C building.

In Rue des Tonneliers stands the Quincampoix tower which was built after the Hungarian invasion in 937; it was part of the wall of enclosure of the old abbey as was the neighbouring tower, called the Tour du Portier.

Refectory – This magnificent 12C chamber (33m - 108ft long and 12m - 39ft high) has no transverse arches but is vaulted with slightly broken barrel vaulting. When the abbey was secularised in 1627 the hall was used for real tennis and was called the Ballon ("ball"). The hall is used for temporary exhibitions.

Storeroom – The storeroom, also 12C, has broken barrel vaulting resting on transverse arches. It is lit by two small windows set high up. The vast cellars below are now occupied by various craftsmen.

ADDITIONAL SIGHTS

Musée bourguignon (**M¹**) ⊙ – This folklore collection, donated to the town by Perrin de Puycousin in 1929, is displayed in a 17C family mansion, formerly the treasurer's house, bequeathed to the town by Albert Thibaudet (1874-1936), the celebrated literary critic, who was born in Tournus. Wax models in Burgundian costume recreate scenes from daily life in past centuries (about forty figures in eight rooms).

The scenes include the interior of a Bresse farm, a local Tournus interior with nine variations of the regional costume, the large room of the Burgundian spinners, collections of headdresses, costumes, and, in the basement, the reconstruction of a Burgundian cellar.

Musée Greuze (**M²**) ⊙ – The museum is mostly devoted to the painter **Jean-Baptiste Greuze** (1725-1805), born in Tournus in the street which now bears his name. His work, sentimental and edifying, is represented here by a fine collection of drawings, a few canvases (including seven original portraits) and many engravings illustrating the genre scenes with which he made his reputation. It also contains a regional archaeological section (prehistoric, Gallo-Roman and Merovingian relics) and rooms displaying 19C Tournusian sculpture.

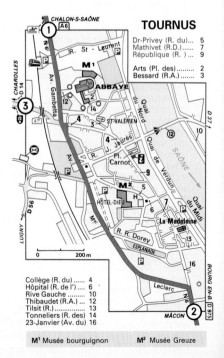

TOURNUS

Dr-Privey (R. du)...	5
Mathivet (R.D.)......	7
République (R.)...	9
Arts (Pl. des).........	2
Bessard (R.A.).......	3

Collège (R. du)	4
Hôpital (R. de l')	6
Rive Gauche	10
Thibaudet (R.A.) ...	12
Tilsit (R.)	13
Tonneliers (R. des)	14
23-Janvier (Av. du)	16

M¹ Musée bourguignon	**M²** Musée Greuze

Old houses – Many old houses and mansions are to be found in Rue du Dr-Privey, Rue de la République and Rue du D.-Mathivet.

View from the bridge and the quays – From the bridge over the Saône at the end of Rue Jean-Jaurès there is a good view of the church of St-Philibert and the town.

La Madeleine ⊘ – This church stands at the heart of the Roman town and, despite the deterioration of the exterior, remains quite attractive. The east end, adjoined by a cluster of houses, should be admired from the banks of the Saône.

The 12C doorway is interesting for the decorative details. The columns supporting the round-headed recessed arches are adorned with beaded braids and overlapping vertical or slanting garlands; the capitals portray foliage or pairs of birds face to face.

The interior, uniformly white since the restoration, has 15C pointed vaulting. Opening off the north aisle is a Renaissance chapel; its vault is adorned with decorative coffers and ribs. The gilded wood statue represents Mary Magdalene and the tabernacle is in the Empire style. The baptismal chapel also dates from the 15C.

EXCURSION

The Region of St-Trivier-de-Courtes – *Approximately 20km - 12 miles southeast.*

This region, which is typical of the Bresse plain, is known for its **Saracen chimneys**, which were built on the estate of the lords of Bagé from the 13C onwards and which are particularly numerous beside the Ain.

The 30-odd which have survived date from the 17C and 18C. Within the house there is an enormous hearth, set away from the wall and covered by a hood, under which a man can stand upright; the flue is lined with wood panels. The chimney pots resemble small belfries or – more rarely – reliquaries built in the Romanesque, Gothic and sometimes Byzantine style; their shapes are round or square (modelled on the belfry of St Philibert in Tournus) or octagonal (the belfry of St-André-de-Bagé); they have one or two bands of vents and are capped by a cone, a pyramid or a Baroque belfry.

They are unusually high (3m to 5m - 10ft to 16ft) and surmounted by a wrought-iron cross. In the past some may have housed a bell, a useful feature in the daily life of these traditionally isolated farms. The adjective "Saracen" does not describe the chimneys' geographical provenance but is a survival of the medieval use of the word Saracen to mean "belonging to a foreign, old or unknown culture"; the term was therefore quite naturally applied to these unusual chimneys.

Saracen chimneys are to be found at:

St-Trivier – *1.5km - 1 mile west by the D 2.* **Grandval** farm.

Vescours – *5km - 3 miles west of St-Trivier; on the left at the entrance to the village.*

Vernoux – *3km - 2 miles northeast of St-Trivier.* **Colombier** farm.

Ferme-Musée de la Forêt ⊘ – *3km - 2 miles east of St-Trivier.* This attractive 16C-17C *(illustration p 17)* farm has been restored and converted into a Bresse farm museum. The small building with the wooden balcony contains a traditional interior; the chimney over the open hearth (4m² - 43sqft) is supported by a beam weighing 4 tonnes. The second building displays a collection of old agricultural implements.

St-Nizier-le-Bouchoux – *6km - 4 miles east of St-Trivier.* **Bourbon** farm *(beware of the dogs).*

VESOUL

Population 17 614
Michelin map 166 folds 5 and 6 or 243 fold 8

Vesoul lies in the delightful valley of the Durgeon, a tributary of the Saône, not far from the border of the Jura region with the southern part of Lorraine. Prehistoric man first settled on the La Motte outcrop overlooking the town to the north. This settlement was replaced by a Roman military camp intended to guard the road between Luxeuil and Besançon. A small market town grew up in the 13C under the sheltering walls of the fort on the plateau. Then the inhabitants moved down into the plain, and Vesoul became an active commercial, religious and military centre. The fort was attacked several times and was finally razed in 1595.

The town was the capital of the bailliage of Amont from 1333 to the French Revolution. In 1678 the Franche-Comté, of which Vesoul was a part, was annexed to France. The coming of the railway in the second half of the 19C transformed the town into a major junction for transport routes and spurred the growth of an industrial zone south of the Durgeon.

Vesoul is the home town of Beauchamps (1752-1801), the astronomer who accompanied Bonaparte to Egypt, and the painter-sculptor Gérome (1824-1904).

The major annual event in Vesoul is the international moto-cross *(see the Calendar of Events at the end of the guide).*

SIGHTS

Musée Georges-Garret ⊙ – This two-storey museum is in the old Ursuline convent (late 17C). The lower floor houses temporary exhibitions and an archaeological department with an interesting collection of Gallo-Roman **funerary steles.** The upper floor is devoted to painting and sculpture, including a large collection of work by local artist Gérome. The 15C representation of Christ Bound near the entrance is particularly eye-catching.

Colline de la Motte – *30 min on foot Rtn.*
The hill of La Motte (alt 378m - 1 240ft) overlooks the valley from a height of about 160m - 525ft. A road twists and turns its way up the hill to some open level ground and a little chapel which houses a number of ex-votos. Further on the road comes to a terrace with a statue of the Virgin Mary, from which there is a beautiful **panorama★** *(bronze viewing table in the shape of the valley)* of the Langres plateau to the west and the Jura mountains, and sometimes even the Alps, to the south.

Église St-Georges – This church is a beautiful 18C classical building. The nave and aisles are the same height, suggesting Rhenish Gothic influence. Note the splendid 18C allegorical marble sculpture of Faith by the Italian Canova and the chapel of the Saint-Sépulcre, which houses a 16C Entombment.

Old houses – Old Vesoul has some houses with particularly lovely façades, for example that of the Hôtel Thomassin (late 15C, Rue Salengro) and of the Maison Baressols (opposite the north wall of the church).

The annual **Michelin Guide Camping Caravaning France,**
offers a selection of campsites with information on
situation and setting and on-site facilities and services.

VÉZELAY★★

Population 582
Michelin map 65 fold 15 or 238 fold 23 – Facilities – Local map under MORVAN

The beautiful setting of Vézelay, the basilica of Ste-Madeleine, the town with its old houses and ramparts, constitute one of the treasures of Burgundy and France.

HISTORICAL NOTES

Girart de Roussillon, the founder – It was this Count of Burgundy, a legendary hero whose exploits were sung in the ballad-chronicles of the Middle Ages, who was the founder of the abbey of Vézelay.
In the middle of the 9C he established a group of monks where St-Père stands today. After the destruction of the monastery during the Viking invasions, Girart de Roussillon decided to establish a new monastery on a nearby hill, a natural position more easily defended, and this time he installed Benedictine monks.
Pope John VIII consecrated the foundation of the abbey of Vézelay in 878.

The call of St Bernard – The abbey was at the height of its glory when St Bernard preached the Second Crusade at Vézelay on 31 March 1146. For a century the church had sheltered the relics of Mary Magdalene, "the beloved and pardoned sinner". Vézelay was then one of the great places of pilgrimage and the start of one of four routes that led pilgrims and merchants across France into Spain and Santiago de Compostella.
It was from the side of this "hill of inspiration" that St Bernard launched his vibrant call for the Crusade, in the presence of King Louis VII of France and his family and a crowd of powerful barons. Such was the authority of the Abbot of Clairvaux that he was considered as the real leader of Christianity. His call was received with great enthusiasm by all present who undertook to leave for the Holy Land without delay. Although the Third Crusade, undertaken in 1190, was not preached at Vézelay, it was there that King Philippe-Auguste of France and King Richard the Lionheart of England met before their departure.
It was also the place chosen by St Francis of Assisi for the first of his monasteries of Minorities in France. In about 1217 two of his friars, whom he had entrusted with the task, chose to settle near to the small church of Ste-Croix, which had been built on the spot where St Bernard had addressed the crowd massed in the Asquins valley; the church was later given into the care of the Franciscans. From 1248, the year of the Seventh Crusade, St Louis, who was a Franciscan tertiary, made several pilgrimages to Vézelay. Vézelay was the birthplace of **Theodore Beza** (de Bèze or Besze in French) (1519-1605) who preached the Reformation with Calvin. **Romain Rolland** (1866-1944), who loved the "breath of heroes" and wished to awaken the conscience of Europe, spent the last years of his life at no 20 Grande-Rue.
Restored after centuries of neglect, the church of Ste-Madeleine is once more the scene of great pilgrimages. The Franciscans have charge of both the church and the chapel of Ste-Croix, which retains some of the original Romanesque arches.

★★★ BASILIQUE STE-MADELEINE ⏱ time: 1 hour

By car from Place du Champ-de-Foire (lower end of the town) via Porte du Barle and a steep one-way street to a parking space near the church. On foot from Place du Champ-de-Foire via Promenade des Fossés returning by Grande-Rue.

The abbey church became a parish church in 1721 but was elevated to a basilica in 1920.

The different stages of the building – The monastery founded in the 9C by Girart de Roussillon came under the control of Cluny in the 11C. The miracles that happened at the tomb of Mary Magdalene soon drew so great a number of penitents and pilgrims that it became necessary to enlarge the Carolingian church (1096-1104); in 1120 a fierce fire broke out on the eve of 22 July, day of the great pilgrimage, destroying the whole nave and engulfing more than 1 000 pilgrims.

The work of rebuilding was immediately begun, the nave was soon finished and, about 1150, the "pre-nave" or narthex was added. In 1215 the Romanesque-Gothic choir and transept were completed.

The discovery at the end of the 13C of other relics of Mary Magdalene at St-Maximin in Provence created misgivings. Pilgrimages became fewer and the fairs and market lost much of their importance. The religious struggles caused the decline of the abbey, which was transformed into a collegiate church in 1538, was pillaged from cellar to roof by Huguenots in 1569 and finally partially razed during the French Revolution. In the 19C **Prosper Mérimée** (novelist: 1803-70), in his capacity as Inspector of Historical Monuments, drew the attention of the public works' authorities to the building, which was on the point of collapsing. In 1840 **Viollet-le-Duc**, who was then less than thirty years old, undertook the work, which he finished only in 1859.

Exterior

The façade – This was reconstructed by Viollet-le-Duc according to plans contained in the ancient documents. Rebuilt about 1150 in pure Romanesque style it was given a vast Gothic gable in the 13C, consisting of a five-light window decorated with statues, also rebuilt in the 19C. The upper part forms a tympanum decorated with arcades framing the statues of Christ Crowned, accompanied by the Virgin Mary, Mary Magdalene and two angels.

The tower on the right – tour Saint-Michel – was surmounted by a storey of tall twin bays in the 13C; the octagonal wooden spire (15m - 49ft high) was destroyed by lightning in 1819. The other tower remained unfinished.

Three Romanesque doorways open into the narthex; the tympanum of the centre doorway on the outside was remade in 1856 by Viollet-le-Duc, who took the mutilated original tympanum as his inspiration: the archivolt, decorated with plant designs, is authentic, but the rest of the arches and the capitals are modern.

Tour of the exterior – Walk round the building anti-clockwise to appreciate its length and the flying buttresses which support it. This side of the church is dominated by the tower of St-Antoine (13C) (30m - 98ft high) which rises above the junction of the nave and the transept; the two storeys of round-headed bays were originally intended to be surmounted by a stone spire.

The chapter house, built at the end of the 12C, abuts the south transept. The gallery of the cloisters *(p 265)* was entirely rebuilt by Viollet-le-Duc. Beautiful gardens *(private property)* now cover the site of the former abbey buildings. Remains of the 12C refectory still stand.

Château Terrace – *Access by Rue du Château.* From this terrace, shaded by handsome trees, situated behind the church on the site of the old Abbot's Palace, there is a fine **panorama★** *(viewing table)* of the valley of the river Cure and the northern part of the Morvan.

Continue round the basilica past the attractive houses built by the canons of the chapter in the 18C.

Interior

Enter the basilica by the door on the south side of the narthex.

Narthex – This "pre-nave", consecrated in 1132 by Pope Innocent II, is later than the nave and the interior façade. Unlike the rib-vaulted church, the Romanesque narthex is roofed with pointed arches and ogival vaulting.

Christ in Glory on the tympanum in the narthex, Basilique Ste-Madeleine, Vézelay

The narthex is so large it seems like a church in its own right. The nave is divided into three bays flanked by aisles surmounted by galleries. The four cruciform pillars of engaged columns decorated with historiated capitals are extremely graceful. The capitals portray scenes from both the Old Testament (Joseph with Potiphar's wife, Jacob, Isaac and Esau, the death of Cain and Samson slaying the lion) and the New Testament (the life of St John the Baptist and St Benedict resurrecting a dead man).

Three doorways in the narthex open into the nave and the aisles of the church. When the central door is open, there is a marvellous perspective, radiant with light, along the full length of the nave and choir.

A detailed examination should be made of the sculptures of these doorways, executed in the second quarter of the 12C, and particularly of the tympanum of the central doorway. This is indisputably a masterpiece of Burgundian-Romanesque art, ranking with that of St-Lazare at Autun.

★★★ **Tympanum of the central doorway** – As the church is a place of pilgrimage, the decoration of the great doorway is devoted to the worldwide evangelical mission which Christ entrusted to his Apostles before His ascension into heaven. All pilgrims arriving at Vézelay, sometimes after a long journey, would learn that God had first approached them. At the centre of the composition a mandorla surrounds an immense figure of Christ Enthroned (**1**) extending his hands to his Apostles (**2**) assembled round him; the Holy Ghost is shown radiating from the stigmata to touch the head of each of the Twelve. All around, on the arch stones and the lintel, are crowded the converts to be received at the feet of Christ by St Peter and St Paul (**3**), symbols of the universal Church. People of every sort are called: on the lintel are *(left)* archers (**4**), fishermen (**5**), farmers (**6**), and *(right)* distant and legendary people: giants (**7**), pygmies (climbing a ladder to mount a horse – **8**), men with huge ears (one with a feather-covered body – **9**). The arch stones show Armenians (wearing clogs – **10**), Byzantines perhaps (**11**), Phrygians (**12**) and Ethiopians (**13**); immediately next to Christ are men with dogs' heads (the cynocephalics converted by St Thomas in India – **14**). The next two panels show the miracles that accompanied the divine word preached by the Apostles: two lepers show their regenerated limbs (**15**) and two paralytics their healthy arms (**16**). Lastly two Evangelists record all that they have seen (**17**).

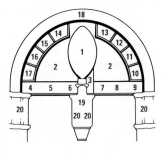

The large-scale composition seeks to demonstrate that the word of God is intended for the whole world. The signs of the zodiac which alternate with the labours of the months on the outer arch stone (**18**) introduce the notion of time: the Apostles' mission must also be transmitted from generation to generation.

On the central pier John the Baptist (**19**) carrying the paschal lamb (unfortunately missing) is shown at the feet of Christ as if supporting Him and introducing Him to His rightful place in the centre. Below Him and on the flanking piers are more Apostles (**20**).

The power of the Holy Ghost which fills the Twelve Apostles is symbolised by a strong wind creating turbulence which ruffles the garments and drapes, and sways the bodies. The linear skill, which is the dominant feature of this masterly work, suggests that in the principal scene the sculptor was following the work of a calligrapher, whereas in the medallions, showing the signs of the zodiac and the months of the year, he felt free to carve humorous interpretations of his contemporaries at work.

Tympana of the side doors – Two recessed arches with ornamental foliage and rosettes frame the historiated tympana on the side doors.

The one on the right represents the Childhood of Christ: on the lintel are the Annunciation, the Visitation and the Nativity; on the tympanum is the Adoration of the Magi. The one on the left represents the apparitions of Christ after His Resurrection; on the tympanum is the apparition to the Apostles; on the lintel is the apparition to the disciples at Emmaus.

Nave – Rebuilt between 1120 and 1135 after a terrible fire *(p 263)*, this Romanesque nave is noteworthy for its huge size (62m - 203ft long), the use of different coloured limestone, the lighting, and above all, the fine series of capitals.

The nave is much higher than the side aisles and is divided into ten bays of groined vaulting separated by transverse arches with alternating light and dark stones. These do much to mitigate the severity of the lines.

The great semicircular arches, surmounted by windows, rest on cruciform pillars ornamented with four engaged columns decorated with capitals. A graceful decoration of convex quarter-section mouldings, rosettes and pleated ribbons goes round the arches, the main arches and the string-course that runs between the windows and the arches.

★★★ **The capitals** – As they are more beautiful than those in the narthex they deserve to be examined in detail *(details and plan below)*.

The sculptors – five different hands have been detected in the work – must have had an astonishing knowledge of composition and movement; their genius is expressed with spirit and malice although their realism does not exclude lyricism, a sense of the dramatic and even of psychology.

Transept and chancel – Built in 1096, when the original Carolingian church was enlarged, the Romanesque transept and chancel were demolished at the end of the 12C and were replaced by this beautiful Gothic ensemble completed in 1215. The arcades of the triforium continue into the transept.

The relics of Mary Magdalene (**a**), preserved in the base of a column surmounted by a modern statue, are to be found in the south transept.

A vast ambulatory, with radiating chapels, surrounds the choir.

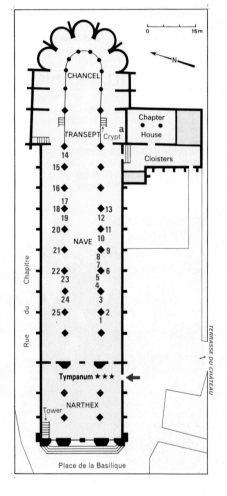

Right side
1) A duel.
2) Lust and Despair.
3) Legend of St Hubert.
4) Sign of the Zodiac: Libra.
5) The mystical mill (Moses and St Paul).
6) The death of Dives and Lazarus.
7) Lamach kills Cain, concealed in a bush.
8) The four winds of the year.
9) David astride a lion.
10) St Martin avoids a tree about to fall on him.
11) Daniel subdues the lions.
12) The angel wrestling with Jacob.
13) Isaac blessing Jacob.

Left side
14) St Peter delivered from prison.
15) Adam and Eve.
16) Two capitals of this pillar are devoted to the legend of St Anthony, a third represents the animals.
17) The execution of Agag.
18) Legend of St Eugenia: thanks to a disguise, she becomes abbot of a monastery of men; accused later of having outraged a woman, she shows her innocence by opening her robe.
19) Death of St Paul the hermit, for whom two lions dig a grave; above, St Anthony prays for him.
20) Moses and the Golden Calf.
21) Death of Absalom: first caught by the hair in the branches of a tree and then decapitated.
22) Two scenes from the fight between David and Goliath.
23) Killing of the Egyptian by Moses.
24) Judith and Holophernes.
25) Calumny and Greed.

Crypt – The Carolingian crypt was completely altered during the second half of the 12C. It used to contain the tomb of Mary Magdalene at the time of the great medieval pilgrimages and still houses part of her relics. The painting on the vaulting is 13C.

Chapter house and cloisters – Built at the end of the 12C, shortly before the choir of the basilica, the chapter house has pointed vaulting. It was completely restored by Viollet-le-Duc. The cloisters, which were razed during the French Revolution, used to have a huge cistern in the centre of the close, the only water reserve for the town. Viollet-le-Duc rebuilt one gallery in Romanesque style.

Ascent of the tower – A staircase *(200 steps)* near the left-hand door, leads to the top of the tower, passing under the rafters above the narthex.

There is a more extensive **view★** from the platform than from the terrace: the old town, the valley of the Cure, the northern part of the Morvan (southeast) and the Auxerrois (north).

ADDITIONAL SIGHTS

Promenade des Fossés – *From Place du Champ-de-Foire at the lower end of the town follow Promenade des Fossés.*
The road is laid out on the line of the ramparts which encircled the town in the Middle Ages and which were punctuated by seven round towers.
The 14C-16C **Porte Neuve,** which bears the coat of arms of the town of Vézelay, is flanked by two rusticated towers with machicolations and opens on to a charming promenade shaded by walnut trees. From (**Porte Ste-Croix** or the Porte des Cordeliers), which provides a good view of the Cure Valley, a path leads down to La Cordelle where St Bernard preached the Second Crusade in 1146; a cross commemorates the great event.
The promenade ends at the château terrace behind the basilica.

Old houses – *Walk up from Place du Champ-de-Foire to the basilica of Ste-Madeleine*
The narrow winding streets still contain many old houses in the picturesque setting of the old town: carved doorways, mullioned windows, corbelled staircase turrets and old wells surmounted by wrought-iron wellheads.

VILLEFRANCHE-SUR-SAÔNE

Population 55 249
Michelin map 99 fold 7 or 244 folds 2 and 3 - Town plan in the current
Michelin Red Guide France – Local map under BEAUJOLAIS

This busy industrial and commercial city is the capital of the **Beaujolais** *(qv)* region. It was founded in 1140 by the lords of Beaujeu *(qv)*, as part of the Anse fortress belonging to the Archbishops of Lyon, to defend the toll house of Limans. The settlement sprang up quickly, and in 1260 Guichard IV de Beaujeu granted the town a charter, which earned it the name of "Villefranche" or "free town".

"La Vague"

"La Vague" – Every year, on the last Sunday in January, army recruits celebrate the **"Fête des Conscrits"**. Those eligible to take part are men between the ages of 20 and 80 years. Dress for the occasion is a black suit and top hat, decorated with a coloured ribbon (different colour for each decade: 20s, 30s etc.). At 1100 the participants form up into a procession, in which they link arms and, clutching colourful bouquets of mimosa and carnations, make their way along the 2km - 1 mile long Rue Nationale close on each others heels, in what is known as the "Friendship wave" *(La Vague de l'Amitié)*.

Modern Villefranche – In addition to its historical role as a wine trading centre, Villefranche now earns its living from the manufacture of sports and work wear (Joannès Sabot founded an overalls factory here in 1887), shirts and hosiery. The metallurgy and mechanical industries are also represented here.

SIGHTS

Old houses ⊘ – Most of the town's oldest houses built between the 15 and 18C are to be found along the **Rue Nationale** (**BYZ**). They have relatively narrow façades, because of a tax imposed on the width of house façades in 1260, to make up for the exemption from taxes and other privileges which had been granted to the town in its charter.

Odd numbered side of the road – Note nos 375 (vaulted passageway), 401 (16C openwork spiral staircase in the courtyard), no 17 Rue Grenette (**BY** – turret staircase with skylights) and 507 (well surmounted by a shell-shaped canopy in the courtyard). No 523,

**VILLEFRANCHE
SUR-SAÔNE**

Nationale (R.).......... **BYZ**

Belleville (R. de)...........BY 5	République (R. de la)..AZ 41
Carnot (Pl.).....................BZ 9	Salengro (Bd Roger)....AY 46
Faucon (R. du)...............BY 19	Savigny (R. J.-M.)........AZ 47
Fayettes (R. des) ....BZ 20	Sous-Préfecture (Pl.)....AZ 49
Grange-Blazet (R.)........BZ 23	Sous-Préfecture (R.).....AZ 50
Marais (Pl. des) ....BZ 32	Stalingrad (R. de).........BZ 52

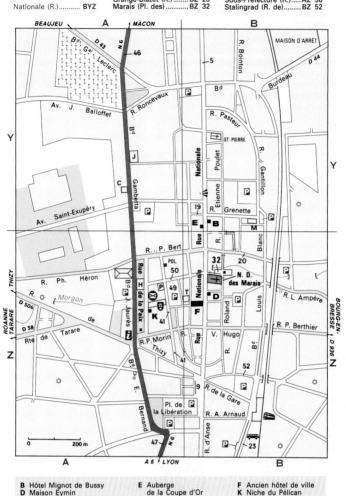

B Hôtel Mignot de Bussy
D Maison Eymin

E Auberge
de la Coupe d'Or

F Ancien hôtel de ville
K Niche du Pélican

the **Hôtel Mignot de Bussy** (**BY B**) is a lovely Renaissance building with a spiral stair-case, mullion windows and shell-shaped niche containing an elegant statue. Behind the 1760 façade of no 561, a vaulted passage with sculpted supports leads to a 16C courtyard surrounded by pink walled buildings. The **Maison Eymin** (**BZ D**) at no 761 has an 18C façade with four levels of arches in the courtyard, hammer-wrought coats of arms (damaged) and an elegant turret housing a spi-ral staircase. No 793, once the residence of the Roland de la Platière family, is indicated by a medallion and a commemorative plaque and features a monumen-tal staircase with a beautiful wrought iron banister.

Even numbered side of the road – From no 400, there is a good view of the polygonal tower and sculpted stone balustrade of the Italian Renaissance house at no 407 oppo-site. A 15C half-timbered house stands on the corner of Rue du Faucon (**BY 19**) and the Rue Nationale (no 476). At no 486, at the back of the alley on the right, a Renaissance bas relief depicts two cherubs with chubby cheeks holding coats of arms with the date 1537.

The **Auberge de la Coupe d'Or** (**BY E**) at no 528 was the oldest inn in Villefranche (late 14C) before being transformed in the 17C. On the corner of Rue Paul-Bert, the façade on the right (no 596) with crocket gables dates from the late 15C and that on the left with moulded mullion windows and medallions is Renaissance. Note the Gothic corner niche at no 706. A passage at no 810 leads to a restored courtyard (well, arcade and turret).

The old **town hall** at no 816 (**BZ F**) was completed in 1660. The façade is built of beautiful warm golden Jarnious stone and has a solid oak door decorated with cast iron nails. The house at no 834 was built in the late 15C and still has a charming courtyard with a staircase turret. The coat of arms is that of Pierre II of Bourbon and Anne de Beaujeu.

Rue de la Paix (**AZ**) – The façade of the building to the south of the Post Office features a "pelican niche" (**AZ K**), a Gothic sculpture decorated with finials and pinnacles. Next to it, set slightly further back, is a pretty Renaissance fountain.

Place des Marais (**BZ** 32) – This pretty square to the north east of the church contains a fountain and is enclosed by modern houses with arcades, painted in shades of pink and ochre. On the corner with Rue Nationale, a ceramic plaque depicts Pierre de Bourbon and Anne de Beaujeu in the same pose as that on the famous triptych by the Master of Moulins.

Notre-Dame-des-Marais (**BZ**) ⊘ – In the 13C a chapel was built in honour of a statue of the Virgin Mary which had been found in a nearby marsh *(marais)*; all that now remains is the small Romanesque tower above the chancel. The magnificent Late Gothic (16C) façade of the church was donated by Pierre de Bourbon and Anne de Beaujeu. Inside, the nave is surprisingly high and has pretty vaulting decorated with sculpture and pendant keystones. The organ was made by J Callinet in 1835. Note the gargoyles on the north façade; one of them represents lust.

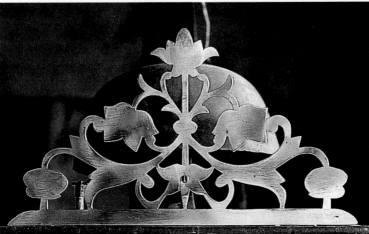

NOVISSIMA TIBI LATET HORA

MAXIMIN CATTIN DU FORT DU PLASNE AN CONTE

Practical
Information

Travelling to France

Before you leave – For information, brochures, maps and assistance in planning a trip to France travellers should apply to the **French Government Tourist Office** in their own country:

Australia Kindersley House, 33 Bligh St, Sydney, New South Wales 2000, ☎ 612 231 52 44.

Canada 30 St Patrick's Street, Suite 700, Toronto, ONT M5T 3A3, ☎ 416-593-4723.
1981 Avenue McGill College, Suite 490, Montreal, PQ H3A 2W9, ☎ 514-288-4264.

Eire c/o 38 Lower Abbey St, Dublin, ☎ 01 300 777.

UK 178 Piccadilly, London WIV OAL, ☎ 0171 499 6911 (24-hour answering service with recorded message and information) or ☎ 0171 491 7622 (urgent enquiries only).

USA France On Call Hotline: 900-990-0040 (US$.50 per min) for information on hotels, restaurants and transportation.
610 Fifth Avenue, New York, NY 10020, ☎ 212-757-1125.
676 North Michigan Avenue, Suite 3360, Chicago, IL 60611, ☎ 312-751-7800.
9454 Wilshire Boulevard, Suite 715, Beverly Hills, CA 90212, ☎ 310-271-2358.

How to get there – You can travel **by air** with scheduled national airlines, or by commercial and package-tour flights, with rail or coach link-ups or Fly-Drive schemes – contact airlines and travel agents for information. France's domestic network (Air Inter) operates frequent services covering the whole country (there is an airport at Dijon).

There are numerous **cross-Channel services** from the UK and Eire (passenger and car ferries, hovercraft, Sea Cat etc.) – for details, apply to travel agencies or:

Brittany Ferries, Millbay Docks, Plymouth, Devon PLI 3EW, ☎ 01752 221 321. The Brittany Centre, Wharf Road, Portsmouth, Hampshire PO2 8RU, ☎ 01705 827701.
Tourist House, 42 Grand Parade, Cork, Eire, ☎ 0121 277801.

Hoverspeed, Maybrook House, Queens Gardens, Dover, Kent CT17 9UQ, ☎ 01304 240241, direct lines from London 0181 554 7061, Birmingham 0121 236 2190 or Manchester 0161 228 1321.

P & O European Ferries, Channel House, Channel View Road, Dover, Kent CT17 9TJ, ☎ 01304 203 388.
Ticket collection: Russell St, Dover Kent CT16 1QB.
The Continental Ferry Port, Mile End, Portsmouth, Hampshire PO2 8QW, ☎ 01705 827677.
European House, The Docks, Felixstowe, Suffolk IP11 8TB, ☎ 01394 604040.
Larne Harbour, Larne, Co. Antrim, Northern Ireland BT40 1AQ, ☎ 01574 274321.

Sally Ferries, 81 Piccadilly, London WIV 9HF, ☎ 0171 409 2240.
Argyle Centre, York St, Ramsgate, Kent, CT11 9DS, ☎ 01843 595566.

Stena Sealink Line, Charter House, Park St, Ashford, Kent TN24 8EX, ☎ 01233 647047.
Newhaven Harbour, Newhaven, East Sussex BN9 0BQ, ☎ 01273 512266.

If you are travelling **by rail**, British Rail offers a range of services to the Channel ports, and the French railways (SNCF) operate an extensive network including many high-speed passenger trains (TGV) and motorail services throughout France. Tickets bought in France must be validated *(composté)* in the orange automatic date-stamping machines at the platform entrance. Information and bookings from French Railways, 179 Piccadilly, London WIV OBA, ☎ 0171 409 3518, and from the main British and American Travel Centres and travel agencies.

The **Channel Tunnel** operates two rail services linking Folkestone and Calais undersea: the "Eurostar" service, with direct high-speed French (SNCF), Belgian (SNCB) and British Rail passenger and goods trains; and "Le Shuttle", with cars, coaches and motorcycles on passenger shuttles, and heavy goods vehicles on freight shuttles. The journey time is 35 min, 28 min of which are in the tunnel itself at a maximum speed of 130kph-80mph. At the Calais terminal, sliproads feed directly into the French motorway network. "Le Shuttle" will eventually operate 24 hours a day throughout the year, the number of departures being determined by the volume of traffic. For information and ticket reservations, call Le Shuttle passenger enquiries on ☎ 01303 271100, or consult the French Telecom videotex service, Minitel *(qv)*, under the code 3615 LESHUTTLE.

Regular **coach services** are operated from London to Paris and large provincial towns – for details, contact:

Euroways/Eurolines, 52 Grosvenor Gardens, Victoria, London SWIW OAU, ☎ 0171 730 8235.

Hoverspeed, Maybrook House, Queens Gardens, Dover, Kent CT17 9UQ, ☎ 01304 240241, direct lines from London 0181 554 7061, Birmingham 0121 236 2190 or Manchester 0161 228 1321.

Customs and other formalities – Despite the new law which came into force on 1 January 1993 authorising the free flow of goods and people within the EC, it is nonetheless advisable that travellers should be equipped with some valid piece of identification such as a **passport**. Holders of British, Irish and US passports require no visa to enter France for a stay of less than three months. Visas may be necessary for visitors from some Commonwealth countries, and for those planning to stay longer than three months. Apply to the French Consulate (visa issued the same day; delay if application submitted by mail). US citizens should obtain the booklet *Your trip abroad* (US$1.25) which provides useful information on visa requirements, customs regulations, medical care etc. for international travellers. Apply to the Superintendent of Documents, PO Box 371954, Pittsburgh, PA 15250-7954, ☎ 202-783-3238.

Apply to the Customs Office (UK) for a leaflet *(A Guide for Travellers)* on **customs regulations** and the full range of duty-free allowances. The US Customs Service (PO Box 7407, Washington, DC 20044, ☎ 202-927-5580) offers a free publication *Know before you go* for US citizens. There are no customs formalities for holidaymakers bringing their caravans into France for a stay of less than six months. No customs document is necessary (although this is currently under review) for pleasure boats and outboard motors for a stay of less than six months, but the registration document should be kept on board.

Embassies and Consulates

Australia	Embassy	4, rue Jean-Rey, 75015 Paris, ☎ 40 59 33 00.
Canada	Embassy	35, avenue Montaigne, 75008 Paris, ☎ 44 43 29 00.
Eire	Embassy	4, rue Rude, 75016 Paris, ☎ 45 00 20 87.
New Zealand	Embassy	7ter, rue Léonard-de-Vinci, 75016 Paris, ☎ 45 00 24 11.
UK	Embassy	35, rue du Faubourg St-Honoré, 75008 Paris, ☎ 42 66 91 42.
	Consulate	9, avenue Hoche, 75008 Paris, ☎ 42 66 38 10.
		16, rue d'Anjou, 75008 Paris, ☎ 42 66 06 68 (visas).
USA	Embassy	2, avenue Gabriel, 75008 Paris, ☎ 42 96 12 02.
	Consulate	2, rue St-Florentin, 75001 Paris, ☎ 42 96 14 88.

Motoring in France

Documents – Nationals of EU countries require a valid national **driving licence**; nationals of non-EU countries require an International driving licence (obtainable in the US from the American Automobile Association for US$10).

For the vehicle, it is necessary to have the **registration papers** (log-book) and a **nationality plate** of the approved size.

Insurance – Insurance cover is compulsory, and although an International Insurance Certificate (Green Card) is no longer a legal requirement in France, it is the most effective proof of insurance cover and is internationally recognised by the police and other authorities.

Certain UK motoring organisations (the AA and RAC; Routiers, 25 Vanston Place, London SW6, ☎ 0171 385 6644) run accident insurance and breakdown service schemes for members. Europ-Assistance (252 High St, Croydon London CRO 1NF) also has special policies for motorists. Members of the American Automobile Association should obtain the free brochure *Offices to serve you abroad*. The affiliated organisation for France is: Automobile Club National, 5 Rue Auber, 75009 Paris, ☎ 44 51 53 99.

Highway Code – The minimum age for driving is 18 years Old. Traffic drives on the right. It is compulsory for front-seat passengers to wear **seat-belts**; all back-seat passengers should wear seat-belts where they are fitted. Children under the age of ten should be on the back seat.

Full or dipped headlights must switched on in poor visibility and at night: use sidelights only when the vehicle is stationary. In the case of a **breakdown**, a red warning triangle or hazard warning lights are obligatory.

In France, **priority** must be ceded to vehicles joining the road from the **right**: it is particularly important to remember this in built-up areas, where there are often no road markings to remind visitors to slow down as they approach little side roads or minor crossroads. Outside built-up areas, however, traffic on main roads (indicated by a yellow diamond sign) and roundabouts does have priority. Having stopped for a red traffic light at a road junction, vehicles may be allowed to filter to the right by a flashing amber arrow; remember that pedestrians crossing the road into which you are turning have priority.

Regulations on **drink-driving** and **speeding** are strictly enforced – usually by an on-the-spot fine and/or confiscation of the vehicle.

Speed limits (liable to modification) are as follows:
- toll motorways *(péage)* 130kph - 80mph (110kph - 68mph when raining);
- dual carriageways and motorways without tolls 110kph - 68mph (100kph - 62mph when raining);
- other roads 90kph - 56mph (80kph - 50mph when raining);
- in towns 50kph - 31mph;
- outside lane on motorways during daylight, on level ground and with good visibility minimum speed limit of 80kph - 50mph.

Parking regulations – In town there are restricted and paying **parking zones** (blue and grey zones); tickets must be obtained from the ticket machines (*horodateurs* – small change necessary) and displayed inside the windscreen on the driver's side; failure to display may result in a heavy fine or the offending vehicle being towed away.

Car Rental – There are car rental agencies at airports, air terminals, railway stations and in all large towns throughout France. European cars usually have manual transmission but automatic cars are available on demand. An international driving licence is required for non-EU nationals. Fly-Drive schemes are operated by major airlines.

Route Planning – For 24-hour road information: dial 48 94 33 33 or consult the Minitel *(see below)* 3615 code ROUTE.
See page 3 for the **Michelin maps** covering the Burgundy and Jura regions.

3615 MICHELIN Minitel Service

Michelin Travel Assistance (AMI) is a computerised route finding system offering integrated information on roads, tourist sights, hotels and restaurants. 3615 MICHELIN is one of the French Telecom videotex services.

3615 MICHELIN: access code to connect with the service.

Route planning: give your point of departure and destination, stipulate your preference for motorways or local roads, indicate the sights to see along the way, and it will do the rest.

Lunchtime or overnight stops: now look for that special restaurant, secluded country hotel or pleasant campsite along the chosen route.

Where to find Minitel terminals: public terminals are usually to be found in all post offices, some petrol stations and hotels (overs six million terminals in France). The cost of consulting 3615 MICHELIN is 1.27F per minute. This user-friendly travel service is available round the clock.

Field of operation: this outstanding European and road tourist data base covers most European countries.

Have a good journey!

Accommodation

See the Places to Stay map in the Introduction.

Loisirs-Accueil is an officially backed booking service which has offices in most French *départements*. For information, contact Réservation Loisirs-Accueil, 17, rue Ingénieur Robert Keller, 75015 Paris, ☎ 40 59 44 12 (Minitel code: 3615 SLA).

Local branches:

Ain, 34, rue du Général-Delestraint, BP 78, 01002 Bourg-en-Bresse Cedex, ☎ 74 21 95 00.

Doubs, 4ter, faubourg Rivotte, 25000 Besançon, ☎ 81 82 80 48.

Haute-Saône - Territoire de Belfort, 6, rue des Bains, BP 117, 70000 Vesoul Cedex, ☎ 84 75 43 66.

Jura, write to: Hôtel du Département, BP 652, 39021 Lons-le-Saunier Cedex, ☎ 84 85 89 82; apply in person to: 8, av. du 44e-R.I., 39000 Lons-le-Saunier, ☎ 84 24 57 70.

Loiret, 8, rue d'Escures, 45000 Orléans, ☎ 38 62 04 88.

Nièvre, 3, rue du Sort, 58000 Nevers, ☎ 86 59 14 22.

Yonne, 1 et 2, quai de la République, 89000 Auxerre, ☎ 86 51 12 05.

The "**Accueil de France**" tourist offices which are open all year make hotel bookings for a small fee, for personal callers only. The head office is in Paris (127, avenue des Champs-Élysées, 75008 Paris, ☎ 49 52 53 54 for information only) and there are offices in many large towns and resorts. The brochure *Logis et Auberges de France* is available from the French Government Tourist Office.

Rural accommodation - Apply to Maison des Gîtes de France, 35, rue Godot-de-Mauroy, 75009 Paris (☎ 49 70 75 75) or 178 Piccadilly, London WIV 0AL (☎ 0171 493 3480) for a list of relevant addresses, including **bed and breakfast** accommodation (*chambres d'hôte*). Consult the Minitel service also, code 3615 Gîtes de France. Those in search of accommodation during walking or cycling tours should refer to the guide *Gîtes, Refuges, France et frontières* by A. and S. Mouraret, Éditions La Cadole, BP 303, 75723 Paris Cedex 15, ☎ 45 75 45 36.

Youth Hostels – There are many youth hostels throughout France. Holders of an International Youth Hostel Federation card should apply for a list from the International Federation or from the French Youth Hostels Association: La Ligue Française des Auberges de Jeunesse, 38, boulevard Raspail, 75007 Paris, ☎ 45 48 69 84.
Hostelling International/American Youth Hostel Association (☎ 202-783-6161) offers a publication *International Hostel Guide for Europe* (US$13.95). The publication is also available to non-members.

Electricity – The electric current is 220 volts. Circular two-pin plugs are the rule – an electrical adaptor may be necessary.

General information

Medical Treatment – First aid, medical advice and chemists' night service rota are available from chemists (*pharmacies* – green cross sign).

It is advisable to take out comprehensive insurance cover, as the recipient of medical treatment in French hospitals or clinics must pay the bill. Nationals of non-EU countries should check with their insurance companies about policy limitations. Reimbursement can then be negotiated with the insurance company according to the policy held. All prescription drugs should be clearly labelled; it is recommended to carry a copy of the prescription.

American Express offers its cardholders a service, "Global Assist", for any medical, legal or personal emergency – call collect from anywhere ☏ 202-554-2639 (available to Amex cardholders only).

British citizens should apply to the Department of Health and Social Security for a **Form E111** which entitles the holder to urgent treatment for accident or unexpected illness in EU countries. A refund of part of the costs of treatment can be obtained on application in person or by post to the local Social Security Office (Caisse Primaire d'Assurance Maladie).

Currency – There are no restrictions on the amount of currency visitors can take into France. Visitors wishing to export currency in foreign banknotes in excess of the given allocation from France should complete a currency declaration form on arrival.

Banks – Banks are open from 0900 to 1200 and 1400 to 1600 and are closed on Monday or Saturday (except if market day); some branches open for limited transactions on Saturday. Banks close early on the day before a bank holiday. A passport is necessary as identification when cashing cheques in banks. Travellers' cheques are exchangeable at banks, or bureaux de change found at airport terminals and larger railway stations and in some hotels and shops. Commission charges vary and hotels usually charge more than banks for cashing cheques for non-residents. Most banks have cash dispensers which accept international credit cards.

Credit cards – American Express, Carte Bleue (Visa/Barclaycard), Diners Club and Eurocard (Mastercard/Access) are widely accepted in shops, supermarkets, hotels, restaurants and petrol stations.

Post – Post Offices open Monday to Friday 0800 to 1900, Saturday 0800 to 1200. Postage via airmail: letter or postcard to UK 2.80F; aerogramme to USA 5.00F; letter (20 g) or postcard to USA 4.30F. Stamps are also available from newsagents and tobacconists.

Poste Restante mail should be addressed as follows: Name, *Poste Restante, Poste Centrale*, postal code of *département* followed by town name, France. The **Michelin Red Guide France** gives local postal codes.

Telephone – Public phones using pre-paid phone cards *(télécartes)* are in opération in many areas. The cards (50 or 120 units) which are available from post offices, newsagents and tobacconists can be used for inland and international calls. Calls can be received at phone boxes where the blue bell sign is shown.

Internal calls – When calling within either of the two main zones (French provinces or Paris and its region) dial only the 8-digit correspondent's number. From Paris to the provinces dial 16 + 8-digit number. From the provinces to Paris dial 16 + 1 + 8-digit number. After a few initial rapid pips, the French ringing tone is a series of long tones (slightly longer than those of the British engaged tone); the French engaged (busy) tone is a series of short beeps.

International calls – For Paris dial the country code 33 + 1 + 8-digit number. For the provinces dial the country code 33 + 8-digit number.

When calling abroad from France dial 19, wait until the continuous tone recurs, then dial the country code and dialling code and number of your correspondent. For international enquiries dial 19 33 12 + country code.

Telephone rates from a public phone at any time are: Paris-London about 4.30F for 1 minute; Paris-New York about 7F for 1 minute. Cheap rates with 50% extra time are available on weekdays between 2230 and 0800, and at weekends starting at 1400 on Saturdays.

Shopping – The big stores and large shops are open Monday to Saturday 0900 to 1830-1930; smaller, individual shops may close during the lunch hour. Food shops – grocers, wine merchants and bakeries – are open from 0700 to 1830-1930; some open on Sunday mornings. Many food shops close between 1200 and 1400 and on Mondays. Hypermarkets are usually open until 2100-2200.

Public Holidays – The following are days when museums and other monuments may be closed or may vary their hours of admission:

New Year's Day	France's National Day (14 July)
Easter Day and Easter Monday	Assumption (15 August)
May Day (1 May)	All Saint's Day (1 November)
VE Day (8 May)	Armistice Day (11 November)
Ascension Day	Christmas Day
Whit Sunday and Monday	

National museums and art galleries are closed on Tuesdays whereas municipal museums are closed on Mondays. In addition to the usual school holidays at Christmas and in the spring and summer, there are long mid-term breaks (10 days to a fortnight) in February and early November.

Tourist information

Local Tourist Offices – These provide tourist information at regional and *département* level:

Comité régional du tourisme de Bourgogne – Conseil régional, BP 1602, 21035 Dijon Cedex, ☎ 80 50 10 20.

Comité régional du tourisme de Franche-Comté – 9, rue de Pontarlier, 25044 Besançon Cedex, ☎ 81 83 50 47.

Comité départemental de tourisme de l'**Ain** – 34, rue du Général-Delestraint, BP 78, 01002 Bourg-en-Bresse Cedex, ☎ 74 21 95 00.

Association départementale de tourisme du Territoire de **Belfort** – Hôtel du Département, place de la Révolution-Française, 90020 Belfort, ☎ 84 21 27 95.

Comité départemental du tourisme de la **Côte-d'Or** – Hôtel du Département, BP 1601, 21035 Dijon Cedex, ☎ 80 63 66 00.

Conseil général, service du tourisme du **Doubs** – Hôtel du Département, 7, avenue de la Gare-d'Eau, 25031 Besançon Cedex, ☎ 81 83 24 31.

Comité départemental du tourisme de **Haute-Saône** – Maison du tourisme, 6, rue des Bains, BP 117, 70002 Vesoul Cedex, ☎ 84 75 43 66.

Comité départemental du tourisme du **Jura** – Hôtel du Département, 8, avenue du 44e-R.I., BP 652, 39021 Lons-le-Saunier, ☎ 84 24 57 70.

Comité départemental du tourisme du **Loiret** – 8, rue d'Escures, 45000 Orléans, ☎ 38 54 83 83.

Comité départemental du tourisme de la **Nièvre** – 3, rue du Sort, 80000 Nevers, ☎ 86 36 39 80.

Comité départemental du tourisme de **Saône-et-Loire** – 389, av. de Lattre-de-Tassigny, 71000 Mâcon, ☎ 85 38 27 92.

Comité départemental du tourisme de l'**Yonne** – 1, quai de la République, 89000 Auxerre, ☎ 86 51 12 05.

Maison de la Franche-Comté – 2, boulevard de la Madeleine, 75009 Paris, ☎ 42 66 26 28.

The addresses and telephone numbers of the **tourist information centres** *(syndicats d'initiative)* of most large towns and tourist resorts may be found among the Admission Times and Charges at the back of this guide, and in the **Michelin Red Guide France**. They can supply large-scale town plans, timetables and information on local entertainment facilities, sports and sight-seeing

Tourism for the Disabled – Some of the sights described in this guide are accessible to handicapped people and are indicated in the Admission Times and Charges section with the symbol ⅃. The booklet *Touristes quand même! Promenades en France pour les Voyageurs Handicapés* published by the Comité National Français de Liaison pour le Réadaptation des Handicapés, 236bis, rue Tolbiac, 75013 Paris, ☎ 53 80 66 66, covers nearly 90 towns in France and provides practical information for people who suffer reduced mobility, or visual or aural impairment. Another useful publication is the *Guide Rousseau des Handicaps* (SCOP, 4, rue Gustave-Rouanet, 75018 Paris, ☎ 42 52 97 00). The **Michelin Red Guide France** and **Michelin Guide Camping Caravaning France** indicate hotels and campsites with facilities suitable for physically handicapped people.

Some books to read

A Concise History of France - R Price (Cambridge University Press)
A Holiday History of France - R Hamilton
Brillat-Savarin: The Judge and his Stomach - G Macdonogh (John Murray)
France Today - J Ardagh (Penguin)
In Beaujolais - M Buller (Thames and Hudson)
Le Corbusier 1910-1965 - W Boesiger and H Girsberger (Artemis)
Long Ago in France - MFK Fisher (Flamingo)
Puligny Montrachet (Journal of a village in Burgundy) - S Loftus (Penguin)
Slow Boat Through France - H McKnight (David and Charles)
The Spirit of Burgundy - R Gibson (Aperture)
The Wine Lover's Guide to France - M Busselle (Pavilion Michael Joseph)

Refreshment

Don't forget to consult the latest **Michelin Red Guide France** when choosing where to stop and eat. It contains a selection of restaurants to suit a variety of pockets and tastes. *See also the chapter on Gastronomy in the Introduction.*

Culinary specialities from Burgundy include *escargots* (snails), *poulet de Bresse* (chicken) and *cuisses de grenouille* (frog's legs), which can be found in charming little inns along the banks of the Saône and the Seille. For those moments when a little something is called for in between meals, try local gingerbread, or sweets made from aniseed or blackcurrant. In the wine-producing region, many producers allow visitors to taste their wines on the spot, sometimes with bread and cheese or meat to soak it up.

Maison régionale des Arts de la table — 15, rue St-Jacques, 21230 Arnay-le-Duc, ☎ 80 90 11 59.

Culinary specialities from the Jura include *jambon de Luxeuil* (ham), *jésus de cerf* (venison sausage), *brési* (smoked beef),

Smoking meat in the Jura

smoked Morteau or Montbéliard sausage, *morilles* (wild mushrooms), cheese such as Bleu de Gex, Morbier, Cancoillotte and of course the famous Comté, which is used to make a rich local fondue dish. All these are washed down nicely by local Jura wines.

Discovering the region

Bird's-eye views

Hang-gliding and paragliding – The Jura region is ideally suited to these air-borne sports. Hang-gliding is the more complicated of the two, requiring a degree of technical understanding of aerodynamics. Beginners should only attempt either under properly qualified supervision.

École de Vol libre du Poupet, St-Thiébaud, 39110 Salins-les-Bains, ☎ 84 73 09 71. Aux Rousses (maiden flights on paraglider for two), Bar le Rousseland, route N 5, 39220 Les Rousses, ☎ 84 60 03 72.

Hot air balloon – Air Escargot, 71150 Remigny. ☎ 85 87 08 84.
Air Adventures, av. du Général-de-Gaulle, 21320 Pouilly-en-Auxois.
Bombard Balloon Adventures, château de Laborde, 21200 Meursanges, ☎ 80 26 63 30.
Bourgogne Tour Incoming, 14, rue du Chapeau-Rouge, 21000 Dijon, ☎ 80 30 49 49.

Helicopter – Helijob, BP 25, aéroport de Bourgogne, 21600 Longvic. ☎ 80 67 88 64.

Tourist plane – Aéroclub beaunois, aérodrome de Beaune-Challanges, route de Seurre, 21000 Beaune. ☎ 80 22 21 93.

Lakes and reservoirs in the Jura

The ideal setting for windsurfing, water-skiing, fishing, rambling around the lake shore and so on.

	Map reference		Altitude	Surface area (in hectares)	Maximum depth (in metres)	Resorts nearby
Abbaye	243	31	887	97	27	
Allement (Barrage)	244	5	267	225	23	
Antre	243	42	800	5	13	
Barterand	244	17	300	19	15	
Bonlieu	243	31	850	22	28	Bonlieu
Chaillexon	243	21	748	80	30	
Chalain	243	30	492	232	45	Marigny
Chambly	243	31	502	33	30	
Champagney (Bassin)	243	9	412	328	25	Champagney
Cize-Bolozon (Barrage)	244	5	283	263	24	
Clairvaux (Grand Lac)	243	30	525	64	25	
Coiselet (Barrage)	244	5	304	380	21	
Divonne-les-Bains	243	44	466	44	3	
Etival (Grand Lac)	243	42	790	17	13	
Genin	243	42	836	8	18	
Ilay	243	31	802	79	30	Ilay
Lamoura	243	43	1050	5	10	
Maclu (Grand Lac)	243	31	700	25	25	Ilay
Malsaucy (Étang)	243	10	390	62	4	
Nantua	244	6	475	141	43	Nantua
Narlay	243	31	800	42	48	Ilay
Rousses	243	32	1075	100	25	Les Rousses
St-Point	243	32	850	398	40	Malbuisson
Sylans	244	6	584	50	22	Nantua
Val	243	31	504	50	28	
Vernois	243	29	740	30	10	
Vouglans (Barrage)	244	6	430	1700	100	Maisod

Leisure cruising

Boating in Burgundy – Three rivers – the Yonne, the Saône and its tributary the Seille – together with several canals or stretches of canal provide about 1 200 km - 1 931 miles of navigable waterway for those who would like to visit Burgundy by boat.
Some of the ports beside the waterways offer organised cruises lasting a few hours or several days (excursion craft, cabin cruisers) or cabin cruisers for hire.

Holiday barge on a canal in Burgundy

H. Gyssels/DIAF

Winter in the Haut-Jura

No licence is required to hire a boat but the helmsman must be an adult; a practical and theoretical lesson is given at the beginning of the hire period. To pilot such a boat successfully one must observe the speed limits and heed the advice of the hirer, particularly when mooring or passing through locks.

For information about cruises and hiring boats *(embarkation ports are marked on the map)* apply to the tourist information centre of the appropriate town or to "Bourgogne Voies Navigables". 1-2, quai de la République, 89000 Auxerre, ☎ 86 52 18 99.

Information such as navigational advice, useful addresses, and tourist information along the waterways is available from Navicartes (9, quai de l'Artois, 94170 Le Perreux-sur-Marne), which publishes navigational maps, and from Guides Vagnon, Les Éditions du Plaisancier, BP 27, 69641 Caluire Cedex.

Boating in the Jura region – The Jura region offers its fair share of rivers (the Saône and the Doubs), canals (Canal de l'Est and Canal Rhin-Rhône) and lakes (Lac de Vouglans) – all in all, over 320km - 200 miles of waterways – to boating enthusiasts, who can either opt for a cruise *(see under Besançon, Gray and Vouglans in the Admission Times and Charges section)* or hire their own craft. Those intending to leave from Dol or Mont-béliard (along the Canal Rhin-Rhône) should enquire at Nicols locations, route du Puy-St-Bonnet, 49300 Cholet, ☎ 41 56 46 56. Those leaving from Corre (Michelin map 66 fold 5) along the Saône and the Canal de l'Est should enquire at Locaboat Plaisance, Port-au-Bois, 89300 Joigny, ☎ 86 91 72 72.

Local history trails

All over France, since 1975, *routes historiques* have been designated by the Caisse nationale des Monuments historiques et des Sites (62, rue St-Antoine, 75004 Paris, ☎ 44 61 21 50), with a view to helping visitors to a region to discover more about its historical monuments. These itineraries are described in leaflets available from the CNMHS. For the region described in this guide, the *routes historiques* are: Route des Ducs de Bourgogne, Route des Trésors de la Puisaye, Route Buissonière (this stretches from the Paris region to the Rhône valley and the Alps).

Nature parks

Parc naturel régional du Morvan – Maison du Parc à St-Brisson, 58230 Montsauche, ☎ 86 78 70 16.

Parc naturel régional du Haut-Jura – Maison du Haut-Jura, 39310 Lajoux, ☎ 84 41 20 37 *(see also under ST-CLAUDE: Excursion)*.

Parc naturel régional des Ballons des Vosges – Mairie, 90200 Giromagny, ☎ 84 29 56 51 (Territoire de Belfort); Mairie, 70440 Château-Lambert, ☎ 84 20 49 84 (Haute-Saône).

Spa towns

Besides traditional spa treatments, these offer various health and fitness courses combining sport, rest... and a supervised diet !.

Divonne-les-Bains – Thermes Paul Vidart, avenue des Thermes, BP 66, 01220, ☎ 50 20 05 70.

Lons-le-Saunier – Thermes Ledonia, Parc des Bains, BP 181, 39000, ☎ 84 24 20 34.

Luxeuil-les-Bains – Établissement thermal, avenue des Thermes, BP 93, 70303, ☎ 84 40 44 22.

Salins-les-Bains – Les Thermes, place des Alliés, 39110, ☎ 84 73 04 63.

For further general information: Association des villes thermales de Franche-Comté, Hôtel de Ville, place du 8-Septembre, 25000 Besançon, ☎ 81 81 87 50.

Tourist trains

Many of these are steam driven and operate along pretty, renovated stretches of railway in the Burgundy region.

Petit train de la Côte-d'Or – APTCO, gare de Plombières-Canal, 21370 Plombières-lès-Dijon, ☏ 80 45 88 51, runs along the Ouche and the Canal de Bourgogne *(journey time: 1 hour 20 min)*, 1 July to 15 September daily.

Train touristique des "Lavières" – 6, rue des Capucins, 21120 Is-sur-Tille, ☏ 80 95 36 36, runs through the pine forest near Is-sur-Tille, mid-June to mid-September on Sundays from 1500 to 1900, 6F.

Chemin de fer de la vallée de l'Ouche – 4, rue Pasumot, 21200 Beaune, ☏ 80 22 86 35, steam or diesel train along the old track between Dijon and Bligny, leaving from Bligny-sur-Ouche.

Chemin de fer des Combes – ☏ 85 55 26 23, May to October at weekends, gives a good view of Le Creusot and surroundings.

Chemin de fer touristique de Puisaye – Avenue de la Gare, 89130 Toucy, ☏ 86 44 05 58, along the old track from Montargis to St-Sauveur.

P'tit train de l'Yonne – ATPVM, 89440 Angely, ☏ 86 33 81 20, 5km – 3 miles through the Serein valley between Massangis and Civry, May to September on Sundays and public holidays from 1500 to 1730 (every half hour), 25F, children: 20F.

Vineyards and wine tasting

In **Burgundy**, the Bureau interprofessionnel des Vins de Bourgogne organises wine tasting *(dégustation)* courses (1 to 5 days) and publishes a leaflet (*Visites et dégustations de vignes en caves*, 15F) on the cellars which are open to visitors and offer wine tasting (available from local tourist offices or the following addresses: Rue Henri-Dunan, 21200 Beaune, ☏ 80 22 21 35; 389, avenue de Lattre-de-Tassigny, 71000 Mâcon, ☏ 85 38 20 15; Le Petit Pontigny, 1, rue de Chichée, BP 31, 89800 Chablis, ☏ 86 42 42 22).

There are a dozen "wine routes" through the Mâcon and Beaujolais regions, signposted "Suivez la grappe", which include churches, abbeys and châteaux as well as wine-growing establishments. Details from Route des vins Mâconnais-Beaujolais, 8, rue Dufour, 71000 Mâcon, ☏ 85 38 09 99.

Tourist offices can also give details on any local wine appreciation societies *(confréries)* which allow visitors to participate in their activities.

The **Maison Mâconnaise des vins**, 484, av. de Lattre-de-Tassigny, 71000 Mâcon, ☏ 85 38 36 70, and the **Maison des vins de la Côte chalonnaise**, promenade Ste-Marie, 71100 Chalons-sur-Saône ☏ 85 41 64 00 offer wine tasting on their premises.

In the **Beaujolais** region, there are numerous wine tasting opportunities, often in the local wine cooperatives *(caves coopératives)*. It is advisable to telephone in advance as some close on public holidays (local tourist offices often have details).

UIV de Beaujolais, BP 17, 210 en Beaujolais, 69661 Villefranche Cedex, ☏ 74 65 45 55.

Maison du Beaujolais, RN 6, 69220 St-Jean-d'Ardières, ☏ 74 68 76 90.

La Cave de Tain-l'Hermitage, Union des propriétaires, BP 3, 26600 Tain-l'Hermitage, ☏ 75 08 20 87.

At Romanèche-Thorins, the **"Hameau de vin"**, in a renovated railway station, presents the various stages of wine production from grape to glass (tasting included!). Further details from Hameau du vin, Dubœuf-en-Beaujolais, 71570 Romanèche-Thorins, ☏ 85 35 22 22.

Recreation

Arts and crafts – A brochure on local artisans and their activities *(Les métiers d'art)* is available from 389, av. de Lattre-de-Tassigny, 71000 Mâcon, ☏ 85 38 27 92. The Puisaye region is well known for its pottery, and lists of potters' workshops open to the public can be obtained from the Maison de la Puisaye (place du Château, 89170 St-Fargeau, ☏ 86 74 15 72) and other local pottery associations.

Canoeing – Information from the Fédération française de canoë-kayak, 87, quai de la Marne, 94340 Joinville-le-Pont, ☏ 48 89 39 89, or from the Comité de l'Yonne de canoë-kayak, av. Yver prolongée, 89000 Auxerre, ☏ 86 52 13 86. Canoes can also be hired from some local tourist offices (Ain, Doubs, Jura).

Caving and pot-holing – The numerous caves and chasms in the Jura (particularly in the Doubs valley) cry out to be explored by keen speleologists. In view of the relative dangers involved, however, it is advisable to go caving or pot-holing with a group, rather than alone.

Fédération française de spéléologie, 130, rue St-Maur, 75011 Paris, ☏ 43 57 56 54.
Comité régional de spéléologie en Franche-Comté, 25310 Pierrefontaine-lès-Blamont, ☏ 81 35 11 12.

Dog-sled race

Cycling – Information and itineraries from the Fédération française de Cyclotourisme, 8, rue Jean-Marie-Jégo, 75013 Paris, ☎ 45 80 30 21. The Morvan and Jura are particularly well suited to mountain biking; contact the Association Les Quatre Chemins for details of mountain bike tracks.

Dog-sled racing – This made its first appearance in France in 1979, when the first dog-sled club was opened. The sport has been increasing in popularity ever since. Races are organised in the Jura region, for example at La Pesse and Les Fourgs.
For details of trips in dog-sleds, contact Jurachiens, les Granges Berrard, 25300 Les Fourgs, ☎ 81 69 48 19.

Fishing – A leaflet *Pêche en France* (Fishing in France) is available from the Centre du Paraclet, BP 5, 80440 Boves, ☎ 22 35 34 70, as well as on sale at local fishing associations. A two-week fishing permit *(pêche en vacances)* is available for holiday-makers from local fishing associations and angling shops. The Doubs and the Loue are particularly good for fly-fishing, being well stocked and maintained.

Horse-drawn caravans – These can be hired for half a day to a week in the Tonnerre and Yonne regions. Contact the Tonnerre tourist office (10, rue du Col-lège, ☎ 86 55 14 48) or the Association Les Quatre Chemins *(see Rambling below)*.

Rambling – Topo-guides, published by the Fédération française de la Randonnée pédestre, which give detailed maps of the short, medium and long distance footpaths and other valuable information are on sale at the Centre d'Information de la Randonnée pédestre (64, rue de Gergovie, 75014 Paris, ☎ 45 45 31 02).
Every summer a 5-day ramble "From Alésia to Bibracte" is organised, retracing the steps of Vercingetorix and Caesar. For details, contact the Association Les Quatre Chemins, 33, Grande-Rue-Chauchien, 71400 Autun, ☎ 85 52 07 91.

Riding – Information from the Fédération des randonneurs équestres, 16, rue des Apennins, 75017 Paris, ☎ 42 26 23 23. An annual handbook is published by the Association nationale de Tourisme Équestre (ANTE), 170, quai de Stalingrad, Ile-St-Germain, 92130 Issy-les-Moulineaux, ☎ 45 54 29 54.
Information on riding in the Jura is available from Association régionale de tourisme équestre de Franche-Comté, 52, rue de Dole, 25000 Besançon, ☎ 81 52 67 40 (Monday to Friday from 1330 to 1730).

Fly-fishing for trout

Skiing – The Jura region is ideal for **cross-country skiing,** because of the variety of relief to be found here. There are more than 2 000km - 1 245 miles of clearly signposted, well maintained ski tracks. There are also a number of small **downhill skiing** resorts, the most notable of which are at Métabief, Les Rousses and Vattay.

The **Grande Traversée du Jura** (GTJ) is a 400km - 250 mile cross-country ski route, with a main track and 5 intermediate tracks, crossing several *départements* following the contours of the Haut-Doubs through evergreen forests. For further details of this and other cross-country ski tracks, contact the Espace Nordique Jurassien, Mairie-annexe, BP 132, 39304 Champagnole Cedex, ☏ 84 52 58 10. Those wishing to book into overnight accommodation en route should contact Étapes Jura, M.-F. Cattani, "Sous les Bois", 39370 La Presse, ☏ 84 42 73 17.

The École nationale de ski de fond et de saut (national cross-country and ski-jumping school) is at Prémanon, near Les Rousses.

For details of training courses, contact Accueil Montagnard, 25240 Chapelle-des-Bois, ☏ 81 69 26 19, or the Comité d'organisation de la Trace-Transjurassienne, place Clemenceau, BP 79, 25301 Pontarlier Cedex, ☏ 81 46 66 00.

Cavemen on skis...?

Some people believe that skiing originated in the Far East (possibly Manchuria) and played a part in migrations from East to West.

The oldest ski yet discovered dates from 3200BC and was unearthed in good condition from marshland near Hoting in Sweden. Ancient rock carvings dating from 2500-2000BC also testify to the existence of this mode of transport in Scandinavian countries in prehistoric times.

The word "ski" itself comes from the Old Norse for "bit" (of wood). Originally, people skiied on two curved bits of wood, of unequal length, with skin tied to the bottom. They used only one ski stick for balance. This mode of transport, used by everyone from soldiers to postmen, was not adopted outside Scandinavian countries for many centuries. It was mainly the Norwegian Fridtjof Nansen's expedition across Greenland on skis in 1888 which stimulated interest in the technique in the rest of Europe.

Despite the swift rise in popularity of downhill skiing, which developed from a need to adapt the sport to the more mountainous conditions prevalent in countries outside Scandinavia, cross-country skiing too remains immensely popular and attracts many skilful sportsmen and women. The first ever Winter Olympic Games were inaugurated at Chamonix in 1924, and included only Nordic ski events: cross-country, ski-jumping and Nordic combination, for which perhaps not surprisingly the Norwegians carried off all the medals!

The most famous cross-country ski race in the world is the Vasaloppet in Sweden, which draws huge crowds to a 89km - 55 mile course. The Jura region, however, has held its own long-distance cross-country ski race since 1979, the **Transjurassienne,** *which covers 76km - 47 miles from Lamoura (in the Jura) to Mouthe (Doubs). Since 1984, the course has been included in the Nordic World Cup series for cross-country ski racing, for which race meetings are held in various countries over a period of several months.*

C. Michel/EXPLORER

Skittles

Calendar of events

The list below is a selection of the many events which take place in this region. Visitors are advised to contact local tourist offices for fuller details of musical events, son et lumière shows, arts and crafts fairs etc. especially during July and August.

22 January

Champlitte .... Festival of St Vincent, patron saint of wine-growers (dating from 1719).

Saturday after 22 January

La Côte .... "St-Vincent Tournante" - rotating festival (venue changes annually) in honour of the patron saint of wine-growers. *Further information from: Confrérie des chevaliers du tastevin, BP 12, 21701 Nuits-St-Georges.*

Last Sunday in January

Villefranche-sur-Saône .... "Fête des Conscrits" and "La Vague" *(qv).*

1st weekend in February

Chablis area............ "St-Vincent Tournante"; ☏ *86 42 80 80.*

10-13 February

Mouthe .... "L'Étoile de Mouthe" husky dog-sled racing; Transalp' Internationale.

3rd Sunday in February

Lamoura-Mouthe ... "Transjurassienne" cross-country skiing race.

27 February

Chalon-sur-Saône ... Annual pelt fair ("Foire aux Sauvagines").

End of February - beginning of March

Chalon-sur-Saône ... Carnival: various parades, children's events, fair and day of the "Goniots"; procession and children's ball; *details:* ☏ *85 43 08 39.*

1st weekend in March

Les Fourgs.............. Dog-sled race.

April to November

Beaune .... "Son et Lumière" every evening at the Hôtel-Dieu; *details from the tourist office:* ☏ *80 22 24 51.*

3rd or 4th week in May

Mâcon .... National French wine fair.

Whit Sunday

Goumois
   66 fold 18 *(1)* ...... International canoe slalom.

31 May

Semur-en-Auxois.... "Fête de la Bague": horse race (dating from 1639).

1st fortnight in June

Vesoul .... International and regional motorbike racing (moto-cross).

3rd Sunday in June

St-Jean-de-Losne ... "Fête de la batellerie" (Boatmen's festival).

Friday and Sunday following Corpus Christi

Paray-le-Monial ...... Pilgrimage in honour of the Sacred Heart.

Sunday nearest 24 June

Mont-St-Vincent .... Celtic bonfire festival in honour of St John the Baptist.

End of June

Mâcon .... French rowing championships on the Saône.

14 July

Clamecy................. Jousting on the Yonne in memory of log-floating.

22 July

Vézelay .... Feast of St Mary Magdalene; pilgrimage.

1st Monday in August

Château-Chinon...... International cycling championship.

1st weekend after 15 August

**Different village
each year** .... Haut-Jura festival (local productions): ☎ *84 41 20 37.*

Saulieu .... Charollais show.

Last Sunday in August

Accolay .... Water jousting.

Cluny .... Draught and stud horse show.

End of August - beginning of September

Dijon .... Wine festival; international festival of music and folk dancing.

A Saturday in September

Beaune .... Wine festival.

Weekend nearest 7 September

Alise-Ste-Reine....... Pilgrimage in honour of St Reina; period pageant and re-enactment
of the miracle of St Reina at the Théâtre des Roches.

8 September

Mont Brouilly........ Wine-growers' pilgrimage to the chapel on Mont Brouilly.

Ronchamp .... Pilgrimage to Notre-Dame-du-Haut.

1st Sunday in September

Arbois.................... "Fête du Biou" wine festival.

1st fortnight in September

Belfort................... French wine and gastronomy fair.

Besançon............... International music festival and best young conductors' competition.

2nd weekend in September

Charlieu................. Folk festival.

September to December

Beaujolais region ... Numerous grape harvest festivals and wine fairs.

1st weekend in October

Auxerre .... Hot-air ballooning.

Sunday nearest 16 October

Paray-le-Monial ...... Festival of St Marguerite-Marie.

1st fortnight in November

Dijon .... International food fair.

3rd Saturday, Sunday and Monday in November

Vougeot .... 1st of the "Trois Glorieuses" at the Château du Clos de Vougeot.

Beaune .... 2nd of the "Trois Glorieuses": wine auction at the Hospices in the
covered market.

Meursault.............. 3rd of the "Trois Glorieuses": the "Paulée" at Meursault.

4th Sunday in November

Chablis .... Chablis Wine Fair.

Last weekend in November and 1st week in December

Belfort................... National young producers' cinema festival.

10 to 24 December

Montbéliard .... "Lumières de Noël" Christmas market.

3rd Saturday in December

Bourg-en-Bresse .... Plucked and drawn poultry show.

---

(1) Map references are given here for places not described in the main text of the guide.

Admission times and charges

Every sight for which there are times and charges is indicated by the symbol ⊙ in the main part of the guide. As times and charges for admission are liable to alteration, the information below is given for guidance only. The information was, as far as possible, correct at the time of going to press; information shown in italics indicates that current details were not available.

Order: The information is listed in the same order as the entries in the alphabetical section of the guide.

Dates: Dates given are inclusive.

Last admissions: Ticket offices usually shut 30 min before closing time; exceptions only are mentioned below.

Charge: The charge is for an individual adult; the charge for a child is given where appropriate.

Concessionary rates may be available for students and old-age pensioners. Large parties should apply in advance. In some cases, admission is free on certain days, eg Wednesdays, Sundays or public holidays.

Disabled tourists: Sights which have comprehensive facilities for disabled tourists are indicated by the symbol &. below.

Guided tours: The departure time of the last tour of the morning or afternoon will be up to an hour before the actual closing time. Most tours are conducted by French speaking guides, but some of the larger or more frequented sights may offer guided tours in other languages. In some cases the term "guided tours" may cover group visiting with a recorded commentary. Enquire at the ticket office or bookstall. Other aids commonly available for non-French-speaking tourists are notes, pamphlets or audio-guides.

Churches and chapels: Admission times are indicated if the interior is of special interest. Tourists are not admitted, other than to worship, during religious services. Some churches and many chapels are kept locked, in which case the key can generally be obtained from the person who keeps it (address usually posted in the doorway/porch), who will often accompany visitors round the church/chapel. A donation is welcome.

Tourist information centres: The addresses and telephone numbers are given under 🖪 below for the local tourist information centres, which provide information on market days, early closing days etc. and also on guided tours of towns or parts of the region of particular interest, which are organised in season.

A

Vallée de l'AIN

Upper valley of the Ain

Champagnole: Musée archéologique – Open 6 June to 3 September from 1400 to 1800 (1715 on Sundays and public holidays); closed Tuesdays, 14 July and 15 August; 15F; ☎ 84 53 01 00.

The Ain reservoirs

Moirans-en-Montagne: Musée du Jouet – Open 1 May to 30 September from 1000 to 1200 and from 1400 to 1800; closed Saturday and Sunday mornings 1 October to 30 April; 25F, 8-18 year olds: 15F, under 7s: 10F; ☎ 84 42 38 64.

Lac de Vouglans: Boat trips – Departures every day from April to October; apply to Jura Croisières Fluviales, pont de la Pyle, la Tour du Meix, 39270 Orgelet; ☎ 84 25 46 29.

ALISE-STE-REINE

Les Fouilles (Mont Auxois) – Open 4 July to 4 September daily from 0900 to 1830, 5 September to 2 November and 26 March to 3 July daily from 1000 to 1730; 23F (joint ticket with the Musée Alésia); ☎ 80 30 54 60.

Musée Alésia – Same opening times as Les Fouilles; joint admission.

AMBRONAY

Ancienne abbaye – Open from 0900 to 1200 and 1400 to dusk (1800 in summer); closed Sunday mornings; ☎ 74 38 29 25.

ANCY-LE-FRANC

Château – Guided tours (45 min) 26 March to 15 November daily from 1000 to 1200 and 1400 to 1800; closed the rest of the year; 42F; ☎ 86 75 14 63.

Musée de l'automobile et de l'attelage – Open 1 April to 1 November daily from 1000 to 1200 and 1400 to 1800; closed the rest of the year; 20 F; ☎ 86 75 14 63.

ANZY-LE-DUC

Church – Open daily from 0800 to 2000.

ARBOIS

🏛 Hôtel de Ville, 39600. ☎ 84 37 47 37

Guided tours of the town – Apply to the tourist office.

Tourist train – Operates April to September daily from 1100 to 1800; journey time: 40 min; 25F, children: 15F; leaves from the Champs de Mars car park.

Maison de Pasteur – Museum currently being reorganised; ☎ 84 66 11 72.

Caves de l'Hôtel de Ville – Temporary exhibitions are held Wednesday to Sunday from 1400 to 1800; closed Mondays, Tuesdays and public holidays; 15F; ☎ 84 66 07 45.

Musée Sarret-de-Grozon – Open 15 June to 15 September from 1500 to 1900; closed Tuesdays; 10F; ☎ 84 66 26 14.

Château Pécauld: Musée de la Vigne et du Vin – Open 1 February to 30 November from 1000 to 1200 and 1400 to 1800; closed Tuesdays; 15F; ☎ 84 66 26 14.

ARC-ET-SENANS

Saline Royale – Open 1 July to 31 August from 0900 to 1900, 1 April to 30 June and 1 September to 1 November from 0900 to 1200 and 1400 to 1800, 1 January to 31 March and 2 November to 31 December from 1000 to 1200 and 1400 to 1700; 29F; ☎ 81 54 45 45.

AUTUN

🏛 3, av. Charles-de-Gaulle, 71400. ☎ 85 52 20 34

Guided tours of the town – Apply to the tourist office.

Cathédrale St-Lazare – Open daily from 0800 to 1900; for guided tours apply to the tourist office.

Belfry – It is possible to climb to the top all year round daily from 0800 to 1830; 30F.

Musée Rolin – Open 1 April to 30 September from 0930 to 1200 and 1330 to 1800, October to March from 1000 to 1200 and 1400 to 1600 (1700 in October), on Sundays out of season open from 1430 to 1700 only; closed on Tuesdays and public holidays; 14F; ☎ 85 52 09 76.

Hôtel de Ville: Library – Open Monday to Saturday from 1400 to 1800 (1700 on Saturdays); closed on Sundays and public holidays; the collections of antique documents are only displayed during temporary exhibitions; no admission charge.

Musée Lapidaire – ♿ Open 16 April to 30 September from 1000 to 1200 and 1400 to 1800, the rest of the year from 1000 to 1200 and 1400 to 1600; on Sundays from 1 October to 31 December open 1400 to 1630 only and from 1 January to 15 April open 1400 to 1600 only; closed in February and on Tuesdays and public holidays; no admission charge; ☎ 85 52 35 71.

Muséum d'Histoire naturelle – Open July to late September from 1000 to 1200 and 1400 to 1800, the rest of the year from 1400 to 1700; closed on Mondays, Tuesdays and public holidays; 14F; ☎ 85 52 09 15.

If time permits...

Monastère tibétain Kagyu-Ling – Open in summer daily from 1500 to 1900, in winter on Wednesdays, Saturdays, Sundays and public holidays only from 1430 to 1800; open daily during school holidays; 10F; ☎ 85 79 43 41.

AUXERRE

🏛 1, quai de la République, 89000. ☎ 86 52 06 19

Guided tours of the town – Available mid-July to late August: guided tours, tours with headsets in *triporteurs* (special three-wheeled tourist vehicles) and boat trips; apply to the tourist office for details.

Cathédrale St-Étienne – Open daily from 0900 to 1200 and 1400 to 1800; closed Sunday mornings; closes early at 1700 on the afternoons of Sundays between 3 July and 5 September (because of organ recitals which take place from 1700 to 1800); ☎ 86 52 23 29.

Ancienne abbaye St-Germain – Open 1 June to 31 October from 1000 to 1830, the rest of the year from 1000 to 1200 and 1400 to 1730; closed Tuesdays, 1 January, Easter Monday, Whit Monday, 1 and 8 May, 1 and 11 November, 25 December; 25F (ticket includes admission to the Musée Leblanc-Duvernoy); NB: maximum group size 30 people, book in advance; ☎ 86 51 09 74.

St-Eusèbe – Open Monday to Saturday from 0800 to 1200 and 1400 to 1830; open on Sundays by appointment; ☎ 86 52 13 85 or 86 51 01 58.

Musée Leblanc-Duvernoy – Open from 1400 to 1800; closed Tuesdays, 1 January, Easter Monday, Whit Monday, 1 and 8 May, 1 and 11 November, 25 December; 10F (joint ticket with the Ancienne abbaye St-Germain: 25F); ☎ 86 51 09 74.

Musée d'histoire naturelle – Open 15 May to 30 September Monday to Friday from 1000 to 1830 and at weekends and on public holidays from 1500 to 1830; open the rest of the year Monday to Friday from 1000 to 1200 and 1400 to 1730 and at weekends and on public holidays from 1430 to 1730; no admission charge; ☎ 86 51 51 64.

B

Massif du BALLON D'ALSACE

Giromagny: Musée de la Mine et des Techniques minières – Open April to 31 October Thursday to Sunday from 1430 to 1800; 5F; ☎ 84 29 03 90.

BAUME-LES-DAMES

Église abbatiale – Open July and August during painting exhibitions; there are also concerts during July and August; for further details apply to the *mairie:* ☎ 81 84 07 13.

If time permits...

Grotte de la Glacière – Guided tours (45 min) 1 March to 30 November from 0900 to 1200 and 1400 to 1800 (1700 September to November); in June, July and August open from 0800 to 1900; 29F, children: 15F; ☎ 81 60 44 26.

BAUME-LES-MESSIEURS

Abbaye – In July and August guided tours (45 min) from 1000 to 1800 or individual tours with headset (deposit required) of the village, the abbey and the abbey church; 25F.

Musée de l'Artisanat jurassien – *Open 1 July to 15 September daily from 1030 to 1230 and 1500 to 1800; 3F per workshop; audiovisual system 20 min per workshop;* ☎ *84 47 26 93.*

BEAUCOURT

Musée Frédéric-Japy – Open Monday to Friday from 1400 to 1700, Sundays and public holidays from 1430 to 1730; closed Mondays, Tuesdays and 1 January, 1 May, 1 November and 25 December; 10F; ☎ 84 56 57 52.

BEAUJOLAIS

The vineyards

St-Julien: Musée Claude Bernard – Open from 1000 to 1200 and 1400 to 1800 (1700 October to February); closed the week between 25 December and 1 January, during March and on Mondays and 1 May; 10F; ☎ 74 67 51 44.

Salles-Arbuissonnas-en-Beaujolais: Museum – Guided tours (30 min) April to October on Saturdays, Sundays and public holidays; 3F; apply to Mme Médal at Salles 2 days in advance; ☎ 74 67 51 81.

Belleville: Church – Guided tours (30 min) 1 July to 15 September on Tuesdays, Wednesdays and Thursdays from 1500 to 1800; contact Mme Chartron (☎ 74 69 63 22) or the tourist office (☎ 74 66 44 67).

Château de Corcelles – Open 1000 to 1200 and 1430 to 1830; closed Sundays and public holidays; ☎ 74 66 00 24; the chapel and the wine cellar are open to groups only.

Romanèche-Thorins: Maison de Benoît Raclet – Guided tours (30 min) on last Saturday in October; the rest of the year apply to the *mairie* (during working week only); ☎ 85 35 51 37.

Romanèche-Thorins: Musée du compagnonnage Guillon – Open Easter to 1 November from 1000 to 1200 and 1400 to 1700; closed on Fridays and Saturdays; 12F; ☎ 85 35 52 48.

Juliénas: Cellier de la Vieille Église – Open from 0930 to 1200 and 1430 to 1800; open on Sundays only during January; closed on Tuesdays from October to May and also on 1 January and 25 December; ☎ 74 04 41 43.

"La montagne"

Beaujeu: Musée des traditions populaires Marius-Audin – Open 1 July to 30 September from 1000 to 1200 and 1430 to 1800, 1 April to 30 June and 1 October to 30 November on Sundays and public holidays at these times and during the week afternoons only; closed Tuesdays and from 1 December to 31 March; 8F; ☎ 74 69 22 88.

In the land of golden stone

Pays des Pierres Dorées: Pavillon du Syndicat d'Initiative – The tourist office is at Châtillon-d'Azergues and is open May to October on weekdays from 1000 to 1200 and 1400 to 1800, on Saturdays from 1000 to 1200 and 1500 to 1800 and on Sundays from 1000 to 1300; ☎ 78 47 98 15.

Châtillon: Chapelle St-Barthélemy – Open Easter to 1 November on Sundays and public holidays from 1430 to 1800; the rest of the year apply to the Association de la Licorne, mairie de Châtillon: ☎ 78 43 91 11.

Chessy: Church – Closed to tourists on Sunday mornings (other than to worship).

Bagnols: Church – If closed, apply to M Boinon in one of the houses in the village square.

Theizé: Château de Rochebonne – *Guided tours (30 min) May to October at weekends;* 10F; ☎ 74 71 22 27.

Theizé: Church – Open early June to mid-September daily; in May and from mid-September to mid-October at weekends only; closed Tuesdays; 10F; ☎ 74 71 25 14.

Oingt: Church – Open May to end of September on Sundays from 1400 to 1900; during the week apply to M. Jean Veilloux; ☎ 74 71 20 88.

Oingt: Tower – Open 1 May to end of September on Sundays and public holidays from 1400 to 1900; 5F; ☎ 74 71 24 38.

Ternand: Church – Guided tours; apply to the *mairie*; ☎ 74 71 33 43.

BEAUNE
🛈 Rue de l'Hôtel-de-Ville, 21200. ☎ 80 22 24 51

Guided tours of the town – 1 July to 15 September daily at 1500; time: 1 hour 45 min; apply to the tourist office.

Hôtel-Dieu – Open Palm Sunday to the third Sunday in November daily from 0900 to 1830, the rest of the year from 0900 to 1130 and 1400 to 1730; 27F; ☎ 80 24 45 00.

Musée du Vin de Bourgogne – Open daily from 0930 to 1730; closed on Tuesdays from 1 December to 30 April and also on 1 January and 25 December; 20F; ☎ 80 22 08 19.

Hôtel de Ville: Musée des Beaux-Arts – Open 1 April to 20 November daily from 1400 to 1800; 20F; ☎ 80 24 56 92.

Hôtel de Ville: Musée Étienne-Jules Marey – Same admission times and charges as the Musée des Beaux-Arts.

If time permits...

Archéodrome – ♿ Open in July and August daily from 1000 to 2000, 1 March to 30 June and 1 October to 30 November from 1000 to 1800 and 1 November to 28 February from 1000 to 1700; 50F; ☎ 80 26 87 00.

BELFORT
🛈 Passage de France, 90000. ☎ 84 28 12 23

Belfort Lion: Viewing platform – Open 1 April to 30 September from 0800 to 1900, April to June and October from 0800 to 1200 and 1400 to 1900 (1800 in April and October), November to March from 1000 (0900 at weekends) to 1200 and 1400 to 1700; 3F; ☎ 84 28 52 96.

Fortifications – Guided tours (30 min) June to September; out of season by appointment at weekends, weather permitting; 12F (joint ticket with the Musée d'Art et d'Histoire); ☎ 84 28 52 96.

Musée d'Art et d'Histoire – Open 1 April to 30 October from 0800 to 1200 and 1400 to 1900 (1800 in April and October), the rest of the year from 1000 to 1200 and 1400 to 1700; closed on Tuesdays from October to April and also 1 January, 1 November and 25 December; 12F, no admission charge on Wednesdays; ☎ 84 28 52 96.

Hôtel de Ville – Open Monday to Friday, apply to reception.

BELLEY
🛈 Place de la Victoire, 01300. ☎ 79 81 29 06

Guided tours of the town – Apply to the tourist office.

Palais épiscopal – Apply to the tourist office.

Château de BELVOIR

Fortress – Open (guided tours available: 1 hour) in July and August daily from 1000 to 1130 and 1400 to 1730, Easter to 30 June and 1 September to 31 October open on Sundays and public holidays only; 25F; ☎ 81 91 06 02.

BERZÉ-LA-VILLE

Chapelle des Moines – Open May to September daily from 0900 to 1200 and 1400 to 1800, in April and October from 1000 to 1200 and 1400 to 1730; ☎ 85 38 57 06.

BESANÇON
🛈 Place de la 1re Armée-Française, 25000. ☎ 81 80 92 55

Guided tours of the town – Apply to the tourist office.

Boat trips on the Doubs – Landing stage for tourist boats *(bateaux-mouches)* on the **Pont de la République (Halte nautique St-Paul)**; departures in July, August and early September (until school starts) on weekdays at 1030, 1430 and 1630 and at weekends and on public holidays at 1030, 1430, 1630 and 1815, in May and June on weekdays at 1530 and at weekends and on public holidays at 1430 and 1630, in September (from when school starts until the end of the month) at 1515; journey time: 1 hour 15 min; 43F, children: 33F; ☎ 81 68 13 25 or 81 68 00 06.

Tourist train – Operates 1 April to 30 September daily from 1100 (1000 in July and August) to 1800; journey time: 40 min; 28F, children: 18F; leaves from Porte Rivotte or the Citadelle; ☎ 81 68 13 25.

Palais de Justice – For details telephone (during the working week) ☎ 81 65 11 00.

Musée du Temps – Currently undergoing restoration work; for further information telephone ☎ 81 81 45 14.

Horloge astronomique – Guided tours (30 min) at 0950, 1050, 1150, 1450, 1550, 1650 and 1750; closed during January, on Wednesdays from 1 October to 1 April and on Tuesdays all year; 23F.

Citadelle – Open 1 April to 30 September from 0915 to 1815, the rest of the year from 0945 to 1645; closed 1 January and 25 December; 22F (includes admission to the 4 museums in the Citadelle), 15F on Tuesdays; ☎ 81 82 16 22.

Musée Comtois and Musée agraire – Open 29 March to 29 September daily from 0900 to 1800, and 30 September to 28 March from 0930 to 1630; closed Tuesdays; 23F; ☎ 81 82 16 22.

Musée d'Histoire naturelle and Musée de la Résistance et de la Déportation – Same admission times and charges as the Citadelle *(above)*.

Musée des Beaux-Arts et d'Archéologie – Open from 0930 to 1200 and 1400 to 1800; closed Tuesdays and 1 January, 1 May, 1 November and 25 December; 20F, no admission charge on Sundays and public holidays; ☎ 81 81 44 47.

Bibliothèque municipale – Temporary exhibitions are held every year.

Jardin botanique – Open from 0830 to 1130 and 1400 to 1600; closed on Saturday afternoons, Sundays and public holidays; ☎ 81 66 56 69.

Hôpital St-Jacques: Pharmacy – Apply to the tourist office.

Chapelle Notre-Dame-de-Refuge – Open daily from 1400 to 1800; closed in winter; ☎ 81 66 96 00.

If time permits...

Nancray: Musée de plein air des maisons comtoises – Open 1 June to 31 August from 1000 to 1800, in April, May, September and October from 1400 to 1730; closed on Tuesdays except during June, July and August; 25F, children: 10F; ☎ 81 55 29 77.

BOURG-EN-BRESSE
🛈 6, av Alsace-Lorraine, 01005. ☎ 74 22 49 40

Guided tours of the town – Apply to the tourist office.

Brou

Church – Open 1 April to 30 September daily from 0830 to 1200 and 1400 to 1830, 1 October to 31 March from 1000 to 1200 and 1400 to 1630; 26F; ☎ 74 22 26 55.

Museum – Open 1 April to 30 September from 0900 to 1230 and 1400 to 1900, the rest of the year from 0900 to 1200 and 1400 to 1700; closed 1 January, 1 May, 1 and 11 November and 25 December; 12F; ☎ 74 45 39 00.

BRANCION

Château – Open Easter to 1 November daily from 0900 to 2000, the rest of the year weekends and public holidays only from 0900 to 1800; 12F; ☎ 85 51 11 41.

St-Pierre – Open Easter to 11 November daily from 0800 to 1800; ☎ 85 51 24 40.

BRIARE

If time permits...

La Bussière: Fresh-water fishing exhibition – Guided tours (40 min) 27 March to 2 November daily from 1000 to 1200 and 1400 to 1800; closed Tuesdays except those during July and August; 28F; ☎ 38 35 93 35.

BUGEY

Haut-Bugey

Grotte du Cerdon – Guided tours (1 hour) 1 May to last Sunday in September from 1000 to 1800, 1 October to 11 November on Sundays and public holidays at these times; 30F; ☎ 50 23 74 06.

Bas-Bugey

St-Rambert-en-Bugey: Maison de Pays – Open from 0900 to 1200 and 1400 to 1800; closed Sunday and Monday mornings; telephone for details on public holidays; ☎ 74 36 32 38.

Château de BUSSY-RABUTIN

Tour – Guided tours 1 April to 30 September at 1000, 1100 and on the hour from 1400 to 1800, the rest of the year at 1000, 1100, 1400 and 1500; closed on Tuesdays and Wednesdays out of season, also 1 January, 1 May, 1 and 11 November and 25 December; 26F; ☎ 80 96 00 03.

Each year
*the **Michelin Red Guide France***
revises its selection of hotels and restaurants
in the following categories

– pleasant, quiet, secluded
– with an exceptionally interesting or extensive view
– with gardens, tennis courts, swimming pool, beach facilities.

C

CHABLIS

St-Martin – *Apply to the tourist office, Le Petit Pontigny, 89800 Chablis,* ☎ *86 42 42 22.*

Lac de CHALAIN

Marigny: Maison des Lacs – Guided tours in July and August from 1430 to 1830; 20F; ☎ 84 25 76 04.

CHALON-SUR-SAÔNE   🛈 Boulevard de la République, 71100. ☎ 85 48 37 97

Guided tours of the town – From 15 June to 15 September, leaving from the Hôtel de Ville, tours of Old Chalon on Mondays at 1000 and of Chalon by Night on Fridays at 2100; apply to the tourist office.

Musée Denon – Open all year from 0930 to 1200 and 1400 to 1730; closed on Tuesdays and public holidays; 10F, no admission charge on Wednesdays; ☎ 85 48 01 70 (ext 4237).

Musée Nicéphore-Niepce – Open July and August from 1000 to 1800, the rest of the year from 0930 to 1130 and 1430 to 1730; closed on Tuesdays and public holidays; 10F, no admission charge on Wednesdays; ☎ 85 48 41 98.

Cathédrale St-Vincent – Open daily from 0700 to 1900; guided tours organised by the tourist office between 15 June and 15 September on Wednesdays at 1600 (leaving from the square outside the main entrance of the cathedral).

Hôpital – ♿ Guided tours (1 hour 30 min) 15 June to 15 September on Wednesdays at 1430, the rest of the year on the last Wednesday of the month only; 10F.

Tour du Doyenné – Open 2 May to 1 September from 1400 to 1630; closed on Sundays and public holidays.

CHAMPLITTE

Musée des Arts et Traditions populaires – Guided tours (1 hour 30 min) from 0900 to 1200 and 1400 to 1800 (1700 October to March); closed on Sunday mornings, Tuesdays (except those in July and August), 1 January, 1 November and 25 December; 30F, under-18s: 20F, children: 10F; ☎ 84 67 82 00.

Musée 1900 – Arts et Techniques – Same admission times as the Musée des Arts et Traditions populaires above; 20F, under-18s: 15F, children: 5F.

La CHARITÉ-SUR-LOIRE   🛈 Place Ste-Croix, 58400. ☎ 86 70 15 06

Guided tours of the town – In July and August at 1000, 1100, 1500, 1600 and 1700; closed on Sunday mornings; apply to the tourist office; 20F.

Notre-Dame – Open daily from 0900 to 1830; guided tours available from 1000 to 1200 and 1500 to 1800 on request at the tourist office.

Musée – Open (45 min guided tours available) 1 July to 15 September from 1000 to 1200 and 1430 to 1830; open on the following public holidays: Easter, 1 May, Ascension Day, Whitsun; 12F; ☎ 86 70 34 83.

CHARLIEU   🛈 Place St-Philibert, 42190. ☎ 77 60 12 42

Guided tours of the town – In July and August on Wednesdays and Saturdays at 1500; 15 July to 15 August evening tours of the historical town centre on Thursdays at 2130; apply to the tourist office; 50F.

Abbey – Open (45 min guided tours available) 15 June to 15 September from 0900 to 1900; 1 April to 15 June and 15 to 30 September from 0900 to 1200 and 1400 to 1900; 1 October to 30 November and 1 February to 31 March from 0900 to 1200 and 1400 to 1700; telephone for details in December and January; closed 1 January and 25 December; no guided tours available on Tuesdays from 1 April to 15 June, or on Tuesdays and Wednesdays from 1 October to 31 March; 20F (joint ticket with Couvent des Cordeliers and Salle Armand-Charnay); the lapidary and sacred art museums can only be visited as part of a guided tour; ☎ 77 60 08 17.

Salle Armand-Charnay – Open during the Easter painting exhibition (Salon de Peinture) and during exhibitions in the summer; ☎ 77 60 08 17.

Couvent des Cordeliers – Open (30 min guided tours available); same times and charges as the abbey (joint ticket); ☎ 77 60 07 42.

Hôtel de Ville – Open all year from 0900 to 1200 and 1330 to 1700; closed on Wednesday afternoons, at weekends and on public holidays; no admission charge; ☎ 77 60 23 55.

Musée de la Soierie – Open daily from 1400 to 1800; 20F, joint ticket with the Musée hospitalier: 30F.

Musée hospitalier – Same admission times and charges as the Musée de la Soierie.

St-Philibert – Open daily from 0900 to dusk; apply to the tourist office for guided tours.

If time permits...

La Bénisson-Dieu: Church – Open Easter to 1 November daily from 0800 to 1900; ☎ 77 66 62 61.

CHÂTEAU-CHINON

Musée du Septennat – ♿ Open 1 May to 31 October daily from 1000 to 1800 (1900 in July and August), the rest of the year open at weekends, on public holidays and during school holidays; closed during January and on 25 December; 20F, joint ticket with Musée du Costume: 30F; ☎ 86 85 19 23.

Musée du Costume – Same admission times and charges as the Musée du Septennat; ☎ 86 85 18 55.

CHÂTEAUNEUF

Château – Guided tours (45 min) 1 April to 30 September hourly from 0930 to 1130 and 1400 to 1700 (1800 on Sundays), the rest of the year at 1000, 1100, 1400 and 1500 only; closed on Tuesdays and Wednesdays out of season and on 1 January, 1 May, 1 and 11 November and 25 December; 20F; ☎ 80 49 21 89.

If time permits...

Commarin: Castle – Guided tours (45 min) 2 April to 31 October from 1000 to 1200 and 1400 to 1800; closed Tuesdays; 35F; ☎ 80 49 23 67.

CHÂTILLON-COLIGNY

Guided tours of the town – Apply to the tourist office.

Musée – Open 1 April to 31 October on weekdays from 1400 to 1730 and at weekends and on public holidays from 1000 to 1200 and 1400 to 1730; the rest of the year open at weekends and on public holidays only from 1430 to 1730; closed Mondays, 1 January and 25 December; 8F; ☎ 38 92 64 06.

CHÂTILLON-SUR-SEINE

Musée – Open 16 June to 15 September from 0900 to 1200 and 1330 to 1800, 1 April to 15 June and 16 September to 15 November from 0900 to 1200 and 1400 to 1800, 16 November to 31 March from 1000 to 1200 and 1400 to 1700; closed on Tuesdays between 16 September and 15 June; 21F; ☎ 80 91 24 67.

St-Vorles – Open 16 June to 15 September daily from 1030 to 1200 and 1430 to 1730 (guided tours at 15.30), 1 April to 15 June on Wednesdays, Saturdays, Sundays and public holidays at these times, 16 September to 11 November on Saturdays, Sundays and public holidays from 1430 to 1630; closed 12 November to 31 March; ☎ 80 91 24 67.

CÎTEAUX

Abbey – The only part open to visitors is the abbey church, open daily from 0600 to 1230 and 1400 to 2000; 20 min audio-visual presentation in English, French and German; ☎ 80 61 11 53.

CLAMECY   🛈 Rue du Grand-Marché, 58500. ☎ 86 27 02 51

St-Martin – Open daily from 0930 to 1900; for guided tours, apply to the tourist office.

Musée d'art et d'histoire Romain-Rolland – Open from 1000 to 1200 and 1400 to 1800; closed on Tuesdays (all year), Sundays (from 1 November to Easter), 1 January, 1 May and 25 December; 15F; ☎ 86 27 17 99.

Château du CLOS DE VOUGEOT

Tour – Guided tours (45 min) 1 April to 30 September from 0900 to 1830 (1700 on Saturdays), the rest of the year from 0900 to 1130 and 1400 to 1730; 15 min audio-visual presentation on the Confrerie des Chevaliers du Tastevin after the tour; 15F; ☎ 80 62 86 09.

CLUNY   🛈 6 rue Mercière, 71250. ☎ 85 59 05 34

Ancienne Abbaye – Open (1 hour 15 min guided tours available) 1 July to 30 September from 0900 to 1900, 1 April to 30 June and in October from 0930 to 1200 and 1000 to 1800 (1700 in October), 1 November to 31 March from 1030 to 1130 and 1400 to 1600; closed 1 January, 1 May, 1 and 11 November and 25 December; 26F; ☎ 85 59 12 79.

Musée Ochier – ♿ Open (1 hour guided tours available) 1 July to 30 September daily from 0900 to 1900, 1 April to 30 June and in October from 0930 to 1200 and 1400 to 1800 (1700 in October), the rest of the year from 1030 to 1130 and 1400 to 1600; closed 1 January, 1 May, 1 and 11 November and 25 December; 13F; ☎ 85 59 23 97.

Tour des Fromages – Open 1 July to 30 September daily from 1000 to 1900, 1 April to 30 June and in October from 1000 to 1230 and 1430 to 1900, the rest of the year from 1000 to 1200 and 1430 to 1830; closed on Sundays in winter and on 1 January, 1 May, 1 and 11 November and 25 December; 6F; ☎ 85 59 05 34.

Haras National – Open all year daily from 0900 to 1900; no admission charge; ☎ 85 59 07 85.

St-Marcel – Open April to November daily from 0800 to 1800; ☎ 85 59 07 18.

Château de CORMATIN

Interior – ♿ Guided tours (45 min) in July and August daily from 1000 to 1830, in June, September and October from 1000 to 1200 and 1400 to 1830 (1730 in September, 1700 in October), in the Easter holidays and at weekends and on public holidays in May from 1000 to 1200 and 1400 to 1730; 30F; ☎ 85 50 16 55.

La CÔTE
The vineyards ①

Chenôve: Cuverie des ducs de Bourgogne – ♿ Guided tours (45 min) 15 June to 30 September from 1400 to 1900, the rest of the year by appointment; no admission charge; ☎ 80 52 51 30 (ask for the *"service culturel"*).

Fixin: Parc Noisot – Open 15 April to 15 November on Wednesdays, Saturdays and Sundays from 1400 to 1800; 6F; ☎ 80 52 45 62 or 80 52 45 52 *(Mairie)*.

Reulle-Vergy: Museum – Open 1 July to 30 September daily from 1400 to 1900, the rest of the year by appointment; 10F; ☎ 80 61 45 31.

The vineyards ②

St-Romain: Local archaeology and ethnology – Exhibition at the town hall: open in July and August on weekdays from 1600 to 2000 and at weekends and on public holidays from 1400 to 2000; the rest of the year open by appointment; closed on Mondays; no admission charge; ☎ 80 21 28 50.

Santenay: St-Jean – Open daily from 1000 to 1200 and from 1430 to 1830; ☎ 80 20 63 15.

Le CREUSOT   🅱 Château de la Verrerie, 71200. ☎ 85 55 02 46

Château de la Verrerie: Museum – Guided tours (1 hour) 1 April to 30 September daily from 0900 to 1200 and 1400 to 1900, the rest of the year Tuesday to Friday from 1000 to 1200 and 1400 to 1800 and Saturday from 1400 to 1800; open on public holidays from 1400 to 1900 in season, and from 1400 to 1800 out of season; closed on Sundays and Mondays out of season and 1 May; 30F; ☎ 85 55 02 46.

Écomusée – Open daily from 0900 to 1200 and 1400 to 1900 (1800 October to March); 15F; ☎ 85 55 01 11.

If time permits...

Montceau-les-Mines: Fossil museum – ♿ Guided tours (1 hour) on Wednesdays, Saturdays and the first Sunday of the month from 1500 to 1800; closed from 14 July to 15 August and on 1 January and 1 May; it is possible to arrange tours by appointment; 15F; ☎ 85 57 38 51 (tourist office: Place de l'Hôtel de Ville, 71300).

Montceau-les-Mines: Blanzy Mine – ♿ Guided tours (2 hours) 15 July to 16 September daily from 1430 to 1800, 15 March to 30 June and 17 September to 20 November at weekends and on public holidays only at these times; 25F; ☎ 85 68 22 85.

CUISEAUX

Maison de la vigne et du vigneron – Open 15 May to 30 September from 1500 to 1900; closed on Tuesdays; 10F; ☎ 85 76 27 16.

The Michelin Green Tourist Guide Portugal
Architecture
Fine Art
History
Geography
Picturesque scenery
Touring programmes
Town and site plans
A guide for the holidays

D

DIJON
🛈 34 rue des Forges, 21022. ☎ 80 44 11 44

Guided tours of the town – Apply to the tourist office. Ticket valid for all museums except the Musée Grévin: 15F.

Musée des Beaux-Arts – Open all year from 1000 to 1800; the modern art department is closed from 1200 to 1330; closed on Tuesdays and 1 January, 1 and 8 May, 14 July, 1 and 11 November and 25 December; 15F; ☎ 80 74 52 70.

Tour Philippe-le-Bon – Open 1 April to 30 November Monday to Friday from 0900 to 1200 and 1345 to 1730, the rest of the year on Wednesdays from 1330 to 1530 and Saturdays from 0900 to 1100 and 1330 to 1530; 15F.

Hôtel de Vogüé – *Only the inner courtyard is open to visitors.*

Bibliothèque municipale – *Courtyard and chapel (reading room): open Tuesday to Saturday from 0930 to 1230 and 1330 to 1830 (no lunch break on Wednesdays and Saturdays); closed on Saturdays in July and August; first floor rooms closed until further notice;* ☎ *80 30 36 39.*

Musée Magnin – Open 1 June to 30 September from 1000 to 1800, the rest of the year from 1000 to 1200 and 1400 to 1800; closed on Mondays; 12F; ☎ 80 67 11 10.

Chartreuse de Champmol – The Puits de Moïse and the chapel doorway can be seen all year round daily between 0830 and 1900; no admission charge; ☎ 80 42 48 48.

Cathédrale St-Bénigne: Crypt – *Open all year from 0900 to 1900 (1800 November to February); 4F;* ☎ *80 30 39 33.*

Musée archéologique – Open 13 June to 30 September from 0930 to 1800, the rest of the year from 0900 to 1200 and 1400 to 1800; closed on Tuesdays and public holidays; 10F; ☎ 80 30 88 54.

Muséum d'Histoire naturelle – Open all year Mondays and Wednesday to Saturday from 0900 to 1200 and 1400 to 1800, Sundays and public holidays from 1400 to 1800; closed Tuesdays and 1 January, 1 and 8 May, 14 July, 1 and 11 November and 25 December; 10F, no admission charge on Sundays; ☎ 80 76 82 76.

Musée Grévin – ♿ Open all year daily from 0930 to 1200 and 1400 to 1900; closed 1 January and 25 December; 30F; ☎ 80 42 03 03.

Musée Rude – Open 1 June to 30 September from 1000 to 1200 and 1400 to 1745; closed on Tuesdays and 14 July; no admission charge; ☎ 80 74 52 70.

St-Michel – Open daily; guided tours available in June, July and August from 1400 to 1800; ☎ 80 63 17 84.

Musée de la Vie bourguignonne – ♿ Open all year from 0900 to 1200 and 1400 to 1800; closed on Tuesdays and 1 January, 1 and 8 May, 14 July, 1 and 11 November and 25 December; 10F, no admission charge on Sundays; ☎ 80 30 65 91.

Musée d'art sacré – Open all year from 0900 to 1200 and 1400 to 1800; closed on Tuesdays and 1 January, 1 May, 14 July, 1 and 11 November and 25 December; 8F, no admission charge on Sundays; ☎ 80 30 06 44.

DOLE
🛈 Place Grévy, 39100. ☎ 84 72 11 22

Guided tours of the town – Apply to the tourist office.

Collégiale Notre-Dame – Guided tours including ascent of the bell tower available 1 July to 15 September; apply to the tourist office.

Maison natale de Pasteur and Musée Pasteur – Open 1 July to 31 August from 1000 to 1800 (1700 on Sundays), 1 April to 30 June and in September from 1000 to 1200 and 1400 to 1800, in October and during the February school holidays from 1000 to 1200 and 1400 to 1700 (on Sundays from 1400 to 1800 only); closed on Tuesdays and 1 January, 1 May and 14 July; 16F; ☎ 84 72 20 61.

Musée des Beaux-Arts – Open from 1000 to 1200 and 1400 to 1800; closed on Tuesdays, 1 May and from 23 December to 2 January; ☎ 84 72 27 72.

Palais de Justice – Open Monday to Saturday.

St-Jean-l'Évangéliste – If church is closed, apply to the parish priest's office *(La Cure)*; ☎ 84 72 05 14.

If time permits...

Auxonne: Napoleon Bonaparte Museum – Open 2 May to 15 October from 1000 to 1200 and 1500 to 1800; closed on Thursdays; no admission charge; ☎ 80 31 15 33.

Vallée du DOUBS

The Gorges du Doubs

Villers-le-Lac: Boat service – From Easter to 1 November daily departures from four landing stages.

In the Foothills of the Jura

Clerval: Church – Apply to the nuns of Notre-Dame-d'Afrique, 3 rue de la Porte-de-Chaux.

E

ÉPOISSES

Château – Guided tours (45 min) of the interior in July and August from 1000 to 1200 and 1500 to 1800; closed on Tuesdays; grounds open all year round; 25F; ☎ 80 96 42 65.

F

FERNEY-VOLTAIRE

Château – Guided tours (2 hours) in July and August on Saturdays at 1500, 1600 and 1700; 5F.

FILAIN

Château – Guided tours (45 min) Easter to 11 November from 1000 to 1200 and 1400 to 1900; 30F; ☎ 84 78 30 66.

FLAVIGNY-SUR-OZERAIN

St-Genest – Open 15 June to 30 September from 1000 to 1200 and 1400 to 1800, the rest of the year by appointment; closed on Sunday mornings and Mondays; ☎ 80 96 25 47.

Crypte Ste-Reine – Open for tours August and September daily at 1530, 1630 and 1730, January to July and September to December Monday to Friday from 0900 to 1130 and 1400 to 1700, on Sundays and public holidays by appointment (a few days in advance); 8F; ☎ 80 96 24 65.

Abbaye de FONTENAY

Tour – Open July and August daily from 0900 to 1300 and 1400 to 1800, the rest of the year from 0900 to 1200 and 1400 to 1800; guided tours (1 hour) available 15 March to 15 November, otherwise open for independent visiting the rest of the year; 38F; ☎ 80 92 15 00.

FOUGEROLLES

Écomusée de la Distillation et du Pays fougerollais – Open for partially guided tours in July and August daily from 1000 to 1200 and 1400 to 1700, 15 April to 30 June and in September open from 1400 to 1700; closed on Tuesdays except those in July and August; 20F; ☎ 84 49 12 53.

G

Barrage de GÉNISSIAT

Salle des machines – Guided tours (30 min) 1 June to 31 August on weekdays from 1000 to 1200 and 1430 to 1830, at weekends and on public holidays from 1000 to 1230 and 1400 to 1830.

GEVREY-CHAMBERTIN

Château – Guided tours available 1 February to 15 November Monday to Saturday from 1000 to 1200 and 1400 to 1800 (1700 out of season), on Sundays and public holidays (all year round) from 1100 to 1200 and 1430 to 1800 (1700 out of season); it is possible to visit by appointment in January; closed on Thursdays, Easter Day, 15 August and 25 December; 20F; ☎ 80 34 36 13.

GRAND-COLOMBIER

If time permits...

Lochieu: Musée rural du Valromey – Open 1 April to 31 October from 1000 to 1200 and 1400 to 1800; closed on Wednesday mornings; 18F; ☎ 79 87 52 23.

GRAY

🗓 Ile Sauzay, 70100. ☎ 84 65 14 24

Guided tours of the town – Apply to the tourist office.

Boat trips on the Saône – To Mantoche, Prantigny, Savoyeux and Pontailler. Departures from Quai Mavia. Apply to CNFS, BP 30, 25130 Villers-le-Lac, ☎ 81 68 05 34, or the Gray tourist office.

Musée Baron-Martin – Open 1 April to 30 September from 0930 to 1200 and 1330 to 1800, the rest of the year from 1000 to 1200 and 1400 to 1700; closed on Tuesdays and 1 January, 1 May, 1 November and 25 December; 13F; ☎ 84 64 83 46.

J

JOIGNY

Excursions

Musée rural des Arts populaires de Laduz – Open in July and August daily from 1100 to 1900, in June and September from 1400 to 1900, Easter to 31 May and 1 October to 2 November open at weekends and on public holidays only from 1400 to 1900; 25F; ☎ 86 73 70 08.

La Fabuloserie – Guided tours (1 hour 30 min) in July and August daily from 1400 to 1800, Easter to June and September to early November at weekends and on public holidays only at these times; 30F; ☎ 86 63 64 21.

St-Julien-du-Sault: Church – If closed, apply to Mlle Cagne, 17, place de la Mairie; ☎ 86 63 25 89.

La Ferté-Loupière: Church – Open daily from 0800 to dusk; for guided tours apply to M. and Mme Breton, Rue Basse, La Ferté-Loupière, 89110 Aillant-sur-Tholon; ☎ 86 73 18 79.

Château de JOUX

Tour – NB There are a lot of steps. Guided tours (1 hour) Easter to the last Sunday in October from 1000 to 1200 and 1400 to 1700; in July and August from 0900 to 1200 and 1330 to 1830; 21F; ☎ 81 69 47 95.

L

LONS-LE-SAUNIER
🛈 Rue Pasteur, 39000. ☎ 84 24 65 01

Guided tours of the town – Apply to the tourist office.

Hôpital: Pharmacie – Guided tours (1 hour 30 min) in July and August on Tuesdays, Thursdays and Saturdays at 1430 (except on 14 July and 15 August); 5F; leave from the gates of the Hôtel-Dieu; details from the tourist office; ☎ 84 24 65 01.

Musée des Beaux-Arts – Open from 1000 to 1200 and 1400 to 1800, on Saturdays, Sundays and public holidays from 1400 to 1700 only; closed on Tuesdays; ☎ 84 47 26 93.

Musée municipal d'archéologie – Same admission times and charges as the Musée des Beaux-Arts; closed on 1 January, 1 May and 25 December; ☎ 84 47 12 13.

Vallée de la LOUE

Cléron: Château – Guided tours (30 min) 10 July to 20 August on Saturdays, Sundays and public holidays from 1430 to 1800; 20F; gardens open to the public mid-July to mid-August in the afternoons: 10F.

LOUHANS

Hôtel-Dieu – Guided tours (1 hour 30 min) 1 March to 30 September Monday to Saturday at 1030, 1430 and 1600, on Sundays and public holidays at 1430 and 1600, the rest of the year on Thursdays and Saturdays at 1030; 20F; ☎ 85 75 54 32.

L'Atelier d'un journal – ♿ Open all year from 1500 to 1900; closed on Tuesdays and (from October to mid-May) at weekends and on public holidays; 15F; ☎ 85 76 27 16.

Excursion

Chaisiers et pailleuses de Rancy – ♿ Open 15 May to 30 September from 1500 to 1900; closed on Tuesdays; 15F; ☎ 85 76 27 16.

LUXEUIL-LES-BAINS

Hôtel des Échevins (Musée de la tour des Échevins) – Open 1 April to 31 October from 1030 to 1200 and 1500 to 1900; 1 December to 31 March open on Sundays from 1430 to 1700; closed on Tuesdays, Sunday mornings and during November; 10F; ☎ 84 40 00 07.

M

MÂCON
🛈 187, rue Carnot, 71000. ☎ 85 39 71 37

Guided tours of the town – In July and August on Saturdays at 1500; apply to the tourist office.

Musée municipal des Ursulines – Open (guided tours available if booked a fortnight in advance) from 1000 to 1200 and 1400 to 1800; closed on Sunday mornings and Tuesdays, 1 January, 1 May, 14 July, 1 November and 25 December; 15F; ☎ 85 38 18 84.

Vieux St-Vincent: Lapidary Museum – Open all year daily, every day except Tuesday; narthex: open from 1000 to 1730 (1900 1 June to 30 September); south tower and intervening bay: open 1 June to 30 September from 1000 to 1200 and 1400 to 1900 (except on Sunday mornings); closed 1 January, 1 May, 14 July, 1 November and 25 December; 10F; ☎ 85 38 18 84.

Musée Lamartine – Open (guided tours available if booked a fortnight in advance) 1 April to 31 October from 1000 to 1200 and 1400 to 1800, the rest of the year from 1400 to 1800; closed on Sunday mornings, Tuesdays, during January and February and on 1 May, 14 July, 1 November and 25 December; 15F; ☎ 85 38 18 84.

Hôtel-Dieu – ॐ Guided tours (15 min) all year, except on Tuesdays, Sundays and public holidays, from 1000 to 1200 by appointment (a fortnight in advance) at the Musée des Ursulines, 5, rue des Ursulines, 71000 Mâcon; ☎ 85 38 18 84.

MÂCONNAIS

La montagne

Lugny: Church – *Apply to the Centre Pastoral, Rue du Pont.*

Site préhistorique d'Azé – Guided tours (1 hour 30 min) 1 April to 30 September daily from 1000 to 1115 and 1400 to 1815, in October on Sundays and public holidays only from 1000 to 1115 and 1400 to 1815; 32F; ☎ 85 33 32 23.

Clessé: Church – Monday to Saturday apply to Restaurant Cossu in the Place de l'Église; ☎ 85 36 90 93; and on Sunday mornings to l'épicerie Sivignon (grocer's) near the church; ☎ 85 36 94 25.

Lamartine heritage trail

Château de Monceau – Courtyard and terrace open all year from 1000 to 1800; to visit the chapel apply to the attendant.

Milly-Lamartine: Maison d'Enfance de Lamartine – Guided tours (1 hour) early May to late September at 1000, 1100, 1500, 1600 and 1700; closed on Tuesdays and Fridays; 25F; ☎ 85 37 70 33.

Château de Berzé-le-Châtel – Guided tours (45 min) in July and August daily from 1000 to 1200 and 1400 to 1800; 27F; ☎ 85 36 60 83.

St-Point: Château – Guided tours (30 min) 1 March to 15 November from 1000 to 1200 and 1400 to 1830; closed on Sunday mornings and Wednesdays; 20F; ☎ 85 50 50 30.

Pierreclos: Château – Open 1 June to 1 November from 0930 to 1200 and 1300 to 18.00, the rest of the year from 0930 to 1200 and 1330 to 1730; 25F; ☎ 85 35 73 73.

MONCLEY

Château – Guided tours (2 hours) on Sundays in July and one Sunday in August at 1500; 30F; apply to the tourist office in Besançon; ☎ 81 80 92 55.

MONTARGIS

🅱 Bd Paul-Baudin, 45205. ☎ 38 98 00 87

Musée Girodet – Open all year from 0900 to 1200 and 1330 to 1730 (1700 on Fridays); concerts on Saturdays in July and August from 1830 to 2030; closed on Mondays, Tuesdays and public holidays; 16F; ☎ 38 98 07 81.

Musée du Gâtinais – Open all year from 0900 to 1200 and 1330 to 1730 (1700 on Fridays); closed on Mondays, Tuesdays and public holidays; 16F; ☎ 38 98 07 81.

MONTBARD

Parc Buffon – Guided tours (1 hour) 1 April to 30 September from 1015 to 1200 and 1415 to 1800, the rest of the year from 1000 to 1200 and 1400 to 1700; evening tours in July and August on Sundays at 2130; closed on Tuesdays in season, and on Fridays and Saturdays out of season; 10F; ☎ 80 92 01 34 (ext 305).

Musée des Beaux-Arts – Open 1 June to 31 August from 1000 to 1200 and 1500 to 1800, in April, May, September and October from 1500 to 1800; closed on Tuesdays; last admissions an hour before closing time; 11F; ☎ 80 92 01 34 (ext 305).

Musée des anciennes écuries de Buffon – Open 1 April to 15 November from 1000 to 1200 and 1400 to 1800; closed on Tuesdays; 10F; ☎ 80 92 01 34 (ext 305).

Excursions

Forges de Buffon – Open in July and August on Wednesdays, Thursdays and Fridays from 1000 to 1200 and 1430 to 1800, on Mondays, Tuesdays and at the weekends from 1430 to 1800; in June and September daily (except on Tuesdays) from 1430 to 1800; 25F; for details of opening times outside these periods, contact ☎ 80 89 40 30.

Château de Nuits – Guided tours (1 hour) 1 April to 1 November from 1000 to 1200 and 1400 to 1730; 20F; ☎ 86 55 71 80.

MONTBÉLIARD

Guided tours of the town – Apply to the tourist office.

Château: Museum – Open from 1000 to 1200 and 1400 to 1800; closed on Tuesdays and 1 January, 1 May, 11 November and 25 December; ☎ 81 94 43 21.

Temple St-Martin – Open to visitors as part of the guided tour of the town, every Saturday from 1 June to 30 September; meet at the tourist office at 1500; 30F; ☎ 81 94 45 60.

Sochaux

Musée Peugeot – Open daily from 1000 to 1800; 30F, children: 15F; ☎ 81 94 48 21.

Tour of the Peugeot factories – Guided tours (2 hours 30 min – group size must be less than 8) Mondays to Fridays at 0830; closed on public holidays; minimum age: 15 years; meet at the Musée Peugeot, Carrefour de l'Europe at Sochaux.

If time permits...

Fort on Mont-Bart – Open 1 June to 30 September daily from 1400 to 1800, in May and October at weekends at these times; 15F; ☎ 81 97 51 71.

MONT-ROND

Télécabine – Operates from the Col de la Faucille 1 December to 30 April and 1 June to 30 September; journey time: 11 min Rtn; 21F.

Télésiège – Operates from 1 December to 30 April; journey time: 15 min Rtn; 21F.

MONT-ST-VINCENT

Musée J.-Régnier – Open 15 April to 15 September on Sundays and public holidays from 1500 to 1900; no admission charge; ☎ 85 57 38 51.

MOREZ

Musée de la Lunetterie – Closed for reorganisation; ☎ 84 33 08 73.

MORVAN

Parc natural régional du Morvan: Maison du Parc (St-Brisson) – Open all year Monday to Friday from 0845 to 1200 and 1345 to 1730, and also weekends between Easter and mid-November from 1000 to 1200 and 1400 to 1800; for details of exhibitions telephone in advance during office hours; ☎ 86 78 70 16.

LE BAS-MORVAN ②

Avallon: tourist office – 6, rue Bocquillot, 89200. ☎ 86 34 14 19.

Avallon: St-Lazare – Open from Palm Sunday to 1 November daily from 0800 to 1800.

Avallon: Musée de l'Avallonnais – Open 15 May to 15 September from 1000 to 1230 (1200 15 May to 14 June) and 1400 to 1830 (1800 15 May to 14 June); closed on Tuesdays; 15F; ☎ 86 34 03 19.

Avallon: Musée du Costume – Guided tours (45 min) 15 April to 1 October daily from 1030 to 1230 and 1330 to 1730; 20F; ☎ 86 34 19 95.

N

NANTUA

Lac de Nantua: Boat trips – Apply to the Hôtel du Lac, 15, avenue de la Gare, 01130 Nantua; ☎ 74 75 00 12.

Musée départemental de la Résistance et de la Déportation de l'Ain et du Haut-Jura – Open 1 May to 30 September from 1000 to 1230 and 1400 to 1800; closed on Mondays; 20F; ☎ 74 75 07 50.

NEVERS

Guided tours of the town – Apply to the tourist office.

Pottery workshops – The Ateliers Montagnon (10, rue de la Porte-du-Croux) are open to visitors every Wednesday in July and the first Wednesday of the month the rest of the year at 1430; closed on public holidays; no admission charge; ☎ 86 57 27 16.

Musée archéologique du Nivernais – Open all year from 1000 to 1200 and 1400 to 1800; closed on Monday afternoons and Tuesdays; 10F; ☎ 86 59 17 85.

Musée municipal Frédéric-Blandin – Open 1 May to 30 September from 1000 to 1830, the rest of the year from 1000 to 1200 and 1400 to 1730; closed on Tuesdays and 1 January and 25 December; 10F; ☎ 86 68 45 62.

Cathédrale St-Cyr-et-Ste-Julitte – The 6C baptistery is not open to the public; guided tours of the cathedral in the summer *("Regards sur la cathédrale de Nevers")*; ☎ 86 59 06 74.

Couvent St-Gildard and Museum – Guided tours (1 hour) 1 April to 31 October daily from 0700 to 1200 and 1330 to 1930, the rest of the year from 0730 to 1200 and 1400 to 1900; no admission charge; ☎ 86 57 79 99.

Ste-Bernadette-du-Banlay – Apply to Monsieur le Curé, 23, rue du Banlay; ☎ 86 57 32 90.

If time permits...

Circuit auto-moto de Nevers-Magny-Cours – Guided tours (1 hour 30 min) all year except on race days and during the last two weeks in December; essential to book, at least a fortnight in advance; apply to Mme C. Picard; ☎ 86 21 80 00.

NUITS-ST-GEORGES

Musée – Open 2 May to 31 October from 1000 to 1200 and 1400 to 1800; closed on Tuesdays; 10F; ☎ 80 61 13 10.

ORNANS   🛈 Rue P.-Vernier, 25290. ☎ 81 62 21 50

Festivities – Events are organised by the Courbet museum in association with the Doubs council and the society of friends of Gustave Courbet; apply to M. Jean-Jacques Fernier for details (3, rue Le Nôtre, 75016 Paris).

Musée Courbet – Open from 1000 to 1200 and 1400 to 1800; closed on Tuesdays from 1 November to Easter, and on public holidays; 20F, 40F during exhibitions which generally take place between the second week of June and the end of September; ☎ 81 62 23 30.

If time permits...

Trépot: Musée fromagerie – Guided tours (1 hour) 1 July to 15 September from 1400 to 1800, and in June on Sundays only at these times; 15F; ☎ 81 86 71 06.

Gouffre de Poudrey – Guided tours (45 min) 1 July to 31 August daily from 0930 to 1900, in May, June and September from 0900 to 1200 and 1330 to 1800, 1 March to 30 April tours at 1100, 1530 and 1700, in October tours at 1400, 1530 and 1700, in November on Sundays and during the school holidays only; closed 1 December to 28 February, on Wednesdays in March, April, September, October and November; 28F, children: 17F; 10 min son et lumière; ☎ 81 59 22 57.

Dino-Zoo – At Charbonnière-les-Sapins. Open 1 May to 30 September from 1000 to 1800, 1 March to 30 April from 1400 to 1800, in October from 1330 to 1730, in November on Sundays and during the school holidays only from 1330 to 1730; 28F, children: 17F; ☎ 81 59 27 05.

Grottes D'OSSELLE

Caves – Guided tours (1 hour 10 min) in June, July and August from 0830 to 1900; in April, May and September from 0900 to 1200 and 1400 to 1800, in October from 1430 to 1700 (Sundays from 0900 to 1200 and 1400 to 17.00); 28F; ☎ 81 63 62 09.

OYONNAX

Musée du Peigne et des Matières plastiques – Open 1 July to 31 August Monday to Friday from 1430 to 1830, the rest of the year Tuesday to Friday from 1400 to 1800; closed on public holidays; 13F; ☎ 74 81 96 82.

P

PARAY-LE-MONIAL   🛈 25, av. Jean-Paul II, 71600. ☎ 85 81 10 92

Guided tours of the town – In season Monday to Saturday at 1000; apply to the tourist office.

Basilique du Sacré-Coeur – Open daily from 0800 to 1900; guided tours available, apply to the tourist office.

Chambre des Reliques – ♿ Open Palm Sunday to 1 November daily from 0900 to 1830; no admission charge; ☎ 85 88 85 80.

Parc des Chapelains – ♿ Open (30 min guided tours available) Palm Sunday to 1 November daily from 0900 to 1830; 10F; ☎ 85 88 85 80.

Chapelle de la Visitation – Open daily from 0700 to 1900; guide tours available by appointment; ☎ 85 88 85 80.

Musée du Hiéron – Temporarily closed for refurbishment.

Musée de la Faïence charollaise – ⅙ Open Palm Sunday to 1 November from 1000 to 1200 and 1400 to 1800 (1500 to 1900 in July and August); closed on Tuesdays; 15F; ☎ 85 81 10 92.

Château de PIERRE-DE-BRESSE

Écomusée de la Bresse bourguignonne – Open 1 June to 30 September daily from 1000 to 1200 and from 1300 to 1900, the rest of the year from 1400 to 1800; closed from the 25 December to 2 January; 30F; ☎ 85 76 27 16.

Excursions

St-Germain-du-Bois: L'Agriculture bressane – Open 15 May to 30 September from 1500 to 1900; closed on Tuesdays; 15F; ☎ 85 76 27 16.

Maison de la forêt et du bois de Perrigny – Open 15 May to 30 September from 1500 to 1900; closed Tuesdays; 15F; ☎ 85 76 27 16.

Abbaye de la PIERRE-QUI-VIRE

Salle d'exposition – ⅙ Open from 1015 (1115 on Sundays and public holidays) to 1230 and 1500 to 1730 (1700 on Mondays); closed during January; audiovisual presentation; ☎ 86 32 21 23.

POLIGNY

🛈 Rue Victor-Hugo, 39800. ☎ 84 37 24 21

Guided tours of the town – Apply to the tourist office.

Typical chalets of the Franche-Comté – It is possible to visit one of 500 typical Comtois chalets; apply to the Comité interprofessionnel du Comté in Poligny (Avenue de la Résistance); ☎ 84 37 23 51.

Église de Mouthier-Vieillard – Guided tours 15 June to 15 September from 1000 to 1700; apply to M. Jeannin, 1 bis, place Notre-Dame; ☎ 84 37 15 91.

Hôtel-Dieu – Guided tours (15 min) Monday to Friday from 0900 to 1200 and 1400 to 1700; closed on Saturday afternoons, Sundays and public holidays; apply to the tourist office; ☎ 84 37 13 30.

Maison du Comté – Open 1 July to 15 September from 0800 to 1115 and 1400 to 1730, the rest of the year Monday to Friday from 0800 to 1115 and 1400 to 1715 (1615 on Fridays); 12F; ☎ 84 37 23 51.

PONTARLIER

🛈 56, rue de la République, 25300. ☎ 81 46 48 33

Musée municipal – Open Monday to Friday from 1000 to 1200 and from 1400 to 1800, on Saturdays from 1400 to 1800 and Sundays from 1500 to 1900; closed 1 January and 25 December; 10F; ☎ 81 46 73 68.

PONTIGNY

Abbey church – Open daily from 0900 to 1900; guided tours available all year, telephone: ☎ 86 47 54 99.

R

Château de RATILLY

Castle – Open 16 June to 15 September daily from 1000 to 1800, 1 April to 15 June on weekdays from 1000 to 1200 and 1500 to 1800, at weekends and on public holidays from 1500 to 1800, 16 September to 31 March daily (except Sundays and public holidays) from 1500 to 1800; closed 15 December to 15 January; 15F; ☎ 86 74 79 54.

Les RECULÉES

Reculée des Planches

Grotte des Planches – Guided tours (1 hour) in July and August from 0930 to 1800, in April, May, June and September from 1000 to 1200 and 1400 to 1700, 1 October to 14 November from 1000 to 1200 and 1430 to 1630; closed 15 November to 27 March and on Fridays between 1 October and 14 November; 28F, children: 14F; ☎ 84 66 13 74.

Cirque de Baume

Grottes de Baume – NB There are a lot of steps. Guided tours (40 min) mid-March to mid-October mornings and afternoons; 17F; ☎ 84 44 61 58.

La ROCHEPOT

Château – Guided tours (30 min) in July and August from 1000 to 1200 and 1400 to 1800, April to June and in September and October from 1000 to 1130 and 1400 to 1730; 26F; ☎ 80 21 71 37.

RONCHAMP

Notre-Dame-du-Haut – Open 15 March to 30 September from 0900 to 1900, the rest of the year from 0900 to 1600; 10F; ☎ 84 20 65 13.

Musée de la Mine – Open Easter to 1 November from 1400 to 1900; closed Tuesdays; 15F; ☎ 84 20 70 50.

S

ST-CLAUDE
🛈 Avenue de Belfort, 39200. ☎ 84 45 34 24

Guided tours of the town – Apply to the tourist office.

Exposition de pipes – Open 1 June to 30 September daily from 0930 to 1830; early February to late May and in October from 1400 to 1800 (except on Sundays and public holidays); closed 1 May; 17F; ☎ 84 45 17 00.

Exposition de diamants et pierres fines – Same admission times and charges as the Exposition de pipes.

ST-FARGEAU

Tour of château – Open in July and August Monday to Friday from 1000 to 1200 and 1400 to 1900, weekends and public holidays from 1000 to 1900; 1 September to 11 November from 1000 to 1200 and 1400 to 1800 (1900 weekends and public holidays); 35F; ☎ 86 74 05 67.

ST-LÉGER-VAUBAN

Maison Vauban – ♿ Open 1 June to 15 September daily from 1000 to 1200 and 1400 to 1900; open at weekends in May, September and October; 18F; ☎ 86 32 26 30.

ST-PÈRE

Notre-Dame – Open Palm Sunday to 1 November daily from 0800 to 1900.

Musée archéologique régional – Temporarily closed.

Fouilles des Fontaines-Salées – Open daily from 1000 to 1230 and 1330 to 1830; closed from 1 November to 1 April and on 1 May; no admission charge.

ST-THIBAULT

Church – Open 15 March to 15 November daily from 0900 to 1800; to visit the chapel of St Giles ☎ 80 64 66 07 or 80 64 62 63.

SALINS-LES-BAINS
🛈 Place des Salines, 39110. ☎ 84 73 01 34

Guided tours of the town – Apply to the tourist office.

Salines – Guided tours (1 hour) from the Easter holidays to 15 September at 0900, 1000, 1100, 1430, 1530, 1630 and 1730; from 1 February to the Easter holidays and 16 September to 30 November at 1030, 1430 and 1600; closed 1 November, and during December and January; 22F, children (12-15 years): 12F; details from the tourist office; ☎ 84 73 01 34.

Hôtel-Dieu – Guided tours (20 min) in June, July and August; 10F; apply to the tourist office; ☎ 84 73 01 34.

SAULIEU

Musée – Open from 1000 to 1230 and 1400 to 1800; closed on Tuesdays and from 25 December to 1 January; 20F; ☎ 80 64 19 51.

SEMUR-EN-AUXOIS
🛈 2, Place Gaveau, 21140. ☎ 80 97 05 96

Guided tours of the town – Apply to the tourist office.

Notre-Dame – Open daily from 0900 to 1200 and 1400 to sunset; open on summer evenings from 2100 to 2230 if the weather is fine.

Tour de l'Orle d'Or and Musée – Guided tours (30 min) 15 June to 15 September daily from 1000 to 1200 and 1400 to 1800; 12F; ☎ 80 97 05 96.

Musée – Open 1 June to 30 September Wednesday to Sunday from 1400 to 1730, the rest of the year on Wednesdays and Fridays only; 25F; ☎ 80 97 24 25.

SEMUR-EN-BRIONNAIS

Château St-Hugues – Open 1 March to 15 November Monday to Saturday from 1000 to 1200 and 1400 to 1900 (1830 1 March to 1 June, 1800 15 September to 15 November); open Sundays 1 March to 15 September from 1300 to 1900 and 16 September to 15 November from 1300 to 1830; 10F; ☎ 85 25 13 57.

SENS

☐ Place Jean-Jaurès, 89100. ☎ 86 65 19 49

Guided tours of the town – Apply to the tourist office.

Museum, Treasury and Palais Synodal – Open 1 June to 30 September daily from 1000 to 1200 and 1400 to 1800, the rest of the year on Mondays, Thursdays and Fridays from 1400 to 1800, and on Wednesdays, Saturdays, Sundays and public holidays from 1000 to 1200 and 1400 to 1800; 18F, no admission charge on Wednesdays; ☎ 86 64 15 27.

St-Pierre-le-Rond – Closed for restoration work.

St-Maurice – Open daily from 0800 to 1700.

St-Savinien – Apply to the priest's house, 71, rue d'Alsace-Lorraine; ☎ 86 65 19 27.

Roche de SOLUTRÉ

Musée – Open 1 June to 30 September daily from 1000 to 1300 and 1400 to 1900, in May from 1000 to 1200 and 1400 to 1800; the rest of the year from 1000 to 1200 and 1400 to 1700; closed on Tuesdays out of season, and during January and February, and on 1 May and 25 and 31 December; 17F; ☎ 85 35 85 24.

SULLY

Château – Guided tours (30 min) of the interior from June to September every afternoon; grounds open from Easter Monday to 1 November every day; 35F; ☎ 85 82 01 08.

T

TAIZÉ

Église de la Réconciliation – Open daily; prayer meetings on weekdays at 0815, 1220 and 2030, and on Sundays at 1700 and 2030; Mass at 1000; ☎ 85 50 30 30.

TALMAY

Château – Guided tours (45 min) in July and August from 1500 to 1700; closed on Mondays; 30F; ☎ 80 36 13 64.

Château de TANLAY

Tour – Guided tours (45 min) 1 April to 15 November at 0930, 1030, 1130, 1415, 1500, 1545, 1630 and 1715 (and 1800 in July and August); 36F; ☎ 86 75 70 61.

TONNERRE

☐ 42, rue de l'Hôpital, 89700. ☎ 86 55 14 48

Guided tours of the town – In July and August on Tuesdays, Thursdays and Saturdays at 1600; apply to the tourist office.

Ancien Hôpital – Guided tours 1 June to 30 September daily at 1000, 1100 and from 1300 to 1800; 26 March to 31 May and 1 October to 13 November during the week by appointment at the tourist office, at weekends and on public holidays from 1300 to 1800; closed on Tuesdays; 20F.

St-Pierre – Guided tours available on request at the tourist office; ☎ 86 55 14 48 (Mme Chambrillon).

TOURNUS

☐ 2, place Carnot, 71700. ☎ 85 51 13 10

St-Philibert – Open daily from 0800 to 1900 (1800 in winter); guided tours available in the summer, mornings and afternoons (times posted at the entrance), and in the winter on request at the tourist office; ☎ 85 51 13 10.

Musée bourguignon – Open 1 April to 1 November from 0900 to 1200 and 1400 to 1800; closed on Tuesdays and 1 May; 10F; ☎ 85 51 29 68.

Musée Greuze – Closed for restoration work, following transferral to the Hôtel-Dieu; for further details contact the tourist office.

La Madeleine – Open daily from 0800 to 1200 and 1400 to 1700; ☎ 85 51 02 70.

Excursion

Ferme-Musée de la Forêt – Open 1 July to 15 September daily from 1400 to 1900; 1 April to 30 June and 16 September to 2 November weekends and public holidays from 1400 to 1900; no admission charge; ☎ 74 30 71 89.

V

VESOUL

☐ Rue des Bains, 70000. ☎ 84 75 43 66

Guided tours of the town – Apply to the tourist office.

Musée Georges-Garret – Open from 1400 to 1800; closed on Tuesdays.

VÉZELAY

Basilique Ste-Madeleine – Open daily; ☎ 86 32 33 61.

VILLEFRANCHE-SUR-SAÔNE

☐ 290, rue de Thizy, 69400. ☎ 74 68 05 18

Guided tours of the town – Apply to the tourist office.

Old houses – Guided tours of the "Vieilles demeures caladoises" (2 hours) in July and August on Saturdays from 1000 to 1200, leaving from the tourist office; 10F.

Notre-Dame-des-Marais – For a guided tour, apply in advance to the parish priest's office *(La Cure)*, 49 rue Roland, ☎ 74 60 05 17.

Glossary

abbaye	abbey	*étang*	lake
barrage	dam	*forêt*	forest
belvédère	viewpoint	*fouilles*	excavations
butte	hill	*gouffre*	chasm
calvaire, croix	calvary, cross	*grotte*	cave
cascade	waterfall	*lac*	lake
chartreuse	charterhouse	*maison*	house
château	castle, palace	*mont, montagne*	mountain
cirque	(natural) amphitheatre	*musée*	museum
		pays	country
cluse	transverse valley in the Jura	*perte*	rift
		pic	summit, peak
col	mountain pass	*pont*	bridge
combe	coomb	*reculée*	blind valley typical of the Jura
confluent	confluence		
corniche	cliff road	*roche, rocher*	rock
côte	slope	*route*	road
crêt	peak, ridge	*saut*	waterfall
creux	dip, hollow	*signal*	beacon
défilé	ravine	*source*	spring
écomusée	open-air museum	*val, vallée*	valley
église	church		

Index

Montargis *Loiret*

Brillat-Savarin, Jean-Anthelme

Isolated sights (caves, châteaux, dams, abbeys etc.) are listed under their proper name.

Towns, sights and tourist regions followed by the name of the *département*

People, historical events and subjects